THOMAS JEFFERSON
Statesman of Science

Portrait of Thomas Jefferson shown with scientific instruments.
Engraving by Cornelius Tiebout, 1801. Courtesy of the Library of Congress.

THOMAS JEFFERSON
Statesman of Science

SILVIO A. BEDINI

MACMILLAN PUBLISHING COMPANY
NEW YORK

Collier Macmillan Publishers
LONDON

The following institutions have graciously granted permission for the use of the following illustrations: Academy of Natural Sciences of Philadelphia, Figures 26, 35; American Philosophical Society, Figure 2; Heye Foundation, Museum of the American Indian, 18; The Historical Society of Pennsylvania, Figures 3, 32; The Library of Congress, Frontispiece, Figures 8, 15, 19, 29, 37; Massachusetts Historical Society, Figures 4, 13; Musée de l'Armée, Paris, Figure 10; National Museum of American History, Smithsonian Institution, Figures 1, 14, 16, 23, 25; Peabody Museum of Archeology and Ethnology, Harvard University, Figure 34; Private collection, Figures 21, 22; Science Museum, South Kensington, London, Figures 9, 20; The Thomas Jefferson Memorial Foundation, Figures 5, 6, 7, 11, 12, 17, 24, 27, 28, 30, 31, 33, 36, 38.

Parts of Chapters IV, V, IX, XIII and XIV have appeared in several of the writer's previous publications: *The Declaration of Independence Desk: Relic of Revolution*, Smithsonian Institution Press, © 1981; *The Great Plains Quarterly*, Winter 1984, reprinted in *Mapping the North American Plains: Essays in the History of Cartography*, edited by Frederick Luebke, Frances W. Kaye, and Gary E. Moulton, University of Oklahoma Press, © 1987; *Thomas Jefferson and His Copying Machines*, University Press of Virginia, © 1984; and *Publication No. 61* of the Virginia Division of Mineral Resources, © 1985. The author expresses his appreciation to each of these publishers for their permission to include this material herein.

Macmillan Publishing Company
866 Third Avenue, New York, N.Y. 10022

Collier Macmillan Canada, Inc.

Library of Congress Catalog Card Number: 89-28345

Printed in the United States of America

printing number
1 2 3 4 5 6 7 8 9 10

Library of Congress Cataloging in Publication Data
Bedini, Silvio A.
    Thomas Jefferson : statesman of science / by Silvio A. Bedini.
        p.   cm.
    Includes bibliographical references.
    ISBN 0-02-897041-1
    1. Jefferson, Thomas, 1743–1826—Knowledge—Science.
    2. Presidents—United States—Biography.   3. Statesmen—United
    States—Biography.   4.   Science—United States—History.   I. Title.
    E332.2.B37   1990
    973.4'6'092—dc20
    [B]   89-28345
                                                                CIP

For my wife Gale,
whose assistance and persistence
were primarily responsible for
bringing this work to completion

By the Same Author

Nature intended me for the tranquil pursuits of science, by rendering them my supreme delight. But the enormities of the times in which I had lived, have forced me to take part in resisting them, and to commit myself on the boisterous ocean of political passions.

Letter from Thomas Jefferson to
Pierre Samuel Du Pont de Nemours,
2 March 1809.

CONTENTS

ILLUSTRATIONS

PREFACE

It must be stated at the very outset that this work is not a comprehensive biography of Thomas Jefferson, but is concerned primarily with a single aspect of his life—his scientific endeavors. Events of his personal, political and diplomatic career are included briefly only as necessary to provide signposts marking the epochs dividing his life.

Possibly no other figure in American history has received such perennial acknowledgement as Thomas Jefferson. He has been the subject of intensive studies as a politician, diplomat, patriot, lawyer, architect, humanist, classical scholar, philosopher, tourist, book collector, "Apostle of Americanism," and even simply as himself. To complete the portrait, it is necessary to study him also in relation to science—not only as a man of science, however, but also in his more important role as statesman of science.

More than that of any other American of his time, Jefferson's life was multifaceted, with the consequence that his biography becomes the saga of the politics, diplomacy, and in fact of world history during the first half century of the American republic.

Of the numerous successful biographies of Jefferson that have been produced from 1837 to the present, none has sufficiently emphasized or detailed his "other life," of science.

One of the most dominant aspects of Jefferson's life, his preoccupation with science, had its beginnings during his boyhood on the Virginia frontier and continued unremittingly to his final years in his planning of the University of Virginia. His interest in all the sciences of his time was not merely that of the dilettante, for he brought more knowledge to each of them than almost any of his contemporaries. In fact, in Jefferson's endeavors can be found reflected the state of the sciences of the period in which he lived, not only in the American colonies and the new republic, but also in Europe, of which he kept himself fully informed.

The search for the man of science from the great mass of his surviving papers and the records of his scientific preoccupations and pursuits has presented a considerable challenge, inasmuch as the total of his papers relating to the last thirty-five years of his life has been published only in part. Nonetheless, the search for and recovery of these science-related records has been particularly rewarding.

In the considerable literature produced about major figures in history, intimate glimpses of the men themselves emerge rarely when separated from the accounts of their careers. This was particularly true of Jefferson. It was primarily in his dealings with his children and grandchildren and a few close friends that the humanizing touches appeared and brought him more warmly to life. It is for this reason that they have been included.

To follow Jefferson's receptive and unceasingly active encyclopedic mind through a lifetime of eighty-three years as it intromitted, or literally inhaled, each innovative idea as it appeared on the scene, and observe the use he made of every grain of knowledge, applying it either for his own uses or for the general well-being, has been a remarkable experience. In his lifetime no thought or fact was wasted.

Probably the ultimately comprehensive scientific biography of Jefferson cannot be undertaken until after all of his papers have been published, studied, and evaluated by future historians. The present work is offered, meanwhile, as a preliminary study, as it were, of "the scientific life of Thomas Jefferson."

In view of his active public life, it was not always possible for Jefferson to keep abreast of scientific activities in all fields, and this factor and his own impulsive preconceptions and reactions led him occasionally into error. His political opponents and detractors lost no opportunity to make much of his few mistakes. Nevertheless their efforts failed to diminish his influence on the American scientific scene.

By means of his scientific interests and worldwide political reputation he was largely responsible for enhancing the reputation of science in his own country and at the same time for bringing recognition of American science to the rest of the world, fulfilling the unique role of a "statesman of science."

As with other published biographies of Jefferson, the primary source of the present work has been his surviving papers. This is by no means the largest collection of personal and public papers of a major American figure, but it is nonetheless sufficiently substantial. Of these the comprehensive edition being produced by the Princeton University Press since 1950 with the remarkably complete notes of the late Julian P. Boyd served as the primary source for the first fifty years. Of the papers of this period, those Jefferson had preserved to 1770 were burned in the fire that destroyed his home at Shadwell. Many of his official papers as Governor of Virginia were lost in 1782 when the British burned Richmond.

Of the papers and correspondence produced during the last thirty-three years of his life, selections have been included in the several published collections produced between 1829 and the first decade of the twentieth century, by Thomas Jefferson Randolph, H. A. Washington, Paul Leicester Ford and A. A. Lipscomb & Albert Bergh. As a consequence, many of Jefferson's letters and papers relating to science have remained unpublished, and the originals have had to be sought from the various collections in which they repose. The only complete index of these papers and their subjects is maintained by the editors of The Papers of Thomas Jefferson at Princeton University Library.

In this work extensive use has been made of quotations from Jefferson's writings, for good reason. Most often his own method of expression has proven to be superior to any possible paraphrasing or summarization. Furthermore, his choice of word and phrase invariably revealed better than any writer's efforts his persona and his philosophy.

Certain characteristics of Jefferson's writing evident in the quotations should be mentioned. For example, his use of "it's" for "its," and his invariable reversal of the letter combinations "ei" and "ie" such as "yeild" for "yield," have been maintained as he wrote them. From his mentor, George Wythe, he adopted the practice of not capitalizing the first letter of each new sentence, which has, however, been corrected in the quotations used for the convenience of the reader.

It has not been possible to include all of Jefferson's communications relating to his scientific pursuits, for which several volumes would have been required, but the most important have been noted in the present study. It is accordingly offered to the reader with the same reservation with which Jefferson prefaced his *Notes on the State of Virginia:* "The subjects are all treated imperfectly; some scarcely touched upon."

SILVIO A. BEDINI
Washington, D.C.

ACKNOWLEDGEMENTS

Any work of substantial scope such as this one inevitably owes a considerable debt to countless librarians, archivists and fellow historians who have provided required reference materials, verified statements, or contributed useful suggestions.

Particularly I am indebted to the custodians of the major collections of the papers of Thomas Jefferson, including Paul Sifton of the Library of Congress; Edmund Berkeley, Jr. and Gregory A. Johnson of the Manuscripts Division of the Alderman Library, University of Virginia; Louis J. Tucker, Director, and Ross Urquart, Curator of Manuscripts, of the Massachusetts Historical Society; and Ms. Popp of the Huntington Library and Art Gallery.

An even greater debt is owed to the past and present "family" at Monticello, with whom I have been closely associated on this and other Jefferson-related research for more than thirty years. The former director in residence, James A. Bear, Jr., assistant director, Charles L. Granquist, Jr., and William L. Beiswanger of the research staff, and the present director, Daniel Jordan, have been of invaluable assistance over a period of many years.

To Lucia Stanton, of the Thomas Jefferson Memorial Foundation, I am particularly indebted for having read the manuscript and for being a constant source of vital research information.

Support has always been forthcoming from Ruth W. Lester, Associate Editor of *The Papers of Thomas Jefferson* at the Princeton University Library.

I have had splendid cooperation from the staff of the Smithsonian Institution Libraries, including the director, Robert M. Maloy, and Ellen B. Wells, Lucien Rossignol, Janette Saquet, H. Scott Berger, Charles G. Berger and James M. Roan, among others. Lela Bodenlos, volunteer in the Libraries, has worked assiduously and endlessly verifying citations and furnishing assistance in other aspects of the research.

Others who have contributed guidance, assistance and suggestions are Jay Gaynor at the Colonial Williamsburg Foundation, Inc. and Ralph E. Ehrenberg, Geography and Map Divsion, Library of Congress; Robert Friedel, Tony Appel, Uta C. Merzbach, Ramunas Kondratas, Margaret B. Klapthor and Brooke Hindle of the National Museum of American History, Smithsonian Institution; Murphy D. Smith, the late Gertrude

D. Hess, Elizabeth Carroll-Horrocks and Whitfield J. Bell, Jr. of the American Philosophical Society; John D. Battle, Jr., M.D. of the Cleveland Clinic Foundation, Richard J. Wolfe, Curator of Rare Books, Francis A. Countway Library of Medicine; the late Harold Jefferson Coolidge; Barbara Narendra, Peabody Museum of Natural History, Yale University; David D. Gillette, New Mexico Museum of Natural History; Clayton E. Ray of the Smithsonian Institution; Frank Whitmore, Jr., U. S. Geological Survey; Charles Smart, Gay Vostreys and Carolyn Spawn of the Academy of Natural Sciences of Philadelphia; C. C. Lamberg-Karlovsky, Peabody Museum of Archeology and Ethnology, Harvard University; John C. Van Horne, Director, The Library Company of Philadelphia; and the late Herman R. Friis, formerly of the National Archives and Records Service.

The interested encouragement of the late Dumas Malone and Daniel J. Boorstin must also be mentioned. The late Julian P. Boyd was particularly interested in this endeavor, and provided the strongest support and assistance with specific aspects of the work over a period of years.

Finally, last but not least must be mentioned my editor, Charles E. Smith, former President and Publisher of Macmillan and Scribner Reference, whose skillful editing of the manuscript made the publication of this work possible.

To my wife Gale I owe the greatest debt, for not only has she produced the index, but has worked closely with me in the preparation of the manuscript from the very beginning.

To all of the foregoing, and others whom I have neglected to mention, I wish to express my most sincere appreciation.

CHAPTER I

FRONTIER GENTRY (1700–1760)

The boys of the rising generation are to be the men of the next,
and the sole guardian of the principles we deliver over to them.

Letter from Thomas Jefferson to
the Reverend Samuel Knox, 1810.

"Science is my passion, politics my duty," explained Thomas Jefferson
to a correspondent in his later years, and in these few words he summarized the preoccupation that spanned more than half a century of
public service, and a lifetime of scientific endeavor.[1]

More than any other public figure in American history, with the
exception of Benjamin Franklin, Jefferson epitomized the Renaissance
man by the range of his interests and activities, particularly in the sciences, in addition to a career in politics and diplomacy.

This lifelong preoccupation was founded on several basic pre-
cepts, one or more of which he promulgated from time to time. Human progress, he contended, was to be achieved only by application
of the sciences, which provided a common ground for engendering
fraternal relations among men. He was convinced that only the practical sciences merited consideration in the service of mankind, and
strongly supported their mandatory teaching in schools and colleges.
He was adamant in the conviction that Americans must and should
profit from the scientific accomplishments of the rest of the world in
order to achieve a true democracy.

He advocated, although he did not always practice, the principle
that in science there must be absolute freedom of inquiry, and that
the only legitimate conclusions were those resulting from careful observation and experiment. Finally, he was dedicated to the premise

that science could and should serve government, and that government must support science.

Jefferson was led to his passionate pursuit of science by a combination of influences brought to bear upon him from childhood. Born far removed from urban life a short distance from the frontier, he grew up in a level of society that had a respect for learning. His surroundings imbued him with an inborn appreciation of the world of nature, natural resources and the importance of the land. The remarkable richness of the Piedmont forests and fields he roamed in his boyhood kindled a lifelong interest in nature which was to direct his future course.

The earliest influence Jefferson experienced came from his father, Peter Jefferson, a land developer and surveyor of the back country. His parent provided him with his first learning and instilled in him a lasting preoccupation with the mystery of the continent's unexplored and unknown regions. An early teacher, the Reverend James Maury, further contributed to his curiosity about the natural sciences.

Despite his lifelong scientific endeavors, Jefferson was not a scientist, by definition one professionally trained in the sciences who earns more than half his income from their pursuit. He was an accomplished man of science, however, with demonstrated capability in surveying, astronomy and mathematics and a greater than ordinary knowledge of botany, medicine and other sciences.

Jefferson was also claimed by others to be an inventor, because of the large number of labor-saving devices with which he was associated. Many of the productions labeled as his "inventions" were in fact modifications of existing devices, which he altered for his own needs. Thus did he gain the titles of inventor and gadgeteer, neither of which he claimed. However, he did conceive of a number of devices that were truly inventions, notably a wheel cipher device and a mouldboard for a plough. He had a love of and competence with hand tools, which he used to advantage in his scientific and technological pursuits as time permitted.

Although during his lifetime Jefferson's scientific activities brought him national and foreign honors, they also brought him constant overwhelming criticism and abuse from his political adversaries, and an unfavorable press attacked him again and again. It has remained for future generations to evaluate properly his achievements as "the philosopher president."

The plantation named Shadwell, the homesite of Peter Jefferson, overlooked the lowlands along the Rivanna River from the flat summit of a gentle ridge that parallels the Southwest Mountains. It was in that small wooden frame house that on April 13, 1743 (April 2, O.S.) was born the future third President of the United States. The Virginia frontier lay to the west, approximately one hundred miles away, in the region that became Virginia's Highland County and the state of West Virginia.

The earliest Virginia plantations were developed along the rivers and creeks of the Tidewater region because the first settlers sought to establish their homes along the water courses, which provided a natural means of travel and transportation of goods. Goochland County, in which Shadwell was located, was relatively late in being settled. The upper streams had dangerous falls and rapids making travel difficult, and the rocky, mountainous hillsides were less productive than the lowlands for the cultivation of tobacco and grain, the standard crops of the time.

"Piedmont" was the name given to the foothills of the Blue Ridge and the Appalachian Mountains. Rivers divided the region into three parts: the Northern Neck between the Potomac and the Rappahannock Rivers, the Roanoke and the James River sections.

The newly formed Goochland County consisted of a large area within the central Piedmont, extending from a point approximately ten miles west of Richmond to the Blue Ridge Mountains. The northern shore of the Appomattox River bounded it on the south, and the South Anna River on the north. The county encompassed all of the drainage system formed by the James River's north and south forks, then known as the Rivanna and the Fluvanna Rivers.

Goochland County was founded by wealthy landowners from the eastern counties. The speculators among them who came for the express purpose of developing the region were not frontiersmen in the true sense. Such a one was Peter Jefferson, an enterprising young planter who was then twenty-six years of age.[2]

In 1735 Peter Jefferson was granted a patent for a tract of one thousand acres south of the Rivanna, which later became Monticello. It was situated across the river from the twenty-four hundred acres acquired several days earlier by his close friend, the wealthy landowner William Randolph. Randolph was a member of one of Virginia's patrician families and had inherited a large plantation called "Tuckahoe" situated across the James River.

Not satisfied that the tract provided a sufficiently suitable homesite, in 1736 he obtained another two hundred acres from Randolph's new holdings north of the Rivanna. Jefferson acquired the acreage from Randolph in exchange for "Henry Weatherborne's biggest bowl of arrack punch." This punch, for which Weatherborne of the Raleigh Tavern was famous, was brewed from a mash of rice or molasses or the juice of the coconut palm. It was on this segment of land that Jefferson later built Shadwell. In 1741 Jefferson added another two hundred acres to his plantation, also purchased from Randolph. The earliest patent in the region had been issued in 1734, making Jefferson one of the first settlers of what became Albemarle County.[3]

Peter Jefferson's grandfather, also named Thomas, a man of property with a plantation in Henrico County, had lived in Virginia in the 17th century. Designated one of "ye surveyours of ye highways," he also served as appraiser, witness of wills, juror and surveyor of the county. His son, Thomas Jefferson, Jr., was one of the "gentlemen justices" of Henrico County, sheriff, and captain of militia. He developed his land holdings chiefly by importing individuals to the colony. He built the church in Bristol parish, owned a racing mare, and was the father of six children, of whom Peter was the youngest of three sons.[4]

As a consequence of the death of his mother when he was only eight years of age, Peter Jefferson did not receive the customary education provided by what was called "the mother's school." In early communities it was generally the mother who taught her children to read and write, and introduced them to basic arithmetic. The Bible was used for reading, recitation and composition, since textbooks were scarce in that period.

As the youngest child, Peter probably was not given as much attention educationally as were the older sons. At the time of his father's death in 1731, Peter Jefferson was named executor and chief beneficiary, his oldest brother having died. Peter's share of the estate consisted of two slaves, some livestock and horses, land in Goochland County and the major part of his father's personal possessions.[5]

After completing his responsibilities as executor during the next several years, Peter moved to the property he had inherited on Fine and Manikin Creeks. While developing a small plantation there, he acquired land elsewhere. According to the standards of England, he would have been classified as a yeoman, a man whose primary profession was the farming of land that he owned.

Yeomen in Virginia rarely had formal education, but were generally skilled in business, and often were mechanically inclined, all characteristics of Peter Jefferson. Despite his frugal education, he was a voracious reader and gradually accumulated a respectable library. He taught himself mathematics, in which he developed considerable skill, and proved to have an aptitude for business and particularly for land development. Like his father, Peter Jefferson was appointed to a number of public offices in his community. He served as a vestryman, was appointed justice of the peace in 1734, and a sheriff of the county three years later.[6]

It was while accompanying William Randolph on a visit to the latter's uncle, Isham Randolph, that Peter met his future bride. The Randolph plantation, called "Dungeness," was situated on the James River some fifty miles below the mouth of the Rivanna. Isham Randolph had served as colonial agent for Virginia in London for some years. Upon returning to the province, he was elected to the House of Burgesses. In 1738 he was appointed Adjutant General of the province, and two years later he became colonel in charge of Goochland County militia.[7]

From the moment he met Randolph's oldest daughter Jane, Peter Jefferson was greatly attracted to her. During the next two years he visited Dungeness often, and in October 1739 they were married. Born in London, the oldest of nine children, Jane was nineteen at the time of her marriage, and Peter was thirty-two years of age. The young couple made their home on the plantation on Fine Creek, and in the next two years they became the parents of two daughters. With a growing family, Jefferson came to the conclusion that the preferable homesite would be on the land he owned north of the Rivanna, and he decided to build a house there.[8]

In about 1741, leaving his family behind, and accompanied by several of his more skilled slaves, Peter Jefferson journeyed to the Rivanna property. He brought with him building materials and prepared for a long stay. After making a study of the property, he selected a plateau along the river for the house site, near a gap in the Southwest Mountains. To the east and south it commanded a view of a great rolling plain, while on the west and north the vista extended as far as the Southwest Range. South of the river was a wooded hill on an elevation of five hundred feet called Little Mountain.

The land was quickly cleared, and Jefferson and his slaves built a small one-story wooden building, divided into four chambers, and one or two essential outbuildings, probably including a smoke-house and slave quarters.

The new homestead was adjacent to one of the major highways connecting the head of the Tidewater at Richmond with the valley of Virginia so that in time it became a natural stopping place for travelers en route to Williamsburg.

Jefferson named his new home "Shadwell," for the parish in London in which his wife had been born. After the buildings were completed, he set his men to preparing the land for planting. Because part of the land proved to be too rocky for cultivation and other areas were densely wooded, he planted the fields along the lowlands with tobacco, and the upper portions of the land with wheat and corn, which could be readily transported by water to Richmond to be ground into flour. Ready at last to return to Fine Creek, he left several slaves and an overseer behind on the premises.[9]

At Fine Creek once more, Jefferson spent most of the following year making preparations for moving his family to Shadwell. The plantation he left behind would also be maintained by slaves under the supervision of an overseer. Then, with his wife, now pregnant with young Thomas, his two daughters and the rest of his household, Jefferson made the journey one more time to Shadwell, which was to become his permanent home.[10]

By necessity, every Virginia plantation had to be completely self-sufficient. All that was consumed had to be grown on the premises and made at home, including fabric, clothing, and other commodities. The wives and daughters of early plantation owners spent some of their time spinning and weaving and preparing food for winter storage.

The presence of an adjacent river or stream was vital to a plantation, for it provided the water power required for mills built along its banks, and it also furnished the primary means of transportation of farm produce and crops to be sold in the lower country. Hogsheads of tobacco were conveyed downstream by barges formed of two canoes lashed together.

Thomas Jefferson was born shortly after the family had moved to Shadwell. His father was now in modest circumstances, but was not yet recognized as either a major landowner or a surveyor. He was impressive in appearance as well as achievement. His contemporaries described him as of gigantic stature and possessing great strength. It was said, for example, that once he had taken two hogsheads of tobacco, each weighing a thousand pounds, and had raised them simultaneously from their sides to an upright position. On another occasion, after watching three of his slaves attempting unsuccessfully to tear down an old building by means of ropes, he pushed them aside and, taking the ropes, pulled down the building single-handed.[11]

Soon after Peter Jefferson's arrival in Goochland County he met William Mayo, a neighboring landowner. Mayo held the position of surveyor of the County and he and Jefferson were soon associated in mutual endeavors, including surveying expeditions into the wilderness. Jefferson may have learned the art of surveying, which was to become one of his major occupations later in life, from his father, but it was with Mayo that he gained professional experience in the field.

Born the son and grandson of middle class clergymen in southwestern England, Mayo worked for ten years as a surveyor in Barbados and produced a map of the island which resulted in his election to the Royal Society of London, and his appointment as one of the surveyors of the long disputed boundary between Virginia and North Carolina. He was named county surveyor in the following year, and became a vestryman of St. James Parish and was appointed a major landowner and a dominant figure in the region.[12]

As the Rivanna region became more and more settled, the inhabitants realized that it was difficult and often impossible to reach the county seat. Accordingly, in September 1744 the General Assembly arranged to separate part of Goochland County to form another to be called Albemarle County. At a meeting held in February 1745 to organize the new county, Peter Jefferson was named a justice of the peace and a judge of the court of chancery. Also appointed to a similar position was a surveyor named Joshua Fry. As the presiding justice of the peace and then county lieutenant—a position formerly designated Commander of the Plantations with authority equivalent to that of governor of the County—Fry exemplified the epitome of wealth, social position and public service. Thereafter he devoted his time fully to surveying, employing four assistants, one of whom was Peter Jefferson.[13]

Two years after young Thomas was born, Peter Jefferson moved with his family to Tuckahoe following the death of William Randolph. In a codicil to his will the latter had specified that he wished Jefferson to remove with his family to his plantation and remain there until Randolph's infant son, Thomas Mann Randolph, was fully grown. It was a considerable imposition, and came at a most inconvenient time for Jefferson. He was reluctant to leave the new plantation he had just begun to develop, but he felt obligated to fulfill his friend's last wish.

Undoubtedly he also foresaw advantages to himself, for the costs of maintaining his growing family and servants, including the education of his children, would be at the expense of the Randolph estate. Before leaving Shadwell, Jefferson appointed an overseer to supervise it in his absence. Tuckahoe was not distant from Fine Creek, and Jefferson planned to visit both of his properties periodically.[14]

Thomas Jefferson later recalled that the earliest memory of his life was the journey from Shadwell to Tuckahoe, more than fifty miles away. He remembered being handed to a servant on horseback and riding the distance with him on a pillow.[15]

At Tuckahoe, Jane Jefferson took over the management of her cousin's mansion and its servants. She had often visited Tuckahoe as a girl and was familiar with the household. She attended to the needs of the four Randolph children and the three of her own as well so that her days were fully occupied.

Randolph had specified that his son was to be educated exclusively by private tutors, and was not to attend the College of William and Mary. Nor was he to be sent to England for his education, as was the practice in wealthy families in that period. Accordingly, a private tutor or schoolmaster was engaged at Tuckahoe, and school classes were held in a separate small building on the premises. It consisted of a single room with a high ceiling, and it was in this schoolroom that Thomas received his earliest schooling. Randolph had also specified that his three daughters were to be educated according to their "quality and circumstances" and presumably were taught at the same time as the boys.[16]

There is ample evidence that prior to entering school Thomas received more of his earliest education from his father than from his mother, possibly because of her preoccupation with the responsibilities of a large household. Insufficient attention has been given by biographers to the influence which Peter Jefferson exercised over his oldest son; there is no doubt that it was considerable.

First of all, the growing boy must have been inspired by his burly father's personality and achievements. At the same time, Peter must have been extremely proud of the promise shown as a child by his first son. Because Thomas would become his principal heir, Peter undoubtedly spent as much time as possible with him.

For example, he taught his son to write, as evidenced by the marked resemblance in their handwriting, suggesting that it was Peter's writing that young Thomas first copied. His father also probably taught him to read, as well as the rudiments of arithmetic, all of which were part of the traditional "mother's school" training of the period.[17] At an early age, Thomas was taught to read music and play the violin, probably by a music master at Tuckahoe, employed in the same manner as a dancing master was hired to teach the five oldest children to dance. Jane, Thomas's oldest sister, also shared his enthusiasm for music and enjoyed singing.

During the time that Thomas was growing up, the violin was virtually the only musical instrument available to the people of Virginia. It was to be found in almost every home, whether rich or poor, and public fiddling contests were held frequently. Occasionally drums, hautboys (oboes) and trumpets were also used in public events, but the violin, or "fiddle" as it was commonly known, was the instrument most often featured for private and public entertainment.[18]

Tuckahoe was divided into seven large farms, each under the management of its own overseer, so that Peter Jefferson had ample time for his own pursuits. He became increasingly involved with surveying, and frequently accompanied Fry on his expeditions, often remaining away for long periods. While at Tuckahoe, Peter Jefferson was appointed, together with Joshua Fry and Robert Brooke, surveyors for the Crown to resolve a land dispute between Lord Fairfax and the Crown. The surveying party set out from Tuckahoe in September 1746 to the headspring of the Potomac River and worked during the next seven weeks until the onslaught of winter weather forced them to abandon the field. The often almost impassable terrain and variable weather made the work difficult; several of their horses were killed in accidents, and the surveyors suffered from lack of food and water. In the next year they continued the survey and brought it to completion in February 1747.[19]

That autumn Fry and Jefferson undertook another important surveying expedition, the continuation of the boundary between Virginia and North Carolina. The expedition proved to be the most grueling of Jefferson's life, for the surveyors were often forced to defend themselves against wild beasts, and at night found uneasy shelter in hollow trees. After exhausting their provisions, Jefferson killed one of the mules to provide food for the men. Fry and Jefferson returned home before the year ended, and their report was favorably received by the Council, which awarded each of them a bonus of 300 pounds sterling in addition to expenses.[20]

Several months later Acting Governor Lewis Burwell selected Fry and Jefferson to prepare for publication a map of the inhabited regions of Virginia. Upon completion it was sent to London and by Act of Parliament was engraved and published by Thomas Jefferys, Geographer to the Prince of Wales. In October 1750 they each were paid 150 pounds sterling for their work. Theirs was the first map of the region made from actual surveys and provided considerable insights into and information about Virginia's geography. The map was acknowledged to be a major achievement and remained in use for years to come.[21]

Thomas Jefferson was three years of age in 1746 when his father set out with Fry and Brooke on the third survey of the Northern Neck. The boy undoubtedly witnessed the important meeting of the surveyors at Tuckahoe in January before they ventured forth and another when they met again after their return. He must have listened with considerable excitement as his father and his companions related their exploits in the wild.

Even though he was too young to have remembered many details of his father's comings and goings, he would have overheard discussions of the surveys and the perils and hardships encountered during the frequent visits of Fry and other surveying associates to Tuckahoe and later to Shadwell.

One can only speculate what young Thomas was like as a boy, for few descriptions were left by members of his family, teachers or youthful associates. It is known that he was always considered tall for his age, slim and lanky and even gawky at times, with large hands and feet. In his youth he had flaming red hair and a thin freckled skin that sunburned and windburned easily. In his heritage he combined the aristocracy of the Tidewater from his mother, including its great pride, refinement and even prodigality and excesses, with the yeomanry of the Piedmont on his father's side, featuring an energetic and healthy body and mind and a sense of independence and opportunism.

As demonstrated by his later interests and activities, Thomas was filled with a boy's natural curiosity about how things worked, and the mysteries of the natural world around him. He undoubtedly inherited a certain amount of dexterity from his father, and from him he learned about tools. Despite Peter's alleged outward austerity and tendency towards taciturnity, he was nonetheless a tender husband and a devoted father. He spent such leisure as he could command in reading, favoring Shakespeare above all other writers, but with an appreciation also for Pope and Addison. He supervised his son's early reading, and repeatedly emphasized the importance of punctuality, perseverence, energy and system.[22]

Peter Jefferson's library was not large but it covered a wide range of subject matter, including law, history, geography, astronomy, religion, mathematics and literature. It also included such practical items as a two-volume "scrivener's guide," and "Bishop of Sadar & Man's Instruction for Indians." He also owned "Maps of the 4 Quarters of the World," "A Map of the City of London," a map of Virginia and "A set of surveyors & other math[ematical] instruments," the last-named valued at £6 at the time of his death. Young Thomas undoubtedly had the freedom to use these books as a boy, as well as the sixteen or more tomes of *The Spectator* and other volumes of *The Tatler* and *The Guardian* which his father owned.[23]

In addition to assisting him with other studies, Peter Jefferson probably taught his son the elements of surveying, perhaps even taking him into the field with him on nearby assignments. It is likely that he also taught him drafting, an art in which Thomas excelled and which he continued to utilize throughout his life.

Young Thomas was born at the edge of the wilderness into a world with natural riches abounding. The overheard conversations of his father with other surveyors must have ignited an already active imagination and aroused an insatiable curiosity about the dangers and delights that lay beyond the beyond. Always before him he had the frontier and the unknown regions which a boyish imagination would fill with ferocious beasts, dangerous mountain rapids, treacherous swamps and other unknown dangers of every kind lurking behind every tree and every rising hill.

The wilderness had more than hazards and hardships to offer, however, for it also held the mystery of great spaces where no white man had ventured. Undoubtedly it was a prospect to inflame the imagination of any impressionable boy, and was to create attitudes considerably different from those of his contemporaries living in urban environments. These attitudes were to remain with him throughout his life and were primarily responsible for his desire to develop and expand the young new republic.

Among Thomas's early interests were the Indians. Although he had heard tales of encounters with treacherous natives, he did not know them, for Indians no longer lived in the forests near Shadwell and Tuckahoe, and the only ones he did encounter were peaceful. His father had met many Indians in the field in the course of his work, and occasionally some of them would stop at Shadwell to visit on their way to the provincial capital at Williamsburg. Young Thomas was greatly impressed by them, and recalled them vividly in later years. Particularly he remembered the great Cherokee warrior and orator, Outacity, also known as Ontassere and Ostenaco, who visited often at his home.

During the years that he spent at Tuckahoe and then after returning with his family to Shadwell in 1752, Peter Jefferson became fast friends with Joshua Fry, not only because of their close association in the field, but also because of a shared love of learning. Fry's home, Viewmont, was some thirteen miles distant from Shadwell, and at least one half day's journey on horseback.

Thomas Jefferson later told one of his grandsons, "My father had a devoted friend, in whose house he would go, dine, spend the night, dine with him on the second day, and return to Shadwell in the evening. His friend, in the course of a day or two, returned the visit, and spent the same length of time in his house. This occurred once every week, and thus, you see, they were together four days out of seven."[24]

In 1752 the governor appointed Fry to serve as a commissioner on behalf of Virginia to negotiate the Treaty of Logstown with the Delaware and Iroquois Indians, and a year later Fry was commissioned commander of the Virginia regiment raised against the French, following the failure of George Washington's mission of peace to the governor of the French. Washington served as lieutenant colonel under Colonel Fry's command on the expedition. Fry's fall from a horse led to an illness from which he never recovered, and he died at Will's Creek on the way from Alexandria.[25]

During the last few years that he served as county surveyor, Fry had performed little of the work himself but left it to his assistants. With Fry's death, his major public offices fell to Jefferson, who succeeded him as county surveyor and county lieutenant. He served during the sessions of the Assembly in 1754, and in 1755 he was elected to the House to represent Goochland County, but did not stand for re-election.

After Fry's death all surveys of the county were made by Peter Jefferson and his assistants, Thomas Turpin, John Smith, and John Staples. Although in most instances the field work was performed by the assistant surveyors, the surveys were filed in Jefferson's name.

Meanwhile Jefferson's new post as county lieutenant of Albemarle County assumed greater responsibility as war with the Indians again threatened. It conferred military command over an extensive portion of the Indian frontier at a time when war with the French in this region seemed imminent. Surveyors were called in from the field to mobilize troops and supplies. They rarely led their men into battle, however, inasmuch as their prime function was recruiting, provisioning, and paying the militia, which required all of their time.[26]

Not long after his return to Shadwell from Tuckahoe, Peter Jefferson placed Thomas in the so-called "Latin school" of the Reverend William Douglas. Douglas had come to Virginia in 1748 or 1749 and had been employed for a time as tutor in the household of Colonel Spence Monroe of Westmorland County. In 1750 he had returned to England to be ordained. He was assigned to St. James Parish in Northam and returned with his wife and infant daughter to settle in Goochland County. He was considered to be a learned man and at the time of his death he owned a collection of books valued at £150, which was a substantial library in that period.[27]

Some concept of the curriculum of the schools taught by clergy may be derived from an advertisement in the *Virginia Gazette* of another young clergyman. In addition to teaching French, Latin, Greek, and English to young ladies and gentlemen, his school offered "Book-keeping, by double entry, Algebra, Geometry, Measuring, Surveying, Mechanicks, Fortification, Gunnery, Navigation, and the use of the Globes and Maps, after a natural, easy and concise Method, without Burthen to Memory."[28]

The Latin school, which may have been selected by Peter because he was a vestryman of Douglas's parish, did not offer such a wide range of subjects, and Thomas later stated that he had not had a high opinion of Douglas's intellectual accomplishments. He considered Douglas to have been but a superficial Latinist and even less informed in Greek. Nonetheless, Jefferson learned the rudiments of both languages as well as French at that school.[29]

During the five years that Thomas attended the Latin school, he spent many of his vacations at Shadwell. He devoted part of each day to riding his horse through the cultivated fields and the deep forests that rose all around the edge of the plantation. His father taught him how to ride and how to cross the Rivanna on horseback.

By his own account, his father gave him a gun when he was ten and sent him out into the forest for the purpose of developing self-reliance. According to the story he later told, he found neither beasts to threaten him nor quarry to shoot. Ashamed that he would have to return without any evidence of his prowess, he reported that at last he found a wild turkey caught in a pen. Thinking this was a prize attesting to his skill with the unfamiliar weapon, he took the turkey, and tying it to a tree with a garter, shot it. Later in life he recommended hunting as a desirable youthful exercise, but did not himself engage in hunting to any marked degree.[30]

It was at an early age that Thomas became a compulsive walker and spent countless hours wandering through the dark deep-carpeted forest, tracking through the lowlands along the lush growth of the Rivanna's borders and climbing its rocky promontories. In marked contrast were the elevated fields and valley farmlands under cultivation in tobacco, wheat and corn.[31]

During these years Peter Jefferson devoted much of his time to the instruction of his oldest son in the landowner's responsibilities. He instilled in him self-reliance, the need for exactness and precision in all things, and the necessity for building his body for the purpose of maintaining good health. He stressed the importance of mathematics, a subject beloved by Peter, and instructed him in the elements of book-keeping and the operation of a plantation. He shared with his son his own love of reading, and took him about the plantation as he taught slaves to perform specialized tasks in carpentry, milling, planting, and the use of tools.

It was undoubtedly from his father that Thomas learned the basic lessons in behavior, which many years later he conveyed to Thomas Jefferson Smith, a young boy who was his namesake, as "A Decalogue of Canons" to be observed in practical life:

1. Never put off until tomorrow what you can do to-day.
2. Never trouble another for what you can do yourself.
3. Never spend your money before you have it.
4. Never buy what you do not want, because it is cheap; it will be dear to you.
5. Pride costs us more than hunger, thirst and cold.
6. We never repent for having eaten too little.
7. Nothing is troublesome that we do willingly.
8. How much pain has cost us the evils which have never happened!
9. Take things always by their smooth handle.
10. When angry count ten, before you speak; if very angry, one hundred.

This set of principles governed Thomas's later life, and he found occasion to repeat them to his own children again and again.[32]

As a boy Jefferson often crossed the Rivanna to climb the round-topped mountain on his father's property called Little Mountain. From it he commanded a view of the entire countryside extending from the great Blue Ridge rising on the west to the rolling green Piedmont stretching into infinity towards the east until the view was lost in the mists arising from the lowlands. The mountain intrigued him, and he thought of it as his own.

During his periods at home, Jefferson's favorite companion was his oldest sister Jane. Together they roamed the fields and the woods, and she became his closest confidant, the one with whom he shared his most intimate thoughts. Jane was an excellent singer, and he often accompanied her on his violin.

In the evenings, while Peter Jefferson read *The Spectator* or one of his favored books, his wife attended to the needs of their children and to the supervision of the servants. She instructed the girls in the principles of housekeeping and may have taken the time to teach them how to sew and churn. It is likely that the parents divided their time in this manner, and that while she cared for the younger children and instructed her daughters, he devoted part of his time to the instruction of his sons.

As the family grew, Peter became increasingly aware that the small house at Shadwell was insufficient to accommodate them, and in 1753 he undertook the enlargement of the dwelling. His accounts with John Biswell, who may have been a millwright in the region, listed materials and labor that suggest that Jefferson enlarged the dwelling substantially and added several more outbuildings. In common with the practice on neighboring plantations, he probably added a brick kiln, and made bricks from the local red clay soil.[33]

In the following year Jefferson paid £15.0.0., "by covering a house," confirmation that he had either enlarged the dwelling at this time or built a new one.[34]

In June 1757 Peter Jefferson became ill. He was visited on June 25th and three subsequent occasions in July by his friend the physician Dr. Thomas Walker. His condition did not improve, and Walker made numerous visits to Shadwell in August to care for his patient, to no avail. Peter Jefferson passed away on August 17, at the age of fifty. His death at such a young age, with a large family to be provided for, came as a great shock to everyone.[35]

Fortunately he had become a man of some means so that there was no concern for his family's future well-being. He was owed £351 in Virginia currency for surveys completed between March 1754 and August 1757, and his estate included considerable property and other items, which his will carefully divided among his survivors.[36]

According to Peter's will, when Thomas reached the age of twenty-one he was to make a selection of lands either on the Rivanna or on the Fluvanna Rivers. He was to receive also a proper share of the livestock, half of the slaves not otherwise disposed of by the terms of the will, and the residue of the estate. The lands not selected by Thomas were to go eventually to his second son Randolph, together with a similar share of the livestock and slaves. Thomas was also bequeathed "my mulatto slave

Tawny, my books, mathematical instruments, and my cherry tree desk and bookcase."

At the time of his death Peter Jefferson possessed, in addition to other furniture, two desks and two bookcases, one each of cherry and walnut. Thomas also inherited all of his father's maps, surveying instruments, and his account books as executor of the Randolph estate and as County Surveyor of Albemarle County.[37]

Thomas returned to Shadwell as soon as he was informed of his father's death, and remained for a brief period while the guardians appointed by his father decided on his future schooling. Then fourteen years of age, he was greatly affected by the loss of his father, who had been the family's pillar of strength, and a parent to whom he was deeply attached. He suddenly found himself nominally the head of the household, although it would be seven years more before he would reach legal age and become the owner of a considerable acreage with farming facilities and a number of slaves.

Meanwhile, he had as his responsibility a mother, six sisters and a younger brother only two years of age. He must have felt suddenly totally lost and incompetent to deal with the present, to say nothing of his future.

Jefferson's guardian was Dr. Thomas Walker, one of the most prominent men of King and Queen County. In addition to practising as a physician, he was a planter, surveyor, importer, soldier and politician. For a number of years he had served as Indian Commissioner for the province, conducting large transactions for the government in the purchase of lands. His estate was often the site of conferences with Indian chieftains. In 1750 he was the first white man to have entered Kentucky with an expedition, preceding those of Christopher Gist and Daniel Boone.[38]

In consultation with the other guardians named by Peter Jefferson for his son—the Honorable Peter Randolph, Thomas Turpin and John Harvie—Dr. Walker selected the school maintained by the Reverend James Maury, the resident rector of Walker's parish on the border of Louisa and Albemarle Counties. Maury was married to Walker's niece. His school was between twelve and fourteen miles from Shadwell, and ten miles from Walker's home.

During the French and Indian Wars, Maury had served as chaplain to the Albemarle troops by their request. Born in Dublin, he had emigrated to Virginia with his father in 1719 and attended the College of William and Mary. He went back to London to be ordained and returned to Virginia to serve a rectorship elsewhere before moving to Goochland. He became rector of King William Parish, which contained three churches and a chapel, and consequently he spent much time on horseback attending to his clerical responsibilities. At the time of Peter Jefferson's death, Maury's school was already well established and considered to be the best in the province. Jefferson's guardians paid £20 annually for Thomas's board.[39]

Maury had collected what was considered to be an impressive library for that period, consisting of more than four hundred volumes. These included works on history, religion, natural philosophy, literature and languages. In his teaching he emphasized a good background in grammar, and a familiarity with history and literature, and considered that "an Acquaintance with the Languages, antiently spoken in Greece & Italy, is necessary, absolutely necessary, for those who wish to make any reputable Figure in Divinity, Medicine, or Law."

> Maury also added a Taste & Relish for the liberal Sciences & politer Arts, by furnishing the Mind with materials to work upon, rescue such from Pursuits, which are either Trivial or unworthy of Man, especially men of elevated Rank, or else criminal, destructive, & flagitious . . . It moreover furnishes such of them as are inspired with a generous Ambition to enlarge the Sphere of their Observation and Knowledge, with all the Means for investigating Science up to her Fountain-head; & it qualifies them for making more than an ordinary Progress in all the initiative Acts, &, indeed, in every Department of Science.[40]

Jefferson moved in with Maury's family of eight children, and soon made close friends of two of them, James, Jr. and Matthew. James was somewhat younger but he became one of Thomas's intimates, and often accompanied him home to Shadwell on weekends.

At school much of Jefferson's time was spent in reading Greek and Latin, and he soon distinguished himself by his scholarship and industry. Maury was claimed to have a fine English style and classical background. Although intolerant of the British government in support of religious freedom, he encouraged Jefferson to familiarize himself with current literature as well as the classics. He particularly stressed the importance of competence in the use of the English language.

Although Jefferson's interest in the natural world had received no encouragement from the Reverend Douglas, it was rekindled by the Reverend Maury, who evinced a similar' curiosity about natural phenomena and the world that lay beyond the forests of the Piedmont which encircled Albemarle County. Maury collected fossils and minerals, and in 1754 his brother-in-law reported having received from him a fossil cockle shell found on the top of one of the Blue Ridge Mountains as well as a lump of sea coal from the same source. Sea shells on mountain tops, where no sea or ocean was known to have existed, proved as intriguing to the master as they later would become a preoccupation for his pupil.

Jefferson enjoyed play as much as study. He was a keen hunter and his strength and fine health contributed to his endurance. One of his favorite diversions was to join other boys on hunting forays on nearby Peter's Mountain that loomed high over Edgeworth. There they hunted deer, foxes and other game. Having learned how to handle weapons from his father, he used them well at home in search of ground squirrels and other small game.[41]

In a region so sparsely settled, with human habitations so far apart, riding was a basic necessity, and each of Maury's young pupils appears to have been equipped with his own horse at school. As reported many years later, Jefferson had a "slow pony" while his friend Dabney Carr had a swift horse. At the Maury school Jefferson was able to pursue his love of walking as well, spending many hours roaming through the woods and along the river.

Another close friendship that Jefferson developed at school was with Dr. Walker's son John. In a letter to James Maury, Jr. written in 1812, Jefferson mentioned that all of his old friends were gone, and spoke of getting together with him, during which time "We would beguile our lingering hours with talking over our youthful exploits, our hunts on Peter's Mountain, with a long train of et cetera in addition . . . Reviewing the course of a long and sufficiently successful life, I find in no portion of it happier moments than those were."[42]

James Maury, Jr., who was later appointed American consul to Liverpool by Jefferson when president, recalled that Thomas had been outstanding among the pupils in his father's school and noteworthy for his diligence and proficiency. He seemed to have been quite shy, however, and often would prevail on the others to initiate actions he desired rather than doing so himself. For example, when he wished for a holiday, he would induce one of his young friends to make the suggestion. If it succeeded, then he promptly retired to master whatever the assignments may have been, and having done so, would rejoin his friends in their activities. These were perforce limited because of the remoteness of the school from community life. Recalling these school days some half a century later, Jefferson reproached himself for procrastination, suggesting that the standards he had set for himself were inordinately high.[43]

Dabney Carr, who became Jefferson's closest friend during his boyhood, had been born in the same year, and they spent much of their time together at school and on vacation. Tradition relates that while at Shadwell the two often studied together beneath a favorite oak tree on the southwest slope of the mountain on which Jefferson would later build his home. It was agreed between them that whichever of them was the first to die, the other would bury him under that tree.[44]

With the completion of his studies the time came to leave the Reverend Maury's school, and Jefferson's mind was filled with many concerns. At the age of seventeen, he became increasingly restless as he contemplated his future. He wished to enter college, as he knew that his father would have planned for him, but without his father's presence, he turned to his cousin and guardian, Colonel Peter Randolph. He visited Randolph at Chatsworth, his home on the James River, and held a prolongued discussion of the condition of his family affairs and of his future plans. Encouraged by this meeting, he then wrote to John Harvie, another of his guardians and the manager of his business matters.

Reporting on his meeting, Jefferson wrote that Randolph "thought it would be to my advantage to go to the college, & was desirous I should go, as indeed I am myself for several reasons." He explained that as long as he remained at home, one-fourth of his time undoubtedly would be occupied in entertaining company that came to Shadwell, a situation that would not prevail if he were absent from the plantation.

Furthermore, if he went to college, it would lessen the expense to the estate. He expected that at college "I shall get more universal Acquaintance, which may be serviceable hereafter to me," and that he would be able to pursue his studies in Greek and Latin as well there as at home, "and likewise learn something of the Mathematics."[45]

Jefferson did not have much choice in the selection of an institution of higher education. He could attend one of the New England colleges, but the expense would be considerable, travel would present an additional problem, and he would acquire a view of life totally different from that of Virginia, where he planned to spend the remainder of his life. Attending college in England was out of the question because of the cost. The alternative remaining to him was to attend the only academic institution in the South, the College of William and Mary.

Taking his violin and possibly some new music from London he had purchased, early in 1760 Jefferson rode off on horseback to Williamsburg, a distance of some one hundred and twenty miles from Shadwell, requiring three or four days of travel. Along the way he visited the homes of friends and relatives and remained overnight before resuming his journey.

CHAPTER II

TOWN AND GOWN (1760-1762)

When your mind shall be well improved with science, nothing will be necessary to place you in the highest points of view, but to pursue the interests of your country, the interests of your friends, and your own interests also with the purest integrity, the most chaste honor.

Letter from Thomas Jefferson
to Peter Carr, 1785.

When Jefferson arrived at Williamsburg, two whole new worlds opened up to him, the world of urban life and that of academe. Until now he had never seen even a village of more than twenty houses, and his first view of the capital of one of the largest British colonies in America impressed him greatly. In actuality, Williamsburg in the mid-eighteenth century remained little more than a small community of one thousand inhabitants including slaves, with about two hundred houses. It was surrounded by a flat expanse of tobacco fields as far as the eye could see.

The capital changed markedly in the winter months, however, when the legislature and general court were in session, and the sleepy community became a scene of intense activity. The country gentry rode or drove in from outlying districts in great numbers, and the streets bustled with activity during the day, and at night a variety of entertainment was provided. When the sessions ended, Williamsburg once again resumed its dormant appearance.[1]

One can only speculate how the strange new sights and sounds and the delights of the capital excited the seventeen-year-old Jeffer-

son. After having spent a childhood and early youth in the austerity
of the virtual wilderness without near neighbors, shops, theatres, or
any of the many conveniences now at hand, the contrast must have
been considerable. To be able to walk into a shop to purchase commodities and luxuries, for example, must have been an intoxicating
experience at first.

To observe distinguished figures of government at close hand as
they went about their business in town or during sessions in the Capitol, or while being entertained at the Raleigh Tavern, must have been
of never-ending wonder to the young student.

Jefferson was related on his mother's side to most of the society
of Williamsburg, and undoubtedly met a number of his kinsmen, and
may have joined them in social events. It is not surprising that at first
he found himself divided between social dalliance and attention to his
studies. Gradually, however, he withdrew to the latter.

Jefferson particularly favored music and riding, and engaged in
them during his leisure. Much of his free time was spent with John
Page, his closest friend in the student body, who would later become
governor of Virginia. This early friendship was to be maintained for
the rest of their lives.[2]

In spite of College regulations prohibiting students from maintaining horses, Jefferson kept one or two horses at Williamsburg after
his arrival, stabling them in town and riding them daily for short trips
to explore the surrounding region on weekends. As time went on,
however, he curtailed the distances and rode less frequently, generally
at nightfall.

He had brought his violin with him and continued to play it for
his own pleasure in the privacy of his room, although not for as long
periods as he had when he was younger. As he became increasingly
immersed in his studies, he reduced his leisure activities to walking for
at least one mile each evening. He had never learned to smoke, and
had good digestion, once remarking he was "blessed with organs of digestion which accepted and concocted, without even murmuring,
whatever the palate chose to consign to them."[3]

Regrettably, Jefferson recorded few of his first impressions of the
town and College, although many years later he commented that the
Capitol was "a light and airy structure" and the Governor's Palace was
large with commodious grounds around it. The hospital and the College, however, he described as "crude, misshapen piles which but that
they had roofs, would be taken for brick kilns." The main building of
the College was a two-story brick edifice in much the same style as
the buildings of the same period of Harvard College. It had a steep
roof, a belfry and long rows of windows. Two solid brick houses occupied by professors were situated nearby and completed the College

premises, which stood within a four-acre square shaded by numerous trees and divided by well-worn paths.[4]

The establishment of the College in 1693 by a grant from the British monarchs William and Mary at first encountered considerable opposition not only in England but also from the governor of Virginia. The College president was a commissary appointed by the Bishop of London and he automatically became a member of the Virginia Council and a judge of Virginia's highest court.

Like most of its counterparts in the American colonies, the College had been founded as a seminary for educating young Southern gentlemen and training them to become ministers of the gospel for Virginia. Therein "the youth may be piously educated in good letters, and manners, and that the Christian faith may be propagated amongst the Western Indians, to the glory of the Almighty."[5]

For almost two centuries, from the first settlement of Virginia until the onset of the American Revolution, no public provision was made in the province for schools of any kind, and almost all the teachers of private schools were ministers of the Church of England. The schools that existed were maintained by most of the incumbents in their parishes, less in the interest of education than in an effort to supplement their own meagre income. A number of the ministers were relatively well educated, and some were graduates of Cambridge and Oxford or of Scottish universities. Except in rare instances, they were generally capable of providing instruction in Greek and Latin and the elements of mathematics, which embraced arithmetic, Euclid, and surveying.

From about 1690 more professional men began to emigrate to Virginia from England and continued to come in some numbers during the second quarter of the eighteenth century. As a consequence, education in the province gained new impetus, and students ventured into the four major professions available at the time; some practised law or medicine, some entered the ministry and others sought careers in politics and became members of the House of Burgesses. They began to exert a strong influence on the vestries of the parishes, for it was in their meetings that the parish schools were sustained, and civilian and religious liberties were argued.[6]

The academic standards at the College of William and Mary admittedly were not of the highest level at the time that Jefferson attended. As a consequence, the wealthier southern families sent their sons to complete their education to universities in England and Scotland which offered a wider range of learning than the relatively specialized fare provided at Williamsburg.

Jefferson later commented "the admission of the learners of Latin and Greek had filled the college with children. This rendering it disagreeable and degrading to young gentlemen, already prepared for entering on the sciences, they are discouraged from resorting to it, and thus the schools for mathematics and moral philosophy, which might have been of some service, became of very little." Furthermore, the revenues, too, were depleted for accommodating those who came only to acquire the rudiments of the sciences.

The sovereigns whose names the College bore had endowed it with £1984 and twenty thousand acres of land as well as the income from certain taxes which yielded an additional resource of £300 a year. From other benefactors the establishment acquired an annual total of £3000, and one estate was given with the proviso that Indian students be maintained at the College. The teaching of Indians was not successful, but remained a requirement.

Since one of the primary purposes for founding the College was to train ministers of the established church, the faculty included a professor of divinity and a professor of moral philosophy. The president was required only to present four theological lectures annually, and as Commissary, or representative of the Bishop of London, he was in charge of Williamsburg's parish church. Since assignments to the Virginia parishes were generally given to English clergymen by the Bishop in London, there was little or no incentive for Virginians to train for the clergy, and few came to the College to study theology.

The student body consisted for the most part of those who came to study Latin and young men whose parents could not afford to send them to school in England. Despite its shortcomings, and there were many, the College exerted considerable influence on the Commonwealth. Its alumni included numerous leaders who directed the destinies of Virginia and were to play important roles in the American Revolution.

The College was divided into four schools, a grammar school for the instruction of boys to the age of fifteen, a school of philosophy, a postgraduate divinity school and an Indian school. The system of instruction was similar to that in England. A student entering grammar school remained for five years and studied Latin and Greek. At the age of fifteen he was given an examination, and if he passed'it satisfactorily he was admitted to the school of philosophy, which corresponded most closely to the modern college.

Its faculty consisted of only two professors, a professor of natural philosophy and mathematics who taught "Physicks, Metaphysicks, and Mathematics," and a professor of moral philosophy who taught natural and civil law, "Rhetorick, Logick, and Ethicks." Following the general form and organization of the two major English universities, when a student completed four years of study he was granted a degree of Bachelor of Arts. Upon satisfactory completion of three more years of study, he was awarded the degree of Master of Arts.

If a student was intended for the ministry, he entered the school of divinity after receiving his Bachelor of Arts degree. The divinity school faculty also consisted of two professors, one of whom taught the Hebrew language and the Old and New Testaments, while the other taught "the commonplace of divinity and the controversies with heretics."

There was no provision for those who intended to pursue the law. They would study in the office of a lawyer, or attend an English university, and those pursuing medicine studied in Europe. Very few Virginians attended a college in the northern American colonies.[7]

The College of William and Mary imposed an entrance'fee of one *pistole*, an old European gold coin commonly in use in the period, and required that an annual fee of £20 sterling be paid to each of the student's professors. Each professor was paid £150 annually by the College and was provided with two rooms for which he was to acquire his own furniture, which had to be purchased in town. This generally was limited to six chairs, a table, a grate, a bed and bedstead. Members of the faculty were not permitted to marry, and they were required to live on the College premises.

The regulations for students were equally strict. They were not permitted to marry, but they had the choice of living in the dormitories or in lodgings in town. They were prohibited from keeping a race horse at the College or in town, forbidden to race horses, gamble at billiards or other gaming tables, or to keep or engage fighting cocks. They were not allowed to attend or be seen in "yᵉ ordinaries, in or about yᵉ town except they be sent for by relatives, or other near friends."[8]

Students were forbidden to leave the College premises or venture beyond the bounds "particularly towards the mill pond without yᵉ express leave of his respective master, or tutor, first had, & obtained." Nor was the student allowed to possess "cards, dice, or other implement of gaming" within the bounds of the College. Furthermore, students were prohibited from telling lies, cursing, swearing, engaging in obscene actions, fighting or quarreling or "to set into drinking," and each such transgression was punishable without respect of persons. Despite these rigid restrictions, when Jefferson enrolled, students frequently kept guns and dogs in their dormitory rooms, and maintained horses in town as was to be expected of Southern gentlemen.[9]

Jefferson was filled with excitement upon his first view of the town, and with great anticipation as he inspected the College premises where he planned to spend the next two years of his life. His high expectations were soon dispelled, however. Upon enrolling on March 25th, he moved into one of the dormitories. It was not long before he discovered that the College was not only poorly governed but was a hot bed of dissension.

Many of his fellow students from wealthy Virginia families had enrolled only because they were forced to do so by their families. They were without interest in study, and upon completion of the two years they returned to their plantations even more dissolute than when they had entered. Most of the faculty were incapable of performing their teaching functions and their lives were filled with scandal. Contention and dissipation prevailed, with frequent riots demonstrating the administration's incapability to exercise authority over either students or faculty.

Some concept of the size and structure of the College'may be derived from a brief review of events occurring just prior to Jefferson's arrival. In 1754 the faculty including the president numbered six professors. Seventy-five students boarded on campus, of whom eight were Indians attending the Indian school, and some forty more resided in town. Eight of the wealthier students kept slave boys to attend them, and fifteen of the students attended on scholarships.[10]

A conflict had arisen between the governor and the clergy over the subject of faculty salaries. The Reverend William Preston and the Reverend Thomas Robinson, who occupied the respective chairs of moral and natural philosophy, resigned and departed for London to bring their appeal for salary increase to a higher authority. As a consequence there was little activity on the campus for such a prolonged period that some parents removed their sons and sent them to the newly-established College of Philadelphia.

It was not until early in 1755 that the Board of Visitors finally took action to fill the faculty vacancies left by the departed professors. The Reverend Goronwy Owen was appointed master of the grammar school and in 1758 William Small was chosen professor of natural philosophy and mathematics.[11]

Owen, a graduate of Jesus College at Oxford, had been acclaimed the premier poet of Wales and a man of considerable learning. Unfortunately, however, he had developed a great fondness for strong spirits. In August 1760, in company with the Reverend Jacob Rowe, he led the students in a "town and gown" confrontation with boys of the community. The Board of Visitors became so exasperated that they ordered Rowe to remove himself and his effects from the College. Owen resigned before he could be dismissed, and was replaced by the Reverend William Webb. The chair of moral philosophy was offered to Andrew Burnaby, who declined it. Eventually it was filled by Richard Graham, who had been removed from the chair of natural philosophy two years previously.[12]

In a letter from London, Philip Ludwell wrote, "I hear many disagreeable things from Virginia, as the battle of the scholars, the regiments laying down their arms, etc., but none with more concern than that the comp.ʸ was presented by the grand jury for drunkeness. How sad a wound does Religion receive, like Caesar, from those who by all Tyes are bound to be her best friends and supporters." The reference was to the Commissary, the Reverend Thomas Dawson, who had been master of the Indian school.[13]

Jefferson soon developed a circle of friends among the students, several of whom he had known from Maury's school, including John Walker and Dabney Carr. Next to Carr, his closest friend was John Page, the son of Mann Page, owner of a large estate in Gloucester County. Described as a young man of sterling qualities, Page boarded with and was tutored privately by Dawson, the College president, as a consequence of his father's influence and wealth. Page's knowledge of Latin was considerably better than that of even the older students, and the president took particular pleasure in introducing him to Lieutenant-Governor Francis Fauquier as his special pupil.

Soon after Jefferson arrived at the College, he was visited in his rooms by the irresponsible and unpredictable Patrick Henry, who told him he had studied law and was now in Williamsburg to apply for a license to practice. He had in fact studied for only six weeks, and George Wythe, who was one of the four examiners, refused to sign the license. Only three signatures were required, however, and young Henry went off with his license to tend his father-in-law's tavern, spending the next four years there before an opportunity came for him to practice law.[14]

For almost half of the time that Jefferson spent at the College, the only professor whose classes he attended regularly was William Small. The only member of the faculty who was not an Anglican clergyman, Small's appointment was due to the Board's dismissal of three of the professors as a consequence of the controversy over salary between the clergymen faculty and local authorities. Although Small had been appointed to teach physics, metaphysics and mathematics, he soon discovered that because of the abrupt dismissal of the Reverend Rowe, he was required to teach all the other courses of the philosophy school as well.

Jefferson and Small took to each other immediately, and a firm friendship quickly developed. The age difference of eight and one-half years notwithstanding, each found in the other an oasis from the chaos existing around them, and Jefferson took every advantage of the friendship. Having little in common with the other members of the faculty, Small turned to the young student who demonstrated such a remarkable degree of self-discipline and dedication to study. Jefferson by the same token was delighted to find among "the licensed champions of orthodoxy" someone who diverged from the established doctrine.[15]

He was extremely well prepared for his college studies, much more so than any of his fellow students, and far more mature than they in years and outlook. It is not surprising, therefore, that he became concerned that the lack of preparedness of other students might be a detriment to the progress of his own education. He found himself spending more and more of his time in Small's company, particularly as the latter unfolded a whole new world before him in the study of mathematics and the sciences.

Jefferson's association with Small is best described in his own words, written many years later.

> It was my great good fortune and what probably fixed the destinies of my life that Dr. William Small of Scotland was then professor of Mathematics, a man profound in most of the useful branches of science, with a happy talent of communication, correct and gentlemanly manners, & an enlarged and liberal mind. He, most happily for me, became soon attached to me & made me his daily companion when not engaged in the school; and from his conversation I got my first views of the expanse of science & of the system of things in which we are placed. Fortunately the Philosophical chair became vacant soon after my arrival at college, and he was appointed to fill it per interim: and he was the first who ever gave in that college regular lectures in Ethics, Rhetoric & Belles Lettres. He returned to Europe in 1762 [1764] having previously filled up the measure of his goodness to me, by procuring for me, from his most intimate friend G. Wythe, a reception as a student of law, under his direction, and introduced me to the acquaintance and familiar table of Governor Fauquier, the ablest man who had ever filled that office. With him, and at his table, Dr. Small & Mr. Wythe, his amici omnium horarum, & myself, formed a parti quarre, & to the habitual conversations on these occasions, I owed much instruction.[16]

Small brought new insights, based on the excellent schooling he had received in Scotland, to the teaching of natural philosophy and mathematics, and a new method. He introduced the lecture system which was already becoming more and more popular in England and abroad. It was extremely successful, and contrasted strongly with the previous system of teaching practised throughout the American colonies.

The traditional method consisted of teaching by the exercise of pure memory and the recitation of answers to questions dictated by the professor or which appeared in published textbooks, a method which continued in use into the 19th century. During his student days, Small had some association with the well-known chemist, Dr. Joseph Black, and as a consequence brought to the College a remarkably enlightened view of science.[17]

It is not possible to determine the nature and extent of the science-teaching and demonstrational instruments and apparatus available at the College during Small's tenure. There were few, if any. Inasmuch as the physical sciences had not been a particularly important part of the curriculum until Small made them so, it is likely that he had brought into the classroom the few instruments he personally owned or borrowed from his friends Wythe and Fauquier. If so, these may have included an achromatic telescope, orrery, barometer, thermometer, microscope, prisms, sector, a set of solids and an electrostatic machine. Realistically, it is doubtful that all of these were available to Small at that time.

Although the teaching of science at the College of William and Mary flourished under Small, it was neither initiated by him nor taught entirely due to his influence, for he had been preceded by several professors having a background in the subject. The fact that importance was originally given by the Board of Visitors to the teaching of the sciences was evidenced by the establishment of the first chair in philosophy in 1712.

From its inception, the College faculty had included a professor of mathematics, but the earliest to teach natural philosophy was the Reverend Hugh Jones, who occupied the position between 1717 and 1729. English-born and with a university education, Jones had served as pastor of a church before his appointment to the College faculty. In 1724 he published *The Present State of Virginia*, a work which remained one of the best sources of information on the commonwealth until late in the century.[18]

Alexander Irvine, who succeeded Jones and taught mathematics for four years, and Joshua Fry who maintained the position for five years, had both been well educated in England or Scotland and had fine backgrounds in the subject. Mathematics as taught in the College at this time was equivalent to that available in the New England colleges. It imparted only the barest rudiments of algebra, geometry, surveying and navigation. Furthermore, the only honorary degree conferred by the College prior to the American Revolution was the degree of Master of Arts conferred upon Benjamin Franklin in 1756 for "the marvellous Discoveries in Natural Philosophy conceived by him and published abroad throughout the entire republic of letters."[19]

By introducing the lecture system, Small brought the teaching of the sciences and mathematics to a new level of effectiveness. In his teaching, he emphasized mathematics as the queen of the sciences, to which all other sciences were related. His students were bombarded by a wide range of subject matter at the same time, a diversity that characterized the Scottish system under which Small had been trained.

The published works used by Small as texts in his classes undoubtedly included *A Course of Experimental Philosophy* by J. T. Desaguliers, first published in London in 1745, several works by George Adams the Elder including *The Construction and Use of Celestial and Terrestrial Globes* first published in 1719 and *Micrographia Illustrata* published in 1746, two works by John Harris, *Lexicon Technicum* and *Astronomical Dialogues* . . .

With A Description of the Orrery, both published in 1704, William Whiston's *Sir Isaac Newton's Mathematical Philosophy More Easily Demonstrated* and Isaac Newton's *Principia*.

He may also have used several works by the lecturer James Ferguson, such as *The Use of the Globes, Description and Use of a New Orrery* and *Astronomy Explained Upon Sir Isaac Newton's Principles*, Edmund Stones's translation into English of Nicolas Bion's *Treatise on Mathematical Instruments* and possibly Charles Leadbetter's work, *Dialling*.

Jefferson particularly delighted in the study of mathematics. He later commented that it became "the passion of my life" and in it he found elements which served him in many other pursuits.[20]

On the weekend, when the president and the divinity professors were attending to their parochial duties off campus, the students spent their time in the neighboring countryside with their hunting dogs and horses, or made the town the scene of their boisterous behavior.

Small and Jefferson avoided these activities by means of long walks and conversation. Small opened his younger companion's mind not only to new concepts in the philosophical world, but also taught him how to observe the living world of nature around him with discovering eyes, and how to subject the physical phenomena to scientific analysis.

Jefferson gained considerably from this association, but Small remained quite unhappy at the College. In addition to the disruption caused by the merry members of the faculty, President Dawson had become a heavy drinker, finally confessing his prediliction when brought before the Board of Visitors. He was pardoned on the promise of improved behavior, but instead he became quite irresponsible and died soon after. Three months passed during which the College remained rudderless, which brought about the deterioration of morale at all levels. The position was subsequently filled by the Reverend William Yates.[21]

Small had other complaints as well. The weather at Williamsburg did not agree with him, and he was constantly unwell. Above all, he was lonely. The closest friend he had was the lawyer George Wythe, and through him he had developed a friendship with the province's lieutenant governor, Francis Fauquier, often called the most elegant gentleman ever seen in Virginia. A fine scholar and a great patron of learning, Fauquier had one fault, a love of "high play" which he introduced into polite society. He was, however, scrupulously honest to a fault in his official dealings, and disdained any of the questionable practises of his predecessors. Despite these associations, Small had much time to himself which he shared more and more with his young student, Jefferson.[22]

As Small's intimate and protegé, Jefferson was admitted to the governor's circle despite the fact that he was much younger than the others. His skill with the violin made him a welcome addition to the musical party the governor held once weekly in the palace. For the first time

Jefferson heard music performed in concert, and brought the concept with him, continuing it with his family at Monticello years later.

Fauquier provided yet another realm of education for Jefferson, that of French and English literature, and Jefferson learned fresh traditions derived from the works of Joseph Addison, Jonathan Swift, Henry St. John Bolingbroke and Alexander Pope, among others. At Fauquier's table he also was kept abreast of current gossip from London as well as news of important events and practises in England, and he began to evaluate by other than parochial Virginia standards. He avoided the governor's penchant for gambling, however. [23]

Wythe, the fourth member of their company, was destined to become a distinguished lawyer, teacher, judge and statesman with whom Jefferson was to remain closely associated for the remainder of Wythe's life. At the time that Jefferson first met him, Wythe was thirty-four years of age, and had the reputation of being the finest Greek and Latin scholar in Virginia. It was their mutual fondness for Greek that helped to bring the lawyer and the student together almost immediately. [24]

Wythe befriended Fauquier soon after the latter's arrival in Williamsburg. According to custom, the appointed governor of the province remained in England while the colony was administered by the lieutenant governor in residence. Fauquier proved to be a particularly successful choice for the position, combining administrative ability with cultural attainments. Although frequently demonstrating a peppery temper, he was nonetheless generous and liberal in manner, and by example and influence he was able to stimulate business and cultivate the arts and sciences. [25]

Shortly after Fauquier's arrival in Williamsburg, Fort Duquesne fell to the British and the tide of the war with the French turned in England's favor. These events were reflected by increased public entertainment and social activities in the Virginia capital. Jefferson arrived at the height of what was called "the golden age" of Virginia's government, attributed largely to Fauquier's administration.

Wythe was as impressed with young Jefferson as Small had been, and invited him frequently to the Wythe table and to participate in the social events at his house. These older friends found Jefferson generally attractive in appearance and dress. His considerable strength and good health belied his thin frame which he had inherited from his mother's side of the family. He was six feet two inches in height and appeared taller because of his sparse build and erect posture.

His angular face with a fair ruddy freckled complexion always bore a bright and cheerful expression, reflecting a vivacious spirit. At this age his hair was said to be in fact not red, as generally reported, but actually auburn or reddish chestnut in color, and it grew thick and silken. His full deepset eyes were light hazel in color, or with flecks of hazel on a grey background, and they easily mirrored each thought that passed through his mind. He had unusually good manners and he was a diverting conversationalist, with a frankness, cordiality and earnestness of tone. Gentle in temper, he was kindly and forgiving. A talented musician, a fine dancer, and a skilled rider, he was capable of any manly sport or exercise. It was not surprising that he became a favored member of the governor's circle.[26]

More than half a century later, Jefferson wrote to a friend about how Small and Wythe had introduced him to Governor Fauquier. "Dr. Small was his [Wythe's] bosom friend, and to me as a father. To his enlightened and affectionate guidance of my studies while at college, I am indebted for everything."[27]

About Wythe, Jefferson was to write,

> his virtue was of the purest tint; his integrity inflexible, and his justice exact; of warm patriotism, and, devoted as he was to liberty, and the natural and equal rights of man, he might truly be called the Cato of his country, without the avarice of the Roman; for a more disinterested person never lived.
>
> Temperance and regularity in all his habits, gave him general good health, and his unaffected modesty and suavity of manners endeared him to everyone. He was of easy elocution, his language chaste, methodical in the arrangement of his matter, learned and logical in the use of it, and of great urbanity in debate; not quick of apprehension, but, with a little time, profound in its penetration, and sound in conclusion. In his philosophy he was firm, and neither troubling, nor perhaps trusting, anyone with his religious creed, he left the world to the conclusion, that religion must be good which could produce a life of such exemplary virtue . . . Mr. Wythe continued to be my faithful and beloved Mentor in youth, and my most affectionate friend through life.[28]

Although primarily preoccupied with his practice and the many political and legal responsiblities thrust upon him, Wythe also manifested an avocation for the sciences. In his study he maintained a collection of instruments of the variety a learned gentleman of his time acquired for his personal edification. There was nothing remarkable about them, and as well as can be determined, they included an orrery or small planetarium, pedestal refracting telescope, a sundial or two, a pair of globes, a portable barometer, a compound microscope, drafting instruments, and possibly an armillary sphere.[29]

It is not known with certainty which or how many instruments Wythe owned when Jefferson was at Williamsburg. By the time of his death he had a useful collection, however, most of which he had acquired after Jefferson's departure. In September 1772 Wythe ordered a telescope from the London merchant John Norton, advising "For a good one I would go as far as eight or ten guineas. I would have a light stand to keep it steady on." Three months later, he sent Norton an order for "a set of [mathematical?] instruments, which . . . may be had for two or three guineas," which he purchased for Jacob Walker, a student then boarding with him. The earliest extant writing of Wythe is a letter or signed order of uncertain date, believed to be 1755, for merchandise including "an aeliopyle a receiver and Naime [sic: Nairne] and Blunt mr. Shermer will be so good as procure for G. Wythe."[30]

Littleton Waller Tazewell, a student who boarded with Wythe while studying law in his office, wrote many years later that in 1787 "About this time Mr. Wythe imported a very complete Electrical Machine together with a fine Air Pump, and sundry other parts of a philosophical apparatus. And when this arrived, most of our leisure moments were employed in making philosophical experiments, and ascertaining the causes of the effects produced."[31]

Late in his life, remembering the interests he had shared with his young student, Wythe specified in his last will and testament, "I give my Books and small Philosophical Apparatus to Thomas Jefferson, President of the United States of America; a legacy considered abstractlie, perhaps not deserving a place in his Museum, but estimated by my Good Will to him the most valuable to him of anything which I have the power to bestow." He also bequeathed his silver cups and gold headed cane to Jefferson.[32]

Jefferson had access also to scientific instruments and apparatus owned by Fauquier, although no mention was made of them in Jefferson's written recollections of the times he spent in the Governor's Palace. The Governor owned a telescope, drafting instruments, a compound microscope, a solar microscope, a camera obscura, a level, a measuring wheel (perambulator) and perhaps others.

Undoubtedly Jefferson participated in experiments and demonstrations made with these instruments both in Wythe's home and in the Governor's Palace, events which were responsible for generating the particular love of scientific instrumentation that Jefferson later demonstrated.

Fauquier had as great an interest in the sciences as Wythe. On July 9, 1758, a few months after his arrival in Williamsburg, the region experienced an unusually heavy hailstorm on an extremely hot Sunday afternoon. The hailstones destroyed the Palace garden as well as all the window panes on the north side of the governor's residence. Fauquier collected a sufficient number of the hailstones to use for cooling wine and freezing cream during the following day. He wrote a careful report of the event, which he sent to his brother in London, reporting the size and shape of the hailstones. The account was subsequently published in the *Philosophical Transactions* of the Royal Society.

Fauquier also maintained a daily record of temperatures, winds and rainfall for the years 1760 to 1762 which was later published in Burnaby's account of his travels in Virginia. It is entirely likely that it was Fauquier's example that inspired Jefferson to begin keeping similar weather records.[33]

Jefferson's association with Wythe and Fauquier and his participation in their discussions continued until Fauquier's death in March 1768 following a lingering illness. Ever preoccupied with the sciences, Fauquier had stipulated in his will that if he should die from a disease of unknown nature, an autopsy could be conducted. After his death, his instruments and other possessions were shipped to his son in England.[34]

Jefferson's love of music was amply fulfilled as a consequence of his regular participation in the weekly concerts held at the palace. He also developed a friendship with Peter Pelham, organist at Bruton Parish Church, whom he often heard play. Occasionally he attended performances of comic operas presented by traveling companies.[35]

Jefferson's interest in books was further influenced in his student years when he and his friend John Walker became members of the restricted campus secret society known as "F.H.C." or the "Flat Hat Club." Membership was limited to six students at a time, and although it "had no useful object," it nevertheless was a most convivial group. With the intention of forming a Club library, the members asked the Reverend Thomas Gwatkin to compile a catalogue of the most useful and valuable books for the purpose. Gwatkin included fifty-nine works on mathematics, natural philosophy and natural history.

Included were such familiar titles as Edmund Halley's *Tables*, Isaac Newton's *Principia*, Smith's *Opticks*, Benjamin Franklin's *Letters*, Joseph Priestley's *Histories of Electricity and of Light and Colours*, Ferguson's *Astronomy*, Cotes's *Hydrostatic Lectures*, Buffon's *Natural History*, Catesby's *Natural History of Virginia*, and works on agriculture, botany and vegetation. The selection, if made during the period that Jefferson was a member, may well have served him as a guide for beginning his own library, which he began to assemble while a student, and which was to include many of the same titles.

Very little has been published about the Flat Hat Club, and although it survives to the present, it remains virtually unknown. An extant certificate of membership of the year 1771 specified that the desire of the membership was "that the youth may learn thoroughly to cultivate virtue, and that studies may grow strong, that eventually it [the youth] may be a great ornament and pillar of things general and particular, to those whose interest it may be to know these things. . . ."[36]

Possibly because of the lack of information about the Club, a general misunderstanding arose that it was a predecessor of the Phi Beta Kappa Society. In 1819 Jefferson replied to two inquiries about the early history of the latter organization, that he knew of the Society's existence by hearsay only and had no information about its origin. In one of his replies he noted "The contrary supposition has probably been founded on an F.H.C. society which existed at Wm & Mary College when I was there, of which I was a member, that was confined to the Alumni of that institution." In a second letter, to Thomas McAuley at Union College, Jefferson reaffirmed that he knew nothing about the Phi Beta Kappa Society. "When I was a student at Wm & Mary college of this state," he went on, "there existed a society called the F.H.C. society, confined to the number of six students only, of which I was a member, but it had no useful object, nor do I know whether it now exists."[37]

Other students who came under Small's influence in this period included John Page, John Walker and Dabney Carr. John Page wrote many years later, "Before I had the benefit of a Philosophical Education at College, with Mr. Jefferson, Mr. Walker, Dabney Carr and others, under the illustrious Professor of Mathematics, Wm. Small, Esq., afterwards well known as the great Dr. Small, of Birmingham, the darling friend of Darwin, History and particularly Military and Naval History, attracted my attention . . . I never thought, however, that I had made any great proficiency in any study, for I was too sociable, and fond of the conversation of my friends, to study as Mr. Jefferson did, who could tear himself away from his dearest friends, and fly to his studies."[38]

Looking back on his college days at the age of sixty-five, Jefferson described to his grandson, Thomas Jefferson Randolph, the difficulties he had experienced. He explained that he had done as much as possible to shield his grandson, but that he himself had had a different experience:

But thrown on a wide world, among entire strangers, without a friend, or guardian to advise, so young too, and with so little experience of mankind, your dangers are great, and still your safety must rest on yourself. A determination never to do what is wrong, prudence and good humor, will go far towards securing to you the estimation of the world. When I recollect that at fourteen years of age, the whole care and direction of myself was thrown on myself entirely, without a relation or friend qualified to advise or guide me, and recollect the various sorts of bad company with which I associated from time to time, I am astonished I did not turn off with some of them, and become as worthless to society as they were. I had the good fortune to become acquainted very early with some characters of very high standing, and to feel the incessant wish that I could ever become what they were. Under temptations and difficulties, I would ask myself what would Dr. Small, Mr. Wythe, Peyton Randolph do in this situation? What course in it will ensure me their approbation? I am certain that this mode of deciding on my conduct, tended more to correctness than any reasoning powers I possessed. Knowing the even and dignified line they pursued, I could never doubt for a moment which of two courses would be in character for them. Whereas, seeking the same object through a process of moral reasoning, and with the jaundiced eye of youth, I should often have erred. From the circumstances of my position, I was often thrown into the society of horse racers, card players, fox hunters, scientific and professional men, and of dignified men; and many a time have I asked myself, in the enthusiastic moment of the death of a fox, the victory of a favorite horse, the issue of a question eloquently argued at the bar, or in the great council of the nation, well, which of these kinds of reputation should I prefer? That of a horse jockey? a fox hunter? an orator? or the honest advocate of my country's rights? Be assured, my dear Jefferson, that these little returns into ourselves, this self-catechising habit, is not trifling nor useless, but leads to the prudent selection and steady pursuit of what is right.[39]

While Jefferson was a student at college, he again had occasion to see Outacity, the Cherokee warrior who had visited his home. He heard him make his great farewell speech to his people at their camp outside Williamsburg before his departure for England. Although he did not understand a word spoken, Jefferson recalled "the moon was in full splendor, and to her he [Outacity] seemed to address himself in his prayers for his own safety on the voyage, and that of his people during his absence; his sounding voice, distinct articulation, animated action, and the solemn silence of his people at their several fires, filled me with awe and admiration."[40]

As Jefferson neared the completion of his second year at the College, he gave serious thought to the selection of a profession, although in fact he had little choice. The Shadwell estate was responsible for the maintenance of his mother and brother and sisters. He had no interest in a military career, and probably would not have been able to obtain a commission even if he were so inclined. Commerce of the province was in British hands and there was no manufacture worth mentioning. In another time and another clime he might have chosen a career in architecture. His indecision was finally resolved by William Small, who encouraged him to choose the law, and George Wythe, who offered him the opportunity to study in his office.

After long deliberation, Jefferson accepted Wythe's offer. He was not certain that he would find career fulfillment in the practice of law, but on the other hand, it would provide splendid training and background for any other career he might choose.[41]

CHAPTER III

LAW AND LEARNING (1762–1772)

The study of the law qualifies a man to be useful to himself, to his neighbors, and to the public. It is the most certain stepping stone to public preferrment in the political line.

Letter from Thomas Jefferson to
Thomas Mann Randolph, Jr., 1790.

Although classes ended in the spring of 1762, and his college career was over, Jefferson remained at Williamsburg for the remainder of that year. Part of that time he spent in George Wythe's office becoming acquainted with the primary requirements of his studies, and the remainder he devoted to social and personal endeavors. It was not until the Christmas holidays approached that he at last began the homeward journey on horseback to Shadwell.

He had every good intention of spending the forthcoming winter months at home pursuing the study of the law. His first assignment was to familiarize himself with *Coke on Littleton*, a monumental volume consisting of the first four parts of Sir Edward Coke's famous commentary, *Institutes of the Lawes of England*. It virtually constituted the lawyer's Bible in the pre-Revolutionary American colonies.

With his volume of *Coke* bulging in his saddle bags, Jefferson followed the custom of the times and called at the homes of friends and acquaintances along the way. As Christmas Day approached, he arrived at the home of one of his friends, and there he remained for several days to participate in the festivities. He had brought his violin with him, and a collection of new minuets he had acquired in Williamsburg, with which he was able to make a substantial contribution to the merriment.[1]

Throughout his visit he was preoccupied, however, with thoughts of Rebecca Burwell, an attractive young lady with whom he had often tripped the light fantastic to the same minuets in the Apollo Room of the Raleigh Tavern. He carried with him what was his most precious possession—a watch paper which Rebecca had cut out and painted and given to him. He placed it tenderly inside the back cover of his pocket watch. As often as he remembered the thick volume of Coke which lay as a heavy burden not only on his lap but on his conscience, his mind would wander to thoughts of his beloved.

He was horrified, therefore, by "an unspeakable event" which marred his visit, and which he reported in a letter to Page, who was privy to his feelings for Rebecca. During the night some "cursed rats," undoubtedly at the instigation of the Devil himself, he claimed, had eaten through his pocket book which he had placed only a foot away from his head as he slept. They had carried off his "jemmy worked silk garters" as well as the new minuets he had brought with him. To add to his distress, it had rained heavily during the night, and in the morning he had found his watch swimming in a pool of water.

"The subtle particles of the water with which the case was filled had, by their penetration, so overcome the cohesion of the particles of the paper of which my dear picture and watch paper were composed, that in attempting to take them out to dry them,—good God! *Mens horret referre!* [My mind shudders to recall it!]—my fingers gave them such a rent as I fear I never shall get over." Then he added, "And now, although the picture may be defaced, there is so lively an image of her imprinted in my mind, that I shall think of her too often, I fear, for my peace of mind; and too often, I am sure, to get through old Coke this winter."[2]

Jefferson remained at Shadwell from the end of December until the following autumn, determined to devote most of his time to his law books. During the winter months he rose at five in the morning and retired at nine o'clock at night. In the summer months he went to bed at ten.

There was little to distract him at home, except occasional visitors. However, he made up for the time spent with them by adopting the practise of spending twice as much time with his books thereafter. In the evening after supper he roamed the premises, enjoying looking over the gardens and the farm, and invariably he took a long walk to the top of his favorite mountain, which later he named "Monticello." Then, before retiring, he played the violin, often accompanying his sister Jane as she sang. He rode horseback every day, and by means of his walking and riding managed to keep himself in fit condition.[3]

The change from the relatively exciting life he had left behind in Williamsburg and the unchanging routine he found in the countryside proved to be considerable, and he soon began to experience increasing boredom. He was separated from his friends and acquaintances, and there was no one with whom he could share his thoughts except his sister. There was little to inspire him in the voluminous *Coke*, and the days passed slowly. He turned to correspondence for relief, and by this means sought out some of his friends.

"I have not a syllable to write to you about," he addressed his friend Page. "All things here appear to me to trudge on in one and the same round; we rise in the morning that we may eat breakfast, dinner and supper, and go to bed again that we may get up again the next morning and do the same; so that you never saw two peas more alike than yesterday and today."[4]

Although it was never stated in his correspondence or other writings or by those who knew him at the time, there is a definite impression that Jefferson may have been uneasy and not entirely happy during the months that he spent at Shadwell. It is possible that this may have been due to his mother, although he left no clue to the degree of warmth or lack of it in his relationship with her. Burdened as she was with the care of a large family, including her children and some thirty slaves on the farm, she undoubtedly felt deeply the loss of her husband and had little time for leisurely pursuits or conversation. Did she perhaps resent her oldest son's complete freedom from these responsibilities, at the same time that she found herself tied to the inexorable routine of maternity, housekeeping and farm management? The answer may never be known.[5]

Jefferson wrote often to Page, who lived in another and wondrous world at "Rosewell," his family estate in Gloucester County. He confided his most intimate thoughts in those letters, and among other things discussed his desire for foreign travel. He wanted to visit England, Holland, France, Spain and Italy. There he would buy "a good fiddle" and then move on to Egypt and return to Virginia by way of Canada. Such an itinerary would require at least two or three years, he told Page. He did not have the means, however, and this was all daydreaming.[6]

During this interlude at Shadwell he remained hopelessly in love with the same Rebecca Burwell, he reported to his friend, although there is no evidence that he saw her during this period. He had met and admired a number of young girls at Williamsburg, including Betsy Moore, a girl named Nancy, Sukey Potter, Judy Burwell and of course the incomparable Rebecca. During these seemingly endless months, *Coke on Littleton* was his constant companion and for a change of pace he occasionally turned to reading in other subjects and refreshed himself in the Greek, Latin and French languages.[7]

Finally, in October 1763, Jefferson packed his clothing and other belongings he would require away from home. Bidding farewell to his family, he rode off to Williamsburg, where he planned to remain until his studies had been completed. After settling himself in his rooms in a house on one of the side streets paralleling the Duke of Gloucester Street, he began work in George Wythe's office. The General Court convened during the month of his arrival, and he dutifully attended its sessions, watching and listening to its proceedings, and then later questioned Wythe about them. He may have also attended sessions of the county courts and hustings, the local courts held in some parts of Virginia.[8]

It is surprising in some ways that Jefferson had chosen Wythe as his instructor in law in preference to John or Peyton Randolph, sons of his great-uncle John Randolph. Both were eminent lawyers living in Williamsburg, and were personal friends and kinsmen. Yet it may have been for the very reason of relationship that he did not select them. He could not have made a better choice of preceptor, however, for Wythe was one of the most respected lawyers of the region, and proved to be an excellent instructor.

From the time of his arrival in Williamsburg, Jefferson's days and nights were totally filled, as he directed his attention to his studies in earnest. He assisted Wythe with the daily drudgery of his office, researching cases which Wythe would later try in court, drawing up papers and briefs as required and spending much of his time in research in the law library in the Capitol.

Thanks to his father's tutelage, Jefferson was gifted with a clear writing hand even as a young man and he was a competent draftsman, so that he was given no end of the writing and copying chores of the office. Wythe customarily wrote in two handwritings until rheumatism later in life forced him to use an amanuensis. One form resembled print, and the other was a cursive hand. He never capitalized the beginnings of sentences unless it was at the beginning of a paragraph, and he used the lower case letter "i" for the first person. It is not surprising, therefore, that Jefferson soon learned to write in the same manner and adopted Wythe's peculiarities, although he wrote with greater correctness and used the capital letter "I" for the first person.[9]

Despite the heavy schedule in Wythe's office, Jefferson'managed to find sufficient time for relaxation. He kept horses and spent his leisure in riding. He lost few opportunities to attend the frequent balls and other social events held at Williamsburg, where he again met some of the young ladies for whom he had pined during his enforced solitude at Shadwell. He met Rebecca again at a ball in the Apollo Room, and when he was alone with her, he began to stammer. It is likely that she was already engaged to another at the time of this meeting, for she was married a few months later. Jefferson made much of his loss in his letters to Page, but in time his ardor diminished.[10]

Works of fiction had not yet become popular during the second half of the eighteenth century and Cervantes was probably the only fiction writer that Jefferson read. He also found great delight in the works of Shakespeare, Moliere, Homer and old English ballads, which provided diversion from the musty law volumes which occupied most of his reading time. Bacon, Locke and Newton he had designated his "trinity of the three greatest men the world has ever produced," and throughout his life their works formed the basis of many of his endeavors, particularly in the sciences.[11]

Jefferson now resumed his association with William Small, and together they participated in the weekly concerts and occasional receptions held by Fauquier in the Governor's Palace. His preoccupation with the sciences, which had been nurtured by Small in the classroom and out of school association during Jefferson's student days, was renewed once more. It was furthered by the exhilarating discussions on natural philosophy, the rights of man and the laws of nature which were part of the table conversation in the Governor's Palace.[12]

Formal instruction in the law was not available in the American colonies until after the American Revolution, and it was the general practice for one aspiring to such a career to spend two or more years reading the law under the tutelage of a practising lawyer. It was not a lucrative profession in Virginia in the colonial period. The fees were sharply restricted by statute, as a consequence of the jealousy of dominant landowners and their desire to discourage petty practitioners. Consequently the law as a career was possible only for landowners like Jefferson, whose income from their plantations supplemented the meagre earnings derived from a law practice.

Law books of the type known today were extremely few. Even English and Continental works on the law were less than plentiful, and there was not a single report or treatise on the subject published in the American colonies. Legal literature for the most part consisted of abridgements of the works of Bacon, Rolle and Viner, the commentaries of Coke, Plowden and Bracken, Coke's notes on Littleton and reports and summaries, which had just begun to circulate, of significant cases before the English courts. Jefferson copied out abstracts of cases in the Equity and Common Law Courts, including Vernon's *Chancery Reports*, the *Principles of Equity* of Lord Kane, the personal reports of William Peere Williams and Finch's *Precedents in Chancery*.

Sir Edward Coke's *Institutes of the Lawes of England*, which first appeared in 1628, was based on Sir Thomas Littleton's treatise on *Tenures*, first published in 1481 and 1482, the earliest treatise on English law.

The copy owned and used by Jefferson was probably the twelfth edition, published in 1738. The *Tenures* was written in the legal French of the reign of Edward III with numerous Latin equivalents. On these Coke discoursed, sometimes devoting more than thirty pages to a passage of several lines. To add to the difficulties of studying this work, it was printed in black letter type. Jefferson's careful perusal of Coke and his familiarity with it was reflected again and again in his later legislative work, such as the particulars of the bill relating to tenants that he proposed to the Virginia House of Delegates.[13]

Jefferson went on to study the texts of English statutes from the Magna Carta to the reign of James I, the treatises on jurisdiction which formed the other three parts of *Coke on Littleton* and criminal law. He moved on from *Coke* to search out the sources on which English law was based in the period preceding the Norman Conquest. Such in-depth study was not required but even as a student he hated superficial knowledge. No one practising law in his time could be said to have had a greater knowledge of the history of law than did Wythe's energetic young student. As a consequence the history of law provided a remarkable training in research, a discipline that would serve him in his scientific endeavors all through his life.

To facilitate his studies, and to help him later in his practise, Jefferson initiated a commonplace book. As he informed a friend in 1814, he became accustomed to making extracts of the technical works he read. "I was in the habit of abridging and commonplacing what I read meriting it, and of sometimes mixing my own reflections on the subject." He lived pen in hand as he studied, abbreviating common terms, inserting references in old French and law-Latin from other authorities as they were applicable.[14]

During the course of these studies, Jefferson was struck by the realization that the Bible had inadvertently become part of the common law of England, and consequently of the common law of the English colonies in America. It was on the basis of this principle that witches had been hanged, for example, and that labor was forbidden on Sunday. He was convinced that this was basically wrong and due to error, which he was determined to trace to its source.

After considerable effort he discovered the source to be in one of the ancient law books in which the author had converted the words "ancient scripture" to "Holy Scripture." He was able to prove that the original statement meant exactly what it had stated, namely, the ancient writings and the old records of the Church, not the Bible. He traced the use of the term back through his law books to Sir Matthew Hale who had written, "Christianity is parcel of the laws of England." He discovered that Hale provided no source for his statement "but rests the opinion on his own; which was good in all cases in which his mind received no bias from his bigotry, his superstitions, his visions about sorceries, demons, etc. The power of these over him is exemplified in his hanging of the witches."

Jefferson traced the error further to the time that it had resulted in the establishment of laws making it criminal to write against Christianity or to utter words implying disbelief of it. The English jurist, Sir William Blackstone, whose four-volume work on English law was published in the late eighteenth century, incorporated the doctrine in his *Commentaries*, and the British judge, William Murray, Earl of Mansfield, in his decisions pronounced "the essential principles of *revealed* religion are part of the common law."

Jefferson noted that as a consequence the public was left "to find out, at our peril, what, in the opinion of the judge, and, according to the measure of his foot or his faith, *are* the essential principles of revealed religion obligatory on us as part of the common law."[15]

As he continued his research, Jefferson traced the error back into antiquity as far as the seventh century, when Christianity was first introduced into England. Examining every source from King Alfred to Henry de Bracton in the thirteenth century, he was unsuccessful in finding any trace of the adoption of Christianity, formal or informal, as part of the common law. The insertion of the chapters of Exodus from the Old Testament among the laws of Alfred were, in his opinion, "an awkward and monkish fabrication." He believed, furthermore, that Alfred's adoption of the Ten Commandments was an express exclusion of the laws in Exodus, which were suited only to Jews. Jefferson wrote, "The adoption of a part proves the rejection of the rest, as municipal law."

Although in this paper Jefferson demonstrated an aversion for the clergy as an order, he nonetheless exhibited veneration for the Christian religion itself. "The fact that Christianity is truth," he explained, "does not make it a part of the law of England, just as the fact that the Newtonian philosophy, *being reason and verity itself*, in the opinion of all but infidels and Cartesians. . . . They are protected under the wing of the common law from the dominion of other sects, but not erected into dominion over them."[16]

In Jefferson's opinion, it was particularly undesirable to combine Church and State in his time. Such a union had already amply demonstrated its potential evils in Virginia. There the clergy had fallen into considerable contempt and as a consequence of their own indolence and dissolute behavior, were placed in a false and demoralizing position.

This was due in part to the fact that the clergy were very poorly paid. A clergyman, if he was considered to be of relatively high quality, received the equivalent of less than £200 a year, paid in tobacco, and his salary could be as little as £60 if he was considered to be otherwise. He was provided with a glebe, revenue-yielding church-owned land, equivalent to a good working farm which might or might not be stocked and provided with one or two families of slaves, depending on the vestry's inclinations. For baptisms, marriages and burials he received fixed fees paid in tobacco.

Too often clergy were appointed without a sufficient review having been made of their experience and fitness, and no supervision was provided. Although geographically the parishes were of considerable size, generally they contained too few families to form even a modest congregation. For these among other reasons, the Virginia clergy in general earned a reputation for drunkenness and licentiousness.[17]

Jefferson moved his lodgings several times during the years that he remained at Williamsburg. For a time he shared a room for study with two other young students, John Tyler and Frank Wallis. Eventually he acquired larger lodgings and brought his black servant Jupiter from Shadwell to attend his needs.

During this period Jefferson was occasionally visited by his friend, Patrick Henry, who often came to the capital when the General Court was in session. From time to time Henry borrowed books from Jefferson's library, including the works of David Hume, and Jefferson noted that he usually returned the books unread. Henry had not yet become well known and moved about the streets of the city unrecognized as a public figure. Certainly he did not go unnoticed, for he dressed in shabby coarse clothes and appeared so countrified that his presence frequently brought comment from those who observed him.

Jefferson had first met Henry before entering college, during Christmas holidays at the home of Captain Nathaniel West Dandridge. Henry was seven years older, but they found much in common and during the two weeks of their stay they shared the pleasant company with dancing and holiday festivities. Henry was a talented fiddler although he played only by ear. Not in the least concerned with fashion in dress, he had manners that reflected those of deer hunters, with whom Henry spent much of his time. Nonetheless, he had an engaging personality and a native genius with which he was able to charm many, Jefferson among them.[18]

It was not until much later that Henry was to manifest his talents as an orator. Despite his appearance, "the forest-born Demosthenes," as he had been described, became "Mr. Henry" when he rose in court. When he appeared before the House of Representatives in 1764, his oratorical powers were demonstrated so forcefully that during the next session of the House a vacancy was made for him, and he was elected to a seat.[19]

When Jefferson attained legal age in April 1764, he spent his birthday preparing to undertake measurements of the height above the creeks at Williamsburg. Presumably he borrowed the instruments required, possibly from Fauquier or Wythe. He wrote to Page and invited him to join in the project. One creek was a tributary of the James River, and the other of the York River, both of which were navigable to within one mile of the capital.[20]

Now that he had come into his inheritance and formally assumed his role as head of his family, he made several financial arrangements. From this time forward he charged the costs of his education and maintenance to his own account and no longer against his father's estate. He reached a decision concerning the lands he and his brother had inherited from their father, and chose the lands along the Rivanna River as being more desirable than those on the Fluvanna River, which then would go to his brother upon his achieving legal age.

The lands Jefferson selected consisted of a tract of two thousand three hundred and fifty acres. Excluded was the family homestead at Shadwell, which had been left to his mother for her lifetime, but he rented it and its slaves from her, and continued to live there. He did not yet have much time to devote to agricultural interests, but he spent many hours maintaining the financial records, keeping careful notes of his business arrangements with his mother as well as a special account for his sister Elizabeth.[21]

In the autumn of 1764 Jefferson was greatly saddened by William Small's departure for England. Various reasons have been suggested for the professor's decision to leave the College of William and Mary. There was the fact that his six year appointment had come to an end. Although he had important close friends in the community of Williamsburg, including Wythe and Fauquier, Small also had powerful enemies on the College's Board of Visitors. In common with most of the faculty, he had strongly opposed the attempt of the Board to require the president and masters to abide by all the regulations which it had imposed, with the threat that failure to do so would result in forfeiture of their posts.[22]

At the time of his departure, Small was given a commission by the College administration to purchase science-teaching instruments and apparatus for the College. For the purpose the Virginia government had appropriated the sum of £450, a surprisingly substantial amount in that period, which would have been equivalent of between three and five thousand dollars and perhaps even more.

Upon his arrival in England, Small contacted Benjamin Franklin in London and obtained from him a letter of introduction to the manufacturer Matthew Boulton in Birmingham. Franklin also took Small to meetings of the Royal Society and introduced him to some of its members.[23]

Small was eminently successful in fulfilling his commission, and in 1767 purchased and shipped back to the College a large collection of scientific instruments and apparatus, at a total cost of £332.4.0. The instruments and apparatus were said to have been among the finest available in England. No complete record survives, except for a folded sheet of paper in Small's handwriting listing more than forty items with individual prices. A large number had been purchased from the leading London instrument makers including Edward Nairne and Peter Dollond. Notable were an achromatic telescope, a double microscope and a solar microscope all made by Peter Dollond, and an electrical machine with numerous attachments made by Nairne. It is apparent from the part of the purchase list that survives, that the selection provided the College with an impressive range of equipment for science teaching, some of which may survive.[24]

In 1767 Jefferson expanded his record keeping by means of a pocket-sized memorandum book which he carried about with him. In it he noted legal memoranda, financial notes concerning expenditures and payments made, fees paid and similar entries relating to property. He also recorded miscellaneous information, filling his memorandum books with many other similar entries derived from personal observation or accounts of his neighbors and friends, or copied from books.

Later, when he began construction of a new home, he filled his memorandum books with an extensive miscellany relating to building materials and techniques with which he was greatly concerned at the time. These were not idle exercises in any sense of the word, but a compilation of information which he fully expected would later be useful. Kept informally, the first entries were made in the summer of 1767, and thereafter he carried these pocket-sized books with him on his travels, each night taking the time to note the expenditures made each day as well as other items that aroused his interest.[25]

Particularly in these memorandum books as well as in a record he called his *Garden Book* he recorded time and motion spent, a habit which became a major preoccupation as he grew older. He became, in effect, a self-trained efficiency expert, always questioning how time and labor could be saved. It was this characteristic that led him later in life to note methods of construction, unusual devices and utilitarian objects which caught his attention during his travels, and many of which he subsequently modified for his own convenience.[26]

During the later years of his study of law, Jefferson was often approached by other law students requesting advice about reading matter, as well as by parents seeking recommendations for the education of their sons. He prepared an outline for a young man about to embark on law studies which was undoubtedly based on the daily schedule he had pursued. First of all, Jefferson specified, it was necessary to master Latin and French as well as natural philosophy and mathematics.[27]

In 1765 Jefferson took the initiative in organizing the clearing of the Rivanna River of obstructions to make it navigable. During a visit to Shadwell he had learned that someone had successfully used a canoe on the lower waters of the river, a report which inspired him to investigate the obstructed sections. By means of a canoe he surveyed the river and came to the conclusion that loose rock could be removed to make transportation on the waterway possible. He estimated that it could be cleared for a distance of twenty-two miles without excessive cost.

He organized a public subscription to fund the project and raised £200. He also aroused the interest of his former guardian, Dr. Walker, who was also his neighbor and a member of the House of Burgesses. With Walker's assistance, an act was passed by the Assembly authorizing the clearing of the great falls of the James River, the Chickahominy and the Rivanna or North Branch of the James, to be achieved by private means. Jefferson was one of the trustees organized to receive subscriptions locally, probably because he was the one who had initated the project.

The clearing of the Rivanna was completed within the next five years. Fallen trees were removed, sluices were cut through rapids, and long dams were constructed by means of rock piles to direct water into the sluices. Thereafter the river provided a useful means of transportation for agricultural produce and other goods.[28]

On the first of October, Jefferson suffered the loss of his oldest sister, Jane, who was twenty-five years of age. Jefferson considered her his equal in understanding, and they shared many hours together. They often sang together at home and along the banks of the Rivanna near Shadwell; he frequently accompanied her with his violin. Two of his sisters had married and moved away, and since he had little in common with the remaining children who were much younger, he continued to feel Jane's loss for many years.[29]

In 1766 Jefferson began to keep records of plantings of the flower and vegetable gardens, trees and shrubs and other details relating to gardening, which he continued for more than a half century. His first entries were for the blooming of various shrubs and flowers in the month of March. Each year he recorded his planting and sowing in great detail, as well as his brickmaking operation after he began his new home on the mountain. Although he kept records of the garden from 1766, it was not until 1774 that he entered them in a new manuscript volume that he named the *Garden Book*.

It was in this volume that Jefferson first noted some of the remarkable statistics for which he later became known. The *Garden Book*, and the *Farm Book* which also was begun in 1774, are almost identical in appearance and binding, and have the same paper and a similar number of pages.[30]

After the passage of the Stamp Act, Jefferson did not again refer to his grandiose plans to visit Europe and England. The political events of the time may have lessened his desire to see the motherland, and since his farms were not yielding an adequate crop of tobacco annually, he did not have sufficient funds for foreign travel. Instead, he decided to make a tour through the colonies during his last summer vacation.

Jefferson's curiosity had been aroused by discussion of inoculation for smallpox which was being performed in Philadelphia by Dr. William Shippen, Jr., and he determined to go there. He was also curious about how people lived outside the commonwealth of Virginia, and planned to visit Annapolis and New York as well. In early May 1766, at the age of twenty-three, he set out in a horse and carriage driven by one of his young black slaves. They crossed endless rivers: the York, Pamunkey, Rappahannock, Potomac, Pawtuxent, Patapsco, Susquehanna, Delaware, Passaic, Hackensack, and the Hudson. The list does not include some fifty smaller streams and the wide shallows of the Chesapeake which they traversed and which had to be forded or crossed by ferry boats propelled by poles.

At Annapolis, where he lingered for several days, he admired the city and particularly the houses. He attended the lower house of the Maryland Assembly, which was in session. He noted that the business of the Maryland Assembly was conducted much more informally than in the Virginia House of Burgesses, and that the Assembly lacked the degree of dignity and decorum which was manifested in the latter. It was during this visit that the first news of the repeal of the Stamp Act came, to much public rejoicing.

At Annapolis Jefferson had his slave return home and he continued alone. Driving through Delaware and Pennsylvania, he observed how the country differed from that of tidewater Virginia and the Piedmont region with which he was familiar. He admired the cultivated fields of grain, clover and flax, and the great orchards he passed along the way. It was the most pleasant part of his journey.[31]

Upon his arrival in Philadelphia he called upon Dr. John Morgan, professor of medicine at the College of Philadelphia. He had brought with him a letter of introduction from his physician, Dr. George Gilmer. Then he had himself inoculated against smallpox, probably by Dr. William Shippen, Jr. The method in use at that time was called "variolation," which carried considerable risk and from which a high mortality resulted. Despite general opposition to the practice, Jefferson decided to take the risk, and suffered no great ill effects as a consequence. It was not until much later that the improved methods of Dr. Edward Jenner were instituted, in which Jefferson was to play a major role.[32]

Philadelphia was much larger than any other city he had ever seen, with a population of between eighteen and twenty thousand residents, and he was consequently greatly impressed. Continuing to New York, he attempted to observe as much of that city as possible. He found it to be somewhat smaller than Philadelphia and less attractive. He made his return to Virginia by boat, arriving home in July, the entire sojourn having taken three months.

He noted that after arriving in Virginia he spent one night in a tavern operated by a lady who had just returned from the funeral of a young man in the neighborhood, who had died after having been bled twenty-six times. This incident remained in Jefferson's memory, and he later voiced strong disapproval of the common practice of bleeding.[33]

It was during the years of his law study that he undertook to build a library for himself. Among the series of records he had begun to maintain when he was of a very early age was his "Literary Bible," in which he recorded passages extracted from books he had read and which provides an invaluable record of his preoccupation with the classical writers and natural philosophy. During these years he often frequented the offices of the *Virginia Gazette* where books were sold and spent time perusing the volumes imported from England, purchasing those to be added to his growing library.[34]

Languages particularly intrigued him. "To read the Latin and Greek authors in their original is a sublime luxury," Jefferson wrote many years later, "and I deem luxury in science to be at least as justifiable as in architecture, painting, gardening, or the other arts. I enjoy Homer in his own language infinitely beyond Pope's translation of him, and both beyond the dull narrative of the same events by Dares Phrygius; and it is an innocent enjoyment. I thank on my knees him who directed my early education for having put into my possession this rich source of delight; and I would not exchange it for anything which I could then have acquired, and have not since acquired."[35]

To his knowledge of Latin and Greek, he added other languages. He perfected his French soon after he had begun the study of law, and then he taught himself Italian. It was probably in February 1764 that he began to study that language seriously. At that time he purchased a volume of Niccolò Macchiavelli's writings, two other historical works in Italian and an Italian-English dictionary. He mastered the language so well that he was able to read Niccolò Macchiavelli's *The Prince* and Giovanni Battista Beccaria's *Dell'Electricismo Naturale ed Artificiale* in the original. Next he attempted to learn Anglo-Saxon which he found useful because of the many legal terms that originated in that language. Wythe, who was himself an accomplished linguist, encouraged him in his language studies.

Jefferson was among the first in the American colonies and in English-speaking nations to make a study of the Anglo-Saxon language. After tracing thousands of English words to their ancient sources in Old English, he arranged the resulting roots alphabetically to form the first Anglo-Saxon dictionary. It was not until the nineteenth century that the study of English philology and Old English became the basis of advanced study in English, American and Continental universities.[36]

In his autobiography, Jefferson later summed up his law career with the brief statement, "In 1767 he [Wythe] led me to the practice of the law at the Bar of the General Court, at which I continued until the Revolution shut up the Courts of Justice."[37]

Having spent approximately three years in law study, he engaged in its practice for seven years, followed by two more years devoted to reforming the laws of Virginia, so that approximately twelve years of his life were devoted to the law. The events of the times were to change the deadly dull prose of the musty law tomes, to which he had dedicated so much of his early years, into living gospel, and convert the principles of the rights of man into familiar language of the day, a conversion in which he was to play a major role.

Jefferson was twenty-four when he began to practice law in Williamsburg, a career which he undertook with the full awareness that it would not be a lucrative profession, particularly in Virginia in that period. The large volume of work provided to the lawyer in New England and the Middle Colonies from trade and commerce were lacking in Virginia, and payment in hard cash was notable by its rarity.

Soon after he had begun his practice, Jefferson was asked by his uncle, Thomas Turpin, who had married Peter Jefferson's sister, to undertake the supervision of the law studies of his cousin Philip Turpin. Jefferson declined on the basis that he did not plan to remain at Shadwell more than two months during that year, after which time he planned to move to the house he was presently intending to build. Nor did he expect to be able to spend a greater proportion of his time at home thereafter, so that it would be an injustice to Philip.

Furthermore, he did not need an assistant and it was his view that placing a young student to study with an attorney might prove to be rather a hindrance than a help. The best assistance that could be provided to the young man would be to direct his reading, and the order in which the works were to be read. Accordingly, Jefferson prepared a study plan which would serve the purpose. The problem remaining was the availability of the books, for "a lawyer without books would be like a workman without tools." Jefferson provided a list of the necessary works which he estimated could be purchased for £100 sterling.

He offered, however, that if Philip should follow his suggestions, "I shall endeavor as often as possible to take your house in my way to and from Williamsburgh [sic] as it will afford me a double satisfaction of observing his progress in science and of seeing yourself, my aunt, and the family."[38]

Jefferson did not have the voice required for court use due to a slight throat defect, which created some diffidence in his manner when he rose to speak before an audience. His voice achieved an odd huskiness when he raised it above conversational level, rendering him almost incomprehensible. Although he spoke well and fluently, this characteristic made public speaking distasteful for him, and he rarely addressed the legislature or similar bodies. Furthermore, his preoccupation with precision of statement was unsuitable to oratory.

However, during his youth his speaking abilities must have been greater than in later life, for Edmund Randolph once commented that Jefferson spoke "with ease, perspecuity, and elegance." He was eminently successful as an attorney, a profession which in his time required constant oratorical display. Undoubtedly his masterful grasp of the fundamental principles of the law and his unsurpassed ability to express himself in writing compensated adequately for any deficiency he may have experienced in public speaking.[39]

Although law was the only practical career open to Jefferson, and he was brilliantly prepared for the practice of law, it was not the career that best fitted his personality. His inquisitive mind would have been best suited for the role of the scholar and the pursuit of the sciences, and dedicated to writing for which his sense of style and ability for clear expression were eminently adapted. Such opportunities were not available to young men in Virginia in the mid-eighteenth century, however, and the law remained the only practical career.[40]

Jefferson's greatest pleasure in the law was not in its practice, but in the opportunity it afforded him to search out colonial records and early statutes from their scattered repositories, tracing existing laws to their origin, copying them and preserving the originals when he could obtain them. Beginning while a law student, he sought out the colony's earliest records and transcribed a great number of them, particularly those originals that were in poor condition.

He also searched out manuscript and printed copies of others. He often wrapped fragile papers in oil cloth and sealed them by sewing to protect them from air and further damage. As he later wrote to Wythe,

"I observed that many of them [early records] were already lost, and many more on the point of being lost, as existing in only single copies in the hands of careful or curious individuals, on whose death they would probably be used for waste paper, I set myself therefore to work, to collect all which were then existing, in order that when the day would come in which the public should avert to the magnitude of their loss in these precious monuments of our property, and our history, a part of their regret might be spared by information that a portion had been saved from the wreck, which is worthy of their attention and preservation."[41]

It was as a consequence of this valiant preservation effort conducted during his years of study and practise of the law, that in 1807 Jefferson was able to lend his collection of documents to William Waller Hening to use as the basis for his compilation of his massive work *Statutes at Large*. Hening's work achieved Jefferson's ambition to save these important documents "from the worm, from the natural decay of the paper, from the accidents of fire, or those of removal when it is necessary for any public purpose . . . [from] ravages of fire and ferocious enemies."[42]

In his first year of practice, Jefferson was involved in 68 cases, and during the next four years his practise steadily increased. In his second year he acted as counsel in 115 cases in the General Court, 198 cases in 1769, 221 cases in 1770 and 237 cases in 1771. Thereafter his practice lessened due to his increasing involvement with political issues; in 1772 he dealt with only 154 cases, in 1773 with 127 cases, and he handled only 29 cases during the early part of 1774. He kept a careful account of them and maintained a separate record book for his fees, noting amounts actually received, and those still owing, which were considerably greater than those received. His practice was successful and unusually active at a time when the economy of Virginia was experiencing a depression and debts had mounted and assets diminished as a consequence of unresolved problems of land tenure, boundary disputes and a criminal law that was long outmoded.

Jefferson's records related only to cases heard before the General Court. It has been assumed by biographers that he also practised in the county courts but he did not do so because in that period it was unlawful for a lawyer who was not a barrister to practise in both the General Court and the county courts. A barrister was defined as a lawyer who had graduated from one of the Inns of Court in London and was qualified to try cases before the superior courts of England. In Jefferson's time several barristers practised law in Virginia, but he did not qualify among them.

Jefferson's casebook contained numerous drafts of deeds, wills and pleadings which were heard before the county courts. There is no doubt that he visited their quarterly sessions particularly in Albemarle and Augusta Counties, since much of his business before the General Court related to appeals from county court cases. These visits were also made to collect money owed, and for consultation with lawyers handling the original cases in county courts before they came to the General Court. He probably also appeared in county courts as executor, guardian or witness as occasion demanded.[43]

The quarterly Court Days were special occasions and brought people from great distances in the countryside, not only to serve as litigants and witnesses, but also to collect and pay debts, and to conduct other business outside the courts. It was a great occasion for trading horses, selling and buying slaves, auctioning property and providing the family with a rare outing. Bands of entertainers performed and peddlers hawked their wares, making it an exciting scene.

Jefferson had other reasons for attending the Court Days at Albemarle County. Since he became a Burgess of that county in 1769, these occasions provided him with an opportunity to meet his constituents.

Land claims and petitions of lapsed land claims pre-empted by new patents and caveats on such claims were heard before the Governor's Council. Other cases before the Council included a dispute over the office of sheriff of Amherst County and a proceeding to remove from office a justice of the peace. Older attorneys also occasionally utilized Jefferson's assistance in the preparation of cases for trial, requiring him to travel to various county seats.

It was most unusual for a young Virginia lawyer to begin his practice in the General Court, the lawyers of which were considered to be the elite among the practitioners of the law. Some of them had practised as barristers in England before coming to Virginia, and others had begun their careers in county courts. Undoubtedly Jefferson was accepted primarily as a result of the good offices of George Wythe, who was highly regarded, and from whom he had received the most thorough preparation before appearing before the examining board.[44]

As had his father before him, Jefferson was appointed justice of the peace. Since it was customary for a landowner to become involved with the politics of the commonwealth, Jefferson stood for representative of his county in the House of Burgesses. According to custom, he solicited votes by visiting his neighbors and others in the county and inviting them to Shadwell for a bowl of cheer. They came and partook of the cakes and punch which he provided, and later voted for him. His electioneering costs totalled four pounds nineteen shillings and threepence, equivalent to approximately twenty-five dollars. Jefferson was elected, and attended the sessions as they were scheduled.[45]

In 1768 Jefferson began the construction of a new home near the summit of his "low mountain." He had originally planned to call his home "The Hermitage," according to an entry in his *Memorandum Book*, but soon changed it to "Monticello." The name "Monticello" was un-doubtedly inspired by his admiration for Andrea Palladio, the sixteenth century Italian architect whose books he owned and studied avidly as he progressed with plans for his estate. In the second volume of Palladio's *Four Books of Architecture*, the author described the surroundings of his most famous structure, the Villa Rotunda near Vicenza. He wrote that it was pleasantly situated on the top of a *monticello* ("low mountain" or "little mountain"), washed by a navigable river at one side of its base and surrounded by hills cultivated with fruit trees on the other to form a *gran teatro* or theatre setting.[46]

He had toyed with the idea of building his own house long before he undertook the project in earnest. Some time previously he had written to Page that he intended to build "a small house, which shall contain a room for myself and another for you, unless Belinda [Rebecca Burwell] think proper to favour us with her company, in which case I will enlarge the plan as much as she pleases." This letter was part of the amusing correspondence which transpired between the two friends and was not to be taken seriously, for Jefferson never proceeded with designs for such a building.[47]

In planning his new home, Jefferson discarded the traditional plans of Virginia plantations. While at college he had purchased his first book on the subject of architecture from an old cabinetmaker who lived near the College gates. Later, in 1764 he purchased copies of Dodsley's *Description of 'The Leasowes'* and Shenstone's *Unconnected Thoughts on Gardening*. In the following year he added the volume by John James on *Gardening*, a translation made in 1728 of a French treatise by Dargenville and Le Blond, who had codified the style of Le Nôtre. There is no doubt that he was strongly influenced by these works in developing his designs for his house and its landscaping, particularly the works of Shenstone, whose house "The Leasowes" had achieved fame as one of the important smaller landscaped estates in England.[48]

The first task in the project was to fell the trees that covered the crest of the mountain and to trim the timber so that it could be used later for building the structure. In 1767 he had already begun assembling building materials. The next part of the work was to level the top of the mountain where the house was to be erected. In May 1768 Jefferson paid Theodorick Munford £84 sterling "to lay out in the best crown glass and 150 yards window line" to be ordered from England.

He also bargained with John Moore, a neighbor, to level a square of two hundred and fifty square feet of the summit before Christmas, in exchange for one hundred and eighty bushels of wheat and twenty-four bushels of corn. The leveling was begun on the northeast end. Seven laborers were then put to work to excavate a foundation for the house.

It was probably during this period that he bought the first of the scientific instruments that were to form a large collection and become an important part of his life. He paid Robert Cobb of Albemarle County to make a spirit level for him, which he probably used for laying out the house site.[49]

An example of Jefferson's statistical method was recorded in his *Garden Book* relating to the earth moved during the construction of the house.

> Julius Shard fills the two-wheeled barrow in 3 minutes and carries it 30 yards in 1-½ minutes more. Now this is four loads of the common barrow with one wheel. So suppose that the four loads put in, in the same time, viz., 3 minutes, 4 trips will take 1-½ minutes—6, which added to 3 filling is—9 to fill and carry the same earth which was filled and carried in the two-wheeled barrow in 4-½ minutes. From a trial I made with the same two-wheeled barrow, I found that a man would dig and carry to the distance of 50 yards, 5 cubical yards of earth in a day of 12 hours' length. Ford's Phil did it, not overlooked, and having to mount his loaded barrow up a bank 2 feet high and tolerably steep.[50]

During the next year, with the ground prepared and his building materials on order, Jefferson turned to refining his house plans. Most of the building materials required had to be taken up the James River by barge, then up the Rivanna to the foot of the mountain, and finally transported by horses up the mountainside.[51]

On the afternoon of February 1, 1770, Jefferson had dinner with his family at Shadwell before proceeding to Charlottesville. At some time after his departure, the house burned to the ground. A few books, his violin, and several beds were all that were saved from the blaze. As he later informed Page, he lost "every paper I had in the world, and almost every book. On a reasonable estimate I calculate the *cost* of the books burned to have been £200 sterling. . . . Of the papers too of every kind I am utterly destitute. All of these, whether public or private, of business or amusement, have perished in the flames."[52]

No mention is made of what happened then or thereafter to Jefferson's mother and the younger children, but there was no injury and they undoubtedly found shelter and continued to live in another building on the premises. The house was probably rebuilt soon after. After his mother's death in 1776, the dwelling house remained uninhabited except by overseers and tenants until 1800, when Jefferson noted that he paid "for repairing the East end of Dwelling house" and for "building the West end."[53]

The greatest immediate loss that Jefferson suffered as a result of the fire consisted of most of his law books and notes he had prepared for cases which were to come before the General Court in the near future. He promptly placed an order with booksellers through his friend Thomas Nelson, but it would be some time before the books could be replaced. His friends all rallied to his assistance and he borrowed £100 from Dabney Carr for book purchases. Fortunately he had managed to preserve his *Memorandum Books*, which have proven to be invaluable sources for historians.

In addition to his books on the law, Jefferson had assembled a fairly well-rounded library with purchases he made at Williamsburg and others he ordered from England. Included were works on the classics, literature, the arts, architecture and the sciences. By 1773 his library consisted of 1256 volumes.[54]

By the time the fire occurred, Jefferson had already acquired a few scientific instruments of his own as well as books. The earliest entry in his records relating to instruments was dated 17 October 1769 noting that he had paid "2.6." to "Craig [James Craig] for mend[in]g microscope & perspect[ive] glasse." There is no record, however, of the purchase of these instruments.[55]

Jefferson's house on top of the mountain was still under construction when the fire occurred at Shadwell, and it was not until later that year that the first or southwestern "outhouse" was ready for occupancy, and he moved into it in November 1770. It was not until quite some time later that more than one room of the main house became habitable. It had not been a simple undertaking to build a house on a mountain top in a primitive community, because roads had to be built to transport tools and building materials to it. The brick had to be made on the premises, space had to be provided for temporary storage of the materials and workmen had to be trained.

Throughout this period Jefferson continued his law practice in Williamsburg and supervised the building project at Monticello on periodic visits. He continued to spend the summer months at Monticello, but progress on the house was inordinately slow. At one point he sought to hire an "architect," by which he meant a builder, for the main building, but without success. The beginning was made with the second or northwest pavilion, which was probably enclosed by the first winter.

The mountaintop eyrie was indeed beautiful, and would enable Jefferson to develop his house, gardens and farm as he had visualized. It also had some practical drawbacks, however, which he may not have anticipated and with which he had to wrestle for the rest of his life. There was a shortage of water, and even the 68-foot well he had dug in 1769 failed to provide a sufficient supply even for just the household during the dry summer months. Water had to be hand carried to the house and other buildings from springs along the sides of the mountain.

Another continuing problem was soil erosion because irrigation was not possible due to the shortage of water. It was not until his retirement years that he was able to resolve the problem by means of contour ploughing. Another difficulty he experienced was in attempting to level the grounds near the house for kitchen gardens and orchards, and he finally resorted to creating a wide terrace around the building and terracing the orchard and vineyard area.[56]

Meanwhile he became active with other aspects of his new home. In 1767 he grafted his first trees, and by September 1768 he had acquired almost thirty-five quarts of clover seed for his fields in addition to grass seed for making his lawn. By the summer of 1771 he had obtained a copy of Thomas Whately's *Observations on Modern Gardening* which was to serve as the inspiration for later development of the grounds.[57]

In early October 1770 Jefferson made the first of many visits to "The Forest" in Charles City County, the home of a wealthy landowner and lawyer named John Wayles. There Jefferson went to call upon Wayles's eldest daughter, Martha Wayles Skelton. The child of a second marriage, Martha at the age of seventeen had married Bathurst Skelton, son of James Skelton, a major landowner and sometime sheriff of Henrico County. Young Skelton had been a student at the College of William and Mary in 1763 and 1764, the period Jefferson was in Williamsburg, and they had mutual friends, so that undoubtedly they too were acquainted.

Skelton apparently was also interested in the sciences, for among his books, which later became part of Jefferson's library, were copies of James Ferguson's *Astronomy* and *Lectures on Mechanics*, Potter's *Mechanics*, Maclauren's *Algebra*, Ward's *Algebra* and *Ladies' Geography*. Skelton married Martha in 1766 and died suddenly in 1768, after less than two years of marriage, leaving a nineteen-year old widow and a small son, who died three years later.[58]

By all accounts, Martha Skelton had extraordinary beauty in form and in face, and was somewhat over medium height, of slight build but fine proportions. She also possessed a fair complexion, abundant hair slightly auburn in color and large dark expressive eyes. A most competent housekeeper, she also played the harpsichord and sang and danced and was an accomplished rider on horseback. A good conversationalist, she demonstrated literary tastes, a neat handwriting and ability to keep accounts, and had a warm and affectionate disposition.

It is not surprising, therefore, that such a beautiful young widow with so many fine attributes and wealth besides, did not lack for attention from young men in the region. During the four years of her widowhood her hand was sought by many, among them young Jefferson, then twenty-eight years of age. He was scarcely handsome, but nonetheless his imposing stature, vigorous carriage and intelligent nature made him outstanding among his competitors.

The story is told that when two of his rivals arrived at the same time at the Wayles residence they were shown into a room together. As they listened they heard the young widow and Jefferson singing and playing together, their voices accompanied by her harpsichord and his violin. Their song was plaintive and tender and they sang as two individuals expressing their feelings to each other. The rivals continued to listen for a few moments, looked at each other, and without exchanging a word they left the house and did not return.[59]

How Jefferson first became acquainted with Martha Wayles Skelton is not certain. Her father was a wealthy man of affairs, very popular in society and an attorney with a large practice in Williamsburg. Jefferson undoubtedly became familiar with him while establishing his own practise. He may have met Martha in Williamsburg while attending social functions, or he might have been invited to "The Forest" by her father on various occasions.

Jefferson visited "The Forest" again in December and during the following year made periodic visits, becoming a familiar of the family. He was a generous tipper to the Wayles servants, as recorded in his *Memorandum Books*.[60]

Late in 1771 Jefferson attended court at Williamsburg and was re-elected to the House of Burgesses. He had been offered the law practice of Robert Carter Nicholas but had refused it, probably because the demands of his own practice, coupled with supervision of the construction of his new home, made it unfeasible.[61]

Towards the end of that year Jefferson asked for Martha's hand and she agreed to marry him. The wedding date was set for New Year's Day. On Christmas Eve he set out on horseback accompanied by his servant, but they did not arrive until after Christmas Day. Friends and relatives gathered at "The Forest," some coming from substantial distances. The wedding bond was signed for Jefferson by his soon-to-be brother-in-law, Francis Eppes, and on December 31st he applied for a wedding license, for which he paid forty shillings. The ceremony took place the next day, New Year's Day, with two clergymen officiating. It was a gay event, with a fiddler providing the music.[62]

Jefferson had planned to leave for Monticello with his bride immediately after the ceremony, but their departure was delayed for two weeks by bad weather. Virginia had been having a record snowfall during the past month. By the time Jefferson and Martha set out at last in a phaeton with two horses for Monticello, a distance of one hundred miles, there was some snow on the ground. As they continued up the slopes of the Blue Ridge, the snow increased in depth, in some places to three feet. Several times en route the vehicle had to be repaired, the last time at

Tuckahoe, where Jefferson had spent part of his childhood. According to family tradition, the story was that the snow had fallen to such a depth that they were forced to abandon the phaeton at Blenheim, the home of Colonel Carter.

Departing Blenheim at sunset on horseback, they left the road and proceeded the last eight miles of the journey through a mountain track over ground covered with from eighteen inches to two feet of snow. They arrived late at night, after the servants had all retired and the fires had gone out. Not a light was burning in the south pavilion and there was not a spark of fire left, nor could they find any food.

Jefferson struck a light, stabled the horses and attended to their needs. Returning to the house, he vainly searched for food, finding a half bottle of wine. This was to be their only supper, and they toasted each other amidst much merriment. The main house was not yet habitable, and the couple made their home at first in the south pavilion, the outbuilding in which Jefferson had maintained bachelor quarters.[63]

Jefferson remained at Monticello until the fields had turned green in the spring. He did not attend the meetings of the House of Burgesses and also absented himself from his practice during this time.[64]

In September their first child, a daughter they named Martha, was born and for the next six months there was considerable concern whether she would survive. But the child recovered miraculously and little Martha eventually developed a robust constitution like that of her father.[65]

CHAPTER IV

CLIMATE FOR GREATNESS (1772–1781)

Liberty is the great parent of science and of virtue; a nation will be great in both in proportion as it is free.

Letter from Thomas Jefferson
to Dr. Joseph Willard, 1789.

During the next several years, Jefferson had little time for scientific endeavors, his attention being fully occupied with his new family, the construction of his new home, membership in the newly formed Society for the Promotion of Useful Knowledge and his legal practise such a long distance away from home in Williamsburg. Then, as the disaffection between the American colonies and the mother country gradually increased, he found himself drawn more and more into the approaching conflict.

A major distraction was the death on May 17, 1773 of Jefferson's closest friend and brother-in-law, Dabney Carr. A promising young lawyer who was rapidly emerging as a prominent political figure, Carr had been elected to the House of Burgesses for Louisa County in that year. Family tradition relates that Carr was buried at Shadwell, while Jefferson was away at Williamsburg. He returned to Monticello, and within the following week he set his laborers to excavating a new grave at the top of the mountain under the great oak where he and Carr had spent so many youthful hours. Honoring their boyhood pledge, he had his friend's remains disinterred and transferred to a plot in the eighty-foot square that had been prepared, which thereafter became the Jefferson family burial ground.

Carr's death was a great personal loss, and Jefferson mourned deeply. He wrote an epitaph for his friend's gravestone and inscribed it as being from "Thomas Jefferson, who of all men living, loved him most."[1]

It was characteristic of Jefferson, who never displayed his private feelings publicly, that even at the moment of his grief, he was nonetheless impelled to record the time required to dig the grave and to calculate how many acres one man could grub at the same rate. On May 23rd he noted in his *Memorandum Book*, "2 hands grubbed the graveyard 80 feet square—⅟₇ of an acre in 3-½ hours, so that one would have done it in 7 hours, and would grub an acre in 49 hours— 4 days."[2]

On May 28th, shortly after Carr's death, John Wayles passed away, and Jefferson was named one of the executors of his father-in-law's estate. When the property was divided in the following year, on his wife's behalf Jefferson acquired more than eleven thousand acres and one hundred thirty-five slaves, among them the Hemings family. Included in Martha's inheritance was her father's collection of 669 volumes, which became part of Jefferson's library. He noted in 1773 that his library now numbered 1256 volumes. Jefferson promptly sold six thousand acres to meet his share of Wayles's debts, and the balance was added to his existing holdings in Bedford County and new lands in Goochland County.[3]

During the autumn of that year, the president and faculty of the College of William and Mary "unanimously agreed that Mr. Thomas Jefferson be appointed surveyor of Albemarle, in the room of Mr. Nicholas Lewis, who has sent his letter of resignation, and that he be allowed to have a deputy."[4]

Virtually nothing is presently known about the qualifications required by the College for the position of surveyor, nor of the method used in examining candidates. The College did not train surveyors, and few of the eighteenth century colonial surveyors in Virginia had attended the College. The College appeared to be more concerned with collecting fees for surveying than in maintaining standards of the art, and the president and faculty exercised no supervision over the practise of the surveyors in the field, nor of the surveys they submitted for land patents. Fees paid by the surveyors were used for the benefit of the College.

There is reason to believe that instead of considering the technical competence of candidates in the art of surveying, the college selected them primarily on the basis of their qualifications as "gentlemen" in the sense that the term was then used in Virginia. The social status of the province's officeholders was judged to be an important consideration.[5]

Jefferson received the appointment at a time when he had become particularly depressed with the practise of law and was contemplating the possibility of pursuing another profession in the future. There is no evidence that he actually engaged in surveying as part of the appointment, however, for no surveys signed by him as county surveyor were filed, nor is there record of his resignation. He allowed the appointment to lapse, for in the following April Anderson Bryan succeeded him to the position.

Nonetheless, Jefferson apparently had prepared for the position, for among the scientific instruments he owned in this period was "Marshall's meridian instrument" for which he had paid twenty shillings in Virginia currency. This is readily identified as "Mr. Marshall's new invented instrument for finding VARIATION of the NEEDLE" offered for sale in 1772 by Edmund Dickinson of Williamsburg. Dickinson described it as "extremely simple and cheap, and will be singularly serviceable to Surveyors if the Act takes Place which obliges them to return Plats and protract their Surveys by the true Meridian."[6]

The amendment to the act to which Dickinson referred was published in the *Virginia Gazette* in an announcement "To the Printer." It was passed by the Assembly to be effective June 1, 1773, by means of which all surveyors in Virginia were required thereafter to correct their plats by using the Marshall instrument before submitting them for file. Plats were maps of portions of land on which topographical or other features were indicated, and might be part of or a complete survey executed by a surveyor in the field. The Act also revealed that this requirement had been suggested by none other than Thomas Marshall himself, the inventor of the instrument, then a member of the House of Burgesses.[7] (Document No. 1)

The problem to which the act was related was a serious one for all surveyors of the period and undoubtedly the Marshall instrument provided a convenient solution. Curiously, nothing is known about it other than the brief description in Dickinson's advertisement, the Act of 1773 and the notation in Jefferson's inventory of scientific instruments.

There may have been several reasons why Jefferson allowed the appointment to lapse. Although at first he had been enthusiastic about its prospects compared with his law practise, reconsideration made him more fully aware of its inherent problems. Most of the desirable public land in the county had already been assigned, and there was no great profit to be made from surveying in the field. Remembering his father's career, he realized he would be required to be absent from his family for long periods. Furthermore, a multiplicity of other unanticipated interests had begun to occupy more and more of his time.

During the next months Jefferson devoted all his efforts to the improvement of Monticello. In the spring of 1774 he laid out an area for a future garden, and planted a great number of vines and vegetables. He had become interested in viticulture through the influence of Philip Mazzei. The Italian patriot had arrived in Virginia in 1773 under the patronage of Thomas Adams with the intention of developing vineyards in the region. At first he stayed with Francis Eppes and planned to go with Adams from there to the Shenandoah Valley, where Adams owned property he considered suitable for viticulture.

Mazzei departed in November, and en route visited Monticello in December and remained overnight. Jefferson became enthusiastic about the Italian's project, and the next morning took him on a tour of his plantation. He pointed out some land adjacent to his which was available for sale, and offered also to lend him the use of some of his plantation. The trip to the Shenandoah was cancelled, and Mazzei instead became a guest at Monticello. He purchased the nearby land, remaining at Monticello until a house was built for him.

Some Italian workers had accompanied Mazzei, and later that year he brought a dozen or more vignerons from Tuscany. Jefferson particularly enjoyed speaking with them and learning their dialect. "Jefferson knew the Italian language very well," wrote Mazzei, "but he had never heard it spoken. Nevertheless, speaking with my men he understood them and they understood him. I was impressed by their demonstrations of joy at the circumstance."

The Italian workmen brought tools from Italy, some of which were hitherto unknown in Virginia, as well as new varieties of grapevines and vegetables, which Jefferson added to his own garden. Despite his enthusiasm, his attempt at viticulture met with disaster due to an unseasonably late frost which also destroyed half of his fruit crop and almost all of his wheat, corn and rye and some of the tobacco plants. As a result, the rest of the year proved to be financially poor for Monticello.[8]

By this time the extent of his land holdings and the number of his slaves made it necessary for Jefferson to expand his record keeping, and he began to maintain another record, which he named his *Farm Book*. In it he noted his farming operations, data about plants he cultivated, records of erosion and excerpts from his readings on agriculture. Its primary purpose was to enable him by means of lists to calculate how much food and clothing were required for his slaves. Meanwhile one of the four "roundabout" roads to the mountaintop had been completed, and bricks needed for building the house were still being made in his kiln.

Jefferson planted a number of fruit trees, and in the spring he designed a permanent vegetable garden on the slope to the southeast between the orchard and the first "roundabout." He made an elaborate operation of planting the new vegetable garden, partly to occupy himself during Martha's second pregnancy, because he was determined to remain close to her during this period. He numbered the planting beds and marked them on sticks and in his records, often using Italian names for the vegetables. Among these were "Cipolle bianche di Tuckahoe" (white onions of Tuckahoe), "Fagiuoli d'Augusta" (beans from Augusta), and "Aglio di Toscania" (Tuscan garlic). The use of the Italian names reflected not only his association with his recently arrived neighbor Mazzei, but also his desire to utilize the language which he had taught himself while studying law.[9]

The spring of 1774 was to be an eventful although unhappy season for Jefferson. Early on the afternoon of February 21st an earthquake shook the region. It was sufficiently strong so that at Monticello "It shook the house so sensibly that everybody ran out of doors." The same phenomena occurred the following day at almost the same time. "So strong were the tremors on the mountain that it was only with difficulty that the servants and farm hands could be induced to return to work."[10]

Meanwhile, Jefferson's sister Elizabeth, who was one and one-half years younger, and who was often inclined to wander in mind and body, disappeared from home and could not be found. She may have been terrorized by the earthquake. An intimate of the family later wrote, "I have always understood that she was very feeble minded if not an idiot— & that she and her maid were drowned together while attempting to cross the Rivanna in a skiff."[11]

The family searched vainly for her in the woods and along the river, and it was not until four days later that her body was found. On March 6th, the day before her funeral was to take place, the Rivanna River flooded, causing considerable damage. Its waters rose "18 I.[nches] higher than the one which carried N. Lewis's bridge away & that was the highest ever known except the great fresh in May 1771." Elizabeth was buried on March 7th in the family graveyard.[12]

A month later Jefferson and Martha became the parents of a second daughter, whom they named Jane Randolph for her paternal grandmother. Martha's life was a relatively happy one, filled with responsibility not only for her immediate family but also for the families of the slaves on the plantation. They came to her for assistance when help was required due to illness or a lying-in, to supervise the making of clothes and for countless other needs. Her husband was devoted to her, and their evenings together were filled with conversation and music as they talked, played the violin and harpsichord and sang together.

Eventually, however, Martha's domestic activities in her own home and on the plantation began to take a heavy toll on her constitution, and the rapidity with which she continued to have children further contributed to her failing health.[13]

Meanwhile, great unrest was developing in the colonies. The problems that had developed intermittently with the mother country had once more come to the fore. The governor of Virginia, John Murray, Earl of Dunmore, had called the House of Burgesses together after having prorogued it for almost a year. By ignoring the resolves of the House, he forced the formation of a Committee of Correspondence. As incidents occurred in other colonies over the tea tax, following the burning of the *Gaspée*, the committee became increasingly active and began to correspond with similar committees in the other colonies.[14]

These events led Jefferson to turn more and more from his law practise to increasing involvement in politics and government. By this time he had become uniquely qualified as an expert on the legal rights of the colonies as well as the natural rights of the individual in relation to government. He was an authority on the jurisdiction of government as a consequence of his extensive research and reading while studying law as well as his experience in its practise.

His study of the history and development of English Common Law led him to distrust laws made by judges. In his view the jury system had practical merits and he admired it because an important function of government was retained by the people. He had even proposed that the jury system be extended into the Courts of Chancery because so great a proportion of the jurisdiction over property was being engulfed by the latter.[15]

As a consequence, his practice suffered and finally, in August 1774 he reached the decision to terminate it. The last case noted in his case book was dated November 9, 1774. He transferred the practice to Edmund Randolph, and the transfer was announced in a circular distributed by Randolph to all of Jefferson's clients.[16]

Having disposed of his law practice, Jefferson could at last pursue his inclinations with greater freedom. He now turned to the prosecution of law in its larger meaning, the natural rights of the individual and the legal rights of the colonies, and identified himself more openly with the aggressive local patriots. On May 5 1774 Lord Dunmore reconvened the Assembly.[17]

News of the closing of the port of Boston in May reached Virginia ten days later while the Assembly was still in session, with the consequence that the younger radical Burgesses proceeded to the Apollo Room of the Raleigh Tavern to sign an Association. Included with Jefferson were Patrick Henry and the two members of the Lee family, among others. It was agreed to set aside June lst, to be "a day of fasting, humiliation, and prayer," to make the people aware of the seriousness of the situation. Robert Carter Nicholas, a senior Burgess, agreed to be the sponsor, and the bill was presented to the full House and passed unanimously.

In retaliation Lord Dunmore promptly dissolved the Assembly, and the Burgesses, once more gathered at the Raleigh Tavern, adopted a series of resolutions declaring that an attack on one of the colonies was an attack on all of them. They agreed to write to all of the colonies requesting the formation of a general congress and appointment of delegates to it. The group then disbanded and many went home.

Dispatches from Massachusetts which arrived two days later, however, caused Randolph to reconvene those remaining in Williamsburg. They met to prepare a communication to inform Massachusetts that Virginia in principle would probably support her in boycotting importations and even exportations, but that definite action would have to await a meeting of the General Congress.[18]

Jefferson had departed for Monticello and he was no longer in Williamsburg on June 1st when the Burgesses marched to Bruton Church in defiance of the governor. Without consulting Lord Dunmore, he and his old school friend John Walker called for a patriotic service of prayer in the local parish of St. Anne's, of which he was a vestryman. The service's purpose was "devoutly to implore the divine interposition in behalf of an injured and oppressed people." When the dissolved Assembly called for the election of delegates to a convention which would concern itself with the fate of the colonies, Jefferson and Walker were chosen as the representatives of Albemarle County.[19]

When the freeholders of Albemarle County met at Charlottesville in late July, they re-elected Walker and Jefferson as their representatives. They adopted a series of resolutions which Jefferson had hastily drafted, and which he was to have presented at the convention. Jefferson then began to prepare instructions to be issued by the forthcoming convention to the delegates to be sent to the General Congress. He presented his ideas in the form of resolutions to serve as instructions to the delegation and which could be embodied in the address of Congress to the king. Written in utmost haste, his language was occasionally intemperate.

Unfortunately Jefferson was stricken with dysentery on his way to Wiliamsburg, and was forced to turn back to Monticello. From his sick bed he forwarded copies of his instructions to Peyton Randolph and Patrick Henry, the delegates who were to go to Philadelphia. Henry either never read his copy or lost it, for he made no use of it. Although Randolph disagreed with the tone of Jefferson's resolutions, he nonetheless presented them to the delegates assembled in his house. They were applauded but not approved entirely, and in the course of events were not acted upon.

Meanwhile, without his knowledge, some of Jefferson's friends arranged to have the resolutions printed privately. They were issued with the title A Summary View of the Rights of British America. The pamphlet had wide distribution, and during the same year it was reprinted in Philadelphia and twice in England. Although his name did not appear on the pamphlet, Jefferson's authorship became known and brought his name, until now unknown except in Virginia, to the attention of political leaders in New England.[20]

In the voting for delegates to the Albemarle Committee, Jefferson headed the list, and he was elected also to the Convention for the Colony of Virginia which convened in Richmond on March 20, 1775. Peyton Randolph was elected president. The Virginia Convention approved the proceedings of the Continental Congress and voted to place Virginia in a posture of defence. A committee, of which Jefferson was named a member, was appointed to raise the militia and to arm it.

Some members vehemently objected, claiming that such an action meant war without having the soldiers, arms or stores with which to fight it. It was at this point that Henry rose and gave his famous speech: "Gentlemen may cry peace, peace, but there is no peace. . . .," he cried. "Is life so dear, or peace so sweet, as to be purchased at the price of chains and slavery? Forbid it, Almighty God! I know not what course others may take, but as for me . . . give me liberty or give me death!"

For the first time in his public career, and one of the few times he was to do so, Jefferson rose in a public assembly to make a speech. He supported Henry, and "argued closely, profoundly and warmly." The resolution was passed, although with only a slight majority. On March 24th Jefferson introduced a resolution to instruct the Virginia committee to investigate the facts concerning the alleged defection of New York from the Association. The following day the delegates to the Congress were elected, and although Jefferson had not been on the original list, his name was added as an alternate in the event that Peyton Randolph was unable to attend.[21]

Jefferson returned from Richmond to Elk Hill, one of his properties in Goochland County which he had acquired in 1774 as part of his wife's inheritance. There his family had been staying for a prolonged sojourn before returning to Monticello. Meanwhile in Williamsburg the confusion mounted as the governor compounded one political error after another. The greatest reaction came from his confiscation of gunpowder from the colonial magazine at Williamsburg and removing it to the armed schooner *Magdalen*. While negotiating with the angered people of Williamsburg for its return, the governor received news of the events at Lexington and Concord, and the American Revolution had begun.

Dunmore sought to make amends by reconvoking the Assembly to report certain concessions recently received from Lord North. Jefferson traveled from Monticello to attend the meeting of the Assembly over which Peyton Randolph was to preside. Although as Randolph's alternate he should have proceeded to Philadelphia to attend the meetings of the Congress, he was anxious to learn what was about to transpire in his own colony.

Lord North's concessions and Dunmore's promises and efforts to soothe the Burgesses met with a cold reception. Upon Randolph's request, Jefferson prepared a reply to Dunmore, but before it could be delivered, the Assembly sent a committee to examine the magazine from which the powder had been confiscated. At the magazine three of the men were injured by a booby trap that the British had installed and unwittingly had forgotten to disarm. Dunmore was accused of deliberately having set the trap, and the Virginians prepared to march.

Dunmore was thoroughly frightened, and gathering his family and possessions together, fled hastily to the British warship *Fowney* lying off Yorktown. From the safety of the vessel he made loud noises and numerous threats but never returned to Williamsburg. The Assembly took no notice of his flight, and the chairman of the committee, Archibald Cary, rose to read the reply prepared by Jefferson to Dunmore's speech just as if the governor were present. Jefferson was developing a polemic style that was direct and wasted no words. The House approved the reply, although recommending "a dash of cold water on it here & there, enfeebling it somewhat."[22]

Jefferson was not present during the reading or the ensuing debate, for he had departed for Philadelphia, to serve in Peyton Randolph's place as delegate to the Congress. He drove to Fredericksburg where for £50 he purchased the horse he named "The General" and which became his favorite mount. After three days he was on the road once more to Annapolis, where he took time to purchase books before moving on to Wilmington, where he was forced to hire a guide. He arrived in Philadelphia after ten days of travel. He obtained lodgings on Chestnut Street at the establishment of Benjamin Randolph, a distant kinsman, cabinetmaker-innkeeper and prominent patriot, where other delegates were also staying.[23]

Jefferson presented his credentials to the Congress and was installed as a delegate from Virginia. The Virginian delegation welcomed him, particularly since he had brought "for use of myself & other delegates of congress £315," their long-awaited back pay. Furthermore, they knew him and respected his achievements, and he made a favorable impression on the other delegations as well. The *Summary View* had brought him advance modest fame, and it was known that he had drafted the response to Dunmore.

Except for John Jay and Edward Rutledge, at the age of thirty-two Jefferson was the youngest member of the Continental Congress. Although he generally remained silent during public debates, his alertness, ability to express himself in writing and his demonstrated decisiveness in committees and in conversation, all served to create a favorable reaction to the young Virginian, particularly from John Adams and other older members. During his stay in Philadelphia he was asked to join other delegates when they dined at the newly completed fashionable City Tavern.[24]

Two days after Jefferson's arrival, one of the questions under discussion concerned the preparation of a statement or declaration to explain to the people why the colonies were taking up arms. It was agreed that George Washington, who was about to proceed to an encampment near Boston, should announce such a declaration to the assembled troops and to the public as well. The task of drafting the statement was first assigned to John Rutledge of South Carolina.

Rutledge produced a draft overnight, the poor phraseology and harsh content of which did not meet with approval. It was resubmitted, and John Dickinson of Pennsylvania and Jefferson were added to the committee to improve it. William Livingston of New York proposed that its revision be assigned to Jefferson.

Jefferson based his version of the statement on the historical and argumentative theses of his *Summary View*. The committee which now met to consider the draft consisted of Rutledge, Dickinson, Franklin, Jay and Johnson. The draft was given once more to Dickinson to rewrite inasmuch as he spoke for the majority, which was not prepared for a permanent break with England. He incorporated much of Jefferson's language, and in this modified form the statement was finally passed.[25]

A committee was appointed on July 22nd with Benjamin Franklin, John Adams, Richard Henry Lee and Jefferson to report on Lord North's conciliatory motion in the House of Commons. Inasmuch as Jefferson had already drafted the reply of the Virginia Assembly on the same proposals, he was asked to repeat his performance for the next Continental Congress.[26]

After the Congress recessed on August 1st, he departed for Monticello, accompanied by Benjamin Harrison until they reached Annapolis, where they parted. Jefferson continued his journey to Williamsburg where the Virginia Convention was in session, and reported on the proceedings of the Congress. At this time he was re-appointed in his own right as a delegate when the Congress would meet again on September 5th. He remained at Williamsburg for a week before proceeding to Elk Hill, and then on to Monticello, bringing with him four butter prints'or moulds which Martha had coveted.[27]

He was still tense upon his arrival home with excitement and enthusiasm for the events in which he had recently participated, but his mood soon changed to sadness. Shortly after his arrival, his daughter, Jane Randolph, died; she was one and a half years old. He remained home for a month, dealing with the most important plantation affairs before he left once more in late September for Philadelphia, where the Congress had already been in session for two weeks. A day after Jefferson's departure, the Virginia Committee of Safety commissioned him County Lieutenant and commander of militia for Albemarle County.[28]

He returned to Philadelphia and resumed his previous lodgings at Benjamin Randolph's, where Peyton Randolph and Thomas Nelson also were staying. On October 22nd Peyton Randolph died suddenly of apoplexy at age fifty-four. Thereafter Jefferson was occupied attending the day-long sessions in the State House.[29]

As time passed, Jefferson could visualize no alternative to the existing crisis except a definite break between the colonies and the mother country to achieve eventual independence. As he wrote to the Loyalist John Randolph, with whom he was negotiating the purchase of a violin and collection of books, "I am one of those, who, rather than submit to the rights of legislating for us, assumed by the British Parliament, and which late experience has shown they will cruelly exercise, would lend my hand to sink the whole island in the ocean." Jefferson succeeded in acquiring Randolph's violin but not his books.[30]

During this period the Congress was concerned primarily with the raising and supplying of armies. He found the sessions unbearably boring and tedious because he could contribute little to the technical military bills under consideration, and his few appointments on committees dealt with relatively minor matters. He was also considerably worried over news that his daughter Martha was ill. She and her sister were away from home visiting the Eppes family. He was also worried about his wife, since neither she nor anyone else at home answered his letters.[31]

Finally, Jefferson could stand the silence no longer and in late December 1775 he departed for home. There he found the family safe, although Martha was still unwell.

Until this time Jefferson had had no reason to be concerned about his mother, but during the interlude that Jefferson was at home she died unexpectedly after an hour's illness, at the age of fifty-seven. His only surviving records of her demise are a terse entry in his *Memorandum Book* merely recording the event, and a mention in a letter to his mother's brother, William Randolph. "The death of my mother you have probably not heard of. This happened on the last day of March after an illness of not more than an hour. We suppose it to have been apoplectic."[32]

Surprisingly, he remained at home for two months, with no explanation for his prolonged absence from events in Philadelphia. Presumably he used the time to make arrangements for the maintenance of his brother and sisters and for the settlement of his mother's estate. As part of his responsibility as County Lieutenant, he compiled a list of militia volunteers from Albemarle, seemingly the only task in that office that he performed.

His departure was postponed by illness, which incapacitated him and for which he was treated by Dr. George Gilmer. It may have been the beginning of one of his headaches, an indisposition which was to plague him for many years. Finally, at the beginning of May, he left Monticello to resume his post in Philadelphia, leaving his wife £10 in cash for household expenses. He arrived in Philadelphia exactly a week later and found that events had been moving at a furious pace, and that the revolt had grown into a revolution.[33]

The movement for outright independence was growing rapidly. Despite the pressures from the liberals to declare independence immediately, the radicals including Jefferson realized that they must proceed more slowly and urged caution.

Meanwhile the city was suffering from increasing heat. Jefferson informed his friend Thomas Nelson, Jr., "I am at present in our old lodgings, tho' I think, as the excessive 'heats of the city are coming on fast, to endeavor to get lodgings in the skirts of the town where I may have the benefit of a freely circulating air."[34]

A week later he fulfilled his resolve and found new accommodations in a brick building on the southwest corner of Seventh and Market Streets, later renumbered 700 Market Street. Jefferson rented the second floor, which included a parlor and bedroom, for 35 shillings sterling per week. He shopped for needed items and paid to see a monkey on display.[35]

Several days before Jefferson's arrival, John Adams and Richard Henry Lee had introduced a resolution of advice to the colonies to adopt "such government as shall in the opinion of the representatives of the people, best conduce to the happiness and safety of their constituents in particular and America in general." Meanwhile Virginia had instructed its delegates to declare for independence at once, and in Williamsburg a new constitution suitable to a sovereign state was being formed.

Edmund Pendleton wrote to Jefferson privately informing him of these events, news which had the effect of galvanizing him into action at last after a period of apathy on the subject of the much discussed independence. He was convinced that the framing of a constitution was premature, for in his view the current Convention did not represent the true sentiments of the people in these matters.

Greatly concerned, within a few days Jefferson drafted his own version of a constitution for Virginia, which he prepared in the form of an act rather than as a definitive constitution, so that later it could be amended. He gave his proposals to Wythe, who was returning to Williamburg, to submit to President Pendleton of the convention.

Wythe arrived too late, for the Committee of the Whole had already reported its version to the House. However, the committee added Jefferson's preamble and some phrases from Jefferson's draft.[36]

Richard Henry Lee rose in the Congress with the instructions of the Virginia Convention before him to move three resolutions: that the American colonies were independent and absolved of all allegiance to the British Crown; that it was expedient to take measures to form foreign alliances; and that a plan of confederation be prepared and transmitted to the colonies. After deliberation the Congress concluded that only a declaration of independence would make it possible for foreign powers to enter into alliances with the colonies.

A committee consisting of Jefferson, Adams, Franklin, Roger Sherman and Robert R. Livingston was appointed to develop the declaration to be available by the adjourned date of June 11th. Because Jefferson had received the greatest number of votes, he was selected as chairman. This came as a surprise since he had remained silent throughout'the great debate. The selection was due in fact to political and personal feuds among the Virginia delegates, whose selection would have split the delegation, and furthermore Adams had become greatly impressed with Jefferson and had worked on his behalf. As Adams later recalled, the Committee of Five met in session, decided on the articles to be included, and assigned Adams and Jefferson as a subcommittee to draft them.

Jefferson proposed that Adams should draft the document but the latter refused for several reasons. He claimed that it would be politically desirable to have a Virginian as the leader, and he was convinced furthermore that he personally was considered obnoxious and suspect and was unpopular with other members of the Congress. Also he pointed out that Jefferson had demonstrated a particular ability for written expression. The actual circumstances are uncertain, for Jefferson later claimed that there was no subcommittee, and he was pressed to draft the document. In his diary, however, Adams had reported that the committee appointed Jefferson alone to draft it.[37]

While still lodging at Randolph's in May, Jefferson took the opportunity to utilize his landlord's skills as a cabinetmaker. He designed a portable lap desk for himself, the first of his so-called "inventions." He intended to use it primarily for dealing with his correspondence while traveling, so that he could utilize what he impatiently'described as wasted time during coach travel between Monticello and Philadelphia, and during his long absences from the conveniences of home.

The desk was designed with a slanted top that when opened doubled the writing surface, and was equipped with a book rest for reading. It would have a lockable drawer for storing written papers and a supply of paper, pens, ink and sand for blotting. Furthermore, it was to be made of wood sufficiently thin throughout to reduce its weight to a minimum. During the last two weeks of May he provided a sketch of his requirements to Randolph, who produced a fine piece of mahogany furniture which met all of Jefferson's requirements. Jefferson kept the desk with him on all his travels and at home and was to continue to use it for the next half century.[38] (*Figure 1*)

It was probably at the same time that he asked Randolph to make for him his second "invention." This was a Philadelphia Windsor chair, possibly made by Francis Trumbull or by Randolph himself, modified to revolve. This was achieved by the addition of a platform and pivot between the seat and leg frame, featuring a central spindle with rollers made from window-sash pulleys.[39] (*Figure 2*)

Because of the frequent misuse of the word "invention" in relation to Jefferson, it must be explained that what have frequently been called his inventions, were in fact modifications of existing devices and equipment, designed to'fit his particular needs. Jefferson did not invent the portable writing desk or the revolving chair, but he devised modified forms of both to suit his personal requirements.

Upon receiving his assignment from his fellow members on the committee, Jefferson retired to the isolation of his rooms so that he could concentrate without interruption on the project before him. It was on this lap desk and while seated in this chair that Jefferson drafted the Declaration, toiling alone for the next seventeen days. He rose each day at dawn, and as was his custom, soaked his feet in chilled water to ward off colds, and then retired to his desk to ponder and write.

He based the form and contents of his document on the written minutes of the Committee's proposals. As he wrote to Henry Lee almost a half-century later, his project was "not to find out new principles, or new arguments, never before thought of, not merely to say things which had never been said before; but to place before mankind the common sense of the subject, in terms so plain and firm as to command their assent, and to justify ourselves in the common stand we are compelled to take. Neither aiming at originality of principle or sentiment, nor yet copied from any particular and previous writing, it was intended to be an expression of the American mind, and to give to that expression the proper tone and spirit called for by the occasion."[40]

Jefferson's method of bringing the document together was to write each thought as it occurred to him on a separate piece of paper, assembling them into proper order, and then rewriting them into final form. He described this process in a letter written many years later, noting "whenever in the course of the composition, a copy became overcharged, and difficult to be read with amendments, I copied it fair, and when that also was crouded with other amendments, another fair copy was made, &c. These rough drafts I sent to distant friends who were anxious to know what was passing."[41]

Among those to whom he sent copies of his drafts were Richard Henry Lee, George Wythe, Philip Mazzei, Edmund Pendleton and possibly John Page. All of these copies, including the "rough draft" he kept for his own files, and the copy he later presented to the Congress, were written on the lap desk.[42]

As he had explained, Jefferson had been instructed merely to say things that had been said before without making original contributions or new philosophies. It was a difficult task, for assuming that Lee's resolution would pass the Congress, the Declaration had to provide justification for it not only to the American people but also to the world. Concurrently, it had to be propaganda couched in particularly pleasing, impassioned argumentation. He welded these together in a convincing manner by the addition of philosophical principles.

After completing a version that met with his entire satisfaction, Jefferson showed it to Adams, who suggested minor changes. Later it was brought to Franklin, who made several other revisions in the draft, after which Jefferson made a fair copy which he submitted to the committee, which promptly approved it.

The Committee of Five reported Jefferson's draft on June 28th, and it was read to the Congress. It had to be tabled, however, until Lee's resolution had been approved, which occurred on July 2nd. While the delegates attempted to reach a decision on the question of independence, they had an opportunity to examine the declaration at their leisure and discussed its strengths and weaknesses and suggested revisions.[43]

On July 4th Jefferson called at Sparhawk's stationery store and purchased a thermometer, and ladies' gloves for his wife. John Sparhawk was a publisher and bookseller who maintained the London Bookstore on Market Street, and imported and sold philosophical instruments, books and stationery supplies. George Washington also was among his clients.[44]

The Congress met at nine o'clock as usual, and later that day Benjamin Harrison, chairman of the Committee for the Whole, reported that the delegates accepted the document that had been presented. Because of the urgency to have the document printed for distribution to the colonies, there was not sufficient time for the secretary of the Congress, Charles Thomson, to make a copy of it with its added amendments, nor to transcribe it into the Secret Journal, but he left space in the volume for the insertion of a printed copy.[45]

It is likely that Jefferson himself delivered the document to the Market Street shop of John Dunlap, the printer to the Congress. Later that evening he was probably joined by Thomson to assist in proofreading. Although it was the subject of intensive search for years, the original copy did not survive because it probably had been cut into sections and distributed to the several printers in the shop to set in type.[46]

On Monday July 8th Philadelphia celebrated the adoption of the Declaration of Independence. By order of the Committee of Safety of

Pennsylvania and under the authority of the Continental Congress, the document was proclaimed at noon from the observatory platform behind the State House, which had been erected in 1769 to observe the transit of Venus. During the morning of the warm sunny day large groups from the city began to gather in the State House Yard and others traveled in from the surrounding countryside. Collected at the foot of the platform were Mayor Samuel Powel and other city officials, who were joined by forty-nine members of the Congress. The Committee of Inspection joined the Committee of Safety and together they made their way to the Yard, where troops were drawn up in formation.

Sheriff William Dewees arrived shortly after twelve o'clock, accompanied by his deputy Colonel John Nixon. As they quickly climbed the steps to the platform, a silence fell over the crowd. "Under the authority of the Continental Congress and by Order of the Committee of Safety," Dewees began, and went on, "I proclaim a Declaration of Independence!" Nixon then stepped forward and proceeded to read the document to an attentive audience. As he finished speaking, the troops saluted and the people rendered three loud huzzahs. Several reports later made by observers described the gathering as "a great concourse of people," but noted the absence of individuals of wealth, family and position.[47]

The event was succinctly described by John Adams in a letter written the following day to the absent Maryland delegate, Samuel Chase. "The declaration was yesterday published and proclaimed from that awfull Stage, in the State House Yard, by whom do you think? By the Committee of Safety,! the Committee of Inspection, and a great Crowd of People. Three cheers rendered the Welkin. The Battalions paraded on the common, and gave us the Feu de Joy, notwithstanding the scarcity of Powder. The Bells rung all Day, and almost all night. Even the Chimers [of Christ Church] chimed away . . . The arms are taken down from every public place." That evening the coat-of-arms of George III was set afire in the Commons before a cheering crowd.[48]

It was during his stay in Philadelphia that Jefferson began to maintain his weather records in a comprehensive notebook style. Of particular interest are his notations of temperatures for the first few days of July:

1776	July 1:	9:00 A.M.	81-1/2
		7:00 P.M.	82
	July 2:	6:00 A.M.	78
		9:40 A.M.	78
		9:00 P.M.	74
	July 3:	5:30 A.M.	71-1/2
		1:30 P.M.	76
		8:10 P.M.	74

July 4:	6:00 A.M.	68
	9:00 A.M.	72-1/2
	1:00 P.M.	76
	9:00 P.M.	73-1/2

The entry for July 4th, the day on which the Declaration of Independence was accepted, is of particular significance. Later writers dramatized the day as one of sweltering heat, but Jefferson's notes indicate that it was a moderately warm day. The following day he returned to Sparhawk's shop to purchase a barometer.[49] (*Figure 3*)

Jefferson remained in Philadelphia and attended meetings of the Congress until the beginning of September, and then returned to Virginia. He was elected to the Virginia House of Burgesses to represent Albemarle County, and during the next two and one half years he directed his energies to the reform of Virginia'a legal system and to the liberalization of its political and social institutions.

He proposed the disestablishment of the Anglican Church, a complete revision of the legal code deriving from colonial administration and the abolition of entail, an ancient British system by means of which the inheritance of property was limited to the owner's lineal descendants or specifically his male children. He was appointed to a committee of the House of Delegates to make such a revision. He soon proved to be the committee's leading spirit by first rewriting all statutes dealing with crime and punishment, and modernizing them to conform with more humane practices.

He then proceeded to draft a series of measures designed to provide the Commonwealth with a sound republican foundation. Included in these were a bill for the abolition of primogeniture, a statute for religious freedom, and three bills in which were comprised a systematic plan for general education. These provided for elementary education for everyone, and university training for superior students. Also considered were the more mundane and local concerns of his constituents.[50]

Not long afterwards Jefferson managed to find time to undertake some meteorological observations. On September 15, 1776 he took barometrical readings. His first reading recorded the height of the mercury to be 29.44 inches at Monticello, at the tobacco landing on the shore of the river 30.06 inches, at "a spring on the N.E. side of Montalto" 29.52, and at the top of Montalto 29.1433 inches. Second readings at the spring were 29.48 inches and 29.445 inches at Monticello. He accordingly calculated the mean of the observations at Monticello to be 29.4615 inches, and at the river shore to be 30.06 inches, leaving a "difference of weight of air" of .5975 inches. The mean of the second and third observations at Monticello was 29.465 inches, and of the top of Montalto 29.1433 inches, yielding differences of .321667 inches, making Montalto 280 feet higher than Monticello and the whole of Montalto a height of 792.17 feet above the Rivanna. These heights were estimated "by Nettleton's table." Jefferson had found the table in the *Philosophical Transactions* for the year 1725 as part of an article on barometrical observations made "at different Elevations above the Surface of the Earth" by a certain Dr. Thomas Nettleton living in or near Halifax, England.[51]

Despite his political activities, there were intervals when he was able to remain at Monticello for several months at a time, particularly while Martha was experiencing difficulty in childbearing. His only son, born in May 1777, lived for one month only, and an infant daughter they named Mary was born a year later.

During one of these periods at home Jefferson actively participated in the formation of a new county to be created from part of Albemarle County. In 1777 a request for having their own county was made by 133 inhabitants situated too far from the county seat at Charlottesville for the convenient conduct of business. A petition was presented to the House by either Jefferson or John Harvie the younger. After consideration, the committee presented a resolution to the House, which was accepted. A bill was prepared in accordance with the usual process, and passed on the third reading. Jefferson was ordered to carry it to the Senate, where it was passed on June 3, 1777.

The bill called for the creation of a new county and a new parish, both to be named "Fluvanna," and provided for a survey to be made of the boundary between Albemarle and Fluvanna Counties, to be based on the line suggested in the petition. It was at this time that Jefferson produced a map of Albemarle County which defined the proposed division shown by a line from the southwest corner of Louisa County to the downstream side of Scotts Ferry on the Fluvanna River. This was Jefferson's earliest first known venture into cartography and mapmaking.[52]

Jefferson occasionally managed to find time to pursue other scientific endeavors, despite his active political life. He corresponded with Giovanni Fabbroni, a young Florentine scholar and friend of Philip Mazzei who had mentioned him and his interest in science. Jefferson apparently had invited Fabbroni to come to the American colonies, possibly communicating at first through Mazzei. Fabbroni was anxious to accept the invitation but found himself unable to do so. Having come under the patronage of Leopold Grand Duke of Tuscany, he was sent to France and England to observe scientific progress.[53]

To Fabbroni, Jefferson explained his meteorological activities. "Tho' much of my time is employed in the councils of America I have yet a little leisure to indulge my fondness for philosophical studies. I could wish to correspond with you on subjects of that kind. It might not be unacceptable for you to be informed for instance of the true power of our climate as discoverable from the Thermometer, from the force and direction of the winds, the quantity of rain, the plants which grow without shelter in the winter &c. On the other hand we should be much pleased with contemporary observations on the same particulars in your country, which will give us a comparative view of the two climates. Fahrenheit's thermometer is the only one in use with us. I make my daily observations as early as possible in the morning and again about 4 o'clock in the afternoon, these generally showing the maxima of cold and heat in the course of 24 hours. I wish I could gratify your Botanical taste; but I am acquainted with nothing more than the first principles in that science, yet myself and my friends may furnish you with any Botanical subjects which this country affords, and are not to be had with you: and I shall take pleasure in procuring them when pointed out by you. The greatest difficulty will be the means of conveyance during the continuation of the war."[54]

During this period Jefferson and the Reverend James Madison, formerly professor of natural philosophy and then newly appointed president of the College of William and Mary, had been conducting comparative weather observations daily for a period of at least five years. Some of these observations, recorded in their correspondence, are of particular interest. For example, it was possible for them to determine "by contemporaneous observations between five and seven weeks . . . the averaged and almost unvaried difference of the height of mercury in the barometer at these two places [Monticello and Williamsburg] was 0.784 of an inch; the pressure at Monticello being so much the lightest—that is to say, about a thirty-seventh of its whole weight."[55]

Most of Jefferson's data on weather in Virginia was later published in his *Notes on the State of Virginia*, in which he stated, "Journals of observation on the quantity of rain and degree of heat being lengthy, confused, and too minute to produce general and distinct ideas, I have taken five years' observations, to wit from 1772 to 1777, made in Williamsburg and its neighborhood, have reduced them to an average for every month of the year, and stated those averages in the following table, adding an analytical view of the winds for the same period."[56]

Elsewhere in the same work he noted that in 1781 both heats and colds were becoming more moderate in the memories of the middle-aged, and the snows less frequent and deep. Even the phenomenon of the rainbow did not escape the two observers.[57]

In January 1778 Jefferson purchased a theodolite from the "rev.d mr Andrews" for the sum of £45. With this surveying instrument, designed to measure vertical and horizontal angles, the altitude and the azimuth, he planned to measure the angle of intersection of the horizon with distant mountains visible from Monticello. Later that year he recorded his observations in his *Memorandum Book*: "Placing the Theodolite on the top of the house, the Eastern spur of the High Mountain [now known locally as Brown's Mountain or Patterson Mountain] intersects the horizon 19° westward of Willis's mountain. Note the observation was made on the intersection of the ground (not the trees) with the horizon." Willis Mountain was an isolated peak and easily visible from Monticello on clear days. Consequently it served him as a focal point for surveying other sites and for making observations.[58]

After observing the solar eclipse of June 24, 1778 at Monticello, he sent copies of his notes to Page and the Reverend Madison, who in turn reported their own experiences. Madison reminded Jefferson that on the following October 5th and October 12th there were to be immersions of a satellite of Jupiter if it would be convenient for him to observe them.

Jefferson also reported his observations to David Rittenhouse, clockmaker, maker of mathematical instruments and astronomer, with whom he had become acquainted in Philadelphia while attending meetings of the Continental Congress. Rittenhouse was a member of the Pennsylvania Assembly and president of the Council of Safety. He had gained a reputation as a leading man of science not only with his astronomical observations but also two orreries he had produced, for the College of New Jersey (later Princeton University) and the College of Philadelphia (which became the University of Pennsylvania). The orrery, a form of planetarium demonstrating the solar system in three-dimensional form, showed the annual as well as diurnal motion of the earth around the sun and of the moon around the earth, and sometimes the motions of other planets as well.

Rittenhouse's clockwork-driven orreries derived their importance in the history of astronomy because of their original concept, the first major innovation since the invention of the orrery in 1709 by the English clock and instrument maker George Graham. Rittenhouse did not duplicate what had been accomplished by his predecessors, but added an entirely new dimension to the representation of the universe in miniature.[59]

To Rittenhouse, Jefferson commented that he found himself at a disadvantage for lack of an accurate timepiece. "We were much disappointed in Virginia generally on the day of the great eclipse," he wrote, "which proved to be cloudy. In Williamsburgh, where it was total, I understand only the beginning was seen. At this place which is in Lat. 38° 8' and Longitude West from Williamsburgh about 1° 45' as is conjectured, eleven digits only were supposed to be covered. It was not seen at all till the moon had advanced nearly one third over the sun's disc. Afterwards it was seen at intervals through the whole. The egress particularly was visible. It proved however of little use to me for want of a time peice that could be depended on; which circumstance, together with the subsequent restoration of Philadelphia to you, has induced me to trouble you with this letter to remind you of your kind promise of making me an accurate clock, which being intended for astronomical purposes only, I would have divested of apparatus for striking or for any other purpose, which by increasing it's complication might disturb it's accuracy. A companion to it, for keeping seconds, and which might be moved easily, would greatly add to it's value. The theodolite, for which I spoke to you also, I can now dispense with, having since purchased a most excellent one."

Jefferson then went on to extol Rittenhouse's achievements and particularly his production of the planetarium in the College of Philadelphia:

> I doubt not there are in your country many persons equal to the task of conducting government: but you should consider that the world has but one Ryttenhouse, and that it never had one before. The amazing mechanical representation of the solar system which you conceived and executed, has never been surpassed by any but the work of which it is a copy. Are those powers then, which being intended for the erudition of the world, like air and light, the world's common property, to be taken from their proper pursuit to do the commonplace drudgery of governing a single state, a work which may be executed by men of an ordinary stature, such as are always and every where to be found? Without having ascended Mount Sina for inspiration, I can pronounce that the precept, in the decalogue of the vulgar, that they shall not make to themselves 'the likeness of any thing that is in the heavens above' is reversed for you, and that you will fulfill the highest purposes of your creation by employing yourself in the perpetual breach of that inhibition. For my own country in particular you must remember something like a promise that it should be adorned with one of them.'[60]

Perhaps inspired by Rittenhouse's achievements, Jefferson returned to his dream of having an astronomical observatory of his own. In about 1772 he had originally contemplated building an astronomical observatory at Monticello consisting of five stages with an overall height of 107 feet. His preliminary design greatly resembled Georgian prototypes of public buildings, such as the State House in Philadelphia, which he had visited several years earlier and may have inspired his design. It was not until several years later that he purchased land adjacent to Monticello which included High Mountain, a name which he then rendered into its Italian version "Montalto." Today it is known as Patterson Mountain, at the northern extremity of the long ridge called Carter's Mountain. Although presently partially wooded, in his time the completely forested uniform slopes of the promontory rose like a smooth round cone to a height of more than four hundred feet above Monticello. It dominated the view from Jefferson's house to the southwest. The land of the mountain was considerably less tillable than the adjacent region and was not a practical investment for farming, and Jefferson used it as a timber source. He purchased what he could see in addition to one hundred yards past that point.

Soon after the acquisition of Montalto, he developed another design for an observatory, undoubtedly his most original and ambitious structure. He may have been inspired to consider such a project in conversations with Rittenhouse, and probably made sketches while sitting through the long and often boring meetings of the Continental Congress. It is not inconceivable that he seriously considered the erection of such a building after peace was restored. (*Figure 4*)

In the two drawings that he produced in this period the character of the building was changed considerably from his first drawing made several years earlier. One drawing is of a tower 107 feet in height having three setbacks. However, he discovered that after the necessary space had been assigned for stairways and wall thicknesses, an insufficient working space of only nine feet by five feet remained. He then designed a crenellated observation tower one hundred and twenty feet in height with three set-backs which served as a filled-in foundation to support an observatory room and instrument room measuring ten by fifteen feet. The rooms were enclosed in a cubical structure of eighteen feet with fortress-like walls of eighteen-inch thickness.

Open galleries in the form of narrow terraces were provided behind the parapet walls. From the observation room, well situated above the haze and fog of the valley and even of low-lying clouds, so that celestial observations would not have been impeded, it may have been possible to glimpse the Rivanna River, flowing almost a thousand feet below.[61]

At the beginning of 1779, approximately four thousand British and Hessian prisoners who had surrendered at Saratoga marched the distance of almost seven hundred miles from Boston to Albemarle County, where they were to be maintained until shipped to England in accordance with the Convention. They arrived during a long period of extremely bad weather and were assigned to a barracks, not yet completed, on a hill outside Charlottesville.

The meat supply which had been set aside for them had been poorly butchered and much of it was spoiled, and it was rumored that the prisoners would have to be moved elsewhere. Returning from a sojourn at Poplar Forest, Jefferson learned of the situation and promptly took action. After he had consulted with Governor Patrick Henry, the troops were moved to completed barracks with their own gardens and poultry. Jefferson wanted these "Convention troops," as they were called, to remain in the County partly for local and for humane reasons, but also for personal interest, for he enjoyed the presence and company of the officers, some of whom became near neighbors.

There was no discussion of politics or public affairs with the foreign officers, but there was a considerable exchange of hospitality. Colonel Carter's plantation, Blenheim, was rented to the ranking British officer, Major General William Phillips, and Philip Mazzei's home during Mazzei's absence abroad was occupied by the ranking Hessian officer, Major General Friederich Adolphus Baron von Riedesel.[62]

Mazzei had undertaken a financial mission for the state of Virginia in Europe. In one way the occupation of his home proved to be an unfortunate arrangement, for during the brief three-week stay of the Baron and his family, horses destroyed Mazzei's vineyards beyond recovery. By this time, however, Mazzei's countless facile enthusiasms had become overwhelming and exhausting to Jefferson, and he considered Mazzei's wife to be particularly ill-mannered, so that he welcomed the Italian's departure. Jefferson enjoyed the company of the Hessian general, however, and Martha Jefferson became particularly attached to the Baroness and her daughters. Included in this new social circle were several other Hessian officers, notably Captain Baron von Geismar who played the violin, to Jefferson's delight, and another named Johann Ludwig von Unger.[63]

On June 1, 1779, Jefferson was elected Governor of Virginia, a position he assumed with considerable reluctance. In fact he had not campaigned for the office but probably allowed his name to be placed in nomination. The next two years proved to be excruciating, and confirmed his original hesitation in accepting the position.

His attempts to organize Virginia's limited human and material resources were greatly hampered by the reluctance of the Congress to provide the support and military leadership which the state required. He found himself presiding over the most extensive territory of the new nation with a weakly defended coastline and a vulnerable western frontier.

The state economy was greatly endangered by the depreciation of Continental currency but also by the inflation brought about by taxation. After Congress voted to cancel the issuance of Continental currency, the burden of supplying the army fell to individual states. To add to his problems, crop failure at the end of 1779 forced Virginia to import provisions.[64]

An account of visits made to Monticello by an unidentified Hessian officer after Jefferson had become governor was published in Germany in a Hamburg newspaper, and provides a valuable and unique view of

Jefferson's home at that time. The officer explained that his only occupation at the time was learning the English language, which was made easier for him than for others because he had access to Jefferson's library. He added:

> The Father of this learned Man was also a Favorite of the Muses. There is now of his a Map of Virginia extant, the best work of the kind. The Governor [Jefferson] possesses a Noble Spirit in Building. He is now finishing an elegant building projected according to his own fancy. In his parlour he is creating on the Cieling [sic] a Compass of his own invention by wich [sic] he can know the Strength as well as the Direction of the Winds. I have promised to paint the Compass for it. He was much pleased with a fancy Painting of mine.[65]

Jefferson's preoccupation with weather-watching had now found tangible expression at Monticello with the installation of the weather vane to enable the reading of wind direction from inside the mansion as well as outdoors. The shaft of the weathervane may have passed from the roof through his library on the second floor and the ceiling of the parlor. It is much more likely, however, that it passed through the portico. It terminated with an index or arrow at the center of the wind rose painted on the ceiling, in such a manner that as the vane moved, the index indicated the wind direction. (*Figure 5*)

Jefferson may have been inspired to some degree by the aviary or *tholus* of the villa of the Roman writer, Marcus Terentius Varro, which was described in considerable detail in Varro's work on agriculture and later in a volume by Robert Castell, both of which Jefferson owned in his library.

The letter of the unidentified Hessian prisoner of war published in the Hamburg newspaper provides the additional evidence that the weathervane was being installed in about 1780, and that the original compass rose was painted by that Hessian, undoubtedly to Jefferson's specifications.[66] (*Figure 6*)

For many years Jefferson hoped that the College of William and Mary would eventually be designated the University of Virginia, but his efforts repeatedly encountered violent opposition in the state. Until he finally turned his attention to the establishment of a separate state university several decades later, Jefferson was devoted to his alma mater. He urged his friends and others not to send American youth to European universities because the College in Williamsburg could provide the same education except in the matter of modern languages.[67]

An achievement of this period that provided Jefferson with considerable satisfaction was the reorganization of the College of William and Mary. As Governor of the state and as a member of the Governing Board of the College, Jefferson modified its entire course of study. By this time the "foreign" element of the faculty, appointed by the Bishop of London, had returned to England.

The existing grammar school and School of Divinity were abolished, and the teaching of Latin and Greek was dropped from the College curricula, although it was restored in 1792. The College was divided into five schools, of philosophy, mathematics and science, medicine, law and modern languages. The School of Law and the School of Modern Languages were the first in America. The School of Medicine was the second, the first being at the University of Pennsylvania. Uniting the faculties of law, medicine and the arts in one institution, the College was the first to attain the character of a university, a name formally acquired in the faculty records of 1781.

Jefferson was responsible for introducing the Lecture and the Honor System as well as the Elective System of Studies, by means of which a student was permitted to select any two of the five established schools. Jefferson had also proposed that the name of the College be changed to University. However, because the College of William and Mary had been the school of the Established Church, the change of name was not approved by the General Assembly.

In his proposal for reorganizing the College, Jefferson included a provision that had little to do with the rest of the bill, but reflected not only his personal interest in astronomy but also his admiration for the achievements of David Rittenhouse.

"And that this commonwealth may not be without so great an ornament," the provision stated, "nor, its youth such a help towards attaining astronomical science, as the mechanical representation, or model of the solar system, conceived and executed by that greatest of astronomers, David Ryttenhouse; Be it further enacted, that the visitors first appointed under this act, and their successors, shall be authorized to engage the said David Ryttenhouse, on the part of this commonwealth, to make and erect in the said college of William and Mary, and for its use, one of the said models, to be called by the name of the Ryttenhouse, the cost and expense of making, transporting and erecting whereof shall, according to the agreement or allowance of the said visitors, be paid by the Treasurer of this commonwealth, on warrant from the Auditors." Despite his spirited endorsement of an orrery for the College, it was not to be realized.[68]

His proposal for the College's reorganization, which was adopted on December 4, 1779 by the College's Board of Visitors, virtually revolutionized American education. The curricula of other American universities were later remodeled with some modification based on the plan executed at the College of William and Mary.

On January 21, 1780 Jefferson was pleased by his election to membership in the American Philosophical Society, at the same time as General Washington, the Chevalier de La Luzerne, John Jay, John Adams and James Madison among others. His election undoubtedly was due to some degree to his authorship of the Declaration of Independence and his position as Governor of Virginia but also to his reputation as a natural philosopher and his interest in the sciences.

At the Society's meeting held on December 17th of the previous year, acknowledgement had been made of a communication from the Reverend James Madison, partly relating to Jefferson's endeavors. It consisted of a series of "Meteorological Observations" by Jefferson and Madison undertaken separately for a year and a half; likewise a set of experiments on what was called the "sweet spring." A continuance of correspondence was requested, which initiated an exchange that was to last for forty-seven years.[69]

For making a comparison with his own observations, Jefferson asked his friend, John Page, for a copy of his meteorological notes ("Journal on the Weather"). Page had loaned it to the Virginia Society for Advancing Useful Knowledge, however, and when he recovered it, he found it to be in a greatly mutilated condition so that it was of little use. He referred Jefferson to David Jameson, charter treasurer of the Society, inasmuch as he had continued weather observations since the beginning of the war.[70]

Late in 1779 Joseph Reed, president of the Pennsylvania General Assembly, proposed to Jefferson the appointment by Virginia of commissioners to meet with those appointed by Pennsylvania to survey the extension of the Pennsylvania-Virginia boundary. On advice of the Council, Jefferson selected the Reverend Madison and the Reverend Robert Andrews, to "determine the extent of the five degrees of Longitude by celestial observation."[71]

His instructions to Madison and Andrews were that the "Commissioners proceed to execute the work from the Termination of Masons and Dixons Line to the Completion of the five Degrees of Longitude and thence on a meridian to the Ohio. We propose that the extent of the five Degrees of longitude shall be determined by celestial Observations." One group of observers was to be in Philadelphia and the other at Fort Pitt. Jefferson felt certain that the necessary instruments could be acquired in Philadelphia, but for those stationed at Fort Pitt, instruments would have to be obtained from their Corporation, namely, the College of William and Mary, noting they they would be replaced if injured.

Jefferson suggested the use of astronomical observations for running the line, a proposal accepted by Reed, because they would serve "not only as determining the present question with more certainty, but as it tends to solve a problem both useful and curious to the Learned World." However, because their instruments were scattered and in need of repair, and so much time would be required to assemble and repair them, the season would be too late for undertaking the survey, and it was postponed to the following May.[72]

On January 5, 1781 Jefferson had been elected a Councillor of the American Philosophical Society for two years, an honor which pleased him greatly. "The busy scene in which I have the misfortune to be engaged," he responded on April 18th, "has kept me too long from acknowledging the receipt of your polite letter notifying this honour to me; and I shall be very happy if the leisure, to which I mean shortly to retire, shall enable me to contribute any thing worthy the acceptance of the society. But too long detached from those objects which come more immediately within their plan, it will scarcely be within my power to recover even the little familiarity I once had with them, and which would be far short of rendering the society any service. I can only assure them that I shall not be wanting in every respect and office which I may have an opportunity of rendering."[73]

As the tempo of the war increased, however, Jefferson had even less time for philosophical pursuits then before. With the beginning of a British campaign against Virginia's southern neighbors, the state capital had to be moved inland to Richmond. The surrender of Charleston and the loss of the Virginia regiments garrisoned there led Jefferson to offer Washington a plan for improvement of military intelligence.

When Cornwallis encamped near the Virginia and North Carolina border, Jefferson had only the state militia to protect the state. After his defeat at Camden, South Carolina, General Horatio Gates retreated with the Virginia troops under his command. Meanwhile the government continued to demand reinforcements from Virginia but failed to provide arms and supplies for them. Cornwallis's advance north from South Carolina and Georgia was finally halted in the fall, and Jefferson contemplated the possibility of expanding military operations on the lands claimed by Virginia on the north and west. The plan could not be implemented, however, for a few days later Benedict Arnold appeared with a fleet in Chesapeake Bay and moved up the James River. Jefferson called out the militia but it was already too late to organize a defense.

Ruin and destruction followed Arnold's repeated raids from the mouth of the James River to the capital at Richmond. Governor Jefferson and those members of the legislature who had appeared for a May session agreed to move the government from the capital to Charlottesville. Jefferson remained behind in Richmond for a time but then joined his family at Tuckahoe. In the interim the legislature had not reorganized at Charlottesville as planned. Five days later, on June 1st, Jefferson's term as governor expired. The legislature failed to act in time to choose a successor, and he remained in Charlottesville to complete official business before returning to Monticello on June 3rd.[74]

Jefferson personally supervised the transfer of public stores and state records from Richmond. He developed a scheme for Arnold's capture and then withdrew to await the next British move, but his strategy did not succeed. Following Arnold's raid, Lafayette was sent with a detachment to Virginia which managed to turn back a British raid on Richmond, but he was unable to protect the capital against a major attack.

Meanwhile, General Cornwallis had been informed that members of the Virginia state government had gathered at Charlottesville, and he conceived the idea of capturing them. He dispatched Colonel Banastre Tarleton there with dragoons and mounted infantrymen. If the mission had succeeded, it would have been a major coup, for with Jefferson at Charlottesville among others were Patrick Henry, Richard Henry Lee, Thomas Nelson, Jr. and Benjamin Harrison. Furthermore, the Continental Army had valuable military stores deposited in the city.

Tarleton, known as "the Hunting Leopard," moved with great speed, planning to cover the last seventy miles of his journey in twenty-four hours. At midday on June 3rd he stopped with his men to rest their horses, then proceeded to the Cuckoo Tavern in Louisa County, arriving between nine and ten that evening. Quite by coincidence Captain John Jouett, Jr. of the Virginia militia saw them passing his father's house on the main highway. Realizing the intent of the British, Jouett mounted his horse and rode towards Charlottesville approximately forty miles away on a little traveled road through the wilderness.

Tarleton and his men rested at a plantation near Louisa Courthouse. As they continued on their way, they encountered a wagon train with arms and clothing for General Greene's army in South Carolina and set it afire. They arrived at Castle Hill, the residence of Dr. Thomas Walker, soon after dawn and delayed for half an hour to refresh the horses, according to Tarleton's account. Local tradition states, however, that he remained considerably longer. Walker had prepared a lavish breakfast for the British with the intention of delaying them as long as possible so that Jefferson and the legislature would be enabled to escape.

Jouett was far in advance of Tarleton, and after crossing the Rivanna at Milton Ford, he rode up the mountain to Monticello, arriving at half past four o'clock in the morning. He awakened Jefferson and his guests, and after taking some refreshment, he rode off again to Charlottesville to arouse the other legislators. Jefferson's guests had a leisurely breakfast and then they rode down to Charlottesville to join their associates. At Charlottesville the members of the General Assembly disbanded hastily upon learning from Jouett that the British were approaching, and agreed to convene again three days later at Staunton. Before they could make their escape, however, seven of them were captured by the British.[75]

After the departure of his guests, Jefferson quickly prepared for the removal of his family to Enniscorthy, the home of Colonel Coles approximately fourteen miles away; they were to travel by way of Blenheim, the Carter estate, where Jefferson planned to meet them.

During the next two hours he collected his most important papers, including memoranda relating to the state of Virginia. He was interrupted by the arrival of Captain Christopher Hudson of the Continental Army, who had come to warn him that the British were already ascending the road up the mountain to Monticello.

Jefferson immediately hurried his family off in their carriage in the care of a young man who had been studying law with him. Then leaving his horse at the gap between the mountains, he took his pocket telescope and proceeded by a cross path to a rock between Monticello and Carter's Mountain from which he could observe Charlottesville. From his observations of the town, nothing appeared to be amiss. As he was about to return to the house, he noticed that he had lost his light "walking sword." Returning to pick it up, he looked again towards Charlottesville through his telescope and was startled to see the green and white uniforms of British dragoons and the red coats of infantrymen in the streets of the town. Hastening to where he had hitched his horse, he barely escaped the British, who had already arrived at Monticello, where a Captain McLeod promptly took possession. He was not pursued, however, and he was able to join his family later that day at Blenheim and had dinner with the Carter family.[76] (*Figure* 7)

Although Jefferson anticipated that the home of the state governor would be a particular target for molestation, Tarleton had given strict instructions that nothing was to be touched or injured in the mansion. His orders were scrupulously followed, and all that was taken were a few bottles of wine from the cellar.

Although Tarleton had acted honorably concerning Jefferson's possessions, Lord Cornwallis did otherwise. He had encamped his army for ten days near Elk Hill, and used the house as his headquarters building. Before his departure he destroyed the growing crops of tobacco and corn, burned the barns, stables and fences as well as one year's crop of tobacco in the tobacco house, confiscated fifty-nine head of cattle, thirty sheep and sixty hogs, killed all the colts and drove away with nine mares. Twenty-nine slaves were taken prisoner to a camp where smallpox and camp fever raged and all but three of them subsequently died. The damage was estimated at three or four thousand pounds. There was no question that Cornwallis had singled Jefferson out for this wanton destruction.[77]

Jefferson's bitter cup was not yet full. The members of the Assembly who had managed to escape the British met at Staunton, reconstituted themselves and met in session under the aegis of Patrick Henry. The Assembly moved for establishing a dictator, for only in this manner, Henry and his supporters argued, would it be possible for Virginia to recapture the leadership among the states that her governors had failed to provide. The scheme failed by a narrow margin, and Thomas Nelson, Jr. was elected Governor.

At this time George Nicholas proposed and it was resolved "That at the next session of the Assembly an inquiry be made into the conduct of the Executive of this State for the last twelve months." Jefferson was required to present an account of his administration of the previous year. Suspecting that Henry had engineered the attack, he demanded from Nicholas to know the specific charges, and prepared to respond to them before the Assembly at its next meeting.[78]

To add to his misery, on June 30th Jefferson suffered a bad fall from his horse, which resulted in a broken arm, and he was confined for six weeks. Several decades later, during the presidential campaign of 1805, the accident was reported in the *Richmond Enquirer* and distorted by his political opponents, who claimed that the fall had occurred while fleeing from the British at Monticello.[79]

It was at this critical point in Jefferson's career that the Congress appointed him to the commission with Benjamin Franklin and John Adams which was to go to Paris to negotiate a peace with Great Britain. Lafayette offered him hospitality in France, and the prospect of visiting Europe at last, of which he had long dreamed, was exciting. He was forced to refuse the appointment, however, albeit with great reluctance and personal anguish, because of the necessity of remaining in Virginia to defend himself before the Assembly.

Jefferson returned to Monticello to recuperate and prepare his defence before the Assembly. December 12th was the day scheduled for the inquiry and Jefferson appeared in person. His friends had rallied meanwhile, and the accuser Nicholas failed to come forward. The committee established to collect evidence found itself with nothing more than unsubstantiated rumors. A resolution was passed unanimously

> That the sincere thanks of the General Assembly be given to our former Governor, Thomas Jefferson, Esq. for his impartial, upright, and attentive administration of the powers of the Executive, whilst in office; popular rumors gaining some degree of credence, by more pointed accusations, rendered it necessary to make an inquiry into his conduct, and delayed that retribution of public gratitude, so eminently merited; but that conduct having become the object of open scrutiny, tenfold value is added to an approbation, founded on a cool and deliberate discussion. The Assembly wish therefore, in the strongest manner, to declare the high opinion which they entertain of Mr. Jefferson's ability, rectitude and integrity, as Chief Magistrate of this Commonwealth; and mean by thus publicly avowing their opinion, to obviate all future, and to remove all former, unmerited censure.

On December 19th the resolution was approved by both houses, after the Senate had removed much of the verbiage of protestation.[80]

CHAPTER V

"MEASURE OF A SHADOW" (1781–1784)

To learn . . . the ordinary arrangement of the different strata of minerals in the earth, to know from their habitual collocations, and proximities, where we find one mineral; whether another, for which we are seeking, may be expected to be in its neighborhood, is useful. But the dreams about the modes of creation, enquiries whether our globe has been formed by the agency of fire or water, how many millions of years it has cost Vulcan or Neptune to produce what the fist of the Creator would effect by a single act of will, is too idle to be worth a single hour of any man's life.

Letter from Thomas Jefferson
to Dr. John F. Emmet,
1826.

At Monticello once more, Jefferson felt mortally wounded, physically and mentally, from these recent events, in what was the darkest period of his life. It would become even darker before the year was out, however, but in the meantime he set to work on a project which was to prove to be one of his major scientific endeavors, namely, the writing of his *Notes On the State of Virginia.*

The routing of the Virginia militia at the battle of Camden had begun to raise serious doubts about the outcome of the American Revolution, and may have been the reason that the French government requested information about the new American nation to which it furnished assistance. Instructions were received by Anne César, Chevalier de La Luzerne, the French minister to the United States, to collect perti-

nent data about the individual states. The project was assigned to the
secretary of the French legation, François Marbois, later Marquis François de Barbé-Marbois.

Marbois prepared a questionnaire on twenty-two topics, based on
a natural progression, as follows:

1. The Charter of your State.
2. The present Constitution.
3. An exact description of its limits and boundaries.
4. The Memoirs published in its name, in the time of its being a Colony,
   and the pamphlets relating to its interior or exterior affairs present or
   ancient.
5. The History of the State.
6. A Notice of the Counties Cities Townships Villages Rivers Rivulets
   and how they are navigable. Cascades Caverns Mountains Productions
   Trees Plants Fruits and other natural Riches.
7. The number of its Inhabitants.
8. The different Religions received in that State.
9. The Colleges and public establishments. The Roads Buildings &c.
10. The Administration of Justice and a description of the Laws.
11. The particular Customs and manners that may happen to be received
    in that State.
12. The present State of Manufactures Commerce interior and exterior
    Trade.
13. A notice of the best Sea Ports of the State and how big are the vessels
    they can receive.
14. A notice of the commercial productions particular to that State and
    of those objects which the Inhabitants are obliged to get from Europe
    and from other parts of the World.
15. The weight measures and the currency of the hard money. Some de-
    tails to the exchange with Europe.
16. The public income and expences.
17. The measures taken with regard of the Estates and Possessions of the
    Rebels commonly called Tories.
18. The condition of the Regular Troops and the Militia and their pay.
19. The marine and Navigation.
20. A notice of the Mines and other subterranean riches.
21. Some sample of those Mines and of the extraordinary Stones. In short,
    a notice of all what can increase the progress of human Knowledge.
22. A description of the Indians established in the State before the Euro-
    pean Settlements and of those who are still remaining. An indication
    of the Indian Monuments discovered in that State.[1]

With the advice and assistance of Charles Thomson, the Secretary
of the Congress, Marbois forwarded copies of his list to prominent men

in each of the states, including Thomas McKean of Delaware, John Sullivan of New Hampshire, John Witherspoon of New Jersey and Joseph Jones of Virginia.

Jones, a member of Congress from Virginia and uncle of James Monroe, turned the questionnaire over to Jefferson, then Governor of Virginia, as the individual best informed and most capable of providing the information. He probably contacted Jefferson on a visit to Richmond. Upon his return to Philadelphia several months later, Jones informed Marbois that Jefferson now had the questionnaire, which prompted Marbois to write to Jefferson early in February.[2]

It was during the relatively quiet period following the withdrawal of British forces from Tidewater Virginia in October 1780, that Jefferson turned to his task. He responded to Marbois,

> Hitherto it has been in my power to collect a few materials only, which my present occupations disable me from compleating. I mean however, shortly, to be in a condition which will leave me quite at leisure to take them up, when it shall certainly be one of my first undertakings to give you as full information as I shall be able to do on such of the subjects which are within the sphere of my acquaintance. On some of these however I trust Mr. Jones will engage abler hands, those in particular which relate to the commerce of the state, a subject with which I am totally unacquainted, and which is probably the most important in your plan.[3]

Jefferson continued to compile data for the questionnaire during what was undoubtedly the busiest time of his life, while serving as governor of Virginia and during a period of intensely troubling personal events that followed. A daughter, Lucy Elizabeth, died at the age of five months, and his wife Martha's health had deteriorated to a precarious state. He attended her diligently during the next several months, finding moments for the questionnaire when he could.[4]

He resumed work on the project after his term of office ended, in the summer and autumn of 1781, resorting to his "commonplace book," in which he had copied excerpts from oral reports and publications, and had made notes from personal observation. At Poplar Forest, his summer retreat, and later at Monticello while recuperating from his fall, he utilized other research resources he had available. The preparation of the answers provided him with "a good occasion to embody their substance, which I did in the order of Mr. Marbois' queries, so as to answer his wish and to arrange them for my own use."

"I had always made it a practice," he wrote many years later, "whenever an opportunity occurred of obtaining any information of our country, which might be of use to me in any station public or private, to commit it to writing."[5]

This compilation was not confined in a bound volume as were most commonplace books, but instead consisted of scattered notes made "on loose papers, bundled up without order, and difficult of recurrence when I had occasion for a particular one." It was a collection of more than one hundred pages of memoranda including tables, notes made as reminders to himself and additional data and sheets with corrections. Much of this information had been gathered during the ten or more years since 1770 after his papers and books had been destroyed in the fire of Shadwell.[6]

Ever since his student days, Jefferson had diligently made notes of the natural world around him and particularly data about his native state of Virginia. As a beginning he had purchased the few books that had been written on the subject; possibly the earliest such purchase was the copy of William Stith's *The History of the First Discovery and Settlement of Virginia*, which he had purchased in Williamsburg in 1764, while he was studying law with Wythe.[7]

Another category of records he had avidly collected at that time consisted of manuscript materials relating to Virginia history, assembling eighteen volumes of legislative, judicial and miscellaneous records of the colony.[8]

Some of the sources to which he now resorted were notations of information he had requested and received from others whom he considered to be reliable sources. He had also recorded related data received orally from friends and others. Often he had urged his younger friends, such as Peter and Dabney Carr, Jr. and Francis Walker Gilmer, to acquire an extensive knowledge of their own "country", by which he meant Virginia, and during his career as a lawyer he constantly sought information about his state which might be useful for his work. It had long been Jefferson's intention to organize all this miscellaneous information into some sort of order when a suitable opportunity offered. The occasion to make use of this material was at last at hand.[9]

He now contacted friends for specific information he required, particularly about Virginia's flora and fauna. Dr. Thomas Walker, for example, reported that he had knowledge of a buffalo weighing eighteen hundred pounds, and John Bolling, a relative by marriage, noted a deer weighing two hundred and thirty pounds, although Jefferson had previously believed that the maximum weight of a deer was one hundred seventy-five pounds.

Colonel Archibald Cary had seen a bear weighing four hundred and ten pounds while a Mr. Miller of Augusta had raised a hog weighing one thousand pounds, and Colonel Ingles had killed a bear weighing more than fifteen hundred pounds. Isaac Zane wrote that he had a horse five feet eight inches in height which weighed 1366 pounds.

One correspondent informed him that the catalpa tree grew "about the north limit of the 37°," or in the region of Halifax County. From others Jefferson collected information about turtles in Ohio, and the prevalence of specific birds, snakes and lizards in various regions.

Archibald Cary provided comparative information about animals of Europe and America. He wrote, "I am sorry I have not been more attentive to the Weights of Many Wild Anamals for except a Ber, an elk and several Bucks, I never waighd any. I saw in England a Panther sayd to be from the Cost of Gania, and a wolf said to be from Germany both full Grown, and I Can assure you I have seen of both Kinds in Virginia much larger."[10]

While at Poplar Forest, Jefferson reviewed the memoranda he had brought with him on his flight from Monticello, digesting it bit by bit and adding to gaps and omissions from his own memory of things seen and heard and read. He made a list of items about which he required more information to be sought from others. Working in the solitude of his retreat, far from potential distractions, Jefferson wrote freely, without great concern for literary style, for at that time he had no intention of making any other use of the data except to respond to Marbois.

Nonetheless, he prepared each reply with excruciating accuracy, and in addition to the data requested, he took the opportunity to correct misinformation, theories and fallacies already published by French writers. As he wrote, he could not refrain from adding some of his own opinions, conclusions, reflections and personal philosophy to the facts.

Jefferson completed the greater part of the work in several weeks during the summer, then began to organize the manuscript in the order of the queries that Marbois had provided. The weeks passed quickly and relatively pleasantly, and for the first time in many months Jefferson had a feeling of substantial achievement.

By the time he returned to Monticello in early August, his manuscript was almost complete. He continued to add to it as time allowed, while preparing for his appearance before the Virginia Assembly. After his hearing ended, he remained in Richmond long enough to seek out more information he was still lacking for his compilation.[11]

Jefferson had an ulterior purpose in responding to Marbois's queries with such detail. Having been appointed a councillor of the American Philosophical Society, which he recognized to be a particular honor, in December he informed Charles Thomson, a fellow councillor, that he did not know either the duties of that office or "the nature of their institution to judge what objects it comprehends."

In preparing the answers to Marbois's queries, he went on,

it occurred to me that some of the subjects which I had then occasion to take up, might, if more fully handled, be a proper tribute to the Philosophical society, and the aversion I have of being counted a drone in any society induced me to determine to recur to you as my antient friend, to ask the favor of you to peruse those answers, and to take the trouble of communicating to me your opinion whether any and which of the subjects there treated would come within the scope of that learned institution, and to what degree of minuteness one should descend in treating it; perhaps also you would be so friendly as to give me some idea of the subjects which would at any time be admissible into their transactions.[12]

Thomson admitted that he was as ignorant as Jefferson of the nature of the duties of a councillor, but assured him that his answers to the Marbois queries would be most acceptable. "And therefore though I regret your retiring from the busy anxious scenes of politics," he wrote, "yet I congratulate posterity on the Advantages they may derive from your philosophical researches."[13]

This was all the encouragement that Jefferson required, and he proceeded to develop the notes accordingly. At this time he had not considered the possibility of publishing the manuscript, planning only to circulate copies to friends and associates to obtain suggestions for additional material and corrections. As with many authors, no sooner had the copy to Marbois left his hands than he became concerned with the need of adding to it and correcting it, which he continued to do during the winter months. His friends and informants complied by sending him additional data supplementing his own continued research.

While he was serving as delegate to the Continental Congress in Philadelphia during the following winter, he undertook further revisions. Realizing that he had produced a useful document which might serve other purposes, he now rearranged his manuscript, not in the order in which Marbois's queries appeared, but instead according to what he visualized a guide book would include.

He began with a description of Virginia's geography and natural aspects, considering in order its boundaries, rivers, seaports, mountains, cascades, flora, fauna, minerals and climate. He then added sections about the nature of its people, its military and marine forces, aborigines, population, counties and towns, constitution, laws, colleges, buildings and roads.

Next he considered Virginia's "Proceedings as to Tories," religion and manners. He then added commercial considerations such as manufactures, subjects of commerce, weights, measures and money, public revenues and expenses, and ended with histories, memorials and state papers.

In certain categories, such as rivers, he was able to include specific information about depths and navigability, harbors and tonnage of ships that could navigate them. He included rivers and bodies of water outside of Virginia such as the Missouri, Ohio, Mississippi and Illinois Rivers and as far as the Hudson River and Lake Erie. In the section on caves he was able to include dimensions, and he provided as well data on distances, winds and temperatures.

The greatly increased size of the manuscript, and the number of requests for copies he received from informants and friends, convinced Jefferson that it should be published. "Some friends who occasionally communicated wishes for copies; but their volume rendering this too laborious by hand, I proposed to get a few printed for their gratification. I was asked such a price however as exceeded the importance of the object." In view of the high costs of printing, Jefferson postponed plans for publication for the time being.[14]

The manuscript of the notes had expanded into a project of such scope as he had never contemplated. It evolved from what at first was a casual endeavor to produce a statistical survey, to what has been considered by historians to be the most important book on science produced in America in the eighteenth century. Not only was it to become one of his major scientific achievements, but it was to cast him in the role of one of the foremost early American men of science. Furthermore, it was to direct Jefferson into a field of study which gained for him the title "father of American vertebrate paleontology."[15]

While compiling data on animals for the section on *Productions Mineral, Vegetable and Animal*, he eagerly took the opportunity to refute the theories of the French naturalist, Georges Louis Leclerc, Comte de Buffon. Buffon was the leading naturalist of his time, director of the Jardin du Roi and of the French royal museum. His advanced evolutionary theory of 1766 had met with less than general approval, however, and the pressure brought upon him by the theological faculty of the University of Paris forced him to retreat from it. He subsequently confined his investigations within the limits of his belief in the absolute fixity of species, as a consequence of their biological grouping by physiological characteristics, habitat and mores, and the survival of the fittest.

In his writings Buffon had asserted that the living animals of America were smaller in size than those of the Old World, and that there were fewer species. Among his claims was that the tapir was the largest of the New World animals.[16]

Jefferson had not only the positive knowledge to refute these claims, but also the temerity to attack a number of the assertions and statements published by Buffon and his associate, Louis Jean Marie Daubenton. To do so required considerable courage, inasmuch as Jefferson had no credentials in the sciences. He was, however, well informed not only of the achievements and writings of the European naturalists of his time, but about American flora and fauna.

Jefferson disputed Buffon's contention that the Old World animals had degenerated due to the supposed adverse influence of the American climate. The French naturalist had stated that a combination of the elements as well as other physical causes were responsible for the lack of aggrandizement of animals. He further contended that heat was conducive and moisture was adverse to the production and development of larger quadrupeds in the New World.

Jefferson considered this hypothesis doubtful, convinced that it was based on insufficient observation, and consequently he felt assured that there was no basis for such a conclusion. He summarized Buffon's contentions into four categories, namely, (1) Animals common to both the Old World and the New were smaller in the latter; (2) Animals peculiar only to the New World were on a smaller scale; (3) Animals that had been domesticated in the Old and New Worlds had degenerated in the latter; and (4) There were fewer species in the New World. He then contrasted the tables produced by Buffon and Daubenton on the four issues with tables of his own, based on live or recently killed animals.[17]

Jefferson identified 89 birds to be found in his state, providing both Mark Catesby's designations as well as their popular names, 26 quadrupeds aboriginal to both Europe and the American continent, 18 indigenous only to Europe, 74 found only in America, and 8 quadrupeds domesticated in both Europe and America. In compiling tables of comparison of animal species, Jefferson noted that they were not intended "to produce a conclusion in favor of American species, but to justify a suspension of opinion until we are better informed, and a suspicion in the mean time that there is a uniform difference in favour of either [continent]; which is all I pretend."[18]

The discovery of gigantic bones in Ohio led him to speculate that large animals such as the mammoth may still be roaming the wilderness. In the eighteenth century the name "mammoth" was in common usage not only for the woolly mammoth, but also to describe the North American incognitum that was eventually defined as the American mastodon.

Taking the "mammoth" as his example, which had been described by Linnaeus and Buffon, Jefferson noted that the "big buffalo" as it was known to the American Indians, was the largest of American mammals. Indian tradition claimed that it was carnivorous and that it survived in the northern regions of America. He related how a delegation of Indian warriors had visited him while he was serving as governor of Virginia and answered his questions about what they knew or had heard of the animal whose bones had been found at the salt licks along the Ohio River.

The chief Indian speaker related that the tradition handed down among his people was that in ancient times a herd of these large beasts had come to the big bone licks and caused great destruction of bears, deer, elks and buffaloes, animals that had been created for the use of the Indians. At that point "the Great Man," who had been looking down from above, became so enraged that he seized the lightning and descended to earth. Seating himself on a mountain, he hurled his bolts among the large beasts until they were all destroyed except for one large bull which was wounded and bounded away to beyond the great lakes where he continued to live to that day.[19]

One of the most valuable derivatives of Jefferson's compilation, later published as his *Notes on the State of Virginia*, was the degree of interest in fossil remains which had been aroused by his research. As a consequence, he personally undertook a systematic collection of fossil bones and established a network of others for the purpose.[20]

Fossil bones had been recovered from various parts of the American continent for centuries past, long before Jefferson became interested in the subject. Since his time, modern archeologists have found evidence that pre-Columbian Indians collected fossil bones and may have used them for Indian "medicine," providing the basis for their legends about great beasts that roamed the earth. The first to write about American fossil remains was the New England minister, Cotton Mather, in a letter of 1712 to Dr. John Woodward of London, published two years later in the *Philosophical Transactions*. Canadians who had come in 1735 to fight the Chickasaw Indians discovered elephant skeletons and mastodon bones along the Ohio River. A few years later the English naturalist Mark Catesby found fossil remains of extinct animals in Carolina. An American fossil was first illustrated in 1756 by the French naturalist Jean Etienne Guettard, and American fossils were first scientifically studied in 1762 by the French naturalist Daubenton.[21]

A major source of fossil bones was the great fossil repository at Big Bone Lick on the banks of the Big Bone Lick Creek in Kentucky discovered in the mid-eighteenth century. Later another was found in Virginia's western territories. It was not until 1784, however, that any descriptions of these repositories were published. A collection of fossil bones from this site was sent to London in 1766, and described with others by the English physiologist, Dr. William Hunter, in a paper published in 1768. A comparable collection was sketched by the Philadelphia artist and museum entrepreneur, Charles Willson Peale, for the Hessian army surgeon Christian Friedrich Michaelis.[22]

Paleontology was not recognized as truly a science even in Europe in this period, but the discovery of as yet unidentified fossils on the American continent triggered the interest of French and British naturalists, and as a plentiful supply of materials for study became available, speculation was engendered also among American men of science. In 1767 the London merchant-naturalist, Peter Collinson, read the first technical report of these finds before the Royal Society, and Dr. William Hunter also reported on the subject to the Society; both papers were published in 1768.[23]

Jefferson was well-informed of the writings of these English and European naturalists, and noted that naturalists in the Old World identified tusks and skeletons recovered from Big Bone Lick as those of elephants and the grinders as those of hippopotami. He commented that the tusks and skeletons and grinders were substantially larger than those of elephants and hippopotami, however, and essentially different in form. Such a division he considered to have been made arbitrarily and he expressed his confusion.

"Whenever these grinders are found there also we find the tusks and the skeleton.... It will not be said that the hippopotamus and the elephant came always to the same spot, the former to deposit his grinders, and the latter his tusks and skeleton.... We must agree then, that these remains belong to each other, that they are of one and the same animal."[24]

Jefferson realized that although he had established the relationship of the tusks, skeletons and grinders, the problem of their identification still remained unresolved. No known elephant had molars remotely resembling those of the hippopotamus, and no hippopotamus had tusks similar to those of the elephant. No agreement was reached by European naturalists about the nature of the animal in question. After examining some of the first fossils recovered from Big Bone Lick, Hunter in London had adopted the view that they were remains of carnivores. When Collinson examined similar remains in the same period, he concluded they were remains of herbivores, an extinct species of elephant.[25]

Jefferson was inclined at first to accept the theory that the fossil bones were remains of the elephant. However, no species of elephant was known to live above the tropics, and he contemplated whether an elephant species adapted to the cold had once lived on the northern American continent. If so, might one still exist in the great unexplored regions? He finally concluded that these remains were of an incognitum resembling the elephant, but not of any species then known. "I find it easier to believe that an animal may have existed, resembling the elephant in his tusks and general anatomy, while his nature in other respects was extremely different."[26]

It was against this background of European interest and conflicting conclusions that Jefferson ventured his opinions. In his description of the animals of Virginia in the Notes, he included the "mammoth" or mastodon among animals existing in America and Europe. He noted that if asked why he had done so, his response would be "Why should I omit it, as if it did not exist? Such is the economy of nature, that no instance can be produced, of her having permitted any one race of her animals to become extinct; of her having formed any link in her great work so weak as to be broken."[27]

In addition to successfully overthrowing Buffon's claims and suppositions, Jefferson disputed Daubenton's contention that the mastodon remains were from two different animals, the elephant and the hippopotamus. He concluded that the incognitum was a carnivore, and that the northern distribution of mammoths and mastodons were not elephants, which were tropical, but a different species adapted to cold climates.[28]

In arguing against Buffon's belief that moisture was deleterious to animal growth, he stated, "The truth of this is inscrutable to us by reasonings *a priori*. Nature has hidden from us her *modus agendi*. Our only appeal on such questions is to experience; and I think that experience is against the supposition."[29]

Jefferson became so intrigued with the challenge presented by fossil remains that in December 1781, shortly before the events culminating in the capture of Richmond by the British, he sent a letter by hand of Daniel Boone to the explorer Colonel George Rogers Clark to arrange for Clark to acquire for him some fossil bones. He suggested that Clark might leave them with someone at Fort Pitt until the surveyors of the Pennsylvania boundary arrived and could bring them back in their wagon. He added, "The retirement into which I am withdrawing has increased my eagerness in pursuit of objects of this kind."[30]

Several months passed before Clark was able to report; he had had a disappointing lack of success in his search for the fossil teeth Jefferson had requested. He had found only a broken thigh bone but expected to obtain other specimens in the spring since a strong outpost was to be established at Licking Creek.

"I shall have the largest and fairest got—a Thigh and Jaw Bone Grinders and Tusk," Clark added. "The Animal had no foreteeth that I could ever discover and by no means Carnivorious [sic] as many suppose…. Their is very Curious Shells found in many parts of this Cuntry. I shall send you a few of them…."[31]

The *Notes*, which confirmed that discoveries of fossil remains had been relatively common and from a large number of localities, was the first comprehensive work on the topography, natural history and natural resources of one of the United States. Although not presented as a formal scientific paper, and hastily prepared in response to a specific need, it was the precursor of the great volume of scientific reports subsequently issued by the United States government.

By means of charts Jefferson listed 129 medicinal, esculent, ornamental and otherwise useful plants, shrubs and trees native to Virginia. He also included vegetables, fruits and ornamental plants introduced by English colonists, and added maize, tobacco, potatoes, pumpkins, cymblings and squashes. His identifications were based on the *Flora Virginica* of Johann Friedrich Gronovius, which in turn had relied heavily upon the works of John Banister and John Clayton.

Jefferson preferred the Linneaen system of botanical classification to the natural system proposed by Antoine Laurent de Jussieu "because it is sufficient as a groundwork; admits of supplementary insertions, as new productions are discovered, and mainly because it has got into so general use that it will not be easy to displace it."

In his opinion, the Linnaean system had the advantage of aiding the memory to retain knowledge of plants; everyone used the same names for the same items, and it enabled one to trace an unknown by its characteristics "up to the conventional name by which it was agreed to be called."[32]

Jefferson was particularly intrigued by the "singular quality" of *Datura stramonium*, commonly known as Jimson weed. "The late Dr. [Thomas] Bond informed me," he wrote in the *Notes*, "that he had under his care a patient, a young girl, who had put the seeds of this plant into her eye, which dilated the pupil to such a degree, that she could see in the dark, but in the light was almost blind." The Aztecs and the Algonquin Indians were familiar with the plant's narcotic properties and both used it as a ceremonial intoxicant. The popular name is a corrupted form of "Jamestown," Virginia, where the plant was found growing in abundance by the early settlers. It was reputed to have derived its name because of the strange behavior, after eating it, of soldiers sent against Nathaniel Bacon in 1678.

The characteristics of this poisonous plant were first described in 1705 by Robert Beverley in his *History of the Present State of Virginia*. A member of the nightshade family, it is also known as thorn apple, devil's trumpet, stinkwort and stinkweed. Extremely poisonous, the drug *stramonium* is extracted from its leaves for use in certain medicines. It is an important source of atropine and has been listed in the United States Pharmacopia from the early nineteenth century.[33]

Greatly influenced by Richard Bradley's work on plant growth, Jefferson noted, "It is by the assistance of heat and moisture that vegetables are elaborated from the elements of the earth, air, water, and fire," a statement made before Lavoisier's ideas had become widespread.[34]

Under "Climate," Jefferson included some of the weather observations he had recorded daily at Williamsburg between 1772 and 1777. To a table of temperatures, and rainfall, he added a table of wind directions "formed by reducing nine months' observations from Monticello and similar observations made at Williamsburg." Included also was a comparison of the average temperature at Monticello and Williamsburg over a period of five or six weeks, indicating that at Monticello the temperature was 6-⅛° lower and the barometer 0.748° lower.[35]

He devoted particular attention to his account of "Aborigines." He listed 29 Indian tribes "Northward and Westward of the United States," and 55 tribes within the United States listed by the regions in which they lived. Another 14 tribes, which "apprehending these might be different appellations for some of the tribes already numerated," were not included in the table. Not the least of the compilation was a bibliography of 346 histories, memoirs and state papers relating to Virginia.

The contents of the *Notes* were not always purely statistical, for occasionally Jefferson permitted his imagination to speculate, such as on geological events of the past. He also shared some of Charles Thomson's visionary conjectures which he included in an appendix to the work. "I am informed that at York town in Virginia, in the bank of York river," Thomson wrote,

> there are different strata of shells and earth, one above another, which seem to point out that the country there has undergone several changes; that is, that the sea has, for a succession of ages, occupied the place where dry land now appears; and that the ground has been suddenly raised at various periods. What a change it would make in the country below, should the mountains at Niagara, by any accident, be cleft asunder, and a passage suddenly opened to drain off the waters of Erie and the upper lakes! While ruminating on these subjects, I have often been hurried away by fancy, and led to imagine, that what is now the bay of Mexico, was once a champaign country; and that from the point or cape of Florida, there was a continuing range of mountains through Cuba, Hispaniola, Porto Rico, Martinique, Guadaloupe, Barbadoes, and Trinidad, till it reached the coast of America, and formed the shores which bounded the ocean, and guarded the country behind; that by some convulsion or shock of nature, the sea had broken through these mounds, and deluged that vast plain, till it reached the foot of the Andes; that being there heaped up by the trade winds, always blowing from one quarter, it had found its way back, as it continued to do, through the Gulf between Florida and Cuba, carrying with it the loam and sand it may have scooped from the country it had occupied, part of which it may have deposited on the shores of North America, and with part formed the banks of Newfoundland. But these are only the visions of fancy.[36]

The *Notes* contain the earliest reference to the presence of gold in the Appalachians. Jefferson described a lump of gold ore weighing approximately four pounds that had been discovered on the north side of the Rappahannock River in Virginia, some four miles below the falls. He reported that the gold was in the form of small flecks interspersed throughout the lump of ore, "which yeilded seventeen pennyweight of gold, of extraordinary ductility." It was the only indication of the presence of gold of which he was aware.[37]

To Jefferson, it was eminently clear that the biological factors limiting the characteristic size of species were to be considered separately from those qualities of environment which affected individual size. Since all derived their dimensions from what he described as "the same nutritive juices," the differences in size were obviously due to causes still un-known. "What intermediate station they shall take may depend on soil, on climate, on food, on a careful choice of breeders. But all the manna of heaven could never raise the mouse to the hulk of a mammoth."[38]

Another of the topics which provided Jefferson with an opportunity to discredit French naturalists related to fossil shells, impressions of which were found in large bodies of schist, a metamorphic crystalline rock, discovered near the eastern foot of North Mountain. Deposits of shells had been found also in the Andes mountains fifteen thousand feet above sea level, all of which was proposed to have been evidence of an ancient universal deluge.

Jefferson was opposed to this conclusion. After providing a calcula-tion of the weight of water and the gravity of the earth, he wrote, "as these waters, as they fell, would run into the seas, the superficial measure of which is to that of the dry parts of the globe, as two to one, the seas would be raised only fifty-two and a half feet above their present level, and of course would overflow the lands to that height only."[39]

Although he agreed that there was evidence of a partial deluge around the Mediterranean, he insisted that it could not account for shells found on mountain strata. To the supposition that the bed of the ocean had at some time suffered a great convulsion and heaved marine beds to those heights where now shells and other marine animals were found, he responded that there was no evidence of a force sufficient to heave such masses to a height of fifteen thousand feet above sea level.

Jefferson also dismissed Voltaire's proposal that such shells were chemical precipitates, that some shells grew unattached to animal bodies in the manner that nature provided an equivalent operation in passing the same materials through the pores of calcareous earth and stones, such as the calcareous drop-stones generated by the percolation of water through limestone.

He found the three hypotheses equally unsatisfactory, and ended with the statement, "We must be contented to acknowledge that this great phaenomenon is as yet unsolved. Ignorance is preferable to error; and he is less remote from the truth who believes nothing, than he who believes what is wrong." The subject of fossil shells continued to intrigue him, and although he found no satisfactory explanation, he eventually somewhat favored the hypothesis that they were a consequence of a con-vulsive activity of nature.[40]

One of the most remarkable parts of the Notes was Jefferson's report of his excavation of an Indian mound. In his account, however, he noted no date for the excavation; it may have been undertaken in the 1770's, but it is far more likely that it occurred at some time between 1780 and 1782. He explained that he knew of no existing Indian monuments, inasmuch as sites of recovery of Indian arrow points, stone hatchets and pipes and occasional images could not be considered such.

He made an exception, however, of the "barrows" or tumulus graves now called "Indian mounds" of which many are to be found all over the country. These were constructed of earth or of loose stones and made in various sizes as repositories for the dead. Nothing was known as fact about them.

It had been conjectured by some that they were graves of fallen Indian braves buried on the site of combat. Others proposed that they were community graves in which the bones of all the Indian dead within a certain period had been collected from numerous individual graves. Yet others, as Jefferson explained, believed that they were "general sepulchres for towns," an opinion supported by the fact they they occurred on the softest ground near rivers.

With his consuming interest in the Indians, Jefferson had long been preoccupied with the puzzle of the mounds. Finding one of these "barrows" as he called them, in his own neighborhood, he determined to resolve the question of their purpose by excavating it. That he had done so is not in the least surprising, but what is remarkable is the systematic method with which he undertook it, and the carefully detailed description he provided of his procedures.

Jefferson found the mound on low-lying ground approximately two miles above the principal fork of the Rivanna River. It was situated opposite several hills where former settlements of the Monacan Indians were known to have existed, and which Captain John Smith had recorded on his map in the seventeenth century.

The mound was "spheroidal" in shape, and approximately forty feet in diameter at the base. Jefferson concluded that originally it may have been as much as twelve feet in height. It was surrounded by a ditch about five feet deep and five feet wide.

Unfortunately, during the preceding twelve years the soil had been ploughed, a circumstance which he estimated had reduced the level as much as seven and one-half feet. He found evidence that trees with trunks as large as twelve inches in diameter had existed on the site before it was ploughed. From all appearances the mound had not been an occupied site, but an accumulation of bones from ancient burials, the first of which had been deposited directly on the ground and to which others had subsequently been added in layers, with a few stones placed over each burial.

After having related the mound to its natural surroundings and surviving evidence of human occupation of the area, he proceeded to record in the most painstaking manner the stratigraphical stages of his excavation. There is no indication that he may have had any hesitation about

desecrating a human burial which had remained undisturbed for many
centuries; presumably he felt that the knowledge to be gained from the
operation would justify it. He reported his procedures in a scientific
manner:

> I first dug superficially in several parts of it, and came to collections of
> human bones, at different depths, from six inches to three feet below the
> surface. These were lying in the utmost confusion, some vertical, some
> oblique, some horizontal, and directed to every point of the compass, en-
> tangled and held together in clusters by the earth. Bones of the most dis-
> tant parts were found together as, for instance, the small bones of the foot
> in the hollow of a scull [skull]; many sculls would sometimes be in contact,
> lying on the face, on the side, on the back, top or bottom, so as, on the
> whole, to give the idea of bones emptied promiscuously from a bag or bas-
> ket, and covered over with earth, without any attention to their order.
> The bones of which the greatest number remained, were sculls, jawbones,
> teeth, the bones of the arms thighs, legs, feet and hands. A few ribs re-
> mained, some vertebrae of the neck and spine, without their processes,
> and one instance only of the bones which serves as a base to the vertical
> column. Ten sculls were so tender, that they generally fell to pieces on
> being touched. The other bones were stronger. There were some teeth
> which were judged to be smaller than those of an adult; a scull, which on
> a slight view, appeared to be that of an infant, but it fell to pieces on being
> taken out, so as to prevent satisfactory examination; a rib, and a fragment
> of the under-jaw of a person about half grown; another rib of an infant;
> and a part of the jaw of a child, which had not cut its teeth. The last
> furnishing the most decisive proof of the burial of children here, I was
> particular in my attention to it. It was part of the right half of the underjaw.
> The processes by which it was attenuated to the temporal bones, were en-
> tire, and the bone itself firm to where it had been broken off, which, as
> nearly as I could judge, was about the place of the eyetooth, its upper edge,
> wherein would have been the sockets of the teeth, was perfectly smooth.
> Measuring it with that of an adult, by placing their hinder processes to-
> gether, its broken end extended to the penultimate grinder of the adult.
> This bone was white, all others of a sand color. The bones of infants being
> soft, they probably decay sooner, which might be the cause so few were
> found here.

In order to examine its internal structure, Jefferson then proceeded
to make a vertical cut through the mound as deep as the surrounding
ground level approximately three feet from its center. At the bottom on
the level of the surrounding ground, he found bones covered with stones,
some of which had been brought from a neighboring cliff and from the
river an eighth of a mile distant. Above these he found a "large interval

of earth," then more bones, an arrangement that was repeated several times.

At one end of the section he had made, there were four strata of bones and at the other end he found three; the strata were not at the same levels at both ends. He failed to find holes in any of the bones which might have been made by weapons. He estimated that the barrow contained approximately one thousand skeletons and concluded that the mound covered not only the bones of those who had fallen in battle but others as well. Furthermore, it was not a town sepulchre, he concluded, in which the bodies would have been placed upright and touching each other.

He reasoned further that the mound derived its origin and growth from the normal accumulation of bones from common burial, the first burial having been made on the ground level with a few stones placed over the bones and then covered with earth as much as required by the quantity of bones. Subsequent bones were placed above these, covered with stone and earth, in a series of burials over a period of time. He noted:

the following are the particular circumstances which give it this aspect

1. The number of bones.
2. Their confused position.
3. Their being a different strata.
4. The strata in one part having no correspondence with those in another.
5. The different states of decay in these strata, which seem to indicate a difference in the time of inhumation.
6. The existence of infant bones among them.[41]

Jefferson's excavation was made not for the purpose of recovering and acquiring artifacts, although he was a compulsive antiquary with a keen historical sense, interested in the artifact for its own sake and as an example of primitive art. Instead he undertook the excavation as a scientific inquiry for the purpose of resolving a problem. In applying his innate sense of order and detail, he anticipated modern archeology's basis and methods by almost a full century. He followed no precedent, for in the eighteenth century there was no established method for excavating ancient sites. It was not until the nineteenth century that the science of archeology began to evolve slowly within the ambience of the academic world.

The importance of Jefferson's experience and his report of it cannot be overstressed, for he introduced for the very first time the principle of stratigraphy in archeological excavation. His principle has become a basic part of the methodology of all archeology, regardless of where in the world it is undertaken. The principle is the method for providing a calen-

dar for establishing the age of remains. As the criterion of scientific excavation, it is the principle in which every student of the science must be
trained.

As C. W. Ceram, the noted author of *Ur of the Chaldees*, commented, Jefferson "not only indicated the basic features of the strati-
graphic method, but also virtually named it, although a hundred years
were to pass before the term became established in archeological jargon.
For in this classic paragraph he uses the word "stratum" for layer no less
than six times."[42]

The distinguished English archeologist, Sir Mortimer Wheeler,
noted the originality of Jefferson's work and wrote, "He describes the
situation of the mound in relation to natural features and evidences of
human occupation. He detects components of geological interest in its
materials and traces their sources. He indicates the stratigraphical features of the skeletal remains. And he relates his evidence objectively to
current theories. No mean achievement for a busy statesman in 1784
[sic]!"[43]

Thomson in his appendix shared Jefferson's particular outrage over
the aspersions cast by Buffon on the masculinity and manhood of the
American Indian, especially since the French naturalist had never seen
an American Indian and his conclusions were based merely on hearsay.
Buffon had written

> The savage is feeble, and has small organs of generation; he has neither
> hair nor beard, and no ardor whatever for his female; although swifter than
> the European because he is better accustomed to running, he is, on the
> other hand, less strong in body; he is also less sensitive, and yet more timid
> and cowardly; he has no vivacity, no activity of the mind; the activity of
> his body is less an exercise, a voluntary motion, than a necessary action
> caused by want; relieve him of hunger and thirst, and you deprive him of
> the active principle of all his movements; he will rest stupidly upon his legs
> or lying down entire days.[44]

Jefferson's response was strong and to the point. He described Buffon's view as "An afflicting picture indeed which, for the honor of human nature, I am glad to believe has no original. The American Indian
is neither more defective in ardor, nor more impotent with his female,
than the white reduced to the same diet and exercise . . . he is brave,
when an enterprise depends on bravery . . . he will defend himself
against an host of enemies, always chusing to be killed, rather than to
surrender . . . his sensibility is keen, even the warriors weeping more
bitterly on the loss of their children."[45]

Jefferson collected such facts as he could on Indians for a rebuttal to
Buffon, and submitted them to Charles Thomson for review. Thomson
responded with a comprehensive report on the social, physical and intel-

lectual characteristics of the Indian, which Jefferson later included as part of an appendix to the published work.[46]

In the closing passage of the *Notes*, Jefferson commented, "Young as we are, and with a country before us to fill with people and happiness, we should point in that direction the whole generative force of nature, wasting none of it in efforts of mutual destruction. It should be our endeavor to cultivate the peace and friendship of every nation, even of that which has injured us most, when we shall have carried our point against her. Our interest will be to throw open the doors of commerce, and to knock off all the shackles, giving perfect freedom to all persons for the vent of whatever they may choose to bring into our ports and asking the same in theirs. . . . Were the money used by a country to wage war expended in improving what they already possess, in making roads, opening rivers, building ports, improving the arts, and finding employment for their idle poor, it would render them much stronger, much wealthier and happier. This I hope will be our wisdom." In these words he foreshadowed the commercial policy which eventually led to the imposition of the Embargo of 1807.[47]

Finally Jefferson packed the completed questionnaire with a letter to Marbois, informing him that he had been retired from public service only since June, and that he had been enabled to collect the desired information only lately due to the confusion of the war. He entrusted the bulky manuscript to Jacquelin Ambler, husband of the former Rebecca Burwell of his schoolboy interest, to forward to Marbois, but it was not until late March or April 1782 that Marbois received it.

Having learned from Thomson and d'Anmours that Jefferson had completed the questionnaire although it had not yet reached him, Marbois wrote in January to inquire. It developed that when Jefferson had left the questionnaire and covering letter with Ambler to deliver, the latter was more concerned about safety than speed and several weeks elapsed before he could find a safe courier.[48]

Jefferson had long ago invited the Marquis François Jean de Chastellux, a major general on the staff of the Comte de Rochambeau, to come to Monticello and spend a few days in his company amidst the mountains. When the Marquis arrived in April 1782, he described the mansion in some detail, noting, "it resembles none of the others seen in this country; so that it may be said that Mr. Jefferson is the first American who has consulted the Fine Arts to know how to shelter himself from the weather."

Jefferson and Chastellux shared many common interests and talked deep into the night, discussing the poems of Ossian and "at other times, natural philosophy was the subject of our conversations, and at still others, politics or the arts, for no object has escaped Mr. Jefferson; and it seems indeed as though, ever since his youth, he has placed his mind, like his house, on a loft height, whence he might contemplate the whole universe."

Chastellux expressed pleasure upon seeing the score of roe deer that Jefferson had raised, which were so tame they came to eat Indian corn from his hand. He also went to see the "rock bridge" joining two mountains—the famous Natural Bridge of Virginia—some eighty miles from Monticello, which at one time was owned by Jefferson. He had purchased it on July 5, 1774 by means of a deed drawn in the name of King George III, acquiring 157 acres of land in Botecourt County.

Jefferson and the Marquis discussed the bridge in an attempt to find an acceptable hypothesis to explain such a curiosity of nature. Jefferson had written in the *Notes* that it was his view that the bridge had "been cloven by some great convulsion."

Later, after having read Buffon's comments on the subject, Chastellux concluded that it had in fact been formed by "the action of waters," an opinion consistent with that of modern geologists. After visiting the bridge again in 1815 with his young protégé, Francis Walker Gilmer, Jefferson changed his mind, agreeing with Gilmer, who later read a paper before the American Philosophical Society presenting the theory that the bridge had been formed by "the chemical and mechanical action" of the waters, a view similar to the one eventually reached by Chastellux.[49]

In the account of his visit, Chastellux provided an (interesting vignette of Jefferson. "Let me describe to you a man, not yet forty," he wrote, "tall, and with a mild and pleasing countenance, but whose mind and understanding are ample substitutes for every exterior grace. An American, who without ever having quitted his country, is at once a musician, skilled in drawing, a geometrician, an astronomer, a natural philosopher, legislator, and statesman. . . . I found his first appearance serious, nay, even cold; but before I had been two hours with him we were as intimate as if we had passed our whole lives together; walking, books, but above all, a conversation always varied and interesting."[50]

Meanwhile the stress of events had taken their toll on Martha Jefferson. During the Revolution she had been forced to flee her home, and after her return to Monticello she continued to mourn the twenty-seven slaves taken prisoner by the British and allowed to die so brutally. The prospect that her husband was constantly liable to be captured for treason during this period also had given her frightening nightmares. She was already weak and ill when she had fled with her family before Tarleton's troops.

In May she again gave birth, to another daughter they named Lucy Elizabeth. It had been a difficult pregnancy, and after the child was born the mother never fully recovered her health, lying bedridden for four months, her husband constantly in attendance. As his daughter Martha later recalled, "For four months that she lingered he was never out of Calling. When not at her bed side he was writing in a small room which opened immediately at the head of her bed."[51]

Jefferson was offered the appointment as delegate of Albemarle County to the House of Delegates, which he refused two days before the birth of his sixth child. The House was reluctant to accept his refusal, and Speaker John Tyler offered to yield his own position to him since he believed that Jefferson was better qualified. Remaining adamant, however, Jefferson explained his reasons in a letter to James Monroe.

"Before I ventured to declare to my countrymen my determination to retire from public employment," he wrote, "I examined well my heart to know whether it was thoroughly cured of every principle of political ambition, whether no lurking particle remained which might leave me uneasy when reduced within the limits of mere private life. I became satisfied that every fibre of that passion was thoroughly eradicated."

He had spent thirteen years in public service, he went on, during which period his private affairs had suffered seriously, and now he had a young family which required his attention, to which he had added the family of his deceased friend and brother-in-law, Dabney Carr. Then he added, "I had been so far from gaining the affection of my countrymen, which was the only reward I ever asked for or could have felt, that I had even lost the small estimation I before possessed." There was no doubt that he had "stood arraigned for treason of the heart and not merely weakness of the head," he added, and although he had been exonerated, Jefferson had been so deeply wounded that he had resolved to abandon public life thereafter.[52]

It was assumed that his decision not to return to public office derived solely from the wrong he had received, an attitude strongly resented by even such close friends as James Madison. Very few knew of his anxiety for his wife's well-being during this period, which was the chief reason for his refusal to serve in the House. Meanwhile rumors of her serious condition were beginning to circulate about Richmond and friends sent their sympathy, to which he did not respond. He remained concerned only with events at home, and for four months he wrote no letters.[53]

Martha Wayles Skelton Jefferson died on September 6, 1782. Jefferson noted the event in his *Memorandum Book* with his customary terseness: "My dear wife died this day at 11:45 A.M." His sister Martha Carr and his wife Martha's sister Elizabeth Eppes were present at the death bed, and for the past four months they had shared the nursing with Jefferson.

For the next three weeks following his wife's death Jefferson did not leave his own room, and his daughter Martha was always beside him. As she later reported, in mid-October he finally emerged from a state of stupor "as dead to the world as she was whose loss occasioned it."[54]

Martha described the inconsolable state of her father and how "A moment before the closing scene he was led from the room almost in a state of insensibility by his sister Mrs. Carr who with great difficulty got him into his library where he fainted and remained so long insensible that they feared he never would revive." He remained in his room, walking incessantly and resting occasionally on a pallet that had been brought in at the time that he had fainted.[55]

Martha was buried in the family graveyard at Monticello and on her gravestone Jefferson had these words chiseled:

TO THE MEMORY OF
MARTHA JEFFERSON,
DAUGHTER OF JOHN WAYLES;
BORN OCTOBER THE 19TH, 1748, O.S.
INTERMARRIED WITH
THOMAS JEFFERSON
JANUARY THE 1ST, 1772;
TORN FROM HIM BY DEATH
SEPTEMBER 6TH, 1782;
THIS MONUMENT OF HIS LOVE IS INSCRIBED.

To this inscription Jefferson added two lines written in Greek from the 22nd book of Homer's *Iliad*, which may be rendered:

If in the melancholic shades below
The flames of friends and loves cease to glow,
Yet mine shall sacred last; mine undecay'd,
Burn on through death and animate my shade.[56]

He kept the few small souvenirs of their marital life but eventually destroyed their letters, fully aware that only in this manner could their intimacies be preserved from the prying eyes of the future. The months that followed were a desolate period for the statesman. Intermingled with the consuming grief over the death of his wife was the bitter conviction that he had been disavowed by his countrymen for his conduct of the resources of Virginia during the Revolution. As he approached his fortieth year, he was troubled by self-doubts about his past achievements and consumed with a restlessness about the years ahead.

Jefferson's great dream of an idyllic future as a farmer living together with his beloved wife and surrounded by his family and his books had been shattered irreparably by Martha's unexpected death. The indecision which filled his days during the next two years was finally to be resolved with the realization that he could again take his place in public life and serve the nation.

When he eventually emerged from his room, he rode constantly about the mountain and through the woods, with his ten-year-old daughter always beside him. During this time of soul-searching and agonized indecision, he rode five or six miles every day. He was greatly depressed, "finding myself absolutely unable to attend to anything like business," as he expressed himself to Elizabeth Wayles Eppes, Martha Wayles Jefferson's half-sister.[57]

His first concern after he had recovered from his partial collapse was for the children. He brought his three daughters and his wards, the children of his sister Martha and Dabney Carr, to Ampthill, the residence of Colonel Archibald Cary, to be inoculated for smallpox. There he remained with the children, acting as their nurse until they had recovered. Mary, then aged four, and the new infant were sent to live at Eppington with Francis and Elizabeth Eppes. Eppington was situated on the Appomattox River in southern Chesterfield County. Mary and Lucy were to know no other early home or parents.

The tragic loss which they shared served to forge a tight bond between Jefferson and young Martha, known at home as Patsy, a bond which grew and strengthened and endured for the remainder of their lives. He was a caring father with maternal as well as paternal characteristics. He loved children, enjoyed having them about him, had a talent for anticipating their wants and exercised infinite patience with them. He easily won their confidence because he treated them as people and gave thoughtful consideration to their most trifling requests as well as to their serious concerns.[58]

It was at Ampthill that he received notice that on November 12th Congress had again unanimously appointed him Minister Plenipotentiary to France to help negotiate the peace. It had been his firm intention to retire permanently from public life, but Martha's death destroyed this dream. Although the war was ended, negotiations for peace were still in progress. Henry Laurens of the commission had become a prisoner of war of the British, and it seemed desirable to provide a fresh outlook with Jefferson's presence.

For Jefferson it came at a most fortunate time. He welcomed the opportunity to leave Monticello with its many painful memories for an interval, because he had become convinced he would no longer find happiness there. The appointment to the House of Delegates did not have any allurement, for it was too close to home. But the promise of seeing the Old World at last intrigued him.[59]

Jefferson returned to Monticello and arranged for Francis Eppes and his overseer Nicholas Lewis to handle his business matters for him during his absence. He then departed with Martha for Philadelphia, where he devoted time to activities of the American Philosophical Society, and purchased a chessboard and chessmen and associated socially with James Madison and other friends. Then he traveled to Baltimore to await the sailing of the French frigate *Romulus* which was temporarily blocked by ice nearby.

Meanwhile he had not yet been given a safe conduct by the British, and Congress seemed reluctant to request it. Furthermore, the negotiations in Paris had progressed so satisfactorily that Jefferson's presence was no longer considered necessary, but nonetheless, Congress still wished him to go. He waited in vain, for it was to be a year and a half before his departure for France.[60]

During this interval, he received from Colonel Arthur Campbell, the county lieutenant of Washington County, Virginia, a large fossil jaw tooth found in the Salina in the county. Campbell had obtained the tooth from Major Alexander Outlaw of North Carolina, the director of the Salt Works. Campbell reported that "Bones of an uncommon size, of which the Jaw Tooth now offered you is one" were found in pits dug to reach the veins of salt water. Campbell had shown the tooth to Colonel Preston, who was of the opinion that it was of the same animal of which bones had been found near the Ohio River and some of which Croghan had sent to England several decades earlier.[61]

Pleased with the gift, Jefferson determined to take other fossils with him to Europe, undoubtedly to show them to Buffon and his associates. Furthermore, he was anxious to collect as much more information as possible for his *Notes* before having them printed, a task to which he set George Rogers Clark.

"A specimen of each of the several species of bones now to be found is to me the most desirable object of Natural history, [he told Clark] and there is no expence of package or of safe transportation which I will not gladly reimburse to procure them safely. Elk-horns of very extrardinary size, petrifactions, or anything else uncommon would be very acceptable. . . . Any observations of your own on the subject of the big bones or their history, or on anything else in the Western country, will come acceptably to me, because I know you see the works of nature in the great, and not merely in detail. Descriptions of animals, vegetables, minerals, or other curious things, notes as to the Indians, information of the country between the Mississippi and waters of the South Seas, &c. &c. will stir your mind as worthy being communicated. I wish you had more time to pay attention to them.

Not having heard from Clark, he wrote to him again repeating his request for bones of every species with instructions for their shipment so that he could have them in hand on his departure.[62]

* * *

The year 1783 had begun well for Jefferson. In January he was inordinately pleased to receive the honorary degree of D.C.L. (Doctor in the

Civil Laws) from the College of William and Mary in acknowledgement of his championship of American liberty and his numerous achievements in the arts and letters.[63]

Early in the same month he was again elected a councillor of the American Philosophical Society, which provided him with an opportunity to have examples of American ingenuity brought to the attention of Europe, to contradict the Abbé Raynal's contentions. In his writings Guillaume Thomas François, Abbé de Raynal, had commented, "America has not yet produced a good poet, a capable mathematician, a single man of genius, in a single art or in a single science."[64]

In his *Notes*, Jefferson had made a classic retort:

"America has not yet produced one good poet." When we shall have existed as a people as long as the Greeks did before they produced a Homer, the Romans a Virgil, the French a Racine and Voltaire, the English a Shakespeare and Milton, should this reproach be still true, we will enquire from what unfriendly causes it has processed, that the other countries of Europe and quarters of the earth shall not have inscribed any name in the roll of poets. "But neither has America produced one able mathematician, one man of genius in a single art or a single science." In war we have produced a Washington whose memory will be adored while liberty shall have votaries, whose name will triumph over time, and will in future ages assume its just station among the most celebrated worthies of the world, when that wretched philosophy shall be forgotten which would have arranged him among the degeneracies of nature. In physics we have produced a Franklin, whom no one of the present age has made more important discoveries, nor has enriched philosophy with more, or more ingenious solutions of the phaenomena of nature. We have supposed Mr. Rittenhouse second to no astronomer living: that in genius he must be the first, because he is self-taught. As an artist he has exhibited as great proof of mechanical genius as the world has ever produced. He has not indeed made a world; but he has by imitation approached nearer its Maker than any man who has lived from the creation to this day. As in philosophy and war, so in government, in oratory, in painting, in the plastic art, we might shew that America, though but a child of yesterday, has already given hopeful proofs of genius, as well of the nobler kinds, which arouse the best feelings of man, which call him into action, which substantiate his freedom, and conduct him to happiness, as of the subordinate, which serve to amuse him only. We therefore suppose, that this reproach is as unjust as it is unkind; and that, of the geniuses which adorn the present age, America contributes its full share. For comparing it with other countries, where genius is most cultivated, where are the most excellent models for art, and scaffoldings for the attainment of science, as France and England for instance, we calculate thus. The United States contain three millions of inhabitants; France twenty millions; and the British islands ten. We produce a Washington, a Franklin, a Rittenhouse. France then should have half a dozen in each of these lines, and Great-Britain half that number, equally eminent.[65]

Although Jefferson had so effectively refuted Raynal's claim in his *Notes*, the Frenchman's words still smarted, and he was determined to bring with him to France a tangible example of American ingenuity, and the best available, in his view, was Rittenhouse's remarkable mechanism.

Ten days after his re-election, he proposed that David Rittenhouse be commissioned to produce an orrery to be presented by the Society to King Louis XVI of France. He suggested that the gift would be intended as an expression of gratitude of the American people to France for its assistance in the Revolution, but at the same time it would serve the purpose of impressing the French with an example of American genius.[66]

Although he may have been unaware of it, the idea was not original with Jefferson. In December 1776, while Silas Deane was in France soliciting supplies from the French for the Continental Congress, he had made a similar suggestion to the Committee of Secret Correspondence and again separately to John Jay. French interest and support of the American colonies would be enhanced, Deane believed, by a gift of suitable "curiosities." His suggestions of such items ranged from insect collections, a pair of bay horses, a Rittenhouse orrery, and barrels of apples or walnuts. No action was taken on Deane's suggestion, and Jefferson's proposal made seven years later was eventually to suffer the same fate.

Jefferson, however, felt it was not a matter with which the American Congress should be concerned, as Deane had proposed. Instead it was a project more appropriately undertaken by the American Philosophical Society as the leading American body of learning.[67]

The Society responded favorably to Jefferson's suggestion by appointing a committee to bring the project into execution. After conferring with Rittenhouse, the committee reported that he agreed to make the instrument for £200. The Society approved the project, and then informed the French Minister, Anne César Chevalier de La Luzerne, who in turn notified the French court. "Mr. Rittenhouse, Sire, works on his planetarium, but with some slowness," he wrote, "he is Treasurer of the Commonwealth of Pennsylvania; he had with regret fulfilled the functions least associated with his talents but those necessary for making a living. He may come himself to France to present his fine work to the King when it is completed."[68]

Minister Luzerne informed the committee in due course that he had received a favorable response from the court in Paris, intimating that the French monarch approved the Society's plan. The Minister indicated that it was "expressive of his Majesty's intention by his royal Patronage to excite an Emulation between the literary Societies of France and the United States."

The response pleased the Society, and its membership looked forward to an early completion of the instrument. Rittenhouse had other priorities, however; he was preoccupied with public concerns as treasurer of the Commonwealth of Pennsylvania, in addition to having to make his own living. For a time he seriously contemplated the pleasant possibility of traveling to France to present the orrery to the king, but his interest languished as other personal problems arose. Although the Society's interest in the project was to lessen with the passage of time, Jefferson nonetheless persisted in pursuing it.[69]

The French were already familiar with Rittenhouse's achievement, which had been reported in France. In November 1780 the orrery at the College of New Jersey had been shown by the college president to the Marquis de Chastellux, and Rittenhouse personally had demonstrated the second orrery to him in Philadelphia several days later. Other members of Rochambeau's staff were present at the demonstration, including the chaplain Abbé Robin, and the chief commissary Claude Blanchard.[70]

Despite the effort that Jefferson expended in developing and pursuing the proposal, all involved should have realized that it was most unlikely that Rittenhouse would ever complete a third orrery. Pleased beyond measure though he was by the honor implied, Rittenhouse should have disenchanted Jefferson and his other supporters by admitting that he was no longer physically or emotionally capable of undertaking the project.

The fact of the matter was that it was extremely tedious work and a major undertaking to reproduce the innumerable delicate and intricate parts. His enthusiasm for his great achievement had been expended in the designing and construction of the first orrery, and duplicating it for the second time offered no challenge or sense of satisfaction. It was with the greatest difficulty, and only because of an unfulfilled promise, that he had completed the second instrument for the University of Pennsylvania. Jefferson was to let the matter rest, but only for the time being.[71]

While waiting for safe passage, Jefferson passed the time by developing a scheme for classifying the scientific works in his library. He devised and described two methods of cataloguing. One was alphabetical, which he considered unsatisfactory because of the occasional difficulty of recalling an author's name, and also because in some instances the author's name was not provided. The other, which he preferred, was an arrangement according to subject, although sometimes it was difficult to determine where to place a work which contained multiple subjects such as geography and natural history.

It was on the principle of subject content that he finally arranged his own library. He was obviously influenced by Sir Francis Bacon's division of man's mental faculties—memory, reason and imagination—which he applied to the three main headings of History (civil and natural), Philosophy (moral and mathematical) and Fine Arts. Books relating to the primary concerns of his public life and which formed the largest segment of his library, Jefferson classified under Moral Philosophy.

Science was divided into Natural History and Mathematical Philosophy. Natural History included materials and facts relating to the animal, vegetable and mineral kingdoms which he designated as "Natural History Proper," but he adopted the broad sense of the term from Pliny's *History naturalis* to include works relating to man's utilization of the materials of nature. Accordingly, in his classification of scientific books under "Natural History," with those on anatomy, botany, mineralogy and zoology, he included practical treatises on agriculture, chemistry, medicine, surgery and the technical arts.

Grouping the theoretical sciences under "Mathematical Philosophy," to the "pure" sciences of arithmetic and geometry he added the "physico-mathematical" sciences of astronomy, dynamics, geography, mechanics, optics, phonics, pneumatics and statics. Gardening he considered to be an art, and was listed under "Fine Arts" together with architecture, criticism, music, oratory, painting, poetry and sculpture. It is of interest to note that his system of classification continued to be used by the Library of Congress for almost a century after his personal collection of 6479 books was purchased by the Federal government in 1815.[72]

Early in June 1783 Jefferson was elected a delegate from Virginia to the Congress, which had moved to Princeton. However, the Congress adjourned on the day of his arrival and was scheduled to meet again at Annapolis three weeks later. The uncertainty of the permanent seat of the Congress was the subject of a letter he wrote to the Governor of Virginia, in which he expressed his personal view that the seat should be in Georgetown rather than Annapolis. The choice was not just a matter of personal preference, however, for he had with his usual practical approach estimated distances and analyzed regional opinion.[73]

While at Annapolis he arranged for Martha to remain in Philadelphia with Mrs. Thomas Hopkinson, mother of his friend Francis Hopkinson, where she was together with the children of Hopkinson and David Rittenhouse. Jefferson had already prepared a course of reading she was to undertake, and arranged through Marbois for a French tutor for her.

At this time, he began the practice of writing to his children. He set the standard for his correspondence with his daughters by always including some event of interest with recommendations for their personal conduct, appearance and work habits. He frequently forgot the age of his young correspondents, however, and often wrote of matters in a way beyond their years.[74]

A short time after his election to Congress, Jefferson had learned of an intriguing new invention available, in England. This was the copying press which made possible the duplication of writings by means of a rolling press. Invented and patented by James Watt in 1780, it was as yet little known outside of England, but he probably saw one or obtained a description of one which had been purchased by Franklin. Accordingly he requested Robert Morris, the government's supervisor of finances, to order a rolling press for him for his own use at Monticello. Not totally confident of Morris's ability to acquire one, however, he also inquired about presses from the Philadelphia merchant, Samuel House.[75]

Instead of attempting to order the press directly from the manufacturer or his agent in England, Morris in due course wrote to Franklin in Paris, enclosing a part of Jefferson's letter; he assumed that Franklin would be best informed where such an item could be purchased.

Seven months passed before Jefferson's order was finally forwarded from Paris to Herries & Company, the Watt agent in London, by Franklin's grandson and secretary, William Temple Franklin. More time passed before the shipment was made and neither Morris nor Jefferson were informed that a press was on its way until Jefferson was about to leave for Paris. Having no use for a press at Monticello while he was in France, he directed Morris to keep it for his own use or dispose of it on Jefferson's account.[76]

Jefferson left Philadelphia for Annapolis with James Madison in the last week of November 1783. More than two weeks passed after the announced date before a sufficient number of members of Congress arrived for a meeting at the State House. During this period Jefferson was actively involved as chairman of a committee for a reception held for Washington and an audience at which the General resigned his commission in what was described as "an affecting scene."[77]

Jefferson did not neglect his interests in astronomy during this period. Late in 1783 he took the time to summarize the two slim volumes of Buffon's *System of Astronomy* for his friend Francis Hopkinson.[78]

He had begun to revise his *Notes*, and sent pages to his friend Thomas Walker, asking him to review them and return revisions and suggestions particularly with relation to the table of animals, for which he needed weights, and matters relating to the Indians. He also queried Colonel Archibald Cary, who sent him the desired information about various animals he had hunted.[79]

In late November Jefferson received fossil shells and some seeds from Clark, and again expressed the hope of obtaining a collection of fossil bones. He mentioned that in England a large sum of money had been appropriated to explore the American continent from the Mississippi to the West Coast. He considered it disturbing news because, "They pretend it is only to promote knolege. I am afraid they have thoughts of colonising into that quarter. Some of us have been talking here in a feeble way of making the attempt to search that country. But I doubt whether we have enough of that kind of spirit to raise the money. How would you like to lead such a party? Tho I am afraid our prospect is not worth asking the question." It is clear from this communication that Jefferson had already assessed the need for exploration of the Western country at least two decades before he was to arrange the Lewis and Clark expedition.[80]

Nor were his meteorological observations neglected. The greatest difficulty experienced by Jefferson and his fellow weather-observers was in the availability of suitable instruments. Glass and optical instruments were not made in the United States until the first quarter of the nineteenth century. Until then they had to be imported, chiefly from England, which had developed an important industry in the production of thermometers and barometers by skilled Italian artisans who had migrated there.[81]

He sent a thermometer to Isaac Zane, "the only one to be had in Philadelphia," and enclosed a record of his recent observations. He then asked for specific observations to be made, including "the temperature of the cave at different distances from the mouth. The temperature of your ice house. That of a good spring. That of a good well if you have one. The observations in the cave should be at every foot or two when you first enter, till you find it's temperature become nearly uniform which will probably be at about 20 feet. The most convenient way of doing this is to let it [the thermometer] down by a string to different depths as far as the whole goes down nearly perpendicular; letting the glass remain till you think it is settled at it's due point and then drawing it up hastily." After having visited Zane's home, he designed a water wheel for Monticello similar to the one he had seen there but which he believed had advantages in the manner in which the buckets had been attached.[82]

At Jefferson's request, the Reverend Madison borrowed a thermometer "which appears very sensible as to Heat and Cold, tho' it is so constructed that I cannot ascertain the Accuracy of the Division by plunging it in boiling water; This appears of Consequence especially when we keep corresponding Observations." This was important inasmuch as he and Jefferson were to make simultaneous observations at Williamsburg and Charlottesville. To test it for the greatest degree of cold, he exposed the thermometer to the night air in an open window. During the day he exposed it as much as possible in the open air. Madison expressed a wish to have a barometer, because "the British robbed me of my Thermometer and Barometer" and he had been unable to find another locally. Although he had ordered others from England, months would pass before they would arrive.[83]

Madison also encountered a further problem because the owner of the borrowed thermometer asked for its return, making it impossible for Madison to continue his observations. At this point his meteorological diary ended and would not be resumed until his instruments arrived from England.[84]

Jefferson recruited as many of his friends and associates for his weather observations as he could. "I wish you had a Thermometer," he commented to James Madison. "Mr. Madison of the college and myself are keeping observations for a comparison of climate. We observe at Sunrise and at 4 o'clock P.M. which are the coldest and warmest points of the day. If you could observe at the same time it would shew the difference between going North and Northwest on this continent. I suspect it to be colder in Orange or Albemarle than here [Annapolis]."

James Madison agreed to become one of the weather watchers but, he noted, "The want of both a Thermometer and Barometer had determined me to defer my meteorological diary till I could procure these instruments."[85]

The degree of accuracy with which the records were maintained is demonstrated in a report from the Reverend Madison after he finally obtained his own instruments the following April. "A Pocket Thermometer which stands on the second floor and the N.W. side of the House was on the 24 inst. at 4 o' Clock, at 77°, on the 25. 78, on the 26. 81-½, to day 27. at 82. The weather during this period has been fair and the wind S. the atmosphere thick NW. . . ."[86]

In February Jefferson became quite ill, scarcely able to read or write. When he was able to be up and about again, he followed his usual custom of browsing in the bookstores. As always he was seeking works about North American geography and it may have been at this time that he found and purchased two volumes relating to the voyages of Captain James Cook who had sailed to the Pacific Northwest. One was *An Authentic Voyage to the Pacific Ocean. By an officer on Board the Discovery* by John Rickman (Philadelphia: 1783) and the other was *A Journal of Captain Cook's Last Voyage to the Pacific Ocean. . . in the Years 1776, 1777, 1778 and 1779* by John Ledyard (Hartford 1783). Whether Jefferson acquired these volumes at this time is not certain, but there is no question that the unexplored Western lands were on his mind by the time he reached Annapolis.[87]

Jefferson continued to be unwell during most of this period, his condition undoubtedly aggravated by the casual performance of the members of Congress. "I have had very ill health since I have been here and am getting rather lower than otherwise," he informed Madison. The peace treaty had been signed in September and had been received by the President two weeks later. Ratification had to be accomplished within six months of the signing, for which nine states were required to be represented. It was not until March 1st, however, that a sufficient number of representatives appeared.[88]

By mid-March Jefferson's health had substantially improved. The most important project with which he was now concerned was the disposition of the Western lands. Although the Ordnance of 1784 is generally believed to have been drafted by Jefferson, he did not in fact have the larger role in its creation. After he took his seat in the Congress in November 1783, he became chairman of a number of committees, and eventually of the committee to prepare "a plan for the temporary government of the western territory." Congress had already discussed the formation of Western states in relation to Indian affairs before Jefferson's arrival, and the long discussions over Virginia's cession and over Indian affairs had already shaped the main outlines of the committee's report of March 1, 1784, when the Virginia delegates laid before Congress the deed cession of its territory beyond the Ohio River. The earlier cession of 1781 had been rejected, and it was not until late 1783 that the Congress specified the terms, and that Virginia complied with them.

After these terms had been accepted, a committee prepared a plan for temporary government of the territory. Jefferson as chairman presented the report, which was recommitted, presented again and finally approved after amendment in late April.

Known as the Ordnance of 1784, it proposed that new states be formed from the Western lands and that each be admitted to the Union on an equal basis with the original states. It provided for governments not merely in the territory northwest of the Ohio, but in all lands that should later be ceded to individual states. At the same time the committee proposed that Virginia should permit the formation of a separate Kentucky and urged further cession of territory somewhat larger than the present state.[89]

Jefferson's principal contribution was probably contained in the paragraph specifying the boundaries of the proposed states, each of which was to extend two degrees of latitude from north to south counting from 31° northward. The east to west dimensions were to be determined by parallels drawn between the Falls of the Ohio River and the mouth of the Great Kanawha River. He delineated boundaries on both lands already ceded and those later to be ceded. He recommended immediate division into the full number of states required by the Virginia amendment of 1780, rejecting the proposal of preliminary government in one or more territories before developing state boundaries.

It was his conviction that in order to retain a republican government, the state should remain of a size small enough to support a homogeneity of interests which would guarantee economic and political bases. However, in proposing specific boundaries for the states, he exceeded the maximum and violated Virginia's stipulations and those of the committee. He had selected his meridian lines for abstract balance and in an effort to avoid conflict between large and small states.

The report provided for boundaries and names of the proposed states, for the establishment of temporary as well as permanent governments, with provisoes on which they were to be formed, and a charter of compact. Jefferson had added two clauses, one prohibiting slavery and the other withholding citizenship to any one claiming hereditary titles.

Although Congress radically revised the proposal, fixing boundaries proceeding southward from 45° instead of at two degree intervals northward from 30° latitude, for example, the final version of the Ordnance retained Jefferson's geographical concept. Before leaving for France he drafted an elaborate plan for disposition of the public domain.[90]

In the first bill Jefferson drew boundaries for fourteen new states, and named ten of them. He arranged them mathematically in tiers, but the plan was never put into effect. He devised names for the new states from translations of Indian names or by rendering geographical features into classical form: "Cherronesus," "Assenisipia," "Pelisipia," "Michigania" (which became Michigan), and, "Illinoia" (which became Illinois), "Metropotamia," etc. The names were included on a map of the United States in Bailey's Pocket Almanac, Being an American Annual Register for the year 1785. (Figure 8)

The names of the new states were deleted from Jefferson's second report, however, and in 1787 it was determined that his boundaries were too small. The specific provisions for government of the new states did not become effective until after the lands had been purchased from the Indians and offered for sale, and in fact the provisions were superseded by those of the Ordnance of 1787.[91]

James Monroe, who was primarily responsible for altering the size of the new states, reported his activities to Jefferson in France. Jefferson did not oppose the idea that at first an arbitrary government should be established with a governor, council and court of five judges appointed by Congress under laws of one of the original states. In the matter of state size, however, he wrote that making them fewer and larger "is reversing the natural order of things. A tractable people may be governed in large bodies; but in proportion as they depart from this character, the extent of their government must be less. We see into what small divisions the Indians are obliged to reduce their societies. This measure, with the disposition to shut up the Mississippi give me serious apprehensions of the severance of the Eastern and Western parts of our con-federacy."[92]

It was during his stay at Annapolis that Jefferson first became inter-ested in ballooning. He was introduced to the subject by the French minister, Chevalier de La Luzerne, who had been informed in a letter from his brother that he had witnessed an ascension in Paris to about three thousand feet. The balloon had traveled some six miles in twenty mi-nutes before returning to the ground, although it could have traveled three times the distance. This was the first manned flight of a free bal-loon filled with air, made on November 21, 1783 by the French scientist J. F. Pilatre de Rozière with the Marquis d'Arlandes as his passenger.[93]

Ever alert to the potential of new inventions, in informing Francis Hopkinson about the event, Jefferson noted, "This discovery seems to threaten the prostration of fortified works unless they can be closed above, the destruction of fleets and what not. The French may now run over their laces, wines &c. to England duty free. The whole system of British statutes made on the supposition of goods being brought into some port must be revised. Inland countries may now become *maritime* states unless you chuse rather to call them *aerial* ones as their commerce is in future to be carried on through the element. But jesting apart I think this discovery may lead to things useful. For instance there is no longer a difficulty how Congress shall move backwards and forwards, and your bungling scheme of moving houses and moving towns is quite superseded, we shall soar sublime above the clouds. It is happy for us too that this invention happens just as philosophy is taking such a start in our own hemisphere: for I find by the last election of members to the Society there are no less than 21 new philosophers found, every one of whom is superior to my countryman Madison."[94]

In the following month Hopkinson informed Jefferson that "a Gen-tleman in Town" [Philadelphia] was making an air balloon having a di-ameter of six feet.[95]

Jefferson discussed ballooning with James McClurg, theologian and scientific lecturer at the College of William and Mary, in a letter now lost. His communication apparently inspired McClurg and the Reverend Madison to attempt to make a balloon at the College. Madison reported that air made from straw was much more inflammable than from wood or other materials, but they had not been able to achieve the levity that was required. They were using a gun barrel to collect the air and asked Jefferson for information of methods used in France.[96]

To his young cousin Philip Turpin, Jefferson wrote that in the event that he had not been informed of the latest discovery of air travel by balloons, he would provide details based on a copy he had obtained of the work by Barthelemy Faujas de St. Fond, *Description des Expériences de la Machine Aérostatique*, describing the experiences of the Montgolfier brothers.

From his reading Jefferson concluded that two desiderata still remained, namely, to discover the cheapest and easiest method of making the lightest inflammable air, and producing a means of enveloping the gas in an enclosure that would be light, strong, impervious to air and waterproof. Finally, it was necessary to devise a means of providing supplies of gas without having to carry fire.

He suggested that the uses of this discovery could include transportation of some commodities; to traverse deserts, enemy territories and countries ravaged by infectious disorders or pathless mountains; to convey intelligence into besieged places or for reconnoitering an army; to throw new light on thermometric, barometric, hygrometric and other climatic or atmospheric phenomena; to discovering the poles, raise weights, lighten ships over sandbars, housebreak and smuggle, among other endeavors. He also compiled a table of the ascensions with related data.[97]

In Philadelphia shortly before his departure for France, Jefferson "had the pleasure of seeing 3 balons here. The largest was of 8 f[eet] diameter and ascended about 300 feet." The American interest in ballooning became so widespread that it led to new fashions in clothing "a la Montgolfier." Hopkinson reported that in Philadelphia the people had been amusing themselves by watching air balloons made of paper and sent aloft by Dr. Foulkes. They rose twice or three times the heights of the houses.

Perhaps inspired by these experiments, John Morgan introduced a motion at a meeting of the American Philosophical Society to raise a subscription for the Society to construct and raise an air balloon.[98]

Jefferson continued to make revisions in his *Notes* and added materials provided by Charles Thomson as an appendix. He finally abandoned any plans to have the work printed in the United States. Aitken, the Philadelphia printer he had consulted, who had formerly estimated a price of £4 a sheet, now raised the price to five pounds ten, which increased the total price of the publication by £18. Worst of all, Aitken admitted that he would be unable to complete the printing in the few weeks remaining before Jefferson's departure. The printer Dunlap was out of the city so that Jefferson had no alternative but to abandon publication until after he was in Paris, where he hoped to find an English printer and less expensive rates.

On May 7, 1784 Jefferson's appointment to France was reinstated, to replace John Jay who was returning to the United States. Because of the imminent departure of the vessel on which Jefferson was to sail, he was forced to leave the city so abruptly that he was unable to visit his two younger daughters before sailing. As a consequence, he never saw Lucy Elizabeth again.[99]

He traveled to Philadelphia and collected Martha at her school, then proceeded with her to Boston, arriving on June 18th. After numerous delays, on July 5th Jefferson and his daughter sailed out of Boston harbor on the new merchantman *Ceres*. The six fellow passengers included the ship's owner Colonel Tracey.

The voyage was pleasant and they enjoyed calm seas. Martha continued her studies under her father's supervision, while Jefferson was learning Spanish "with the help of a Don Quixote lent him by Mr. Cabot, and a grammar" during the nineteen days they were at sea. They landed at Portsmouth, where they were detained a week by Martha's illness; she had contracted a fever resulting from the effects of the voyage. Jefferson then hired a vessel to take them to Le Havre, where they disembarked and traveled overland to Paris.[100]

CHAPTER VI

"THE VAUNTED SCENE" (1784–1786)

Behold me at last on the vaunted scene of Europe! . . . you are, perhaps, curious to know how this new scene has struck a savage of the mountains of America. Not advantagdeously I assure you.

Letter from Jefferson to
Charles Bellini, 1785.

On August 6, 1784, one month and one day after his departure from the United States, Jefferson arrived in Paris with eleven-year-old Martha and his black servant James Hemings. Jefferson established himself with his entourage in temporary quarters at the Hotel d'Orléans on Rue Richelieu, and several days later moved to the Left Bank to another hotel, also called Hotel d'Orléans, on the Rue des Petits Augustins. In the autumn of 1785 he moved to the Hotel de Langeac where he resided for the remainder of his stay in Paris.

John and Abigail Adams had been living in Paris since 1778 in a fine house at Auteuil, four miles outside the city. They soon came to the assistance of Jefferson and his daughter to make them feel more at home, and they frequently dined together.[1]

A major concern was finding a proper school for Martha. After consulting with the Marquis de Chastellux, he enrolled her with the nuns of the Abbaye Royale de Panthemont in the Rue de Genelle. Martha brought with her a long list prepared by her father of instructions on behavior including recommendations for extra study. Always concerned for making the best use of time, he admonished her, "Determine never to be idle. No person will have occasion to complain of the want of time who never loses any. It is wonderful how much may be done if we are always doing."

It was a lonely period at first for the young girl, for she knew little French and the other students knew no English. Jefferson visited her daily to make her feel more at home until her French improved. When official functions prevented his visit to the Abbaye, he wrote letters to her instead.[2]

Although he could converse with the numerous French individuals he met in his own country, Jefferson experienced difficulty in understanding the language as spoken in Paris. He felt that in general the people appeared to be sullen and unhappy, resigned to the conditions in which they were forced to live under a burden of heavy taxation.

His first impressions of Paris were disappointing and did not meet his expectations of the great romantic European capital, "the city of light." The streets were poorly paved if at all, were much too narrow and without provision for pedestrians, and frequently covered with deep mud that made walking difficult. Accustomed as he had been to the serene pastoral existence he had enjoyed at Monticello and even in Richmond, the constant noise and confusion of the French city distracted him from his work.[3]

Eventually he solved the problem by renting rooms in the Carthusian monastery on Mont Calvaire, situated on a hilltop above the town of Suresnes beyond the Bois de Boulogne. There he retired when requiring concentration for preparing state papers and official correspondence, often remaining for a week or more until his work was finished. He maintained excellent relations with the lay brothers, known locally as the "Hermites," who worked in their vineyards and stocking manufactory and also sold wood and honey. They occasionally visited him when they came into Paris.

Jefferson's work and study habits remained much as they had been before. He rose early and devoted the morning hours to business following a brief interlude for breakfast. At one o'clock he always rode or walked into the country, sometimes covering a distance of as much as seven miles.[4]

One of his priorities had been to call upon Dr. Benjamin Franklin to pay his respects, which he did almost immediately after his arrival. The elder statesman was housebound with the gout "and a stone" in his home in Passy. Although they met frequently thereafter, and were mutually cordial, they were greatly separated by age and did not share a social life.

The first meeting of the commission, consisting of Franklin, Adams and Jefferson, took place at the end of August. The instructions Jefferson had brought with him were for the negotiation of treaties of commerce with almost all the European nations, and their first project was to draft a general form for the treaties to be shown to those nations willing to negotiate. However, the requirements imposed by Congress were not acceptable to the maritime nations for the most part, and there was a lack of confidence in the emerging new republic. The development of the treaties kept Jefferson and his fellow commissioners greatly occupied, and meanwhile Jefferson was also dealing on those commercial matters with which a treaty already existed.[5]

Negotiations proceeded slowly with long lapses. Consequently Jefferson discovered that since his duties as American minister were not exacting, he had much leisure for observing the country and the people and for his own pursuits. Although he admired the French arts, he took a dim view of all else in the country. He was particularly depressed by the crowded conditions and the poverty he observed on all sides. He urged Monroe to come for a visit to France, for "it will make you adore your own country, it's soil, it's climate, It's equality, liberty, laws, people and manners. My god! How little do my countrymen know what precious blessings they are in possession of, and which no other people on earth enjoy."[6]

Of French achievements, he wrote to a young Italian professor at the College of William and Mary, "In science the mass of the people are for centuries behind ours; their literati, a dozen years before us. Books, really good, acquire just reputation in that time, and so become known to us, and communicate to us all their advantage in knowledge." This delay, he believed, had the advantage of placing the Americans out of the reach of European presses and their countless useless publications, which perished quickly.

As to the behavior of the people, he reported, "Intrigues of love occupy the younger, & those of ambition the more elderly part of the great. Conjugal love having no existence among them, domestic happiness . . . is utterly unknown."[7]

Almost immediately after his arrival, Jefferson made provision for conditions at work as well as at home. He ordered a Watt copying press for his own office, negotiating it through William Temple Franklin. The order was placed with Woodmason's, agent in London for the Watt firm, and it was to be forwarded by a shipping agent named Moore. The order underwent a series of incredible misadventures, and it was not until mid-March that the press arrived at Rouen. It remained unclaimed for more than six months at a depot after its arrival because the cases had been improperly labeled. An organized search finally brought the order to light.

New difficulties arose before Jefferson could claim the new press because at that time British products were prohibited in France. Exceptions were made only for the members of the foreign diplomatic corps, but since Jefferson was a relatively new arrival, his name had not yet been included in the list. Finally it was arranged to have the packing cases redirected to Franklin, and then they were permitted to be forwarded, arriving in mid-May.[8] (*Figure 9*)

Jefferson quickly learned how to operate the press himself and was immensely pleased with it, for it enabled him to complete the files of his official papers and outgoing personal correspondence. No longer would there be the need to write out summaries or to make handwritten duplicates of papers. Two years later, when his younger daughter Mary joined him in France, he taught her how to use the press to make copies of letters.[9]

He sought to share his pleasure in the invention with his friends and urged them to purchase presses for themselves. "Have you a copying press?" he queried James Madison several months after he had obtained his own. "If you have not you should get one. Mine (exclusive of the paper which costs a guinea a ream) has cost me about 14 guineas. I would give ten times that sum that I had it from the date of the stamp act." Madison responded cautiously that he did not have such a press and that it must wait until he could afford one. "I am led to think it would be a very economical acquisition to all our public offices which are obliged to furnish copies of papers belonging to them," he added.[10]

Jefferson described his new acquisition also to the Reverend Madison, commenting, "you must have learned long ago of the machine for copying letters at a single stroke, as we have received them in America before I left."[11]

In actuality, the copying press was not as well known outside of England as Jefferson assumed. When Franklin returned to the United States in 1787 and brought his Watt press with him, it was still relatively unknown among Americans. Among the few who owned one was George Washington, who had received it as a gift in 1782 from the Dutch outfitters of the *Bon Homme Richard* for John Paul Jones, but there were not many others.[12]

Jefferson's quest for new ideas and inventions ended abruptly although only temporarily in late January 1785, when Lafayette returned from the United States bringing letters for Jefferson. Among them was a letter from Jefferson's family doctor, Dr. James Currie, informing him that his two-year-old daughter, Lucy Elizabeth, had died of whooping cough three months earlier, on October 13th. The youngest Eppes child also had died from the same malady at the same time.[13]

Jefferson was prostrate with grief, possibly harboring a sense of guilt for having left his children such a great distance away that he could not be with them in their need. He was solaced by the Adamses and the Lafayettes in his immediate sorrow, and throughout his period of poor health that followed. It was not until the following spring that he was fully recovered.[14]

Despite his many occupations and preoccupations, the distance that separated him from his second daughter Mary was now constantly in his mind, and made him uneasy. Since the death of Lucy Elizabeth, Jefferson had become extremely anxious to reunite his remaining family and to bring Mary to join him in Paris. Having finally reached a decision, he sent explicit instructions to Francis Eppes, with whom Mary was staying. He specified that Mary was to sail on a good vessel but only during the periods between the beginning of April and the end of July to avoid the equinoctial storms. The vessel must have made at least one good voyage because "I think it would be found that all the vessels which are lost are either on their first voyage or after they are five years old." She was to travel on a French or English ship only, because they alone would be immune from attack by the Algerian pirates. If "some good lady passing from America to France, or even England," could not be found, "a careful gentleman would do. In this case some woman who has had the small-pox must attend her." He proposed "a careful negro woman," who need come no further than Le Havre, l'Orient or Nantes, where Jefferson would meet them, and then the woman could return to Virginia.[15]

Jefferson continued to worry about the hazards of travel. As he wrote to Elizabeth Eppes, "to be exposed to all the sufferings and risks, great and small, to which a situation on board a ship exposes every one, I drop my pen at the thought—but she must come."[16]

Meanwhile, however, six-year old Mary had become stubborn in her determination not to leave the Eppes family and her young friends at Eppington, and so informed her father. Every means was used to entice her but without success. Finally Jefferson was reduced to considering extremes, and proposed that his daughter might actually have to be shanghaied.[17]

In a communication from John Jay, Jefferson was notified that the Congress had elected him to succeed Dr. Franklin as minister to France. Two days later John Adams was appointed the first American ambassador to the Court of St. James and soon moved to London.[18]

Now came the time for formalities, and Jefferson presented his credentials to the French Minister of Foreign Affairs, the Count de Vergennes. When the Minister asked, "You replace Monsieur Franklin, I hear?" Jefferson responded, "I *succeed* him. No one can *replace* him."[19]

Jefferson had been one of the first Americans to purchase a copy of the remarkable *Encyclopédie* produced in 28 volumes by Diderot-d'Alembert in 1781–1782, and he was also among the early subscribers to the voluminous *Encyclopédie méthodique* begun in 1782 by Charles Joseph Panckoucke, which was finally completed in 1832. A copy of the Diderot-d'Alembert work had been purchased at Jefferson's request while he was governor for the use of the state of Virginia. When it arrived, he became so intrigued with the work that the Council had to take action to have it removed from him for the use of others. Meanwhile, he had arranged to purchase a copy of the Encyclopédie méthodique by contacting Panckoucke directly, but it did not arrive until after his arrival in France. Soon thereafter he took subscriptions for it for his friends.[20]

One of Jefferson's early concerns now that he was in Paris was for the printing of his *Notes on Virginia*, and eventually he found time to inquire about printers. He was pleased to discover that the cost would be approximately one fourth of the price he had been quoted in Philadelphia, but before sending his work to press he decided to correct and expand it.

There is some question about the identity of the printer he selected, inasmuch as no written communication concerning the printing of the *Notes* has survived and it is probable that the work was negotiated in person. It is generally assumed that the printer was Philippe-Denis Pierres, then considered to be the finest in Paris.[21]

Jefferson had another reason other than cost for having the *Notes* printed in Paris instead of the United States. The work contained an exceedingly frank exposition of his views on the Constitution of Virginia and concerning the abolition of slavery, views which differed greatly from those of many of his Virginia contemporaries. There was no doubt that when published they would engender controversy at home. It was for this consideration that he intended to have only a discreet number of copies printed, which he would personally distribute and only to selected friends.[22]

In the guidebook format of the *Notes* the text followed an "Advertisement" notifying the reader that the "subjects are all treated imperfectly; some scarcely touched upon." The first eight sections related to geography, a discussion of military strength, Indians, counties and towns, Constitution, laws, religion, manufactures, manners, weights and measures, commerce, histories and state papers. The work concluded with three appendices and a long addition "Relative to the Murder of the Logan Family." The book is less than a masterpiece of order and organization, to be sure, but when taken in its entirety, it proves to be an impressive compendium of information.

Printing arrangements for the *Notes* were finally completed, and as he informed Madison, "They yesterday finished printing my notes. I had 200 copies printed, but do not put them out of my own hands, except two or three copies here & two which I shall send to America, to yourself and Colo. Monroe, if they can be ready this evening, as promised."[23]

In sending a copy to Monroe, Jefferson noted, "I have taken measures to prevent it's publication [distribution]. My reason is that I fear the terms in which I speak of slavery and of our Constitution may produce an irritation which will revolt the minds of our countrymen against reformation in these two articles, and thus do more harm than good." He added that he had asked Madison to sound out others on the matter, and that if in his opinion it would not cause a great reaction, he then planned to send copies to each of the students at the College of William and Mary as well as to his friends.[24]

Two of the first copies off the press he sent to the French general, Marquis François Jean de Chastellux, one of which was to be forwarded to the Comte de Buffon, since Jefferson had not yet made Buffon's acquaintance. He told Chastellux that he left it up to the general's personal knowledge of America to recognize the obvious erroneous contentions made by the French historian and philosopher, Guillaume Thomas François, Abbé de Raynal, concerning the comparative merits of education in Europe and the United States.

Despite the precautions he had taken to restrict distribution of his Notes, Jefferson discovered that the copy he had given Charles Williamos, a Swiss-born one-time intimate of Jefferson's household, had upon his death fallen into the hands of the bookseller, Louis François Barrois. The bookseller promptly made plans to publish what Jefferson described as "a very abominable translation."

Consequently, as Jefferson informed C. W. F. Dumas, the American diplomatic agent at The Hague, he was induced to agree to the request of the Abbé André Morellet, who had arranged with Barrois to publish his (Morellet's) translation, subject to Jefferson's review and revision. Morellet had received a copy from Jefferson originally and had already translated some passages for his own purposes. Morellet had great prestige in intellectual circles, was elected to the Académie Royale des Sciences in 1785, and was a fellow member with Franklin of the Société d'Auteuil.[25]

While Morellet was engaged in translating the Notes, he suggested that sales would be enhanced with the addition of a map of the country it described. Jefferson concurred, for this provided him with an opportunity to supplement also the copies of his own private printing that he had already distributed.[26]

Although he was not an experienced cartographer, Jefferson had made at least one map for public use earlier in his career. He had considerable experience in surveying and as part of his law practise had already drawn land plats used in litigations. His plan was to combine the several existing maps of Virginia and supplement them with new information he expected to obtain from various sources, thus creating a new map. He laid out his map with the prime meridian, or 0° longitude, established at Philadelphia, in accordance with common usage of the time. He included an area of approximately 1° east to 8° west of Philadelphia, and from 36° to 42° north latitude.

Regions added were that part of North Carolina north of Albemarle Sound, all of the states of Virginia, Maryland, Delaware and Pennsylvania, the western regions of New York and New Jersey and the territory westward just beyond where the Ohio and Great Kanhawa Rivers met.

He utilized recent cartographical works available to him, which he knew with certainty had been made from actual surveys and consequently were the most reliable. Among these was one of the several available versions of the William Scull map of 1770 for the section on Pennsylvania, and for Virginia he utilized the map produced in 1750 by his father and Joshua Fry. He revised it with additions of more recent data from the 1778 survey made by Thomas Hutchins. It is probable that he also used M. Mouzon's map of North Carolina to update the Fry and Jefferson version of that region. He also acquired a copy of the Lewis Evans map of the British Colonies for comparison with his own composition.

Finally he added information about the western regions he had collected from some of the explorers and land developers with whom he was acquainted, including Thomas Hutchins, John Page, Isaac Zane and Thomas Walker. He incorporated data from the notes of the survey of the Pennsylvania boundary he had obtained from Page and he looked forward to receiving a copy of the line that had been run.

He included geographical phenomena which had not been previously recorded cartographically, such as the Natural Bridge, the caves described by Zane and Madison and the Indian mound he had excavated. He also divided the western lands into five new states, of which he labeled three: "A New State," "Kentuckey" for the western county of Virginia already known by that name and "Frankland" for the state which became Tennessee. Finally, he indicated what he believed to be the correct western boundary of Virginia.

For plotting latitude, he used observations he had made at Monticello, which was situated 38° 8′ 17″, and for that of Williamsburg he utilized latitudes provided by the Reverend Madison. The latitudes of the western limits of Pennsylvania he obtained from Rittenhouse.[27]

Using a scale of one inch to twenty miles, Jefferson worked on the map for more than a year, noting in February 1786 that he hoped to have it completed within the next several weeks. He asked Edward Bancroft at the American embassy in London to investigate potential London engravers for the map, of which he planned to order 1800 copies.[28]

Meanwhile, Morellet's published translation proved to be a great disappointment to Jefferson. Furthermore, the edition was printed on paper of mediocre quality with unattractive type, and contained numerous misprints and errors of translation. To add insult to injury, the order of the contents was transposed. It was inevitable, he wrote, that a book-seller would arrange to have the work translated in an edition that was "interverted, abridged, mutilated . . . I found it a blotch of errors from beginning to end."

Two separate errata lists were issued, but Jefferson remained greatly disappointed. He compiled an extensive memorandum entitled "Errors in the Abbé Morellet's translation of the *Notes on Virginia* the correction of which is indispensable." He prepared it after the issuance of the first short errata list but before the publication of the second and longer one, so that unfortunately it did not fulfill his purpose of including all the corrections.[29]

Jefferson's interest in ballooning, first aroused by witnessing several unmanned ascensions in Philadelphia, was revived by an opportunity to attend the historic manned balloon ascension of the Roberts brothers from the gardens of the Tuileries.

On Sunday morning he joined the great mass of people crowding through the six entrances that admitted ticket holders to the Château des Tuileries. He observed that the balloon was made in an oval shape, not a sphere. It had already been filled with hydrogen the previous day, and was brought to the platform erected for it over the oval pool in front of the Château.

As the crowd pushed its way forward to obtain a better view of the interior of the balloon's gondola, they accidentally broke the rudder at the stern. Nonetheless, the Roberts brothers and their cousin, Colin Hullin, having arrived as scheduled, climbed into the ship and rose into the air one minute before noon, amidst the excited cries and hurrahs of the tightly packed crowd.

The balloon was out of sight of Paris shortly before two o'clock and established a new distance record, eventually coming to earth once more twenty minutes before seven o'clock that evening at the village of Beau-vray near Béthune.[30]

The subject fascinated him, and Jefferson kept himself informed of all ballooning ascensions and experiments. He obtained copies of a pam-phlet published by the Roberts brothers the previous year and sent them to several of his American friends. While in Philadelphia before his de-parture, as he had reported to Monroe, "I have had the pleasure of seeing 3 balons here. The largest was of 8. f.[eet] diameter and ascended about 300 f.[eet]." Several months after having observed the ascent of the Rob-erts brothers, he informed Francis Hopkinson, "Mr. Blanchard of this country and Dr. Jeffries of Massachusetts arrived here the day before yesterday from Dover, having crossed the channel on the 7th, in a Bal-loon. They were two hours from land to land. It was filled with inflam-mable air. We are told of a method of extricating this from pit coal, cheaply and speedily, but it is not yet reduced to experience." He considered the event of sufficient importance to inform a number of his other friends of it, including Neil Jamieson, St. John de Crèvecoeur and James Monroe.[31]

Jefferson was the first to report the death of the world's first airman. The earliest news to reach the United States was provided by Jefferson in June 1785, to Monroe and Joseph Jones in a description of the fatal accident of Jean Francois Pilatre de Rozière. After having waited for several months at Boulogne for a suitable wind which would enable them to cross the Channel, Rozière with a companion, Pierre Romain, finally ascended in his balloon. Shortly after the balloon was in the air, the wind changed and returned them to the French coast. At a height said to be approximately six thousand feet an accident occurred and the balloon of inflammable air burst, dropping the voyagers to earth, killing both. Rozière had combined a Montgolfier balloon with the one filled with inflammable air and it was presumed that the heat from the Montgolfier unit ignited the gas in the other.

In summarizing the accident to Thomson, Jefferson noted that the earlier account of the ascension had been in error and that it had now been reported to have been to a height of about sixteen hundred feet, not six thousand. He also mentioned the accident in a letter to Abigail Adams, adding, "This will damp for a while the ardor of the Phaetons of our race who are endeavoring to learn us the way to heaven on wings of our own."[32]

Jefferson was hopeful that some progress in ballooning was being made in the United States, for he foresaw the potential use of air travel in the future. He informed Ralph Izard, Charles Thomson and others of the experience of Messrs. Alban and Vallet, directors of the Manufacture de Javel, a chemical laboratory and factory of the Comte d'Artois, where experimentation was being undertaken with hydrogen gas for balloons. "Two artists at Javel, about 4 miles hence, are pursuing the art of directing the baloon," he wrote. "They ascend and descend at will, without expending their gaz, and they can deflect 45 degrees from the course of the wind when it is not very strong. We may certainly expect that this desideratum will be found. As the birds and fish prove that the means exist, we may count on human ingenuity for its discovery."[33]

It was not long before Jefferson became intrigued to find in Paris new inventions which were not known in the United States, and which he hastened to confide to James Madison, Charles Thomson, and other friends. He was particularly curious about the "cylinder lamp" which had been "invented here lately which with a very small consumption of oil (of olives) is thought to give a light equal to six or seven candles. The wick is hollow in the middle in the form of a hollow cylinder, and permits the air to pass up thro' it. It requires no snuffing. They make shade candlesticks which are excellent for reading and are much used by studious men."[34]

Thomson expressed a wish to have such a lamp, and Jefferson later sent him one which he had obtained from England; it was produced by a Quaker maker named Meigs who had managed to evade the patent of the original inventor, a Swiss physicist named François Pierre Ami Argand. "There is but one critcal circumstance in the management of it," Jefferson warned Thomson, "that is the length of the wick above the top of the cylinder. If raised too high it fills the room with smoke, if not high enough, it will not yeild it's due light. The true medium is where it ceases to a sensible smoke in the room. Two or three experiments will set you to rights in this." Some years later he provided a hanging Argand lamp to the American Philosophical Society through its librarian, John Vaughan.[35]

Equally fascinating to him were "Phosphoretic matches", consisting "of a small wax taper, one end of which has been dipped in Phosphorus, and the whole is enclosed in a glass tube hermetically sealed. There is a little ring on the tube to shew where it is to be broken. First warm the phosphoretic end (which is the furthest from the ring) by holding it two or three seconds in your mouth, then snap it at or near the ring and draw the phosphorized end out of the tube. It blazes in the instant of its extraction. It will be well always to decline the tube at an angle of about 45°, (the phosphorized end lowest) in order that it may kindle thoroughly. Otherwise though it blazes in the first instant it is apt to go out if held erect."

The matches cost about 30 *sous* per dozen, Jefferson reported, and they were convenient for lighting a bedside candle at night or for softening sealing wax, and in the woods they replaced flint and steel. He warned, "if the phosphorus dropped on the hand, it is inextinguishable and would burn through to the bone. It is said that urine would extinguish it." The matches were in fact already known in the United States, as Thomson informed him, and were sold in toy shops in Philadelphia.[36]

Jefferson found and purchased a model of a hydraulic engine which he thought might have application at home. As well as can be determined, however, he made no use of it later at Monticello. The possibility exists that he contemplated using it to pump water up into reservoirs on the roof, from which the water would flow by gravity into the house. If he did in fact attempt it, no record survives, and the only evidence is a drawing of the engine with a description in French.[37]

He learned of yet another invention which appeared to have potential for application in the States and to which he devoted considerable attention. He informed Hugh Williamson that he had seen "a simple invention in mechanics here which may be of some use. It is nothing more than the application of the screw to the air, water, or any other fluid. The screw pulling itself through a solid, will evidently do the same through a fluid, only allowing a loss in it's effort proportioned to the want of tenaciousness or resistance in the fluid. If it draws itself along, it will draw also bodies tacked to, or connected with it. I saw the screw. It is about 8. feet long, it's axis is about 9. Inches diameter and the spiral vane [thread] of about two feet radius. Being fixed on a couple of light boats and turned rapidly on its axis (by means of a wheel, band, and pulley) it carries them across the Seine very quickly. The screw lies horizontal. If it's axis coincides with that of the boat, it moves it directly forward. But turning it on a pivot so as that it shall intersect the axis of the boat, it changes her direction. If made to work in water it's effect will still be greater as the fluid yeilds more resistance. It is thought applicable to a vessel becalmed, to submarine navigation so as to give motion in any direction horizontally or vertically, to aerial navigation for raising or lowering a balloon, moving it in a calm, and influencing it's direction even in a current of air by the combination of it's effect with that of the wind. If so, I wish we knew it, the precise construction of the Connecticut turtle and its actual performance." The "Connecticut Turtle" was the submarine invented by David Bushnell of Connecticut during the American Revolution.[38]

Some time later he reported the same invention to the Reverend Ezra Stiles, as "a method of moving a vessel in the water by a machine worked within the vessel . . . [the inventor] did not know himself the principle of his own invention." He had gone to see it and described it as "a screw with a very broad thin worm, or rather it is a thin plate with it's edge applied spirally round an axis. This being turned operates on the air as a screw does, and may be literally said to screw the vessel along; the thinness of the medium and it's want of resistance occasions a loss of much of the force. The screw I think would be much more effectual if placed below the surface of the water." He suspected that Bushnell had made a prior discovery of the same principle and again expressed a desire to obtain an account of the "Turtle."

He forwarded some published works which he believed Stiles would find useful, including a four-volume set of the *Bibliothèque Physico-oeconomique* which provided an account of the advancement of the arts during the past few years. He also included five volumes of the *Connaissance des Temps* for the years between 1781 and 1785, because they contained Nicolas Louis de La Caille's catalogue of fixed stars, Charles Messier's catalogue of nebulae, John Flamsteed's catalogue of stars, Leonhard Euler's lunar tables with corrections, the tables for the planet Herschel [Uranus] and Johann Tobias Mayer's catalogue of zodiacal stars.

He acknowledged the information that Stiles had provided concerning the large fossil bones discovered on the Hudson River, which he agreed appeared to be of the "mammoth" [mastodon]. He had seen a piece of the ivory from one of the tusks which he pronounced to be very good. He also asked about a plant which Abigail Adams had found in Connecticut and brought to Paris. Its unusual feature was that it "vegetates when suspended in the air"[39]

Stiles later forwarded a letter he had received from General Samuel Holden Parsons, a Connecticut speculator in Western lands, which included a sketch of a formation made by the mound builders at the mouth of the Muskingum River, in which Parsons had reported the presence of brick and pottery. Jefferson concluded from the great height of the structure that the mound builders were superior to the American Indians in their knowledge of the arts, but doubted whether there was in fact any connection between the mound builders and the American Indians, a conclusion with which Stiles appeared to agree.

He was confident that the Indians could make mounds and entrenchments, but he questioned whether they could make brick. No evidence had been found of the use of iron by the aborigines along the eastern coast, although they were said to have used brickwork fortifications along the Ohio River. He was eager to learn whether Parsons had personally observed actual bricks among the ruins.

Jefferson commented on the similarities between the American Indians and those of eastern Asia, and contemplated that the American aborigines undoubtedly were descended from those of Asia or vice versa. He noted that among the red inhabitants of eastern Asia "there are but a few languages radically different" but that the American Indians had an infinite number of languages and so radically different from each other that no evidence could be found of a common source. Consequently he concluded that the period of time required to have developed so many languages must have been considerable.

If the mound builders of the Mississippi valley had an advanced culture, then either the Indians were not connected with them and constituted a separate later civilization, or else they had suffered a great decline. In questioning the observations of Parsons to Stiles, Jefferson had substantial evidence to support his contention, but his suggestion that the mound builders might have been ancestors of the Indians was criticized by several writers, including Thomas Ashe in his book of travel. Barton, Rush and Williamson concurred in the opinion that the Indian civilization had declined due to lack of tillable soil and access to hunting, and that consequently they had lost the use of a written language and knowledge of their religion.[40]

Of the numerous scientific endeavors which Jefferson observed in France, none aroused his interest more than the experimental astronomical instruments being developed by the Abbé Alexis Marie de Rochon and his assistant Herbage. Having first achieved renown as a physician and then as an astronomer, Rochon presented several papers on optics before the Académie Royale des Sciences in 1766.

On one of Rochon's maritime voyages, he collected some rock crystal in Madagascar from which he later made telescope objectives. Working in the Cabinet de Physique de la Muette, he undertook a long series of experiments with prisms and attempted to replace the mirrors of sextants with achromatic prisms.

Rochon also succeeded in combining two prisms cut from rock crystal into a micrometer by means of which two images could be produced and made to coincide by moving an achromatized rock crystal plate along the axis of a refracting telescope. He experimented also with the development of reflecting telescopes. In association with Noel Simon Carochez he constructed a mirror of "platina" [platinum] which brought him a prize of 400 *livres* and earned for him the title of "*astronome de la marine.*"[41]

When he first came to Jefferson's atttention, Rochon was already well known as one of France's foremost optical inventors. He had already produced his achromatic object-lens from double-refracting rock crystal and had used it with a new form of heliometer of his own design. Jefferson visited Rochon and sought to bring his work to the attention of all at home concerned with astronomy. He first reported to Rittenhouse on Rochon's application of natural crystals for telescope lenses and his use of the recently discovered metal, platinum, for telescope specula.

"The Abbé Rochon has lately made a very curious discovery in optics," he commented. "He has made lenses with a chrystal from Iceland which has a double focus, perfectly distinct and at considerable distances from each other. I looked through a *telescope* to which he had adapted one of these and saw at the same instant an object on the banks of the Seine and a house half a mile further back with equal precision, the intermediate object being dim as not at a proper distance from either focus. He supposes this chrystal composed of two substances of different refracting powers, not so united as to single their effect. He proposes by it a method of deciding in time whether the obliquity of the ecliptic really changes, and he thinks it will be more accurate than those hitherto known."[42]

The Reverend Madison, having also been informed of the invention, responded with enthusiasm, had some questions concerning the means by which the effect was produced, the specific gravity of the crystal, and how it differed from other rock crystals. Jefferson was unable to provide the information at that time inasmuch as the Abbé lived some distance outside of Paris.[43]

Rochon's other discoveries also intrigued Jefferson, and he described "platina" to Hopkinson as a metal which had been found only in South America, and like gold and silver, was not liable to rust, nor was it affected by any of the acids except aqua regia, a mixture of nitric and hydrochloric acids. "It also admits of as perfect a polish as the metal hitherto used for the specula of telescopes," he commented. "These two properties have suggested to the Spaniards the substitution of it for that use. But the mines being closed up by the government, it is difficult to get the metal."

Rochon believed that this new metal could receive as high a polish as any previously used, he added, and that the polished surface would not be affected by air nor by the touch of a finger. Jefferson had examined the mirror on a dull day so that he was unable to judge its reflective capability. He also informed Franklin and Stiles of the new discovery, noting that he was not certain whether the use of platina for telescopes was original with Rochon; he thought that perhaps it had been first used by the Spanish.[44]

"Platina," later known as the precious metal called platinum, may have been known in Europe as early as the first part of the sixteenth century as a metal incapable of being fused which had been found in Mexico and Darien. It first achieved recognition after an account of the voyage of the Spanish explorers, Don Jorge Juan y Santacilia and Antonio de Ulloa, was published in 1748. A means for melting platinum was achieved in the mid-eighteenth century, but it was not until the early nineteenth century that its special qualities were fully exploited.[45]

Meanwhile the Reverend Madison had researched the double-refracting crystal and was able to tell Jefferson something about the "Icelandic Chrystal as [being] long known to Opticians for its singular refracting Powers. It is described as a kind of Talc, found in the form of an oblique Parallelopiped, and composed of Lamina which will cleave parallel to either of its Sides; from which Constitution, its Property may properly be derived."

He mentioned that Franklin had given a piece of the crystal to a friend in Philadelphia and that there was also a telescope using the crystal already in Philadelphia, "by which the Suns apparent Diameter is readily measured, and small Distances accurately determined."[46]

Many years later, Jefferson described his association with Rochon to Robert Patterson. He had recently received copies of Rochon's pamphlets and his book, and explained that he had become fairly intimate with him. In conversation, the Abbé had provided additional explanations of what had appeared in his published works.

Jefferson added that he also owned one of Rochon's telescopes which the inventor had originally given to Franklin and which had come to him from Hopkinson. "The graduated bar on each side is 12 Inches long. The one extending to 37° of an angle, the other to 3,438 diameter in distance of the object viewed. On so large a scale of graduation, a nonias might distinctly enough sub-divide the divisions of 10″ to 10″ each; which is certainly a great degree of precision. But not possessing the common micrometer of two semi-lenses, I am not able to judge of their comparative merit."[47]

Throughout his absence from home Jefferson maintained contact with his nephew Peter Carr and sought to counsel him on his studies and about life in general. Young Carr, now fifteen, admitted that he had not progressed in his studies as well as had been expected. In advising him, Jefferson emphasized "the possession of science is, what (next to an honest heart) will above all things render you dear to your friends, and give you promotion in your own country. When your mind shall be well improved with science, nothing will be necessary to place you in the highest points of view, but to pursue the interests of your country, the interests of your friends, and your own interests also, with the purest integrity, the most chaste honor. The defect of these virtues can never be made up by all the other acquirements of body and mind. Make these, then, your first object. Give up money, give up fame, give up science, give up the earth itself and all it contains, rather than do an immoral act. And never suppose, that in any possible situation, or under any circumstances, it is best for you to do a dishonorable thing, however slightly so it may appear to you."[48]

From time to time Jefferson urged his friends to take advantage of his presence in France to obtain instruments or other items they required. James Madison had described several in which he was interested.

> I have seen a *pocket compass* of somewhat larger diameter than a watch, which may be carried in the same way. It has a spring for stopping the vibration of the needle when not in use. One of these would be very convenient in case of a ramble into the Western Country. In my walks for exercise or amusements, objects frequently present themselves, which it might be matter of curiosity to inspect, but which it is difficult or impossible to approach. A portable glass would consequently be a source of many little gratifications. I have fancied that such an one might be fitted into a Cane without making it too heavy. On the outside of the tube might be engraved a scale of inches &c. If such a project could be executed for a few Guineas, I should be willing to submit to the price; if not, the best substitute I suppose will be a *pocket telescope*, composed of several tubes so constructed as to slide the lesser into the greater. I should feel great remorse at troubling you with so many requests, if your kind and repeated offers did not stifle it in some measure.[49]

It was not until several years had passed that Jefferson was able to fulfill Madison's requests and forward "your pocket telescope, walking stick, and chemical box. The two former could not be combined together. The latter could not be had in the form you referred to."[50]

It was in the summer of 1785 that Jefferson first became aware of the achievements of a French gunsmith named Honoré Blanc, who had developed a new method of manufacture for military weapons. He made them with interchangeable parts for greater economy of production and for ease of repair in the field. Visualizing the potential value of such a process to the United States, he visited Blanc at the weapons manufactory at St. Etienne. He was intrigued with the revolutionary mechanical process and convinced of its military importance. His interest in new inventions included those useful in warfare, and it should be remembered that his earlier speculations on the future of ballooning included its potential value in warfare, for traversing enemy territory, conveying military intelligence for reconnoitering an army, the destruction of fortified works and "of fleets & what not."

He returned from his visit with great enthusiasm, eager to share his experience with John Jay, Minister of Foreign Affairs. Jay reported:

> An improvement is made here in the construction of the musket, which it may be interesting to Congress to know, should they at any time propose to procure any. It consists in the making every part of them so exactly alike that what belongs to any one, may be used for every other musket in the magazine. The government here has examined and approved the method, and is establishing a large manufactory for the purpose. As yet the inventor has only completed the lock of the musket on this plan. He will proceed immediately to have the barrel, stock, and their parts executed in the same way. Supposing it might be useful to the U. S., I went to the workman, he presented me the parts of 50. locks taken to pieces, and arranged in compartments. I put several together myself taking pieces at hazard as they came to hand, and they fitted in the most perfect manner. The advantages of this, when arms need repair, are evident. He effects it by tools of his own contrivance which at the same time abridge the work so that he thinks he shall be able to furnish the muskets two *livres* cheaper than the common price. But it will be two or three years before he will be able to furnish any quantity. I mention it now, as it may have influence on the plan for furnishing our magazine with this arm.[51]

The concept of military weapons with interchangeable parts had been first attempted in 1722 by the French government for the production of gun locks. Abandoned after a decade of unsuccessful experimentation, the project was initiated anew by Blanc for the purpose of providing weapons to the French military.[52]

Although credit for the system of manufacture with interchangeable parts is properly due to Blanc, it was Inspector General of French Artillery, Jean Baptiste Vaquette de Gribeauval who was responsible for adopting the system on a large scale for the artillery.

Together with Blanc, in 1783 they devised a program by means of which all French artillery materiel was thereafter standardized to enable the interchange of like parts in all its elements. This "Gribeauval method" made possible expeditious assembly and disassembly during repair in the field of field guns, fore carriages, caissons, vehicles, etc. and to develop gauges for every part, notably for the ironwork.[53] (*Figure 10*)

Jefferson quickly realized the potential of Blanc's system for application in the United States, and was determined to promote it. Having received no response from Jay, he next informed Patrick Henry, then Governor of Virginia, ostensibly to advise him that he had been informed that the order of French arms that had been purchased for the state would be ready in eight months. He then went on to describe Blanc's system in virtually the same words he had used in his earlier letter to Jay.[54]

So enthusiastic had he become in fact, that he purchased a group of weapons incorporating Blanc's gunlocks to be shipped back to the United States for testing by the American government. Included in his purchase were "six Officers fusils for the U. S."[55]

Determined to pursue the matter despite the lack of response from Jay and Henry, Jefferson next turned to Secretary of War Henry Knox. Referring to his earlier communication to Jay, he described Blanc's achievements as those of "a workman here."[56]

"If the situation of the finances of this country should oblige the government to abandon him [Blanc]," he went on, "he would prefer removing with all his people and implements to America, if we should desire to establish such a manufacture, and he would expect our government to take all his implements on their own account at what they have cost him. He talked of about 3,000 guineas. I trouble you with these details, and with the samples (1) That you may give the idea of such an improvement to our own workmen, if you think it might answer any good end. (2) That all the arms he shall have for sale may be engaged for our government, if he continue here and you think it important to engage them. (3) That you may consider and do me the honour of communicating your determination whether, in the event of his establishment being abandoned by this government, it might be thought worthwhile to transfer it to the United States on conditions somewhat like those he has talked of."[57]

There is no evidence that Jefferson received replies from any of his communications concerning Blanc to government officials. Still undaunted, however, he arranged to have the Blanc weapons he had purchased packed and shipped to Jay. Although complete when shipped, by

FIGURE 1. Declaration of Independence desk. Portable writing desk designed by Jefferson on which he drafted the Declaration of Independence. Courtesy of the National Museum of American History, Smithsonian Institution.

FIGURE 2. Jefferson's revolving chair made to his specifications by Benjamin Randolph in 1776, and in which he probably sat while drafting the Declaration of Independence. The writing arm was added later at Monticello. Courtesy of the American Philosophical Society.

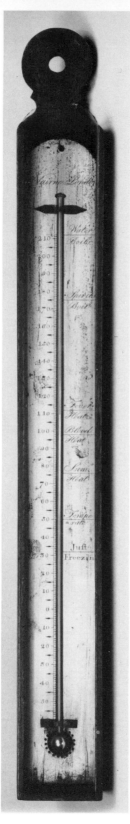

FIGURE 3.   Thermometer made by Nairne & Blunt of London, formerly owned by Jefferson. Courtesy of the Historical Society of Pennsylvania.

FIGURE 4. Sketch of observatory tower with Georgian steeple, planned for Montalto. Ink and wash, c. 1771. Courtesy of the Massachusetts Historical Society.

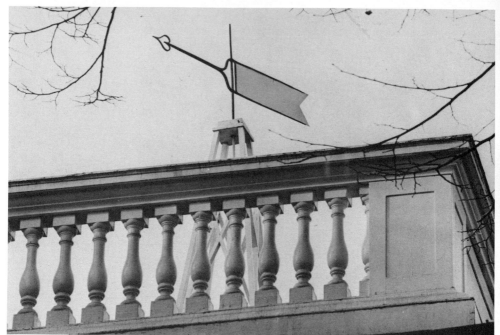

FIGURE 5.   Wind vane, installed over the East Portico of Monticello, which indicated wind directions on a compass rose on the ceiling below. Courtesy of the Thomas Jefferson Memorial Foundation.

FIGURE 6.   Wind rose painted on the ceiling of the East Portico indicating wind directions by means of a wind vane on the roof. Courtesy of the Thomas Jefferson Memorial Foundation.

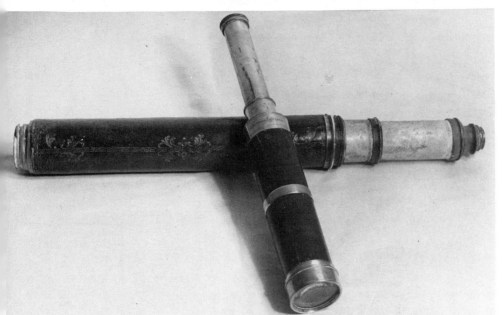

FIGURE 7.   Hand telescopes owned by Jefferson, one with leather main tube and parchment draw-tubes, and the other with wooden main tube and silver plated draw-tubes, the outer of which is inscribed "Thomas Jefferson." Courtesy of the Thomas Jefferson Memorial Foundation.

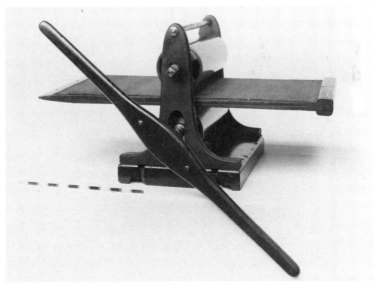

FIGURE 9.   Stationary form of the Watt copying press, similar to those Jefferson purchased for his use in France and later as Secretary of State. Courtesy of the Science Museum, South Kensington, London.

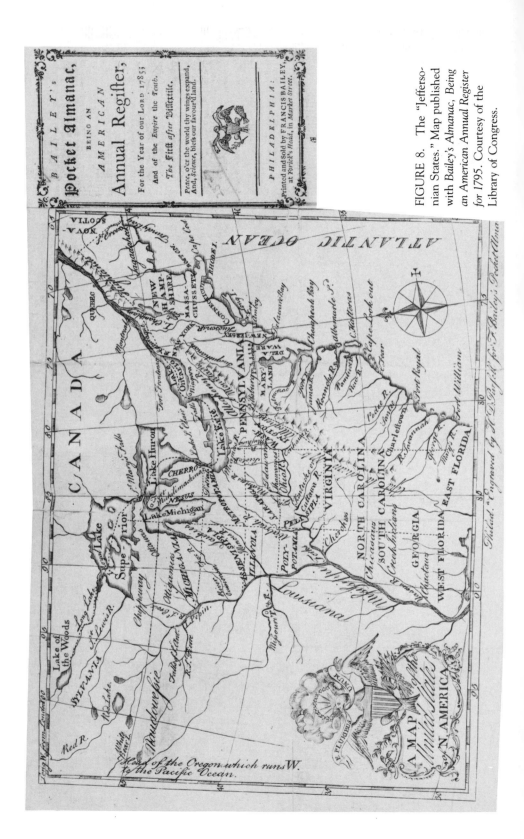

FIGURE 8. The "Jeffersonian States." Map published with *Bailey's Almanac, Being an American Annual Register for 1795.* Courtesy of the Library of Congress.

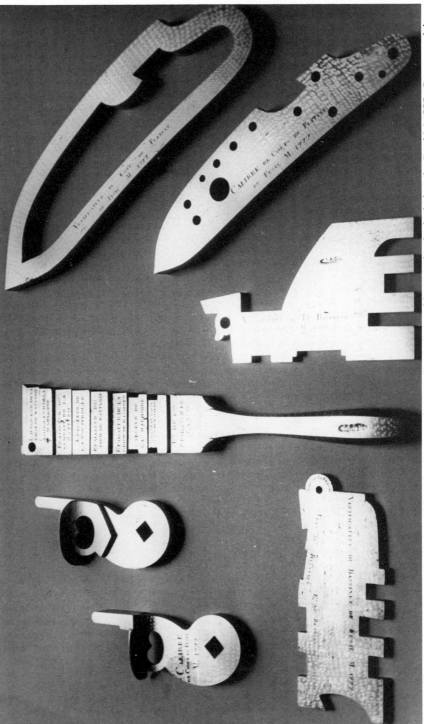

FIGURE 10. Gauges developed by Honoré Blanc for the manufacture of interchangeable parts for the lockplate for Fusil M 1777. Courtesy of the Musée de l'Armée, Paris.

FIGURE 11. Theodolite made by Jesse Ramsden of London owned and used by Jefferson. Courtesy of the Thomas Jefferson Memorial Foundation.

FIGURE 12. Achromatic refracting telescope made by Dollond of London used by Jefferson at Monticello. Courtesy of the Thomas Jefferson Memorial Foundation.

the time they arrived in New York the lockplates and other critical parts were missing. Jefferson, by then again in the United States, promptly ordered replacement parts through William Short in Paris. After calling upon Blanc, Short reported that Blanc's "machine is not mounted at present," and that it could not be mounted for such a small order. Within the next two weeks, however, the gunsmith collected and forwarded six gunlocks, but they failed to arrive at Short's apartment.

It was not until much later that the gunlocks were delivered, including a gunlock for a soldier's musket sent as a sample. Also in the package was a printed memoir by Blanc explaining his improvements and procedures, which Jefferson forwarded to Knox.[58]

Jefferson's efforts to interest the American government proved to be completely futile, despite his strong convictions that he was presenting a unique opportunity not to be overlooked. Blanc's offer to migrate to the United States apparently evoked no interest from either the Secretary of Foreign Affairs or the Secretary of War. It is conceivable that the long delay experienced by Jefferson in having the sample weapons shipped to the United States may have been responsible for the lack of interest, but there is no reasonable explanation for the absence of any response from the two government departments most involved.

Jefferson persisted in seeking support for Blanc in the United States, but nothing more occurred in the matter. Nonetheless, the subject remained alive in Jefferson's mind, and long after he became President of the United States, he thought he had found someone who could adapt and apply Blanc's principles of manufacture for the good of the American people, in the person of the American inventor Eli Whitney.[59]

Always alert to new instruments and devices which could be made useful for himself or others, Jefferson was intrigued to read in the *Encyclopédie des Arts et Métiers* a description of a musical instrument invented by a certain Renaudin for determining the true time of musical movements, such as Largo, Adagio, etc. Renaudin, not to be confused with the violin-maker of the same name, was a harpist. The instrument he had designed, which he named a *plexichronometre*, was constructed for him by his brother who was a clockmaker.

Curious about the instrument, Jefferson visited Renaudin, and the latter showed him three versions he had developed. The first had sold for twenty five guineas, and a second version was available for half that price. Both were powered by means of a mainspring and regulated by a balance wheel.

Renaudin then showed Jefferson the most recent version he had devised, which was motivated by a descending weight and regulated by a pendulum like a common clock, and cost only two and a half guineas.

Its dial plate was divided into 52 equal degrees inscribed at appropriate points, and marked with the names of the musical movements—Largo, Adagio, Andante, Allegro and Presto. Largo was at 1, Adagio at 11, Andante at 22, Allegro at 36 and Presto at 46.

These were selected by turning the index at the center of the dial to the appropriate name. The string by means of which the pendulum with its bob was suspended was shortened or lengthened so that the pendulum's vibrations represented the vibrations for the movement selected. The machine included an audible click and operated somewhat like a music box of small size. The instrument was approved by the Ecole Royale de Chant, and the Academy of Music at Paris found it so useful that it had ordered that all music to be printed in Paris thereafter should have the movements numbered in accordance with the *plexichronometre*.[60]

Jefferson described the instrument in detail to Hopkinson, noting "the numbers between two movements, as between 22 and 36, give the quieter or slower degrees of the movements, such as the quick Andante, or moderate Allegro." Although in his opinion the instrument was useful, he felt it could be considerably simplified. He ordered one of the *plexichronometres* from Renaudin, and attached to it a seconds pendulum according to several movements. He found the pendulum regulated to

	Largo	[vibrates	52]	
	Adagio	[	60]	
[DRAWING]	Andante	[	70]	times a minute.
	Allegro	[	95]	
	Presto	[	135].	

Accordingly, he felt that anyone could make a chronometer adapted to Renaudin's instrument. He suggested that for the harpsichord one might drive five little brads or nails into the wall, marking them 1 through 5 as shown in a sketch which he enclosed, attach a string pendulum with a ball bob so that if it were hung at brad No. 1 it would vibrate 52 times in a minute (Largo), etc. Such a pendulum could also be attached to the music stand of someone playing the violin.[61]

The recent astronomical discoveries made in England by the German-born musician turned astronomer, Friedrich Wilhelm Herschel, also attracted Jefferson's attention, and that of the whole scientific world. As Jefferson informed the Reverend Madison, the most recent issue of *Connaissance des Temps* provided tables for "the planet Herschel" [first named "Giorgium Sidus" and later "Uranus"].

He noted the curious circumstance that thirty years earlier the German astronomer, Tobias Mayer, had actually observed the planet, but considering it to be a fixed star, included it as the 964th in his catalogue of zodiacal stars, and that in 1781 a later German astronomer, Johann

Elert Bode, had observed that the star was missing. Jefferson was also impressed that Herschel's discoveries of double stars now exceeded 900, twice the number noted in the *Philosophical Transactions*.

"You have probably seen that a Mr. Pigott [Edward Pigott] had discovered periodical variations of light in the star Algol. He has observed the same in the *n* of Antinous, and makes the period of variation 7D. 4H. 30', the duration of the increase 63 H. and of the decrease 35 H. What are we to conclude from this? That there are suns which have their orbits of revolution too? But this would suppose a wonderful harmony in their planets, and present a new scene where the attracting powers should be without and not within the orbit. The motion of our sun would be a miniature of this. But this must be left to you Astronomers."[62]

Jefferson had happened to notice the absence of the American grouse and pheasant in the King's Cabinet of Natural History, of which Buffon was the superintendent. He asked Hopkinson to purchase for him both males and females of these birds in the Philadelphia market and to have them prepared and packed "by some of the Apothecary's boys" for shipment to him. He advised that methods for preserving the birds could be found in the first volume of the *Encyclopédie* or in Buffon's work on natural history.

He also wished to obtain two or three hundred "Peccan nuts from the Western country." He thought that they might be available in Pittsburgh. He specified that they should be as fresh as possible, and were best packed in a box of sand. They were to be a gift to the royal botanical garden.

In his *Notes* Jefferson had provided the first scientific description of the pecan, a year before Humphrey Marshall included it in his *Arbustum Americanum*, which is considered by many to be the first mention made of it. Jefferson noted that it had not been described by Linnaeus, nor by the botanists Philip Miller and John Clayton, but that it was mentioned as *Pacanos* by Don Ulloa in his *Noticias Americanas*.

In actuality, Bartram and others had known of the species for a quarter of a century. The British officer, Colonel Henry Bouquet, had brought some pecans to Bartram from Pittsburgh, who in turn had distributed them to Peter Collinson and probably also to John St. Clair in 1760 or 1761. Collinson thought at the time that they might be seeds of the "Bouduc tree" or Kentucky coffee tree.

Neither Bartram nor others had attempted to give the tree a botanical name, however, and it remained for Jefferson to provide it with scientific recognition. He specified it as *Juglans alba, foliolis lanceolatis, acuminatis, serratis, tomentosis, fructu minorie, ovata, compresso, vix insculpto, dulci, putamine tenerrimo* ["Juglans alba, with lanceolate leaflets, acuminate, serrate, tomentose, small fruit, ovate, compressed, little sculptured, sweet, thin shell"]. He had planted seeds of the pecan at Monti-

cello not long before his departure for France, in 1779 or 1780, although
he did not record it in his *Garden Book*. Some years later he again planted
pecan from seed he had received from William Clark and Dr. Samuel
Brown.[63]

To Hopkinson he again posed the inevitable question: "What is
become of the Lunarium for the king?" Jefferson had probably decided
by this time to simplify the commission for Rittenhouse from a complete
orrery to an instrument demonstrating only the motion of the moon
around the earth, for his references now were to a "lunarium" and no
longer to an "orrery."

Seven months later Jefferson inquired once more about the instrument for the king. "Could you prevail on him [Rittenhouse] to answer
this also, When will the Lunarium be done?" Hopkinson responded
somewhat facetiously: "The Lunarium is still in Contemplation, and will
I believe, be executed some Time or other. The particular Aera may be
within the Ken of inspired Prophecy, but is certainly not within the
Reach of Astronomical Calculation." In a more serious vein he added
that Rittenhouse had been in poor health. It is believed that Rittenhouse
had in fact begun work on the orrery, albeit half-heartedly, in response
to repeated urgings. He was quite ill during the last few years of his life,
and probably for that reason no mention of the project was made thereafter by the principals who had ordered the instrument.[64]

In his correspondence with Rittenhouse, Jefferson refrained from
mention of the orrery, but discussed among other topics the survey of
the southern and western lines of Pennsylvania, inquiring how far beyond the meridian of Pittsburgh the western boundary extended. This
information he required to enable him to trace the boundary on the map
he was preparing for the *Notes*.

He also requested information about Rittenhouse's observations and
opinions on fossil shells. "It will not be difficult to induce me to give up
the theory of the growth of shells, without their being the nidus of animals. It is only an idea, and not an opinion with me." He reminded
Rittenhouse that in the *Notes* he had stated that there were three opinions on the origin of the shells: that they had been deposited on even
the highest mountains by an ancient universal deluge; that they were
animal remains, as were all calcareous stones and earths; and that the
shells grew in the same manner that crystals did.

He was somewhat inclined to favor the third opinion, but ventured
a fourth possibility, that some convulsive activity of nature had forced
up some of the items living on the bed of the ocean. However, no such
convulsion of nature had occurred in recent times or since recorded history. He found it impossible to believe any of these hypotheses, and
would have to await some other explanation which was more consistent
with what was known of the operations of nature.[65]

Jefferson lost no opportunity to report technological advances he observed in France. The fire engines constructed in Paris which supplied water for most of the city, he discovered, were capable of raising four hundred thousand French cubic feet of water in twenty-four hours, which impressed him. The engines had been described in William Owen's *Dictionary of Arts and Sciences* based on Denis Papin's *Digester*. He also sent copies of the *Bibliothèque physico-oeconomique* and the *Connaissance des Temps* containing the tables of Herschel's planet, to be distributed to Wythe, Peter Carr and Page. He again described the screw invention, suggesting it could be applied to move the balloon through the air.[66]

Discovering that he could have a pocket watch made to order for him "by the best & most faithful hand in Paris," he hastened to inform Madison. "It has a second hand, but no repeating, no day of the months, nor other useless thing to impede and injure the movements which are necessary. For 12 *louis* more you can have in the same cover, but on the back side & absolutely unconnected with the movements of the watch, a pedometer which shall render you an exact account of the distances you walk." He offered to purchase a similar one for Madison if he wished.[67]

An innovation Jefferson observed at about this time was a new method of engraving known as the "polytype" process. It utilized a special ink for writing upon copper plates, and made possible the production of as many copies from the plate as desired. He called upon the inventor, François Hoffman, who presented him with a copper plate and writing materials so that he could make his own polytype. Jefferson wrote a note on it as a sample, and in less than an hour Hoffman presented him with a hundred copies. Polytype, and its later adaptation by Hoffman for stereotype printing, aroused considerable interest in Jefferson's circle. For a time he considered the possibility of having his *Notes* printed by such a method and obtained an estimate of cost, but did not proceed with it.[68]

Despite his self-appointed role as American observer of the European scientific scene, Jefferson did not neglect his scientific preoccupations at home. From the Indian agent Benjamin Hawkins he requested information about the Indians, particularly their languages, of which he continued to compile vocabularies. He also asked for various plants and seeds he wished to give to others. From Hawkins he sought seeds of the Venus Fly-trap (*Dionaes muscipula*) which he believed was also called the "Sensitive Plant," presumably as a curiosity to donate to the royal botanical garden. It was not until several years later that Hawkins was able to provide the seeds.[69]

Informed that he had been elected a member of the Agricultural Society of South Carolina, Jefferson offered to send the society some new materials for cultivating, including seeds. To William Drayton he forwarded seeds of a grass cultivated almost entirely in Malta which had proven useful also in southern Europe. Known locally as "Sulla," the

Spanish called it "St. Foin," and Linnaeus identified it as *Hedysarum coronarium*. He explained that it was generally sown in the autumn. He was also attempting to obtain acorns of the cork oak from southern France which he promised to send.[70]

From time to time Jefferson was asked to provide information about the United States for several French publications. He contributed information for the four-volume work by François Soulès, *Histoire des troubles de l'Amérique anglaise,* and one of his new friends, Louis-Alexandre, Duc de la Roche-Guyon et de la Rochefoucauld, introduced him to Jean Nicolas Démeunier, author of the *Encyclopédie méthodique.* In a meeting with Démeunier, and later in correspondence, the latter asked countless questions concerning the United States for inclusion in his work. Realizing the importance of such a publication, which would have wide distribution and permanence, Jefferson prepared his data with considerable care and responded in a report of seventy-three pages.

Démeunier incorporated the information into a general article on the United States as well as in separate articles about individual states, which he sent in draft to Jefferson for review and correction of errors. Jefferson was appalled to find it "was indeed a mass of errors and misconceptions from beginning to end." He made the necessary corrections, expecting that they would be incorporated into the published version, but was greatly chagrined to discover that many of the errors remained when it appeared in print.

"He has still left a great deal of the Abbé Raynal," he complained, "that is to say a great deal of falsehood, and he has stated other things on bad information. I am sorry I had not another correction of it. He has paid me for my trouble in the true coin of the country, most unmerciful compliment. This, with his other errors, I should surely have struck out had he sent me the work, as I expected, before it went to press." The article on Virginia appeared to have been based for the most part on the *Notes.*[71]

After becoming involved in a discussion with Jean Baptiste LeRoy on the subject of sea breezes, Jefferson produced a long discourse on the range of sea breezes prevailing in Virginia during the warm part of the day in the summer months, and their causes. "We know too little of the operation of nature in the physical world," he cautioned, "to assign causes with any degree of confidence."[72]

As time allowed, Jefferson continued to pursue his interest in fossil remains, and utilized every opportunity to inform himself on the subject in visits to the Royal Cabinet of Natural History and collections of informed amateurs. He became personally acquainted with the leading young naturalists in Paris, and in addition to Buffon and his associate Daubenton, he met Barthélemy Faujas de St. Fond and André Thouin, as well as Bernard Germain Étienne de LaVille-sur-Illon, Comte de Lacépède. With some he was to continue association by correspondence for years to come.

At Annapolis prior to his departure for France, Jefferson had made the acquaintance of Major John Sullivan, governor of New Hampshire. They had discussed Buffon's erroneous comments about the American moose, one of America's largest living animals, and concluded that some means of correcting the errors should be taken. Jefferson gave Sullivan a list of questions to be answered about the moose, which the latter circulated to some of the region's most experienced hunters after his return to Durham. He forwarded data including measurements to Jefferson, but more information would be required to convince Buffon.

Sullivan suggested that a real specimen would be most convincing, and Jefferson agreed. He asked Sullivan to proceed to obtain a moose and other large animals regardless of cost, and carefully specified how the skins, skeletons and horns were to be preserved so that when reassembled "we should have its true form and size." Knowing, however, that the animals were too rare to be obtained in perfect condition, he was willing to accept what they could furnish, emphasizing once more his desire to have a moose. During the next year Sullivan and the Revolutionary patriot, General William Whipple, attempted to find animals in Maine and elsewhere but their efforts were unsuccessful. Jefferson was persistent, however, and a year after his previous request, he again urged Sullivan and others to try to obtain the animals for him.[73]

Before leaving the United States, Jefferson had had the forethought to bring with him to France some tangible evidence in the form of actual specimens to strengthen his written arguments with Buffon. As later recounted by Daniel Webster, Jefferson told him, "being about to embark from Philadelphia for France, I observed an uncommonly large panther skin at the door of a hatter's shop. I bought it for half a Jo [sixteen dollars] on the spot, determining to carry it to France, to convince M. Buffon of his mistake in relation to this animal, which he had confounded with the cougar. He acknowledged his mistake and said he would correct it in his next volume." Buffon added that his health prevented him from venturing out at that time, but invited Jefferson and Chastellux to come to the Jardin des Plantes.[74]

At one of the social gatherings in Paris after he and Buffon had finally met, they found themselves in an argument about the characteristics of the moose. The French naturalists were strongly promulgating their theories of the degeneracy of animals in America, and consequently Jefferson found it imperative to have the evidence in hand to disprove their theories.

Almost a full year passed before word came at last from Sullivan that a moose had been found and would be forwarded as soon as weather permitted. Another obstacle was to interfere, however, because the moose had been obtained before the arrival of Jefferson's instructions. Sullivan reported "The bones not being left in the skin or proper care taken to preserve or dress the skins with the hair on, so that no resemblance of the animal could be had."[75]

Undaunted, however, Sullivan arranged with a Captain Colburn of Lebanon, New Hampshire to hunt for another moose which would be shipped with only the skin opened and the entrails removed. The second moose was found in Vermont by Colburn, but unfortunately it had been killed in the heavy snows of late winter at a site in the deep woods some twenty miles from the nearest road. Almost two weeks were required to haul the large heavy carcass to Sullivan's house.

Sullivan arranged with local Indians to prepare it according to Jefferson's instructions and to preserve the skin with the hair and hoofs. They were not totally successful, however, possibly due to the time lapse since the animal was shot. The skin came off the head, and the moose had no antlers, but Sullivan had already expended great effort and expense in the project, and he decided to send it nonetheless. It was late May before a ship could be found to transport it. With the carcass of the moose Sullivan included horns of deer, elk and caribou, and roebuck. He also forwarded an invoice of costs, totaling $61.17.2 lawful money, which was equivalent to £46.7.10-1/2 sterling.

The trials and tribulations of the moose were not yet ended. The ship destined to carry the shipment was delayed, and when it finally set sail the crates inadvertently were left behind. However, Sullivan managed to have them transported to Boston, whence they were shipped to Havre de Grace. In August Jefferson received Sullivan's accounting of costs but neither the moose nor Sullivan's letters had yet arrived. The invoice both surprised and chagrined Jefferson, for it was far in excess of what he had anticipated, but he paid it promptly nonetheless.

After almost six months in transit, the crates with the carcass and horns of other animals arrived in Paris in late September. There was further disappointment after the shipment's arrival, for much of the hair had fallen off the hide, although sufficient remained so that Jefferson hoped that Buffon would have it mounted on its legs in the King's Cabinet.[76]

Although Buffon was absent from the city at the time, Jefferson had the moose assembled and sent it to him with a note and a copy of the published Notes. He wrote, "I wish these spoils, Sir, may have the merit of adding anything new to the treasures of nature, which have so fortunately come under your observation, and of which she seems to have given you the key: they will in that case be some gratification to you, which it will always be pleasing to me to have procured."[77]

The moose was mounted and placed in the King's Cabinet as Jefferson had hoped. It was judged to have been almost seven feet high. Buffon had known the animal only by name and had in fact assumed it to be identical with the very small Lapland deer. Many years later, when the elder statesman was visited at Monticello by Daniel Webster, Jefferson recounted his discussion with Buffon, which Webster recorded from memory. He was able to convince Buffon at last, Jefferson said, and "He promised in his next volume to set these things right also, but he died directly afterwards," and the corrections were never made.[78]

In requesting from the jurist and legislator Archibald Stuart the horns, skeleton and skin of an elk if possible, Jefferson again demonstrated his familiarity with taxidermy. "The most desirable form of receiving them," he advised, "would be to have the skin slit from the under jaw along the belly to the tail, and down the thighs to the knee, to take the animal out, leaving the legs and hoofs, the bones of the head, and the horns attached to the skin. By sewing up the belly &c. and stuffing the skin it would present the form of the animal." If this was not possible, however, he would accept the parts detached.[79]

Jefferson had long contemplated visiting England, and the opportunity came at last in the spring of 1786, when he was invited to London to join John Adams to assist him in negotiating a treaty with an envoy from Tripoli. He made the journey on March 6th accompanied by Adams's son-in-law, Colonel William Stephens Smith, and arrived in London five days later. He remained in England more than seven weeks, during which he visited a number of country seats and historic sites.

He derived great pleasure in calling at the shops of the major English makers of mathematical instruments, and purchased a substantial number. He met John Jones on the day of his arrival and ten days later visited the shop of Peter Dollond, from whom he purchased a telescope, a hygrometer and a solar microscope. On a visit to Jesse Ramsden the same day he purchased a thermometer, globe, protractor, theodolite, pocket dividers and a circular draw-pen. Some time later he purchased a chest of hand tools from Thomas Robinson, a pocket level and "pantographer" from Shuttleworth's shop, and from Jones he acquired a compound microscope, a botanical microscope, an air pump and apparatus and a small electrostatic machine. He also purchased paper for his copying press from Woodmason's stationery shop, which served as agent for the Boulton & Watt firm. He also visited the Royal Observatory and hospital at Greenwich.[80] (*Figures 11, 12*).

When Lafayette later reproached him for purchasing English goods, Jefferson replied that he had purchased only what was not available in France. "It is not for a love of the English but a love of myself that I sometimes find myself obliged to buy their manufactures," he added.

Jefferson was always greatly annoyed by the wasteful time spent in traveling, during which he was unable to pursue his reading and writing. Although he used his portable writing desk which he always kept with him, he particularly felt the need for his copying press. While on his journey to England, he spent his leisure designing a portable version based on the Watt stationary press. Upon his arrival in London, he visited the physicist, Tiberius Cavallo, with whom he was acquainted. Since Cavallo was familiar with London craftsmen, Jefferson enlisted his assistance to have the press he designed made for him by an English toilet case maker. He then arranged with Smith, who was secretary of the American legation in London, to have it shipped to him in Paris. Jefferson later reported that he was delighted with the portable model and informed Smith "it is perfectly made. Be so good as to present my compliments and thanks to Mr. Cavallo for his attention to it."[81] (*Figure 13*)

Later, after his return to France, Jefferson sought a craftsman in Paris capable of duplicating the portable press because he intended to present some to friends as gifts. Jean Baptiste LeRoy of the Académie Royal des Sciences recommended François Philippe Charpentier, a talented engraver and mechanician known for his inventive talents. Jefferson provided Charpentier with specifications and the latter constructed several of the presses, one of which Jefferson presented to Lafayette.[82]

Realizing the potential value of such an instrument in the American diplomatic service, Jefferson described the press to William Carmichael, the acting charge d'affaires in Madrid. "The itinerant temper of your court," he wrote, "will, I think, render one of these useful to you. You must therefore do me the favor to accept one." He shipped the press in the care of Don Miguel de Lardizábel y Uribe, to whom he first demonstrated its use so that he in turn could instruct Carmichael.[83]

Jefferson's enthusiasm for his new device was particularly evident in a description he provided to Madison of how and why he had devised it. "Having a great desire to have a portable copying machine," he wrote, "and being satisfied from some experiments that the principle of the large machine could be applied to a small one, I planned one when in England and had it made. It answers perfectly. I have since set a workman to making them here, and they are in such demand that he has his hands full. Being assured that you will be pleased to have one, I send you one by Colo. Franks."

He then casually added that the machine cost 96 *livres*, the appendages another 24 *livres*, and the paper and ink 12 *livres* more. At that time 6 *livres* was equivalent to approximately one American dollar, so that the total investment was about 22 dollars, a substantial expenditure. Although Madison had already explained that he could not afford the luxury of a copying press, Jefferson persisted, for his philosophy was first to obtain the convenience desired, and worry about costs later.[84]

Unknown to Jefferson at the time he had designed his portable press, another version of it was being made and marketed illicitly in London in violation of the Watt patent by the cabinetmakers William and Frederick Fleming. William Temple Franklin became aware of the Fleming presses during a visit to London. In a letter to his grandfather, he mentioned having seen "a new Invented Press—on the same Principle as that we have, but so contrived as to be convenient for Travelling. The Whole forms a small writing Desk—about the same size with that given me by Mrs. Lawrens—and answers every purpose of the old one, and is less expensive."[85]

James Watt was not aware that his invention had been exploited until it was brought to his attention by Andrew Cabrit, head of the foreign department of the mercantile house of Matthew Boulton. The news must have come as a shock to Watt, who was always excessively concerned with the protection of his inventions by patent, having undergone long litigation relating to his patents for the steam engine. (*Figure 14*)

Despite the obvious market for a portable copying press, however, the firm of James Watt and Company did not begin manufacture of portable presses until after the patent for the stationary model had expired in 1794. Curiously, the portable version it produced was never patented by the firm.[86]

Whether Jefferson realized that he was violating the Watt patent with his portable version is not certain. He probably considered the portable model to be a new form quite different from the stationary version. Furthermore, his disapproval of monopolies in general may have played a role. Finally, since he was not having his portable model made for commercial exploitation, in his mind it probably did not constitute a violation.

Some time later Jefferson's friend, Louis Dominique Ethis de Corny, Procurateur du Roi et de la Ville, asked him to examine a portable copying press which he owned and which no longer functioned properly. This may have been one of the Fleming products, possibly purchased by Madame de Corny during a visit to England. After studying the instrument, Jefferson reported that it required considerable modification to render it useful again, and recommended that the work could be performed by Charpentier.[87]

Jefferson was to make extensive use of his portable press during his travels in southern France and Holland, and again during his return voyage to the United States. He also used it later on his tour of the northern United States with Madison in the spring of 1791.

After returning to the United States he instructed his former secretary William Short to "Set Charpentier immediately to make a copying press according to the drawing sent. He is so dilatory that he will need to be frequently enquired of as to its progress, in order that it may be ready." The mail traveled slowly, and it was a considerable time before the Charpentier press was delivered.[88]

While in England, Jefferson discussed the production of the map for his *Notes* with William Faden, publisher of maps, globes and atlases, and then negotiated with the engraver Samuel Neele with whom he made final arrangements for producing a plate. However, his draft of the map had not yet been completed, and it was not until August after his return to Paris that he sent his final drawing to Colonel Smith to be forwarded to Neele. Jefferson arranged to provide the engraver with copies of the other maps he had consulted because the manuscript was not too clearly written.

Neele completed the plate by the end of December and Jefferson received it early in January. He was disappointed by the great number of orthographical errors it contained, and engaged the French engraver Guillaume Delahaye to make the corrections. These were completed two months later, and 250 copies in proof were printed.

The delay in producing the map imposed no hardship on the printing of the *Notes* because Barrois worked slowly. Although Morellet's translation was published early in 1787, it bore the date "1786" on the title page.[89]

In London Jefferson visited the publisher, John Stockdale, with whom he also discussed the production of his map for the *Notes*. When the English bookseller approached Jefferson for permission to print an English edition of the *Notes*, the statesman came to the conclusion that it would be in his best interests to do so, "to let the world know that it was not really as bad as the French translation made it appear."

After he returned to Paris, Jefferson sent Stockdale a corrected copy of the manuscript. When the preparation of the map plate was again delayed, Stockdale became considerably annoyed because he had already printed the edition quickly on the promise of the plate, and had already advertised the work for sale. Now he had to postpone issuing copies until the map could be included. (*Figure 15*)

Jefferson meanwhile was experiencing considerable exasperation in attempting to have the plate returned by Barrois, and it was not until he had threatened him with the police that the plate was relinquished so that he could mail it to Stockdale. Morellet had been out of the city during the argument with Barrois, and later complained that an insufficient number of copies of the map had been produced before the plate was surrendered to Jefferson.

When the plate arrived, Stockdale discovered that it was in poor condition and estimated that Barrois must have pulled at least 1500 prints from it. An argument then ensued over the price to be paid to Jefferson for all the copies of the map pulled in England, and he had as much difficulty reclaiming the plate from Stockdale as he had had with Barrois. It was not returned to him until February 1788.[90]

Jefferson received 450 copies of the map and had them colored in outline. He made them available to three booksellers in the United States and 200 copies were sold. Seventeen editions or reprintings of the work were to be produced during his lifetime. The *Notes* had a wide distribution in many countries. The geographical sections in particular remained a standard reference for the next several decades.

The *Notes* was highly praised and also severely criticized by many in the United States for the statements about slavery, the Virginia Constitution and the account of the Logan-Cresap incident. Nonetheless, scholars are of the opinion that the *Notes* was the most important political and scientific work produced in America prior to the end of the eighteenth century.[91]

Jefferson had frequently expressed a dim view of the value of the artisan, which was confirmed for him by what he observed in England. It was a feeling mixed at the same time with admiration, for in London he observed that the mechanical arts had been brought to an impressive state of perfection. As he commented to Madame de Corny after his return to Paris, "The English mechanics certainly exceed all others in some lines. But be just to your own nation. They have no patience, it is true, to sit rubbing a piece of steel from morning to night, as a lethargic Englishman will do, full charged with porter. But do not their benevolence, their cheerfulness, their amiability, when compared with the growing temper and manners of the people among you, compensate for their want of patience?"[92]

He had to admit that he had seen many achievements in England which he admired and envied. Among the most impressive was the application of steam to operate grist mills. He had observed eight pairs of millstones being operated by steam, and noted that there were plans to set up thirty stones in the same mill. One hundred bushels of coal were consumed for the operation of the eight stones. The use of steam impressed him considerably, and he commented on it to several correspondents.[93]

In midsummer 1786 the American artist, John Trumbull, whom Jefferson had first met in London, arrived in Paris, and Jefferson invited him to be his house guest at the Hotel de Langeac. Trumbull had brought some of his paintings with him which were greatly admired by the Baron von Grimm and others, and he planned to paint the events of the American Revolution. The thirty-year old Trumbull and Jefferson became fast friends, and they often took long walks together. The young painter became part of what Jefferson called "our charming coterie in Paris."

Through Trumbull he met the English miniature painter, Richard Cosway and his wife, Maria Hadfield Cosway, when they arrived in Paris in the fall. He immediately became intrigued with Maria's talents, her modesty, her beauty and her coquettishness. They soon went everywhere together, sometimes accompanied by Trumbull, frequently alone. They visited the Halle aux Bleds, where Jefferson sought some ideas for a market he contemplated establishing in Richmond, went to dinner at St. Cloud, and to hear the composer Krumpholtz.

For a month and more Jefferson was almost constantly in Maria's company, often cancelling official appointments in order to be with her. Richard Cosway, meanwhile, was busy with commissions for painting portraits and left his wife to her own devices much of the time.[94]

This was a period of unusual adventure for the statesman, now forty-three, and he had not for some time been as happy as when he was in Maria's company. There is no doubt that he had fallen in love with the attractive young flirtatious beauty who had once wanted to be a nun. Whether their warm friendship developed into an illicit love affair is not known, for he later spoke of his association only with friendship and sentiment, never with emotion that could be described as passion. Yet Jefferson was invariably reticent about his personal feelings and private life, relating to his mother and his wife, for example, and it is entirely possible that the relationship with the young English artist was much more than met the eye.

Their ventures into the city and the countryside terminated abruptly on or about September 18th, when Jefferson was returning from a long walk with a companion. Still about four miles from home, he fell and dislocated his right wrist. Tradition reports that it happened when he attempted to jump over a fence. Grasping his damaged wrist with his other hand behind his back, he did not interrupt the conversation nor mention the damage. It was not until he arrived home that he told his companion what had happened. When a surgeon was summoned, he found the wrist to be considerably swollen.

Jefferson's walking companion is not identified. Could it have been Maria? The possibility that she was involved is reflected in his letter to William Stephens Smith. "How the right hand became disabled would be a long story for the left to tell," he wrote. "It was by one of those follies from which good cannot come, but ill may." It was a long story which he never told.[95]

On the day of the accident Jefferson paid the fees of two surgeons, but their ministrations were not very helpful. The wrist had been improperly set and remained swollen. Its refusal to heal caused Jefferson considerable pain in addition to frustration in attending to his official duties and correspondence. The burden of transcribing replies to his correspondence fell to William Short, while Jefferson slowly taught himself to write with his left hand. He consulted other surgeons in the next four months, who suggested he should bathe the wrist in mineral water. Of the several resorts recommended for the purpose, Jefferson selected Aix. He no longer was able to play the violin, and to all intents and purposes the wrist remained weak and useless thereafter.[96]

Maria wrote to him during this period of incapacitation, hoping that he would be well enough to join her and others at dinner on the following day, when she would "divert your pain after with good music." He was unable to attend, and remained confined to his home by the pain. He also was forced to miss the ceremonies honoring his friend Lafayette with the presentation of the French patriot's bust to the City of Paris.

It was not until October 4th that he ventured forth once more. The Cosways were to leave Paris on the following day, and wishing to see them, he set out in his carriage. However the roughness of the pavement caused the carriage to jolt to such a degree that his wrist became extremely painful, and he was forced to turn back home. He spent a sleepless night, and sent Maria a note written with his left hand informing her with considerable regret that he had had to forego the pleasure of her companionship for that of a surgeon.[97]

Despite his shattered wrist, which had never been set properly, he passed the frustrating hours of his confinement correcting the text of his *Notes*. In December he still was having new pages printed. Ever reluctant to expose them to the public eye, he asked the recipients, including Chrétien Guillaume de Lamoignon de Malesherbes, to "put them into the hands of no person on whose care and fidelity he could not rely, to guard them against publication."

He was not yet satisfied with the work, and as long as a year after the *Notes* had been printed, he advised Wythe, "But of the numerous corrections they need, there are one or two so essential that I must have them made, by printing a few new leaves & substituting them for the old."[98]

CHAPTER VII

THE VIRGINIAN ABROAD (1786–1789)

But even in Europe, a change has sensibly taken place in the mind of man. Science has liberated the ideas of those who read and reflect, and the American example has kindled feelings of right in the people. An insurrection has consequently begun, of science, talents, and courage, against rank and birth, which have fallen into contempt ... Science is progressive, and talents and enterprise on the alert.

Letter from Thomas Jefferson
to Charles Bellini, 1785.

The next three years were crucial ones in the development of the young republic, and all of Jefferson's wisdom and experience were required during this period that would witness the debate over the ratification of the Constitution, the fashioning of the Bill of Rights, renegotiations with troubles allies and the beginning of the French Revolution. The year 1787 could be said to mark a turning point in the future of both France, where the Assembly of Notables initiated a chain of events that led eventually to the revolt of the people, and of the United States with the framing of a new Constitution.

Despite the distance separating him from the scene and the demands of his diplomatic duties in Paris, Jefferson kept abreast of events at home, through reports from his friends. Because of his absence, he was again denied an opportunity to share in the formulation of a Federal Constitution, as once before when the Virginia Assembly adopted the constitution of 1776. Nonetheless, he was able to contribute, by providing Madison with a library of published works on ancient and modern confederacies which the latter used in his remarkable research in developing the ideas of republic federalism. He also commented on the outline of the purposes of the Federal Convention which Madison sent him, and advanced his own ideas to him.

In particular Jefferson objected strenuously to the omission of a Bill of Rights which he believed was required to impose restraints on the Federal government against abuse of the rights of the people, such as had been included in the constitution of Virginia. He insisted that provision must be made to guarantee freedom of religion and of the press, protection against standing armies, restriction against monopolies, and to provide the habeus corpus laws and trial by jury. He was adamant that the Constitution must also allow for prohibition of re-election to office.[1]

Not the least of his accomplishments while abroad was the preparation of a plan for the state capitol of Virginia which he modeled upon the Maison Carrée and which may be said to have begun the classic revival in the United States.[2]

Eager "to promote the general good of mankind by an interchange of useful things," he devoted much of his time while in France to seeking out the best achievements of the civilization of the Old World and to report them to the new. At the same time he attempted to have Europe benefit from the best achievements of the mind and spirit of his country. Not merely a promoter of American interests, he was anxious that the French have correct information about the United States, its appearance and history and the accomplishments of its people. In this endeavor his boundless curiosity led him to investigate and report every new invention and process that came to his attention, particularly in the sciences, by which American could benefit, and in this manner served both continents as a "statesman of science."

Never far from Jefferson's mind, even after he became well established in French society, was his interest in the Pacific Northwest. It was rekindled once more after meeting John Ledyard, an intrepid young American soldier of fortune who had come to Paris with a plan to establish a fur company. The son of a Connecticut sea captain, he had abandoned Dartmouth College shortly after matriculation to wander through the New Hampshire and Canadian wilds to study the Indians. After sailing the Mediterranean, he joined Captain James Cook on his third voyage around the world seeking the Northwest Passage. During an excursion into Alaska, Ledyard discovered a Russian settlement collecting furs for sale. Realizing the monetary potential of furs in the world market, he planned to exploit it.

Returning to England, Ledyard signed with the British Navy, but

with the advent of the American Revolution, he jumped ship and returned to Connecticut. There he wrote and published an account of
his travels with Cook. It was the first work by an American known to
have set foot in the North Pacific and to have met Russians there. In
all likelihood Jefferson had read Ledyard's account before he met him,
and it may in fact have provided the incentive that led him to propose to George Rogers Clark that Clark undertake an expedition to
the West.[3]

Jefferson became extremely fond of the charismatic young adven-
turer full of exciting ideas, and often invited him to dine at his table
with other Americans in Paris. He introduced Ledyard to John Paul
Jones, who was also enthusiastic about the potential of fur trading and
attempted to assist him in his enterprise.[4]

Meanwhile a French expedition commanded by Jean François de
Galaup, Comte de la Pérouse, set out to search for the fabled Northwest Passage, explore the coasts of America, penetrate the waters of
Siberia, China and the South Sea islands, and determine whether a
river or other water source connected with Hudson Bay. Included in
the itinerary was the Pacific Northwest. Jefferson was unaware of the
French expedition until it was about to sail, and instantly became suspicious, voicing his concern to John Jay. Although the French
claimed the object of the mission was to add to their knowledge of geography, "some other circumstances appear to me to indicate some
other design; perhaps that of colonizing the Western coast of
America, or perhaps only to establish one or more factories there for
the fur trade."[5]

Despite Jones's efforts, Ledyard was unsuccessful in finding a suitable vessel for his enterprise. He determined instead to traverse Russia
as far as the north Pacific and then cross the American continent
from the west to the east. Jefferson enthusiastically endorsed the plan,
providing money to Ledyard on several occasions. He also helped him
devise a system of confidential record-keeping by the use of symbols
tattooed on various parts of his body, including a method of measuring the latitude by means of a distance of twelve inches marked off on
his arm.[6]

Although Lafayette, Baron Friederich von Grimm and Jefferson
joined together in interceding with the Russian ambassador in Paris
on Ledyard's behalf, they were unsuccessful. Jefferson immediately informed Ledyard by letter, "I saw the Baron von Grimm yesterday at
Versailles, and he told me he had received an answer from the Empress, who declines the proposition made on your account. She thinks
it chimerical. I am in hopes your execution of it from our side of the
continent will prove the contrary." Whether Ledyard received the let-

ter is not known, but several months later he wrote to Jefferson that he was leaving for St. Petersburg to begin his journey overland to the Bering Sea, Nootka and the Pacific Northwest.[7]

Departing from St. Petersburg in June 1787, Ledyard was arrested eight months later on the orders of the Empress, and sent home by the route he had come, under threat of hanging if he returned.

"He promises me if he escapes through this journey [through Russia], he will go to Kentuckey and endeavor to penetrate Westwardly from thence to the South Sea," Jefferson had informed the Reverend Madison. In London once more, Ledyard undertook a voyage of exploration to Africa, during which he became ill and died.[8]

In his *Autobiography*, Jefferson later wrote about Ledyard, "I suggested to him the enterprise of exploring the Western part of our continent, by passing thro St. Petersburg to Kamschatka, and procuring a passage thence in some of the Russian vessels to Nootka Sound, whence he might make his way across the continent to America; and I undertook to have the permission of the Empress of Russia solicited. . . . The Empress refused permission at once, considering the enterprise as entirely chimerical. But Ledyard would not relinquish it."[9]

Although Ledyard and his adventures had ignited once more Jefferson's long-standing dream of exploring the unknown western lands of the North American continent, his failure to enlist the cooperation of George Rogers Clark, and the demise of John Ledyard, forced him to wait several decades more before his dream could be realized.

It was a busy period, during which Jefferson was preoccupied with a variety of diplomatic negotiations, with the French minister of foreign affairs, Charles Gravier, Comte de Vergennes. The statesman's hatred for England was instrumental in providing French support of the American colonies, and he had negotiated the Treaty of Paris in 1783. Jefferson claimed that the assignment to the farmers-general of a monopoly on American tobacco imports discouraged trade, and another subject of contention was the importation of whale and fish oils. He also was greatly concerned by the seizure of American ships by Barbary pirates, about which he corresponded with John Adams. With Virginians at home he also corresponded about plans for the Virginia state capitol.[10]

In Jefferson's controversy with the Comte de Buffon concerning the relative humidity in Europe and the United States, in which the French naturalist "makes this hypothesis one of the two pillars whereon he builds his system of the degeneracy of animals in America," the statesman expressed doubt of the fact, although he was then unaware of evidence which might have supported his denial of it.

It occurred to him that a solution might be found in the use of a hygrometer to measure the relative humidity. In conversations with Dr. Franklin he had learned of the latter's experiments with magnets produced for him by the English instrument maker, Edward Nairne. These were described in a letter from Franklin to Nairne published in the second volume of the *Transactions* of the American Philosophical Society. Therein Franklin requested Nairne to make for him on the principle he had explained a hygrometer "which, taking slowly the temperature of the Atmosphere, shall give its mean degree of moisture" that would enable the comparison of the humidity of various climates with more accuracy.[11]

Jefferson asked Benjamin Vaughan, a British diplomat in London, to verify whether Nairne had made such a hygrometer according to Franklin's idea. If so, he wished to order several of them made identically so that he could send one to the United States, the readings of which he could compare with one he would retain in Paris. He also requested a set of magnets from Nairne like those he had made for Franklin, so that he could repeat the experiment.

Contemplating the possibility that the hygrometer might resolve his controversy with Buffon on relative humidity, he described to Vaughan such an instrument designed by David Rittenhouse, no account of which he believed had ever been published, which provided a record of the actual moisture in the air.[12] (*Document 2*)

Vaughan promptly placed the order with Nairne & Blunt, and the instruments were conveyed to Paris by Colonel Smith. Vaughan commented that European philosophers seemed to have formed their opinions about humidity on the basis of three sources, "the excessive vehemence of the rains which fall at times in the colonized parts of Eastern America, especially to the Southward. Next from the cultivated parts of the West Indies . . . and lastly from the inhabitants of our colonies having generally chosen for the seat of their plantations and settlements the banks of the sea or of rivers; or else low lands, swamps, and mill ponds; either for the sake of cheap carriage, and easy cultivation, or of the advantages for machinery afforded by such situations."

Nairne had advised Vaughan that he had made the hygrometer according to Franklin's plan. Vaughan objected to the fact that the motion of the pin resulted in greater changes in the position of the smaller arm and consequently of the index, when the smaller arm was at right angles to the pin's line of motion.

Accordingly, he simplified Franklin's design and had one made by Nairne & Blunt which he sent to White, principal surgeon on the expedition of convicts to Botany Bay. He had a second one made which he sent to Jefferson with "precautions" for its use. Also included was the set of magnets he had ordered, and which arrived after Jefferson's departure for southern France.

Vaughan also enclosed a thermometer he had had made. It consisted of a thin tube that initially made it difficult to read the elevation of the mercury. To overcome this problem he first placed white paper behind it, but then was able to improve the reading even more by adding a strip of black paint on the back of the tube. The paint was not visible when viewed sideways, and made the front of the thermometer appear dark so that the column of mercury became readily visible. (*Figure 3*)

He had noted also that in some thermometers the same result was obtained by flattening the bore in which the mercury was inserted, but although he had not used such an instrument, he knew that others who had used them deemed them unsatisfactory. He concluded that the best results were obtained by bringing light into the tube from the back of the scale, or by using a transparent scale.[13]

Always alert to any mention of inventions, one morning Jefferson was somewhat disturbed and considerably annoyed to read in the *Journal* that an Englishman claimed priority of invention and had obtained a patent for making the circumference of a wheel in a single piece. The newspaper writer assumed it was a revival from the Greeks, but as Jefferson wrote, it had in fact been first achieved by farmers in New Jersey. The inventor who had obtained the patent had learned of it from Franklin during one of the latter's visits to London. Franklin had become intrigued by the idea, and had assisted the man to develop it in his shop, laboring some weeks to "give old wood the pliancy of young."[14]

Jefferson was still awaiting some of the scientific instruments he had ordered while in London, among which was a perspective machine. John Jones, the instrument maker, informed him that it was in progress, and that he had been adding a number of requisites, such as a drawing board, and a place for a glass panel mentioned by the science lecturer, James Ferguson. "I made the frame square for an obvious reason vis to admit the whole of the board," he explained, "as the drawing of a Machine &c. when placed near the Instrument may require a larger space, than the Arches admit of." Jefferson was not destined to receive the perspective machine without difficulty, however, for it was stolen en route and it was not recovered until some time later.

Jones also informed Jefferson of the recent publication of a three-volume work he knew would delight him, the *Récréations physiques et mathématiques* by Guillaume Germain Guyot.[15]

Almost five months after his accident, Jefferson still was unable to use his wrist, as he informed Madison. "I have great anxieties lest I should never recover any considerable use of it. I shall by the advice of my Surgeons, set out in a fortnight for the waters of Aix en Provence. I chose these of several they proposed to me, because if they fail to be effectual, my journey will not be useless altogether. It will give me an opportunity of examining the canal at Languedoc and of acquiring knowledge of that species of navigation which may be useful hereafter: but more immediately it will enable me to make the tour of the ports concerned in commerce with us."[16]

Although Jefferson had planned to leave earlier on his voyage to southern France, he was delayed by the illness and death of Vergennes. Finally, on February 28th, he departed from Paris by carriage with post horses. He proceeded up the Seine through Champagne and Burgundy and then down the Rhone River to Aix, where he tried the effect of the waters on his wrist. The problem was that the bones had never been set properly, however, and consequently the wrist never healed entirely.

Although Jefferson did not succeed in finding a cure for his wrist, the journey was nonetheless fruitful in that it enabled him to study crops, soils and agricultural methods, to collect statistics on manufactures and to observe chimneys, bridges, forests, sidewalks, aqueducts, canals, pumps and other items that he found ingenious and practical.[17]

Jefferson kept in contact with his office through William Short, whom he also informed of his progress and the cities and regions he visited. "I am now in the land of corn, wine, oil, and sunshine," he reported from Aix en Provence. "What more can a man ask of heaven? I am sure it will bring me to life again."[18]

To Chastellux he wrote from Marseilles, requesting an introduction to someone at Tours in Touraine, where he planned to investigate the mystery of fossil shells described in that region by Voltaire in an article in his *Questions Encyclopédiques*.[19]

To Lafayette he wrote, "I have been pleased to find among the people a less degree of physical misery than I had expected. They are generally well clothed, and have a plenty of food, not animal indeed, but vegetable, which is as wholesome. Perhaps they are over worked, the excess of the rent required by the landlord, obliging them to too many hours of labor, in order to produce that, and wherewith to feed and clothe themselves . . . It will be a great comfort to you to know, from your own inspection, the conditions of all the provinces of your own country, and it will be interesting to them at some future day to be known to you. This is perhaps the only moment of your life in which you can acquire this knolege. And to do it most effectually you must be absolutely incognito, you must ferret the people out of their hovels as I have done, look into their kettles, eat their bread, loll on their beds under pretence of resting yourself, but in fact to find if they are soft."[20]

As he drove through southern France, Jefferson made careful notes about the countryside through which he traveled, observing the women and children "carrying heavy burdens, and laboring with the hoe," an indication of the poverty of the region. He particularly observed the soils of the regions through which he passed, noting in Burgundy "a good red loam and sand, mixed with more or less grit, small stone, and sometime rock." From la Baraque to Chagny the plains extending to the Soane were of "reddish-brown, rich loam, mixed with much small stone" and the plains along the Soane between Chalons and Mayon of "a dark rich loam, in pasture, and corn."[21]

He was anxious to reach Touraine, where his primary concern was to investigate "the growth of shells unconnected with animal bodies" in Tours at the chateau of a writer on the antiquities of Touraine named Felix François de La Sauvagère, which had been described by Voltaire.

In his *Notes* Jefferson had included the several popular explanations for the presence of fossil shells found on mountaintops. In the Paris edition of the *Notes* printed in 1785 he presented a chemical theory: "Besides the usual process for generating shells by the elaboration of earth and water in animal vessels, may not nature have provided an equivalent operation, by passing the same materials through the pores of calcareous earths and stones? . . . Is it more difficult for nature to shoot the calcareous juice into the form of a shell, than other juices in the form of crystals, plants, animals, according to the construction of the vessels through which they pass? Have not naturalists brought themselves to believe much stranger things?"[22]

The passage had brought considerable criticism because it was inconsistent with the Biblical account of Noah's flood, and accordingly he deleted it in later editions. In the English edition published two years later, he presented three hypotheses, including the deluge of Noah, convulsions of nature and the theory proposed by Voltaire.

When Voltaire had flippantly proposed that fossil shells found high in the Alps may have been dropped by pilgrims returning from the East, he had demonstrated little interest in geology and had discarded the popular theories of how the earth was formed. Later in his life, however, he wrote extensively on geology, directing more attention to the question, and collecting his own evidence.

Jefferson took issue with Buffon's theory that mountains were formed by the continuous movement of water, and disagreed also with the French geologist, Benoit de Maillet, who suggested that mountains were formed by the heaping of material under the sea and then by the drying up of the seas.

Voltaire dismissed such theories as hydrostatically impossible, favoring the speculation of the seventeenth century Jesuit polymath, Athanasius Kircher, that mountains were primordial features of the earth's surface. Voltaire undertook personal investigation of fossil shells near Geneva in his own district, and compared them with modern terrestrial shells. He later noted that they were not marine shells, and that rock samples from Touraine contained fragments of fresh-water shells non-marine in origin. All of which, he concluded, argued against marine inundation. Jefferson reasoned however, that "the three hypotheses are equally unsatisfactory, and we must be contented to acknowledge, that this great phaenomenon is as yet unsolved. Ignorance is preferable to error; and he is less remote from the truth who believes nothing, than he who believes what is wrong."[23]

When Jefferson arrived at Tours, he called upon M. Gentil, a local official with whom Chastellux had arranged a meeting for him. Gentil had corresponded with Voltaire on the subject and was acquainted with La Sauvagère, whom he considered to be reliable although over-imaginative, but commented that he agreed with him concerning the shells.

Gentil had not himself observed the growth of the same identical shells as had La Sauvagère, but he admitted he had often seen such masses of those shells of all sizes, and had once made a collection of them for the Emperor's cabinet and kept duplicates for himself. Gentil gave Jefferson a copy of La Sauvagère's new book.[24]

Jefferson wrote, "What are we to conclude? That we have not materials enough yet, to form any conclusion. The fact stated by La Sauvagère is not against any law of nature, and is therefore possible; but it is so little analogous to her habitual processes, that, if true, it would be extraordinary; that to command our belief, therefore, there should be such a suite of observations, as that their untruth would be more extraordinary than the existence of the fact they affirm. The bark of trees, the skins of fruits and animals, the feathers of birds, receive their growth and nutrition from the internal circulation of a juice through the vessels of the individual they cover. We conclude from analogy, then, that the shells of the testaceous tribe, receive also their growth from a like internal circulation. If it be urged, that this does not exclude the possibility of a like shell being produced by the passage of a fluid through the pores of the circumjacent body, whether of earth, stone, or water; I answer, that it is not within the usual economy of nature, to use two processes for one species of production. While I withhold my assent, however, from this hypothesis, I must deny it to every other I have ever seen, by which their authors pretend to account for the origin of shells in high places. Some of these are against the laws of nature, and therefore impossible; and others are built on positions more difficult to assent to, than that of de La Sauvagère. They all suppose the shells to have covered submarine animals, and have then to answer the question, How came they fifteen thousand feet above the level of the sea? And they answer it, by demanding that cannot be conceded. One, therefore, who had rather no opinion than a false one, will suppose this question one of those beyond the investigation of human sagacity; or wait till further and fuller observations enable him to decide it." The subject would continue to preoccupy Jefferson in future years.[25]

Jefferson sent a copy of La Sauvagère's memoir to Rittenhouse, explaining that his informant told him that he had seen sufficient evidence of the growth of shells around Tours to convince not only him but even the most incredulous unbeliever. Nonetheless, Jefferson found it questionable. "It is so unlike the processes of nature, to produce the same effect in two different ways, that I can only bring myself to agree it is not impossible."[26]

While in France, Jefferson had observed that the annual consumption of rice was considerable, and that in Paris alone approximately 2,200,000 pounds were consumed. Curious about how much of the rice came from the United States, he learned that two kinds of rice were sold in France, rice from the Carolinas purchased through England, and "Piedmont rice" from Italy. The latter was preferred to American rice, although imports of each were approximately equal.

The rice dealers indicated the difference in quality resulting in preference for Italian rice was due to the difference in techniques in preparing the rice for the market. The Carolina rice appeared to be husked with a machine that broke the grains to a greater degree than did the Italian machines, and the Americans apparently exercised less care in separating the broken grains. Consequently the French rice dealers had to sort whole grains from broken, making the cost greater to the consumer.

Jefferson thereupon determined to discover the differences in the machines used to husk the Piedmont rice. When he inquired at Marseilles, however, he received contrasting reports. Seeking the location of the rice fields of the Piedmont, he discovered that the nearest were in fact in Italy near Milan.

Crossing the Alps into Italy, he traveled to the rice country between Vercelli and Pavia, visiting the Venellese and Milan rice fields to observe their machines in operation. He was surprised to discover that the process and machinery in use there were already well known and not new after all. They were in fact the same as those used in Carolina, made somewhat like a powder mill, some of them having an iron tooth on each pestle. As many of their machines were made without teeth as with them. At Casino he found a rice machine consisting of a beater arm with six serrated pestles, and he described the details of the machine to the South Carolina jurist and gentleman farmer, William Drayton.[27]

The secret of the superiority of Italian rice, Jefferson discovered, lay not in its processing but in the fact that it was of a different species. It varied substantially in color, form and quality from that of Carolina.

Wishing to send some of the Italian rice to the United States, he was immediately informed that the government in Turin was well aware of the fact that the Italian rice was unique to the region and that consequently "they prohibit the export of rough rice on pain of death."

Not above breaking the law a little in his good cause of providing European agricultural improvements to the United States, even at considerable risk, he was determined nonetheless to bring away with him some of the rice. On his return to France, he divided the several pounds of rice from his pockets into three separate parcels, which he shipped to Drayton for the Agricultural Society of South Carolina by three separate routes to ensure they would arrive safely.

Meanwhile a mule driver named Poggio whom Jefferson had hired to obtain some of the rice had managed to complete his mission. When they met again in Genoa, Jefferson shipped off the rice to experimental farmers of his acquaintance in Georgia and South Carolina.[28]

Shortly thereafter he reported his adventures in the rice country to his old friend, Edward Rutledge at Charleston. From across the Alps he wrote,

> I found the machine exactly a one as you had described to me in Congress in the year 1775. There was but one conclusion then to be drawn, to wit, that the rice was of a different species, and I determined to take enough to put you in seed . . . The little therefore which I brought myself must be relied on for fear we should get no more; and because also it is genuine from Vercelli where the best is made of all the Sardinian Lombardy, the whole of which is considered as producing a better rice than the Milanese. This is assigned as the reason of the strict prohibition.[29]

As he observed the groves of olives and the cultivation of capers during his tour of southern France and northern Italy, Jefferson became convinced that there were many regions in the southern United States in which they, as well as the breadfruit tree, could be successfully cultivated.

In a letter to Wythe he commented, "I do not speak of the vine, because it is the parent of misery. Those who cultivate it are always poor, and he who would employ himself with us in the cultivation of corn, cotton, &c., can procure, in exchange for them, much more wine, and better than he could raise by its direct culture."[30]

The fig and the mulberry were already well known in the United States, but his efforts to introduce the olive were less successful. "The olive is a tree the least known in America," he reported, "and yet the most worthy of being known. Of all the gifts of heaven to man, it is next to the most precious, if it is not the most precious. Perhaps it may claim a preference even to bread, because there is such an infinitude of vegetables which it renders a proper and comfortable nourishment."

He discussed the uses of olive oil, which was not being produced in sufficient quantity for export, so that little was imported by the United States, and consequently Americans had not learned its use and value. As a result of Jefferson's enthusiastic encouragement, several wealthy South Carolina land owners determined to undertake olive culture, and the Agricultural Society of South Carolina eventually employed a contact in Marseilles to raise and ship olive trees to them.

Meanwhile, from Jefferson they received seeds and cuttings which they attempted to propagate. Several hundred olive trees were shipped to Charleston in 1793 as a consequence of Jefferson's involvement, but olive culture in South Carolina did not succeed, despite of all his efforts. In 1813 he complained that of about five hundred olive plants he had had shipped from Aix, few if any were then surviving, and those were grown merely as curiosities.[31]

He had also investigated other plants that could be exported. The almond tree he thought to be too precarious, while the caper, although more tender, could easily be grown and required little cultivation. The pickled flower buds of the *Capparis spinosa* were a favored condiment and used as an ingredient in sauces in Europe, and he had watched women collecting caper buds every day in the French countryside.

He imported some *Capparis* bushes from Marseilles and sent them to Drayton in Charleston to propagate, convinced that their culture would be commercially profitable. He warned that the detailed instructions for their cultivation which he enclosed were not to be relied upon, however, because "in the canton where this plant is cultivated, the inhabitants speak no written language, but a medley, which I could understand but very imperfectly."[32]

During his travels through the seaport towns along the southern and western coasts of France, Jefferson took every opportunity to collect information not only about crops and plants, but also on other aspects of agriculture. He noted the effects of prevailing winds on plant life. "These provinces, calculating on the poverty of their soil and their climate by its latitude only . . . should have been the poorest in France. On the contrary . . . spurs or ramifications of high mountains, making down from the Alps . . . give to the valley the protection of a particular enclosure to each, and the benefit of a general stagnation of the northern winds produced by the whole of them, and thus countervail the advantages of several degrees of latitude."[33]

He observed that olive trees did not thrive on the plain between Avignon and Orgon, presumably because of the lack of similar protection, and that orange trees thrived only where protected from heavy winds. He recorded an unusual phenomenon he had observed when crossing three mountain ranges of the Alps at Col de Tende. As he traveled up the mountain, the plants disappeared in a particular order and then reappeared in reverse order as he descended the mountain on the other side, and that it occurred each time. He specified order of disappearance to be caper, orange, palm, aloe, olive, pomegranate, walnut, fig and almond.

He correlated soil types with the forms of plant life they supported, and observed how grapevines thrived when exposed to the sun. He was puzzled to discover that the countryside of the Languedoc canal had later seasons, and conjectured that possibly the Cervennes mountains to the east advanced the warm season, and that the proximity of the Mediterranean may also have had some effect on the seasons.[34]

On the return journey to Paris, Jefferson made another detour through the Canal du Midi, or Canal of Languedoc, which had been built by King Louis XIV to unite the Mediterranean with the Atlantic Ocean, where he encountered the nightingale. He could not contain his rhapsodic appreciation of the nightingales, which enthralled him. He had been sailing along the canal, he reported to his daughter Martha back in Paris, "as I have been for a week past, cloudless skies above, limpid waters below, and on each hand a row of nightingales in full chorus. This delightful bird has given me a rich treat before, at the fountain of Vaucluse . . . It gushes, of the size of a river, from a secluded valley of the mountains, the ruins of Petrarch's chateau being perched on a rock two hundred feet perpendicular above. To add to the enchantment of the scene, every tree and bush was filled with nightingales in full song. I think you told me you had not yet noticed this bird. As you have trees in the garden of the convent, there might be nightingales in them, and this is the season of their song. Endeavor, my dear, to make yourself acquainted with the music of this bird, that when you return to your own country, you may be able to estimate its merit in comparison with that of the mocking bird. The latter has the advantage of singing through a great part of the year, whereas the nightingale sings only about five or six weeks in the spring, and a still shorter term, and with a more feeble voice, in the fall."[35]

Despite his euphoria, Jefferson was less than pleased with his examination of the state of canal locks and boat navigation, for he found the reversal of roles of men and women intolerable. "The locks are mostly kept by women," he reported, "but the necessary operations are much too laborious for them. The encroachments by the men on the offices proper for the women is a great derangement in the order of things. Men are shoemakers, tailors, upholsterers, staymakers, mantua makers, cooks, door-keepers, house-keepers, housecleaners, bedmakers. They coeffe the women, and bring them to bed: the women, therefore, to live are obliged to undertake the offices which they abandon. They become porters, carters, reapers, wood cutters, sailors, lock keepers, smiters on the anvil, cultivators of the earth, &c. Can we wonder if such of them as have a little beauty prefer easier courses to get their livlihood, as long as that beauty lasts? Ladies who employ men in the offices which should be reserved for their sex, are they not bawds in effect? For every man whom they thus employ, some girl, whose place he has taken, is driven to whoredom."[36]

From the end of the canal at Toulouse, Jefferson continued to Bordeaux to observe the viniculture of the region, and then went on to Nantes and Lorient to investigate the commerce of those seaports. He arrived in Paris at last on June 10, 1787, after an absence of three months and ten days.

He summarized his experience in a letter to Lafayette, "In the great cities, I go to see what travellers think alone worthy of being seen; but I make a job of it, and generally gulp it down in a day. On the other hand I am never satiated with rambling through the fields and farms, examining the culture and cultivators, with a degree of curiosity which makes some take me to be a fool, and others to be much wiser than I am."[37]

Although Jefferson had long promulgated the concept that only an agrarian nation could provide personal liberty and public virtue, he eventually came to the realization that in order for the United States to achieve true national independence, commercial and industrial development were necessary, despite the associated dangers he could foresee.

When asked about the expediency of encouraging commerce in the United States, he responded,

> Were I to indulge my own theory, I should wish them to practice neither commerce nor navigation, but to stand, with respect to Europe, precisely on the footing of China. We should thus avoid wars, and all our citizens would be husbandmen . . . But this is theory only, and a theory which the servants of America are not at liberty to follow. Our people have a decided taste for navigation and commerce . . . and their servants are in duty bound to calculate all their measures on this datum: we wish to do it by throwing open all the doors of commerce, and knocking off its shackles. But as this cannot be done for others, unless they will do it for us, and as there is no great probability that Europe will do this, I suppose we shall be obliged to adopt a system which may shackle them in our ports, as they do us in theirs.[38]

Throughout his stay in France, Jefferson persistently sought manufacturing processes which could be developed in the new nation and that would achieve what he considered to be an acceptable balance between agriculture and commerce. He was opposed to the establishment of permanent monopolies, as he called them, for new inventions and manufacturing developments, because they limited their benefits for the common good. At the same time he recognized the need to support and encourage creativity in manufacturing and related fields of endeavor.

"Every discovery which multiplies the subsistence of man must be a matter of joy to every friend of humanity," he had commented.

> As such, I learn with great satisfaction that you have found the means of preserving flour more perfectly than has been done hitherto. But I am not authorized to avail my country of it, by making any offer for its communication. Their policy is to leave their citizens free, neither restraining nor aiding them in their products. Tho' the interposition of government in matters of invention has its use, yet it is in practice so inseparable from abuse that they think it better not to meddle with it. We are only to hope therefore that those governments who are in the habit of directing all the actions of their subjects by particular law, may be so far sensible of the duty they are under of cultivating useful discoveries, as to reward you amply for yours which is among the most interesting to humanity.[39]

Jefferson maintained what was for his time a most advanced view of intellectual property. He claimed that there was no natural property right in an invention, and that such rights were created by society. He proposed that it was a moot question whether the origin of any kind of property could be claimed to be derived from nature at all. He argued that there was no basis for admitting a natural or even hereditary right to inventors.

"Stable ownership is the gift of social law," he claimed, "and is given late in the progress of society. It would be curious, then, if an idea, the fugitive fermentation of an individual brain, could, of natural right, be claimed in exclusive and stable property."[40]

It seemed unlikely to Jefferson that large scale manufacturing processes could succeed in the United States because of the relatively high cost of labor resulting from the great demand for men in agricultural activities.

"A manufacturer going from Europe will turn to labor of other kind if he find more to be got by it, & he finds some emploiment so profitable that he can soon lay up money enough to buy fifty acres of land, to the culture of which he is irresistibly tempted by the independence in which that places him, & the desire of having a wife & family around him." He believed that if any manufacture could succeed there, it would be cotton, although he was aware that the plant did not grow north of the Potomac and not in any quantity except in the deep South.

In Virginia, the state with which he was the most familiar, he reported there was no manufacture of wire or cotton cards, used for preparing cotton for spinning, or if any, not worth mentioning. There was no stocking weaving, nor weaving of cotton cloths of any kind; the only stocking weaving was in cottage industries. As a matter of policy, the Virginia government did not aid manufactures, and it generally allowed matters to take their own course.[41]

Jefferson continued to send his friends and associates at home "the crumbs of science on which we are subsisting here . . . in proportion as they are dealt out." He was often severely critical of the scientific activities he observed.

To the Reverend Madison he reported on the discoveries of some, or the lack of discoveries of others, including William Herschel and the Dutch physician and plant physiologist Jan Ingenhousz. "Herschel's volcano in the moon you have doubtless heard of," he concluded, "and placed among the other vagaries of a head, which seems not organized for sound induction. The wildness of the theories hitherto proposed by him, on his own discoveries, seems to authorize us to consider his merit as that of a good optician only."

He was as dubious about the achievements of Ingenhousz. "You know also, that Dr. Ingenhous has discovered, as he supposed, from experiment, that the vegetation might be promoted by occasional streams of the electrical fluid to pass through a plant, and that other physicians have received and confirmed this theory. He now, however, retracts it, and finds by more decisive experiments, that the electrical fluid can neither forward nor retard vegetation. Uncorrected *still* of the rage of drawing general conclusions from partial and equivocal observations, he hazards the opinion that light promotes vegetation. I have heretofore supposed from observation, that the light affects the color of living bodies, whether vegetable or animal; but that either the one or the other receives *nutriment* from that fluid, must be permitted to be doubted of, till better confirmed by observation. It is always better to have no ideas, than false ones; to believe nothing, than to believe what is wrong. In my mind, theories are more easily demolished than rebuilt."[42]

Jefferson erred in his dismissal of Ingenhousz and his discovery that plants exhale carbon dioxide and that light promotes vegetation. Ingenhousz was in error in proposing that plants received nutriment from light, as he supposed, because in truth, sunlight enabled plants to resume their beneficial operations upon the air. Despite his interest in and understanding of the sciences, Jefferson was occasionally prone to fallacious observations, such as those with which he dismissed the work of Herschel and Ingenhousz.

After his return to Paris, Jefferson had found awaiting him a communication from John Churchman 3rd, a land surveyor and cartographer of Nottingham, Maryland, who claimed to have conceived a new theory on the variation of the magnetic needle which he proposed to apply for determining longitude.

His longitude proposal was first announced in the press in 1777, and described as being based on the theory that two satellites revolved around the earth, one at the North Pole and the other at the South Pole. Although invisible from the lower latitudes, Churchman estimated the period of revolution of the northern satellite to be 463 years.

He presented a revised paper on his theory before the American Philosophical Society ten years later. The committee appointed to review it concluded that the theory was inconsistent with known principles and recorded observations, and dismissed it as "groundless whimsy."[43]

Francis Hopkinson also commented on Churchman to Jefferson. "As to Philosophy—We abound with Schemers and Projectors," he wrote. He mentioned a number of them, including "a Mr. *Churchman*, who has found out the Longitude by means of the Variation of the Needle. All he asks to be allowed him is that there are two invisible Moons, one revolving around the North Pole and the other round the South Pole, in small Circles, and in Times of his own contriving. These Moons by their attraction occasion the Phenomenon called Magnatism, and their periodical Revolutions form the magnetic Meridian and cause the Variations of the Compass. This learned Man understands as much of Philosophy as can be acquired by practical Surveying; and as much of Navigation as can be obtain'd from padling in a Canoe."[44]

Although he knew of Churchman's theory in general, Jefferson had not yet seen the proposal itself, and until then he remained non-committal on the theory.[45]

Undeterred by the rebuff from the American Philosophical Society, Churchman now asked Jefferson to use his influence to bring a written presentation, of which he enclosed a copy, before the Académie Royale des Sciences. The Académie had already received another copy and on review reported that the proposal was found to be insufficiently explicit for the Académie to render an opinion.

As well as he and the Académie had been able to determine, Jefferson wrote to Churchman, "we imagine you to make a table of variations of the needle, for all the different meridians whatever. To apply this table to use, in the voyage between America and Europe, suppose the variation to increase a degree in every one hundred and sixty miles. Two difficulties occur: (1) a ready and accurate method of finding the variation of the place; and (2) an instrument so perfect, as that (though the degree on it shall represent one hundred and sixty miles) it shall give the parts of the degree so minutely, as to answer the purpose of the navigator. The variation of the needle at Paris, actually, is 21 west." He felt certain that Churchman would have provided explanation of the doubts expressed.[46]

Undaunted by the general lack of appreciation and support his proposal encountered, Churchman went on to publish a request for financial assistance. He then contacted Sir Joseph Banks of the British Board of

Longitude, and attempted to enlist Benjamin Franklin's endorsement as well. To all he explained that further study now made him uncertain that the satellites were situated above the earth, and he considered that they might be rolling on its surface or beneath it.

Each refusal made him all the more determined. Churchman now cleverly took advantage of the clause in the Constitution granting power to the Congress "to promote the Progress of Science and the useful Arts" by the issuance of patents. He interpreted the clause to mean that more than patents was intended. Accordingly, not only did he apply for patents for his claimed solution for determination of longitude at sea, but he also petitioned for Congressional support of a voyage he proposed to make to Baffin's Bay, where he assumed the North Pole was situated, to enable him to make magnetical experiments.

He managed to enlist the support of James Madison, but the proposal was nevertheless rejected, not because of any concern about the lack of validity of the project, but because the government was then in financial difficulties. It left the possibility open, however, for Churchman to make another application later. This he proceeded to do in 1791. Although his project had been disputed by Rittenhouse and virtually every other American man of science informed of it, Churchman obtained strong support for his second application in the House of Representatives in the person of the Virginia Congressman, John Page.

Likening the Churchman project to the Parliamentary support provided to Edmund Halley and the English prize offer for anyone venturing an expedition to the North Pole, Page urged "whatever can contribute to the discovery of longitude must be worthy of encouragement." Other supporters of Churchman warned that caution should be exercised before totally rejecting it, to avoid the same embarrassment experienced by other nations in the past upon prematurely rejecting scientific projects.

A committee chaired by Page reported that Congress could appropriately support proposals such as Churchman's. The decision whether to make a grant was left to the House of Representatives, which eventually returned a negative decision. The important consequence of the Churchman application was the decision of Congress that the Federal government could indeed appropriately support scientific projects by application of the patent clause. It was never successfully invoked, however, and it remained for Jefferson to undertake the first scientific endeavor with government support during his Presidency. Although the scientific world scorned his proposal, Churchman published his *Magnetic Atlas*, which appeared in four editions and was widely distributed.[47]

Jefferson meanwhile was looking forward to the arrival in France of his second daughter, Mary. The *Arundel*, Captain Andrew Ramsay's ship, was anchored on the James River not far from Eppington, and Mary was enticed on board with her young cousins to spend the day. Exhausted after a day of hide and seek, Mary fell asleep on deck. The Eppes family quietly went ashore, and the ship sailed with eight-year-old Mary and her fourteen-year-old black maid, Sally Hemings, on board. The child Sally was the daughter of a mulatto slave named Betty Hemings and John Wayles, the father of the late Martha Jefferson and was inherited by Martha with 152 other slaves from her father's estate. Jefferson had taken Sally's brother James to France with him to learn French cooking. When the ship docked in London, Mary was placed in the care of Abigail Adams, with whom she remained for two weeks before continuing on to France in company with Sally.[48]

After such a long absence, Mary did not recognize her father or sister, nor did they recognize her at first. Periodically Martha took her to the convent school so that she could become acquainted with the faculty and students a little at a time. When she had finally familiarized herself sufficiently with the Abbaye, she was enrolled as a student. There she was known at first by her nickname "Polly," then as "Marie," and finally as "Maria," the name she continued to use for the remainder of her life.[49]

The new Federal Constitution being proposed in the United States was of vital interest to Jefferson and he attempted to keep himself informed long distance, chiefly in correspondence with Madison. He made clear his concern over the absence of a bill of rights, stating that such a bill should provide "clearly and without the aid of sophism . . . for the restriction of monopolies." He relied on Madison to correct the omission.[50]

In the next year he wrote to Madison expressing his rejoicing with "the general voice from north to south which calls for a bill of rights . . . The saying there shall be no monopolies, lessens the incitements to ingenuity, which is spurred on by the hope of a monopoly for a limited time, as of fourteen years; but the benefit of even limited monopolies is too doubtful to be opposed to that of their general suppression."[51]

He found himself weakening, however, and later in 1789 wrote to Madison that he approved of the declaration of rights as far as it went, but that he would like to have the addition of an Article 9 specifying "Monopolies may be allowed to persons for their own productions in literature, and their own inventions in the arts, for a term not exceeding—years, but for no longer term and for no other purpose."[52]

Several of the American colonies continued the practice begun in the seventeenth century of granting patents, and there was obvious concern for adopting a similar procedure for the national government. However, no proposals for providing power to Congress to grant patents were included in the early proceedings of the federal convention, neither in the "Virginia Plan" submitted by Edmund Randolph which opened the business of the convention on May 29, 1787, nor in the draft of a federal government submitted by Charles Pinckney.

It was not until August 18th, almost three months after the convention had been in session, that James Madison submitted "certain powers," for consideration by a committee of detail, to be added to those of the general legislature. These suggested "powers" were "to secure to literary authors their copyrights for a limited time," and "to encourage by premiums and provisions the advancement of useful knowledge and discoveries." The same day Pinckney followed suit by submitting several other proposals, which included "to grant patents for useful inventions," and "to secure the author's exclusive rights for a certain time."[53]

Both proposals were submitted to the committee of detail, and on August 31st those parts of the Constitution which had not been acted upon were sent to a committee consisting of one member from each state. On September 5th the committee made its report, recommending that Congress be provided with powers "to promote the progress of science and useful arts, by securing for limited times to authors and inventors the exclusive right to their respective writings and discoveries."

This received unanimous agreement, and in due course and after final revision, this clause became Paragraph 8 Section 8 of Article I. Consequently, it was to Madison and Pinckney that credit is due for adding to the powers of Congress the protection of creative efforts of its people.

Earlier in *The Federalist No. 43*, Madison commented "the utility of this power will scarcely be questioned. The copyright of authors has been solemnly adjudged, in Great Britain, to be a right of common law. The right to useful inventions seems with equal reason to belong to the inventors. The public good fully coincides in both cases with the claims of individuals. The States cannot separately make effectual provision for either of the cases, and most of them have anticipated the decision of this point, by laws passed at the instance of Congress."[54]

This Constitutional provision is the first substantive of law in history that affirmatively recognized property rights in the result of the type of mental activity productive of inventions. Although the framers of the Constitution were thoroughly familiar with the British system of patents, neither the word "patent" nor the word "grant" was used in the provision. There seemed to have been a deliberate intention by using the word "securing" to emphasize the rights of authors and inventors.

The British patent system, on the other hand, did not appear to recognize such rights, but implied that the rights were vested in the

Crown which then granted them "as special acts of the sovereign grace." The granting of patents was to figure largely in Jefferson's life within the next few years.[55]

Resuming his correspondence after his return to Paris, Jefferson mentioned that he had not written to the Reverend Madison in such a long time because "the genius of invention and improvement in Europe seems to be absolutely taking a nap. We have nothing to communicate to you but of the small kind, such as making the axletree turn with the wheel, which has been proposed here, adopted by some, and thought to be proved best by experiment, though theory has nothing to urge in its favor."

He mentioned that a "hydrostatic waistcoat is lately announced, which a person puts on either above or below his clothes in a minute, and fills with air by blowing with the mouth in twelve seconds." It had not yet been demonstrated, however, so that he knew no details of its construction. He ventured that it would be useful when a shipwreck was anticipated.

Madison had sent him some shells, about which Jefferson commented "because their identity with marine shells and their vicinity to the sea, argue an identity of cause." Nonetheless, in his view, shells found on mountains have not been accounted for, even after reading the memoir on petrifaction mixed with shells by La Sauvagère, and after having visited the region in France where they had been found. "This fact is so curious," he added, "so circumstantially detailed, and yet so little like any known operation of nature, that it throws the mind under absolute suspense."

He commented on Herschel's discovery of Oberon and Titania, two of the satellites of the planet Uranus, which he believed was already known in the United States. He concurred with Madison's suggestion that the periodical variation of light in certain fixed stars resulted from Maculae, a suggestion he found more acceptable than that of Pierre Louis Moreau de Maupertius, who supposed that the bodies were flat, or the opinion that the star had an orbit of revolution so large as to vary its amount of light.[56]

Looking forward to the arrival of the recently published third volume of the *Transactions* of the American Philosophical Society, Jefferson cautioned Rittenhouse that the Society should be more rigid in acceptance of papers for publication. Of new inventions he mentioned that someone in Paris had invented a process for converting sea water to potable water and had some evidence of its success. The same inventor also had devised a varnish for coating biscuit barrels to maintain them in good order and keep them free from insects. Since the inventor was willing only to sell his secrets, Jefferson anticipated that it would be some time before they became known and useful to the public in general.[57]

Having received from Wythe suggestions for constructing geometrical models made of ivory and wood for teaching, Jefferson concluded that wood would serve as well as ivory. He suggested using a sheet of veneer, or possibly of the cardboard of which ordinary cards were made. "The difficulty is, how to reconcile figures which must have a very sensible breadth to our ideas of a mathematical line, which, as it has neither breadth nor thickness, will revolt more at these than at simple lines drawn on paper or slate." He suggested that if Wythe wished to have them made in France, he would be able to arrange it.[58]

The Indians and their origins continued to preoccupy Jefferson, particularly the preservation and recording of antiquities found in the Western lands. "I wish," he commented, "that the persons who go tither would make very exact descriptions of what they see of that kind, without forming any theories. The moment a person forms a theory his imagination sees in every object only the traits which favor that theory. But it is too early to form theories on those antiquities. We must wait with patience till more facts are collected."

He expressed the hope that the American Philosophical Society would develop a program for collecting data about the Indian monuments already known and publish them "naked" in the *Transactions*, and continue their attention to those hereafter to be discovered.

"Patience & observation may enable us in time to solve the problem whether those who formed scattered monuments in our Western country, were colonies sent off from Mexico, or the founders of Mexico itself? Whether both were the descendants or progenitors of the Asiatic redmen."

He commented also on the stratification of rock, recalling that those to be found between the Blue Ridge and the North Mountain in Virginia were parallel with the pole of the earth. He observed the same phenomena in most of the Alps between Cette and Turin during his return journey to Paris. Along the precipices of the Pyrenees [he meant the Apennines] where rock ledges overhung the Mediterranean, he noted that their direction was not consistent and that they differed.

Thomson had mentioned that in the West the stratification was horizontal. "Their variety proves they have not been formed by subsidence as some writers of the theories of the earth have pretended, for then they should always have been in circular strata, & concentric. It proves too that they have not been formed by the rotation of the earth on its axis, as might have been suspected had all these strata been parallel with that axis. They might indeed have been thrown up by explosions, as [John] Whitehurst supposes, or have been the effect of convulsions.

But there can be no proof of the explosion, nor is it probable that convulsions have deformed every spot of the earth. It is now generally agreed that rock grows, and it seems that it grows in layers in every direction, as the branches of trees grow in all directions. Why seek further the solution of this phenomenon? Everything in nature decays. If it were not reproduced then by growth, there would be a chasm."

He spoke also of the use of steam which he had observed in England. He mentioned that Matthew Boulton at first had made a secret of his mill, and that consequently during his visit to London he had been permitted to see it only superficially. He had seen no water wheels and in fact there were none. However, at the steam mill at Nîmes which he had gone to see, the steam raised water, and that water turned a wheel.[59]

Even while overseas Jefferson kept frequent contact with several of the young men in whose education he maintained an interest, particularly his nephew Peter Carr and Thomas Mann Randolph, Jr. Young Randolph, who was studying at the University of Edinburgh, wrote to Jefferson concerning his decision of a choice of a future career. He enclosed a certificate naming Jefferson an honorary member "in a society instituted here for the encouragement of the study of natural history among the students of this university [University of Edinburgh]." Jefferson was pleased with the honor, but modestly explained that his only contribution to the subject of natural history had been his *Notes* prepared only in response to Marbois, of which he forwarded a copy.[60]

Traveling, he noted to Peter Carr, made men wiser but less happy. "When men of sober age travel," he counseled, "they gather knowledge, which they may apply usefully for their country; but they are subject ever after to recollections mixed with regret; their affections are weakened by being extended over more objects; and they learn new habits which cannot be gratified when they return home. Young men, who travel, are exposed to all these inconveniences in a higher degree, to others still more serious, and do not acquire that wisdom for which a previous foundation is requisite, by repeated and just observations at home. The glare of pomp and pleasure is analogous to the motion of the blood; it absorbs all their affection and attention, they are torn from it and the only good of this world, and return to their home as a place of exile and condemnation."[61]

Jefferson's attention was attracted to the prospect of cutting a canal through the isthmus of Panama, which was then under consideration by the Spanish government. It had often been contemplated in the past and was considered to be feasible. In his view, the boring of a canal through the isthmus of Panama appeared to be less difficult than cutting through some of the inferior French canals. He further proposed that the

Gulf Stream, "that tropical current, entering it [the Panama Canal] with all its force, would soon widen it sufficiently for its own passage, and thus complete in a short time that work which otherwise will still employ it for ages."[62]

A year and a half later he commented to William Carmichael on the proposal, and told him that he had been informed by the Chevalier Jean François, Baron de Bourgoing (Burgoyne) that a survey and topographical examination of the isthmus of Panama had already been completed, which indicated that "a canal appeared very practicable, and that the idea was suppressed for political reasons."

He expressed the hope that Carmichael, as diplomatic and commercial representative of the United States, could obtain a copy of the survey report. He also suggested others who could provide additional information, noting that he was eager to have as much detail as possible on the subject.[63]

Preparing well in advance for the end of his sojourn in France and return to the United States, Jefferson periodically made provision for equipping himself with scientific instruments and other items that were not readily available at home. (*Document 3*)

He maintained acquaintances he had formed during his visit to London among the leading makers of mathematical instruments and he contacted them again. Early in 1788 he received two thermometers he had ordered from John Jones, who apologized that because the order had arrived during the Christmas season when he was greatly rushed, he had been unable to provide "that peculiar attention to the process of the fabrication of your Thermometers, as I wished." Jones informed him that he had made some minor additions to the small orrery he had ordered, and sent along a printed description. He expected to be in Paris in the near future so that if Jefferson had any special requests he could fulfill them.

He also sent Jefferson a description of the *Dictionary of Arts and Sciences,* to which Jones had contributed articles. This was the third edition of the *Encyclopaedia Britannica,* the first volume of which had appeared in October. In the entry for *America,* Jones had included mention of Jefferson's *Notes:*

> As ranging on the same side with the Abbé Clavigero, the ingenious Mr. Jefferson deserves particular attention. This gentleman, in his *Notes on the State of Virginia,* &c. has taken occasion to combat the opinion of Buffon; and seems to have fully refuted them both by argument and facts.

The item included the table from the *Notes* reviewing the quadrupeds of North America and Europe. In the American edition published in 1798, the statement was modified to say that Jefferson had refuted Buffon's opinions "in many instances" instead of "fully."[64]

John Trumbull, who had become one of Jefferson's constant associates in Paris, was planning a visit to England, and he asked the artist to do several favors for him. He was to inquire whether it was possible to purchase there a triangular odometer to be placed between the spokes of a carriage wheel, and to determine the price. He was also to call upon Stockdale the bookseller-publisher to determine the cause of the delay in shipping books he had ordered.[65]

Although Jefferson maintained an ongoing interest in chemistry, and considered it to be one of the most important sciences, he did not then seem to be fully aware that during the period of his residency in Paris he was actually a witness at the birth of the new science of modern chemistry. Although the phlogistic theory of the German physicist and chemist, Georg Ernst Stahl, continued to be supported by chemists of the old tradition, the French chemist Antoine Laurent Lavoisier had effectively destroyed Stahl's theory for the next decade or more. He had also just announced to the French Academy of Sciences that water, which had been long regarded as a basic constituent of matter, was not an element after all, but a compound of Joseph Priestley's dephlogisticated air and of Henry Cavendish's inflammable air, which Lavoisier now renamed oxygen and hydrogen.

Thereupon a dispute raged concerning priority of discovery which Jefferson described to several of his American correspondents. Experiments of the chemists were contradictory and inconclusive, he reported, and it was his opinion that adequate means had not yet been invented to enable the necessary investigation to be conducted.

He reported how, when speaking with Buffon one day on the current enthusiasm for chemical inquiry, he was shocked to hear Buffon comment that he considered chemistry as no more than cookery and that he placed the endeavors being carried out in the laboratory on the same footing as those of the kitchen.

"I think it [chemistry], on the contrary," Jefferson went on, "among the most useful of sciences, and big with future discoveries for the utility and safety of the human race. It is yet, indeed, a mere embryon. Its principles are contested; experiments seem contradictory; their subjects are so minute as to escape our senses; and their result too fallacious to satisfy the mind. It is probably an age too soon, to propose the establishment of a system."[66]

It was his view that "The contradictory experiments of chemists, leaves us at liberty to conclude what we please. My conclusion is that art has not yet invented sufficient aids, to enable such subtle bodies to make a well-defined impression on organs as blunt as ours; that it is laudable to encourage investigation, but to hold back conclusion."[67]

In 1787 four of the leading French chemists presented a new simplified chemical nomenclature, which provides the basis of that used today. Jefferson objected to Lavoisier's attempt to reform chemical nomenclature because in his view it was premature. "One single experiment may destroy the whole filiation of his terms, and his string of Sulphates, Sulfites, and Sulfures may have served no other end than to have retarded the progress of the science by a jargon from the confusion of which time will be requisite to extricate us. Accordingly it is not likely to be admitted generally." Despite his objections to Lavoisier's new system, Jefferson nonetheless purchased a copy of his two-volume work when it was published in 1789.[68]

He reported on other discoveries—Bertholet's development of a fulminating powder, the application by M. Puymarin of Toulouse of a spathetic acid to corrode flinty substances which could be applied for engraving on glass, and the discoveries of the French astronomer and mathematician, Pierre Simon Marquis de Laplace, of the secular acceleration and retardation of the moon's motion caused by the sun's action in proportion to the change of its eccentricity, that is, as the earth's orbit increased or diminished.[69]

Jefferson did not neglect other scientific topics current in France at the time. He became greatly intrigued by a new explanation of the rainbow proposed by an unidentified French abbé. It demolished the theories of Marcantonio de Dominis, Descartes and Newton, that a cone of rays from the sun falling on a cloud in the opposite part of the heavens was reflected back in the form of a smaller cone, with the apex in the eye of the observer so that his eye had to be in the axis of both cones and equally distant from every part of the rainbow.

The abbé reported he had observed rainbows with one end close to him and the other at a very great distance. Jefferson commented that he had often observed the same phenomena, but he had never seen what the abbé reported, namely, several rainbows at the same time intersecting each other. According to his own theory, when the sun was on the horizon, the horizon intercepted the lower half of the bow, if above the horizon, it would intercept more than half, in proportion, so that generally the rainbow would never appear as more than a half-circle, despite the fact that the abbé claimed to have seen more than the half circle of a rainbow.

Jefferson noted that he had in fact himself seen the leg of the rainbow below the level at which he stood because the topography of Monticello made it possible, with a mountain in the direction opposite the afternoon sun, and the valley more than five hundred feet in depth between Monticello and the other mountain.

Although the facts appeared to demolish the Newtonian theory of light, Jefferson felt that neither did they support the abbés conclusions, that the rays of the sun passed through some opening in a cloud between the sun and the observer to form an iris on the opposite side of the sky. He reached the conclusion that as a consequence "we are wiser than we were, by having an error the less in our catalogue; but the blank occasioned by it, must remain for some happier hypothetist to fill up." He reported also on the death of Buffon which had occurred some time previously.[70]

With Vaughan's assistance, Jefferson made other purchases of instruments from London makers, including "[Benjamin] Martin's portable air pump & apparatus [from] Jones . . . £12-12-0." Always alert to promote American achievements, he informed Vaughan, "A considerable improvement in the Air pump has taken place in America. You know that the valves of that machine are its most embarrassing parts. A clergyman in Boston has got rid of them in the simplest manner possible. The alteration he has made is described in the philosophical transactions of Boston. I put this description into the hands of Mr. Jones, instrument maker in London, when I was there. But he has not tried it. I have since wished I had made an acquaintance there with Mr. Nairne, and communicated it to him." The Boston clergyman was the Reverend John Prince of Salem, Massachusetts, who designed and constructed a scientific apparatus for several of the New England colleges. Meanwhile Jefferson had learned of a modification to the air pump that had been made in Holland, but was not aware of the details.[71]

"The invention you allude to respecting the air pump," Vaughan responded, "was long ago used by Mr. Nairne, as Mr. Cavendish has confirmed to me; but Mr. Nairne says he has laid it aside, finding the great object was not so much to free the receiver from the air, as the barrel in which the piston moves. A Mr. Heurter [Hurter] has moved the lower valve in that barrel by a power distinct from the air in the receiver, & it is said with great advantage."[72]

While Jefferson had been traveling, the Nairne & Blunt hygrometer based on Franklin's principle had arrived, as well as one designed by Jean André DeLuc. He compared the operation of the latter with a hygrometer by H. B. de Saussure which he had been using, and he made several suggestions for improvement of the one based on Franklin's principle to make it achieve more precise recording. He had his hygrometer modified by a craftsman in Paris to meet his requirements. He was having these modifications adapted to several more of the Nairne & Blunt hygrometers so that they would be suitable for making comparative records of humidity in Paris, England and in two parts of the United States to which he planned to distribute them.

"I verily believe," he added, "it will turn out in event that the atmosphere of our part of America is less humid than that of this part of Europe: and that this furnishes an instance the more wherein philosophers, as you justly observe, hasten the general conclusions from too few observations, and on false testimony of these observations. I must do justice to those of your country [England] to say they have given less than any others into the lies of Paw [Cornelius de Pauw], the dreams of Buffon & Raynal, and the well-rounded periods of their echo: [William] Robertson."[73]

Vaughan noted that Nairne had experienced the same degree of variation of his hygrometer in London as Jefferson had in Paris. He suggested that hygrometers should be returned to the country of their origin for checking their accuracy of registration. He asked Jefferson to send him one of the hygrometers he had modified, in a manner which appeared to be most ingenious.[74]

In due course Jefferson ordered several of the hygrometers to be made for him, at least one of which he planned to use in Paris and another to send to the United States. However, as he informed Vaughan, "I have not yet had time to try the execution of the wood hygrometer proposed by Dr. Franklin. Though I have most of the articles ready made, I doubt now whether I shall be able to do it before my departure for America, and I shall go off the instant I receive it." The instruments were not produced in sufficient time, however, for Jefferson to distribute them and make use of them before his departure.[75]

While Jefferson was absent from Paris, Thomas Paine had arrived with letters of introduction from Franklin, and he probably met Jefferson before again leaving Paris for London. Jefferson foresaw great potential in Paine's invention of an iron bridge "which promises to be cheaper by a great deal than stone, and to admit a much greater arch."[76]

Paine obtained a patent for his bridge in England and was now executing the first example with an arch of between 90 and 100 feet. Jefferson's interest in Paine's invention led him to study the subject of bridges at some length. In correspondence with Paine, he discussed details of construction and the relative merits of various ways for installing rails.

He cautioned "the practical iron men are much better judges than we theorists," and in the course of a disquisition on equilibrium and catenaries, he mentioned that he had obtained a treatise on the equilibrium of arches by the Italian Abbé Lorenzo Mascheroni.

He reported that an Abbé Etienne d'Arnal of Nîmes recently had obtained a patent or exclusive privilege for navigating the rivers of France with the steam engine. However, d'Arnal had not been in a position to use it himself and furthermore had been so unsuccessful with a steam mill at Nîmes that he was not likely to venture into new projects.[77]

Jefferson was surprised and delighted to receive the diploma of an honorary degree from Harvard College forwarded to him by its president,

Dr. Joseph Willard. "Conscious how little I merit it," he responded, "I am the more sensible of their goodness and indulgence to a stranger who has had no means of serving or making himself known to them. I beg you to return them my grateful thanks, and to assure them that this notice from so eminent a seat of science is very precious to me."[78]

He listed the most important recent French and Italian publications, and then went on to report that "the chemical dispute about the conversion and reconversion of air and water, continues still undecided. Arguments and authorities are so balanced that we may still safely believe, as our fathers did before us, that these principles are distinct. A schism of another kind has taken place among the chimists. A particular set of them here have undertaken to remodel all the terms of the science, and to give to every substance a new name the composition, and especially the termination, of which shall define the relation in which it stands to other substances of the same family. But the science seems too much in its infancy as yet for this reformation: because in fact the reformation of this year must be reformed again the next year, and so on, changing the names of substances as often as new experiments develop properties in them undiscovered before. The new nomenclature has accordingly already proved to need numerous and important reformations. Probably it will not prevail. It is espoused by the minority only here, and by a very few indeed of the foreign chymists. It is particularly rejected in England."

He spoke also of the patent for steam navigation obtained in England by James Rumsey, who was building a vessel which would be ready for experimentation in May. He was awaiting with considerable anticipation the return of La Pérouse who "will probably add to our knowledge in Geography, botany and natural history."

Jefferson expressed himself as being greatly impressed with the recently published *Méchanique analytique* of Joseph Louis Lagrange, whom he considered to be the greatest mathematician then living, and who in his work proposed to reduce all the principles of mechanics to the simple principle of equilibrium and to provide a practical formula that would be applicable to all. Jefferson also kept current with other new scientific developments, such as the works of the Italian anatomist, Lazzaro Spallanzani, on digestion and generation, and the history of Mexico by the Mexican historian, Abbé Francisco Javier Clavijero. He took advantage of the opportunity to comment once more on the new chemical nomenclature that had been proposed which had aroused such controversy in the French scientific community. Finally, in his reply to Willard, he went on to rhapsodize somewhat on the future of American science:

> What a field have we at our doors to signalize ourselves in. The botany of
> America is far from being exhausted, its mineralogy is untouched, and its

natural history or zoology totally mistaken and misrepresented . . . It is for such institutions as that over which you preside so worthily, sir, to do justice to our country, its productions, and its genius. It is the work to which the young men you are forming should lay their hands. We have spent the prime of our lives in procuring them the blessing of liberty. Let them spend theirs in showing that it is the great parent of science and of virtue, and that a nation will be great in both always in proportion as it is free."[79]

Early in 1788, John Adams received permission to return to the United States from London. He had been commissioned to negotiate loans for the United States from Dutch bankers but upon learning of his scheduled imminent return, he referred the bankers in the Netherlands to consult with Jefferson on future difficulties.

This proved to be a most unpleasant position for Jefferson, for American Treasury commissioners had recently informed the Dutch bankers that the United States might have to default on interest payments on old loans. The principal bankers for the United States in Amsterdam proposed a plan which would meet the crisis, but would at the same time provide profit at the expense of the United States. The matter was entirely out of Jefferson's province.

He arranged to meet Adams in Amsterdam, and they prevailed on the bankers to abandon the proposal, and Adams was able to negotiate the loan of another million before returning to England. Jefferson proudly reported that American credit had been secured at last for at least two years more.[80]

Jefferson had set out for Amsterdam to meet Adams on March 4, 1788 in his own carriage with post horses. He traveled through Valenciennes, Brussels, Antwerp and Rotterdam and reached The Hague on March 8th. There he was joined by Adams, and they rode together to Amsterdam. Business was concluded by March 20th and Jefferson decided to take advantage of his sojourn to see parts of Europe he had not previously visited.

On his return journey he proceeded up the Rhine into Germany. During his travels he kept minute records of what he observed relating to agriculture, topography, population, mechanical arts and architecture of the countryside through which he passed. In Amsterdam he had observed "Joists of houses, placed, not with their sides horizontally and perpendicularly, but diamond wise . . . Windows opening so that they admit air and not rain . . . Dining tables letting down with single or double leaves . . . A lanthern over the street door, which gives light equally into the antechamber and the street . . . A bridge on a canal turning on a swivel," and many other items of interest.[81]

At Coblenz he noted the use of a central heating system by means of which "large rooms very well warmed by warm air conveyed from an oven below, through tubes which open into the rooms." In Westphalia he observed the hogs, "tall, gaunt, and with heavy lop ears" from which the "celebrated ham" was produced. At Cologne he became interested in a stove which he later purchased.[82]

At Frankfort he observed "The neighborhood of this place is that which has been to us a second mother country. It is from the palatinate on this part of the Rhine that those swarms of Germans have gone, who, next to the descendants of the English, form the greatest body of our people. I have been continually amused by seeing here the origin of whatever is not English among us. I have fancied myself often in the upper parts of Maryland and Pennsylvania."[83]

Here he met his old friend the Baron von Geismar, who had been a prisoner of war during the Revolution and whose release Jefferson had been instrumental in obtaining. Together they took side trips to other German cities, meeting former Hessian officers who also had been stationed in Albemarle during their captivity. He was particularly impressed by the castle of Heidelberg. He measured the celebrated monster cask called the "Heidelberg tun" built in 1751 by the Elector Charles Theodore capable of containing 49,000 gallons. Jefferson estimated its capacity to be 283,200 bottles. He crossed the Rhine at Strasbourg and traveled across the northwestern part of France on his return to Paris.

At Epernay he visited the localities where champagne was produced and studied the vintner's methods, as he did also at Coblenz. From there he followed the Marne River to Paris where he arrived on April 23rd.[84]

Between Strasbourg and Nancy he had occasion to observe French farmers, noting that oxen with collars and hames were used for ploughing. It was "the awkward figure of their mould-board" of their ploughs which led him to consider what its form should be. His resourceful mind immediately analysed the purposes of the mouldboard to be "to receive the sod and after the share has cut under it, to raise it gradually and to reverse it." In order to enter the ground under the sod, the mouldboard's fore end should be horizontal while the hind end should be perpendicular in order to throw over the sod, with the intermediate surface gradually changing. He estimated that the mouldboard should be as wide as the furrow and of a length suitable to the manner in which the plough was made. He immediately set to work to design a practical mouldboard including the details of his calculations, with sketches in his *Memoranda* of his travels for later development. Once again Jefferson demonstrated his wide-ranging mind that often led to invention, not necessarily always of new devices, but also the improvement of existing ones.[85] (*Figure 16*)

To add to the miseries of the French people, he noted, the winter of 1788–1789 proved to be extremely severe, and many died of cold and starvation. A mood for revolt was running through the people, and

Jefferson was well aware of the situation. He often traveled to inspect the homes of the poor. The conditions he observed horrified him.

To Adams he reported, "All the tongues of Paris have been let loose and never was license in speaking against the government exercised in London more freely or more universally . . . Mobs of ten, twenty & thirty thousand people collected daily, surrounded the parliament house, huzzaed the members, even entered the doors & examined their conduct, took the horses out of the carriages of those who did well and drew them home . . . the king, long in the habit of drowning his cares in wine, plunges deeper and deeper."[86]

Trade had come to a virtual standstill and the currency had become greatly inflated. Mobs of hungry people roamed the city, having long lost their faith in their king and the Assembly of Notables.

Now that he had his two daughters with him, Jefferson found himself well satisfied with the state of his domestic affairs. He expected life to go on pleasantly, since the girls were studying in the finest school in Paris. Then suddenly, without any warning, Martha now sixteen, wrote to her father that she wished to remain in the convent and become a nun. The family account was that she had become enamored of the serenity and seclusion of the Abbaye, and after considerable meditation, had reached the decision to dedicate herself thereafter to a religious life.

According to one of Martha's granddaughters, Jefferson had been startled by her request to join the Church, but reacted with his usual tact. He did not respond to her note but several days later he suddenly appeared at the Abbaye and had a private interview with the abbess. He greeted his daughters affectionately and told them he had come to take them home with him, and drove away with them in his carriage. He made no mention of Martha's note and according to family tradition, the possibility of her taking the veil was never again mentioned between father and daughter, although she spoke of it freely to her children in later years.[87]

The product of an entirely Protestant society, Jefferson's own religious views tended towards deism, advocating natural religion based on human reasoning rather than revelation, and not accepting interference with the laws of nature by a Creator. He felt that it was preferable for a country to have numerous sects than merely one. He emphasized that human happiness depended on freedom of the mind which included freedom of religious thought. Although he never expressed himself on the subject, it is likely that he was not opposed to having his daughter convert to Roman Catholicism, but rather to her proposed withdrawal from society to the religious life.

His concerns were occasionally reflected in his correspondence, however, including in a letter to Ralph Izard, the South Carolina patriot and senator, in which he recommended that he send his son to be educated in Europe only after he had reached the age of fifteen, in order that he would be more capable "to resist the attempts to change his religion." It appears to be confirmed also in the account of the papal nuncio Antonio Dugani, who in the summer of 1789 noted Jefferson's policy towards his daughter's religious views until she reached the age of eighteen, meanwhile directing her attention elsewhere by involving her more with life outside the convent.

Martha was soon distracted because insofar as her age made appropriate, Jefferson now established her as the hostess of his household. His *Memorandum Books* recorded new expenses, for her clothing, her lessons on the harpsichord and guitar and payments to her dancing master. She was soon introduced into society, where her blue eyes and bright red hair made her an immediate success. She helped to tutor Maria, who received private lessons as well.[88]

President Washington, meanwhile, had become concerned with the navigation of the Potomac and Ohio, and with the possibility of effecting a union of the two by means of a canal which would add to the commerce of upper Virginia. Jefferson agreed to its importance, commenting "I have ever considered the opening of a canal between those two watercourses [the Cayohoga and Big Beaver Rivers] as the most important work in that line which the state of Virginia could undertake. It will infallibly turn thro the Potomack all the commerce of Lake Erie and the country West of that, except what may pass down the Mississipi. And it is important that it soon be done, lest that commerce should in the mean time get established in another channel." He sent Washington a copy of the notes he had made describing the canal of Languedoc in the event that they would be useful.[89]

Although he made no mention of it to President Washington, as has been noted, Jefferson was interested in the possibility of developing a passage through the isthmus of Panama. He mentioned it in a long discourse with Jean Baptiste Le Roy of the Academie des Sciences on the subject of sea winds and ocean currents. He speculated on the advantages of the passage for European and American trade and, at the same time, the problematical natural changes and their deleterious effect.[90]

One of Jefferson's last favors for his friends before leaving France was the purchase of a pedometer which had been requested by Madison several years before, and which had finally become available. He accompanied it with detailed instructions. "To the loop at the bottom of it you must sew a tape, and at the other end of the tape, a small hook (such as we use under the name of hooks and eyes.) Cut a little hole in the bottom of your left watch pocket, pass the hook and tape through it, and down between the breeches and drawers, and fix the hook on the edge of your knee band, an inch from the knee buckle. Then hook the instrument itself by its's swivel hook on the upper edge of the watch pocket. Your tape being well adjusted in length, your double steps will be exactly counted by the instrument, the shortest hand pointing out the thousands, the flat hand the hundreds, and the long hand the tens and units. Never turn the hands backward. Indeed it is best to set them to any given place, but to note the number they stand at when you begin to walk. The adjusting the tape to its exact length is a critical business, and will cost you many trials. But once done, it is done forever. The best way is to have a small buckle fixed on the middle of the tape, by which you can take it up and let it out at pleasure. When you chuse it should cease to count, unhook it form the top of the watch pocket and let it fall down on the bottom of the pocket."[91]

Before leaving Paris, Jefferson took advantage of an opportunity to have his portrait made by a popular new process called the "physionotrace." The invention of Edmé Quenedey, it traced the sitter's profile life-size with crayon on paper stretched on a vertical frame. It was later reduced to a small size by means of a pantographic device. It was then rendered on a copper plate, from which multiple engraved copies were produced by Quenedey's partner, Gilles Louis Chrétien. He probably sat for the portrait because he was intrigued with the mechanical process, as he was with any new method for duplicating writings and drawings.[92]

Fifteen years later, during his first term as President, he again had his portrait made by a similar process in the United States by the French artist, Charles-Balthazar-Julien Fevret de Saint Mémin. The artist had been associated with Quenedey and Chrétien in their enterprise in France for a time before emigrating to the United States. He brought with him a portable version of the physionotrace, with which he produced profile portraits on his travels through the country.[93]

With the development of the domestic crisis in France, Jefferson experienced considerable difficulty in directing the attention of French ministers to American interests. To John Jay he reported the major events taking place which were to lead to revolution, the unprecedented meeting of the Assembly of Notables to discuss the approaching bankruptcy of the royal treasury, and later of the Estates-General. He reported also on the political situation in the United Netherlands, with the conflict that arose between the supporters of the Prince of Orange and the patriot party. In May 1788 he described Paris as "a furnace of politics." He negotiated a consular convention revising the terms of the 1784 convention and which proved to be beneficial for the United States and was the first foreign treaty presented by the American president to the first Congress.

On July 4th 1789 Jefferson held a dinner at four o'clock for all the Americans then in Paris. Martha served as hostess at his home with its garden at the corner of the Champs Elysée and the Neuve de Barry. Marquis de Lafayette and his wife were among the notable guests, who also included French army and naval officers.[94]

Ten days later, on the memorable July 14th, the Bastille fell after the mob had collected arms from the Hôtel des Invalides. Maria, after having witnessed the behavior of the mob on her return from a visit that day to the Lafayette home, was ill from fright. Jefferson and his household remained prisoners in their home, for it was not safe to venture abroad, and in time the supplies of candles and food diminished and the servants vanished. He went to see the demolition of the Bastille and later contributed to the widows of those slain in taking the fortress.[95]

During that tumultuous summer Jefferson accompanied by Short spent his time among the people, in "the character of a neutral and passive spectator," inasmuch as nothing reported could be believed without being seen. Inevitably as the author of the Declaration of Independence and an architect of the American Revolution, Jefferson found his counsel being sought by members of the National Assembly. He was optimistic about the outcome, "having so much confidence in the good sense of man, and his qualifications for self-government that I am never afraid of the issue where reason is left free to exert her force; and I will agree to be stoned as a false prophet if all does not end well in this country. Here is but the first chapter of the history of European liberty."[96]

Due to his position as a member of the diplomatic corps and his friendship with Lafayette, he was well informed of events as they occurred and was able to report objectively to John Jay, American minister of foreign affairs. He noted the people's impatience with the slothfulness of the Assembly, the dissension wrought by the aristocrats, and the divided ranks in which the patriots found themselves. He warned that there was talk of civil war as a consequence of the lack of food due to ruined crops by the cold of the previous winter, public bankruptcy and the potential flight of the king from Versailles.[97]

The previous November, Jefferson had written to John Jay requesting leave to return home, and again in the spring he had appealed to Washington, then President. Now he was concerned for the safety of his daughters and was anxious to leave Paris as soon as possible. Washington's approval of leave did not arrive until August, however.

It was not until October that Jefferson with his family and retinue could depart the city. He said few farewells, for he planned to return.

He was not to witness the executions and havoc which were soon to follow.

In retrospect, the years he had spent in France were happy ones, and he wrote of his fondness for the country and the people, which he retained for the remainder of his life:

> And here I cannot leave this great and good country without expressing my sense of its preeminence of character among the nations of the earth. A more benevolent people, I have never known, not a greater warmth and devotedness in their select friendships. Their kindness and accomodation to strangers is unparalleled, and the hospitality of Paris is beyond any thing I had conceived to be practicable in a large city. Their eminence too in science, the communicative dispositions of their scientific men, the politness of the general manners, the ease and vivacity of their conversation, give a charm to their society, to be found no where else. In a comparison of this with other countries we have the proof of primacy, which was given to Themistocles after the battle of Salamis. Every general voted to himself the first reward of valor, and the second to Themistocles. So ask the travelled inhabitant of any nation, In what country on earth would you rather live?—Certainly in my own, where are all my friends, my relations, and the earliest & sweetish affections and recollections of my life. Which would be your second choice? France.[98]

After five years France had become Jefferson's second home. Greatly awed by European culture, excited by its scientific activities, but depressed by the poverty of the French people, this most questioning of Americans fully expected to return again to "the vaunted scene" after a sojourn at home. Jefferson and his retinue departed from France in the early hours of October 8, 1789 on board the *Anna*, sailing from Le Havre to Cowes, where they transferred to the *Clermont*. With him were his two daughters and his young servants James and Sally Hemings. He also brought with him his "chien bergere, big with pup," a pregnant shepherd dog that gave birth to puppies aboard ship.[99]

A puzzling aspect of Jefferson's long stay in France was that the single American who was the lifelong disciple of French philosophies, with a love of all things French, received less acknowledgement during his lifetime from the French than did either Benjamin Franklin or George Washington. He was rarely mentioned in contemporary French memoirs. He was almost totally ignored by the French press during his stay, a circumstance, however, which was due primarily to his own shunning of publicity and his insistence on personal privacy.

Upon his arrival in France and after introduction to Franklin's own circle of friends, he apparently made little impact on French society at first. He was not unsocial, but he was still mourning the loss of his wife, and maintained a deep reserve. Playing the role of observer, he invariably left center stage to Franklin out of respect for the elder statesman. Another reason for his self effacement was his determination that as an American plenipotentiary, it was important that he not become involved in the political activities that was then agitating all France. In time, however, he developed a wide circle of friends in French society and had many intimates among them.

Most surprisingly, the French failed to recognize him as the scribe of American freedom, and author of the document which had so greatly electrified French opinion in 1776. In fact, in 1787 he was forced to write to the *Journal de Paris* to protest an erroneous account of the Declaration of Independence in which Dickinson was credited as the author. Typically, on this occasion he failed to mention that he had been a member of the committee that had drafted the document.[100]

He was equally reticent about mentioning his authorship of the bill establishing religious freedom, which had been enacted while he was in France. After he had agreed to the publication of a translation, it appeared hidden in the article by Démeunier about the United States in the *Encyclopédie méthodique*, in which Jefferson was briefly mentioned jointly with Wythe as the authors.[101]

CHAPTER VIII

THE SHIP
OF STATE
(1789–1792)

Science is more important in a republican than in any other government. And in an infant country like ours we must depend for improvement on the science of other countries, longer established, possessing better means, and more advanced than we are. To prohibit us from the benefit of a foreign light, is to consign us to long darkness.

Letter from Thomas Jefferson to an
unidentified correspondent, 1821.

On November 23, 1789, almost a month to the day after they left the harbor at Le Havre, Jefferson, his daughters, and the rest of his traveling party disembarked at Norfolk. As they neared land, the coast was obscured by mist. Unable to see the Virginia capes, the ship managed to reach Lynhaven Bay. There strong winds beat against the vessel and it lost its topsails and almost collided with a brig leaving port. But their adventure was not yet over.

Immediately upon docking, a fire broke out on shipboard which seriously threatened the vessel. The passengers were quickly removed to safety, and "they were in the act of scuttling her," later wrote Martha, "when some abatement in the flames was discovered, and she was finally saved . . . So great had been the activity of her crew, and of those belonging to other ships in the harbor who came to their aid, that everything in her was saved. Our trunks, and perhaps also the papers, had been put in our state-rooms, and the doors incidentally closed by the captain. They were so close that the flames did not penetrate; but the powder in a musket in one of them was silently consumed, and the thickness of the travelling-trunks alone saved their contents from the excessive heat. I understood at the time that the state-rooms alone, of all the interior partitions, escaped burning."[1]

Jefferson and his party were met and greeted by a committee appointed by the Virginia legislature, but in spite of this fine token of welcome, they experienced difficulty in obtaining accommodations in Norfolk for the night. Finally several gentlemen relinquished their rooms at Lindsay's Hotel in their favor.

It was while reading the newspapers at Norfolk that Jefferson learned that in September President Washington had nominated him for the position of Secretary of State, and that he had been confirmed by the Senate. President Washington had informed him in a letter written in October, which, however, did not reach him until three weeks later.

During his absence abroad Congress had combined foreign affairs and all of domestic administration other than defense and finance into one department under the Secretary of State. Of those solons with experience in foreign affairs Franklin had become too old for public office, Adams was now vice president, and John Jay, his predecessor in the office was now chief justice. Consequently Jefferson appeared to be the inevitable choice not only to Washington but to the Congress.

He promptly borrowed horses for his carriage from friends in order to proceed to Richmond, where he was welcomed by the Virginia Assembly. From Richmond he went to Eppington to visit with the Eppes family, and it was there that on December 12th an express rider brought him President Washington's communication offering him the position of Secretary of State. He responded to Washington that he preferred to keep his present post as Minister, and that he wished to return to France, but that he would spend the next several months reaching a decision.[2]

Jefferson and his family again were reunited with his young second cousin, Thomas Mann Randolph, Jr. either in Richmond or Tuckahoe. Wherever they may have met, Martha and young Randolph soon fell in love with one another. Jefferson approved of the match, and spoke of Randolph as "a young gentleman of genius, science, and honorable mind." "Science" was never far from Jefferson's mind as a desirable attribute.[3]

Arriving at Monticello two days before Christmas, the statesman was greeted with great rejoicing by all the slaves on the plantation.[4]

The statesman found much awaiting his attention upon his return. Farming had not been profitable during his absence, and he attempted to borrow funds from Amsterdam money lenders. He had brought apricot trees from France which he planted, and immediately plunged into resolving the many problems of the plantation which were facing him. Undoubtedly he often visited his wife's grave, and sometimes spent the evenings playing his violin while Martha played on her mother's pianoforte with young Randolph and John Eppes singing to their accompaniment. During the Christmas season Randolph began to court Martha, and by the end of January they were engaged.[5]

Meanwhile President Washington was becoming impatient as he waited for Jefferson's decision. Finally he asked James Madison to visit him at Monticello and obtain an answer. As Jefferson had written to Madison before leaving Paris, he had no intention of accepting any other appointment after the present one. "My object is to return to the same retirement. Whenever, therefore, I quit the present, it will not be to engage in any other office, and most especially any one that would require a constant residence from home."[6]

Despite these words, however, he was unable to refuse Washington anything he wished. On February 14th he reluctantly accepted the exalted position, with a mental reservation which he later expressed, "When I came into this office it was with the resolution to retire from it as soon as I could with decency."[7]

He began to make plans for his departure to New York, and possibly because of his forthcoming absence, Martha and Randolph decided to marry sooner than they ordinarily might have done. The wedding took place at Monticello on February 23rd. Jefferson duly recorded the event in his *Memorandum Book*, "My daughter Martha is this day married to Thomas Mann Randolph junr."[8]

Now that the plantation was in relatively good order once more, Jefferson left it in the charge of his overseer, Nicholas Lewis, with assistance from his new son-in-law, and rode off to Richmond en route to New York. Maria was left in Martha's care, and during the next several months the young couple, taking Maria with them, wandered about Virginia in a prolonged honeymoon.[9]

Although Jefferson had few illusions about the difficulties he would be facing in his new appointment, he could not have visualized an imminent war between France and England, a worsening national financial situation, the increased burdens derived from the first Patent Act and the Residence Act, and international problems relating to foreign commerce first with England and then with France and Spain.

Jefferson's assumption of his new office proved to be much more difficult than he had anticipated, for there was no centralized site for the new government in the city of New York. It was with some difficulty that he found suitable accommodations for his own home and offices. He sorely missed the ready conveniences to which he had been accustomed at Monticello and in Paris.

Particularly he missed his books and other personal possessions, and it was not a simple matter to find others in New York, which was more of a commercial than a cultural center. As a consequence of these circumstances, his style of living became much more austere than he had previously enjoyed.[10]

From the first moment of his arrival in New York, he was feted constantly with dinners for twenty to thirty guests. The conversation revolved always around the French Revolution and recent changes in the American government. There was also much sentiment for the monarchy and open admiration for England, which Jefferson found puzzling and alarming.

Foreseeing that the war in Europe might spread widely, he took steps to profit from it. He instructed Nicholas Lewis at Monticello to lay aside the production of tobacco on his plantations for the time being and plant as much wheat as possible because he believed it would become at a premium in Europe.

He advised Lewis to grow also hemp, flax, cotton and wool. These were items usually imported from Europe and he anticipated that they would become scarce commodities. "If we may decide from past experience," he wrote, "we may safely say that war and domestic manufacture are more gainful than peace and store supplies."[11]

In his new office, most of all Jefferson missed his copying presses and the advantages they made possible. One of his first official acts was to purchase a stationary copying press for the Department of State so that he could continue to make copies of his correspondence and state papers. The copying press also proved to be useful as a duplicating machine when circumstances demanded more than a single copy of a document. In establishing this procedure in his own office, he introduced into government the practice of making multiple copies of documents for distribution and file, a practice which became routine thereafter in public offices and mercantile houses.[12]

Much remained to be resolved of his affairs in Paris, and Jefferson sent his former secretary, William Short, specific instructions concerning many matters. In addition to directions relating to transportation of his furniture, household items and other supplies, he also enclosed a drawing of his "pyramid clock" which "was the form of the little clock which was stolen from the chimney of my study. The parts a.b. c.d. were parts of a cone, being round and tapering to the top, where a gilt head was put on. I would wish one to be made like that, as to the pedestal part, but with obelisks as is represented here a.b. c.d. instead of conical columns as the former had. No gilt head to be on the obelisk, but to be in plain marble, cut off obliquely as is always done in the obelisk. The section of an obelisk, you know, is a square; I mean it's ichnography. The clock to have a pendulum vibrating half seconds exactly. To have a second hand, but none for the days of the week, month, or moon. To strike the hours and half hours. The dial plate to be open work, or as the French work-men say, le cadran a jour, of black marble." *(Document 4)*

He recalled that the superintendent of the Salle des Ventes, where he had purchased his clock, had undertaken to have such a timepiece made for him at a price of either 12 or 15 guineas and it required three or four weeks to complete. He was anxious to have the clock ordered as soon as possible so that it could be included with the shipment of other items.

He ordered an ivory-leaved pocket book with twelve leaves and ivory covers similar to others he had had made for him previously. Among the books he included two copies of the *Encyclopédie ancienne*, the *Tacitus* of the Abbé Brotier "(or some such name)," Buffon's works, containing the parts of Daubenton's works also, and the *Bibliothèque phys-ico-oeconomique* for 1790.

Short was to arrange for Adrien Petit, the manager of his household in Paris, to come to the United States to work for him in New York. He was instructed that Petit was to bring plants of the Burée pear, the Doyennois, seeds of Phaseolus Caracalla, alpine strawberries, and "as many sky larks and red legged partridges as he can, 2 or 3 pair of Bantam fowls, a pair of Angora cats, d[itt]o of Angora goats (these last can only be had of the king's stock)." He noted also "In packing the chest of tools, almost every piece must be wrapped up separately and the chest be then put into an external box." The pyramid clock was eventually delivered and was featured at Monticello during Jefferson's later years and has been restored to the mansion in recent times.[13] *(Figure 17)*

Inevitably one of Jefferson's first priorities was the maintenance of weather records. He now had an unusual opportunity to compare those he maintained in New York with those in Virginia, and he enlisted his new son-in-law to keep records at Monticello. He noted that ever since his arrival, the city had experienced a period of very disagreeable weather, with considerable rain and snow.

He carefully explained his method of record-keeping to Randolph. The records were to be kept for each day, with observations made twice daily, as early as possible in the morning and again between three and four o'clock "because I have found 4 o'clock the hottest and day light the coldest point of the 24 hours."

He made his initial entries on the leaves of one of his ivory pocket books and then once weekly copied them into his record book for perma-nent record. In addition to temperatures, he also entered abbreviated indications for clouds, rain, hail, snow, the first appearance of birds, the leafing and flowering of trees, frosts, occurrence of the aurora borealis and other climatological notes.[14]

Randolph was unable to begin the observations immediately because "I have not a thermometer even, at present, but shall provide
myself directly with one, and as soon as possible with a Barometer. The
addition of the Meteorological phaenomena, observations with respect
to the migrations of birds, and the changes in plants ought to render it
a pleasing task to the Philosopher, the Sportsman and the Farmer,
equally." Randolph eventually attempted to record weather data in accordance with his father-in-law's instructions, and did in fact send him
a copy of the weather diary he had maintained. He had been able to
find only a single thermometer available for sale in Richmond, however,
"which was short, badly graduated and at an exhorbitant price." He did
not purchase it, and instead he used "the old Spirit Wine Thermometer
in the Study."

Jefferson also prevailed on Rittenhouse in Philadelphia to maintain
records of thermometerical and barometrical readings in Philadelphia,
which the latter submitted early in May.[15]

Jefferson's major task as Secretary of State was the formulation of a
national foreign policy. At the same time his office served as the major
communication link between the president and all the Federal offices as
well as the governments of the thirteen states. Although responsible directly to the president and not to the Congress, Jefferson nonetheless
was required to draft reports to that body.

It was not long before he found himself in increasing conflict with
Alexander Hamilton. In time the two men became symbols of a conflict
of ideas that was to continue through American history. Hamilton was
a monarchist in spirit and advocated national power and rule by a favored
few, believing in "the necessity for either force or corruption to govern
men." Jefferson, on the other hand, promoted self-government and the
freedom of the individual. As Secretary of the Treasury, Hamilton hitherto had considered himself to have the position of first place in the
counsel to the president.

During the first presidential administration, particularly during the
New York period, the two rivals generally agreed on policy and Hamilton
appeared to hold the older statesman in high respect. It was not until
the subject of the public debt arose that the first major conflict emerged.
One serious difference after another developed between the two men, in
the matter of foreign policy as well as of the Bank of the United States,
and their hostility grew with each new major issue.[16]

During his absence from home, Jefferson kept in constant communication with his son-in-law concerning events at Monticello. He inquired

about the acquisition of Foster's boring machine [drilling apparatus] for the farm, and also reported that he had been unable to begin his weather studies due to the fact that he had not yet been able to move into the house he had leased. As well as he could determine, however, "there will not be one position to be had for the thermometer free from the influence of the sun both morning & evening," but when he moved in he hoped to find a better position. He had already maintained comparative weather diaries with James Madison recorded at the latter's father's house in Orange and at his own at Monticello.

He noted that the air became warmer as one ascended a mountain both morning and evening and he assumed "on a mountain it should be warmer in the morning & cooler in the heat of the day than on the common plain; but not in so great a degree as these observations indicate." He planned to investigate the phenomenon further.[17]

Despite his participation during the early months after his arrival, he found New York's social climate not as pleasing as the wonderful years he had spent in France. He particularly missed his Parisian circle of erudite friends, and he wrote them many letters of thanks and farewell. His social activities came to an abrupt halt with the onslaught of a massive headache which effectively confined him to his home for a month of sheer frustration. During the same time President Washington became ill with a cold that turned into pneumonia. For a time the president's life was despaired of, but he eventually rallied and made a remarkable recovery. Early in June he took Jefferson with him on a three day fishing trip off Sandy Hook. Although Jefferson's headache continued, he was able to deal with the business of his office once more.[18]

By now the new government had been sufficiently administratively structured and resolved into three Departments—State, Treasury and War—with the Attorney General as legal advisor. The Executive branch was headed by the President with the three Secretaries and Attorney General responsible primarily to him and not to the Congress, for they acted only in his name and with his approval. Although the Department of the Treasury had a considerably larger staff, the Department of State was nonetheless the most important of the three. Consequently Jefferson achieved a closer relationship with the president than did the other Cabinet officers.

Upon his arrival, Jefferson was informed that the House of Representatives had imposed as an official duty of the Secretary of State the drafting of "a proper plan or plans for establishing uniformity in the Currency, Weights and Measures of the United States." Jefferson was hampered in this endeavor by the fact that his library, including the valuable resource material he had assembled for preparing his *Notes*, was far away at Monticello, and that in New York few of the books he needed were available for consultation or purchase. It was this lack of books that eventually led the Congress to reconsider the feasability of developing a library for the use of the legislative and executive branches of the government.

To add to his difficulties, Jefferson had to compile his report "under a severe attack of periodical head ach which came on every day at Sunrise, and never left me until sunset. What had been ruminated in the day under a paroxysm of the most excruciating pain was committed to paper by candlelight, and then the calculations were made." The most violent attack occurred during the first week of May.[19]

Until this time, the weights and measures used in the American colonies were almost all of English origin, and copies of the yard, gallon, bushel and avoirdupois pound had been adopted by individual colonies at various times. Eventually the growing inter-colonial commerce found the lack of uniformity in these standards so confusing and inconvenient that after the end of the Revolution the establishment of a uniform standard became an urgent priority.

Congress was assigned the sole and exclusive right by the Articles of Confederation to undertake this task. Since no legislation was enacted to provide such a system, a clause was inserted in the Constitution giving Congress the power. During his administration, President Washington urged that action be taken in the matter, and on January 15, 1790 Jefferson was requested by Congress to produce such a report.

Jefferson considered that a standard of length should be based on a natural phenomenon which would be commonly known with the intention that it would be as readily reproducible as possible. He proposed that the common pendulum would best serve the purpose. He specified a simple pendulum consisting of a cylindrical iron rod of such length— about 58.7 regular inches divided into five new feet, each foot to be further divided into ten new inches—that a swing from one end of its arc to the other and back again would require two seconds.

The Philadelphia clockmaker Robert Leslie had suggested the adoption of a vibrating rod as the standard of measure, and described it in a manuscript pamphlet which had been sent to John Jay. When Jefferson learned of it he considered it most favorably, and asked Leslie's permission to propose to Congress adoption of the vibrating rod instead of the pendulum. If it were approved, he added, it was possible that Leslie's assistance might be required in its adjustment.[20]

On July 13th, six months almost to the day after receiving the assignment, Jefferson submitted to Congress an elaborate plan for uniformity, a system by means of which all the weights, measures and coins "will be derived altogether from mechanical operations, viz., a rod vibrating seconds . . . subdivided and multiplied . . . for every measure of length, surface and capacity and these last filled with water to determine the weights and coins." The standard for measurement was to be "a uniform cylindrical rod of iron of such length as in latitude 45 degrees, in the level of the ocean and in a cellar or other place the temperature of which does not vary through the year, shall perform its vibrations in small equal arcs in one second of mean time."

This standard rod was specified to be divided into 587-⅕ equal parts, each of which was to be declared a line of one-tenth of an inch. The measure of capacity was to be based on the bushel having a cubic capacity if a decimal system was to be adopted, or on a gallon of 270 cubic inches and a bushel of 2160 cubic inches if the old system was to be retained. The unit of weight was to be the ounce, which was "the weight of a cube of rain water of one-tenth of a foot; or rather, that it is the thousandth part of the weight of a cubic foot of rain water weighed in the standard temperature."

Jefferson submitted two proposals—the first of which was to use such a pendulum to define the weights and measures of the English Customary Service and to define and render them uniform. His second proposal was to establish a new system of weights and measures based on decimal ratios such as had already been adopted for the coinage. For frequently used units, he recommended retaining some of the old names, and that sizes of new units should be as close as possible to the old ones. The "foot," for example, would be nearly as long as the old foot, but divided into ten new "inches."

As an alternative to the establishment of all weights and measures on the decimal system, he suggested that the system already in existence be re-defined and made uniform. Whichever was adopted, he proposed, should be introduced gradually to lessen inconvenience. It might be first introduced in the counting houses, and later into all legal proceedings, then for merchants and traders dealing in foreign commodities, and eventually it was to be brought into common use for everyone. During the next six years, there was considerable discussion of the system in Congress, with various committees reporting, but no legislative action was taken. It was not, in fact, until several decades later that the standards were established.[21]

The first consideration of the subject of coinage in the new nation had been a report compiled by a committee consisting of George Wythe, Roger Sherman and James Duane, which was submitted to the Continental Congress in 1776. It recommended a table of values of the gold and silver coins then in common use throughout the colonies. Jefferson was added to the committee, and when the report was recommitted, he prepared a new version with careful estimates of the values of each "expressed by decimal notation in Dollars and parts of a dollar." He submitted the report on the day that he left Congress and it was tabled and not revived until 1782.

In 1784, the subject of coinage was still one of the issues before Congress, and he learned that Robert Morris as superintendent of finance had reported on the subject. Jefferson proceeded to compile his own notes and recommendations, "Notes on the Establishment of a Money Unit, and of a Coinage for the United States." Submitting the proposal to Morris, he hoped it would be considered at the next session of Congress. It played an important role, and he subsequently recommended the dollar as the standard unit and subdivisions thereof which would coincide with other familiar coins, a proposal which Congress finally adopted. By an act of Congress of April 2, 1792, the United States Mint was established at Philadelphia with David Rittenhouse as its first director, and Henry Voigt as the Chief Coiner.[22]

The first several months proved to be hectic for Jefferson, with the enactment by Congress of two acts the fulfillment of which was to become his personal responsibility while in office. The first of these was the first Patent Act which Congress had approved on April 10, 1790, establishing a system based on the British prototype. On May 31st of the same year, the first copyright law was passed, based on the British Statute of Anne of 1710. The second major project was the Residence Act which was passed in the same month to establish a Federal City situated on the banks of the Potomac River, to be the permanent seat of the Federal government.[23]

The first Patent Act provided for a three-man board having power to grant patents, consisting of the Secretary of State, the Secretary of War, and the Attorney General. An inventor, be it "he", "she," or "they," was required to present a petition to the board which was empowered to grant the patent in the name of the United States, "if they shall deem the invention or discovery sufficiently useful and important." The petition was to include a specification in writing, and a drawing and a model if possible. These had to be so exact and detailed that the invention could be distinguished from other objects before known and used, and that persons skilled in the art would be able to construct, make, or use the invention.

Infringement was to be punishable by damages assessed by a jury, and forfeiture of the infringing devices to the patentee. Patents could be repealed within one year by the judgement of a district court, on the complaint of any person, who, however, was required to pay all costs if he lost. Fees were nominal. The cost of filing was fifty cents, plus ten cents for each hundred words of specification, two dollars for making out the patent document, one dollar for affixing the Great Seal and twenty cents for all endorsements and other services, so that the overall cost totaled between four and five dollars. The fees received were divided between the clerk in charge of the department and another clerk as part of their salaries.

The issuance of patents was the responsibility of the Secretary of State, and Jefferson assumed this assignment with mixed feelings. Although he took great pride in this duty, he nonetheless had serious reservations and doubts concerning the constitutionality of the practise. First of all, the new patent law was based on the British system, and he entertained a great dislike for anything that was British. More importantly, although he agreed that inventors should have full rights to their inventions, he was strongly opposed to the granting of monopolies which might withhold technological progress from other inventors and from the general public.

Finally, he questioned whether the standard period of fourteen years for which the law protected each invention was sufficient in a nation that was as large and as sparsely settled as the United States when compared to the smaller European countries. In the new republic the communication of ideas would be considerably slower, he claimed, than in a densely populated country such as England, for example.[24]

Despite the philosophical concerns that continued to bother him, Jefferson was nonetheless pleased with the public response to the new law, and in the manner in which American genius began to emerge as a consequence of its protection. Two months after the law was enacted, he wrote to Benjamin Vaughan, "An Act of Congress authorizing the issuing of patents for new discoveries has given a spring of invention beyond my conception. Being an instrument in granting these patents, I am acquainted with their discoveries. Many of them indeed are trifling, but there are some of great consequence which have been proved by practice, and others which if they stand the same proof will produce a great effect." He mentioned as an example a proposal for a new pile engine submitted by Lemuel Cox, who had constructed the bridge between Boston and Charleston, Massachusetts.[25]

A separate Patent Office had yet to be established and in the interim each patent application had to be individually examined by each member of the board. The process was slow and tedious, due largely to the absence of a body of patent law to provide guidance, and also to the conservative policy of the first examining board. Jefferson's insistence that each application must be examined in detail made the procedure even more time-consuming. Each application was submitted to severe scrutiny, the first criterion being whether the invention or discovery would be sufficiently useful. There was no appeal procedure in this early period. Those applications that were approved were then issued patents by the Secretary of State.[26]

In the beginning, the first patent board, which Jefferson named "the

Board of Arts," customarily met on the last Saturday of each month to review all the applications received, and acted only upon those that which had met all requirements. After July lst, 1791 a preliminary review of all applications was made by the Attorney General to determine the propriety of the application, then read by the individual board members in their own offices or lodgings to save time. Each reader noted criticisms and amendments, which were then compiled by the chief clerk of the Department of State and considered by the entire board in joint meeting.

An oversight in the first patent act was the lack of provision for simultaneous rival claims for the same invention. In such instances, the practise was to issue patents to all claimants. A notable case occurred when John Fitch, James Rumsey, John Stevens and Nathan Read all applied for patents for the invention of the steamboat and other inventions relating to the steam engine. The dilemma was solved by holding a number of hearings with the applicants and eventually granting patents to all of them. The decision did not meet with general satisfaction from the applicants, however, although from their titles it is unlikely that identical patents were issued.[27]

Jefferson had the major responsibility, and discarded those applications he considered impractical or frivolous. Gradually the board was forced to develop rules and regulations concerning matters of form and substance, leading to the establishment of standards for the required specifications and drawings.

The definition of what constituted an invention that was patentable became a major issue facing the board. Frequently they were confronted with situations for which there was no established precedent, and found it difficult to promulgate general rules that would be applicable to all submissions. The procedure matured only by a slow process. However, as Jefferson later reported, they did reach some useful conclusions. Among them was the decision that

> A machine of which we are possessed, might be applied by every man to any use of which it is susceptible, and that this right ought not to be taken from him and given to a monopolist, because the first perhaps had occasion to apply it. Thus a screw for crushing plaster might be employed for crushing corn-cobs. And a chain-pump for raising water might be used for raising wheat; this being merely a change of application.
>
> Another ruling was that a change of material should not give title to a patent. As the making of a ploughshare of cast rather than wrought iron; a comb of iron instead of horn or ivory, or the connecting buckets by a band of leather rather than of hemp or iron. A third was that a mere change of form should give no right to a patent, as a high-quartered shoe instead of a low one; a round hat instead of a three-square; or a square bucket instead of a round one. But for this rule, all the changes of fashion

in dress would have been under the tax of patentees . . . But there were still abundance of cases which could not be brought under rule until they should have presented themselves under all their aspects.[28]

Jefferson was particularly concerned about what he described as "frivolous" patents and the problem they represented. "The abuse of frivolous patents is likely to cause more inconvenience than is countervailed by those really useful," he commented to a correspondent. "We know not to what uses we may apply implements which were in our hands before the birth of our government, and even the discovery of America."

A rule to protect the citizen against such abuses which suggested itself to him "is to consider the invention of any new mechanical power, or of any new combination of the mechanical powers already known, as entitled to an exclusive grant; but that the purchaser of the right to use the invention should be free to apply it to every purpose of which it is susceptible." Jefferson undoubtedly had the inventor Oliver Evans in mind when he wrote these lines, for he was to become the source of many of Jefferson's concerns with the patent system.[29]

Evans emerged in the late eighteenth century as a typical American inventor and entrepreneur with many fields of interest and claims to invention in each of them. He was particularly concerned with the movement of materials in manufacturing processes, the best example of which was the automated flour mill which he constructed in 1785. In it he featured a number of conveyors and other apparatus for the transfer of the raw materials through the processes, including some conveyors he had conceived and used for the first time, as well as other types long known in principle but which he adapted to milling for the first time.

Between 1786 and 1789 he applied for and was granted a patent for his invention in flour mill machinery from the states of Pennsylvania, Maryland and New Hampshire. On December 18, 1790 the same invention was granted the third patent to be issued by the United States government, "for Manufacturing Flour and Meal." This patent achieved importance because it served to test the patent system, and later became the subject of considerable litigation and political controversy.[30]

At least 114 applications for patents were made during the first two years, although only 49 were granted. The actual number of applications filed was probably considerably greater, inasmuch as no record was kept of those that were refused outright due to failure to present properly compiled specifications, drawings or models. Only three patents were granted in the first year.[31]

The amount of work for Jefferson was considerable, added to his primary political and diplomatic responsibilities. This led him to formulate a new patent bill, "to Promote the Progress of the Useful Arts." The new patent law was submitted to Congress on February 7, 1791, but it was not acted upon until two years later. When enacted, the new law incorporated some of Jefferson's provisions and was far more liberal in its application than he had proposed. It effectively suspended the first patent act and provided a registration system specifying certain formalities which were all that was required for the granting of patents. The liberality of the new law particularly benefited New England and was advocated by the Federalists, as well as by President Washington.[32]

Despite Jefferson's continuing objections, the country's growing manufacturing interests, having the support of General Washington, enabled the law to be enlarged. Jefferson construed the new law to have made the issuance of patents a merely ministerial act. "Instead of revising a patent in the first instance," he wrote, "as the board was formerly authorized to do, the patent is now issued of course, subject to be declared void on such principles as may be established by the courts of law. The previous refusal of a patent would better guard our citizens against harassments by law suits, but England has given it to its judges, and the usual predominancy of her example carries it to ours."[33]

Ironically, the new patent act brought the extremely rigid examination of applications by high government officials to the other extreme of having no examination at all, a situation which was not resolved until forty-three years later. One advantage of the system which remained, however, and which Jefferson was quick to realize, was that it served as a link between the government and the scientific and technological development of the nation.[34]

During his tenure as Secretary of State, Jefferson approved a total of sixty-seven patents. The last patent he granted was issued on December 31, 1793, for a "Disputed claim for a Machine to Work in a current of Water, . . . etc., decided in favor of John Clark."[35]

Jefferson's role as examiner of patents sometimes required more than merely reading the specifications and examining models submitted by inventors. On occasion he found it necessary to test personally the invention. In 1791, for example, at the request of the House of Representatives, he investigated a claim made by Jacob Isaacs of Newport, Rhode Island that he had developed a new method for distilling potable water from salt water by means of "the common iron caboose."

Such a process, if successful, would be invaluable for ships at sea and castaway seamen. Jefferson called upon several fellow members of the American Philosophical Society to assist him, including David Rittenhouse, Caspar Wistar, and Professor James Hutchinson from the University of Pennsylvania. As he explained to Wistar, it was necessary to proceed promptly because Isaacs claimed to be poor and consequently it was important not to detain him in Philadelphia any longer than was necessary.[36]

Experimentation with Isaacs's process was undertaken on March

21st and 24th in Jefferson's office with apparatus that Isaacs had erected there. A control distillation without the apparatus was also assembled. A large still and a small still were used to save time in determining proportions.

As the others observed, Isaacs

> fixed the pot, a small caboose, with a tin cap and straight tube of tin passing obliquely through a cask of cold water; he made use of a mixture, the composition of which he did not explain, and from 24 pints of sea-water, taken up about three miles out of the Capes of Delaware, at flood-tide, he distilled 22 pints of fresh water in four hours with 20 lbs. of seasoned pine, which was a little wetted by having lain in the rain.

To determine whether Isaacs's mixture contributed to the operation, other experiments varying the ingredients were made. It was concluded that Isaacs's mixture provided no advantage either to the process or the result. The results favored straight distillation instead of use of the mixture proposed by Isaacs, but in general the process seemed successful. In spite of the negative results of the tests, Jefferson considered it desirable to have had such a demonstration made and publicized because it provided convincing evidence to the public that fresh water could be distilled from salt water by distillation.[37]

The report submitted by Jefferson to the House of Representatives was an exemplary scientific paper, providing a review of the process proposed and the results obtained, with recommendations. It also included a history of the advances made in conversion of salt water into fresh from the sixteenth century to that time. In his search of the literature on the subject Jefferson discovered that similar experiments made previously by others had amply demonstrated that pure water could be obtained from salt water by ordinary distillation.

Jefferson's remarkable scholarship, as well as the comprehensive library at his disposal, were reflected in the report. He summarized the various methods attempted in history prior to that proposed by Isaacs. The report was published by the House of Representatives for distribution, and is believed to be the first scientific paper published under government auspices.[38]

The other major project which Jefferson in his Cabinet position was required to supervise was the Residence Act of 1790. The Act specified that within the next ten years the new permanent seat of government was to be established in the region beside the Potomac River, the exact site to be selected by President Washington. Jefferson served as the president's delegate from the very beginning, and was intimately involved in every aspect and detail not only of the survey of the territory and the design of the city, but also in the acquisition and sale of property.

The problems of creating a new city from a wilderness by a recently formed government were enormous and unanticipated, and it was only the experience and skill of Jefferson and his intimate supervision in close cooperation with President Washington, that brought it to a successful completion. Their mutual intense interest in the development of the capital and its public buildings brought them together in a strong bond of friendship that continued throughout Jefferson's term as Secretary of State.

Jefferson prepared a series of notes to serve as proceedings under the Act. He proposed the size of the territory to consist of one hundred square miles, that three commissioners be appointed to be subject to the president's direction and who "should have some taste in architecture." He carefully outlined each step that was to be taken in the city's development, including plans for receiving gifts of land and for their sale.[39]

The surveyor Major Andrew Ellicott was designated by the president on February 2, 1791 to undertake the survey of a ten-mile square to be known as the "Federal Territory." At the time Ellicott was engaged, with two brothers as his assistants, on a survey in upper New York State. He responded promptly to Washington's summons, however, leaving the work in New York to be completed by his brothers. Three commissioners to supervise the formation of the capital city were selected and a month later the French engineer, Major Pierre Charles L'Enfant, was appointed by Washington to assist Ellicott particularly with the location and design of the buildings.

The *Georgetown Weekly Ledger* commented on another of Jefferson's appointments. Announcing Ellicott's arrival, it alluded to Jefferson's statements about the blacks in his *Notes On the State of Virginia* by adding that Ellicott was "attended by Benjamin Banniker [sic], an Ethiopian, whose abilities as a Surveyor and Astronomer clearly prove that Mr. Jefferson's concluding that race of men were void of mental endowments was without foundation."[40]

First named the "Federal Territory" or "Territory of Columbia," the region eventually became the "District of Columbia." It was Jefferson who selected the Indian name "Anacostia" for the Eastern Branch, verified by Ellicott, which was to be featured in the Territory, and the direction in which Jefferson anticipated the city would develop.[41]

The city's precise location along the Potomac and its development were to be determined by the president. The Residence Act authorized the acquisition of sufficient lands on the eastern side of the Potomac to form a ten mile square. Jefferson interpreted the Act to mean that the new territory could include the Potomac's opposite shore, and the boundaries first drawn placed the Potomac in the middle of the square. From the first, Washington and Jefferson visualized the national capital as a town, not a city. Jefferson's architectural and surveying interests and experience proved to be of considerably value in the early stages of building the new city. He had cultivated a knowledge of foreign architecture in his years abroad, and he was familiar with the work of foreign architects. He had collected a large number of plans of European cities and architectural designs of important Old World buildings. He was also aware that there were too few trained architects in the United States.

He provided L'Enfant with his collection of foreign city plans, and advised him also on the design of the Capitol building and the President's House, using much of the same language he had employed several years before in relation to the capitol of Virgnia. "Whenever it is proposed to prepare plans for the Capitol," he noted, "I should prefer the adoption of some one of the models of antiquity, which have had the approbation of thousands of years and for the President's House, I should prefer the celebrated fronts of modern buildings, which have received the approbation of all good judges."

Jefferson suggested that the streets should be laid out at right angles, and should be made wide, straight and spacious, not narrower than one hundred feet and with a fifteen foot walkway (sidewalk) for pedestrians. He recommended long rows of trees to border the streets and avenues, and eventually provided the trees for Pennsylvania Avenue. He noted that brick would be preferable to stone for building construction. He proposed that a maximum height of buildings be established, such as he had seen in Paris.

The Capitol building was to be the focal point of the design. One square should be allotted to the Capitol "building and government offices, another for a Market, and nine for public walks. He insisted that the commissioners to be appointed should be subject to the president in all matters and that the plan for public buildings must have the approval of the president. He drafted a proclamation issued by Washington early in 1791 defining the boundaries and appointing the commissioners. He instructed both Ellicott on the surveying and mapping of the district, and L'Enfant on laying out the topographical features of the region and selection of sites for public buildings. L'Enfant did not follow Jefferson's plan entirely, and added a series of radiating spaced circles on the rectangular street pattern.[42]

It was not long before conflicts on procedures developed. The arrogant and short-tempered L'Enfant, hoping to have the major features of his plan developed simultaneously, objected to the early sale of lots urged by Washington. After Jefferson and Madison met with the commissioners, they reached the decision not to postpone the sale of lots. They agreed to name the capital city "Washington" in honor of the first president, and the region in which it was to be situated was designated "the Territory of Columbia." The first auction of lots took place in October 1791 and another was planned as soon as a map of the territory could be engraved.[43]

Meanwhile L'Enfant had developed a controversy with the commissioners, refusing to furnish them with copies of his map. Then without
their authority he ordered the demolition of a house which unfortunately
belonged to a nephew of one of the commissioners. Jefferson placed
L'Enfant under the direction of the commissioners, but conflicts continued between L'Enfant and not only the commissioners but also President
Washington. Jefferson finally was forced to terminate L'Enfant's employment and placed Ellicott in charge. Quarrels which later developed between the commissioners and Ellicott eventually led to the surveyor's
dismissal as well.[44]

When the commissioners announced a competition for the design
of the Capitol building, Jefferson made several suggestions, visualizing it
first as a temple and then as a central dome with balancing wings, based
on the Pantheon in Rome. He conveyed his suggestions to Stephen Hallet, a French architect who submitted several plans. An amateur named
William Thornton also joined the competition and developed the concept in a design of his own that was accepted. In practice the Thornton
design proved to be impractical, however, and Jefferson called together
Thornton, Hallet, Hoban and a builder to decide on the procedure to
be followed. They settled on modifications of the Thornton plan, and
the cornerstone was laid by Washington in 1793.[45]

When the time came for selecting a design for the President's
House, various architects competed, and Jefferson also prepared designs,
one of which he submitted anonymously, based on Palladio's Villa Rotunda. It did not meet with a favorable response, however, and the design of James Hoban was the one selected by Washington. Despite the
tempestuous events that marked the early years of the city's planning,
work continued although with spasmodic interruptions and by 1799 the
city of Washington was at last ready for occupancy by the government.[46]

In June Jefferson received a letter from Maria Cosway, written two
months earlier, reproaching him for not having written even a line to
her since his departure from France. He replied promptly, assuring her
that her letter "gives me a foretaste of the sensations we are to feel in
the next world, on the arrival of any new-comer from the circle of friends
we have left behind. I am now fixed here, and look back to Europe only
on account of that circle. Could it be transferred here, the measure of
all I could desire in this world would be filled up, for I have no desire
but to enjoy the affections of my heart, which are divided now by a wide
sea. You know I always ranted about your bringing your pencil and harp
here. They would go well with our groves, our birds, and our sun."

He mentioned that he had been informed that she had given birth
to a child, and "You may make children there, but this is the country to

transplant them to. There is no comparison between the sum of happiness enjoyed here and there. All the distractions of your great Cities are but feathers in the scale against the domestic enjoiments and rural occupations, and neighborly societies we live amidst here. I summon you then as a mother to come and join us." Maria Cosway did not respond to his summons, nor did Jefferson actually believe that she would do so.[47]

Once again he began to suffer from blinding headaches. He complained to his daughter, Martha, of "the periodical headach which had attacked me. It has indeed been remarkably slight since that, but I am not yet quite clear of it. I expect every fit to be the last."

Monroe wrote "Your friends have been made uneasy by a report of your indisposition, but flatter themselves it has been remov'd ere this, as they hear it was a periodical complaint you have had before and which was never accompanied by any dangerous symptoms."

Later he informed his daughter, Maria, "I have been these three weeks confined by a periodical headach. It has been the most moderate I ever had: but it has not yet left me."

To Randolph he explained, "A lingering head-ach still prevents me from answering fully your favors of April 23. and May 3. Having taken the bark till it ceased to produce any effect, I discontinued for some days. I shall resume it today, and hope it will remove the small and feeble returns which still keep me from business." To William Short he reported the same, that for almost a month he had been unable to attend to any business public or private.[48]

Hoping that a voyage on the water would dissipate his malady, Jefferson joined President Washington, Governor Clinton of New York, Congressman William Loughton Smith of South Carolina, and other government notables on a vessel in Long Island Sound sailing to Rhode Island to honor that state's decision to accept the Constitution and become part of the United States. It was also a diplomatic necessity for him to be present.

Ten days later he again departed for Monticello to resolve business and family affairs. He made a side journey to Philadelphia, where he remained for a few days to arrange additions and alterations to the house he was renting when the capital moved from New York to Philadelphia. Arriving at Monticello, he remained there for a month and a half.[49]

It was not until two years later that Jefferson recorded a prescription for the relief of headaches. This was not a remedy for his "periodical headachs", however, but for what he described as "the sun-pain":

Recipe for the head-ach called the Sun-pain. 6. grains of Calomel taken at night, without any thing to work it off, or any other matter whatever.

Mr. A F Willis of Georgia has had this head-ach to a dangerous extremity, and tried bark ineffectually. A drunken Doct.r recommended the above dose of Calomel. It relieved him from the next fit. He had it some years after, and the same medecine relieved him again as quickly. He has cured his son of it also, and was obliged to give it twice at an interval of 2 or 3 days. He communicated it to Mrs. Broadnax a sister of Colo. Fieldg. Lewis who had the same species of headach. it cured her. She has communicated it to others who have tried it with never failing success. April 10, 1792.

To this he added another incident that had come to his attention:

Sep. 1. 96. A negro man had been 3 weeks laid up with the periodical headach or eyeach: I gave him a dose of salts in the morning and in the night 3. drachms of bark. Recollecting then the above prescription I gave no more bark, but the next night gave 6 grs. of calomel. He missed his fit the next day, but note, I was not perfectly satisfied that his sickness was genuine.[50]

Calomel, known also as mercurous chloride, is a white tasteless compound used widely in Jefferson's day as a purgative and fungicide.

After a restful period at home for a month and a half, Jefferson returned to Philadelphia to resume his duties. He had planned to move into the house he had rented from Thomas Leiper at 274 High (now Market) Street, a short distance from his office. Leiper was a prominent Philadelphian wholesale and retail tobacco merchant and manufacturer of snuff and other products and also operated stone quarries. Among his projects were the construction of an experimental railroad with horse-drawn vehicles and a tramway for his quarries. He became a substantial subscriber to the development of turnpikes and canals, and occupied many positions of trust in the city.[51]

Upon his arrival, however, Jefferson found that the alterations he had ordered in September had not been completed. At the end of the year the house was still not ready for occupancy except for one room. "That," wrote Jefferson, "will be my bed-room, study, dining-room and parlor." His furniture had already arrived from France in eighty-six packing cases, with a freight bill of $544.53, and there was no place in which he could unpack them. In a recess between the library and breakfast-room he installed a bed which could be hoisted to the ceiling by means of pulleys in the morning so that the space could be used for other purposes during the day, and let down at night.[52]

The advent of Jefferson's first grandchild, the daughter of Martha and Thomas Mann Randolph, born at Monticello in February 1791, greatly pleased the statesman. When asked to select a name for her, he chose Anne Cary because it related to both sides of the family. It was not until September, however, that he was to see his granddaughter for the first time, when she was eight months old.[53]

* * *

Constantly preoccupied with measurement of distances traveled, Jefferson had attempted to purchase odometers for the purpose while in France. Before leaving Philadelphia he purchased an odometer from the clockmaker Robert Leslie and on his return to Monticello in September he attached an odometer to the wheel of his phaeton to measure the distance traveled. He noted, "These measures were on the belief that the wheel of the Phaeton made exactly 360 revolutions in a mile. But on measuring it accurately at the end of the journey it's circumference was 14. f[eet] 10-$\frac{1}{2}$. I[nches] and consequently made 354.95 revol[utio]ns in a mile. These numbers should be greater then in the proportion of 71 : 72 or a mile added to every 71." The next month he had a box constructed for containing the odometer.[54]

Early in the same year Jefferson was elected one of the three vice-presidents of the American Philosophical Society. With the seat of government now in Philadelphia, he was able at last to attend meetings and spend time with fellow members.[55]

For some time Jefferson had been at work compiling his report for Congress on the cod and whale fisheries, an industry of vital importance to New England coastal states, which were requesting government subsidies to enable them to compete with foreign fishing interests. Although not a fisherman and not particularly fond of the water, while in France Jefferson nonetheless had researched the history of the whaling industry while seeking concessions from the French for the importation of American whale and fish oils, and he now developed his studies further.

His report was extremely supportive of the plight of the fishermen of New England, viewing the fisheries as nurseries for future seamen. Although he opposed granting of government aid, he suggested they should be absolved from customs duties on articles they used. Most of all, he advised, they required free markets for their products possibly obtainable by arrangements with friendly nations, and he emphasized the need to revive the carrying trade. The report was scholarly and powerful, and generally was viewed as anti-British, a circumstance that served Jefferson's intention, for there was strong anti-British sentiment in the Congress and led to anti-British legislation.[56]

Despite the fact that he was busier than ever during this period, Jefferson continued to find time for his scientific interests. He commented to Robert R. Livingston on the latter's experiment made to verify his calculations. "The diminution of friction is certainly one of the most desirable reformations in mechanics. Could we get rid of it altogether we should have perpetual motion. I was afraid that using a liquid for a ful-crum, the pivot (for so we may call them) must be of such a diameter as to lose what had been gained."[57]

He urged his son-in-law to investigate "the great question relative to the Opossum. The proper season is now coming on, and you can easily procure them in any number you please. If you can obtain satisfactory evidence of the whole process of gestation & parturition it would be an acceptable thing to the philosophical society here to receive a paper from you on the subject."

Little was known about the life cycle of the opossum, and Ran-dolph's observation that the pouch in which the animal carried its young disappeared after weaning did not satisfy Jefferson. Jefferson contem-plated the possibility that it contracted rather than disappeared; as a boy he had tried to open the pouch of an animal carrying no young, and remembered that it had been hard to find and more difficult to open.[58]

Jefferson also continued to pursue his interest in the Indians. An old acquaintance, Judge Harry Innes of Danville, Kentucky, sent him an "Image carved of Stone of a naked Woman kneeling: it is roughly exe-cuted, but from the coarseness of the Stone the instrument with which it was probably carved and its antiquity I think shews the maker to have had some talent in that way, the design being good . . . about nine or ten Inches high."

The carving had been found along the Cumberland River by a farmer while ploughing a corn field, and Innes had attempted unsuccess-fully to discover whether there was evidence of an Indian settlement in the area. Innes also enclosed a plan of a fortification, one of many in the region which Innes believed were made by former inhabitants and not by Europeans.

Jefferson agreed that the fortifications recently found must have been the work of aborigines. He had never heard of the use of iron or even of burnt bricks among them. He particularly admired the ability of the Indians as artists and painters, and was delighted to have the small statue. "The Indians will crayon out an animal, plant, so as to prove the existence of a germ in their minds which only wants cultivation. The Indian often carves figures on their pipes not destitute of design or merit."

In his estimation, the statue "would, because of the hardness of the stone, be a better proof of the use of iron [to carve it] than I ever yet saw; but as it is a solitary fact, and possible to have been made with implements of stone, and great patience, for which the Indians are re-markable, I consider it to have been so made. It is certainly the best piece of worksmanship I ever saw from their hands. If the artist did not intend it, he has very happily hit on the representation of a woman in the first moments of parturition." (*Figure 18*)

Several months later he presented the statue to the American Philosophical Society. The statuette was transferred with other Indian artifacts from the Society to the Academy of Natural Sciences of Philadelphia in the latter part of the nineteenth century. It is now in the Fitzhugh collection of the Heye Foundation at the Museum of the American Indian in New York City.[59]

Jefferson also experimented with sowing some rice which had come from Timor. While in France he had become greatly interested in introducing various types in the United States. Rice was already one of the major products of South Carolina, where it had been introduced in the 1680's. Within the next two decades it had become commercially popular, and coastal grown rice became the leading export of the region during most of the colonial period.

Jefferson frequently corresponded with South Carolina planters on agricultural subjects, and while in France he attempted to introduce upland rice (*Oryza mulica*). He first learned that it would grow in mountainous regions with ordinary rainfall from a published work by Pierre Poivre, a former governor of the Île de France. Poivre had noted that rice introduced into Africa from Cochin China was grown successfully all along the African coast.

It was just at this time that Jefferson met a prince from Cochin China visiting Paris, and asked him to send him some of the rice. Despite the prince's promises, it never materialized. Later, as he was about to return to the United States, Jefferson became acquainted with a shipmaster, Captain Nathaniel Cutting, who was planning a voyage around the coast of Africa. He arranged with Cutting to obtain some rice for him, and the shipmaster eventually provided Jefferson a thirty gallon cask of African rice. Jefferson distributed it, dividing it between the Agricultural Society of South Carolina and some planters in Georgia. If this variety could be successfully grown in these locations, he suggested, it would eliminate the problems derived from the summer diseases of swamp rice grown there.

The African rice did not succeed in South Carolina, however, although it flourished in the hilly regions of Georgia. It was later grown in Kentucky and elsewhere as well, chiefly for home use, for it did not compete in quality with coastal rice. Jefferson had grown plants of the rice in pots while in Philadelphia but they had produced no seed. When Jefferson planted it at Monticello he obtained good crops for several years, but lacking conveniences for husking, he allowed its cultivation to decline.[60]

In the spring Jefferson had been appointed chairman of a committee of the American Philosophical Society to study the history of the Hessian fly, an insect which was causing more damage to wheat crops throughout the country "than an army of twenty thousand Hessians." This insect, *Phytophaga destructor*, was said to have been introduced into the American continent in about 1778 in hay or straw bedding materials brought by Hessian mercenaries during the American Revolution to fields on Long Island, New York; hence the name. During the next century it was to spread across the entire continent and become the most serious pest to cereal crops with which American farmers ever had to contend.[61]

Eager to make a contribution to resolving the problem but having no time to spare just then, Jefferson asked his son-in-law to turn his attention to the study of the insect which would enable him to submit its history to the Society. He explained that it would require observations over the period of several summers. The botanist John Bartram had informed him that it was one and the same insect which deposited its eggs on young trees of plum, apricots, nectarines and peaches and made them gummy and worthless. Bartram promised to show Jefferson the insect during the summer.[62]

Jefferson frequently held meetings of his committee at dinner in his home, with Barton, Hutchinson and Wistar attending, as they sought a solution for destroying the pest. At one of the formal meetings, Barton presented a list of questions which were incorporated in a circular distributed the next year to farmers requesting them to report on damage and to make suggestions for its prevention. The Hessian fly continued to cause damage for the next several decades, however, despite the Society's efforts. No report was ever made by the Committee.[63]

With the limited leisure available to him, Jefferson frequently went riding along the banks of the Schuylkill, accompanied by Madison or Monroe or both. Sometimes they forsook their horses for long walks, even venturing out in inclement weather. In mid-May Jefferson and Madison took a long holiday journey up the Hudson River through New York and New England, traveling a total of 920 miles, 256 of them by water, before returning to Philadelphia a month later. It was an enticing prospect, for it provided Jefferson with an opportunity for relaxation, which he greatly needed, and at the same time it enabled him to make some scientific observations.

They fished on Lake George and sailed on Lake Champlain, traversed the state of Massachusetts, and traveled on the Connecticut River. They visited Long Island, where he collected plant materials for Monticello, and throughout the trip he made careful notes, particularly of botanical matters.

From Lake Champlain Jefferson sent his daughter Maria a letter written on birch bark. He compared the beautiful natural surroundings of Lake George with the relatively muddy water of Lake Champlain. He wrote, "On the whole, I find nothing anywhere else, in point of climate, which Virginia need envy to any part of the world . . . When we consider how much climate contributes to the happiness of our condition . . . we have reason to value highly the accident of birth in such a one as that of Virginia."[64]

In Vermont he observed the cultivation of sugar maples and the production of maple sugar, which intrigued him. He was eager to introduce this industry in Virginia and arranged to have seed of sugar maples sent to him. Later on his journey, he purchased an entire stock of young sugar maple trees and several other varieties he found in a nursery on Long Island. His enthusiasm for new plantings at Monticello continued after his return, when he ordered more than two dozen plants including roses.[65]

Characteristically, Jefferson was unable to give himself up totally to relaxation. During this sojourn he successfully completed a systematic study on the Hessian fly and the means of its prevention. This required frequent interruptions of their itinerary, while he stopped to interview farmers and others along their route. It was not an idle enterprise, for he had long been concerned with the subject of agriculture, and the prevalence of the insect had seriously reduced the production of American wheat since 1788.

Furthermore, to avoid the possibility of infection of their own crops, the British had prohibited importation of American wheat, a circumstance that seriously affected American farmers. From the time of their arrival in Poughkeepsie, Jefferson queried not only farmers but also tavern keepers, blacksmiths and local men of prominence for information about the prevalence of the Hessian fly.

He also took advantage of every opportunity to pursue other scientific interests, and on Long Island he met and interviewed several members of the remnant of a tribe of Unquachog Indians to further supplement his Indian vocabularies.[66]

Both Madison and Jefferson derived great enjoyment from the excursion. The sojourn was refreshing, and Jefferson resumed work well rested. "I returned four days ago," he informed Martha, "having enjoyed through the whole of it very perfect health. I am in hopes the relaxation it gave me from business has freed me from the almost constant headach with which I have been persecuted during the whole winter and spring. Having been entirely free of it while traveling, proves it to have been occasioned by the drudgery of business." Despite the innocuous intent of the trip, which was for relaxation and nature study, Jefferson's suspicious political opponents ventured that it had been made with the ulterior purpose of unifying the widely scattered anti-Federalist groups throughout New England and New York for political purposes, although there is no evidence that such was the case.[67]

It was after his return that Jefferson received from Benjamin Banneker of Baltimore County, Maryland, a manuscript compilation of the ephemerides for the year 1792. These were tables of the assigned places of celestial bodies for regular intervals, eclipses and other astronomical data.

Banneker was a free black tobacco planter who had taught himself in mathematics and astronomy from books and instruments lent by a neighbor, George Ellicott. Without instruction or assistance from others, he successfully made astronomical observations and calculated ephemerides for inclusion in almanacs. He had assisted Major Andrew Ellicott as astronomical assistant in the early stages of the survey of the Federal Territory.

In an accompanying letter he pleaded with Jefferson as Secretary of State for the equality of races, offering his calculations as proof that human capability was not related to racial differences. He had chosen Jefferson to be the recipient because he was known to be "measurably friendly and well disposed" to black people.

Jefferson appeared to be impressed by this unusual achievement of an unschooled black man, and in his acknowledgement he stated, "No body wishes more than I do to see such proofs as you exhibit, that nature has given to our black brethren talents equal to those of the other colors of men, and that the appearance of a want of them is owing merely to the degraded condition of their existence in Africa & America. I can add with truth, that no body wishes more ardently to see a good system commenced for raising the condition both of their body & mind to what it ought to be, as fast as the imbecility of their present existence, and other circumstances which cannot be neglected, will admit."[68]

He forwarded the calculations to Marie Jean Antoine Nicolas de Caritat, Marquis de Condorcet in Paris, explaining, "I am happy to be able to inform you that we have now in the United States a negro, the son of a black man born in Africa, and of a black woman born in the United States, who is a very respectable mathematician. I procured him to be employed under one of our chief directors in laying out the new federal city on the Potowmac, & in the intervals of his leisure, while on that work, he made an Almanac for the next year, which he sent me in his own handwriting, & which I inclose to you. I have seen very elegant solutions of Geometrical problems by him. Add to this he is a very worthy & respectable member of society. He is a free man. I shall be delighted to see these instances of moral eminence so multiplied as to prove that the want of talents observed in them is merely the effect of their degraded condition, and not proceeding from any difference in the structure of the parts on which intellect depends."[69]

This letter demonstrates that Jefferson had more knowledge of Banneker than was derived from the calculations and accompanying letter he had received from this black man of science. Undoubtedly he had been informed of Banneker's skill with mathematical puzzles, possibly of his successful construction of a striking clock without previously having seen one, and his mastery of complicated astronomical texts, probably from Major Ellicott, whose family was Banneker's neighbor.

Jefferson's communication to Condorcet reflected a mellowing of attitude when compared with his earlier writings on black slaves. In his *Notes* he had expressed his hatred of the system of slavery in America despite the fact that as a plantation owner his livelihood depended on it. He wished to change the status of the black man from slave to tenant, but was never enabled to do so because of his own usually precarious financial status, except in occasional instances.

Having a great fear of a slave rebellion, he had refused to become part of the antislavery movement in the United States because he honestly believed that the involvement of a public figure would be detrimental to the movement. In France he had refused membership in an abolitionist group, the French Société des Amis des Noirs, for the same reasons.[70]

By sending the Banneker manuscript of astronomical calculations to Condorcet, it was clear that Jefferson wished to provide Banneker with the best possible exposure if he was deserving of it. He hoped to have the manuscript reviewed by one of the committees of France's leading scientific body, the Académie Royale des Sciences, of which Condorcet, one of France's foremost scholars, was perpetual secretary. If the committee rendered a favorable report, it would shed honor on the scientific work in the new nation.

From Condorcet Jefferson had recently received a report on the unit of measure adopted by the French. "Candor obliges me to confess that it is not what I would have approved," he responded.

> It is liable to the inexactitude of mensuration as to that part of the quadrant of the earth which is to be measured, that is to say as to one tenth of the quadrant, and as to the remaining nine tenths they are to be calculated on conjectural data, presuming the figure of the earth which has not yet been proved. It is liable too to the objection that no nation but your own can come at it; because yours is the only nation within which a meridian can be found of such extent crossing the 45th degree & terminating at both ends in a level. We may certainly say then that this measure is uncatholic, and I would rather have seen you depart from Catholicism in your religion than in your Philosophy.[71]

It is not known whether the Marquis ever received Jefferson's letter and the Banneker enclosure, which had been mailed in late August

1791. In the following month Condorcet was appointed secretary of the Legislative Assembly, and in the political turmoil that ensued, he was among the first to support a republic. It was he who drafted the memorandum that led to the suspension of King Louis XVI and summoned the national convention. These events occurred just at the time that Jefferson's letter and enclosure would have arrived. Condorcet then went into hiding for a time. Believing that he was being watched, he left his refuge, was arrested and imprisoned. The next morning he was found dead, and the question of whether his death was due to exhaustion or poison was never resolved.[72]

Banneker's astronomical calculations were published in an almanac for the year 1792 by the Baltimore printers, Goddard and Angell. It was the first of a series of almanacs bearing Banneker's name, which continued through the year 1797, and for which he provided the calculations. The almanacs were supported by the Pennsylvania and Maryland abolitionist societies, and were widely distributed in the United States and England. Banneker's letter to Jefferson and the latter's reply were published as part of Banneker's almanac for 1793 as well as in a separate pamphlet, both of which reached a wide audience.

The publication of the exchange of letters added fuel to an attack by Jefferson's political opponents, who lost no opportunity to point out the disparity between his position on the black man as he had expressed it in his *Notes* and his reply to Banneker. Among the first to comment was Congressman William Loughton Smith during Jefferson's candidacy for President. "What shall we think of a *secretary of state* thus fraternizing with negroes, writing them complimentary epistles, stiling them *his black brethren*, congratulating them on the evidence of their *genius*, and assuring them of his good wishes for their speedy emancipation." The attacks continued, invariably unjustly criticizing Jefferson's endorsement of Banneker's achievement as evidence of moral eminence, not as an example of intellectual activity.[73]

Years later the great French libertarian Henri Grégoire, Bishop of Blois, published a work on Negro literature based on previously published materials. He included biographical sketches of distinguished black individuals including Banneker, intended to prove their intellectual capability. To the poet Joel Barlow Jefferson described Gregoire's book and his correspondence with him in somewhat derogatory terms, pointing out that Grégoire had collected every possible story about men of color

> The whole do not amount in point of evidence, to what we know ourselves about Banneker. We know he had spherical trigonometry enough to make almanacs, but not without the suspicion of aid from [George] Ellicot, who was his neighbor and friend, and never missed an opportunity of puffing him. I have a long letter from Banneker, which shows him to have had a

mind of very common stature indeed. It was impossible for doubt to have been more tenderly or hesitatingly expressed than that was in the *Notes on Virginia*, and nothing was or is further from my intentions, than to enlist myself as the champion of a fixed opinion, where I have only expressed a doubt.

Jefferson's revised estimation of Banneker may have been due in part to Banneker's implied rebuke for maintaining black slaves in "inhuman captivity" while promising freedom in the words of the Declaration of Independence. It undoubtedly also reflected a strong reaction to the criticism his widely publicized letter to Banneker had engendered during his candidacy for the presidency.[74]

Jefferson as always spent his month's leave at Monticello and returned to Philadelphia two days before Congress convened. This time he took Maria with him so that he could enroll her in a school close by where he could visit her frequently. Thereafter, as he traveled between Philadelphia and Monticello several times a year, he always took his daughter with him.[75]

For the past several years he had been experiencing considerable financial difficulties because the season's crops at Monticello had proven to be less than anticipated, and his English creditor refused to accept his bonds for his Cumberland properties. He was unable to collect his rents from his Elkhill plantation, and he was finally forced to sell it. However, he ordered that his name be omitted as the owner, "which as long as I am in public I would wish to keep out of view in every thing of a private nature."[76]

From 1790 to 1793 he was constantly bedeviled with debts, some imposed upon him by others, and others of his own making. He was forced to sell a considerable number of his slaves in a sale which did not reach his expectations, and he realized barely enough to pay installments for only one of his outstanding accounts.

His plan to sell some of his land to French refugees seeking to settle in the region did not materialize, and he had to resort to selling more of his slaves instead. His family provided an additional burden, because they all relied on him for subsidy for one purpose or another. His sister and nephews in particular expected him to assume their debts, and even his friend, John Page, called upon him to endorse a note at a time when, as Jefferson explained to him, he would not be able to meet it if required.[77]

Characteristically, this financial crisis did not in any way limit his personal expenditures. He replenished his wine cellar with an order for five hundred bottles of the finest *vin rouge* of Bordeaux to be shipped from France. He did not hesitate to order a complete set of Piranesi's drawings of the Pantheon and a clock for fifteen guineas. He agreed to pay Petit's salary of $100 when he came to the United States plus room and board. He also commissioned a new coat and three pair of silk and satin breeches.

He planned major construction operations at Monticello in anticipation of his retirement in the near future, and he sent instructions to hire a number of workmen to initiate a major new building project and to order building materials for it. He planned to decorate the interior walls of the mansion with fresco paintings, and negotiated with a friend in New York to arrange for an artist to come to work at Monticello. When he learned that the artist would charge him two dollars a day, however, Jefferson reluctantly cancelled the project. His salary as Secretary of State was three thousand five hundred dollars a year, while his living expenses in Philadelphia, not including the costs of operating Monticello and his plantations, was five thousand two hundred and forty dollars.[78]

By this time Jefferson abandoned cultivation of tobacco on his farm in Albemarle. He had long been opposed to the growing of tobacco, and was aware that its culture in the state had declined considerably by the beginning of the Revolution and was being replaced by wheat.

"I suspect that the change in the temperature of our climate has become sensible to that plant, which to be good, requires an extraordinary degree of heat. But it requires still more indispensably an uncommon fertility of soil; and the price which it commands at market will not enable the planter to produce this by manure.

"Was the supply still to depend on Virginia and Maryland alone as its culture becomes more difficult, the price would rise so as to enable the planter to surmount those difficulties and to live. But the western country on the Mississippi, and the midlands of Georgia, having fresh and fertile lands in abundance, and a hotter sun, will be able to undersell these two States and will oblige them to abandon the raising of tobacco altogether." Jefferson proposed that the growing of wheat was far more desirable because "its herbage preserved the soil's fertility at the same time that the grain provided plentiful food for men and beast in exchange for modest toil."[79]

To Samuel Biddle, whom he hoped to employ as an overseer, Jefferson described the farm at Monticello. At that time it consisted of from five to six hundred acres of cleared hilly land which although originally rich, had been depleted by the cultivation of maize and tobacco. There were from twelve to fifteen laborers to work on the farm who were well clothed and well fed. Having abandoned tobacco growing, Jefferson now wished to banish the cultivation of Indian corn as well. Some years later he returned periodically to the cultivation of tobacco, but only when the price of tobacco escalated.[80]

Early in 1792 Jefferson was appointed a member of the Board of Visitors of the Peale Museum, and at the meeting in February he was elected president of the Board. The Museum was an enterprise in which he maintained considerable interest. It had been established in 1784 by his friend, the notable naturalist and portrait painter, Charles Willson Peale, first as a gallery for his historical portraits, to which he later added displays of natural and artificial curiosities.[81]

At this time also, the same three vice presidents of the American Philosophical Society were re-elected, with Jefferson in first place. He was particularly honored when the following spring Dr. Benjamin Smith Barton read a paper on "A Botanical Description of the *Podophyllum dyphyllum*, now called *Jeffersonia Virginica*," changing the name of a plant genus in his honor. It was later re-named the species *Jeffersonia diphylla*, a name which remains current.[82] (*Figure 19*)

The year was fraught with many problems resulting from the impending war between England and France. Jefferson submitted his report to the Senate on negotiations with Spain, in which he nominated William Short and William Carmichael commissioners. Hamilton's policies came into more vigorous attack and his association with the British Ambassador George Hammond in particular were under scrutiny. Meanwhile Jefferson was yearning to return to his home and hearth and family. As he wrote to Martha, having no particular subject to write about, he had been reflecting on his love for her and their past wanderings together.

"These reveries alleviate the toils and inquietudes of my present situation," he wrote, "and leave me always impressed with the desire of being at home once more, and of exchanging labour, envy, and malice for ease, domestic occupation, and domestic love and society, where I may once more be happy with you, with Mr. Randolph, and dear little Anne, with whom even Socrates might ride on a stick without being ridiculous." Thus Jefferson contemplated how even the most eminent of philosophers would be willing to put aside the problems of the world to relax in domestic tranquility playing "horsy" on a child's hobby horse.[83]

During this busy period, Jefferson was approached by Joseph Gaston Chambers concerning his invention of a repeating weapon. A Pennsylvania farmer, teacher, and language reformer as well as inventor, Chambers had experimented with several military inventions while a student at New Jersey College. Among them were "a Vessel in the nature of a Row Galley which should be sufficient to combat and destroy a whole

Fleet," a form of scuba underwater gear to enable divers to attach explosives to the hulls of enemy vessels undetected (gear which failed for lack of a means of pressurizing the air supply), a new phonetic alphabet and a set of new rules of spelling.

In 1792 Chambers had begun work on a new invention, a repeating firearm. It consisted of an arrangement by means of which ten or more charges and bullets could be placed one on top of another so that the weapon would fire at intervals of from one to eight seconds, each discharge setting off the next charge in turn. In bringing it to Jefferson's attention, he explained, "I feel myself highly interested for the Friends of Liberty and the Rights of men in Europe and throughtout the world," and asked how he could bring his invention secretly to France or rather to Poland. He was willing to take it to Europe himself, but felt it would be advantageous if he had the support of highly placed individuals at home. Months passed with no reply from Jefferson, and Chambers wrote again asking for assistance. After communicating with Congressman J. W. Kittera of Pennsylvania to inquire about Chambers, Jefferson's response to the inventor was non-committal.[84]

Turning then to General Washington and Henry Knox, Chambers eventually aroused sufficient interest so that in a visit to Philadelphia he was given several muskets, shot and powder from government stores to make a demonstration. In a second test he fired his "gun of seven shots" for Jefferson "at his seat near Schuylkill in the spring of '93." However, Chambers failed to obtain a government contract at that time, and during the next few years devoted himself to teaching and farming.

In 1801 he wrote to congratulate Jefferson on his Presidency, and in 1807 when he learned that Robert Fulton was developing a submarine, he sent Jefferson a report on his own early experiments with diving equipment. With the advent of the War of 1812, Chambers resumed his experiments with firearms and in 1813 obtained a patent for his repeating weapon, which utilized multiple touchholes and a movable lock. It was manufactured by Philadelphia arms makers for a contract with the United States Navy, and later for another with the state of Pennsylvania.[85]

Before leaving Philadelphia, Jefferson learned of the availability of a Universal Equatorial Instrument, which he was determined to acquire. Despite his financially straitened circumstances, he negotiated for its purchase. It belonged to John William Gerard De Brahm, formerly of Philadelphia but now living in Bristol. De Brahm, a Dutch military engineer and a surveyor of the province of Georgia, also founded a colony there. He was one of the surveyors appointed to survey the boundary between New Jersey and Delaware. In 1765 he undertook the survey of the coastline from St. Augustine to the Cape of Florida.

The instrument was made by Jesse Ramsden of London, and was the most important item of De Brahm's professional equipment. Being in dire need of money, he decided to sell it in the hope that it would realize a better price than any of his other possessions. He left the instrument with Rittenhouse to be sold, where it came to Jefferson's attention.[86] (*Figure 20*)

In a letter from Monticello, Jefferson informed Rittenhouse that at the time of his departure from Philadelphia he had not mentioned the instrument because after he had paid his bills he was left with scarcely enough money for his return home. However he enclosed a note from Leiper for $238.58 which he had just received, and asked Rittenhouse to hold and use it only if another purchaser for the instrument appeared. If no other offer was made for the instrument, he preferred to wait until his return at the end of September to purchase it.

"I am here indulging in reverie & rural occupations," he added, "scarcely permitting anything to occupy my mind seriously. When I count the days I have still to remain here, I wish I could see at their end only the pleasure of meeting you again, & keep behind the curtain the table piled with papers, & the eternal sound of the door bell." According to an entry in his account books, Jefferson paid less than the asking price for the instrument, giving Rittenhouse an order on his bank account for $102.67. To an unknown correspondent in 1821, Jefferson mentioned that his Equatorial Instrument cost "thirty-five guineas in Ramsden's shop a little before the Revolution."[87]

The instrument was based on the principle of the helioscope designed by Christoph Scheiner in the seventeenth century. A century later, James Short utilized the principle for developing a mounting in the form of a fork equatorial for some of his larger telescope tubes, and in about 1749 he produced a "universal" portable equatorial mount for smaller telescopes, which had little success. During the 1770's Jesse Ramsden turned his attention to the equatorial mount, and for the first time added circles and counterpoises of correct sizes and weights. By 1773 he had completed at least four examples of his improved instrument. It was made portable with an elaborate mounting which could be set by clockwork to follow the course of an observed celestial body across the sky and thus provide a continuous record. Ramsden's "Universal Equatorial Instrument," as it was called, was unquestionably the most sophisticated astronomical instrument in the United States, and the one acquired by Jefferson is believed to be the only example in the country at that time.[88]

After having experimented with his universal equatorial instrument, not surprisingly, Jefferson devised a means of improving it, by the addition of a 12-inch telescope. This he ordered from the London instrument maker, William Jones, together with apparatus required for mounting it on his instrument, enclosing sketches showing the manner in which it was to be attached.[89]

Jefferson meanwhile found himself the focus of a growing conflict between the Federalists and the Republicans for the control of the government, a struggle which became particularly active in individual states. Although the Congressional elections in 1792 returned a majority of Republican Congressmen to the House, the Senate nevertheless remained a Federalist stronghold. It was a presidential election year as well, and although there was no doubt that Washington would be re-elected, there was considerable question about the selection of the Vice President.

Jefferson was determined to retire from public office at the end of the term, however, and planned to have no part in the coming elections. He had already sold his excess furniture in anticipation of his return to Monticello. He had also found a new tenant for the house in Philadelphia and had begun packing.[90]

Meanwhile, on the last day of the year 1792, the famous French aeronaut, Jean Pierre Blanchard, had arrived in Philadelphia and planned to make a balloon ascension within the next few days. He had already made his famous balloon voyage across the English Channel with Dr. John Jeffries of Boston in 1785. Jefferson looked forward with great interest to the event.[91]

CHAPTER IX

THE VEILING
OF
DIPLOMACY
(1792–1793)

*I am for encouraging the progress of science in all its branches,
and not for raising a hue and cry against the sacred name of
philosophy; for aweing the human mind by stories of raw head and
bloody bones to a distrust of its own vision, and to repose implicitly on
that of others; to go backward instead of forward to look for
improvement; to believe that government, religion, morality and every
other science were in the highest perfection in the ages of darkest
ignorance, and that nothing can ever be devised more perfect than
what was established by our forefathers.*

Letter from Thomas Jefferson
to Elbridge Gerry, 1799.

While in France, Jefferson had become intrigued with the future commercial and military potential of the balloon, and continued to follow
the developments of ballooning with avid interest. He was delighted
to have an opportunity to witness the first ascent to be made in the
United States by the intrepid French aeronaut, Jean-Pierre Blanchard
on January 9, 1793. It was a cold day as Jefferson and his daughter
Maria turned out with thousands of others in Philadelphia to observe
the aeronaut. Wearing a cocked hat decorated with white feathers,
and boldly waving both the French and American flags, Blanchard
confidently entered the blue-spangled boat under the balloon of varnished yellow silk.

Against the noisy background of band music and thundering cannon, the huge crowd cheered wildly as the balloon rose from the yard

of the Walnut Street jail at Sixth Street, and bore aloft its solitary passenger. Blanchard remained in the air forty-six minutes and traveled only about fifteen miles, descending in Deptford, New Jersey, but it was an impressive event.

To Martha, Jefferson reported after the event, "The security of the thing appeared so great, that everyone is wishing for a balloon to travel in. I wish for one sincerely, as instead of ten days I should be within five hours of home."[1]

This was a time when Jefferson was torn between official responsibilities and personal endeavors. By now most of the stone required for the foundations of his remodeled mansion at Monticello had been brought up the mountain, and construction was ready to proceed. Although anxious to be at Monticello to supervise the work, he reluctantly responded to President Washington's urging and agreed to continue in office for the time being.[2]

Once again the same panel of officers of the American Philosophical Society was elected. In the previous year Jefferson had proposed that an expedition be undertaken under the Society's auspices, led by a competent individual, to explore the northwestern territory by ascending the Missouri River and crossing the mountains and then descending to the Pacific Ocean. This was the project which Jefferson had hoped that Ledyard would be able to accomplish.

Young Army Captain Meriwether Lewis had applied for the position of leader of such an expedition, but when the French botanist, André Michaux, proposed to the Society a similar expedition westward to the Pacific to Sitka later in the same year, the latter was chosen instead.[3]

Jefferson made use of his membership to help promote the project, in which he was greatly interested. In the next few months he undertook a subscription to finance the expedition, and prepared detailed requirements that the expedition was to achieve. He mapped out the route as a "literary enterprise" and formulated specific instructions for the botanist. He also suggested the possibility that Michaux could travel with a delegation of Indians returning westward. His priority was to be to find the shortest and most convenient route of communication to the Pacific within the temperate latitudes. He was to cross the Mississippi and proceed by land to the nearest part of the Missouri River above the Spanish territory. (*Document 6*)

Jefferson asked Michaux to note and record the country through which he passed, its soil, mountains, rivers, any new flora and fauna and mineral productions, and the latitudes of places. He was to note also the names, numbers and dwellings of inhabitants, their history, language, manners, arts, commerce, and state of society. "Under the head of Animal history, that of the Mammoth is particularly recommended to your enquiries, as it is also to learn whether the Lama, or Paca of Peru is found in those parts of the continent, or how far North they come."[4]

Although Michaux appeared to have had the best intentions to adhere to the Society's instructions, the undertaking changed in nature with the arrival of the French diplomat, Edmond Charles Genêt, as minister of France. Genêt sought to use the project to serve his own intrigues. Michaux was no longer to attempt to reach the Pacific, but to serve as a filibustering agent into Spanish territory in an attempt to free Louisiana and the Mississippi region from Spanish occupation.

The intrigue was discovered before it had actually begun, however, and Michaux returned to Philadelphia by December. Despite his political charge, botany had nonetheless remained his major concern during the five or six months of his journey. The aborting of the expedition was a great disappointment to Jefferson, but the ultimate aim continued to command his attention as he awaited future opportunities.[5]

During his appointment as Secretary of State, Jefferson became increasingly concerned with the apparent lack of security of communications intended to be secret between his office and government representatives overseas. The war between England and France threatened again and again to bring the United States into the fray, and there were other serious diplomatic problems as well.

He had begun negotiations with the Spanish government relating to his concerns with the navigation of the Mississippi River, which required delicate diplomacy. He began to review cryptographic methods which would provide greater security, and it was almost certainly during this period that he invented the wheel cipher.[6]

By the time of the American war for independence, the importance of cryptography for military and diplomatic uses had led to the maintenance of deciphering offices by most of the European nations, with England and France having the best facilities and the greatest degree of expertise. Their cryptographic offices prepared and tested military and diplomatic cryptographic systems not only for their own country's needs, but they also trained and employed cryptanalysts to decipher intercepted communications to and from representatives of other countries. British military figures in North America were customarily equipped with three types of cryptographic systems of varying security. Sympathetic or "secret" inks were also used, although ciphers were preferred because inks required extreme care of handling.

The colonial Americans were admittedly novices in the art of secret communication, and relied heavily upon the use of secret inks. General Washington's secret agents used an ink devised by Sir James Jay and conveyed to Washington by Jay's brother, John. Sir James was a physician sufficiently familiar with chemistry to devise a new type of sympathetic ink after some experimentation.[7]

The most competent of the colonial American cryptographers during the Revolution was a former grammar school teacher from Boston named James Lovell. Considering the state of the art, he was well versed on the subject and became the cryptographic expert of the Continental Congress. He managed to decipher nearly all of the intercepted British code messages, and he created a code for the use of the Continental Army. He solved communications of Lord Cornwallis enciphered in a monoalphabetic method which proved to be the same system used by all British commanders.[8]

Lovell introduced a cipher utilizing a keyword and constructed columns of alphabets beginning with the letters of a keyword numbered from 1 to 27. This was first utilized in 1781 while he was serving as a member of the Committee of Foreign Affairs in his letters to John and Abigail Adams and to others, including General Gates. When Robert Livingston became minister of foreign affairs he used the same method for his correspondence with Adams. Jefferson also employed it in earlier correspondence with William Short. Others who used the method on Lovell's recommendation included James Madison and Edmund Randolph.

Problems arose when Randolph proved unable to decipher messages he received, and it was not until modern times that some of the messages were read. The difficulty was due partly to the number of errors made by Madison in enciphering his messages. Later a code utilizing miscellaneous words and syllables was adopted and used in correspondence among several members of the Continental Congress.

Eventually, after he became minister of foreign affairs, Robert Livingston had printed code forms produced. Printed on both sides of the paper, the forms had on one side letter groups from 1 through 1700, with blanks for random addition of appropriate words and syllables. On the other side were the words and syllables listed alphabetically. Individual correspondents could compile their own arrangements with each of their correspondents. This was the first official American cipher code.

It was used in a variant form by Jefferson and Madison from the spring of 1785 until about 1793. Another variant was used by James Monroe while he was minister to England in 1805, and yet another by James A. Bayard while negotiating a treaty with England after the War of 1812.[9]

Prior to adopting the Livingston cipher code table, Jefferson used a variety of methods. In early 1783 he employed an English-French lexicon as a codebook for correspondence with James Madison, and from April 1783 to May 1785 Jefferson and Madison used a numerical key cipher of which the key has never been found. From May 1784 to March 1785 Jefferson and Monroe also used three different ciphers, examples of which have survived in Jefferson's papers.

In May 1784 Monroe sent a cipher proposal to Jefferson which he used for a period and which was subsequently replaced by two other ciphers prior to early 1785. It presented difficulties, however, and Jefferson found it impossible to decipher Monroe's letter of November 1, 1784. Several months later, in March 1785, he provided Monroe with an explanation and correction of the system.[10]

In 1784 Beverly Randolph sent Monroe a scheme for a cipher and in March 1785 he proposed that they use another which would render their communication more flexible. In 1801 Monroe received a letter from an unidentified correspondent composed of words and figures. In 1803 he was provided with a copy of a method used by the minister for the Louisiana treaty.

It was not a simple matter for these central figures in American diplomacy to keep in order the numerous systems they employed with various correspondents. Jefferson prepared a new and more extensive code on the printed form devised by Livingston for corresponding with Monroe and Madison.[11]

William Carmichael, the American head of mission in Spain, was the first to suggest the adoption of a standard American cryptographic system for diplomatic use, and proposed it to Jefferson in June 1785. "It has long been my surprise," he wrote, "that Congress hath not instructed those they employ abroad on this head. For this purpose a common cypher should be sent to each of their Ministers and Chargé Des Affaires." His concern and that of other American diplomatic personnel, however, brought no action until later.[12]

Despite the wide range of his scholarly interests, cryptography had not been a subject which is known to have preoccupied Jefferson to any degree before the advent of the war for independence, when he first had need for concealing certain communications. He did not own any of the few published works on the subject in his library, and during the war and the period that immediately followed, he relied primarily on hand conveyance of confidential correspondence and not on the security derived from cryptographic means. The methods then known were at best insecure and tiresome in execution, and consequently Jefferson reduced the enciphered portions of his correspondence to a minimum.

Now, however, in his position as Secretary of State, the increasing need for security in diplomatic communication became one of Jefferson's priorities. A new method was urgently needed that was relatively simple to use and at the same time provided the utmost security for multiple correspondents. Although undocumented, it was undoubtedly during the period between 1792 and 1793 that Jefferson characteristically decided to take action and set his mind to the problem, and developed his invention of the wheel cipher.

Jefferson devised a method that could be used simultaneously by many correspondents without reducing the security of the system because it was based on individually assigned keywords. His device proved to be incredibly ingenious. He may have begun by experimenting with a number of alphabets written on separate slips of paper and arranged and rearranged in various ways. The letters in the alphabets on each of the strips were randomly mixed with no two of them having the same order. Based on the number of letters in the alphabet, he had twenty-six of these separate alphabets. The individual slips could be arranged in any order up to twenty-six variations.

Each slip was numbered from 1 to 26 near its center, and was assembled according to the letters of a pre-arranged numerical key, which was generally based on the numerical value of the letters contained in a phrase agreed upon by the two correspondents. The pre-arranged key could be changed periodically by mutual agreement of the correspondents. It was possible to select any one of the twenty-six letters to represent each letter of the message.

The system could be operated with relative ease by printing the alphabets on thin wooden strips that could be moved back and forth within a frame. A similar multiple random-mixed alphabet cipher system had been devised in 1586 by the French cryptographer, Blaise de Vigénère. It is almost a certainty, however, that Jefferson was unaware of Vigénère's system. [13]

Assuming that Jefferson may have mounted the individual alphabets on strips of stiff paper and that he used a rule to line up the letters of the message to be conveyed, he undoubtedly realized that it remained too cumbersome for use in the field. Even with the best organized arrangement, the strips required considerable care and attention in use because they could become separated or lost. Once convinced of the validity and security of the system, Jefferson then reviewed various means available for organizing its components.

The solution was readily at hand on his office desk, in the form of the small locks used to secure the leather-covered dispatch boxes in which diplomatic communications of state were commonly conveyed in Europe and the United States. These iron and brass padlocks, called "letter locks" or "word locks," were the precursors of the modern combination lock, and their history can be traced to at least the fifteenth century and possibly earlier.

Such a lock consisted of four or more brass disks fitted on a central spindle, each inscribed on their circumference with a series of letters randomly selected. They were operated by means of a keyword containing as many letters as there were disks, each letter of the keyword appearing on one of the disks. These had to be aligned in order to open the lock.[14]

In addition to the small padlocks which Jefferson saw almost daily on the dispatch boxes on his desk, he was undoubtedly familiar with the description and illustration of such locks in the *Encyclopédie ancienne* and *L'Encyclopédie méthodique*, both of which he owned in his library. It was probably several examples of these word locks that he purchased in 1784, after having read in the Paris press about the such locks made by LaFontaine and described as "secret locks".[15]

After further experimentation, Jefferson conceived the idea of pasting the strips on cylinders segmented into 26 disks. He had a model, or more probably two identical models, turned in wood. At first the letters may have been inscribed along their peripheries in ink. In two surviving manuscript descriptions of the wheel cipher in Jefferson's hand, one a draft and the other a finished copy, he specified exactly how the models were to be made and of what materials, although he did not specify how the letters were to be inscribed.

After making certain that the arrangement was operable, he probably had the letters impressed along the edges of the disks with steel letter punches. The most permanently secure results would have been achieved with the last-named procedure, and Jefferson would have sought the best means available.[16]

Consequently, it is not surprising to find recorded in his *Memorandum Book* that on April 21, 1792 he had "p[ai]d Frederick Gayer for a set of punches by order on b[an]k US 23.20." These were either steel punches of the type used by type founders to punch brass matrices, or more likely, letter punches used by bookbinders for lettering titles. Gayer was an unemployed type founder residing in Philadelphia with whom Jefferson continued to correspond during the next several years.[17]

Did Jefferson purchase the punches for use at Monticello to mark his tools, for example, or were they acquired specifically for producing the wheel cipher models? The answer may be that they were intended for both. Realizing the need for punches to inscribe the wheel cipher, which he undoubtedly intended to undertake personally to preserve its security if indeed it would prove to be useful for diplomatic correspondence, he purchased the punches with the intention that they would be added to his tool chest.[18]

Although the lack of documentation or correspondence relating to the wheel cipher makes the dating of the invention difficult, the absence of such documentation may be a clue in itself. Produced while he was serving as Secretary of State in Philadelphia, and intended for secret diplomatic correspondence, Jefferson would have avoided putting into writing any more than was absolutely necessary.

The production of the cylinders required considerable skill. After each cylinder had been turned, a hole was drilled through its center to accommodate an iron spindle. It was finished with a boss at one end and terminated in a threaded projection at the other to receive a nut to keep the disks tightly in place. The cylinder would then have been segmented by means of a veneer saw to assure close alignment of the disks when assembled. Furthermore, the disks had to be slightly dished to enable them to fit closely together. (*Figures 21* and *22*)

It is not impossible that Jefferson would have undertaken this work himself, for he owned an elaborate collection of hand tools, and enjoyed using them for small projects. In this way, knowledge of the device by others would be limited to a minimum. However, if he did not have time to do the work himself, or if it was undertaken when he was away from Monticello, he undoubtedly sought a skilled craftsman in the city. Among those he may have employed was his kinsman, Benjamin Randolph, who had produced the lap desk for him in 1776. He would have taken the project to the craftsman's shop and discussed it with him in person, and would have called again for the finished work.[19]

To test the device, Jefferson would have kept one of the models and provided the other to a trusted associate having some knowledge of or competence with cryptography. That correspondent was most likely Robert Patterson, professor of mathematics at the University of Pennsylvania, for it is a matter of record that Jefferson consulted him on cryptographic systems some years later. Jefferson valued Patterson's knowledge, and would have accepted his recommendations and evaluations without further question.

No correspondence concerning the wheel cipher between Jefferson and Patterson survives, and it is entirely likely that none existed; Jefferson would have discussed it with him in person. There is no evidence that the wheel cipher was put into use, nor is there any indication that it was not.

The only reference to it made by Jefferson occurred in a letter to Patterson written a decade later, on March 22, 1802, relating to a new cipher system which Patterson had devised and submitted for President Jefferson's consideration. "I have thoroughly considered your cypher," Jefferson wrote, "and find it much more convenient in practice than my wheel cypher, that I am proposing it to the secretary of state for use in his office."[20]

In selecting Patterson's cipher system over his own, Jefferson was deferring to what he believed to be Patterson's superior knowledge in all things mathematical, and he probably did not test the system thoroughly. It was a columnar transposition system incorporating nulls at the beginning of each column, and had not nearly the security of the wheel cipher. It had the advantage, however, that written instructions for using the system without the need of devices such as the cylinders could be sent by safe courier to the correspondents.[21]

Jefferson suggested several modifications which Patterson approved and then added another of his own, to utilize keywords instead of a series of digits as the key. When Jefferson prepared the cipher for submission to Secretary of State Madison for use by his office, he encountered a further difficulty. He advised Patterson, "it often happens that we wish only a cypher 2 or 3 lines, or only one line, or half a line, or a single word. It does not answer for this. Can you remedy it?"[22]

Patterson promptly responded with a solution, explaining how each letter of a short message should be considered as a column or a vertical line, and with supplementary letters prefixed and adjoined, then transcribed into a horizontal line. He also suggested a simpler variation. Jefferson found the improvements acceptable, and sent by hand of his trusted friend, Du Pont de Nemours, a confidential communication to Robert Livingston, American minister to France.

He enclosed an explanation of the Patterson cipher explaining that it was to be used for private communications not intended for file in the State Department. The cipher keys he chose consisted of Livingston's name and his own and the names of their homes, which could be remembered and required no written form.[23]

Among Jefferson's papers are to be found a number of descriptions of codes and ciphers, including a cipher table devised by Hugh Williamson, former Congressman from North Carolina who later attained recognition for his scientific endeavors, which has some similarities to the arrangement of the wheel cipher.[24]

The possibility exists that Jefferson developed the wheel cipher over a period of time, and that he may have worked on it again and again from its first concept to final refinement, for it appears in his notes as a sophisticated instrument requiring no further modification.

One of the two descriptions which have survived, both of which are in Jefferson's own handwriting, is entitled "The wheel cypher" and consists of two closely written small sheets of instructions for its construction. The second is entitled "Project of a cypher," and written on one and one-half sheets, and the writing is blurred and dim. The paper on which the descriptions of the wheel cipher were written provides no clues, for it does not bear watermarks which might be useful in establishing the date the paper was made. Believed to have also survived is a drawing of the wheel cipher, but it has not been found among the Jefferson papers.[25] (*Document 7*)

Historian Julian P. Boyd conjectured that it was in about July 1790 that Jefferson might have attempted to resolve the problem of providing secure diplomatic communication because it was at this moment that war with Spain and England seemed inevitable. Jefferson persuaded President Washington to send David Humphreys on a secret mission to Madrid, a mission that was probably the best kept secret of Washington's first administration, for it was known only to James Madison, John Brown, Alexander Hamilton, Washington and Jefferson.[26]

This was the beginning of a period of extreme bitterness of partisan politics when the mails were not to be trusted. Knowing that Humphreys would have to work closely with Carmichael in Madrid, and aware of the insecurity of existing cryptographic systems, Jefferson realized that a new cipher was urgently required. He had just completed his elaborate study for a universal system of standard weights and measures based on decimal notation, which would easily have led him to consideration of mathematical principles for cryptographic communication.

He could not have used the wheel cipher at the time even if he had perfected it, however, because of the urgency of Humphrey's departure and the hurried preparation of documents to accompany him. Consequently Humphreys was equipped with a conventional cipher system similar to one he had already been using.[27]

As well as can be determined, Jefferson put the wheel cipher aside after having tested it with Patterson, and never returned to it, for no mention appears in his surviving later papers. His apparent loss of interest in the device constitutes somewhat of a mystery, for he was not one to abandon anything which appeared to be practical, despite any lack of enthusiasm from Patterson. However, the pressures of his office in this period may have prevented him from dealing with matters other than those of the highest priority.

Fortunately the usefulness of Jefferson's invention was not lost to posterity. It was re-invented twice again, the first time after almost a century had passed. It was independently invented in about 1890 by Commandant Étienne Bazeries, the chief of the cryptographic bureau of the French Ministry of Foreign Affairs. In an effort to replace the official French ciphers as part of his work, he devised two new polyalphabetic ciphers employing twenty random-mixed alphabets and incorporated them in a mechanical device he described as a "cylindrical cryptograph." It was identical in form to Jefferson's wheel cipher except for the number of alphabets used. He subsequently published a description with an illustration of his device in a slim volume which appeared in 1901.[28]

Although each might have been developed independently of the other, the similarities between the wheel cipher and the cylindrical cryptograph are too great to be ignored. It is remotely possible that after he abandoned use of his wheel cipher for government use, if indeed it was actually put into service, Jefferson may have described it to one of his friends in France, and that Bazeries found a record of it. If so, there is no evidence.

Credit for having re-invented the wheel cipher for the second time is given to Captain Parker Hitt of the United States Infantry. In a proposal of December 19, 1914 addressed to the director of the Army Service Schools, Hitt explained "this device is based, to a certain extent, on the ideas of Commandant Bazeries of the French Army," and he did not at that time claim the invention to be totally his own. He had in fact converted the mixed alphabets of the Bazeries cryptograph into strip form, rendering them on twenty-five long strips of paper, inscribing each alphabet twice continuously. After numbering the strips, he arranged them by means of a pre-arranged numerical key in a holder made for the purpose.[29]

Hitt subsequently rendered the strip alphabets on disks turned from apple wood which combined to form a cylinder similar to the one used by Jefferson. The proposal was forwarded to Joseph O. Mauborgne, then assistant commandant of the Army Signal School at Leavenworth, at some time between September 1916 and August 1917.[30]

Mauborgne later reported that the messages enciphered with the method were too readily deciphered because the letters had not been sufficiently mixed or scrambled. According to his own account, in early 1917 he converted Hitt's strips into a cylinder consisting of twenty-five separate disks each inscribed with the twenty-six letters of the alphabet randomly mixed, so arranged that the fewest possible number of repetitions of pairs of letters would occur.

He accomplished this by preparing a table of pairs of letters and marking out those pairs that appeared until all possible pairs had been used. When this laborious task was completed, he discovered that he must use three letter pairs twice—DE YA UB—so that the first name he assigned to the device was the combination of these pairs, or the "DEYAUB Cipher."

In arranging the mixture of letters on the disks, Mauborgne used the phrase "ARMY OF THE U. S." on the R disk, in which the letter R followed the letter A. He then had two models of the disk constructed for him by M. S. E. Dusenbury in the Army Signal School shop in Kansas in 1917. Dusenbury made one of the disks of red fiber and the second of hard rubber, each having the same diameter as the rubber patten of Mauborgne's typewriter, so that the paper strips of alphabets would exactly join and register when pasted on the perimeter of the disks.

The cylinder and disks were turned on a precision lathe, and the exact spacing of the 26 holes in each, "in one of which in each disk was placed a tiny pin which went only half way into the disc and projected so as to engage in any disc placed next to it. Alignment of all letters followed," wrote Mauborgne.[31]

When Mauborgne was transferred to Washington, he brought one of the models with him and had a series of test messages set up which were sent out for testing to other cryptographers in government service. No one was able to decipher the messages. Mauborgne accordingly proposed the device for use, and had it accepted in 1918. It was not until three years later that the wheels of bureaucracy succeeded in issuing specifications for manufacture of the device, which was officially named "Cipher Device, M-94" of the U. S. Army Signal Corps. The bid was awarded to the Doler Die Casting Company to produce it in aluminum alloy.[32]

Ironically, in 1922, the same year that Cipher Device, M-94 was put into service, Jefferson's notes for the construction of his wheel cipher were discovered for the first time among his papers in The Library of Congress. The discovery was made by Edmund C. Burnett, a historian engaged in editing the journals of the Continental Congress.

The editing project required decipherment of some still unsolved cryptographic communications between members of the Congress, necessitating consultation with the correspondents's original papers. In the course of this work Burnett frequently communicated for technical advice with Professor John M. Manly of the University of Chicago, who had served as a cryptanalyst in the Military Intelligence Division during World War I.

Burnett later was able to provide Manly with more information. He listed the exchange of correspondence between Jefferson and Patterson relating to the latter's cryptographic method, two closely written sheets of description of the Jeffersonian "wheel cypher," and one and one half pages of a handwritten description of the "project for a cypher," in a very blurred and dim press copy. He added, "Besides the description of the wheel cipher, found in the group of material in vol. 232 [of the Jefferson Papers], there is elsewhere the figure of the cipher wheel; but I do not find a memorandum of its location."[33] (*Document 7*)

Burnett subsequently provided Manly with photostatic copies of the material, and he in turned sent a description of Jefferson's wheel cipher to the foremost cryptanalyst in the United States, Col. William F. Friedman, then Chief Signal Officer of the U. S. Army Signal Corps. Friedman in turn provided Manly with a photostatic copy of the "wheel Cypher," after a personal visit to the Library of Congress to arrange to have the copy made. "I have not yet recovered from my astonishment," he added, "at your discovery of Thomas' perspicacity."[34]

The military community was astounded by the discovery in the Jefferson papers, that among his many other achievements Jefferson more than a century earlier had the ingenuity to invent the cryptographic device which the Army's trained cryptographers had finally developed, and that a description of it had been available in public papers. No effort was made to withdraw Cipher Device, M-94, and it had a long career in service. The Signal Corps relied on the testing which had been undertaken by several agencies, including the Riverbank Research Laboratory, to establish its security and convenience. The 1919 annual report of the Chief Signal Officer noted "they tried to break this cipher but to date have been unsuccessful, notwithstanding the fact they were given 25 messages in the same key."[35]

Cipher Device, M-94 remained in use for official U. S. military communication at least two decades after its adoption. It was declared obsolete in 1943 but was used by tactical units in the Far East in World War II, and continued in use for training purposes thereafter.[36]

Although Jefferson had informed President Washington long ago of his intentions to retire, he found it important not to leave an impression that he was retiring under fire, so he reluctantly returned to work. It was a critical time in world affairs. The war which had been threatening in Europe became reality with the declaration of war between England and France in February 1793, a war that threatened to involve the United States. In the meantime the country was undergoing a financial panic, and Jefferson viewed the war overseas as a means of increasing foreign trade and partial recovery of the economy.

President Washington attempted to heal the schism between Jefferson and Hamilton, but it continued to widen as Jefferson and Hamilton disagreed over the terms of the Proclamation of Neutrality after the outbreak of war overseas. Jefferson particularly disapproved of Hamilton's views of the powers of the executive and legislative branches of government, and Hamilton continued his campaign of vilification of Jefferson in the press, questioning his patriotism. Jefferson and his supporters counter-attacked by accusing Hamilton of dereliction of office. He nimbly defeated the charge and managed to vindicate himself. Jefferson then undertook a program to weld the Republicans into a tighter body by attempting to reduce the power of the Secretary of the Treasury.[37]

As the yellow fever epidemic in Philadelphia increased, the fear of contagion affected the government as well as the community. Although Jefferson lived in the suburbs, he was nonetheless forced to spend his days in the city. Hamilton became seriously ill, Knox fled, and only his pride forced Jefferson to remain, although he moved his office to the house he rented from Moses Cox in Germantown on the Schuylkill.[38]

General Washington had departed from the city in early September, just at the time that there was a heavy incidence of mortality. A week later Jefferson also found it necessary to leave, and due to his worsening financial circumstances, he had to borrow one hundred dollars from the Bank of the United States in order to return to Monticello. He arranged to have his furniture and books shipped home since he planned to retire from office at the end of the month.[39]

Always seeking new ways to promote the sciences among the people, Jefferson contemplated the value to the public of a more useful almanac. He had a comprehensive knowledge of the almanacs produced in his time, and had strong convictions concerning their content and purpose. "I have often wished," he commented to Ellicott, surveyor of the Federal Territory, "we could have published in America an Almanac, which without going beyond the purchase of the people in general, might answer some of the purposes of those a little above them in information. The declination and right ascension of the Sun, the equation of time, places of those of the remarkable stars which are above our horizon in the night, and some other useless articles, without increasing the bulk or price of the almanac. I know no body but yourself from whom we could hope such a thing. What say you to it?"[40]

It was during his last year as Secretary of State that Jefferson contracted for the construction of what he called "the Great Clock" to be installed over the doorway of the Entrance Hall at Monticello, where it survives to the present time. He conceived a timepiece which would serve the entire household and the farm as well, and designed it to be equipped with a great bell to be installed on the roof which could be heard throughout the grounds.

For many years there was speculation about the identity of the maker of the clock, and it was generally attributed to the Swiss watchmaker, Louis Leschot, who had emigrated to Charlottesville with Jefferson's patronage. The fact that Leschot and his wife are the only nonfamily members buried in the Jefferson graveyard appeared to confirm his employment on the estate. However, documentary evidence revealed that the clock already existed before Leschot's arrival in the United States.[41]

The Great Clock was designed by Jefferson and made to his own requirements in 1793. Jefferson had ordered it from the well-known clockmaker of his acquaintance, Robert Leslie of the Philadelphia clockmaking firm of Leslie & Price. He provided specifications and measurements of all details, noting that the movement was also to "turn an hour hand on the reverse face of the wall on a wooden hour plate of 12. I[nches] radius. There need be no minute hand, as the hour figures will be 6. I[nches] apart, but the interspace should be divided into quarters and 5 minute marks." (*Document 8*)

In other words, it was to be a two-faced clock, with one face in the Entrance Hall, and the other under the East Portico outside the building. His order to Leslie included also a second, smaller, clock.[42]

When he received Jefferson's order, Leslie was on the verge of moving to London with his family. Accordingly, he assigned the work to Peter Spurck, a journeyman clockmaker in his employ. Soon thereafter, in 1794, Spurck established his own shop at 2 North Front Street. Several months after his arrival in London, Leslie inquired from Jefferson about the clock. "I am very anxious to learn how your great Clock goes, and also your timepiece, if either or boath do not gone right, if you will be so obliging as to let me know I will send you others from this place, as I can have them mad[e] much better here."

Later in the same year Jefferson responded to several of Leslie's letters. "My great clock could not be made to go by Spruck [sic]. I ascribe it to the bungling manner in which he had made it. I was obliged to let him make the striking mo[ve]ment anew on the common plan, after which it went pretty well. . . ."[43]

As Leslie later explained the circumstances to Jefferson, "before I went to England I experienced too much of the evil of employing Apprentices and Journeymen, to have recourse to it again, one striking proof of it comes within your knowledge, and which hurt my feeling more than all the rest. It was the employing the man who made your large Clock, and the small one intended for you (and who by your letter of last spring I find was Knave enough to charge both you and my Partner for doing the same work) as both of those Clocks were made on a plan different from the common, and neither of them answered, it must have been natural for you to suppose the defect lay in the construction, which was not the case as I have had several made on the same plan which answers every purpose wished for these circumstances with a variety of similar ones, have long ago convinced me of the impossibility of extending the work part of the Clock & Watch business to any degree in this Country at present." Jefferson paid Leslie for the clock in April in the amount of $113.80.

Although the clock was intended for installation eventually at Monticello, it was delivered to Jefferson while he was living in the house in Germantown that he rented from Moses Cox. There he had it installed, using square weights, in order to test the timepiece.

When he vacated the rented house, Jefferson had the clock packed with his other furnishings and brought it back with him to Monticello. He may have installed the clock somewhere in the house on a temporary basis, but it was not until after 1796, when the Entrance Hall had been completed, that the Great Clock was installed in its permanent location.

The timepiece operated unsatisfactorily from the beginning, and Jefferson ordered some changes made in the mechanism. It continued to require repair again and again during the next several years. Despite its shortcomings resulting from the maker's incompetence, it nonetheless has continued to operate to the present time. It was not until recent years, when one of the gears had to be replaced, that it was discovered that Spurck had made the movement with one tooth short in the gear for winding up the weights.[44]

When on July 31 Jefferson had officially submitted his resignation to become effective at the end of September, President Washington was greatly distressed by his decision, and went to visit him at his home hoping to make him change his mind. The President urged him to take leave if he needed it, but to postpone his resignation at least until the end of the year so that the issues before the government that were most pressing could be resolved. Jefferson agreed, but with reluctance.[45]

In the war between England and France, there was never any doubt that Jefferson favored France, based largely on his realization of the parallels between the American and French revolutions, and the the relationship of the fates of the two peoples.

The pressures brought upon the American government during these months, first by the British ambassador and then by Genêt, placed it in a difficult position. It was a particularly unhappy time for Jefferson, whose sympathies were well known. Genêt continued to create more and more dissension until a point was reached at which his expulsion was seriously considered by the President and the Cabinet. Jefferson was sick at heart with the difficulties created by the French minister, which had begun to affect not only everything for which he stood, but also the position of the Republicans. Increasingly he yearned for peace and quiet in the privacy of his family.[46]

By the end of November, the yellow fever epidemic had subsided sufficiently to enable Congress to reconvene in the city. From Germantown, Jefferson informed Thomas Pinckney, American minister to Great Britain, that the spread of the illness "in Philadelphia, became . . . far more destructive than had been apprehended . . . on the lst day of this month the President & heads of the departments assembled here, on that day also began the first rains which had fallen in some months . . . & from that moment the infection ceased, so that the disease terminated almost suddenly. . . ."[47]

Before moving back into the city, Jefferson engaged on another of his spending sprees for scientific instruments to use in his planned retirement at Monticello. He again contacted the London mathematical instrument maker John Jones, and was informed that Jones had retired to the country but that the firm was being carried on by his sons, William and Samuel, under the firm name of W. & S. Jones.

Concerning his earlier order for a twelve-inch telescope and apparatus for attaching it to his universal equatorial instrument, he was informed that "it was undoubtedly a curious contrivance but interferes too much with the construction of the instrument subjecting it to be deranged, and to be out of order somewhat, in shifting occasionally the parts. None of that construction are now made but we could easily make you one if desired." The cost, including a fishskin pocket case, would not be more than four or five guineas.

Jefferson was assured "Jupiter's Moons and Saturn's ring can be distinctly seen by them. A tweve-inch reflector would be much more perfect, and magnify more, but not suitable for the pocket." In the firm's opinion, a three-foot six-inch achromatic refractor was the best telescope being made. Jefferson nonetheless proceeded with his order, and inquired also about globes, for which he was referred to the firm's published catalogue, recommending their new eighteen-inch globes, which were up to date with the most recent discoveries.[48]

Meanwhile he turned to Rittenhouse for the loan of an instrument for another purpose. He asked to borrow his camera obscura because he had "two young ladies at his house whose time hangs heavily on their hands, & the more so, as their drawing master cannot attend them." If the instrument could be borrowed for a few days, it would enable them to "take a few lessons in drawing from nature." The instrument was used for bringing an image, such as a landscape or a portrait, to a piece of paper by means of a lens to enable the viewer to draw the outline. He later purchased a camera obscura made by Rittenhouse.[49]

As the year 1793 drew to a close, Jefferson began to pack for a permanent return to Monticello. Although President Washington made one more attempt to dissuade him from his plan, this time Jefferson was not to be swayed. He spent his last month in office completing various projects. President Washington submitted to Congress the report Jefferson had prepared on dealings with France and England, as well as Jefferson's report on foreign commerce. At this time Jefferson also developed financial arrangements whereby Thomas Mann Randolph, Jr. could save his plantation at Varina, which he was in danger of losing.

On December 23rd Jefferson had the last fifty to sixty packages of his belongings placed aboard a packet bound for Richmond, and on December 31st he formally resigned his office. He left Philadelphia on January 5th, arriving at Monticello on January 16th.[50]

Although Jefferson's achievements as Secretary of State were not commensurate with the effort he devoted to the position and to his dedication to the government, he nonetheless justified Washington's confidence in him. Furthermore, his unending controversy with Hamilton had the effect of directing public attention to the latter's dangerous policies—his tendency towards a monarchial government, his inclination to use force instead of persuasion—and was instrumental in effecting their restraint.

One of Jefferson's last official acts as Secretary of State was to correspond with Eli Whitney concerning his application for a patent for the cotton gin. Jefferson responded with enthusiasm, informing him "the only requisite of the law now . . . is the forwarding of a model, which being received, your patent may be made out & delivered to your order immediately. As the state of Virginia, of which I am, carries on household manufactures of cotton to a great extent, as I also do myself, and one of our great embarrassments is the cleaning the cotton of the seed, I feel a considerable interest in the success of your invention for family use. Permit me therefore to ask information from you on these points. Has the machine been thoroughly tried in the ginning of cotton, or is it as yet but a machine of theory? What quantity of cotton has it cleaned on an average of several days, & worked by hand, & by how many hands? What will be the cost of one of them made to be worked by hand? Favorable answers to these questions would induce me to engage one of them to be forwarded to Richmond for me."

Whitney delayed submitting the required drawings and model while he again reviewed each detail of his design to ensure that enlarged models would not incur weaknesses not existent in the small version, and that the machine could be duplicated without difficulty. He was aware that once the gin was patented and became available to others, there would be a great demand for it.

Since they would have to be manufactured by hand, it was necessary to simplify the process as much as possible. He responded to Jefferson that the yellow fever epidemic in Philadelphia had interrupted business to such a degree that he was forced to delay sending the drawings. Only a model remained to complete the requirements.

Although Whitney's query was typical, Jefferson responded with greater interest than usual. The cotton gin intrigued him not only on its own merits but also because of its potential application to his needs at Monticello, and he intended to purchase one. He had learned of a similar machine advertised in Paterson, New Jersey the previous year, and wondered whether it was the same. Whitney was prompt in replying that the New Jersey gin was, he believed, of a common type with small rollers.

He continued to experience difficulties in modifying his gin and it was not until early 1794 that he completed his miniature model for the Patent Office, as well as a large version to bring to Georgia. By the time that the model was submitted, and the patent was issued on March 14, 1794, Jefferson was out of office, having resigned at the end of the previous year. Seven years would pass before their paths were to cross once more.[51]

CHAPTER X

ROSINANTE STABLED (1794–1796)

Agriculture . . . is a science of the very first order. It counts among its handmaids the most respectable sciences, such as Chemistry, natural Philosophy, Mechanics, Mathematics generally, Natural History, Botany. . . .

Letter from Thomas Jefferson
to David Williams, 1803.

Jefferson departed from Philadelphia bound for home on January 5, 1794. Believing he was finished with public life, he turned to farming with enthusiasm. He was appalled, however, to discover the amount of damage his lands had suffered in his absence. Spending the first several months in reviewing the situation, he wrote to General Washington that he had found, "on a more minute examination of my lands than the short visits heretofore made to them permitted, that a ten years' abandonment of them to the ravages of overseers, has brought on them a degree of degradation far beyond what I expected."[1]

He owned more than ten thousand acres of land at this time, half of which was in Albemarle County, and he possessed holdings as well in Bedford County. Approximately one-fourth of the Albemarle lands were cultivated. His first priority was to salvage his fields by developing a system of crop rotation. This included the use of legumes such as peas, beans and clovers, fertilizers and deep ploughing. He personally maintained contact with all aspects of the work on the farms, and exchanged information with some of the leading planters of his time, including George Washington, James Madison and the political writer and agriculturist of Caroline County, John Taylor.

He was interested in soil-improving plants, such as red clover, to offset the exhausting effects of wheat crops and which at the same time would provide good pasture. He planned to experiment with several varieties of vetch which were fodder and soil-building plants, but never managed to do so, and substituted crops that would preserve the fields as much as possible from erosion. Seeking substitutes for corn and tobacco, he turned to potatoes, clover and sheep, the last-named providing manure which served as fertilizer.

He recommended manuring in addition to other measures he had taken, and later, during his Presidency, he also experimented with the use of gypsum plaster. He made tests to determine how many cattle were needed to fertilize the soil with manure and how much time was required, by comparing the yield of wheat from manured areas to production from similar areas without manure.

As he had indicated in the *Notes*, he considered the cultivation of tobacco "a culture productive of infinite wretchedness. Those employed in it are in a continued state of exertion beyond the powers of nature to support. Little food of any kind is raised by them, so that the men and animals on these farms are badly fed, and the earth is rapidly impoverished."

With a new overseer he had recently hired, he developed a plan of crop rotation with red clover as its keystone to improve soil conditions. He abandoned tobacco growing for wheat. He advocated the culture of red clover to fulfill a number of objectives. It covered the ground with herbage, preserved the soil's fertility, fed those who labored on it requiring less toil, raised animals for food and service and diffused happiness through the economy.

He continued to grow tobacco at Poplar Forest in his Bedford County lands, however, for he relied on it for his major cash income, although he was constantly faced with the problem of marketing. He owned about one hundred and fifty slaves in this period, two-thirds of whom were employed in the Albemarle lands.[2]

Although his fields were divided and enclosed by rail fences, which he considered "a great & perishable work," he replaced some of the internal divisions with rows of peach trees, building a road between them so that they served as dividers for the fields, planting 1157 trees for this purpose. It was necessary to retain the fences required to keep out pigs and cows.

Later, during his years in the Presidency, he also substituted "live fences" of thorn hedges for the rail fences at the summit of Monticello Mountain, and he enclosed other areas with dry walls.

The appearance of his property was greatly enhanced by elimination of the rail fences which became so readily overgrown with wild growth, and furthermore he was provided with abundant fruit. At this time he also made a list of the plants he planned to include in his garden and farm.[3]

Jefferson was relieved and happy to be at home once more, despite the problems he found there. As Isaac, a former Monticello slave, reported, he was "always singing when ridin or walkin; hardly see him anywhar out doors but what he was a-singin; he had a fine clear voice, sung minnits [minuets] and sich: fiddled in the parlor."[4]

Jefferson informed Mazzei and others that now he had "returned home with an inflexible determination to leave it no more." To Henry Knox he described his new way of life, asking "have you become a farmer? Is it not pleasanter than to be shut up within 4. walls and delving eternally with the pen? I am become the most ardent farmer in the state. I live on my horse from morning to night almost. Intervals are filled up with attentions to a nailery I carry on. I rarely look into a book, and more rarely take up a pen. I have proscribed newspapers, not taking a single one, nor scarcely ever looking into one. My next reformation will be to allow neither pen, ink, nor paper to be kept on the farm. When I have done this I shall be in a fair way of indemnifying myself for the drudgery in which I have passed my life."[5]

To Washington he commented,

> The difference of my present and past situation is such as to leave me nothing to regret, but that my retirement has been postponed four years too long. The principles on which I calculated the value of life, are entirely in favor of my present course. I return to farming with an ardor which I scarcely knew in my youth, and which has gotten the better entirely of my love of study. Instead of writing ten or twelve letters a day, which I have been in the habit of doing as a thing in course, I put off answering my letters now, farmer-like, till a rainy day, and then find them sometimes postponed by other necessary occupations.[6]

In order to direct his attention and channel his slim resources to the needs of his farms, it became necessary to delay construction on the mansion for the next two years. As he informed Wythe, "We are now living in a brick-kiln, for my house in its present state is nothing better."[7]

One of his early concerns was for the acquisition of farm machinery. The first priority was a threshing machine, several versions of which had been invented in England and Scotland earlier in the eighteenth century. They were stationary machines and it was necessary to bring the sheaves to them. After having read of them in the writings of the English agricultural writer, Arthur Young, Jefferson had first seen such a machine in 1791, on a visit he made with Washington to a Pennsylvania farm. It was of local manufacture, not a Scottish import.

He requested the American minister to Great Britain, Thomas Pinckney, to have a model made in England for him if possible and to provide him with measurements of wheels and cogs, etc. of the machine described by Young. Pinckney located a Leith threshing machine not far from London and employed a mechanic to construct a model, from which Jefferson could have a full-size machine constructed at Monticello.

He was encouraged in this endeavor by Washington, who advised "If you can bring a movable threshing machine, constructed upon simple principles to perfection, it will be among the most valuable institutions in this Country, for nothing is more wanting, & to be wished for on our farms."[8]

By the time the construction of Jefferson's threshing machine was almost completed, he had added several modifications to the original design. "I have put the whole works (except the horse wheel) into a single frame," he wrote, "movable from one field to another on the two axles of a wagon. It will be ready in time for the harvest which is coming on, which will give it a full trial."[9]

Although the full-scale machine had been completed earlier, it was not until August 1796 that it was in use. Operated by horse power, it was based on the Scottish model and could be moved from field to field. The machine was an eminent success, but Jefferson was not totally satisfied with it. He collected information about the operation of other machines and then made further additions and revisions to his own. The modified version worked well and Jefferson reported that it threshed 13-½ bushels of wheat an hour.[10]

At harvest time Jefferson followed the common practice of laying out a threshing floor on which the wheat was threshed out by horses. Threshing floors for separating the straw from the chaff using horses or oxen to trample out the grain had existed from Biblical times. The practice continued into the eighteenth century, but was often replaced by the flail. Noticing that much time was lost by this means, Jefferson had the floor laid out before harvest thereafter. After he acquired his own threshing machine, he abandoned the use of the floor.[11]

Another piece of equipment he sought was a new grain drill. The first drills for planting small grain were produced in Great Britain and sold in the United States. They were generally not adaptable for planting corn, however, which had to be planted less profusely than wheat, and it was not until later that drills for planting corn were developed.[12]

Now without a salary from public service, and with limited profits from his crops, Jefferson sought an additional means of income that would provide rapid returns to pay the cost of restoring his lands. He wished at all costs to avoid having to sell any part of his properties or his slaves, and manufacturing appeared to provide the best solution.

His first inclination was the manufacture of potash, which was used in the production of soap and glass, and was in fact the sixth largest national export. Jefferson had familiarized himself with the process several years earlier by means of an English translation of Lavoisier's "The Art of Manufacturing Alkaline Salts and Potashes." Samuel Hopkins was an authority on the subject, and had sent Jefferson copies of his patent and his address to the potash and pearlash manufacturers.

Jefferson soon realized that potash manufacture had serious drawbacks as well as potential for profit. He learned that potash manufacture would require cutting a great extent of his forests, burning great masses of timber, rendering their ashes, leaching them of their potassium and boiling down the chemical-laden water to form potash into a solid.

From those he consulted he derived the impression that skilled workers also would be required, which would be costly, even if only for a limited period of time to train his farm hands. Furthermore, equipment also was essential, imposing another expense which he could ill afford. Potash manufacture had other disadvantages. It would leave many of his forest areas virtually denuded, diminish the available stock of firewood and charcoal required for the ongoing operations of the plantation, and generate great clouds of smoke and disagreeable fumes that would constantly envelop Monticello.[13]

These considerations led him to seek other resolutions to his financial problems, and he finally concluded that the manufacture of nails offered a more lucrative prospect. He recalled the tour he had taken with John Adams through the English Midlands to the Black Country. There, in addition to the fine English gardens, he had observed northeast of Birmingham numerous nail-making shops clustered around small villages. He had taken particular notice of the architecture and the arrangement of forges and other features of the shops, and realized that he could duplicate them quite easily at Monticello.

Nailmaking was not a totally new enterprise for Jefferson, for nails had been produced in his blacksmith's shop on the Shadwell Branch since at least 1774 for plantation use. During his stay in Philadelphia, he had visited the iron mongery of the merchant Caleb Lownes in order to inform himself about sizes and prices of nailrod, the methods of shipment, and the terms of credit that would be available.

"If I understand you yesterday," he wrote to Lownes, "it is your custom to furnish nailrod to customers at 60 to 90 days credit. I suppose one ton will serve me the first quarter of the year by the end of which I shall be ready to work up two or three times as much every quarter. I will therefore be obliged to you to send a ton by these vessels to Richmond, payable at three months."

He explained that he would take the lowest rate of credit inasmuch as so much of the time would be required for the slow transportation from Richmond to Monticello. When the nailrod arrived in April, Jefferson paid for it in tobacco shipped to Philadelphia.[14]

Reviewing the availability of labor on the plantation to work in the nailery, he realized that the sons of the slaves constituted an idle work force which could be utilized to advantage. Slave child labor was commonly being used after the Revolution in shops, factories, iron furnaces and similar enterprises throughout the South, and in Europe he had observed women and children employed in rural blacksmith shops. He concluded that slave children would solve the problem of his nailery labor.[15]

With such assistance as he could obtain from his overseer, Samuel Biddle, he established his nailery in a rectangular wooden building in the area of the premises referred to as Mulberry Row on the Upper Roundabout. As an experiment, Jefferson recruited several of his slaves's sons aged ten to sixteen to work in the nailery. He maintained close scrutiny daily of their rate of production, and compared it with production of nailers working in commercial centers in the northern states. To achieve maximum efficiency, he established a military form of working discipline, short of whipping, to maintain order in the shop. "It would destroy their value in my estimation to degrade them in their own eyes by the whip," he commented, "This therefore must not be resorted to but in extremities." During the periods he remained in residence at Monticello, Jefferson assigned responsibility for the nailery to hired overseers, but personally overviewed the operation.[16]

In addition to the food, clothing and housing supplied to the slave families, Jefferson felt it necessary to provide additional incentive and compensation for the nailers. Most of the boys in the nailery were detailed to the fields during harvest season to assist with the crops. When they attained the age of sixteen, they were permanently transferred from the nailery. Most of them entered the trades of smiths, carpenters, etc. rather than to work tending the gardens, orchards and field crops.

He maintained extensive records of the nailery operation, including records of costs of materials, sales to private purchasers and retailers and prices charged. In these records, his preoccupation with statistics is particularly well demonstrated. He went to extreme lengths in analyzing his nailery operation, constructing a table of weights and measures to demonstrate the number of pounds of nails per thousand, the number of nails per pound in the various sizes, and the average lengths of nails produced in naileries in New York, Baltimore, Richmond, Fredericksburg and Great Britain. He repeated the figures for each of the various nail sizes, and they were set against another series of figures for his own nailery in which weights, quantities and lengths were again listed.

According to his chart, his nailers were placed at a level of count-to-weight efficiency close to that of the nailers in the industrial centers of the North. Elsewhere he compiled a chart for a "man-versus-boy versus Baltimore-nailer" comparison for the production of all seven sizes of nails, in which his nailers compared favorably.

The sizes produced in largest quantity at Monticello were eight and ten penny nails, made with faceted heads suitable for housebuilding, wagon-making and cabinetry, although nails of smaller sizes also were produced. The maintenance of such elaborate records made it evident that he viewed his nailery as a most serious venture, the success of which was of considerable importance to him.[17]

The nailery met all of Jefferson's expectations. To several friends he wrote that his newly established nailery promised to "provide completely for the maintenance of my family, as we make from 8. to 10,000 nails a day & it is on the increase." He boasted that "My new trade of nail-making is to me that an additional title of nobility or the ensigns of a new order are to Europe."[18]

He preferred to exchange his plantation's products of tobacco and nails for commodities including food, clothing and other domestic necessities, not only because of a lack of liquid capital, but also because of an aversion to dealing with paper money, which in his mind seemed to be associated with moral corruption.

Advertising of the Monticello nailery was achieved for the most part by word of mouth. To enhance sales, Jefferson distributed specially printed "nail cards" on which types, sizes and prices of nails available were noted, and on which he even inserted nail samples.[19]

So successful was the operation that he decided to expand the nailery's capability by the purchase and installation of a nail-making machine, as he informed his friend, the inventor Henry Remsen. He decided to accept the offer of a certain Mr. Burrel to make a nail-making machine for him for forty dollars rather than await other offers which might have been less expensive. Accordingly, he arranged with Remsen to obtain one of Burrel's machines and have it forwarded to Richmond by water together with 5000 pounds of the iron rod for cutting 4, 6 and 8 penny cut nails as a sample. The machine arrived in due course and by February 1796 it was in operation.[20]

Eventually the Monticello nailery met strong competition from the importation of nails from Great Britain. In 1796 Jefferson commented on "a deluge of British nails" arriving at two import houses in nearby Milton "with a view as it is said of putting down my work." To combat this incursion, and to recover the monopoly of the market in his region, he began to retail his nails in Richmond at wholesale prices.

He arranged with merchants in Milton, Charlottesville and Staunton to serve as distributors, for which they received a five per cent commission on sales. At about the same time at the suggestion of James

Madison, who was a purchaser of his nails, he changed nailrod suppliers from Lownes to Samuel Howell, possibly because of the availability of hoop iron for use with his machine. Howell and his partner Benjamin Jones remained his suppliers until almost the termination of the nailery project in 1823.[21]

Jefferson considered these home industries to be a part of agriculture, and continued to maintain the view that among all occupations, agriculture was the first in utility and should be the first in respect.[22]

Just as he found much to extol of the agrarian way of life, he found as much to criticize about manufacturing on an industrial scale. He feared particularly "the powerful fascination of the great cities." He commented, "The general desire of men to live by their heads rather than their hands, and the strong allurrements of great cities to those who have any turn for dissipation, threaten to make them here, as in Europe, the sinks of voluntary misery." He deplored as well the advent of factories. As time went on, he increasingly supported home industries as a means to supply common needs, such as those he pursued at Monticello.

He fulfilled the clothing requirements of his plantation by gradually increasing the machinery that was necessary and by training those he employed in requisite skills. In time he was able to report that as many as thirty-five spindles were in operation in his weaving house, and was able to come to the decision that no matter what the difference in price might be, he would never again purchase foreign manufactured goods if they were available from American sources.[23]

During his retirement, Jefferson said, he had forbidden himself to think or speak about national affairs. He claimed that he did not read the newspapers. He was totally involved with the operation of his farms and the building projects at Monticello. However, he received newspapers from friends from time to time. In this manner he learned about major issues, such as John Jay's treaty with Great Britain, which greatly distressed him.

Always avidly anti-British, he had become even more so with the passage of the years, and was appalled by the terms presented in the treaty. The Senate had already approved it conditionally but it had not yet been signed. He strongly denounced the treaty in letters to friends and with others who shared his views. Meanwhile opposition to the treaty was growing apace, particularly in Virginia. A series of meetings was held, some of which Jefferson may have attended, but he did not participate.

"It was not in my power to attend at Fredericksburg according to the kind invitation in your letter," he explained to Mann Page, "and in that of Mr. Ogilvie. The heat of the weather, the business of the farm, in which I have made myself necessary, forbade it; and to give one round reason for all, *mature sanus* [being seasonably healthy]. I have laid up my

Rosinante in his stall, before his unfitness for the road shall expose him faultering in the world."[24]

The only problem that clouded Jefferson's new lease on life during his first year of retirement was an attack of rheumatism. In the eighteenth century, "rheumatism" was a catch-all for a great variety of aches and pains including strained muscles, injuries, inflammatory conditions, neuritis, arthritis and osteoarthritis, among others.

It has been suggested that Jefferson's current disability may have resulted from a strain or injury shortly after his return to Monticello. Having found the farms deplorably neglected and being unable at first to hire a competent overseer, he personally took charge and attempted to teach the slaves how to plough. It is suspected that he may have injured a disk when lifting, which was the cause of the condition that persisted for years thereafter. It was not until early December that he was again able to be "in my farmer's coat, immersed soul & body in the culture of my fields."[25]

During the winter months Jefferson was alone at Monticello because Thomas and Martha Randolph were spending the winter at their home at Varina. He directed most of his attention to the establishment of the nailery, and also experimented with seed germination which advanced his knowledge of planting considerably. It was a bitter winter with many little snows and no ploughing could be done from Christmas to early March.[26]

While Jefferson was in Paris, a proposal was being developed to establish an institution of higher learning in Richmond by the Chevalier Alexandre-Marie Quesnay de Beaurepaire. Grandson of the famous French philosopher of the same name, Quesnay had come as a volunteer to fight in the cause of the American colonies. While in the United States, he traveled extensively and conceived the idea of introducing French culture and fine arts. It was John Page who suggested to him the establishment of an academy in Richmond.

Quesnay obtained the support of many subscribers in Virginia to the project, and a cornerstone was laid in 1786. Returning to Paris, he undertook an intense campaign for the academy with favorable results from the highest circles, including Jefferson. In 1787 in order to raise funds, Quesnay published a tract about his proposed academy, but in the following year the political situation brought about the demise of the project. The building which had been completed in Richmond thereafter served as the place of assembly of the Virginia Convention, which in 1788 ratified the Constitution.[27]

Meanwhile, as a consequence of the events of the French Revolution, hard times had come to the College of Geneva, which Jefferson ranked among the best in Europe. He had met some of its professors while in Paris, and one or more of them presumably communicated to him the dissatisfaction of the faculty and its search for a location more conducive to learning.

Jefferson seized on the idea of transferring the College to the United States. He proposed to the Virginia legislature that provision be made for establishing the College in the state, the concept of a cosmopolitan university equipped with Europe's finest scientific talent having long been in his mind.[28]

François d'Ivernois, a Swiss writer, was among those who proposed the transfer of the College of Geneva. D'Ivernois's proposal intrigued him because it was "too analogous to all my attachments to science, & freedom the first-born daughter of science, not to excite a lively interest to my mind, and the essays which were necessary to try its practicability." The decision was in the hands of the legislature, to a member of which Jefferson had forwarded d'Ivernois's papers.

Although the legislature was in general well disposed towards the project, it concluded that it could not be achieved, for several reasons. For one thing, American youth was not inclined to learn a new language, and for another its expense would cause uneasiness and would endanger its permanence. Furthermore, its extent was disproportionate with the narrow state of the Virginia population.

Regretfully Jefferson noted, "I should have seen with peculiar satisfaction the establishment of such a mass of science in my country, and should probably have been tempted to approach myself to it, by procuring a residence in its neighborhood, at those seasons of the year at least when the operations of agriculture are less active and interesting."[29]

Jefferson then turned to General Washington, who had recently received the gift of some shares in the Potomac and James River Companies, and was seeking an appropriate project in which they could be used for the public good. Jefferson suggested that the shares be used to transfer the College of Geneva to the United States, establishing it near the Federal City to become the nucleus for a National University of America. Washington doubted the expediency of importing a foreign faculty unfamiliar with the English language, and the prospect of transferring the College of Geneva to the United States dimmed to extinction.[30]

Despite the intensity of Jefferson's involvement with farming and his nailery, he did not neglect his other scientific pursuits, corresponding with others on various subjects. He received a copy of an address on the meridian, longitude and latitude, that had been delivered before the

Académie Royale des Sciences, and a letter from Patterson to Ritten-house, which had been read before the American Philosophical Society, concerning the adjustment of the glasses of the octant for use on land for back observation.[31]

He was particularly interested in a paper which Jonathan Williams had read before the American Philosophical Society, on "Barometrical Measurement of the Blue-Ridge, Warm Spring, and Allegheny Mountains, in Virginia, taken in the summer of 1791."

Williams explained that the journal would have been submitted much earlier except that he had not been completely satisfied with the accuracy of the barometrical calculations when applied to the measurement of heights in that climate. In the course of his experiments he had found considerable variation when repeated on a known height.

He had finally submitted the journal despite the errors, which, since they related to local circumstances and small elevations, possibly did not affect the principle of barometric measurement on a larger scale. After having used the table to make comparative calculations of the height of the Andes, noted in the account of the voyages of the 18th century Spanish naval officer and scientist, Antonio de Ulloa, and the balloon ascent of Jean-Alexandre Césare Charles in Paris, he concluded that the accuracy of the table to be sufficiently well confirmed.

Williams went on to note some circumstances which appeared to be peculiar to the United States. He made comparisons of the barometer's rise and fall in the course of a year between Europe and Williamsburg, Monticello, Staunton and Red Springs, Virginia, and concluded that the barometer was less susceptible of change in Virginia than in England, and still less the higher the location. He commented that he believed that the height of the Blue Ridge mountains should be greater than estimated. He added that Jefferson supposed the Peaks of Otter to be approximately 4000 feet in height.[32]

Williams sent a copy to Jefferson requesting any additional facts that he may have established by experiment. Jefferson responded that he had estimated the height of the Blue Ridge to be a little greater than had Williams, explaining how he had established it. He noted that the late Thomas Lewis had also measured the height with a quadrant, and he had concluded "the mountain estimated by him & myself is probably higher than that next Rockfish gap. I do not remember from what principles I estimated the peaks of Otter at 4000. f[eet].; but some later observations of Judge Tucker's coincided very nearly with my estimate. Your measures confirm another opinion of mine, that the blue ridge, on its south side, is the highest ridge in our country compared with its base. I think your observations on these mountains well worthy of being published."[33] The appearance of objects, Williams had observed, is affected by the refraction of light rays which tend to increase the apparent height, pointing out Jefferson's mention in his *Notes* "of a phenomenon resembling, in some measure, an appearance which seamen call *looming.*"[34]

In his *Notes* Jefferson had commented that the physical situation of Monticello "affords an opportunity of seeing a phaenomenon which is rare at land, though frequent at sea. The seamen call it *looming.* Philosophy is as yet at the rear of the seamen, for so far from having accounted for it, she has not given it a name. Its principal effect is to make distant objects appear larger, in opposition to the general law of vision, by which they are diminished."

He referred to an incident that occurred in Yorktown, with its endless eastward expanse of water, during which three men in a canoe observed at some distance what was taken to be a three-masted ship. He noted that the phenomenon was familiar at Monticello and mentioned a solitary cone-shaped mountain some forty miles distant which, by the effect of looming, often subsided almost entirely into the horizon. At other times it rose more acutely and higher and sometimes appeared hemispherical and at other times perpendicular with the top as fat and as broad as its base. It could assume various whimsical shapes, all within the period of a single morning. "This phaenomenon begins to shew itself on these [Blue Ridge] mountains, at about 50 miles distance, and continues beyond that as far as they are seen. I remark no particular state, either in the weight, moisture, or heat of the atmosphere, necessary to produce this. The only constant circumstances are, its appearance in the morning only, and on objects at least 40 or 50 miles distant. In this latter circumstance, if not in both, it differs from the looming on the water. Refraction will not account for this metamorphosis. That only changes the proportions of length and breadth, base and altitude, preserving the general outlines. Thus it may make a circle appear elliptical, raise or depress a cone, but by none of its laws, as yet developed, will it make a circle appear a square, or a cone a sphere."[35]

Williams urged Jefferson to publish the result of his "philosophical researches" made after his retirement to Monticello, but Jefferson replied that he had not undertaken any that were not connected with agriculture. "In this way," he wrote, "I have a little matter to communicate, and will do it ere long. It is the form of a mould-board of least resistance. I had some time ago conceived the principles of it, and explained them to Mr. Rittenhouse. I have since reduced the thing to practice and have reason to believe the theory fully confirmed. I only wish for one of those instruments [dynamometer] used in England for measuring the force exerted in the drafts of different plows, &c. that I might compare the resistance of my mould-board with that of others. But these instruments are not to be had here."[36]

Jefferson's combined mathematical and mechanical skills were particularly well demonstrated in his invention of a plough with mouldboard of least resistance. Always interested in agricultural implements and constantly seeking means to achieve greater utility, while he was in France he had paid to observe a plough drawn by a windlass without horses or oxen. It utilized a complicated rig which enabled four men to do the work of two horses, which he pronounced to be "a poor affair."

It was while traveling from the Rhine back to Paris that his attention had been drawn again to the plough, observing French peasants near Nancy tilling the soil with clumsy rudimentary ploughs drawn by oxen. He became preoccupied with the possibility of designing a mouldboard that would be more effective and that could be reproduced simply.

The plough in Jefferson's time had changed little from ancient forms. Generally it consisted merely of a crooked stick having an iron tip, sometimes attached by means of rawhide. Few of them were designed to turn a furrow, and generally were made with rough mouldboards having curves of which no two were alike. Ploughs made by blacksmiths were better but of limited patterns. They were capable of turning a furrow on soft ground but required several men and oxen when ploughing in hard soil.

For the most part ploughs were produced by wheelwrights from traditional patterns suitable for their own localities. The mouldboard was hewn from wood with the grain running as nearly as possible along its shape. To this were nailed blades of old tools or iron straps, or even worn horseshoes, to prevent too rapid wearing.

Improved mouldboards were occasionally produced by smiths, but generally they were too complicated to be reproduced by the average farmer. When a mouldboard split or broke while in use, the farmer generally cut a section of a tree, studied the grain and cut it into shape with an adze. Although attempts to modify the mouldboard had been made in the past, in general they followed traditional designs of the Saxons and were too complicated for easy duplication.[37]

Jefferson first mentioned that he was designing a mouldboard in April 19, 1788 in his notes of travel. He sought to develop a simple formula by means of which a farmer could construct a mouldboard which would operate to the greatest advantage with the simple tools he would ordinarily have at hand, such as the saw and an adze.

He consulted the works of the English mathematician, William Emerson, for a formula that would be useful to him. Basing his work on a study of geometrical solids, he concluded that if the mouldboard's function was to pass through the soil with least friction, the wedge was the optimum form to use. Since the mouldboard's other function was to lift and turn the sod, it "operates as a transverse or rising wedge."[38]

He then defined a geometrical shape consisting of a series of wedges operating in several intersecting planes in which "a curved plane will be generated whose characteristic will be a combination of the principle of the wedge in cross directions, & will give what we seek, *the mould board of least resistance*."

Having noted that other mouldboards were "being copied by the eye, so no two are alike," he set himself the task of producing one that could be readily copied with exactitude. He developed a series of construction diagrams which provided "this great advantage that it may be made by the coarsest workman, by a process so exact that its form shall never be varied by a single hair's breadth."[39] (*Figure 23*)

Upon his return home from France, he discussed the mouldboard with his son-in-law, and constructed one on his design which when tested, proved to be eminently successful. He sent it to Rittenhouse for his opinion, and the latter commented favorably, as did Professor Robert Patterson to whom he had later submitted it. He also described the mouldboard to John Taylor, the political writer and agriculturist.

Jefferson sketched a block of wood cut in such a manner with wedgelike surfaces, which he illustrated with drawings in the detailed description which followed, to show how such a mouldboard might be cut from a block of wood. The block of wood he used was 9 inches bottom width, 13-½ inches top width, 12 inches high, and 36 inches long.[40]

He produced several models of it which he distributed to the American Philosophical Society, the Société d'Agriculture de la Seine in Paris, and others. He gave a demonstration of it in use at Monticello before an English visitor, William Strickland, who presented a favorable report on the invention to the Board of Agriculture on his return to England. Jefferson also sent a model, enclosing a detailed description and copies of his drawings, to Sir John Sinclair, president of the Board, noting that he planned to have it cast in iron. The text of his letter to Sinclair was subsequently published in the *Transactions* of the American Philosophical Society with the title "The description of a mould-board of the least resistance and of the easiest and most certain construction."[41]

Always alert to opportunities to introduce new and useful plants to the United States, Jefferson was pleased to receive seeds of the breadfruit tree from France, and he set about to introduce it to planters in the southern American states. As he advised his French correspondent, "One service of this kind rendered to a nation, is worth more to them than all the victories of the most splendid pages of their history and becomes a source of exalted pleasure to those who have been instrumental to it."[42]

He experimented with the Albany pea, which he called "the white boiling pea of Europe," until he could obtain some hog peas from En-

gland, which in his opinion were the most productive. He was also anxious to obtain some winter vetch. He tested a seed drill developed by C.
T. Martin in the field and pronounced that it worked extremely well. It
was simple in operation, and when used for a single row it operated perfectly. He planned to modify it so that it would sow four rows of wheat
or peas twelve inches apart at one time.[43]

Jefferson now had uninterrupted leisure to enable him to proceed
with his plans for completing construction of the house. He began the
remodeling in the spring of 1796 and continued it through the autumn.
As he noted at this time, "My house which has never been more than
half finished, had during the war of 8. years and my subsequent absence
of 10. years gone into almost total decay . . . and for the present one
you will endeavor to find comfort in a comparison of our covering with
that of an Arab tent and what in Arabis and it's dust, sands, cannot
show, groves of poplars, towering mountains, rocks and rivers, blue skies
balsamic air yet pure and healthy."[44]

By mid-December the region experienced such severe bad weather
that construction work had to be terminated, although another week
would have completed the walls and permitted them to be roofed over.[45]

He took the opportunity to add to the mansion some of the refine-
ments he had observed in France. Tradition claims that it was Jefferson
who introduced the dumb-waiter to the United States, and it was during
this interval that he had a double dumbwaiter built into the two ends of
the fireplace in the dining room. The fireplace was constructed in such
a manner that it projected sufficiently into the room to provide space for
the dumbwaiters, which extended into the service dependencies situated
on the basement level. (*Figure 24*)

Each of the fireplace's end spaces was divided by a central partition
over the entire length of the shaft. A rope pulley passed through an
opening near the top of the spaces a short distance below the mantel,
and terminated in a wooden platform with bottle holders on which full
bottles were placed by servants. In the dining room the full bottles were
removed from one side of the mantel and brought to the dining table,
and empty bottles were returned on the other side of the mantel. These
were let down into the cellar by means of the rope, where a servant
replaced them with filled bottles and returned the platform to the dining
room level. There it remained in position until needed. There is no
record of the date of this installation, and Jefferson may have in fact
added this facility before he went to France.

Although the genesis of this device is not known with certainty, it
was probably inspired by a similar device Jefferson undoubtedly had observed in Paris, at the restaurant called the Café Mécanique at No. 121

Nouveau Palais-Royal. It was the manager, M. Tancres (or Taures), who conceived a novel means of attracting the public—to provide service without visible personnel.

The restaurant featured marble-topped tables, each supported by two truncated hollow columns reaching to the basement below the restaurant's dining area. The host's counter was equipped with a speaking trumpet connected with the kitchens below. As soon as a table of guests had made their selections from the menu, the host relayed their orders by means of the speaking trumpet to the kitchen.

In a short time, a small iron panel flush with the table top opened rather noisily, and from the column there then emerged a dining service almost eighteen inches in height complete with the diners' order. When the diners had finished their meal, and the plates were returned to the center of the table, they disappeared into the lower depths.

This manner of service was unique in a public restaurant. Great crowds of those unsuccessful in obtaining a table invariably collected and waited for hours outside, enviously watching through the windows as the orders ascended and descended at the tables. The concept of service without personnel would have greatly appealed to Jefferson, who had a fetish about the presence of servants who would overhear the conversation while dining.[46]

Another convenience he installed in his dining room may have been inspired by the same restaurant, or another, or possibly even the convent which his daughters attended. At the exit from the dining room which opened out to the stairs leading to the kitchen, which was situated on the north passage belowstairs, he installed a door that pivoted at the center. The door could be opened from either side by means of the pivot hinge. On the passage side, the door was fitted with a series of shelves having strong supports at their centers.

Dishes of food were brought up from the kitchen and placed on the shelves. There the food awaited the convenience of the host, and when he was ready to have it served, he turned the door easily on its pivot so that the side with the dishes faced the dining room, and the food was brought to the table.[47]

There was yet another dumbwaiter on the premises, either in Jefferson's bedroom or in the adjacent study. "Had a dumb-waiter," Isaac, Jefferson's slave, noted in his reminiscences, "when he wanted anything he had nothin' to do but turn a crank and the dumb-waiter would bring him water or fruit on a plate or anything he wanted."[48]

A visitor to the President's House during Jefferson's administration described a similar contrivance, although no tangible evidence now survives of it. When the visitor admired a particular piece of furniture, Jefferson smiled and touched a concealed spring upon it, causing little doors to open and disclose a decanter of wine, a goblet of water, a plate filled with light cakes and a night candle. He explained that he used this table when he was forced to remain up late at night and did not wish to bother the servants.[49]

Jefferson had a great love of hand tools, and collected them even though he had infrequent opportunity to use them. He maintained one of the rooms at Monticello as a workroom. It was the room he and his family called variously the "Greenhouse," "South Piazza" or "Workshop," adjacent to his library, from which it was separated by glass doors. It was in this room that he kept his collection of plants and seeds, and fitted it up with a wide variety of tools for woodworking, carpentry and gardening. (*Figure* 25)

When at Monticello he frequently spent some of his leisure hours in this room, particularly when inclement weather prevented him from being outside. There he made small objects and repaired others, constructing a small case for books or a simple scientific instrument, or possibly producing models from which full scale items were to be constructed.

As Randall noted, "With him manual labor was the amusement, mental labor the occupation. He had, however, a decided fondness for nearly all mechanical pursuits (as well as agricultural ones) and great handiness in acquiring their manipulations. He could turn off his bits of cabinet ware with neatness and dispatch, and tradition is disposed to claim that he could have successfully aspired to the mystery of shoeing his horse, had occasion demanded."[50]

Jefferson received various visitors at Monticello during the summer. A particularly pleasant interlude was occasioned by a visit from his old friend, the Duke de la Rochefoucauld-Liancourt, who stayed for a week at Monticello. In his account of his *Travels through the United States of North America*, he devoted several pages to his visit, in which he described Jefferson's agricultural and other activities.

He added, "In private life, Mr. Jefferson displays a mild, easy and obliging temper, though he is somewhat cold and reserved. His conversation is of the most agreeable kind, and he possesses a stock of information not inferior to that of any other man. In Europe he would hold a distinguished rank among men of letters, and as such he has already appeared there; at present, he is employed with activity and perseverence in the management of his farm and buildings; and he orders, directs and pursues in the minutest detail every branch of business relative to them."

He related how on his arrival he had found Jefferson in the midst of harvesting despite the scorching sun. He commented that the slaves were nourished, and treated as well as white servants. The children were employed in the nail factory while the young and old women spun cloth for clothing for the rest.

"He animates them by rewards and distinctions; in fine, his superior mind directs the management of his domestic concerns with the same abilities, activity, and regularity which he evinced in the conduct of public affairs, and which he is calculated to display in every situation of life."[51]

Jefferson's dream of an idyllic existence as a Virginia farmer was not to survive the march of national events, however. Washington had confided that he would not accept a third term as President. Although it was not public knowledge, his decision was known to political leaders who thereupon began to arrange "tickets" for the election in 1796. The publication of Washington's farewell address in September brought forth additional candidates.

Jefferson's name was prominent among the potential candidates of his own party, and John Adams was the choice of the Federalists. It was Jefferson's opinion that Madison was the best choice for his party, but Madison had recently married and would not even stand for re-election to the House.

Madison was aware that although Jefferson would lend greater prestige to the party, he might discourage his would-be supporters. Madison had all he could do to keep the farmer-statesman from doing so. Meanwhile Jefferson was struggling to have the walls of his residence completed and covered before the onslaught of winter, and paid little attention to the elections.

As the campaign progressed, Jefferson was once again severely criticized by his political opponents, particularly because of his scientific pursuits. Late in the election William Loughton Smith, the Congressman from South Carolina, published a pamphlet entitled *The Pretensions of Thomas Jefferson to the Presidency Examined* in which he violently attacked Jefferson's conduct as Governor of Virginia and Secretary of State, noting that "of all beings, a philosopher makes the worst politician." Jefferson was also attacked for his religious views and was unjustly charged as well with plagiarism in his report on weights and measures.[52]

As Jefferson awaited the results of the November elections, which would not be made public for several weeks, he made it known that he was willing to accept the second position. Consequently it came as no surprise to him, nor were his ambitions or vanity disappointed, when he learned that he had received 68 votes while Adams received 71 and the third contender, Thomas Pinckney 59. In fact he appeared to be relieved that he had not won the presidential election, for he had no illusions about the position.

"I know well that no man will ever bring out of that office the reputation which carries him into it," he wrote of the Presidency. "The honey moon would be as short in that case as in any other, & its moments of extasy would be ransomed by years of torment & hatred."

Upon further consideration, the office of Vice President appeared to be ideal, for he could attend the meetings of the American Philosophical Society, and he would be able to spend a great part of his time at Monticello. As he commented to Benjamin Rush, "I have no wish to meddle again in public affairs . . . If I am to act however, a more tranquil & unoffending station could not have been found for me . . . It will give me philosophical evenings in the winter, & rural days in the summer."[53]

To Madison he explained, "no arguments were wanting to reconcile me to a relinquishment of the first office or acquiescence under the second. As to the first, it was impossible that a more solid unwillingness settled on full calculation, could have existed in any man's mind, short of the degree of absolute refusal. The only view on which I would have gone into it for a while was to put our vessel on her republic tack before she should be thrown too much to leeward on her true principles."[54]

Accordingly, he began to make arrangements for moving to Philadelphia. He would be gone during the spring planting, he knew, but he planned to remain away only a few weeks each year for the next four years so that he could continue to fulfill his schedule for the restoration of the residence and the farms.

It was during this period that his preoccupation with remains of prehistoric animals was revived by the former scout and Indian fighter John Stuart, who sent him an account of unknown beasts roaming the wilderness which had been reported to him by two other scouts, George Wilson and John Davis:

> They were living on cheat river some time in the year 1765 in the nighttime something approached their Camp with astonishing roaring and very much allarmed them, their dogs also srunk and lay down at their feet refuseing to bark, as it drew nerer its cry became in their opinion as loud as thunder, and the stomping seemed to make the ground shake, the darkness of the night prevented their seeing their enemy tho they stood long with their arms to defend themselves, they hoped to see its tracks in the morning, but in this they were disappointed, not a sign was to be found.[55]

Stuart also described bones of a "Tremendous animal of the clawed kind lately found by some saltpetre manufacturers" in a limestone cave a short distance from Stuart's home in Greenbrier County, Virginia. They were found at a depth of two or three feet under the earthen floor of a limestone cave, where they had probably been preserved by what Jefferson described as "the nitreous impregnation of the earth" and some petrifaction. The find included other Bones of Human Creatures . . . of a surprizing size & uncommon kind."

Stuart shipped the bones on to Jefferson, who confirmed that they appeared to be of a species hitherto unknown. He asked Stuart for other remains that might have been found. Some had been dispersed, but Stuart forwarded all that remained of those that had been recovered. The total consisted of a femur, a broken ulna, a radius, three claws, and several bones of the feet.[56]

Excited by this new find, Jefferson planned to donate the bones to the American Philosophical Society, and contemplated describing them in a paper for publication in the Society's *Transactions*. Before doing so, however, he sought a thigh bone so that the animal's height could be estimated.

"I cannot help believing," he commented to Stuart, "that this animal as well as the Mammoth are still existing. The annihilation of any species of existence is so unexampled in any parts of the economy of nature which we see, that the probabilities against such annihilation are stronger than those for it." A thigh had in fact been found in the cave but was subsequently mislaid and lost.[57]

This was an unanticipated opportunity and Jefferson intended to take every advantage of it. He planned to publish an account of the incognitum in the *Transactions* of the American Philosophical Society, where it would receive the attention of the scientific community at home and abroad. He relished the fact that the discovery provided him with an opportunity to make another rebuttal to Buffon to be added to the other proofs that he had already amassed.

Jefferson promptly informed Rittenhouse, the Society's president, of the discovery of the "bones of an animal of the family of the lion, tyger, panther &c. but as preeminent over the lion in size as the Mammoth is over the elephant." He immediately began to prepare his paper to be read before the Society, and hoped it would be in time for inclusion in the new volume of the *Transactions* then in preparation. He also arranged to have Stuart rewarded for his find by election to the Society.[58] (*Figure 26*)

He named the newly found incognitum "the Great Claw" or *Megalonyx*, and classified it as a predator. He compared it to the lion, the largest clawed animal of which he knew, concluding that they were of the same species. He estimated that the animal was more than five feet in height and had weighed slightly more than eight hundred pounds, based on a comparison of the bones. In his paper he also concluded that it still existed inasmuch as its remains had been found:

> In the present interior of our continent there is surely space and range enough for elephants and lions, if in that climate they could subsist; and for mammoths and megalonyxes who may subsist there. Our entire ignorance of the immense country to the West and North-west, and of its contents, does not authorize us to say what it does not contain. In fine, the bones exist: therefore the animal has existed. The movements of nature are in a never-ending circle. The animal species which have once put into

a train of motion, is still probably moving in that train. For, if one link in nature's chain might be lost, another and another might be lost, till this whole system of things should vanish by piecemeal.[59]

It was at this time that Jefferson attempted to provide assistance to Louis, the hereditary Prince of Parma and heir to the Spanish throne. He was only twenty-two years of age and was developing a "cabinet of natural history" or personal museum, and was anxious to augment it "by an addition of all American subjects of the 3 departments of nature," as he informed Thomas Pinckney, who was then American envoy extraordinary to the court of Spain. Pinckney forwarded the request to Jefferson as the one best informed to assist in the endeavor.

Prince Louis offered to exchange European specimens of which he had duplicates or which he could procure. Jefferson referred the prince's proposal to Charles Willson Peale in Philadelphia. He suggested that if he entered into such an arrangement, it might be possible to enlist the cooperation of the minister of Spain with shipments to and from Genoa and Leghorn, and that at other times Jefferson himself might be of assistance.[60]

To the prince, Jefferson replied that he had never himself actually formed a museum or cabinet of natural history, nor was he informed of methods of preparing and preserving such specimens. He explained that he had referred the request to Peale and that he had responded, "I have it in my power to make an exchange of animal subjects generally, of minerals in a small number, but as to vegetables [plants] I have not had time to pay much attention to them as yet. However, by the help of Mr. Bartram and some others of my acquaintance in that line, the subjects wished for may be obtained." Jefferson added that the American botanist John Bartram was the keeper of a botanical garden near Philadelphia, and suggested that he might negotiate with him for plants and trees through Peale.

He then explained that in the matter of compensation Peale was a private citizen with no fortune, and that his sole income was from his "cabinet" or Museum so that the Prince would have to be responsible for transportation costs for specimens sent and received. He suggested that the prince should send a list of desiderata and if the requests were beyond the capabilities of Peale, Jefferson would try to find other sources for him.

Meanwhile he paid his "personal tribute to science and to your Royal Highness's dispositions to promote it, by depositing in your cabinet a tooth of the great animal called in Europe the mammoth, of which we find remains in the interior and inhabited parts of this country; this great distance from us renders them rare and difficult to be obtained." Jefferson forwarded the tooth through the Spanish minister to the United States, and promised to send a copy of the volume of the *Transactions* which would include his article on the *Megalonyx*.[61]

Peale immediately sent off a consignment to the prince and explained that he preferred exchange of artifacts, since he earned funds for his Museum "by my Pensil with less labour." Prince Louis sent long want lists of specimens of fish, birds, and other items for which European specimens would be exchanged. The prince's requests proved to be much greater than Peale was able to supply due to his limited resources.[62]

Jefferson was reluctant to go to Philadelphia at that time to take the oath of office. He considered that making the journey during February with its inclement weather would be difficult, and furthermore he believed that any senator could administer the oath anywhere even at Monticello. However, the suspicion voiced among many that he considered the second office to be beneath his acceptance changed his mind and he quickly made plans for the journey. Furthermore, he had just been elected president of the American Philosophical Society to succeed Rittenhouse, who had passed away in June. It would provide him with an opportunity to deliver his *Megalonyx* bones to the Society as well as his paper on the subject.

Accompanied by his servant, Jupiter, he set out in his carriage and at Dumfries, Virginia, he sent Jupiter back to Monticello with the horses in order to spare them the long journey, and he continued by stage coach. Jefferson brought with him in his carriage and then on the stage a carefully packed box containing the bones of the *Megalonyx* as well as the paper to be read. He wished to escape ceremony and fanfare if possible, and it was at Alexandria that he received his certificate of election.

He arrived at Philadelphia after ten days on the road, and two days before the inauguration was scheduled. In spite of his hope for lack of fanfare, he was met by an artillery company and his arrival was heralded by cannon salvos. A flag prominently displayed bore the motif "Jefferson the Friend of the People." He lodged with the Madisons upon arrival until he could find permanent accommodations for himself.[63]

Following his customary habit, during moments of leisure during the next two days he visited the bookstores. While browsing through the September 1796 issue of the British *Monthly Magazine*, he was startled to find therein an engraving of the skeleton of a great clawed animal, characteristics of which greatly resembled the *Megalonyx*.

The skeleton had been discovered near Buenos Aires and had been added to the Spanish royal cabinet of natural history at Madrid. In the accompanying article by the French naturalist, Georges Cuvier, it was classified among the edentates—mammals having few or no teeth—and a relative of the sloth. Cuvier named it the *Megatherium*.[64]

With remarkable perspicacity, Jefferson immediately concluded that his identification of the *Megalonyx* as a member of the cat family was probably in error. He quickly revised his paper, deleting sections and adding others before submitting it to the Society. He made reference to the article in the *Monthly Magazine,* cautiously noting that it was a condensed translation of Cuvier's *Mémoire* published earlier that year, and that the representation of the skeleton might not be completely reliable.

In a postscript which he added to his paper, he mentioned having seen Cuvier's description of the *Megatherium* after having completed his own paper, and added that after seeing the similarities between the two quadrupeds, he concluded that probably the *Megalonyx* was not carnivorous. Positive identification, he believed, should be left to future study.[65]

Ironically, in 1789 William Carmichael, the chargé d'affaires in Madrid, had sent him a drawing of the *Megatherium* with a measured description. He had enclosed another document as well and noted "I suppose these to be objects of Curiosity to you, the Latter [drawing and description of the Megatherium] however is merely for yourself, for the Academy of natural history here, will soon publish an account of this Animal and the person who furnishes me with the inclosed Sketch and notes desires that his Observations should not be made public."

The description and drawing were in an unidentified hand and stated that the skeleton was almost complete except for "The Tusks and the extremity of the head, the snout are Wanting" as well as other minor bones. Jefferson had thanked Carmichael for the interesting enclosures, and filed the drawing and description. Carmichael's letter had arrived in Paris in April when Jefferson was packing his books and possessions in expectation of his imminent departure for the United States.

He may have read the enclosures hastily, packed them with the rest of his possessions, intending to give them more attention later, and forgot it thereafter in the confusion of travel and his appointment as Secretary of State. Had he remembered the drawing, he would have had the honor of preceding the Spanish naturalists and Cuvier in identifying and naming the quadruped.[66]

On March 3rd, 1797 Jefferson was installed as president of the American Philosophical Society, and on the following day, a Saturday, he was inaugurated Vice President of the United States during the national presidential inauguration ceremonies. Wearing a long single-breasted blue frock coat buttoned to the waist and with his lightly powdered hair in a queue tied with a black ribbon, Jefferson presented a brief speech in the Senate chamber on the second floor of Congress Hall and took his oath. Then with the assembled senators he descended to the chamber of the House where at high noon the major ceremonies began.[67]

At the March 10th meeting of the Society, Jefferson was in the chair as the newly-elected President. As the Society's secretary read to the assembled members the paper Jefferson had prepared, carefully laid out upon the table before him were the bones of the *Megalonyx*. Later Jefferson completed the revisions for publication in the *Transactions*.

In his postscript reporting his discovery of the description and illustration of the *Megatherium*, he left in question the relationship between the *Megalonyx* and the *Megatherium*. He also left open the possibility that the former might have, after all, been a member of the cat family.[68]

In the same issue of the *Transactions* the anatomist, Caspar Wistar, contributed a description of the bones deposited by Jefferson. He concluded that the *Megalonyx* was related to the *Bradypus* or sloth illustrated in Buffon's work on natural history, and in some respects to the *Megatherium*, but that it was not the same species as either, concluding that it was not possible at that time to reach a decision.[69]

On his return to Philadelphia again in May, Jefferson saw a copy of the work by the Spanish naturalist, José Garriga, published in Madrid in 1796, in which the skeleton of the *Megatherium* was illustrated. He realized that Garriga's work pre-dated the article by Cuvier which he had read in the English periodical.[70]

In his memoirs on the *Megalonyx* and *Megatherium* published seven years later, in 1804, Cuvier credited Jefferson as the discoverer of the former. In 1822 the French naturalist, Anselm Desmarest, named the Virginia incognitum *Megalonyx jeffersonii*, by which name it is known today.[71]

Meanwhile it was time for Jefferson to direct his attention to the major responsibilities of the position to which he had been elected, Vice President of the United States.

CHAPTER XI

"HONORABLE
AND EASY"
(1797–1801)

The second office of the government is honorable and easy; the first is but a splendid misery.

Letter from Thomas Jefferson
to Elbridge Gerry, 1797.

The duties and responsibilities of the office of Vice President had not as yet been clearly defined in the Constitution, and consequently Jefferson's views of the office were at best modest and uncertain. He was to preside over the Senate and to succeed the President in the event of his death, resignation or removal. That was to be the extent of his role, "honorable and easy" to be sure, but less than satisfying to the incumbent.

Adams, the first Vice President, had been greatly frustrated in the position, although Washington had occasionally consulted him. In an early meeting with the newly elected President, it became eminently clear that President Adams visualized no change and did not plan to consult Jefferson on state matters.

Nor was the Vice President to become involved with Cabinet proceedings, inasmuch as they were not specified to be part of his responsibilities. Chiefly a survival from Washington's administration, the Cabinet consisted largely of Federalists who viewed Hamilton as the leader of their party. As a consequence, although elected Vice President, Jefferson found himself in fact to be virtually an outsider in the government, and free to pursue his own affairs except when the Senate was in session. For one so constantly active, it was a frustrating prospect.

During the week after his inauguration, Jefferson filled his time by visiting an exhibition of an elephant and some elks, by purchasing a copy of the Nautical Almanac, and some clothing and a pair of spectacles for Francis Eppes and by ordering a bust of himself from the Italian sculptor Giuseppe Ceracchi.[1]

His initial enthusiasm and intention to participate in the activities of the American Philosophical Society since he would now be in Philadelphia was reflected in his letter of acceptance when elected president of the Society. He had written,

> The suffrance of a body which comprehends whatever the American World has of distinction in Philosophy & Science in general, is the most flattering incident of my life, and that to which I am the most sensible. My satisfaction would be complete, were it not for the consciousness that it is far beyond my titles. I feel no qualification for this distinguished Post, but a sincere zeal for all the Objects of our institution, and an ardent desire to see knowledge so disseminated through the mass of mankind, that it may at length reach the extremes of Society, beggars, and kings. I pray you, Gentlemen, to testify for me, to our body my sense of their favour, and my dispositions to supply by zeal what I may be deficient in the other qualifications proper for their service, and to be assured that your testimony cannot go beyond my feelings.

He also conveyed his feelings about the death of Rittenhouse. "Genius, Science, modesty, purity of morals, simplicity of manners, marked him one of Nature's best examples of the Perfection she can cover under the human form. Surely, no Society, till ours, within the same compass of time, ever had to deplore the loss of two such members as Franklin & Rittenhouse. Franklin, our Patriarch, whom Philosophy & Philanthropy announced the first of men, and whose name will be like a star of the first magnitude in the firmament of heaven, when the memory of those who have surrounded & obscured him, will be lost in the Abyss of time."[2]

The Society was to undertake a new mission, brought about by Jefferson's presentation of the fossil remains of the *Megalonyx*, which had aroused considerable interest among the membership. To Jefferson's delight, a special committee was appointed to promote research on American antiquities and natural history. It urged the importance of acquiring one or more skeletons of the American mammoth and remains of any other unknown American animals, the location of which was known or to be discovered.

Particularly it directed attention to discoveries of fossil remains already made at Big Bone Lick in Kentucky and also in Orange and Ulster Counties in New York. Jefferson was enthusiastic about this turn of events and determined to assist the project as much as he was able.[3]

The continued silence from Adams after their initial meeting confirmed his early suspicion that he would have no more than a minimal role in affairs of state. He concluded, therefore, that there was little purpose in remaining in Philadelphia, and decided that he would be able to support the Society's activities as well from Monticello. Accordingly, after Congress recessed within ten days of his inauguration as Vice President, and President Adams had departed for his home in Massachusetts, Jefferson returned to Virginia where much work awaited him at home.

In preparation for continuing weather observations after his return, Jefferson visited the Philadelphia instrument maker and dealer, Joseph Gatty, and purchased thermometers for himself and Randolph.[4]

He had been home not more than six weeks before a special session of Congress was called, requiring him to return to Philadelphia. He was already being considered as a party leader, although he had never consciously sought the role. James Madison probably deserved it as much for his successful organizing of Republican interests in the House during the past several years, and for increasing the party's support among state officeholders.

It was Jefferson, however, who had for a long time been viewed as the symbol of Republicanism, and with Madison's retirement, he became the dominant figure, and assumed the leadership of the party. Jefferson later explained how two major political parties had been developing, and their differences.

"It is now well understood that two political Sects have arisen within the U. S.," he wrote, "the one believing that the executive is the branch of our government which the most needs support; the other that like the analogous branch in the English Government, it is already too strong for the republican parts of the constitution; and therefore in equivocal cases they incline to the legislative powers: the former of these are called federalists; sometimes aristocrats or monocrats, and sometimes tories, after the corresponding sect in the English Government of exactly the same definition: the latter are styled republicans, whigs, jacobins, anarchists, disorganizers &c. these terms are in familiar use with most persons . . . both parties claim to be federalists and republicans, and I believe with truth as to the great mass of them."[5]

When the Congress convened, President Adams informed it of the deterioration of relations with France and the need to plan for defensive measures. Elbridge Gerry was selected to serve with C. C. Pinckney and John Marshall on a commission to France. Jefferson was pleased with Gerry's selection, and urged him to make every effort to avoid war.

"Peace is undoubtedly at present the first object of our nation," he wrote. "Interest & honor are also national considerations. But interest, duly weighed, is in favor of peace even at the expence of spoilations past & future; and honor cannot now be an object."[6]

Jefferson expressed his views on foreign policy and on science to Elbridge Gerry. "I am for free commerce with all nations, political connection with none; and little or no diplomatic establishment. And I am not for linking ourselves by new treaties with the quarrels of Europe; entering that field of slaughter to preserve their balance, or joining in the confederacy of kings to war against the principles of liberty. I am for freedom of religion . . . for freedom of the press, and against all violations of the Constitution to silence by force and not by reason the complaints or criticisms, just or unjust, of our citizens against the conduct of their agents."[7]

He wrote particularly about science. "And I am for encouraging the progress of science in all its branches; and not for raising a hue and cry against the sacred name of philosophy; for aweing the human mind by stories of raw-head and bloody bones to a distrust of its own vision, and to repose implicitly on that of others; to go backwards instead of forwards to look for improvement; to believe that government, religion, morality, and every other science were in the highest perfection in ages of the darkest ignorance, and that nothing can ever be devised more perfect than what was established by our forefathers."[8]

Jefferson waited impatiently through the month of June for the Senate to adjourn so that he could leave Philadelphia once more, and "exchange the roar & tumult of bulls & bears, for the prattle of my grandchildren & senile rest."

Early in July he returned home by way of Montpelier where he stopped for a brief visit. At Monticello once more, he invited Madison to visit him. "I am anxious to see you here soon, because in about three weeks we shall begin to unroof our house, when the family will be obliged to go elsewhere for shelter."[9]

Maria had become engaged to John Wayles Eppes, familiarly known as "Jack," the oldest of the Eppes children at Eppington and her half first cousin and childhood playmate. Jefferson was inordinately pleased at the prospect, for he had fostered young Jack almost from infancy and had directed his boyhood schooling in Philadelphia.

Possessive of his daughters as ever, he proceeded to advise Maria, "harmony in the marriage state is the very first object to be aimed at . . . . Nothing can preserve affections uninterrupted but a firm resolution never to differ in will." Maria was quite unlike her sister and as she grew into womanhood, she became increasingly retiring and desultory and without interest in society. Her awareness of her sister's closer relationship with their father never lessened her fear of losing his affection.[10]

The young couple was married at Monticello on October 13th. One unfortunate incident that marred this idyllic period in Maria's life occurred as a result of the state of the building. Some months earlier she had fallen through the floor of one of the rooms into the cellar, but was not seriously injured. Then she fell out of a door and sprained her ankle so that she was unable to travel.

Maria and John Eppes did not accept Jefferson's offer of his property at Pantops, one of his farms in Albemarle County, because they preferred the tidewater area at Bermuda Hundred in Chesterfield County, a property which was a gift from the groom's father.[11]

At the beginning of December, Jefferson returned to Philadelphia once more because Congress was in session, leaving his home empty and unattended for the winter. The building still remained uncovered except for the parlor and the study. He found lodgings as before at Francis's Hotel. He was reminded by the secretary of the American Philosophical Society that it would meet at its usual time, six o'clock in the evening, adding, "It is a measure of sincerest pleasure to every well-wisher of science that one deep in its researches, and distinguished for its diffusion, is to honour its chair again in this city, invited thereto by an unanimous suffrage."

These were welcome words to Jefferson, for the political scene of which he was a part was rapidly deteriorating and brought him less than pleasure. At the meeting of January 19th, his letter to John Sinclair, president of the British National Board of Agriculture, describing his mouldboard was read to the Society and later published in the *Transactions*.

Fascinated as ever by the subject of fossil bones, he took pleasure in presenting the Society with one of the "mammoth" found in his state, and several months later donated a model of a hand-operated threshing machine invented in Virginia.[12]

More and more as he was forced to assume the leadership of the opposition he found himself in a state of virtual ostracism by Federalists out of government as well as in. Adams appeared to be under the complete control of his Federalist advisors. As a consequence, Jefferson's evenings were generally spent with a few close personal friends and political associates including Albert Gallatin, and with members of the American Philosophical Society.

He was by no means antisocial but it became necessary to avoid social events to prevent political embarrassment. He often used the excuse of health, as he did in a letter to Thomas Willing written in the third person concerning an invitation to a ball. "He hopes his no-attendance will not be misconstrued," Jefferson wrote. "He has not been at a ball these twenty years, nor for a long time permitted himself to go to any entertainments of the evening, from motives of attention to health. On these grounds he excused to Genl. Washington then living in the city his not going to his birthnight; to Mrs. Washington her evenings; to Mr. Adams his soirees; and to all and sundry who have been so good as to invite him to tea and card parties. Tho desirous to go to them it is an indulgence his age and habits will he hopes obtain and continue to him. He has always testified his homage for the occasion by his subscription to it."[13]

This was a period of considerable dissention, during which Jefferson suffered from much criticism on several fronts. Political factionalism had reached new heights filled with political animosities. A letter he had written to Mazzei in 1796 in which he reported changed attitudes in government was made public in garbled form and claimed to contain an attack on George Washington.

To protect himself and correct the distortion, Jefferson wrote, "for a moment concieved I must take the field of the public papers. I could not disavow it wholly, because the greatest part was mine in substance tho' not in form. I could not avow it as it stood because the form was not mine, and in one place the substance very materially falsified. This then would render explanations necessary. Nay, it would render proofs of the whole necessary, & draw me at length into a publication of all (even the secret) transactions of the administration while I was of it; and embroil me personally with every member of the Executive, with the Judiciary, and with others still."

He decided to follow his usual policy of silence, because any explanation he could make would result in creating a difference with Washington, which had never occurred previously. Some time later a personal letter Jefferson had written commenting on public affairs to Peregrine Fitzhugh, a friend and political supporter, was communicated to the recipient's Republican friends with all good intention. One of them repeated part of the substance which reached the ears of one of the opposing party. It was misquoted and exaggerated in the press as a criticism of the administration. When reported to Adams, he began to suspect Jefferson of working against him, and the President's coolness towards him became even more apparent.

To add to these problems, Luther Martin, who for many years had been attorney general of Maryland, launched an attack on Jefferson which was to last over three years. It concerned a speech of the Mingo chief Logan which Jefferson had included in his *Notes* as part of his defense of the American Indians against Buffon's aspersions.

Logan had claimed that Michael Cresap had destroyed his family. Martin, who was married to Cresap's daughter, stated that Cresap had never killed either the Logan family or friendly Indians and that furthermore the Logan speech never took place.

He contemptuously attacked Jefferson as a philosopher, stating "When we see him employed in weighing the rats and mice of the two worlds, to prove that those of the new are not exceeded by those of the old—when, to establish that the body of the American savage is not inferior in form or in vigor to the body of an European, we find him examining minutely every part of their frame, and hear him declare that, though the wrist and the hand of the former are smaller than those parts of the latter . . . when we see him so zealous to establish an equality in such trifles, and to prove the body of his savage to be formed on the same modula with the *"Homo sapiens Europeus,"* how much more solicitous may we suppose him to have been to prove that the mind of this savage was also formed on the same modula?"

Although Jefferson considered the possibility that Martin may have been a tool of the Federalists, it is more likely that the lawyer was acting entirely on his own initiative. Jefferson's response was to proceed immediately to obtain more information about the Logan-Cresap incident, and he was able to confirm the authenticity of Logan's speech.

Greatly angered by Jefferson's "obstinate, stubborn silence," Martin continued his attack with subsequent public letters. Jefferson eventually had copies printed of a letter of general explanation which he circulated to individuals whom he was certain would not let them get into the newspapers, and continued to collect information on the incident for publication in the future. Early in March, Jefferson returned to Monticello and continued to refrain from involvement with political affairs.[14]

As an escape from these problems, in the spring he engaged with the Reverend Madison in making comparative experiments with magnetic declination. Of his dipping needle Madison wrote, "The Instrument is delicate & appears well formed . . . I had every part of the Instrument examined, & touched the Needle with a Magnet of considerable power." After numerous repetitions of his experiment, Madison reported a magnetic declination at Williamsburg of 66° 15'.[15]

Meanwhile the threat of war with France had escalated and the Federalists launched a campaign against the Republicans by means of the Alien and Sedition Acts. The Alien Bill provided power to the government to arrest or deport aliens, while the Sedition Bill made any attacks on the government, its policies or officials criminal libels subject to prosecution in the Federal courts. Jefferson viewed the first to be aimed directly at such men as Comte de Volney, then residing in Philadelphia, and the Swiss-born Albert Gallatin, leader of the Republicans in Congress. He suspected that the Sedition Bill was aimed to destroy the Republican press, particularly the *Aurora* edited by Benjamin Franklin Bache. The temper of Congress had reached almost the point of hysteria, and Jefferson chose this moment to return to Monticello.

During this interlude he drafted his now famous set of Kentucky Resolutions, an appeal from the authority of the Federal government to that of the States, proclaiming the rights and duties of the States to declare unconstitutional measures promulgated by the Federal government. As Vice President, he could not submit the resolutions under his own name, for in the present climate they could have been considered treasonable, especially if generated by an individual of his position. For this reason he prepared resolutions for introduction into one of the state legislatures.

Jefferson dispatched the resolutions to Wilson Cary Nicholas, who turned them over to John Breckinridge on his way to Kentucky. The resolutions were adopted by the state legislature and resolves that were more moderately stated were also passed by the Virginia legislature.

Jefferson was one of the earliest proponents of archeological research in the United States. In 1799, his third year as president of the American Philosophical Society, he had been responsible for the issuance of a circular encouraging the pursuit of research in the natural sciences, archeology and ethnology, with special emphasis on the study of Indian mounds. The circular read as follows:

> The American Philosophical Society have always considered the antiquity, changes, and present state of their own country as primary objects of their research; and with a view to facilitate such discoveries, a permanent committee has been established, and recommends
>
> 1. To procure one or more entire skeletons of the Mammoth, so called, and of such other unknown animals as either have been, or hereafter may be discovered in America.
>
> 2. To obtain accurate plans, drawings and descriptions of whatever is interesting, (where the originals cannot be had) and especially of ancient Fortifications, Tumuli, and other Indian works of art: ascertaining the materials composing them, their contents, the purposes for which they were probably designed, &c.
>
> 3. To invite researches into the Natural History of the Earth, the changes it has undergone as to Mountains, Lakes, Prairies, &c.
>
> 4. To enquire into the Customs, Manners, Languages and Character of the Indian nations, ancient and modern, and their migrations.
>
> The importance of these objects will be acknowledged by every Lover of Science, and we trust sufficiently apologize for thus troubling you; for without the aid of gentlemen who have taste and opportunity for such researches, our means would be very confined. We therefore solicit your communications, now or in the future, on these subjects; which will be at all times thankfully received, and duly noticed in the publications of the Society.
>
> As to the first object, the committee suggest, to Gentlemen who may be in the way of enquiries of that kind, that the Great Bone Lick on the Ohio, and other places where there may be mineral salt, are the most eligible spots for the purpose, because animals are known to resort to such places.

With respect to the second head, the committee are desirous that cuts in various directions may be made into many of the Tumuli, to ascertain their contents, while the diameter of the largest tree growing thereon, the number of its annulars and the species of the tree, may tend to give some idea of their antiquity. If the works should be found to be of Masonry; the length, breadth, and height of the walls ought to be carefully measured, the form and nature of the stones described, and specimens of both the cement and stones sent to the committee.

The best methods of obtaining information on the other subjects will naturally suggest themselves to you, and we rely on a disposition favourable to our wishes.[16]

The committee consisted of the Society's president, Thomas Jefferson; James Wilkinson, Commander of the Army at Headquarters; George Turner of the Western Territory; and Caspar Wistar, Adam Seybert and Jonathan Williams, officials of the Society.

Artifacts recovered from Indian tumuli had already found their way into the Society's collections even before the issuance of the circular. Winthrop Sargent, administrator of the Northwest Territories, had excavated a mound in Ohio in 1794 which produced numerous important relics. They were described by Benjamin Smith Barton in a letter to Dr. Joseph Priestley, which was subsequently printed with illustrations in the *Transactions* in 1799. Some of these artifacts have survived in the Society's collections.[17]

Now having learned from the Reverend Ezra Stiles that some large fossil bones had been recovered in New York State, and encouraged by the Society's interest, Jefferson was eager to acquire some for the Society. Recalling that Robert Livingston lived in the region, he wrote asking whether the bones were indeed of the mammoth and whether some could be obtained.

Livingston responded that the bones had been discovered at Shawangunk in Ulster County, but that they had been declared common property so that they could not be removed until the excavation project had been completed. Although frustrated in this effort, Jefferson continued his search, with the assistance of others, for new evidence and remains of unknown and extinct animals.[18]

One of Jefferson's most constant correspondents was the noted agriculturist and statesman, Colonel John Taylor of Caroline County, Virginia. He had been a Presidential Elector in 1797 and it was he who had introduced Madison's Virginia Resolutions relating to the Alien and Sedition Acts in the Virginia House of Deputies in 1798. For many years

Jefferson and Taylor exchanged long letters relating to details of farming, crops, land conservation and the mouldboard.[19]

Taylor had enabled Jefferson to purchase one of Martin's grain drills and later Jefferson learned that Taylor had seen and approved Martin's greatly improved version of the Scottish threshing machine. "Being myself well acquainted with the original *geered* machine and Booker's substitution of *whirls & bands* (as I have one of each kind), it will perhaps give you but a little trouble to give me so much of an explanation as will be necessary to make me understand Martin's and let it apply, if you please, to the movements by horses or by hand."[20]

Taylor attempted to provide the description Jefferson requested, noting, however, that when he made his own, Martin had not seen either the Scottish threshing machine nor Booker's version. However, inasmuch as Martin planned to apply for a patent, Jefferson would then be able to have a full description.

There was some problem with the patent, requiring revision of the first specifications submitted by Martin with his application for a patent. Taylor appealed to Jefferson for help, asking him to become the patron of his application, and forwarded the model and description to him. The statesman was able to resolve the problem by rewriting the specifications. Martin obtained the patent, for a "wheat-threshing machine," and Jefferson sent it to Taylor with an explanation.

"A patent had actually been made out on the first description," he explained, "and how to get this suppressed and another made for a second invention, without a second fee, was the difficulty. I practised a little art in a case where honesty was really on our side, and nothing against us but the rigorous letter of the law, and having obtained the first specification and got the second put in its place, a second patent has been formed, which I now inclose with the first specification." The patent was issued to T. C. Martin on June 2, 1798 without a residence being listed. Jefferson noted that his mouldboard had been highly approved in his area, where he had been using it for five years with entire satisfaction and approbation.[21]

Despite Jefferson's interest and concern for the successful operation of the Monticello nailery, his absence from the scene led it into financial difficulties. Nailrod shipments from Philadelphia were occasionally late in arrival, bringing the nailery to a standstill.

The finished nails were prepared for transport in casks made by the Monticello cooper, and often the unavailability of a driver or wagon delayed shipments. Most of all, payments for shipments made were excessively delayed by his distributors and direct clients. This necessitated correspondence requesting payment, a chore he found excessively unpleasant, particularly when it became necessary to dun individuals with whom he wished to maintain continued pleasant relationships.

As an example, in 1798 a shipment of nails amounting in value to several hundred dollars sent to his Staunton distributor, William Clarke, remained unaccounted for. Jefferson was always patient with such delays, as reflected in his letter to Clarke. He stated "I am under a necessity of solliciting your remittance of the balance at the first possible moment. I shall be much pressed by a paiment to be made at our next court . . . when receipt of your balance would be particularly acceptable, however, then, or as soon after as you can make it convenient." Nevertheless, several years passed before he received payment, and the unsold nails were returned by Clarke and his successor. This led to Clarke's voluntary resignation as distributor, and Jefferson's need to find another.[22]

The application of steam as a source for power intrigued him, and he was particularly interested in a description of the steam engine from Chancellor Robert R. Livingston early in 1799. He explained that although he was "deterred by the complexity of that hitherto known," he was nonetheless impressed with the superior simplicity and economy of Livingston's engine. He brought the information to the attention of the American Philosophical Society.

At this time Jefferson sought advice from Livingston on domestic water reservoirs which were customarily installed on tops of houses to provide a water supply through pipes, but which could also serve as a reservoir in the event of fire, which was particularly prevalent in rural areas. He was contemplating whether there might not be a common agent by means of which the water could be conducted into such a roof reservoir, and it occurred to him that the kitchen fire might be arranged by means of steam to accomplish it.

He considered "if it's [the fire in the kitchen stove] small but constant action could be accumulated so as to give a stroke from time to time which might throw ever so small a quantity of water from the bottom of a well to the top of the house (say one hundred feet), it would furnish more than would waste by evaporation, or be used by the family."

Jefferson had considered the use of the iron back of the chimney as a cistern to hold water, which could supply steam and be maintained constantly at a boiling temperature by the fire. In view of Livingston's familiarity with the subject, Jefferson considered him the one most likely to be able to invent such a facility. It was probably for this purpose that he had purchased a model of a hydraulic machine in Paris, although there is no evidence that he developed it at Monticello.[23]

During each of the Congressional recesses, Jefferson hurried back to Virginia to deal with the great number of projects always underway in the house and on the grounds, or farming activities of the plantation. One of these was the construction of a new mill house. Jefferson consulted his lawyer at Richmond, David Call, concerning the suit Call was conducting on his behalf for water rights against rival claimants, the heirs of Bennett Henderson.

He was trying to prevent the Henderson heirs from raising their dam at Milton on the Rivanna because it would flood his mill installation at Shadwell. Among the questions to be resolved were "Who is to abate the dam & at whose expense? Who is to fix on the autient level of the water?" Four years after a decree was issued in 1799 in his favor, Jefferson had the Henderson dam demolished. The stone with which Henderson had built the dam had been removed from Jefferson's premises, and he now considered whether and how he could reclaim it in order to re-use it later.[24]

Jefferson had long been contemplating the prospect of a new state university ever since he had made his famous revision of Virginia's laws to reform its educational system. Although his plan to import the faculty of the College of Geneva to Virginia had failed, Jefferson continued to be concerned about the state of higher education in Virginia. He had originally proposed that the College of William and Mary could be revitalized if moved to Albemarle County and modernized. This met with great opposition from those who were concerned with its Episcopal tone so that nothing had come of the proposal.

He was ready to try once more, and consulted with Dr. Joseph Priestley for assistance in planning a science curriculum. When Priestley, discoverer of phlogiston (oxygen) whose experiments with electricity and gases had brought him great renown, left England in 1794, he had established himself in Pennsylvania. However, the persecution which had forced his departure followed him, as Federalists labeled him "atheist" and "Jacobin."

To Priestley, Jefferson described the College of William and Mary as "just well enough endowed to draw out the miserable existence to which a miserable constitution has doomed it. It is moreover eccentric in its position, exposed to bilious diseases as all the lower country is, & therefore abandoned by the public care, as that part of the country is in a considerable degree by it's inhabitants."

His plan was to establish a university in upper Virginia where a healthier location prevailed, and which would be more centrally located in the state. It was to be designed on a liberal and modern plan so that it would attract students from other states as well. To achieve this, it was necessary to develop a good curriculum which included "a judicious selection of the sciences practically grouped together in an institution meant chiefly for use." He felt that no one was as familiar with subjects to be taught as Priestley and for that reason requested his cooperation. He again consulted Priestley about the teaching of languages, which Jefferson did not consider essential in teaching the sciences except as they might be useful in studying them.

"The Gothic idea that we are to look backwards instead of forwards for the improvement of the human mind," he confided to Priestley, "and to recur to the annals of our ancestors for what is most perfect in government, in religion & in learning, is worthy of those bigots in religion & government, by whom it has been recommended, & whose purposes it would answer." Priestley promptly forwarded his "Hints Concerning Public Education" based on his experiences abroad, which had met with less than approbation when published.[25]

Jefferson also consulted Pierre Samuel Du Pont de Nemours, a French official he had known in Paris and who had recently arrived on a commission from the Institut de France to report on the state of scientific research in the United States. Jefferson, who had always considered him to be "the ablest man in France," welcomed him gladly. Du Pont's son had preceded him and established a gunpowder factory in Delaware, where the father also settled.

Because of the limited resources available, Jefferson considered it best to leave the study of the liberal arts to private schools, but wished to emphasize studies in the sciences. Requesting a short sketch of Du Pont's views on science teaching, he received instead a manuscript of several hundred pages entitled "National Education in the United States." Although it included excellent theoretical considerations, it did not fulfill Jefferson's requirements.[26]

It was while he was about to assume his position as Vice President and would have to preside over the United States Senate, that Jefferson became aware of the need for a manual incorporating the rules of procedure and standard parliamentary practice. He had first begun to think about such an undertaking shortly after his appointment and while still at Monticello.

Realizing that he would be called upon to superintend a legislative chamber as Vice President, and that he was "entirely rusty in the Parliamentary rules of procedure," he began to collect examples of pertinent precedents. Soon after having been elected to the position, he had asked George Wythe for any information he might have on the subject of parliamentary procedures, for he found himself uncertain concerning the required procedures.

He considered his old mentor to be the one most knowledgeable in the country on the subject. He hoped that Wythe had kept notes on them and if so asked to borrow them. Although an authority on the subject, Wythe had little to offer, however, and thereupon Jefferson began the task of compiling his own manual.[27]

This undertaking provides an example of Jefferson's remarkable talent for research, which he had demonstrated so ably while studying law in Williamsburg. Although he did not think so, he was already an acknowledged expert on parliamentary procedures gained during his career in the Virginia House of Burgesses. He had copied the rules and precedents in use in the Virginia House, which were derived from those of the British Parliament, into what he called his "Parliamentary Pocket Book," a leather-bound commonplace book. Now, however, he found no one else knowledgeable enough to assist him nor any published references that would be useful.

His predecessor, then Vice President Adams, had not felt the need while in the chair for a specific guide upon which to base his decisions on disputed points of procedure. He relied on British Parliament as a precedent in most such instances, as a consequence of which there had been criticism of his conduct in the chair. For these reasons and because of his perpetual preoccupation with organization, Jefferson felt the necessity for reference to "some known system of rules, that he may neither leave himself free to indulge caprice or passion nor open to the imputation of them."

First of all, he rejected the precedents of the 1776 rules of the Continental Congress, many of which were now in use in the Senate. He continued his work alone, collecting and digesting pertinent British precedents, and collating them with the provisions of the Constitution and the rules of the Senate to which they related.

Despite the fact that he was a committed Anglophobe, he nonetheless found that the rules and precedents of the British parliament were "wisely constructed for governing the debates of a deliberate body," and furthermore that they were in use in various states throughout the country and appeared in publications to which others could refer.[28]

Originally he had no intention to publish his compilation, intending it only for his own use, but he changed his mind as he applied these rules and precedents while in the chair. He determined to prepare them in the form of a parliamentary manual and have it printed as a standard for present and future use.

When the compilation of procedures was completed, he sent it to Wythe to verify the contents for him. Wythe corrected the manuscript as well as he was able, and additional corrections were made by Edmund Pendleton, to whom Jefferson had also sent a copy.

It was Jefferson's plan to prepare the procedures in the form of a work "which I shall deposit with the Senate of the U.S. and may thence possibly get into the public possession . . . It may do good by presenting to the different legislative bodies a chaste Praxis to which they may by degrees conform their several inconsistent & embarrassing modes of proceding."[29]

Just before his term as Vice President ended, Jefferson took his manuscript to Samuel Harrison Smith, publisher of the *National Intelligencer*, who arranged for its printing in February 1801, the year Jefferson was elected to the Presidency. The *Parliamentary Manual* was adopted not only by the Senate at that time, but in 1837 it was adopted by the House of Representatives as well.[30]

In addition to its importance because of its long use in the legislative body, the *Manual* is a particularly fine example of Jefferson's sound scholarship based on careful historical research in a great range of manuscript and published sources. His *Manual* still forms the basis of procedure in the Senate and "in certain parts of the *Manual* are to be found the foundations of some of the most important portions of the House's practice."

The present manual of the House of Representatives also reprints Jefferson's Manual omitting those sections referring exclusively to the Senate. It continues to be used as the nucleus of the larger number of precedents developed and added since his time.[31]

The year 1800 was an election year and the Federalists were becoming concerned about the outcome. The angry reaction from the public to the Alien and Seditions Acts brought about a division within the ranks of the Federalists that threatened their dominant position. Adams refused to grant top military command to Hamilton and ousted his henchmen, Timothy Pickering and Oliver Wolcott, from the Cabinet. These combined actions made Hamilton determined to keep Adams from winning a second term at any cost.

The control of the state of New York became a pivotal factor in what would be a close election. Aaron Burr saved the day by building a formidable Republican opposition with a strong party machine which swept the city and gained control of both houses of the New York legislature. Burr's place on the national ticket was ensured, and it was generally acknowledged that Jefferson was the Republican candidate for President, with Burr as the Vice President.

The Federalists lacked unanimity, and Hamilton desperately sought to shift the selection of New York electors from the legislature to direct popular vote in order to keep Jefferson, that "atheist in religion and a fanatic in politics from getting possession of the helm of state."

Jefferson left for Monticello in mid-May, traveling along the eastern shore where he would be more or less incognito so that he could avoid public demonstrations by supporters along the way. He was not to be spared comment from the press, however. Hamilton's voiced epithet of "atheist", supported by Jefferson's own statements on religion in his *Notes*, and the fact that his household was "French," escalated into countless charges brought against him thundered from pulpits and voiced in scurrilous pamphlets.

Jefferson maintained that the subject of one's religion was a most private matter between oneself and one's God and all his life he refused any public discussion of his religious convictions. As a young man he had rejected his ancestral Anglican, substituting a God of nature in place of a God of revelation. He attended church in Washington and in Charlottesville. Realizing that nothing he could say would silence his critics, he steadfastly refused to respond to his detractors during the election of 1800 on the principle that he was accountable only to God alone for his beliefs. In his view, the Nazarene Jesus was the outstanding moral reformer of the Jews, and he believed that his teachings were of universal importance due to his highly developed moral sense and not to his divinity.[32]

He was again re-elected president of the American Philosophical Society, but when the seat of government was transferred to Washington, he considered his usefulness to the Society to be at an end because of the distance. He offered his resignation, which was declined, and he obviously was pleased to continue in the position.[33]

As the political storm continued to rage all about him, Jefferson to all appearances ignored it and directed his attention to his scientific preoccupations. He made a comparison of the meteorological diaries he had received from an observer in Quebec and from William Dunbar in Mississippi, and noted "the lowest depression of the thermometer" in both.

To Hugh Williamson, he marveled "the result was a wonder that any human being should remain in a cold country who could find room in a warm one." Harry Hill had told him that the temperature at Madeira was generally from 55 to 65°; "If I ever change my climate for health, it should be for that Island." He was interested in learning whether any study had been made on the coincidence between the appearance of the new moon and increased cold, and the full moon and lesser cold, or that the reflected light of the moon affected weather in any way.[34]

To Dunbar he commented, "I have no doubt but that cold is the source of more sufferance to all animal nature than hunger, thirst, sickness, and all the other pains of life and of death itself put together. I live in a temperate climate, and under circumstances which do not expose me often to cold. Yet when I recollect on one hand all the sufferings I have had from cold, and on the other all my others pains, the former preponderate greatly. What then must be the sum of that evil if we take in the vast proportion of men who are obliged to be out in all weather, by land and by sea, all the families of beasts, birds, reptiles, and even the vegetable kingdom! for that too has life, and where there is life there may be sensation."

Intrigued with the phenomenon of the rainbow, he remarked on the fact that in his location Dunbar was able to see the rainbow as "a great portion of the circle." Jefferson noted that he had had a similar experience because of the topography of Monticello, situated on a mountain "five hundred feet perpendicularly high," where a rainbow would span the great distance to the river at the foot of the mountain. He remarked that he had also observed moonbows on several occasions, which were "of the color of the common circle round the moon, and were very near."[35]

He was pleased to have a letter from Andrew Ellicott, who had just returned to Philadelphia after an absence of almost four years. Ellicott had been engaged on a survey of "the southern boundary" with Spanish territories including the Floridas. It had been an arduous experience, but he had made more than four hundred astronomical observations for establishing the boundary.

He had hoped to meet with Jefferson in Washington, and had missed him by only several days. He reported that the lunar distances used by the compilers of the Nautical Almanac were so accurate that now longitude on land could easily be determined by the use of a good sextant and a timepiece and more easily than by observations of eclipses of the Jovian satellites. He wished to publish some of his observations, but had been unable to obtain a reply to his request for permission from the State Department.

Jefferson saw no objection to such a publication, commenting, "My own opinion is that government should by all means in their power deal out the materials of information to the public in order that it may be reflected back on themselves in the various forms into which public ingenuity may throw it."

"The election is under dilemma," Jefferson added. "The two Republican candidates are probably even; and the states in Congress which are Federal are disposed to take advantage of that circumstances, to prevent an election by Congress, and permit the government of the Union to be suspended for want of a head. This tells us who are entitled to the appellation of anarchists with which they have so liberally branded others."[36]

The Presidential campaign of 1800 was filled with bitter charges and countercharges, many heaped on Jefferson, particularly by the Federalist press. He would not make a reply to any of them. As he commented to Samuel Smith, a Maryland Republican leader, "At a very early period of my life, I determined never to put a sentence into any newspaper. I have religiously adhered to the resolution through my life, and have great reason to be contented with it. Were I to undertake to answer the calumnies of the newspaper, it would be more than all my own time, & that of 20. aids could effect. For while I should be answering one, twenty new ones would be invented. I have thought it better to trust to the justice of my countrymen, that they would judge me by what they *see* of my conduct on the stage where they have placed me, & what they *knew* of me before the epoch since which a particular party has supposed it might answer some view of theirs to vilify me in the public eye."[37]

Taking advantage of the election, in late 1800 George Helmbold, Jr. of Philadelphia announced his plan to publish a full-length portrait of Jefferson, a project which he continued to advertise for the next nine months, issuing the portrait in late 1801. At about the same time another engraver named Cornelius Tiebout issued an engraved portrait of Jefferson, featuring his scientific interests with the presence of an electrostatic machine and a pair of globes. The portrait was not produced from life, but incorporated a copy of Rembrandt Peale's portrait of the President attached to a full-length figure. It is the only portrait of Jefferson associating him with science.[38] (See *Frontispiece*)

In late November Jefferson left Monticello for the last time as Vice President and proceeded to Washington, to which the government had moved in June. He immediately took lodgings in the boardinghouse recently opened by Conrad and McMunn on New Jersey Avenue. It was conveniently situated a few steps away from the Capitol, and Jefferson remained in this location throughout the winter until mid-March. As yet there were few boardinghouses and few other accommodations available in the infant city for members of Congress and other government officials.

Despite the popular conception that the new capital city was swampy, "the lands within and surrounding the District of Columbia are as high, as dry, as healthy as any in the United States," pronounced George Washington in 1791. "The major part of the area was covered with trees—tall umbrageous forest trees of every variety, among which the superb tulip poplar rose conspicuous; the magnolia, the azalea, the hawthorn, the wild rose and many other indigenous shrubs grew beneath the shade, while violets, anemones and a thousand other sweet wood flowers found shelter among the roots," wrote Margaret Bayard Smith, who was among the earliest to settle there.

Within the next two decades, however, a great number of the trees were removed to make room for building programs of the growing city, and as a consequence the natural drainage was destroyed and led to occasional floodings of Tiber Creek.

It was in part due to his love of nature that Jefferson had selected Conrad and McMunn's, so that he could enjoy the expanse visible from the windows of his drawing room. He particularly deplored the waste, however, as groves of tulip trees and other forest trees which dotted the plain were being girdled and then cut up by the people for firewood. He noted, "The unnecessary felling of a tree, perhaps the growth of centuries seems to me a crime little short of murder, it pains me to an unspeakable degree."[39]

During his winter in Washington, Jefferson attended the only church in the city. It was a small frame building which had formerly been a tobacco house, and was later purchased by Episcopalians and fitted up as a rude church for its congregation of some fifty or sixty parishioners. The only other building of religious worship in the city was a small Roman Catholic chapel. After the custom of preaching in the House of Representatives on Sunday was instituted, Jefferson regularly attended there accompanied by his secretary. The seats he had chosen on the first occasion were thereafter always left vacant for him while he remained in office.[40]

By mid-December, his victory and that of Burr were confirmed in the state vote for electors. However, a tie occurred in the Electoral College, with Jefferson and Burr each receiving 73 votes, while Adams and Pinckney received 65 and 64 votes respectively. The final decision would rest in a vote in the House of Representatives by state delegations. The first weeks of 1801 were fraught with intense political excitement. The tie vote of the electors kept the rival candidates in high state of suspense about the decision.

Jefferson maintained a calm mien throughout, and gave the impression that he was totally disassociated from the events around him. He spent his time writing letters on scientific matters to friends and associates in the American Philosophical Society.

With Jonathan Williams he discussed changes in climate. William Dunbar of Natchez, Mississippi, offered to exchange information about meteorological observations and Indian vocabularies, an offer that Jefferson welcomed. He was fascinated with the study of languages, and realized their importance in tracing historical origins. He had been collecting Indian vocabularies far and wide with this end in mind.

As he had noted to Benjamin Hawkins, former senator and Indian agent who was on the Creek frontier, "I have long believed we can never get any information of the antient history of the Indians, of their descent & filiation, but from a knowledge & comparative view of their languages. I have, therefore, never failed to avail myself of any opportunity which offered of getting their vocabularies." He sent a similar inquiry to David Campbell in Tennessee for information about the Cherokee dialect. He had already collected a large number of vocabularies, and contemplated having them published.[41]

To William Dunbar he acknowledged having received the vocabularies of the Bedais, Tankawis and Teghas tribes. "I have it much at heart," he wrote, "to make as extensive a collection as possible of the Indian tongues. I have at present thirty tolerably full, among which the number radically different, is truly wonderful. It is curious to consider how such handfuls of men, came by different languages, and how they have preserved them all to one orthography, but I soon became sensible that this would occasion two sources of error instead of one."

He considered it desirable to keep them in the form of orthography in which they were taken, only noting whether they were English, French, etc. It was Jefferson's long-range plan to produce a comprehensive compilation of all the Indian languages, a project which never materialized.[42]

Although Livingston had informed Jefferson that the fossil remains discovered in Shawungunk were not available because they were considered property of the community, inasmuch as "the whole town having joined in digging for them until they were stopped by autumnal rains," Jefferson nonetheless persisted in pursuing the matter.

There were great hopes that a complete skeleton would be recovered because the bones were found covered in a stratum of clay which protected them from the air and water and consequently were better preserved than those found in other sites. Livingston noted that among the remains recovered were vertebrae, part of a jaw with two grinders, tusks, sternum, scapula, tibia and fibula, tarsus and metatarsus and part of a skull. The bones appeared to be of a claw-footed animal, he reported, and "the arm or fore-leg, had a greater motion than can possibly belong to the element or any of the large quadrupeds with which we are acquainted."

Jefferson suggested that in view of the difficulties of obtaining any of the bones, the residents of Shawungunk might be willing to part with a few. He suggested to Wistar that it would be wise for him to compile a list of those bones of which the American Philosophical Society had no examples, and to send the list on to him for forwarding.[43]

Shortly before Jefferson left office, Eli Whitney came to Washington seeking another extension of his contract with the government. He had defaulted on his agreement of 1798 to produce 10,000 muskets in two years, failing to produce a single weapon within the period specified. He then ingeniously "conceived" of the manufacture of interchangeable parts. He brought with him a musket on which ten different gunlocks could be fitted interchangeably.

He arranged for a demonstration of his claimed system before government officials, including Jefferson. Taking parts he had brought with him, Whitney demonstrated that gunlocks could be assembled and disassembled and parts substituted without difficulty. As Connecticut Congressman Elizur Goodrich later reported to the New England gunsmith, Simeon North, Jefferson "did not hesitate to say that he in no instance seen any work of specimens equal to Mr. Whitney's, except in one factory in France." Undoubtedly reminded of his experience in Blanc's manufactory, Jefferson offered to recommend to Monroe, then governor of Virginia, that Whitney be commissioned to make muskets for the Virginia militia. Whitney declined the offer with thanks, however, until his prior committments had been fulfilled.

Despite Jefferson's enthusiastic response, there is every evidence that the locks were made especially for that particular demonstration. Extensive examination of Whitney weapons in collections reveal that they were not in fact made with interchangeable parts. Further evidence is that all lock parts of Whitney muskets are individually numbered to match the numbering of their other parts, which would have been unnecessary if they were interchangeable.

Whitney succeeded in obtaining a contract for muskets to be produced for the Federal government over a five year period but was unable to obtain the advance he requested until Jefferson intervened, and replaced Samuel Dexter as Secretary of the Treasury with Albert Gallatin. Whitney was further delayed in fulfilling his contract by the need to go to South Carolina to promote his cotton gin with the legislature. Calling upon Jefferson on his way South, Jefferson reassured him about the delay. It is likely that in their meetings Jefferson provided Whitney with details of Blanc's operations and his use of gauges. He also informed Monroe of Whitney's "invention," and suggested that it might be possible to employ him in the gun manufactory at Richmond.

The Secretary of War provided Whitney with the time extension he requested, and by the end of 1802 Whitney had completed another thousand muskets. Having to return once more to the South, where he remained for five months, another extension of his contract became necessary. All went well until the summer of 1808, when it was discovered that samples of a Whitney musket selected at random had serious defects. The pan was set too far from the barrel, the ramrod was easily bent and the breechplate was inferior. A new inspection of the weapons already delivered confirmed that many were defective.

Whitney defended the quality of his work by comparing it to that of other armories, which he claimed was equally defective. He did not complete the requirements until early 1809.

Whether Whitney ever achieved mass manufacture with interchangeable parts remains in serious doubt, and is still debated by historians of technology. It was well established that Simeon North did so in about 1815, however. Nonetheless, Whitney's reputation, built with skillful self-promotion and ably supported by his Yale associates and other friends, enabled him to continue to obtain other government contracts.[44]

Meanwhile, as Jefferson occupied himself with peaceful pursuits and ignored the political conflict that raged around him, the House was in bitter turmoil while the Federalists schemed to find some way to turn their defeat into a victory. Wiser heads prevailed, however, and after the balloting had stretched over six days, Jefferson received the majority, on the thirty-sixth ballot.

Shortly after he learned the results of his election to the Presidency, Jefferson wrote to Meriwether Lewis to offer him a position as his secretary. He had known Lewis since the latter's childhood and was well informed of his career. Following a grammar school education, Lewis had joined the militia in 1794 during the Whiskey Rebellion and served in Pennsylvania and western Maryland. He joined the United States Army in the following year and later transferred to the First Infantry Regiment. Much of his work was in recruiting activities and as paymaster, requiring extensive travel among military posts in the Ohio Valley.[45]

Jefferson desired to have Lewis on his staff not only because of his personal acquaintance with the young man, but also for his knowledge of Western lands. He was still thinking about the westward passage, a project which remained one of his priorities, despite Ledyard's aborted journey and Clark's lack of interest in undertaking an expedition. He sent his offer through channels, explaining to Lewis's superior, General Wilkinson, that by employing as his secretary "one who possessing a knolege of the Western country [Ohio Valley], of the army & it's situation, might sometimes aid us with information of interest, which we may not otherwise possess."[46]

To Lewis he wrote, "Your knolege of the Western country of the army and of all it's interests and relations has rendered it desirable for public as well as private purpose that you should be engaged in that office."[47]

Lewis promptly accepted the position offered, and it was during his employment as secretary that he compiled a roster of officers in the Army which enabled Jefferson to achieve his aim of converting the military forces to a minimum standing army.[48]

Jefferson ended his term as Vice President on February 28, 1801. In his farewell address to the senators, he commented that his task as presiding officer of the Senate had been rendered with little difficulty because of the "habits of order and decorum" which distinguished that body. It was in fact his efforts which had brought order and organization to the Senate by means of his *Parliamentary Manual.*[49]

The two weeks remaining until his inauguration were busy ones for Jefferson, as he contemplated new appointments and removals in the important offices. In addition to having selected Levi Lincoln for Attorney General, he planned to appoint Albert Gallatin as Secretary of the Treasury and Robert Livingston as minister to France.

In this period, the transfer of the government from one administration to another took place at midnight on March 3rd, just before the inauguration of a new President. Federalists attempted to hurry through Congress a law that would enable the number of United States district courts throughout the country to be substantially increased. The new law, known as the Judiciary Act, creating new judge-ships, was enacted on February 13, 1801. However, it was passed at such a late hour of the day that there had not been sufficient time for the Department of State to issue commissions to the appointees. In order to ensure that the newly created offices would be filled by Federalist appointees while the Adams administration was still in power, the acting Secretary of State, Chief Justice John Marshall, was busily engaged during the evening of March 3rd writing out the commissions.

Jefferson was aware of the entire proceedings, and strongly disapproved. Because of the haste in which the law was enacted and the appointments were being made, he considered the whole matter unconstitutional. According to some sources, which are not thoroughly documented, however, he took action with his customary boldness. Having already selected Lincoln to be his new Attorney General, he called upon him late that evening and presented him with his own silver pocket watch. He then instructed Lincoln to take possession of the Department of State at midnight, and not to permit a single piece of paper to be removed from the premises after the stroke of midnight. According to tradition, Lincoln followed instructions precisely, and entered Marshall's chambers at the appointed hour. Presumably this apocryphal conversation ensued:

"I have been ordered by Mr. Jefferson to take possession of this office and its papers," he told the surprised Marshall.

"Why, Mr. Jefferson has not yet been qualified," retorted the indignant Chief Justice.

"Mr. Jefferson considers himself in the light of an executor," explained Lincoln quietly, "bound to take charge of the papers of Government until he has been duly qualified."

"But it is not yet midnight!" protested Marshall, drawing forth his watch. Whereupon Lincoln took Jefferson's silver watch from his pocket and showed its face to Marshall.

"But indeed it is!" responded Lincoln. 'This, Sir, is the President's watch, and rules the hour."

Marshall had no recourse but to concede. Taking one last rueful look at the stack of commissions piled upon his desk, and which now lay beyond his action, he left the room.

Years later, when Marshall recounted the incident, it is said he laughed as he described how Lincoln did not permit him to pick up anything in the room except his hat as he made his departure. Marshall had managed to conceal several of the commissions in his pocket, however, and the fortunate judges who received them were known thereafter as "John Adams's midnight judges" or "Midnight Appointments." Some months later, Jefferson was able to demonstrate to Congress that the need for more courts, as claimed by the Federalists, did not in fact exist inasmuch as there was not enough work for those already appointed.[50]

When his younger daughter Maria died several years later, Jefferson was deeply touched by an expression of sympathy from Abigail Adams. It was the first communication following the long harsh silence that had separated him from the Adamses since they left Washington after so many years of intimate friendship. In his response, he mentioned the warm relationship that had existed between his daughter Maria and Abigail in Europe, and then spoke of his long and enduring friendship with John Adams, and assured her that his feelings had never changed.

"I can say with truth," he went on, "that one act of Mr. Adams's life, and one only, ever gave me a moment's displeasure. I did consider his last appointments to office as personally unkind. They were from among my most ardent political enemies, from whom no faithful cooperation could ever be expected; and laid me under the embarrassment of acting thro' men whose views were to defeat mine, or to encounter the odium of putting others in their places. It seemed but common justice to leave a successor free to act by instruments of his own choice. If my respect for him did not permit me to ascribe the whole blame to the influence of others, it left something for friendship to forgive; and after brooding over it for some little time, and not always resisting the expression of it, I forgave it cordially, and returned to the same state of esteem and respect which had so long subsisted."[51]

Although he owned several gold watches and gave them as gifts to others, Jefferson preferred and customarily carried a silver pocket watch, which may have been the one made by the eminent Geneva watchmaker Jean Paul Barral. It was this timepiece that figured in the famous "Midnight Appointments" to which Jefferson referred in his letter to Abigail Adams. In his will be bequeathed it to his grandson, Thomas Jefferson Randolph. Years later, an article in the *Jeffersonian Democrat* of Charlottesville reported, "We have been shown by Mr. . . . Terrell the watch which was bequeathed by Thomas Jefferson to Thomas Jefferson Randolph, and which bears an inscription to that effect. It is a massive piece of machinery, in a silver case, and what is known as a French Pin Escapement. There is an interesting bit of history connected with it which makes it particularly valuable as a relic." Then followed an account of the incident of the Adams's "Midnight Appointments" and the announcement, "this watch is for sale to the highest bidder." All trace of the watch was lost thereafter.[52]

As Jefferson left the the Vice Presidency and prepared to assume office as third President of the United States, there was a general feeling that one era had ended and that a new one was beginning. While the embittered Federalists foretold doom and disaster, the victorious Republicans looked optimistically to the future. Jefferson wrote, "The storm through which we have passed has been tremendous indeed. The tough sides of our Argosie have been thoroughly tried. Her strength has stood the waves into which she was steered, with a view to sink her. We shall put her on her republican tack, & she will now show by the beauty of her motion the skill of her builders."[53]

CHAPTER XII

"SPLENDID MISERY" (1801–1804)

I am not afraid of new inventions or improvements, nor bigoted in the practice of our forefathers . . . Where a new invention is supported by well-known principles, and promises to be useful, it ought to be tried.

Letter from Thomas Jefferson
to Robert Fulton, 1810.

On March 4, 1801, the morning of the inauguration, there was considerable confusion in the Jefferson camp. Although his lodgings were only several hundred yards from the Capitol, and he could easily have walked the distance, it was planned to hire a coach-and-four for such an auspicious occasion. However, his son-in-law, John Eppes, who was to obtain the horses, was not able to deliver them in time.

The occasion was described by the chief of the British legation, Edward Thornton, in a dispatch written on that day to the British foreign secretary, Lord Grenville. "Jefferson," he wrote, "came from his own lodgings to the House where the Congress convenes, and which goes by the name of the Capitol, on foot, in his ordinary dress, escorted by a body of military artillery from the neighboring State, and accompanied by the Secretaries of the Navy and Treasury, and a number of his political friends in the House of Representatives." Over the years other legends arose stating that Jefferson either walked alone or rode horseback to his first inauguration.[1]

A contemporary account of the inaugural ceremonies related that at an early hour the city was filled with crowds of people who had come from adjacent regions. The official ceremonies began with a volley from the company of Washington artillery, which at ten o'clock paraded with the Alexandria company of riflemen in front of Jefferson's lodgings. Promptly at twelve o'clock noon, Jefferson, attended by an entourage of fellow citizens including members of Congress, arrived at the Capitol. He was dressed as a plain citizen without any distinctive badge of office.

As he entered the Capitol building, there was another volley of artillery, and it was estimated that more than a thousand onlookers were in attendance. The members of the Senate were assembled on one side of the Senate chamber and the Representatives and their wives on the other, with Aaron Burr in the chair.

When Jefferson entered the chamber, the members rose, Burr left the chair, and Jefferson seated himself in it. After a few minutes of silence, Jefferson delivered his address before the largest number ever gathered there. He spoke in so low a tone, however, that few heard him clearly. He then sat again for a short period, and finally rose once more to approach the clerk's table to have the oath of office administered by the Chief Justice.

With the end of the official ceremonies, Jefferson left the Capitol to return to his lodgings, accompanied by the Chief Justice, heads of government departments, and the Vice President. Again there was a discharge of artillery as Jefferson left the building.

At his lodgings he was awaited by a number of distinguished citizens. The day was given over to festivity, and at night the whole city was brightly illuminated. Neither John Adams nor the Speaker of the House, Theodore Sedgwick, was present at the ceremonies, having left the city that morning.[2]

Jefferson did not occupy the President's House immediately, and retained his lodgings until mid-March. At the time that he became the second occupant of the President's House, the executive mansion was still in an unfinished state indoors and out, and lacked almost every convenience. The roof and gutters had been leaking since first erected, causing considerable damage to ceilings and any furniture in the rooms. The timbers of the building were found to be in a state of decay due to the fact that the wood was green when first used, and had then been long exposed to weather before the roofing had been completed.

The single enclosure for the grounds was a rough makeshift post-and-rail fence, which remained as late as seven years after the mansion was occupied. The grounds within were littered with rubbish, dotted with pits left unfilled, the remains of brick kilns, abandoned piles of brick and stone cutters's sheds. During Jefferson's tenancy, he managed to arrange some leveling and clearing of the grounds, but they remained unfinished for a long time to come.[3]

Jefferson immediately set a tone of informality as President which was considerably in contrast to previous custom. He had dispensed with wearing a wig after 1800, although others continued to do so. He customarily wore breeches and stockings instead of pantaloons, although he later lamented not having switched to the latter which were so much more comfortable.

He was determined to establish what he termed "Republican simplicity" in government, because in his opinion his Federalist predecessors had established practices not in keeping with the principles of democracy. He replaced the formality of the weekly levees and drawing room receptions of former administrations by assigning only two days annually for public receptions, one on New Year's Day and the other on July 4th.

He also abolished the formal opening of Congress by the President, which in the past had been attended with much dignified pomp. Jefferson was opposed to the display favored by his predecessors, and at the opening of Congress in 1801 he did not appear personally to deliver his message, as had been the custom, nor did he plan to do so in the future. Instead he sent his message to be read before the Senate and House by their respective clerks.

His reason for taking such an action was generally unclear at the time, and assumed by many to have been due to the fact that he was not a successful public speaker. In actuality he was seeking every means at his command to reduce taxes and eliminate the national debt. As he explained to Dr. Benjamin Rush, if he had appeared in person to present his address, Congress would have been required to make a speech in return, requiring more time. He had been informed that each day that Congress was in session the cost to the taxpayer was one thousand dollars.

"I have prevented the bloody conflict to which the making of an answer would have committed them," he informed Rush. "They consequently were able to set into real business at once, without losing 10 or 12 days in combatting an answer." The practice he established was continued by succeeding Presidents until Woodrow Wilson, who reinstituted the earlier practice of delivering important messages to Congress in person.[4]

Jefferson's simplification of procedures was not welcomed in government circles, and was particularly resented by the diplomatic community. While en route to Bermuda from England, the Irish poet, Thomas Moore, had accompanied the British minister to Washington, where he was presented to Jefferson. He wrote bitingly about his reception. About the embryonic capital city, he wrote:

> Infancy now beneath the twilight gloom,
> Come let me lead thee o'er this second Rome,
> Where tribunes rule, where Davi Bow,
> And what was Goose Creek is Tiber now,

This fam'd metropolis, where fancy sees
Squares in morasses, obelisks in trees,
Which second-sighted soars e'en now adorn,
With shrines unbuilt and heroes yet unborn.[5]

When admirers planned a public birthday party for Jefferson for the following April, he informed them "The only birthday I ever commemmorate is that of our Independence, the Fourth of July." Nonetheless, others had different ideas. Jefferson had emerged as "the People's President," voted in by working men, mechanics and farmers who had become dissatisfied with the Federalist government.

The farming town of Cheshire, Massachusetts in particular had rejoiced at the news that the Republicans had triumphed, and were determined to acknowledge it. In the summer of 1801, the ladies of the Baptist church suggested to their minister, Elder John Leland, that they honor the new President in a special manner, with the gift of the largest cheese ever made, to be presented on the country's birthday. When the cheese, utilizing milk from nine hundred cows at a single milking, was well dried, it weighed 1235 pounds, and measured more than four feet in diameter and fifteen inches in thickness. In late November the cheese was conveyed by sleigh to the Hudson River, and from there by the sloop Astrea to New York and then to Baltimore, from whence it proceeded to Washington by wagon.[6]

Jefferson had been informed of the forthcoming presentation, and early on New Year's Day he took the time to write to his son-in-law, Thomas Mann Randolph, Jr., about the event. "The Mammoth Cheese is arrived here and is to be presented this day . . . It is an ebullition of the passion of republicanism in a state where it had been under heavy persecution."

Later that morning he stood in the doorway of the President's House to receive the gift, while Leland read a prepared address in which all the citizens of Cheshire vowed their loyalty to the Constitution. He then preached a sermon on the text "And behold, a greater Solomon is here," extolling the virtues of the new President. After accepting the cheese with suitable expressions of gratitude, Jefferson had it placed in the unfinished audience hall which he named "the Mammoth Room." It amused him to do so because the press had frequently jeeringly referred to his interest in fossils and often spoke of him as "Mr. Mammoth." Now he was able to feature a veritable "mammoth" in the room.

At eleven Jefferson received the New England Congregationalist clergyman and botanist, the Reverend Manasseh Cutler, who was a Representative from Massachusetts, and a group of other Federalists. He treated them to cake and wine, and invited them to view the great cheese "in the Mammoth Room."

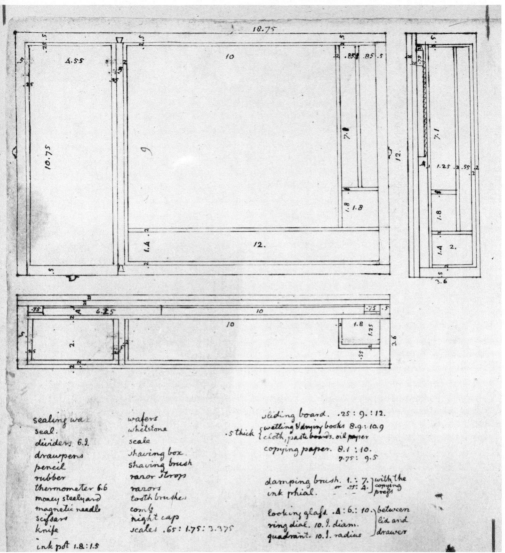

FIGURE 13.   Jefferson's measured drawing for a multi-purpose traveling convenience including a portable copying press. From the *Jefferson-Coolidge Papers*. Courtesy of the Massachusetts Historical Society.

FIGURE 14. Portable copying press, manufactured by James Watt & Co. of London, late 18th or early 19th century. Similar to the version previously designed by Jefferson and produced for him by various makers. Courtesy of the National Museum of American History, Smithsonian Institution.

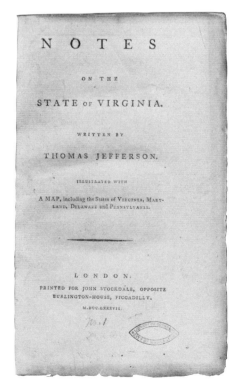

FIGURE 15. Title page of Jefferson's *Notes On the State of Virginia*, the first edition in English. Courtesy of the Library of Congress.

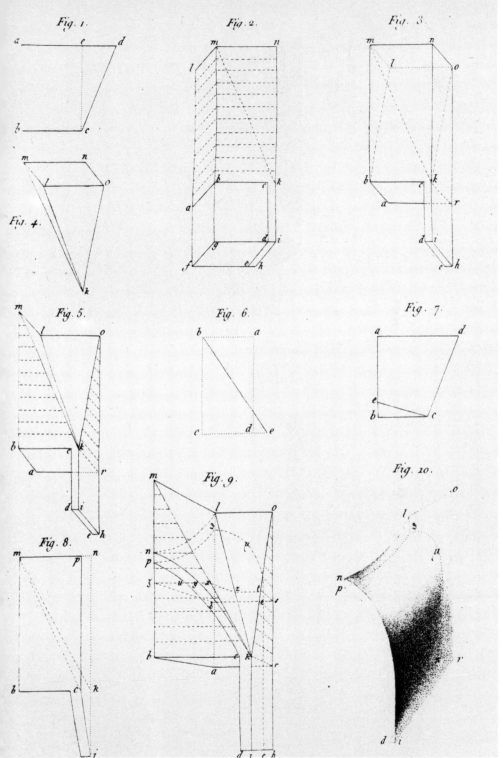

FIGURE 16.   Drawings of the mathematical principles upon which Jefferson designed the mouldboard for the plough. Courtesy of the National Museum of American History, Smithsonian Institution.

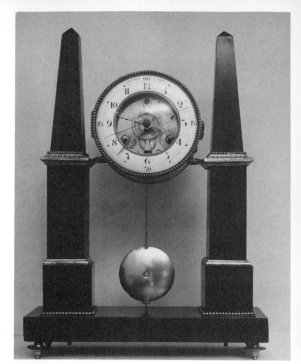

FIGURE 17. The "Pyramid Clock" made by Chantrot of Paris in accordance with Jefferson's design. Polished black marble with gilt ormulu decorations, visible escapement, half-seconds pendulum. Courtesy of the Thomas Jefferson Memorial Foundation.

FIGURE 18. Carved stone statuette of a "pregnant woman kneeling" of Indian origin sent to Jefferson by Judge Innes in 1790. Courtesy of the Heide Foundation, Museum of the American Indian.

FIGURE 19. The plant *Podophyllum diphyllum* re-named *Jeffersonia binata* by Benjamin Smith Barton in 1791 in honor of Jefferson's scientific endeavors, and re-named by Christian Persoon. Engraving from *Curtis's Botanical Magazine*, 1811. Courtesy of Smithsonian Institution Libraries.

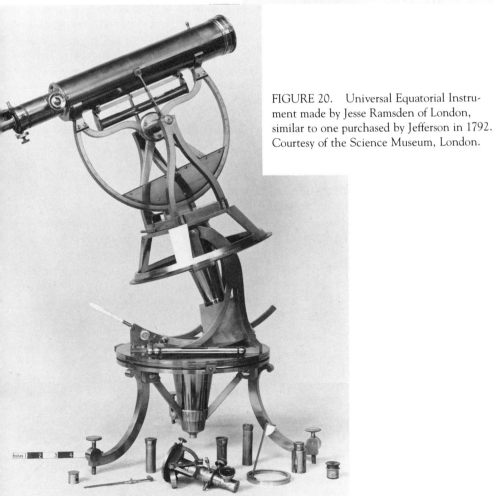

FIGURE 20. Universal Equatorial Instrument made by Jesse Ramsden of London, similar to one purchased by Jefferson in 1792. Courtesy of the Science Museum, London.

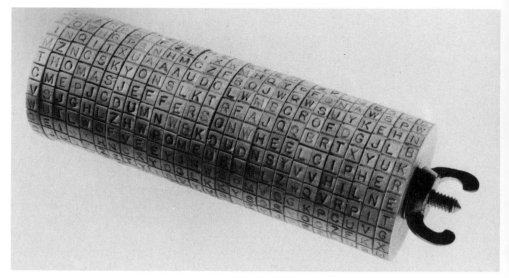

FIGURE 21.   Full scale model of Jefferson's wheel cipher, made exactly from his specifications. Author's collection.

FIGURE 22.   Wheel cipher model dismantled. Author's collection.

FIGURE 23. Reduced-scale model of a plough with Jefferson's mouldboard. Courtesy of the National Museum of American History, Smithsonian Institution.

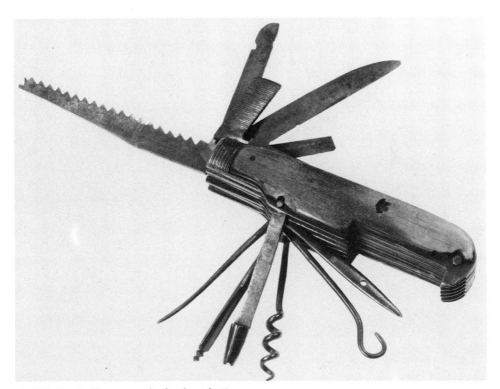

FIGURE 25. Jefferson's pocketknife with 11 blades or tools. Courtesy of the National Museum of American History, Smithsonian Institution.

FIGURE 24.   Dumbwaiter inside the dining room fireplace at Monticello for bringing wine from the basement. Courtesy of the Thomas Jefferson Memorial Foundation.

At noon the Marine Band played "Jefferson and Liberty" while large groups collected, of government officials and citizens of the city, army and navy officers, diplomats and chieftains of the Miami and Pottawatomie Indian tribes, all who came to pay their respects. The president greeted each guest upon arrival, and invited them to go to the Mammoth Room.

Jefferson had made a rule never to accept gifts while in office, and he could not receive the cheese as a gift from the poor farmers who had produced it without providing some exchange or compensation. A few days later, as Leland was about to leave on his return journey, Jefferson prevailed upon him to accept two hundred dollars, probably as a donation to his church, and considerably more than the market value of the cheese.[7]

The event did not pass without comment from opposing political factions. Although the press ridiculed the President's repute among the "American peasantry," it only had the effect of increasing his popularity.[8]

Jefferson's greatest pleasure in Washington was to drive behind his beautiful bays or to ride his then favorite horse "Wildair." A superb horseman, he went riding every afternoon. On Sunday he rode to divine services, and enjoyed singing old psalms. He often visited the nursery gardens of Theophilus Holt on the Eastern Branch [Anacostia River], and of Thomas Main above Georgetown. He ventured out to the Great Falls of the Potomac, and along Rock Creek. He was a regular attendant at the little theatre on Pennsylvania Avenue to see the plays offered.[9]

As he rode about the emerging new city, Jefferson made botanizing expeditions along the banks of the Potomac or into the surrounding hills. Margaret Bayard Smith, wife of the publisher of the *National Intelligencer* who was a good friend and frequent guest at the President's House, reported that no plant or tree escaped his notice; often he would dismount from his horse and "would climb rocks, or wade through swamps to obtain any plant he discovered or desired and seldom returned from these excursions without a variety of specimens of plants he had met with."[10]

Jefferson's informality shocked not only the ladies of Washington and the diplomatic corps, but also the newly elected Federalist senator from New Hampshire, William Plumer. Calling upon the President soon after his arrival in Washington in the company of Congressman General Joseph Varnum, they were admitted through the north door to the reception room.

"In a few minutes, a tall highboned man came into the room; he was drest, or rather undrest, with an old brown coat, red waistcoat, old corduroy small clothes, much soiled—woolen hose—& slippers without heels. I thought this man was a servant; but Genl Varnum surprized me by announcing that it was the President. Never, never rally me again upon my inattention to dress—I certainly dress as well as the first officer of the nation. I tarried about twenty minutes—he is easy of access, & conversed with great ease and freedom."[11]

Despite his abandonment of the former levees and receptions, Jefferson entertained much more frequently than had any President before or many since. He used the dinner table for political and diplomatic negotiations, and individuals he wished to meet were invited on the spur of the moment instead of following protocol with lists of guests to be invited in sequence.

He maintained rigid rules for his dinner guests, insisting on his "Republican simplicity," and his dinners invariably enjoyed a democratic informality. Some guests, such as the British minister, Anthony Merry, and his wife, complained that the treatment they received was boorish and rude, and they were offended because the minister's rank was not properly acknowledged in the seating at dinner.

Jefferson is considered to have been one of the greatest epicures of his time, and accounts of his dinners in the President's House bear ample testimony to confirm it. During his sojourn in France, he had become an aficionado of French cuisine. His French chef, Julien, prepared elaborate dishes, many unknown to his American guests. These ranged from macaroni, then virtually still unknown in the United States, a soup called "bouilli," blancmange or meringue and ice cream. Jefferson was not the first to introduce the last-named delicacy to the United States, as is often claimed, but he had his own recipe. They were described as his "ice creams . . . produced in the form of balls of the frozen material inclosed in covers of *warm pastry*, exhibiting a curious contrast, as if the *ice* had just been taken from the oven."[12]

He is credited with having been the first to introduce both vanilla and macaroni into the United States. After his return from France, he missed many of his favorite foods, and asked his former secretary, William Short, who was still in Paris and was about to return soon, to send him macaroni, Parmesan cheese, Marseilles figs, anchovies, mustard, almonds and a number of other items. He commented that his chef had been all over the city looking for vanilla but discovered that it was not known there. He suggested that Short should send him a packet of it from Paris hidden perhaps in the midst of newspapers. On a visit to Naples, Short managed to obtain for him a "Maccaroni mould," and informed him that the one he purchased was smaller in size than those used in macaroni factories but that it was of the same diameter as others sold to private purchasers.

Despite the pleasure that his guests took in the meals at the President's House, Jefferson was severely criticized for them by his political opponents. Patrick Henry, once a friend who had become one of his foremost antogonists, criticized him in a political speech for having "abjured his native Victuals" and ignoring old-fashioned roast beef.[13]

Jefferson used the smaller of the two dining rooms on the main floor of the residence. It was elaborately furnished with a large mahogany table, a sideboard, a smaller table, two glass cases containing the silver and plated ware, fifteen chairs in black and gold and an oval breakfast table. Chintz curtains screened the windows, and two girandoles and two mirrors decorated the walls. Jefferson was much concerned about protecting the floor, and before each meal he had a green canvas cloth laid to protect it from spilled beverages and grease.

While in Paris, Jefferson had purchased five identical pieces of furniture he called "dumbwaiters," although in fact they were serving tables, and he used them in his dining room in the Hotel Langeac. They were rectangular in shape with three tiers or shelves with galleries, made of mahogany, with marble tops and brass casters and pulls. When he left France, he did not ship these items to the United States, but had others produced to his design by cabinetmakers in either New York or Philadelphia. One of these which he later used at his summer residence, Poplar Forest, was made without a marble top, and probably was produced at Monticello by his master builder, James Dinsmore.[14]

Margaret Bayard Smith described one of the dinners. "When he had any persons dining with him," she wrote, "with whom he wished to enjoy a free and unrestricted flow of conversation the number of persons at table never exceeded four, and by each individual was placed a dumbwaiter, containing everything necessary for the progress of the dinner from beginning to end, so as to make the attendance of servants entirely unnecessary, believing as he did, that much of the domestic and even public discord was produced by the mutilated and misconstructed repetition of free conversation at dinner tables, by these mute but not inattentive listeners."[15]

Another visitor commented on a contrivance incorporated in a wall of the dining room of the President's House, consisting of a set of shelves which by "touching a spring they turned into the room loaded with the dishes placed on them by the servants without the wall." As noted, Jefferson installed a similar arrangement on the pantry door of his dining room at Monticello, presently a reconstruction based on the one at Bremo, the country estate in Fluvanna County of the progressive agriculturist and publicist, John Hartwell Cocke.[16]

When Jefferson moved into the President's House, among his priorities was the improvement of the appearance of the official residence, and he planned to furnish it according to his own taste. There were serious and immediate problems which required urgent attention. So much rainwater had been leaking through the roof, for example, that the ceiling of the East Room collapsed. The roof slates had been fitted so poorly that they forced the front and back walls of the mansion to spread, and Jefferson had to have the walls secured by means of iron ties.

Then he had the slates removed and substituted sheet iron for them in order to reduce the weight load of the roof, which had been estimated to be 82 tons. He hired Benjamin Henry Latrobe as "Surveyor of the Public Buildings," and the latter moved ahead with the modifications that Jefferson proposed. Among these was the addition of low pavilions on the east and west sides to provide dignity to the building.[17]

Jefferson found the presidential furniture brought from Philadelphia to be much worn and shabby. He quickly spent the Congressional appropriation of fourteen thousand dollars for furniture, but the sum was totally inadequate for the need.

Jefferson took advantage of the unfinished state of the mansion's interior, and found another use for the room that had been designed as a "Public Audience Chamber" but remained unfinished. Abigail Adams, the first occupant, had installed two ten-plate stoves to heat it and used it as a drying room for her laundry. At first Jefferson divided the space into two rooms, one for the use of his secretary, and the other for his own workroom. The latter he named the "Mammoth Room." When the ceiling fell, however, Meriwether Lewis was forced to find quarters elsewhere in the mansion.[18]

Jefferson devoted particular attention to his study, which provided him with a refuge from public activities. There he stored his books, scientific instruments, hand tools, paints and palette, maps, globes and gardening tools. He filled the window recesses with potted plants and stands for his roses and geraniums.

Smith related "This he had arranged according to his own taste and convenience. It was a spacious room. In the centre was a long table, with drawers on each side, in which were deposited not only the articles appropriate to the place, but a set of carpenters' tools in one and small garden implements in another from the use of which he derived much amusement. Around the walls were maps, globes, charts, books, &c. In the window recesses were stands for flowers and plants."[19]

There also he hung the cage of his pet mocking bird, "the constant companion of his solitary and studious hours." When he was alone he frequently would open the cage door to enable the bird to fly about the room freely. It often perched on his shoulder as he worked, or alighted on his table and sang, and received food from his lips. When he left the study to go to his bedroom, the mocking bird would hop up the stairs after him. "He could not live without something to love," Smith wrote, "and in the absence of his darling grandchildren, his bird and his flowers became the objects of tender care."

Jefferson favored the mocking bird above all other birds. In writing to Martha one spring about the return of mocking birds to Monticello, he noted that he hoped all the new trees and shrubs that had been added to the plantings around the house would attract more of them "for they like to be in the neighborhood of our habitations if they furnish cover."[20]

He also devised modifications in his chambers to serve his personal needs. Among them was an "odd but useful contrivance for hanging up jackets and breeches on a machine like a turnstile," as reported by a visitor escorted through the President's House by Dolley Madison. This was a closet which Jefferson designed with a circular rack pivoted at the center so that when the door was opened, the rack could be revolved to display the clothing suspended from it. He incorporated a similar closet for his bedroom at Monticello. Although subsequent modifications of the White House have erased all trace of the closet, vestiges of the one at Monticello remain.[21]

A practical device which he designed and installed in his study was an unusual map case, in which a number of maps were rolled on cylindrical shafts. It was built into the wall and designed in such a manner that any one of a variety of maps could be pulled out and remain suspended for study, then released and rolled back on its shaft. It was to prove extremely useful later when he began the planning of his several "corps of discovery" to explore and map the western lands. In more recent times the same type of map case was commercially produced for use in schoolrooms and other facilities.[22]

His preoccupation with the affairs of the nation did not prevent Jefferson from constant contact with activities at Monticello, which were under the supervision of his son-in-law. Events proved that Randolph did not always have the same degree of enthusiasm as his father-in-law for the latter's enterprises. In a report to Jefferson, he commented, "I scarcely look to the nailery at all. George (the overseer) [blacksmith, a slave] I am sure could not stoop to my authority & I hope and believe he pushes your interests as well as I could."[23]

Jefferson also maintained contact with his correspondents on scientific matters. He reacted with enthusiasm when during the summer he was informed by Peale that there was a possibility of obtaining a complete skeleton of the "mammoth" or American mastodon for his Museum in Philadelphia. Seeking some means of bringing his Museum to wider attention, Peale found inspiration in two letters published in the *Medical Repository*, which reported the discovery made in Orange and Ulster Counties in New York of the bones of "an animal of uncommon magnitude."

The remains had been found in some numbers in swamps where farmers had been digging white marl for fertilizer. Wistar and Jefferson had been in correspondence on the subject, and both had obtained specimens from the region. Until this time, however, no one had seriously contemplated the possibility of recovering and reassembling a complete skeleton, and the prospect appealed to Peale.

Jefferson congratulated Peale as well as the world "on there being a person at the critical moment of the discovery who has zeal enough to devote himself to the recovery of these great animal monuments." He instructed the Secretary of the Navy, Robert Smith, who was also acting as Secretary of War, to instruct the Navy agent at New York to lend Peale a pump and several tents.

"It has been a great mortification for me," he informed Peale, "to find myself in such a state as to be unable to come forward and assist you in resources for this enterprise" to a greater degree because of the constraints upon his office, but hoped to be able to do so before the project was completed.[24]

Peale succeeded in retrieving a sufficient number of fossil bones, with the addition of some parts to be carved from wood, to complete a skeleton. Due to inexperience, the excavators had broken important bones, but had recovered enough for two skeletons.

One of these was assembled, with the assistance of Wistar and others, in a room in Philosophical Hall and admission was charged. The great skeleton became one of the world's wonders, and the word "mammoth" entered the language in many forms. "Mammoth bread" was advertised by a Philadelphia baker, and the "mammoth cheese" had been sent to Jefferson by the residents of Cheshire. Questions remained about the mammal's structure, with which Jefferson among others offered to help. A short time later he learned of the recovery of a frontal bone of the "mammoth" in the West and offered to acquire it for Peale.[25]

Encouraged by his success with the mammoth skeleton, Peale now seriously considered the possibility of a state-supported or national museum. His friend, Latrobe, had provided designs for a museum building. The Pennsylvania legislature would be asked to authorize a lottery to fund its construction, and he planned that it would be operated as his Museum. Such a museum would have national benefit beyond state boundaries. Before making his application, however, he was anxious to learn Jefferson's feelings on the subject, and inquired "whether the United States would give an encouragement and make provision for the Establishment of this Museum in the City of Washington."[26]

Jefferson's response was sympathetic but not favorable. Despite his expressed great admiration and respect for Peale's perseverance and skill in developing his Museum, and his wish that it could be made a publicly supported institution, he felt certain that the Congress was not authorized to expend public monies for any purpose except those specified in the Constitution. There were those who have always denied that Congress had power to establish a National Academy, he noted.

"Some who are of this opinion, still wish Congress had power to favor science, and that an amendment should be proposed to the constitution, giving them such power specifically, if there were an union of opinion that Congress already possessed the right, I am persuaded the purchase of your Museum would be the first object on which it would be exercised, but I believe the opinion of a want of power to be that of the majority of the legislature."

He went on to explain that for a considerable time he had been considering a plan for establishing a general university for the state of Virginia. Once that were established, "I should have made your Museum an object of the establishment, but the moment is not arrived for proposing this with a hope of success." Accordingly, he advised that for the time being the Pennsylvania legislature appeared to provide the best possibility for support.[27]

Peale took Jefferson's advice, and without waiting for the latter's grand plan for Virginia, he submitted his proposal to the Pennsylvania legislature. There was considerable opposition to losing the city's only park with the construction of a Museum building, and instead Peale was granted the use of the upper floors and tower of the Pennsylvania State House, later re-named Independence Hall, as well as the east room on the first floor.[28]

Learning that two of Peale's sons were about to set off for Europe to exhibit the second mammoth skeleton, Jefferson offered Peale advice for their behavior and safety in the European cities. To ensure the maximum return from their exhibition, he suggested that they have showings at three different times of the day with escalating prices of admission.

The lowest class of society would attend at the earliest time, he advised, the merchants and respectable citizens during the second showing later in the day, and the third time of showing with highest prices should be selected for "when the beau monde could most conveniently attend." In this manner Peale's sons would ensure that by avoiding mixing "pick pockets, chimney sweeps, etc." with the wealthy, they would have the best possible public response.[29]

One of the scourges of the eighteenth century was smallpox, of which epidemics periodically recurred in both the Old and the New World since 1650. In 1752 6000 of Boston's 16,000 inhabitants had contracted the disease, with the case fatality rate estimated to be from twenty to eighty per cent. While epidemics were ravaging white communities, others occurred also among the Indians in Canada and various parts of the American West, devastating the tribes again and again, sometimes eliminating as much as half their population.[30]

The recurring epidemics followed in the wake of the African slave trade, and were particularly decimating among the American Indians and the black populations. Inoculation was introduced in England and at almost the same time in the American colonies early in the eighteenth century. Opposition by most physicians to inoculation resulted in a battle between the medical community and the clergy, with mob violence. Inoculation for smallpox was forbidden in one colony after another; the belief generally prevailed that it spread the disease instead of preventing it, so that the measure was not widely practiced.

Smallpox became more prevalent during the period of the Revolution, and particularly in the Continental Army after the Yorktown campaign, when it was claimed that the British had spread smallpox in Virginia as part of their campaign to terrorize the people. The Virginia authorities exercised greater leniency towards inoculation during and after the Revolutionary period because of the greater prevalence of the disease.[31]

Stimulated by reports of the work that had been done in England by Dr. Edward Jenner, Dr. Benjamin Waterhouse, a professor of the Medical School of Harvard College, became interested in the subject of vaccination as a preventative against the disease. In 1799 he had received a copy of the publication by Dr. Jenner on the causes and effects of "the Variolae Vaccinae, or Cow-Pock," a disease unknown in the New World. Waterhouse saw the advantages of applying the same technique to smallpox.

After collecting everything that had been printed on the subject and consulting with other doctors, he published a report in the Boston press on the method and its effectiveness. Waterhouse attempted to promote the procedure, but encountered considerable argument and controversy from the medical community.[32]

Undaunted and determined, Waterhouse developed a plan for distributing the vaccine and published articles in newspapers on the subject. He also appealed to then President John Adams, a close personal friend, for assistance in making the procedure known throughout the country. Although Adams promised to inform the American Academy of Arts and Sciences, he took no other action in the matter. Waterhouse's attempts to enlist the support of the Massachusetts Medical Society were strongly resisted by the medical profession, meanwhile, and in fact he was persecuted.[33]

If he were to succeed, it was necessary for Waterhouse to diffuse knowledge of his procedure among the medical profession and the public throughout the country. Having long admired Jefferson as one of the nation's foremost patriots and philosophers, he concluded that a work intended for the general good could not fail to enlist his support. On December 1, 1800 he sent Jefferson a copy of his "A prospect of exterminating the small-pox" with a covering letter.

Jefferson received Waterhouse's letter and pamphlet on Christmas Eve, and responded promptly the next day, explaining that he had kept himself informed of Waterhouse's work and that he had been interested in it even before his letter arrived. It is to be noted that Jefferson frequently wrote letters on Christmas Day, for although his family observed the occasion in a mild way, he did not celebrate the event in the same manner it is done today.[34]

By this time Waterhouse had become confident of his methods, and was anxious to introduce them in the South. Knowing no physicians in those states, he used Jefferson as his contact. He sent him some vaccine which the latter turned over to the chaplain of the Congress, the Reverend Dr. Edward Gantt.

Gantt's first inoculations were unsuccessful, however, as Jefferson reported to Waterhouse, because "it [the vaccine] had been too long unemployed," and asked for more "matter" to be sent two and three times successively until he could report that the inoculation had taken effect.[35]

Waterhouse sent Jefferson descriptive materials, including an illustration of how the smallpox would appear on the skin of blacks. He forwarded a manual by the surgeon of London, with exact illustrations of the kine-pox pustule in all its stages, as well as representations of the small-pox. He also provided carefully detailed instructions for the procedure.[36]

Jefferson forwarded the printed publications he had received to Dr. William Wardlaw, his family physician, asking him to make himself familiar with the subject. He wrote about it also to his daughter Martha. "I shall probably be able to carry on some infectious matter with a view of trying whether we cannot introduce it here . . . If the matter be genuine there is no doubt it prevents the small pox."[37]

To Waterhouse he proposed that it might be possible to improve the transportation of vaccine by modifying the container. "How might it answer to put the matter into a phial of the smallest size, well corked & immersed in a larger one filled with water & well corked, it would be effectually preserved against the air, and I doubt whether the water would permit so great a degree of heat to penetrate to the inner phial as does when it is in the open air. It would get cool every night, and shaded every day under the cover of the stage, it might perhaps succeed." This means proposed by Jefferson was of considerable importance, and was of great value in transporting the vaccine thereafter.

Jefferson planned to depart for Monticello and remain there until September, and arranged for future shipments of vaccine to be forwarded directly to Dr. Gantt, who in turn would send some of it to him at Monticello, where he would endeavor to introduce it.[38]

The vaccine virus was taken by Waterhouse from a young and healthy subject, and prepared on a needle and thread or on a toothpick. Jenner sent vaccine from England between two plates of glass covered with lead; the vaccine adhered to the glass like gum and could be diluted with hot water or warm steam. Jefferson sent the vaccine from Jenner to Dr. John Shore of Petersburg, Va. Meanwhile Dr. Wardlaw inoculated six members of Jefferson's family.

To Waterhouse, Jefferson mentioned that Virginia law permitted inoculation of smallpox, "but under such conditions of consent of the neighborhood as have admitted not much use of the permission." A short time later he reported successful inoculation achieved with the vaccine by both Gantt and Wardlaw. Throughout the correspondence, the vaccine obtained by Jefferson appears to have come only from Waterhouse.[39]

Dr. Wardlaw became the first physician in Virginia to vaccinate for smallpox by the Jenner method, but he was too busy with his practice, and Jefferson and his two sons-in-law personally continued the process. Jefferson reported that during the summer months he had personally inoculated from seventy to eighty members of his own family and household, and his two sons-in-law vaccinated as many of their families, including neighbors. The entire project included approximately two hundred persons who had been vaccinated. He reported in detail to Waterhouse, noting that of the total, only one case was attended with much fever although there were many sore arms.

Upon his return to Washington, Jefferson brought some of the vaccine to the Reverend Dr. Gantt. The latter provided Jefferson with "variolous matter" to be forwarded to Waterhouse, and requested some fresh variolous matter for use in Washington. Waterhouse transmitted to Jefferson those requests for vaccine that he received from Maryland, Pennsylvania and Virginia, and the President accommodated them promptly. He also sent vaccine to Richmond, Petersburg and several other parts of the state. He kept Waterhouse informed of the progress of inoculation in Washington and Virginia by considerably detailed periodic reports, including reactions of individuals.[40]

Jefferson now took action to expand the sphere of inoculation, and sent some of the vaccine to John Vaughan in Philadelphia for the use of Dr. John Redman Coxe, a prominent Philadelphia physician. Coxe introduced vaccination in Philadelphia with the vaccine from Jefferson and with additional serum he received from England a few days later.

Coxe planned to publish an account of vaccine inoculation based on his own experiences, which delighted Jefferson. "I think it an important object in such a work," he stated, "to bring the practice of the inoculation to the level of common capacities; for to give to this discovery the whole of its value, we should enable the great mass of the people to practice it in their own families & without an expence, which they cannot meet. To do this I conceive but a single point essential, which is to enable them to be sure that the matter is in a proper state; and I question if unexperienced people can be guided in this by anything but the date, or distance in time from the inoculation at which the matter is *always* good, but is there such a point of time? I thought from my trials there was, but more extensive observations are necessary to ascertain that, and what the true point of time is."

He commented that when John Vaughan had wished to publish his letter on the subject, Jefferson had objected because inasmuch as he was not a medical man he would be exhibiting himself before the public in a science in which he might be exposed to just criticism. However, if the letter could be useful as a matter of testimony, he would not oppose it.[41]

Later in November, Jefferson again enclosed some variolous matter to Vaughan from a patient inoculated by Gantt, and asked him for more vaccine for Dr. Gantt and for Dr. Wardlaw. Meanwhile Jefferson had forwarded some matter on a quill and thread to Waterhouse, who reported successful use of it.

Jefferson informed Waterhouse that the effort to inoculate with smallpox those who had been inoculated with cowpox had proven successful and he had preserved the cowpox matter in its genuine form. He believed that Dr. Coxe had ascertained the same, since the vaccine he used had come from Jefferson, and Waterhouse had shown by test that the same vaccine produced cowpox.

He then asked Waterhouse to state again the certain rule for distinguishing between genuine and spurious matter. This request in brackets with Waterhouse's response was published without Jefferson's name in the *Medical Repository* for 1802. It was entitled "On the Necessity of establishing a Point of Time for taking the Vaccine Virus for the Purpose of Inoculation, as a Popular Criterion."[42]

In December, an Indian delegation under the Miami chieftain, Little Turtle, arrived in Washington, and met with Congress and later with the president. At various times Congress had provided Little Turtle and his people with equipment and tools for farming, husbandry and home industries besides establishing blacksmiths, bricklayers, &c. The Miami Indians had been taught to plant orchards, to breed and manage horses, and to use scales and weights and measures instead of measuring by using the foot and right hand.

Jefferson invited Little Turtle and his interpreter to the President's House because he said he had a matter to communicate to him of importance for the whole Indian nation. As Waterhouse later recounted the incident to Dr. Jenner, Jefferson explained to the chieftain "that the

GREAT SPIRIT had lately made a precious donation to the enlightened white men over the great water, first to a single person, and from him to another on this side of the waters." He then explained to him the history of the cow or kine-pock as a gift from Heaven to preserve them from the small-pox, and even to banish it from the earth.

"The chief listened to him with marked attention, and desired first to receive the benefits of it himself. This was performed soon after by the Rev. Dr. Gantt, not only on Little Turtle, but also upon nine or ten more warriors of his train. On their departure the President caused them to be supplied with the virus; and the interpreter (a white man) took a copy of the directions for conducting the process." The account continued, "Not long after, fifteen more warriors came down to Washington to receive the same blessing from the Clergyman who had inoculated Little Turtle and his followers."[43]

When Coxe's book about his experiences with smallpox vaccination was published, he sent a copy to Jefferson for deposit in the office of the Secretary of State. Jefferson acknowledged it with thanks and assured Coxe "it will contribute much to the public satisfaction as to this salutary discovery, and to their information as to the manner of treating it."[44]

He went on to inform Coxe, "The vaccine virus being at present lost in this part of the country Dr. Gant has sollicited me to endeavor to recover it for him & his brethren of the profession here. The difficulty of keeping up a constant succession of inoculated subjects, and the uncertainty of success from matter which is not fresh, will probably expose every part of the U. S. to the accident of losing the matter, and render it a thing of common interest to all the Medical gentlemen, while they possess it, to distribute it far & near, in order to multiply their own chances of recovering it whenever the accident of loss may happen to themselves." In the event that Coxe retained some of the vaccine in Philadelphia, he asked him to send some in the mail to him which he would promptly give to Dr. Gantt.[45]

In the spring of the following year, Waterhouse sent Jefferson a copy of Part II of his "Treatise on the Kine-Pox," noting that the President had been mentioned in a published work for his support of the enterprise. Jefferson was mentioned also in the tribute paid to Dr. Edward Jenner in the British press in 1803, which wrote, "this beneficial practice is patronized by JEFFERSON in the New World, & by the EMPEROR OF GERMANY, the EMPRESS DOWAGER OF RUSSIA in the old."[46]

It is no exaggeration that Jefferson was probably as well informed on matters of health, if not even more so, than most physicians of his time. His library contained many books on medical subjects which he read with care. He studied the two volumes by Cuvier on comparative anatomy, about which he commented that it was "probably the greatest work in that line that has ever appeared. His comparisons embrace every organ of the animal carcass; and from man to the rotifer."[47]

Jefferson personally took charge of the health of his family and the slaves in his household. While in Paris his household was attended by an English physician named Dr. Richard Gem, and he described the doctor's very conservative treatment. "I have had this fever in my family 3. or 4. times since I have lived at home," he went on, "and have carried between 20. & 30. patients thro' it without losing a single one, by a rigorous observance of Dr. Gem's plan and principle." Jefferson maintained a correspondence with Gem for some years after his return.[48]

Although he retained a personal physician, Jefferson frequently treated himself for his occasional ailments. One time it was for a "stricture of the ileum" for which he took a dose of calomel with some eight or nine grains of jalap, which brought on salivation. During his first year in the Presidency he suffered from diarrhea, and from his experiments with diet, he concluded that the condition was brought on by fish, although less so by crabs and oysters. For diarrhea he recommended riding as a remedy.[49]

To Caspar Wistar, Jefferson described the state of medicine of his time and the possibility of future improvement. "The only sure foundations of medicine are, an intimate knoledge of the human body, and observation on the effects of medical substances on that. The anatomical & clinical schools, therefore, are those in which the young physician should be formed. If he enters with innocence that of the theory of medicine, it is scarcely possible he should come out untainted with error. His mind must be strong indeed, if, rising above juvenile credulity, it can maintain a wise infidelity against the authority of his instructors, & the bewitching delusions of their theories. . . ."[50] (*Document 10*)

As to governmental interference with medical practice, it was his strong conviction that it should extend only to such acts as were injurious to others. "Reason and free inquiry are the only effectual agents against error," he wrote. "It is error alone which needs the support of government; truth can stand by itself." It was reported that at another time he remarked to President Monroe's physician, Dr. Charles Everett, "whenever he saw three physicians together he looked up to see if there were buzzards in the neighborhood."[51]

During his second year in office, Jefferson was informed by Thomas Moore of Montgomery County, Maryland, of his new invention of a refrigerator. Moore was a cousin of Isaac Briggs, surveyor and personal friend of Jefferson. Shortly after their correspondence, Moore advertised his invention in the New York press.

The inventor claimed that the machine was useful for carrying butter to market in hot weather, and he described it as "very simple and cheap; by the proper arrangement of one conductor, and several non conductors of heat, (which are common cheap materials) a comparatively small quantity of ice made use of, is almost entirely prevented from receiving any heat, but what it extracts from the butter, and this effects with great facility, without being brought in contact with it."

Moore was granted a patent in 1803. The first refrigerators were small in size, consisting of an oval cedar tub about eighteen to twenty inches deep, in which was placed a tin box with square corners which could contain twenty-two prints of butter of one pound each. Space was provided on both sides for ice placed between the tin box and the outer wall. The outer surface was covered with rabbit fur over which a covering of coarse cloth was placed.

Moore claimed that a relative, Thomas McCormick, used the container to carry butter to market in Georgetown twenty miles away, and even in warm weather the butter remained hard and firm. Moore planned to publish a small pamphlet providing directions for constructing his refrigerators, and also his advice on the construction of ice houses. Several named residents of Georgetown who had frequently seen his machine attested to the accuracy of Moore's description of it.[52]

The subject of fossil bones was never far from Jefferson's mind, and when he learned from Peale that some more remains believed to be of the *Megalonyx* had been found in a cave in Greenbrier County, he promptly contacted Michael Bowyer, owner of Sweet Springs, for assistance in shipping them to Peale's Museum.

If they could not be sent directly, he suggested that they be shipped to him and he would pay all transportation costs. Elsewhere half of a head of a mammoth had been acquired by Dr. Samuel Brown, which also was destined for Peale's Museum. In order to complete the mammoth skeleton, Jefferson suggested that it might be useful to publish a list of the bones Peale already had and those he was still seeking.[53]

Having learned of the advertised auction sale of the late George Washington's effects at Mount Vernon, and after reviewing the catalogue, Jefferson asked William Thornton to attend the sale and act as his representative. Although Thornton followed instructions, he was unsuccessful in purchasing Washington's terrestrial globe which Jefferson wanted.[54]

Because of public pressure to deactivate the American Navy following the close of the undeclared war with France, the Federalist Congress attempted to place it on an economical peacetime basis. Concerned that Jefferson's new Republican government might take adverse action, the Federalist Congress passed the Naval Peace Establishment Act in the closing days following Jefferson's re-election. It specified that thirteen of the largest of the thirty vessels in service were to be retained, and the remainder to be sold. Of the thirteen, six were to remain on active duty on the Navy list, and seven were to be laid up "in ordinary."[55]

It was this provision that activated Jefferson to propose his famous dry docks project. He developed a plan to lay up the seven inactive frigates in a roofed facility so that in case of another war, they would be as sound as if new and ready to sail. As his new Secretary of the Navy he had appointed Robert Smith, a man he knew would support Navy legislation. He then conceived of a plan to build a large fleet of gunboats to serve as a floating coastal defense in conjunction with a mobile land force of "flying artillery" to be developed, which could move instantly to any point where danger threatened. Congress was favorably inclined to these suggestions, at least in part, and funds were appropriated for building the gunboats, which were to be housed in small dry docks during peacetime.[56]

The proposal to construct the large dry docks was still liable to encounter opposition, however. Accordingly, Jefferson laid his plans with extreme care. First, he requested a report on the water supply available for the operation of locks required for his dry docks for housing large vessels. The report was favorable, excepting that the water would have to be conducted a substantial distance, for which reservoirs would be required. Jefferson then rationalized that the power to establish the system of dry docks did indeed rest with him, as part of the power given him by Congress for maintaining military preparedness.

He proceeded to design what he considered the project would require, and then communicated with Latrobe, providing him with the details of his concept. He asked Latrobe to furnish the final plans for the project which he could submit to Congress. Latrobe surveyed the Washington region and recommended that the most suitable site would be where Ninth Street S. W., if extended, would meet the harbor. He suggested two possible means of filling the locks with water, one by extending the Potomac Canal beneath Capitol Hill as far as the Navy Yard, and the other to combine the capacities derived from Stoddart's Spring and Tiber Creek. In three weeks Latrobe had not only completed the designs and calculations of cost, but also had prepared an extensive report, which he submitted to the President. As a final touch, he produced an elegant scale model of the dry dock which Jefferson kept on display in his office in the President's House for inspection by the Congressmen.[57]

Now that he had all the information he required readily at hand, Jefferson presented his annual message to Congress in December, advising that if Congress deemed it expedient to spend sums annually for providing naval defence, the first appropriations for that purpose might be used for saving the existing Navy, for there was no way of preserving vessels, lying in water and exposed to the sun, from deterioration. He suggested that such wasteful expenditure of resources could be avoided by adding to the Navy Yard "a dock, within which our vessels may be laid up dry and under cover from the sun." Adequate running water could be provided "at heights far above the level of the tide, if employed as is practised for lock navigation, furnishes the means of raising and laying up our vessels on a dry and sheltered bed." If such a method proved to be successful in Washington, he suggested that similar installations could be built at navy yards elsewhere in the country.[58]

Meanwhile Jefferson had communicated his proposal to the Philadelphia clockmaker, Robert Leslie, recently returned from London, and requested his comments. Latrobe had called upon Leslie and when he described what he proposed, Leslie expressed skepticism. In his view, he informed Jefferson, Latrobe's plan contained a great defect which because of the architect's sensitivity he was hesitant to express to him, but perhaps Jefferson could explain it to him with propriety. Latrobe had indicated that if the project was approved he planned to use the same workmen he had employed for building the Pennsylvania Bank and the waterworks in Philadelphia. Leslie was concerned about what he termed "useless extravagance" demonstrated on those projects. He went on to point out that if all the ships were in the same dock, it would be impossible to take one ship out without floating all the rest. This would be injurious to those that were not in good condition, while others might have their props, stays and stanchions loosened and displaced. Furthermore, it would not be practical to attempt to build a ship in such a dock as designed because it might be inundated every high tide. Finally, the amount of water required for such a large dock would make its filling tedious, to say the least.

Leslie forwarded a sketch he had made for a dry dock which he believed would better serve the purpose at considerably less cost. It consisted of twelve separate docks with a single wet dock in their center. Only such docks as were required at any one time need be filled. Leslie offered to prepare detailed drawings of his proposal, but meanwhile Congressional action made it unnecessary.[59]

The section of the President's message dealing with the Navy was sent by Congress to a Committee on the Navy Yard and Docks for study. It reported favorably and the House formulated a resolution authorizing building of the dry dock. Dr. Samuel Mitchill, Congressman from New York, and others, however, voiced hesitations about the soundness of such a visionary project, which was then referred to a new committee.

It was never brought before the House again, and presumably the proposal died without legislative comment. Although it never came to fruition, it was nonetheless the earliest consideration of an American "moth ball navy."[60]

During the period that he was concerned with the subject of dry docks, Jefferson noted in his *Memorandum Book* that he had "p[ai]d expences going to see the Mud-scoop work." This appears to have been a horse-drawn dredge for clearing dock areas, such as were prevalent in France.[61]

Two decades later Jefferson described the project to John Adams, in an account of his recollections of the American Navy. He added, "We are now, I understand, building vessels to remain on the stocks, under shelter, until wanted, when they will be launched and finished. On my plan they could be in service at an hour's notice. On this, the finishing, after launching, will be a work of time."[62]

In 1825 he again described his proposal for dry docks in some detail to Lewis M. Wiss. In conclusion, he commented, "the advocates for the navy did not fancy it, and those opposed to the building of ships altogether, were equally indisposed to provide protection for them. Ridicule was also resorted to, the ordinary substitute for reason, when that fails, and the proposition was passed over." He remained convinced nonetheless that the proposal was a good one, although "I have thought no more of it since."[63] (*Document* 12)

It was at about the same time that Jefferson also became interested in an attempt to develop the steam boat by Richard Claiborne of Virginia. He had corresponded with Claiborne on and off since the latter had been appointed Deputy Quartermaster for Virginia in 1781. Claiborne later lived in England, and he also corresponded with Jefferson while the latter was in France. After his return to the United States in 1795, he kept in contact with the president.

Claiborne constructed a boat propelled by a "duck-foot paddle" which he patented in February 1802. Later that year he demonstrated it on the Anacostia River in Washington with President Jefferson, the Secretary of the Navy and other government notables on board. Secretary of War Henry Dearborn operated the vessel part of the time as it crossed and re-crossed the river.

The demonstration was eminently successful, and the passengers presented Claiborne with a certificate citing the potential utility of his invention, and subscribed their financial support. On that date Jefferson's *Memorandum Book* recorded that he had given an order to his agent for payment of fifty dollars to Claiborne "in charity." During that summer Claiborne published an announcement of his invention in the New York press.[64]

The "duck-foot paddle" or "palmipede paddle" was not a new concept as a means of boat propulsion, and had already been the subject of experiment in France and England as well as the United States.[65]

After obtaining employment in the Mississippi Territory early in the following year, Claiborne continued with the development and promotion of his "Machine Boat." In 1817 he complained bitterly to Jefferson that a patent had been granted to someone in New York for a "Goose Foot," making him unable to use his invention with a "Duck's foot" for which he had received a patent during Jefferson's administration.[66]

Jefferson's dream of a national university kept surfacing from time to time. Among others, he described his earlier plans to Marc August Pictet, who had emigrated from France with Jefferson's encouragement. He explained that the Virginia legislature had not been ready for the proposal to transfer the College of Geneva, but meanwhile he asked Pictet for information about the science curriculum in his college. He wished to know how the teaching load of subjects was distributed among the faculty, and the time allowed for the teaching of each. He desired this information for an optimum curriculum he was developing for the future.

Apologizing for the imposition, he went on, "I believe every man of science feels a strong and disinterested desire of promoting it in every part of the earth." He explained that there was little new in science in the United States, where "Our citizens almost all follow the same industrious occupation [agriculture], and therefore have little time to devote to abstract science. In the arts, and especially in the mechanical arts, many ingenious improvements are made in consequence of the patent-right giving exclusive use of them for fourteen years. But the great mass of our people are agricultural; and the commercial cities, though, by the command of newspapers, they make a great deal of noise, have little effect in the direction of government. They are as different in sentiment and character from the country people as any two distinct nations, and are clamorous against the order of things established by the agricultural interest. Under this order, our citizens generally are enjoying a very great degree of liberty and security in the most temperate manner."[67]

In 1800 Jefferson had met Joseph Carrington Cabell, a young Virginian who shared his views on education and who hoped to improve the College of William and Mary. Jefferson dissuaded him, noting, "If the amelioration of education and the diffusion of knowledge be the favorite objects of your life, avail yourself of the favorable disposition of your countrymen, and consent to go into the legislative body. Instead of wasting your time attempting to patch up a decaying institution, direct your thoughts to a higher and more valuable object. *Found a new one that will be worthy of the first State of the Union.*"[68]

Cabell followed his advice, became a member of the legislature in 1809, and dedicated himself to Jefferson's vision. Subsequently he played an important role in developing funding for and effecting the establishment of the University of Virginia.[69]

Another national educational need Jefferson supported was for the training of engineers; the American effort during the American Revolution had been supported by trained engineers from France. It was George Washington who had first proposed the germinal idea of a national military academy in his messages to Congress in 1793 and again in 1796, but it was not until more than five years later that Congress enacted a bill to establish the United States Military Academy at West Point, New York. Made part of the Army Corps, it was not as yet conceived as a separate institution for scientific studies.

The Academy existed on a small scale at first, where officers of the Army engineers might give and receive instruction when not otherwise assigned. William H. Barron was a member of the faculty, and Jefferson appointed Jared Mansfield a captain of engineers so that he could become an instructor of mathematics at the Academy. In 1807 Barron was relieved and replaced by the Swiss-born engineer, Ferdinand Rudolph Hassler, and the following year Jefferson appointed Mansfield Surveyor General of the Northwest Territory.[70]

Jefferson was influential not only in bringing to realization Washington's concept, but he was also personally responsible for establishing at the Academy a rigid course in the study of mathematics. He endorsed the French method, which he considered to be a more progressive system than that taught in English schools. The French were the primary exponents of the Continental method of dealing with differential and integral calculus as opposed to the fluxionary or Newtonian tradition of the English.

Later in life, Jefferson made a comparison of the French and English mathematics to Patrick K. Rogers, professor of mathematics at the College of William and Mary, following a discussion of mathematics at the College and of the latter's recently published work, *Mathematical Principles of Natural Philosophy.* He disagreed with Rogers particularly about the work of the English scientist, Tiberius Cavallo, with whom he was personally acquainted.

"The English generally have been very stationary in later times," he went on, "and the French, on the contrary, so active and successful, particularly in preparing elementary books, in mathematics and natural sciences, that those who wish for instruction without caring from what nation they get it, resort universally to the latter language. Besides the earlier and invaluable works of Euler and Bezout, we have latterly that of Lacroix in mathematics, of Legendre in geometry, Lavoisier in chemistry, the elementary works of Haüy in physics, Biot in experimental physics and physical astronomy, Dumeril in natural history, to say nothing of many detached essays of Mongé and others, and the transcendant labors of Laplace, and I am informed by a highly instructed person recently from Cambridge, that the mathematicians of that institution, sensible of being in the rear of those of the continent, and ascribing the cause much to their long-continued preference of the geometrical over the analytical methods, which the French have so much cultivated and improved, have now adopted the latter; and that they have also given up the fluxionary, for the differential calculus."[71]

Jefferson was familiar not only with current developments in mathematics, but while in Paris had become personally acquainted with notable French mathematicians, particularly Joseph Louis Lagrange. Mathematics had always been one of his favorite studies, learned under the tutelage of William Small, who taught that mathematics was the hub from which all other sciences branched out. He continued his interest particularly during his years of retirement, and he was responsible for giving mathematics a more important place in the curriculum of the University of Virginia than it was given at any other university at that time.[72]

With rapid expansion of the country, Jefferson conceived of the establishment of a new office, that of Surveyor General of the United States. No one was better qualified for the position on the basis of training and experience than Major Andrew Ellicott, who had surveyed the Federal Territory, and later the southern boundaries. During a visit from Ellicott, Jefferson offered him the position, without consultation with Congress.

Ellicott was greatly interested, but decided he could not accept it unless another clerk was furnished to the office by the government. Consulting with Gallatin, Secretary of the Treasury, Jefferson assured Ellicott that clerks were paid by the government and not by the incumbent and again offered the position, asking Ellicott, if he were to accept, not to mention it "to any mortal being however confidential until I send you the commission."

"I consider it as one of the most honourable, and flattering incidents of my life," Ellicott responded, "and were my own feelings and inclination, alone concerned, I should not hesitate one moment in accepting the place you offer." A few days later he wrote again specifying his requirements for the position.

The Surveyor General was to be responsible for determining every geographical position necessary for the production of maps and charts, Ellicott specified, by means of which vacant lands were to be divided and the surveying executed. He was also responsible for appointing a sufficient number of deputies for each of the districts to execute the surveying.

The incumbent was to reside in Washington where he would be in charge of arranging and correcting all public charts, surveys, and drafts of the country and its coasts and be able to furnish copies as required. Finally the Surveyor General was to receive the surveys returned by the deputies and arrange them properly with other documents for the use of the government department of which he would be a part. In other words, Ellicott provided a framework for the establishment of the entire office of the Surveyor General with definitions of its responsibilities.

"In this country I have not a single Astronomical correspondent," he added, "neither is it a science which has ever been patronized by either of the States, or by the general government.—A science in this country which cannot support itself must perish!—the economy of public money is considered as the standard of merit, and supposed to include every thing necessary for the honour, dignity, or reputation, of a nation.—From this circumstance there is not within the United States a single Observatory, nor a single citizen except myself, who is paying any attention to practical astronomy, and what I do is at my own expense.—The President of the United States is both a lover of Science, and a man of science himself; but he has no power by his Constitution to aid any branch of philosophy, mechanics, or literature unless it be done at his cost." Ellicott was fully justified in his criticism, one with which Jefferson agreed wholeheartedly and which he would attempt to ameliorate, if not correct entirely, during his tenure in the Presidency.[73]

Ellicott was disappointed that his proposal for the operation of the office was not "consistent with existing laws" for as long as he could live in the Atlantic states, "It would have been a singular pleasure to serve my country under your administration in any capacity which would afford a decent living for myself and my family," he informed Jefferson.

He had long wished to be able to live in Washington, but even so he foresaw problems, because in the position he had outlined he felt it would have been his duty "to attend to the determination of every necessary geographical point within the United States. But in that extensive territorial country claimed by the public, it would be impossible to attend to, and superintend the work in detail, even by a residence in any part of it."

He hoped that his plan for the office would be adopted at some future date because the great number of maps and charts that would be developed in the course of time would require a central facility under government supervision. Had there been such a facility, he commented, "the valuable charts that were burned in the War Office would probably have been preserved." It was not until 1803 that the post was finally established, and Jefferson appointed Jared Mansfield the first Surveyor General of the United States, with the rank of lieutenant-colonel, to survey Ohio and the Northwest Territory.[74]

Jefferson's well-known proclivity to respond to new scientific ideas made him the recipient of many proposals, quite a few relating to the invention of astronomical instruments. Although some proved to be useful, others were not. Among those who contacted him were James Call of Tredell County, North Carolina, who devised an instrument to serve as a lunar or solar dial, for example, and another was Captain Matthew C. Groves, a Boston shipmaster, who had invented an instrument for determining longitude at sea by observation of eclipses of the Jovian satellites. Not having time to examine the proposal himself, Jefferson forwarded it to Patterson, then vice president of the American Philosophical Society, for consideration by the members. He explained that he was unfamiliar with the Society's procedures with such matters, but asked Patterson in any event to render a personal opinion so that he could respond to Groves.

He noted that basically the proposition was to replace the telescope of the octant with one of greater power for the purpose of observing the Jovian satellites. "Take your observation at sea, by drawing the planet & satellites down to or near the horizon, in which situation the body being erect can preserve its position by humoring the motion of the ship and have a steady view of the immersion or emersion of the Satellite. This seems to be a substitute for the marine chair, and being a simple, easy & cheap thing, instead of a complicated, expensive & bulky one, several observers may act at the same time, the better to ascertain the instant of immersion, for the true time of the immersion he depends, as the marine chair does, on the time keepers in use." Jefferson explained that Groves was not a man of science, and incapable of estimating the merit of his invention. Furthermore, he claimed to be extremely poor and anxious to obtain from the invention whatever its worth might be.[75]

Patterson responded that it was not the Society's policy to provide an opinion on a communication before it published it, but commented on it as an individual. He pointed out that a telescope to observe the Jovian satellites required considerable magnifying power, and that consequently it would have a very small field of vision. Any angular motion would throw the object out of the field, a problem that would not be obviated by Groves's contrivance for bringing the image of the object down to the horizon by two previous reflections.

The loss of light from these two reflections, furthermore, would be so great as to render any instrument inadequate for making such observations. He added that as Ellicott had already proven, observations of lunar distances would provide the longitude far more accurately than would observations of the Jovian satellites.[76]

This instance is a particularly useful example of the futility of much that was being attempted by many at the same time to no purpose. Unable to find support for his invention from any source, Groves was nonetheless tenacious, and advertised his invention in the New York press.[77]

Six years later, Groves was still seeking support for his proposal, and eventually returned once more to Jefferson for assistance. The President acknowledged the communications, but explained "the indispensable duties of my office engross my whole time, that I could not give a deliberate reading to two letters so voluminous as these, and not relating to my particular functions, without withdrawing time from objects having stricter claims on me."

Groves explained he had written a play to raise funds for his project and asked Jefferson to circulate a subscription for it and to print his letters describing his proposal. Jefferson responded that although he would be willing to purchase copies, he never permitted himself to be the circulator of any subscription nor undertake printing.

Although sympathetic to Groves's endeavors, he gently suggested "I should think them better applied to the comfort of your family." Once more he explained the scientific flaws inherent in Groves's proposal, noting, "I have gone into these details with the most friendly view of dissuading you from wasting time, which you represent as so much needed for your family, in a pursuit which has baffled every human endeavor as yet, and has lost so much of its importance." Nonetheless, feeling sympathetic towards the shipmaster, he contributed fifty dollars from his own funds.[78]

Despite his preoccupation with national affairs, Jefferson also kept abreast of activities at Monticello. He planned to construct a stone building for the nailery, and now he felt the need to improve his nailmaking equipment. He consulted with the inventor, Thomas Perkins, concerning the possibility of adding some means of automatic feeding of the raw materials to streamline the operation.[79]

Jefferson's equipment was comparatively up to date, for he used a foot-operated lever vise. By this time he had three forges in operation, attended by as many as ten nailers. The shop was also equipped with a cutting machine and a nail-heading machine. Despite his absence from the scene, he nonetheless still found it necessary to undertake personally such routine procedures as ordering nailrod from Philadelphia and assigning specific nail types and sizes. Great quantities of the nails produced were used in building construction on the premises, which in itself justified the operation of the nailery.[80]

CHAPTER XIII

PHILOSOPHER PRESIDENT (1805–1807)

*America, though but a child of yesterday, has already given
hopeful promise of genius, as well as of the nobler kinds, which arouse
the best feelings of man, which call him into action, which
substantiates his freedom and conduct him to happiness.*

Thomas Jefferson, Notes
On the State of Virginia.

During the spring of 1804, considerable planting was accomplished at
Monticello. Forty hemlocks and white pines were planted near the
aspen thicket, and Jefferson made elaborate plans for improving the
gardens at about this time. The toll mill on the Rivanna which he
had inherited from his father had washed away in 1771, and Jefferson
began the construction of another in 1803, the cost of which added to
the canal which he had been building since 1790, would total more
than $30,000 before completion. He received seeds of the Venus fly-
trap from Timothy Bloodworth, the first he had ever been able to acquire, and from Algiers came a pair of bantam fowl which he hoped
to propagate.[1]

Through the intermediary of Isaac Briggs, Jefferson had recently
purchased a clock for $70 from the clockmaker, Benjamin Ferris of
Baltimore, which he had shipped to Monticello where it was put into
use in the kitchen. He also had the Great Clock installed at last
where he had originally planned, over the main doorway to the Entrance Hall.[2]

The Great Clock operates for a period of seven days with each
winding. A pendulum with brass bob swings directly over the main
door. The movement consists of wheelwork of iron and brass encased

within a wrought iron frame. The housing is made of wood with a painted chapter ring with numerals marking the hours and minutes; the seconds were indicated on a small dial within the other.

The motive power is provided by a set of fourteen iron weights, each consisting of two hemispherical halves assembled together in pairs to resemble cannonballs. They are strung on bell wire to opposite corners of the front wall and allowed to drop into the basement through openings cut through the floor.

The wall along which one set of the weights descend is marked with tablets on which the names of the days of the week are inscribed so that the current day is indicated by the top of the first weight, the weights therefore serving the household as a daily calendar. When the weights have dropped the full length of the wire and descended to the basement, power is restored by winding them up again around a drum inside the clock housing by means of a special crank or "key" made for the purpose. The eight "cannonballs" on the left side power the striking mechanism while the weights on the right wall power the time train.

The calendar is arranged so that the top weight indicates the current day and almost the hour as it descends against the names marked on the wall. There was not sufficient room from ceiling to floor to include Saturday, which is marked on the basement wall. Jefferson made it a practice to wind the Great Clock as well as all other clocks in the house every Sunday morning.

The clock was installed during Jefferson's absence by James Dinsmore, his master builder. He experienced difficulties with the descent of the weights, however, which fell upon a projection of the wall in the basement, and he wrote to Jefferson for advice. "I do not approve of cutting the wall," Jefferson responded, "to make a space for the descent of the weights; but would have them advanced into the room so as to descend clear even of the cellar wall. Should the box in this case encroach too much on the window, we may avoid the eye sore by leaving them unboxed, to descend naked till they get to the floor where they may enter a square hole & go on to the cellar floor."[3]

Jefferson also designed an unusual ladder by means of which the clock face could be reached for setting the hands or winding up the weights. He was inspired by the principle of the draftsman's parallel ruler, of which he owned and used several examples. The sides of the ladder were made of wooden angle rail with wooden rungs attached on opposite sides of the rails by means of wooden rivets so that they could be pivoted into position to open and so that the rails fitted into one another when the ladder was closed to form a pole. It was a most ingenious contrivance, remaining inconspicuous in the Entrance Hall until it was used. (Figure 27)

The clock was to activate a sounding device on the roof of the house. Jefferson ordered a Chinese gong "of the shape & size of a camp oven, about 20. I[nches] diameter & 5. I[nches] deep, and weighs about 40 lb. very coarsely made, being merely hammered out. It therefore can cost little and performs the effect of a very large & expensive bell. I wish for one to serve as the bell to a clock, which might be heard all over my farm." The "camp oven bell" was not as successful as Jefferson had anticipated, and subsequently required replacement.[4]

Spurck was required to repair the clock but even the revisions he made were not completely successful. Two years later Jefferson was still seeking "a watch & clock mender" in Staunton to clean and fix "a large clock for the top of my house" as well as a chamber clock. In 1804 he paid for a set of clock weights of a different type and during the next few years he paid several clockmakers to come to Monticello to mend a timepiece which appears to have been the Great Clock.[5]

In 1809 Dinsmore installed a bell system for summoning the servants, and encountered the same problem as he had with the clock weights. He informed Jefferson, "I am now hanging the Bells & find that we will have to use a single crank in each of them owing to the offset in the wall at the bottom of the cellar joist, it gives a great deal of trouble in getting the holes through."[6]

Throughout this period during which the President was preoccupied with planning the exploration of the western lands, he was concerned as well with other governmental projects. At the same time he did not neglect his personal scientific interests. It was in February 1804 that Jefferson first learned of a new device that intrigued him and which was to play an important part in his life for the next two decades. In 1803 John Isaac Hawkins, a young English inventor living in Philadelphia and Bordentown, New Jersey, had produced, among other inventions, one which he named the "polygraph." This was an apparatus utilizing multiple pens to produce simultaneously one or more exact copies of letters and documents being written with one pen. Hawkins assigned the American rights to the invention to Charles Willson Peale, who enthusiastically began its manufacture in early 1803. He visualized great profits from the devices, which would be useful for government and business offices, and he felt certain that they would become instantly popular. He described the invention to Jefferson, hoping to enlist his interest, but without success at first.[7]

The first of the polygraphs Peale produced he sold to Latrobe; it was an instrument with two pens, enabling an original and a copy to be made at the same time. The architect immediately became an enthusiastic supporter and promoter of the device. In his enthusiasm he demonstrated it to Jefferson, who promptly pre-empted it as a loan and continued to use it, meanwhile having asked Latrobe to order one for himself from Peale.[8]

Characteristically, Jefferson instantly visualized several improvements that could be made in the apparatus, which he requested to be incorporated in the polygraph to be produced for him. Immediately there was a problem, however. When Jefferson asked Latrobe to order a polygraph for him, he indicated he would pay for it upon its arrival. Latrobe, as he informed Peale, was "ashamed to say that I had not the Courage to ask for it [payment] beforehand."

Peale was willing to comply with all the changes required, but not with producing an instrument on credit, even for a friend and the President of the United States. "I will not break a Law I have made, as this would be almost as bad as suicide for a Lawmaker to be the breaker of the Laws, he ought to have weighed every objection before he drafted the act. [I plainly] have a squeamish stomach to fear telling the President that I am a strange animal that will not follow my custom, however fashionable it may be, which my observation teaches me to be a bad one. I esteem the President that I could with pleasure present him with one of my best Polygraphs. Yet I cannot sell him one without injuring my feelings on any other terms than I've made to others." Despite his admiration for Jefferson personally and the respect he had for his position, Peale remained curiously stubborn, with the outcome that he sent the polygraph to Jefferson as a gift.[9] (*Figure 28*)

The production of the polygraph underwent a continuing process of trial and error, and with each improvement Peale recalled and replaced those already sold. He refused to place any on the market that were not as perfect as they could be made. As a consequence, his polygraph manufactory represented a major investment, and it was only the income from his Museum that enabled him to keep his family fed and his shop in operation.

Peale was forced to design and make special tools for many parts of the instrument at considerable cost in time and materials. The problem with the product, even when improved, was that it was extremely delicate and required fine adjustment, which the ordinary purchaser was unwilling, incapable or afraid of doing.

At first Peale had equipped the polygraphs with goose quill pens, which left much to be desired in the writing produced. Then he began experimenting with making pens of various metals. Jefferson meanwhile experimented with glass pens, which proved to be unsatisfactory with the polygraph. Then one of Peale's sons sent him a sample of a steel pen nib manufactured by an English pen-maker named Joseph Wise, which proved to have considerable merit. Peale improved upon it, and he was probably the first to manufacture steel pen nibs in the United States.[10]

Always seeking greater perfection, and dedicated to the purpose of retaining copies of all his papers, Jefferson experimented with other writing devices as well and compared them to the polygraph. He made a trial of a similar writing machine invented by the British engineer, Isambard Brunel, of which several examples had been purchased in the United States, but concluded that the Hawkins/Peale polygraph had definite advantages and was easier to use.

From William Lyman, American consul to Great Britain, he obtained one of the earliest examples of the Wedgwood Manifold Stylographic Writer, which incorporated the first commercial use of carbon paper. Ralph Wedgwood's early versions consisted of powdered carbon made to adhere to paper with grease, rendering it malodorous. After experimenting with it, Jefferson reported "It is not pleasant in its use, and I think will not take the place of the Polygraph." Later he wrote, "The single advantage of Wedgwood's Manifold Writer is its being so portable it takes very little room in one's baggage, and may be resolved to in a moment on the road, for copying as well as writing a hasty letter, but fetid copying paper makes the copies a perfect nuisance on your shelves, nor can it bear any comparison in any other point of view with the Polygraph, which I consider as one of the greatest inventions of this age."[11]

Although he acknowledged the Peale instrument to be superior to any other portable copying device, Jefferson nonetheless repeatedly requested further improvement. He wished it to be made lighter in overall weight and reduced to the smallest size possible, similar to the dimensions of the portable writing desk he had designed and on which he had drafted the Declaration of Independence. Peale valiantly attempted to accommodate the President's suggestions, despite the occasional frustration he experienced in doing so. With each new modification that Jefferson proposed, Peale did his best to incorporate it and sent the President a modified instrument. Jefferson then promptly returned the one he had been using and kept the newer model until he conceived more changes to be made.[12]

Many of the suggestions constituted useful improvements of the instrument, simplifying its operation. In the course of the two decades during which he used the polygraph, Jefferson owned at least twelve, although because of his exchange program he paid for only several of them. Peale was unable to sell the returned machines, which added to the cost of the operation of the manufactory. At least 139 letters relating to the polygraph and its improvements were exchanged between Jefferson and Peale.[13]

Despite the combined efforts of Peale, Latrobe, and Jefferson to popularize the polygraph, it failed to attract sufficient public attention to make it a profitable venture. Although Peale placed advertisements in the press, they did little to increase sales. Then on December 4, 1804, the day before Jefferson's re-election to the Presidency, Jefferson permitted Peale to use part of a letter he had written in an advertisement:

> On five months full tryal of the Polygraph with two pens, I can now consci-entiously declare it a most precious invention. Its superiority over the copy-ing press is so decided that I have entirely laid that aside; I only regret it had not been invented 30 years sooner, as it would have enabled me to preserve copies of my letters during the war, which to me would have been a consoling possession.[14]

An endorsement from none other than the President of the United States succeeded in bringing much favorable attention to Peale's poly-graphs, and sales improved for the time being. It was probably the only time that Jefferson permitted himself to become part of a commercial enterprise, but his dedication to the polygraph as "a most precious inven-tion," in his mind justified his involvement.

In addition to the polygraphs he ordered for his own use, Jefferson used the instrument also as gifts to others and as state gifts. He had made it a rule while in public office never to accept gifts of substantial value. "A pamphlet, a new book, or an article of new curiosity," he wrote to one admirer, "have produced no hesitation, because below suspicion. But things of sensible value, however innocently offered in the first ex-amples, may grow at length into abuse, for which I wish not to furnish a precedent."[15]

Consequently, when he was presented with the gift of a hogshead of Marsala wine from Sicily by Commodore Edward Preble, commander of the third squadron who was sent to the Mediterranean in the war against Tripoli, Jefferson was faced with a dilemma for which the poly-graph provided a solution. To refuse the wine outright would be offen-sive, for the gift had been given as a friendly gesture without intent of gaining favor, and refusal would imply that the sender had ulterior mo-tives. Accordingly, he ordered a polygraph from Peale which he would send as a counter-gift to Preble.

"Having determined never while in public office to accept presents beyond a book or things of trifling value," he informed Peale, "I am sometimes placed in an embarrassing dilemma by persons whom a rejec-tion would offend. In those cases I resort to counter presents. Your poly-graph, from its rarity & utility, offers a handsome instrument of retribu-tion to certain characters. I have now such a case on hand. . . ."[16]

Preble was overwhelmed by the unexpected and unusual gift of "an additional specimen of the Mechanical and Inventive genius of our

Country . . . The present coming from the Chief Magistrate of our Nation, whom I esteem and venerate, will render it invaluable to me."[17]

Jefferson also sent one of them to his friend, Count Volney, who had visited him at Monticello in 1796, and another to James Bowdoin when he became commissioner to Spain.[18]

Early in 1806 Jefferson had occasion to call upon Peale again for polygraphs to be used as "counter presents." This order was to be state gifts. It was a time when the troubles with the Barbary States had been occupying his mind. A Tunisian vessel which had attempted to run the blockade into Tripoli had been seized by the American Navy, and after six weeks of negotiation, two well-placed shots from American warships convinced the Bey of Tunis that the Americans meant business.

The Bey hurriedly announced that he planned to send an ambassador to the United States, and three months later the Tunisian ambassador Siddi Suliman Mella Menni, generally referred to as Mellimelli, arrived in Washington amid great fanfare and cannon salvos and was greeted by a large crowd which had assembled to view the curious visitors.

The nation's capital underwent a considerable change during the visit of the Tunisian mission. Mellimelli brought with him a retinue of eleven persons, including two Turkish officers, a secretary, three huge black bodyguards, a cook, a barber and a steward, in addition to other servants most of whose functions were never defined. One was a bearer for the ambassador's four-foot tobacco pipe. An Italian band was later hired by the ambassador which added to the color and confusion that attended him always.

A striking figure of about fifty years of age, sporting an eight-inch black beard, Mellimelli appeared in public arrayed in rich gold-embroidered scarlet silks, white silk blouse and bright yellow Moroccan shoes. Wound about his head was a twenty-yard turban of white muslin upon which was perched a red skull cap. His retinue sported equally colorful attire.[19]

Jefferson's first embarrassment with the mission developed from gifts which the ambassador had brought for the President and Secretary of State. Among them were four Arabian horses, one of which had died during the voyage. A beautiful black horse was intended for Jefferson and a fine bay mare for Madison. For the ladies of Jefferson's family Mellimelli had brought rare cashmere shawls, rich robes, costly fabrics, perfumes and a silver dressing case.

Jefferson found himself with a dilemma, for he could not accept the gifts nor could he refuse them without giving offense. He resolved the problem by placing the gifts on public display during the ambassador's stay and temporarily installing the horses in the Presidential stables. Martha and her daughters coveted the shawls in particular, but Jefferson refused to allow the gifts to be dispersed. Later he arranged to have them sold at public auction.[20]

The antics of the Tunisian mission instantly made them the talk of the town, and Congressmen and government employees in great numbers called upon them at Stelle's Hotel to satisfy their own curiosity. The avidity of the general populace for a glimpse of the strangers led them to storm the hotel gates so that Jefferson had to order a corporal's guard to stand watch to protect them.[21]

Not long after the advent of the Tunisian mission, Colonel Benjamin Hawkins arrived in Washington, bringing delegates of Indian tribes from the Southwest. Both Cherokee and Osage delegations paid a visit to the Congress, which had convened in the north wing of the Capitol, where both the House and Senate were temporarily sharing quarters.

The presence of the Osage chiefs was announced by the jingling of small bells attached to their clothes and they came ornamented with feathers, bones, fox tails, ivory trinkets, shells and bits of polished wood. A small piece of silver was suspended from the nose, each ear was decorated with a fishbone or other ornament and their faces were painted in lurid colors.

When the Indians appeared before the Congress, a number of young ladies were required to vacate their seats on the floor and move to the gallery to make room for the special guests. The Indians listened attentively to the business before the House, and then they silently rose as one and departed in the same order in which they had come.[22]

That evening the Western Indians presented a dance in Washington's only theatre, on Pennsylvania Avenue, an event which had been widely advertised with handbills. The performers received half the proceeds from the box office in addition to a generous supply of rum.

Charles William Janson later commented, "The war-dance exhibited something of the terrific; and the scalping scene was a dreadful picture of that inhuman practice among savage nations. The act of taking off the scalp of the supposed victim was executed with such adroitness, a false scalp being substituted, that the deception was not to be perceived . . . Before the conclusion of the entertainment, the greatest part of them were intoxicated and the audience became anxious to quit the house."[23]

The next morning an Osage chief, who had played an important role in the performance, was found dead in bed, his death attributed to the combination of his exertions and excessive drinking the night before. The chief was ceremoniously laid in a wooden coffin and taken in a hackney carriage to the city burial ground, followed by a procession of all the Indian visitors and a dozen marines. The marines fired three volleys over the grave while the Indians observed in strict silence, without uttering a word.[24]

On New Year's Day, Jefferson held the first of his two annual receptions in the President's House, and invited both the Tunisian mission and the Indian delegations. Other guests included the members of the diplomatic corps and government officials. It was a remarkably fine day, there was a large attendance, and the event proved to be a great success. Jefferson was accompanied by his daughter Martha on this occasion as well as by Dolley Madison and her sister.

Outstanding among the guests inevitably were the Tunisian ambassador and his brilliantly dressed entourage. They excited comment immediately upon their arrival by leaving their shoes and slippers at the door. Their rich garments and their lavish display of gold and pearls contrasted sharply with the painted faces and bodies of the Indians dressed in deerskin moccasions, cloth leggings and blankets. Mellimelli was fascinated with the aborigines, and removed his turban to show them that his head was shaven similarly to theirs.

The Tunisian ambassador was convinced that the Indians were not a native American race, but that they must have come from Gemen Arabia several centuries ago. Convinced that they were in reality followers of Moses, Christ or Mahomet, he had great difficulty in understanding their description of their Great Spirit.[25]

After dinner was over and the last guests had departed from the President's House, Jefferson retired immediately to his study to write to Peale. Informing him "we have to make up some presents for Tripoli, & being desirous to compose it as much as we can of things rare, the produce of our own country, I propose to make the Polygraph an article." He ordered three of them, one for the Bey of Tunis, another for the Tunisian secretary of state, and a third for the ambassador.

All the parts which were customarily made of brass were to be made of silver, he specified, and each of the completed units was to be provided with a lockable packing case. The instruments were to be of the utmost perfection, the President cautioned, because in Tunis there would be no one capable of repairing them.[26]

Peale promptly engaged the Philadelphia silversmith, Abraham Dubois, to execute the silverwork, and he proceeded to produce the other components. When the project was completed, he forwarded the three units in their specially designed cases to Secretary of State Madison with his invoice. The price of each of the polygraphs was $190 in addition to $10 for its packing case. The total of $600 was "paid out of the appropriations for Barbary intercourse."[27]

Several days after the reception, the Indian delegations called formally upon the President, who welcomed them warmly. Addressing them as "My friends & children, Chiefs of the Osages, Missouri, Kansas, Ottos, Panis, Ayowas, & Sioux," he impressed upon them that "We are your fathers, and you shall not lose by the change" from the French,

English and Spanish, who had agreed to retire from the Indian lands between Canada and Mexico.

He urged the chiefs to be at peace with one another as well as with the Americans, and he promised that their wants would be fulfilled by American traders. He invited them to visit Baltimore, New York, Philadelphia and other cities so that they could learn more about their American friends, for which he would provide companions and transportation. "By the time you come back, the snows will be melted on the mountains, ice in the rivers broken up and you will be wishing to set out on your return home."[28]

One of the chiefs responded at even greater length than Jefferson's oration, addressing the President as "My Grandfather," and the Secretary of War as "My Father." He declared it was their wish to become acquainted with "our Fathers & Brothers of the Rising Sun," and again offered the hand of friendship. The Indians were later entertained at the apartment of Samuel Latham Mitchill, Congressman from New York, and they returned his hospitality by singing one of their songs. The poetical articles were published in the press in translation.[29]

A visit was arranged for the Indian delegations to the frigate *Adams*, and they boarded it in the company of the President and the Secretaries of War and Navy. As they were toured through the vessel, cannon saluted, but they demonstrated little emotion at the firing of the great guns. While some of their number remained in Washington, others took advantage of the offer to visit American cities.

Upon their return they reassembled in Washington in April, and Jefferson again addressed them before their departure. Several of the chiefs had died during the course of the visit, and he expressed his condolences. Finally they boarded five stage coaches which conducted them back to their tribes.[30]

The Tunisian mission, meanwhile, remained in Washington throughout the spring, much to Jefferson's frustration. They finally set out in May on a grand tour of major American cities in anticipation of their return home. As they made their way from Baltimore to New York, one problem after another arose. The mission had been placed in charge of James Leander Cathcart of the Department of State, and almost immediately after their departure he sent one letter after another back to Washington complaining about Mellimelli's behavior.

The ambassador blatantly demanded more and more gifts for the Bey. He resisted Cathcart's efforts to keep the mission moving on its way, using every possible excuse to delay along every stop. He demanded reimbursement of a large salary as well as for taxes on all gifts he had received, refusing to leave until this had been done. He purchased numerous items for himself in Boston, and when demanding reimbursement from Cathcart, overcharged him outrageously. He threatened to report

Cathcart's lack of cooperation to Washington, and after an argument, he stormed off by himself on the stage from Boston to Providence intending to return to Washington.

Arriving at Providence, Mellimelli wrote to Madison accusing Cathcart of drunkenness, of maligning the Barbary States and of many financial offenses. He changed his mind about going on to Washington, however, and a week later he returned to Boston. The Tunisian mission was finally embarked on its return voyage to the Barbary States without further mishap, to the great relief of the American government.[31]

Despite the enthusiasm and efforts of its three primary promoters, Peale, Latrobe and Jefferson, the polygraph did not live up to its promise nor did it achieve the popularity which they were firmly convinced it deserved. Its failure to sell can be attributed to several reasons. Banking establishments and houses of business continued the tradition of using clerks and were reluctant to replace them with equipment that appeared to be extremely intricate. The polygraph's complicated and fragile appearance suggested the need for constant adjustment and repair, which were major deterrents for the general public.

Duplicating technology was not to come into its own until after the mid-nineteenth century, except for the Watt copying press, which continued in use to the end of the century. Finally, in 1807, after four years of dedicated effort and considerable expenditure, Peale was forced to discontinue production, and attempted to dispose of the numerous units still unsold.

According to Peale's son, Rubens, who maintained records of all polygraphs made and sold, a total of 60 instruments had been sold and 20 more remained in the manufactory's stock. Peale estimated that each one had cost him $100 to manufacture, yet he had been unable to sell them for more than $50 and $60 each. In time polygraphs had been procured for use in government offices in Washington, undoubtedly upon Jefferson's urging, but it appears that they were rarely if ever used.[32]

Ten years after Peale had discontinued production, Latrobe commented to Jefferson that he had found polygraphs in government offices neglected and forgotten. Latrobe continued to use his polygraph for his own correspondence until about 1817, when he was forced to sell it with other possessions in a bankruptcy sale.[33]

Jefferson maintained two of the instruments, one at Monticello and later another at Poplar Forest, and continued to use them until a few months before his death. It is due largely to the use of the polygraph that such large volumes of his correspondence and papers have survived.[34]

Agriculture, which Jefferson categorized among the sciences, continued to preoccupy him during the Presidential years. He was greatly exercised over the lack of encouragement which public opinion seemed to provide to agriculture, and the lack of education and training currently available in the subject. Society was making great efforts to increase learning, and schools were being founded "to transfer to science the hardy sons of the plough," he noted. He was alarmed because the young were being dazzled by the attractions of the large cities, so that agriculture was left in the lurch. By the pursuit of agricultural endeavors they would increase national productivity instead of consuming it.

Furthermore, the "gradual abolition of the useless offices, so much accumulated in all governments, might reduce the drain also from the labors of the field." The attractions of the city which would result from the increasing exodus from the country, Jefferson felt, could only lead to the same problems of overpopulation and misery which were to be found in the countries of Europe. He summarized it as "the general desire of men to live by their heads rather than their hands, and the strong allurements of great cities to those who have any turn for dissipation, threaten to make them here, as in Europe, the sinks of voluntary misery."[35]

CHAPTER XIV

"THE CORPS OF DISCOVERY" (1804–1807)

A great deal is yet wanting to ascertain the true geography of our country; more indeed as to its longitudes than latitudes. Towards this we have done too little for ourselves and depended too long on the ancient and inaccurate observations of other nations.

Letter from Thomas Jefferson
to Andrew Ellicott, 1812.

The determination of the character and expanse of the western regions of the American continent, a dream that Jefferson had nurtured for more than two decades, was finally to be brought to fulfillment by means of what became known as "Corps of Discovery." The first was to be led by Meriwether Lewis and William Clark, followed by others under Isaac Briggs, William Dunbar, Thomas Freeman and Zebulon M. Pike. It was a venturesome plan, which succeeded largely due to the third President's personal knowledge of national geography and of the scientific practices and instrumentation that would be required.

In early December 1802 Jefferson consulted with the Spanish minister, Carlos Martinez de Yrujo, and several months later with Louis André Pichon, the French legation's secretary in Washington. To both he suggested the possibility that the American government might send an exploring party through their territories for the purpose of collecting scientific information, for which the explorers would require passports. He explained that the party was to explore the course of the Missouri River, cross the Rocky Mountains, and descend the western watercourses to the Pacific Ocean.[1]

Privately, Jefferson had already selected the leader of the expedition to be Meriwether Lewis, then employed as his secretary and whom he had known as a youth. Lewis was a lover of the out-of-doors, self-taught in natural history, had traveled extensively during his military service, and was familiar with the lands beyond the Allegheny Mountains. During his army service he had, moreover, extensive experience in the handling of men in the field. When Lewis had accepted the President's offer of the position of secretary, he had retained his rank of captain in the U. S. Infantry.

Lewis had long been eager for such an assignment as the expedition offered. In 1792, when only eighteen and while stationed with the Army at Charlottesville, he had in fact unsuccessfully applied to Jefferson to permit him to lead the proposed expedition for the American Philosophical Society which was later undertaken by Michaux and subsequently aborted.[2]

Secretaries in the President's House during Jefferson's administration generally enjoyed considerable leisure. Since Jefferson personally handled his own correspondence and filing, secretaries were not required to fulfill ordinary clerical functions, but instead served primarily as aides who dealt with Congressional and diplomatic visitors. Lewis eagerly accepted the leadership of the expedition, and after some delay, Jefferson replaced him in the position of secretary with Lewis Harvie.

During the period prior to Congressional approval, Lewis spent many hours in Jefferson's library perusing the wealth of volumes on the practical arts and sciences and on American exploration and geography. It is likely that he also spent a substantial amount of time with the President discussing preparations, scientific data to be observed and recorded, equipment required and provisions to be made for the potential dangers and hazards to be encountered.[3]

Although Jefferson was not a practical astronomer and had not himself used the octant, nonetheless he had a good understanding of the principles involved and was able to convey them to Lewis. Lewis practised taking altitudes of the sun with the octant and further informed himself from astronomical texts in Jefferson's library. It was obvious, however, that in order to record the data required of him while in the field, professional training would be necessary, which Jefferson promptly arranged.

In preparation for informing the Congress of his proposal, Jefferson assigned Lewis the task of compiling a list of potential requirements of the projected expedition, including the number of men, quantities of equipment and appurtenances, food and clothing and other needs, with an estimate of cost. This list later provided a useful outline for making purchases. Lewis estimated the total cost to be

$2500. It was later erroneously identified by historians as the actual cost of the expedition, which in fact totaled $38,722.25.[4]

Having obtained tentative approval from the Spanish and French diplomats for the exploring party to travel through their regions, Jefferson drafted a message to Congress which he first circulated among the members of his Cabinet for comment and suggestions. On January 18, 1803 he sent a confidential message to Congress. He requested the modest appropriation of $2500 "for the purpose of extending the external commerce of the United States by means of an expedition."

He justified it on the basis of the need to counteract the uneasiness existing among Indian tribes because of the repeated diminution of their territories and their growing policy of refusal to sell lands. This could be achieved by providing an extension of territory, and encouraging the Indians to abandon hunting and instead undertake the pursuit of agriculture and domestic manufactures.

He attempted to keep the project as secret as possible for fear of potential intervention and criticism from his political opponents. Congress benignly approved his request, enacting it into law on February 28, 1803, and Jefferson moved rapidly to implement the project. He drafted a preliminary set of instructions for its leaders, which was revised and supplemented by members of the Cabinet, several of whom provided useful suggestions.[5]

In addition to the privileges of his office, Jefferson had another resource to serve him in undertaking such an endeavor at this time. As president also of the American Philosophical Society, he could call for advice and assistance upon the most eminent American men of science knowledgeable in many of the subjects which such an expedition would involve.

Scarcely a week after Congress gave its approval to the project, Jefferson began communicating with fellow members of the Society as well as others, requesting advice and cooperation in making preparations. Among those Society members whom Jefferson enlisted was the botanist Benjamin Smith Barton; Caspar Wistar, professor of anatomy at the University of Pennsylvania and knowledgeable on zoology; Robert Patterson, professor of mathematics at the University, who was to be consulted on astronomy and instrumentation; and Dr. Benjamin Rush, to advise on medical practice and medical supplies required in the field. En route to Philadelphia to meet with these consultants, Lewis was to visit another Society member, Major Andrew Ellicott, then secretary of the Pennsylvania Land Commission at Lancaster, who would train him in surveying and mapping.[6]

Jefferson also sought advice further afield, from William Dunbar, a Scottish planter and scientist in the Mississippi Territory; the surveyor Isaac Briggs; and John Garnett of New Brunswick, New Jersey, publisher of nautical almanacs and astronomical tables. Meanwhile in Washington Jefferson received enthusiastic support and cooperation from two members of his Cabinet, the Secretary of War Henry Dearborn and the Secretary of the Treasury Albert Gallatin.[7]

In explaining his selection of Lewis to lead the exploring party, Jefferson informed Barton that it would have been preferable to have found someone "perfectly skilled in Botany, Natural History, Mineralogy and Astronomy, joined to the firmness of constitution and character, prudence, habits adapted to the woods, and familiarity with the Indian manners and character, requisite for this undertaking. All the latter qualifications Captain Lewis has. Although no regular botanist, etc., he possesses a remarkable store of accurate observation on all subjects of the three kingdoms, and will, therefore, readily single out what presents itself new to him in either; and he has qualified himself for taking the observations of longitude and latitude necessary to fix the geography of the line he passes through." He asked Barton to prepare some notes for Lewis on botany, zoology and Indian history "which you think most worthy of enquiry and observation."[8]

To Patterson he wrote virtually in the same words describing Lewis, who, he noted, "for some time has been qualifying himself by taking observations of longitude & latitude to fix the geographical points of the line he will pass over, but little means are possessed of doing that; and it is the particular part in which you could give him valuable instruction, & he will receive it thankfully & employ it usefully. The instruments thought best to be carried for this purpose are a good theodolite and a Hadley." A "Hadley", also known variously as a "Hadley's reflecting quadrant" or "octant," was an instrument for making observations of the altitude of the sun or a star at sea or on land.[9]

From Ellicott, Jefferson requested assistance in instructing Lewis in the use of astronomical and surveying instruments beyond Jefferson's own capability and experience. Ellicott agreed to cooperate, and stressed the primary need for Lewis "to acquire a facility, and dexterity, in making the observations" which could be achieved only by practice.[10]

In anticipation of Lewis's arrival, Patterson set to work at once to prepare astronomical formulae for field use, including a table for computing the longitude from observations of lunar distances, and another for calculating the time, altitudes, etc. expressed in the same manner by algebraic signs, which, he assured Jefferson, "renders it easy enough for boys or sailors to use."[11]

Ellicott advised Jefferson that instrumentation required for the forthcoming venture was relatively simple, such as he had identified in his published account of the survey of the southern boundary with the Spanish territory, a copy of which he had given to the President. In this volume he had specified that all that was needed for determining both latitude and longitude was a good sextant, a well-made watch with a seconds hand and an artificial horizon, all of which could be packed into little space.

He also provided Jefferson with instructions for making an artificial horizon according to his personal preference, using water instead of the other liquids commonly used. He cautioned the need to have the container for liquid separate from the cover, to avoid potential motion of the liquid which could be caused by the wind. He then provided specific instructions for determining the meridian altitude of the sun by the method of taking equal altitudes, which he had used successfully for many years, although it was not generally practised by other surveyors.

Finally, Ellicott warned Jefferson that the final calculations of latitude and longitude could not be compiled in the field, but would have to be calculated after the expedition's return because of the considerable amount of reference material that would be required. As an example, he noted that the calculations for Arrowsmith's map of North America had been made in England after Arrowsmith's return from the field.[12]

With these preliminary arrangements completed and a schedule compiled for his meetings with the various advisers, on March 14th Lewis departed from Washington. He took with him an order from the chief clerk of the War Office, Joseph Wingate, Jr., to Israel Whelen, the U. S. Purveyor of Public Stores at Philadelphia. The latter was to purchase such articles as Lewis required that were not already available from military stores, since Jefferson had specified that all preparations were to be vested in the War Office. The principals involved were all friends and supporters of the President; Wingate was Dearborn's son-in-law, and Whelen was "the fighting Quaker" of Revolutionary War fame.[13]

Lewis's first port of call on his journey of instruction was Harpers Ferry, where he arranged for the acquisition of weapons and the supervision of the construction of an iron-frame folding boat for use on the upper Missouri River. Lewis was occupied at Harpers Ferry longer than he anticipated before he was able to move on to Lancaster. Upon arrival there he reported to Jefferson that he had "this day commenced, under his [Ellicott's] direction, my observation, &c., to perfect myself in the use and application of the instruments."[14]

Lewis remained with Ellicott for two weeks, profiting considerably from the instruction. At Lancaster he also arranged for the manufacture of some of the weapons intended for the exploring party. He spent part of each day with Ellicott, who drew from his own experiences in the field in making astronomical observations, and "particularly of the needs and difficulties to be encountered and of the substitutes offered by a woodland and uninhabited country." While surveying in the wilderness, Ellicott frequently had known want and privation, illness and unexpected danger, and had learned how to deal with them. His wise counsel was to prove of immeasurable value to Lewis and his companions during the next several years. [15]

From Lancaster, Lewis traveled to Philadelphia where he consulted with Barton, Wistar, Rush and Patterson in turn as Jefferson had arranged. He devoted part of his time to the procurement of reference works, maps, instruments and other equipment and supplies. The General Land Office, responsible for surveying public lands, was part of the Department of the Treasury and under Gallatin's administration, who had volunteered all resources at his command and had arranged to provide a "blank" map for Lewis's use in the field. It incorporated all information known about the region to be traveled, compiled from existing maps with blank areas which Lewis was to complete with new data as he obtained it.

Noted on the map was the Ohio River as charted by Ellicott, the Pacific coast taken from maps compiled by James Cook and George Vancouver, the upper reaches of the Missouri copied from the maps of Arrowsmith and Mackenzie and the Rio Grande taken from the charts of Jean Baptiste D'Anville and Guillaume Deslisle. All known reliable latitudes and longitudes were added to serve as guideposts for the exploring party. [16]

Lewis was also to be provided with the maps of Mackenzie and Vancouver, Thornton's map of 1798 and Arrowsmith's map of North America including additions made in 1802. He also assembled a small library with purchases of the best available works on botany, zoology, astronomy, the practical arts and mineralogy. Jefferson provided a copy of Mackenzie's *Travels From Montreal*. [17]

Jefferson had very definite convictions not only about the scientific data to be collected, but also stubborn views concerning the instrumentation required for the purpose. The two most common methods for determining the longitude were by observation of the immersions and emmersions of the Jovian satellites, and by observation of lunar distances.

The method of observing the Jovian satellites was easier to use than the observation of lunar distances, but their eclipses were infrequent and uncertain, while the moon was visible daily although its distances were more difficult to calculate. The moon's position changed rapidly as a consequence of its motion in relation to planets and fixed stars, and for that reason could serve as a timekeeper. If the moon's position at a prime meridian could be forecast, an observer at another geographical location could calculate the difference in time and establish his longitude.

Jefferson chose the latter method to be used by the expedition, for, as he wrote, "the moon's change of place (about a half second of space in a second of time) is rapid enough to be ascertained by a good instrument with sufficient precision for the object." [18]

The universal equatorial instrument, which Jefferson had purchased in Philadelphia more than a decade ago and which he recommended for the expedition, was most accurate for the measurement of horizontal angles such as between a heavenly body and a fixed point on earth. As the most sophisticated astronomical instrument of the time, it appealed to him as the best means to make the most accurate observations. However, very few of the instruments had been produced, and would have to be ordered from England, which required more time than was available.[19]

Since the only example of the instrument known to be in the country was Jefferson's, it is doubtful that either Ellicott or Patterson was familiar with it, although they may have known of it. In Jefferson's opinion, the "equatorial theodolite" [universal equatorial instrument], had distinct advantages over the sextant and Borda reflecting circle. (*Document 9*)

Because its telescopes were more flexible, they could be directed sufficiently in advance of the moon's motion to permit noting its place on the equatorial circle before the moon had attained that point in its passage. Then, the instant the limb touched the cross-hairs, the observer was to direct the telescope to the star to complete the observation. The equatorial instrument's apparatus for correcting refraction and parallax rendered the notations of altitudes unnecessary, and in his opinion, dispensed even with the use of a timekeeper or portable pendulum.

So convinced was he that the equatorial would satisfactorily replace a timekeeper for observing lunar distances, that he communicated the proposal not only to Ellicott and Patterson but also to others who made astronomical observations, including Dunbar, Garnett, Briggs and William Lambert. Ellicott and Patterson, in responding, proposed alternatives requiring timekeepers but diplomatically did not comment that in their opinion the equatorial instrument would not serve the purpose.[20]

Later Jefferson explained to an unidentified correspondent, who probably was William Lambert, that since a timepiece would be required for making observations of lunar distances, "it occurred to me that during a journey of two, three, or four years, exposed to so many accidents as himself and the instrument would be, we might expect with certainty that it would become deranged, and in a desert country where it could not be repaired."

It was for this reason that as a substitute he again recommended the use of the universal equatorial instrument. It was true, he admitted, that the instrument's maker, Jesse Ramsden, had in his instructions for its use specified the requirement of a timepiece, but Jefferson added "this cannot be necessary for the margin of the equatorial circle of this instrument being divided into time by hours, minutes, and seconds, supplies the main functions of the time-keeper, and for measuring merely the interval of the observations, is such as not to be neglected. A portable pendulum for counting, by an assistant, would fully answer that purpose."[21]

Jefferson may have begun to have some doubts about the suitability of the instrument, however, for he subsequently advised Lewis, "I would wish that nothing that passed between us here should prevent your following his [Ellicott's] advice, which is certainly the best. Should a time-piece be requisite, it is possible Mr. Garnet could furnish you one. Neither Ellicot nor Garnet have given me their opinion on the substituting the meridian at land instead of observations of time, for ascertaining longitude by lunar motions. I presume therefore it will not answer."[22]

Whereas Ellicott and Patterson had been diplomatic, Lewis was explicit in his comments, informing Jefferson that both Ellicott and Patterson disapproved the use of the equatorial instrument for the expedition because it was too delicate and difficult to transport, and could easily be rendered out of order. In short, Lewis reported, "in its application to my observations for obtaining the Longitude, it would be liable to many objections, and to much more inaccuracy than the Sextant."

Instead, Patterson and Ellicott had recommended that Lewis take two sextants, one or two artificial horizons, a good "Arnold's watch" or chronometer, a plain surveying compass with ball and socket joint, a two-pole chain and a set of drafting instruments.

"As a perfect knowledge of the time will be of the first importance in all my Astronomical Observations," Lewis explained to the President, "it is necessary that the Time-keeper intended for this expedition should be put in the best possible order, if therefore Sir, one has been procured for me and you are not perfectly assured of her being in good order, it would best to send her to me by safe hand." Henry Voigt, a reputable Philadelphia mechanician and clockmaker, had agreed to clean the time-piece to be acquired for the exploring party, and Ellicott had offered to regulate it. Lewis added that in his instructions, the President had mentioned that instruments for celestial observation had already been provided, and accordingly Lewis would not proceed to purchase others until further instructions were received.[23]

By return post Jefferson assured Lewis that his instructions had been in preliminary draft and that no instruments had been purchased. In fact, it was Lewis's specific mission in Philadelphia to do so. He was to be governed entirely by the advice of Ellicott and Patterson, and if he had not already purchased a timepiece, Garnett had informed him he still had a few on hand that might be suitable.[24]

"The idea that you are going to explore the Missisipi," Jefferson had noted in the rough draft of instructions for the conduct and performance of the expedition he had sent on to Lewis, "has generally been given out: it satisfies public curiosity, and masks sufficiently the real destination." There were many similarities between these instructions and those which he had provided to Michaux a decade earlier. In them he emphasized the scientific data to be collected, reflecting his remarkable comprehension of the information necessary to provide a complete view of the unexplored lands so that their resources could be utilized.[25]

As a consequence of the many to whom Jefferson had written for advice and assistance, it was inevitable that there would be some duplication. One such correspondent consulted John Vaughan, librarian of the American Philosophical Society, who in turn then passed the request on to Ellicott. The latter responded that a brass sextant was infinitely superior to the wooden octant, and that a fine sextant could be acquired for between eighty and one hundred dollars. He was planning to make an artificial horizon for the expedition meanwhile, for which he required a slice of the block of talc in the Society's mineral collection. The use of talc for the reflecting surface of the artificial horizon was an innovation evidently not used by others.[26]

By hand of Lewis, Ellicott had sent letters and an artificial horizon he had made to Vaughan and Patterson. In his letter Ellicott asked Patterson to provide Lewis with his own "formula's for the longitude."[27]

Lewis also had with him the list of instruments he had compiled while still in Washington, and with which the President had undoubtedly cooperated. The list included most of the instruments later recommended by Ellicott and Patterson in addition to a number of others which these advisers considered unnecessary. Of particular interest in Lewis's original list was an:

> Instrument for measuring made of tape with feet & inches marked on it, confined within a circular lethern [sic] box of sufficient thickness to admit the width of the tape which has one of its ends confined to an axis of metal passing through the center of the box, around which and within the box it is readily wound by means of a small crank on the other side of the box which forms a part of the axis, its tape when necessary is drawn out with the same facility & ease with which it is wound up.[28]

The common surveyor's measuring tape which was thus described was not commercially produced until almost the mid-nineteenth century. The description suggests that because of the detailed description such an instrument did not then exist, and that it was to be constructed for the expedition. It seems extremely likely that the description had been compiled by Jefferson, for it is very much in his style of writing, and he would have visualized the need for such an item. Expedition records mention a "tape line" to measure the size of fishes, indicating that some form of tape measure had been provided.[29]

Lewis obtained as many as possible of the listed items from military stores, and others he purchased from various sources, chiefly from the Water Street shop of Thomas Whitney, an English-born and -trained maker of mathematical instruments. Whitney provided Lewis with some instruments of his own manufacture as well as others that were imported. He also made modifications of several instruments as required.[30]

From Thomas Parker, a clock and watchmaker on South Third Street, Lewis purchased an "Arnold's watch", which Ellicott had recommended, a gold-cased chronometer for two hundred and fifty dollars; the winding key cost an extra seventy-five cents. As Lewis described it, the chronometer had a balance wheel and escapement of "the most improved construction." Voigt cleaned and adjusted it and constructed a new mahogany box to contain it in which he suspended the instrument by means of "a universal joint." Lewis sent the chronometer to Ellicott by hand so that it could be adjusted, and the latter kept it for two weeks to observe its rate of going.

The chronometer was a timepiece designed to keep time with considerable precision, made with a compensated balance to overcome temperature-caused irregularity. The invention made in the third quarter of the eighteenth century by John Harrison, an English carpenter turned clockmaker, it was subsequently modified by several other clockmakers, including Larcum Kendal, Thomas Earnshaw and John Arnold. Arnold's improvements included a bimetallic balance, an improved detent escapement and a helical balance spring. Chronometers were not manufactured in the United States prior to 1820, and had to be imported from England or France.[31]

The practical-minded Ellicott had specified as "a necessary precaution, to have the Chronometer, with its case, tied up in a bladder when not in use,—it will privent its being injured if by accident it should be thrown in the water by the overturning of a canoe or other accident."[32]

In the final version of Jefferson's instructions, which he provided to Lewis on June 30th after having made more revisions and drafts, he included a multitude of other requirements, then specified the instruments to be used "for ascertaining by celestial observations the geography of the country thro' which you will pass. The object of the mission is to explore the Missouri River and such principal streams of it as by its course and communication with the waters of the Pacific Ocean, may offer the most direct & practicable water communication across this continent, for the purpose of commerce."

Lewis was to take "*careful*" observations of latitude and longitude at all notable points along the river beginning at the mouth of the Missouri, and especially at distinguishable points such as mouths of waterways, rapids, islands and natural landmarks that could be recognized thereafter. The river courses between these points were to be determined by means of the compass and the log-line and with observations of time which were to be corrected by the observations themselves. Variations of the compass at various points also were to be noted. Also to be fixed by means of observations were points of interest on the portage between the heads of the Missouri and water offering the best communication with the Pacific.

Jefferson was particularly insistent that all "observations are to be taken with great pains & accuracy" and that they were to be recorded distinctly and in such a manner that others as well as the observers would be able to comprehend them later, and by using the requisite tables, be able to establish the latitude and longitude for the locations at which they had been taken. Upon their return these records were to be submitted to the War Office in order that the final calculations could later be made by several qualified individuals at the same time.

The President directed that in their leisure time the explorers were to make several copies of their notes and give them to keep to their most trustworthy men to insure against possible loss of records. "A further guard," he wrote, "would be that one of these copies be on the paper of the birch, as less liable to injury than common paper." He had made the same suggestion to Michaux.[33]

Lewis was urged by the President to send back copies of their journals and notes at periodic intervals by engaging Indians to convey communications for the government to Cahokia or Kaskaskia. Realizing that there might be need to communicate confidentially concerning activities observed, he also provided Lewis with a cryptographic system for "putting into cypher whatever might do injury if betrayed."[34] (*Figure 29*)

A stock of baubles and other gifts was provided to the exploring party in addition to smallpox vaccine and peace medals for distribution among the Indians they would encounter on their journey. The government issued "peace medals" to selected chiefs to encourage peace and establish friendship with the Indians. The earliest of these had been produced in 1757 for a Philadelphia association consisting chiefly of members of the Society of Friends. The obverse depicted a medallion portrait of King George II and the reverse featured a scene with a white man offering an Indian a peace pipe. After the Revolution, peace medals always depicted the portrait of the President in office at the time of issue. During Jefferson's administration, the medal bore a medallion bust of Jefferson on the obverse with the legend "Thomas Jefferson, President of the U. S., A.D. 1801," and the reverse featured clasped hands, a peace pipe crossed with a battle axe, and the words "Peace and Friendship." Lewis and Clark presented a number of these medals to Indian chiefs in the course of their journey. Such presentations were noted on September 21 and September 23, 1805 and on May 10, 1806 to a chieftain of the Nez Perce Indians.[35]

Natural phenomena in all its forms was worthy of the explorers's notice and was to be recorded. In addition to "the face of the country," they were to observe and record the soil, flora and fauna. Jefferson particularly urged them to note "the mineral productions of every kind; but more particularly metals, limestone, pit coal, & saltpetre; salines & mineral waters, noting the temperature of the last, & such circumstances as may indicate their character."

He specified that observations were to be made and recorded of "the climate, as characterized by the thermometer, by the proportion of rainy, cloudy & clear days, by lightning, hail, snow, ice, by the accession and recession of frost, by the winds prevailing at different seasons, the dates at which particular plants put forth or lose their flower, or leaf, times of appearances of particular birds, reptiles, or insects."

As the best-informed on the subject of climatology, Jefferson anticipated that valuable information about the new lands would be derived from knowledge of its climate alone. The requirement for detailed records of climatological data is not surprising, for he considered such information to be of considerable importance. He had personally maintained similar records since he studied law at Williamsburg, and was to continue to do so for the remainder of his life, encouraging friends and associates living in other regions to do likewise so that records could be compared.[36]

Although the expedition originally was to be under the sole direction of Lewis, as plans developed Jefferson realized the need for a second leader to replace Lewis if illness or accident befell him. He left the selection of a second leader to Lewis, inasmuch as it would have to be someone congenial to him and with whom he would be living and working in close quarters for several years.

Of necessity the second leader had to be a practical soldier who was accustomed to leading and experienced in the field. He also must be capable of making maps and drawings, for although the President had not specified this requirement, it was implied in his instructions.

Accordingly, Lewis selected one of his former Army friends, William Clark, a younger brother of the frontiersman George Rogers Clark. William had considerable military experience and was knowledgeable about the region where the Ohio and Mississippi Rivers met, a knowledge that was to prove useful. Jefferson approved the choice, being well acquainted with the Clark family, and future events proved the selection to have been an excellent one.[37]

Since there was little time between the date of his selection and Lewis's departure for Pittsburgh, Clark had no role in the conceptual planning of the expedition. Inevitably there were further unexpected delays caused by suppliers in procuring equipment and by the boat builder, and it was not until August 31st, 1803 that Lewis's boat was at last completed. It was instantly loaded and at ten o'clock in the morning Lewis and his men left Pittsburgh and made their way to Wheeling en route to the Mississippi Territory. They left Wheeling on September 9th, no longer able to wait for Dr. William Ewing Patterson, son of Robert Patterson, who had agreed to join the expedition as its physician, but who failed to fulfill his promise.[38]

Not long after his departure, Lewis reported back to Jefferson that during a stop in Cincinnati he had met Dr. William Goforth and seen his collection of fossil remains recovered from Big Bone Lick in Boone County. He thereupon made his way by land to Big Bone Lick where he searched for mammoth remains, particularly for a skull. He noted his finds in great detail and sent Jefferson the bones he had collected. The shipment was lost at Natchez, however, and never recovered. Clark and his Kentucky recruits joined the expedition at Louisville, and the official party of twenty-nine, in addition to several followers, was finally underway.[39]

Jefferson meanwhile had turned his attention to other parts of the master plan he had conceived for exploring and mapping not only the territory acquired by the Louisiana Purchase, but the remainder of the continent as well. With the consummation of the Louisiana Purchase, he now found it necessary to become better acquainted with the region and its inhabitants. He sought to make treaties with many of the tribes to achieve better mutual understanding and trade relationships, and to prevent as much as possible the inter-tribal warfare which limited trade.

As part of his plan, Jefferson appointed Isaac Briggs surveyor of the lands south of Tennessee. Informing Governor Claiborne of the appointment, he described Briggs as a Quaker, a sound Republican, and a man of pure character. "In point of science, in astronomy, geometry, and mathematics, he stands in a line with Mr. Ellicot, and second to no man in the United States." He added, "For the office of surveyor, men of the first order of science in astronomy and mathematics are essentially necessary."

He failed to add that part of Briggs's assignment was to collect and report to him intelligence about the political situation and other conditions in the region. He intended to appoint yet another surveyor for the northwestern department, and to charge him with the establishment of latitudes and longitudes of points on Lake Michigan and Lake Superior, and to make an accurate survey of the Mississippi River from St. Anthony's Falls to the mouth of the Ohio River. He anticipated that by means of these several surveys, an accurate map of the outlines of the entire United States eventually could be produced.[40]

Later in the year Jefferson confided to Ellicott that he expected to receive additional authorization from Congress to "explore and ascertain accurately the geography of the great rivers running into the Mississippi & Missouri, in order to fix their course & their sources, because their sources are the points which give the contour of what will now be the U. S. and having these & the whole course of the great rivers taken astronomically we have an accurate outline & skeleton which can be filled up with details hereafter."

He anticipated sending one party to explore the Red River from its source to the beginning of the Arkansas River and then down that waterway. He planned that another party was to explore up the Padoucas and down the Panis. For such a project he would require several men like Lewis, who would be capable of making astronomical observations for determining the latitude and longitude and should be otherwise well qualified.[41]

He invited the Great Osage chiefs to come to Washington, ostensibly to enter into trade treaties but actually to encourage peace among them. The press, however, implied that an ulterior motive may have been to have the chiefs serve as hostages for the safe return of the Lewis and Clark expedition. In the early spring of 1804, chiefs and warriors of the great Osage, Little Osage and Mandan tribes embarked for Washington, arriving in mid July.[42]

Two notable members of the Lewis and Clark expedition who made significant contributions in the expedition's march across the land were a black slave named York and an Indian woman known as Sacagawea. Possibly because they were not white, their role and contributions have been much distorted and they have erroneously developed into legendary figures. York was a body servant inherited by William Clark from his father. The claim that he was a man of superb physique and great strength who womanized and clowned his way across the continent appears to have been somewhat exaggerated.

Upon reaching the villages of the Mandan Indians, the leaders of the expedition hired a French Canadian half-blood named Toussaint Charbonneau and his wife Sacagawea, a Shoshoni Indian. Although it has often been erroneously claimed that it was she who led the party through the wilderness, she was nonetheless very helpful to the expedition because she was the only member of the party who could speak the language of the Shoshoni, from whom Lewis needed to purchase horses. Furthermore, her presence on the expedition with an infant indicated that it was a friendly and not a war party. A fortunate circumstance was that Cameahwait, one of the first Shoshoni chiefs they met, proved to be her brother. She identified for the explorers topographical features in her home country, and her knowledge of edible plants and how to procure and prepare them was of great value to the men. She traveled with Clark's party to explore the Yellowstone on their return journey, her infant child on her back. Clark became fond of the woman and her child and commented favorably in his journals on her fortitude during the arduous journey.[43]

Meanwhile, as Isaac Briggs began making preparations for his work in the South, he was experiencing difficulties in acquiring an astronomical transit, the most important of the instruments he required for making celestial observations. It was a relatively sophisticated instrument, of which only three existed in the country. Other than one made by John Bird of London used on the Mason and Dixon survey, which was owned by the Pennsylvania Proprietors, the only others were instruments made for their own use by Rittenhouse and Ellicott.

Neither of these instruments appeared to be available, since the Rittenhouse transit was placed on deposit in the American Philosophical Society after his death, and Ellicott was occupied with the Pennsylvania Land Commission. Briggs thereupon ordered a transit from the Philadelphia clock and instrument maker, Henry Voigt. Voigt failed to complete it on time, however, possibly because of other projects to which he gave priority.

Briggs expressed his concerns to Jefferson over the consequent delay of his work. "I must have misunderstood Henry Voight," he commented, "or he must have deceived himself, in the probable time when my Transit instrument would be finished; as he advanced in the work, the period of its completion seemed to be removed to a distance far beyond my expectation. Upon his informing me that it would probably require several months to complete it, I immediately packed up the remainder of my outfit."

Briggs then approached Ellicott and attempted to purchase his transit instrument, but the latter refused to sell it. Made desperate by now for the instrumentation he required to fulfill his assignment, Briggs applied to the American Philosophical Society through Jefferson for a loan of the Rittenhouse transit, requesting its removal to Washington. Inasmuch as it was not owned by the Society but only on deposit from the Rittenhouse family, it was not available for field use. Briggs had no recourse but to continue pressuring Voigt, and he finally arranged with him to ship the transit to him at Natchez as soon as it was completed, together with a chronometer.[44]

Briggs's first surveys had to be made along the southern Louisiana rivers and bayous through forests with lush, almost tropical, undergrowth. In addition to the difficulties of the terrain, he also had to contend with Indian, French and Spanish claimants so that the work progressed slowly, and his health and that of his men suffered considerably. In the summer season the region became so wet and extremely unhealthy that Briggs was forced to return to Washington for a respite, making the long laborious journey on horseback.[45]

Continuing development of his master plan of exploration, Jefferson intended also to investigate the great headwaters of the riverways flowing eastward across the Great Plains from the base of the Rocky Mountains abutting the eastern fringe of New Spain, now known as the American Southwest. There was no first-hand knowledge of the region, and accordingly Jefferson corresponded with anyone having intimate knowledge and collected voluminous notes from every source available.

Consequently, it was with considerable interest and pleasure that he learned that the young Prussian scientist and geographer, Baron Alexander von Humboldt, planned to visit him en route from Cuba on his return journey to Germany. Humboldt had completed an extensive survey of Latin America and Mexico and his notes and maps on New Spain would be of considerable value to Jefferson's endeavor. His visit would be most timely, for with the acquisition of the Louisiana Purchase, information about the Mexican realm on the new border was vitally required, and Jefferson hoped to include it in the message he was preparing for Congress.

The Prussian geographer was uniquely qualified to inform Jefferson, for he had compiled new maps and statistics, as well as geographical, political and economic information which had not been accessible to Americans. Humboldt, meanwhile, was just as anxious to meet the statesman whose writings and ideas had inspired him from his boyhood. He was particularly interested in learning Jefferson's plans for exploring the western lands, and looked forward to discussing with him various topics in Jefferson's Notes, and the state of American science.

A visit to the United States had not been included in Humboldt's original itinerary, but it may have been suggested to him by Vincent Gray, the American consul in Cuba, who made his travel arrangements. Humboldt also sent a lengthy letter to Madison describing his travels and expressing an interest in seeing the United States.[46]

The Baron landed at Philadelphia on May 23, 1804, accompanied by the young Ecuadorian, Don Carlos Montufar, and the French botanist Aimé Bonpland. Thirty-five years of age at this time, Humboldt was described by Jefferson's secretary, William Burwell, as "of small figure, well made, agreeable looks, simple unaffected manners, remarkably sprightly, vehement in conversation and sometimes eloquent."[47]

Immediately after his arrival in Philadelphia, Humboldt wrote to Jefferson. Impressed with the great adventure of American independence, he looked forward to meeting the scribe of freedom. He described his expedition through Central and South America, and requested permission to come to Washington to present his respects. Jefferson promptly invited him to the President's House.

"The countries you have visited," he responded, "are of those least known, and most interesting, and a lively desire will be felt generally to receive the information you will be able to give. No one will feel it more strongly than myself, because no one perhaps views the new world with more partial hopes of its exhibiting an ameliorated state of the human condition." He explained, however, that in Washington the visitor would find nothing curious to attract his attention.[48]

In Philadelphia Humboldt and his companions were warmly received by members of the American Philosophical Society, of which he was promptly elected a member. When he made known his plan to visit Washington, Charles Willson Peale offered his services as guide, being a member of the Society and a friend of the President. Peale welcomed the opportunity for other reasons of his own. It provided him with an opportunity to call upon the President, whom he had not seen in some time, and he would be enabled to deliver a new polygraph he had just completed to Jefferson's order. They were joined by the physician, Dr. Anthony Fothergill, and the pastor of the Old Swede Church, the Reverend Nicholas Collin. They drove through the city across the Schuylkill River into Delaware to Baltimore. There they spent several days before proceeding on to Washington, arriving on the evening of June 1st, and found lodgings in Stelle's Hotel.

On June 4th Humboldt and his party were at dinner at the President's House, with other guests including possibly also William Thornton and Albert Gallatin. The next evening they were the guests of the Secretary of State. The Baron presented an account of his travels over the past five years from which, Gallatin wrote, "he has brought a mass of natural, philosophical, and political information which will render the geography, productions, and statistics of that country better known than those of most European countries . . . I must acknowledge, in order to account for my enthusiasm, that he was surrounded with maps, statements, &c. all new to me and several of which he has liberally permitted us to transcribe."[49]

Jefferson, Gallatin and Madison were amazed at the volume of new data that Humboldt had collected, and Jefferson requested the loan of certain maps and other notes, which would supplement the data he had already collected on the territory of the Louisiana Purchase. The map of Mexico, which Humboldt presented to Jefferson, was said to have been later surreptitiously copied by Aaron Burr.

While the visitors remained in Washington, Jefferson sent a note to the Baron for assistance with a particular problem: "Th. Jefferson asks leave to observe to Baron de Humboldt that the question of limits of Louisiana between Spain & the U.S. is this, they claim to hold to the river Mexicana or Sabine & from the head of that Northwardly along the heads of the Red river & so on. We claim to the North river from its mouth to the source either of its Eastern or Western branch, then to the head of Red river & so on. Can the Baron inform me what population may be between those lines of white, red or black people? And whether any or what mines are within them? the information will be thankfully received."[50]

Jefferson compiled a table of "Louisiana-Texas by Pages, Nolan, Sibley, Humboldt" in which he tabulated information obtained during the visit. Humboldt responded in a 19-page manuscript which was summarized in his table of contents:

Tableau statistique du Royaume de la Nouw. Espagne
Tableau géologique du pays pp. 1–5
Population pp. 5–8
Division politique pp. 8–11
Agriculture, manufactures, commerce, p. 11
Routes de U. Etat p. 12
Mines p. 13
Forces militaire p. 14
Extrait des Tables statisticas del Reyno de
    Nueva Espagna presentadas al Exs. Sr. Virey
    Dn. Toset (?) de Yturrigaray en Enero 1804
    par F. A. Humboldt"[51]

This compilation was to be an extremely valuable resource, particularly on the geography of New Spain, which enabled Jefferson to improve his plans for the expeditions he proposed to send into the fringes of the region.

Jefferson was still convinced of the merits of his plan for taking lunar distances on land without the need of a timepiece, despite the lack of a favorable response from Ellicott and Patterson. During Humboldt's visit, he asked the geographer's opinion, and sent his comments on to Isaac Briggs. Humboldt had stated that there was no doubt concerning the validity and accuracy of the method, "but that it was not new, that even De la Caille had proposed it and De la Lande had given all explanations necessary for it. I think he said in his 3rd vol. I have not the book here but presume you can consult it in Philadelphia and will think it advisable to do so before you address a paper to the P[hilosophical] Society on the subject. Altho the idea was original with myself, yet if it is already known there is no occasion to repeat it."[52]

In the spring of 1804 Jefferson asked William Dunbar at Natchez to organize and advise still another exploring party, this one to proceed up the Arkansas River to its source and then along the highlands to the source of the Red River and then follow it to its mouth and its tributary, the Washita River. He explained "These surveys will enable us to prepare a map of La. which in its contour and main waters will be perfectly correct." He assumed that Congress would authorize funding.[53]

The naturalist Constantin Samuel Rafinesque visited Jefferson in the early summer of 1804 at the President's House, shortly before Jefferson was seeking a botanist to accompany the expedition up the Red River. A short time later Rafinesque sent him seeds of the *Jeffersonia diphylla*. He explained that he was collecting information about the flora of the Middle Atlantic States, and wished to consult Jefferson about plants new to him. He also planned to continue his research in parts of Kentucky and Ohio. Jefferson responded that he planned to send an expedition up the Red River for which he was seeking a botanist. He would welcome Rafinesque's participation but was unable to propose a position that would have sufficient remuneration for him. Before his letter arrived, Rafinesque had already departed for Italy, where he spent the next ten years. Upon his return, however, he applied repeatedly to Jefferson for a position in the new University of Virginia, but without success, presumably because of lack of funds for faculty salaries.[54]

This was not the only incident in which failure of the mails presented a problem on the projected Red River expedition. The well known ornithologist, Alexander Wilson, wrote to Jefferson in February 1806 requesting the position of naturalist on the expedition and gave the letter to William Bartram for forwarding. It is believed that it never reached Jefferson. Finally a medical student named Peter Custis was selected.[55]

Jefferson had visualized that Dunbar would serve only as adviser of the project and direct it, but not accompany the explorers, and had suggested that the surveyor Colonel Thomas Freeman be chosen as the leader of the expedition. He experienced considerable difficulty in finding a botanist to accompany the expedition, and informed Dunbar that Dr. George Hunter had been selected as the scientific member of the party "to make observations, to note courses, and inquire into the same subjects," and recommended him to the leader of the expedition. He assured Dunbar that although Hunter was not a trained botanist and had specialized in chemistry, he was nonetheless capable of making astronomical observations.[56]

Secretary of War General Dearborn, meanwhile, had assumed that Dunbar would lead the expedition and would select the other members of the party, and he offered that a military escort would be provided. Hunter was instructed to consult with Professor Patterson at Philadelphia "to inform you what instruments are in his opinion necessary for exploring the interior of Louisiana in order principally to ascertain the following points, viz. The Latitude & Longitude of the most important sources & junctions of the largest rivers below the Missouri & their courses—It is also the wish of the President that (after having obtained of Mr. Patterson the above information) you will be pleased to purchase such instruments as shall be deemed necessary and repair therewith to Natchez, for the purpose of accompanying such persons as shall be appointed by Mr. Dunbar of that place to explore the Red & Arkansas Rivers & to their sources."[57]

Meanwhile Dunbar, having had no further word from Jefferson, assumed, as Dearborn had, that he was expected to lead the exploring party. He wrote to Jefferson again to assure him that he would do everything possible to promote the expedition. He cautioned, however, that the Spanish should be informed and their consent obtained. He also expressed concern about a band of Osages in Arkansas reported to be unfriendly.

He suggested that the trader Pierre Chouteau be employed as guide and interpreter since he was known to the tribe. He also proposed that the Red River be ascended to enable more scientific data to be collected than would be possible otherwise. Jefferson meanwhile had prepared a set of instructions for the exploring party similar to those he had provided to Michaux and Lewis, which he forwarded to Dunbar. Hunter, he explained, was to be coadjutor and successor in case of accident to the principal.[58]

Having learned from the Osage delegation sent by Lewis from St. Louis that the splinter group of Osages in Arkansas might be troublesome, as Dunbar had predicted, Jefferson arranged to have Chouteau sent to Arkansas to attempt to obtain their cooperation. Dunbar had expressed personal interest in exploring the Ouachita River, and Jefferson agreed to the project as an interim measure. It would provide him with time to negotiate with the Spanish and for Chouteau to deal with the unfriendly Osages, while at the same time the Red River project would remain active.[59]

Dunbar and Hunter set out up the Red River to the mouth of the Ouachita, ascended it as far as Ouachita Post, which later became Monroe, Louisiana, crossed into Arkansas a month later, remained at Hot Springs for a month and then returned to Natchez. Dunbar made a chemical analysis of the waters of Hot Springs, and provided the first account of it after having explored the region of the Ouachita River in 1804. Detailed journals were maintained by both Dunbar and Hunter and forwarded to Washington. The expedition proved to be instructive for later undertakings. A map was later compiled from Dunbar's field notes by Nicholas King, Surveyor General of Washington.[60]

The Red River and its tributaries westward across the plains to a point 635 miles above its mouth were surveyed in 1806 by an expedition under the command of Thomas Freeman and Captain Sparks. Again a map was compiled from Freeman's field notes by King.[61]

The availability of suitable instrumentation was a problem not only for Briggs, but also for Benjamin Hawkins, who wrote to Jefferson from Tockaulatchee in the Creek Agency. "I do myself the pleasure to send you a specimen of my tours through the agency in my journey down the Tennessee with the map of the river. I have made it a habit to travel with a pocket compass and timepiece and have in like manner noted every journey through the country; several of which are plated [platted] and the whole will be sent to the War Office as soon as I have paper and leisure to copy them. I intended them in the first instance as military route only, as I had no rule to reduce the curve of paths taken of time to the same exactness as those of a river, but they will be useful to the delineation of the part of the United States. I could not get a portable instrument to take the latitude or I would have made it more complete."[62]

Another of the great undertakings during Jefferson's Presidency was led by Zebulon M. Pike from St. Louis up the Mississippi to chart the river and adjacent countryside, to purchase sites for military posts from the Indians and to inform Indians and Canadians that the region was now under the new authority of the United States. Although he did not reach the Mississippi's headwaters—his mission did not in fact require that he search for them—the map of his route produced from his notes was a landmark in the history of Western exploration. When Jefferson saw Pike's journals and maps, he found therein much of value upon which to base future expeditions. Nicholas King was assigned to consolidate Pike's maps into one, and after the journal and map were printed, Jefferson ordered copies to be distributed to some members of Congress, to the American Philosophical Society and to others.[63]

Upon being recalled to St. Louis early in 1806, Pike set out on a second expedition west and south across the Rocky Mountains and then southwest towards Santa Fe with a party of twenty men. Observing, describing and sketching the terrain of the Colorado region, he discovered the peak that bears his name. It was primarily a military reconnaissance of which the War Department was informed, but not an expedition authorized by Jefferson.

The purpose of the expedition was primarily to escort some Osage Indians who had been prisoners of the Potawatomi back to their village, to try to effect peace between some Kansas Indians and the Pawnees and to locate the Comanches and bring them into the national fold. Pike and his party were also to explore the Arkansas River, to reach the headwaters of both the Arkansas and Red Rivers and to descend the Red River to Natchitoches. While a small detachment descended the Arkansas River, Pike and his remaining men proceeded up the river to the Rockies. While his men were building a temporary stockade at the confluence of the Purgatoire and Arkansas Rivers, Pike with a companion explored a peak in the northwest. Pike and his men were lost on three separate occasions and eventually were detained by the Spanish, into whose territory they had wandered.[64]

Despite the productive activity that occurred between 1804 and 1806, it ended in the following year. Thereafter, with Jefferson's retirement from office, there was no one who appeared to understand the importance of the West for the country's future development. It was not until 1818 that a Topographical Bureau was established, headed by Major Isaac Roberdeau, who produced a composite map of the West, the first of many others to follow.

Jefferson was still stubbornly convinced that his method of determining longitude with the use of a universal equatorial instrument without a timekeeper was practical, and found occasion to discuss the subject also with William Dunbar. "I set myself to consider whether in making observations at land, that furnishes no resource which may dispense with the time-keeper, so necessary at sea," he informed Dunbar. "It occurred to me that as we can always have a meridian at land, that would furnish what we want of it at sea obliges us to supply by the time-keeper. Supposing Captain Lewis then furnished with a meridian, and having the requisite tables and nautical almanac with him,—first, he might find the right ascension of the moon, when on the meridian of Greenwich, on any given day; then find by observation when the moon should attain that right ascension (by the aid of a known star), and measure her distance in that moment from his meridian. This distance would be the difference of longitude between Greenwich and the place of observation. Or secondly, observe the moon's position over his meridian, and her right ascension at the same moment. See by the tables the time at Greenwich when she had that right ascension. That gives her distance from the meridian of Greenwich, when she was on his meridian. Or thirdly, observe the moon's distance from his meridian any moment, and her right ascension at that moment; and find from the tables her distance from the meridian of Greenwich, when she had that right ascension, which will give the distance of the two meridians. This last process will be simplified by taking, for the moment of observation, that of an appulse of the moon and a known star, or when the moon and a known star are in the same vertical."

Jefferson went on to relate that recently he had proposed this procedure to Isaac Briggs, who considered it correct and practicable. Furthermore, Briggs suggested that Jefferson should communicate it to the American Philosophical Society. However, Jefferson took the view that it was too obvious and consequently already known, but had not been used because it was not practical at sea, where there was the greatest need for it. He explained that before he had been able to confirm the practicability of the method, Lewis had already departed on his expedition.

In conversations later with Humboldt, the latter had informed him that the idea was indeed correct but not new and had already been published by de Lalande in his third volume. Having recently received the third and fourth volumes of Jean Étienne Montucla's history of mathematics edited by de Lalande, Jefferson discovered that both Jean Morin and M. F. Van Langren had already in the seventeenth century proposed making observations of the moon on the meridian, but that it was not clear whether they proposed dispensing with a timekeeper.[65]

After reviewing Jefferson's proposal, Dunbar cautioned that there would be some serious difficulties in using it. It would require two observers, as well as a fine instrument superior to the sextant, such as a Troughton astronomical circle. In addition to describing the difficult calculations to be made, he explained that it would be preferable to make such observations by the sun because of the difficulty of taking double altitudes of a star with an artificial horizon. He sent Jefferson an explanation of the method he used for finding longitude without a timepiece by a single observer, which was considerably simpler.[66]

Jefferson was not about to abandon his cherished proposal and almost a year later he again commented on it to Dunbar. "You will have perceived," he noted, "that my suggestion of a method of finding the longitude on land without a time piece was that of a theorist only, not a practical astronomer. It was founded too in the use of an Equatorial the only instrument with which I have the [least?] familiarity. I never used the Quadrant at all; and had thought of importing three or four Equatorials for the use of those [exploring] parties. They get over all difficulty in finding a meridian. The suggestion however of my imperfect method has had the good effect of producing those less so." He noted that from Joshua Moore he had received a description of yet another method of determining longitude.

As to Dunbar's observations of the currents of the Mississippi, Jefferson stated he was not informed on the subject, although he had studied Torricelli's doctrine of the velocities at different depths. Referring to his grand plan for exploration of the American unknown lands, he added, "The work we are now doing is, I trust, done for posterity, in such a way that they need not repeat it." He expressed his indebtedness to Dunbar for the time and manner in which he had devoted himself to this endeavor, and also "for the excellent method of which you have set the example, and which I hope will be the model to be followed by others. We shall delineate with correctness the great arteries of this great country. Those who come after us will extend the ramifications as they become acquainted with them, and fill up the canvas we begin."[67]

Undoubtedly influenced by his preoccupation with continental exploration during this period, Jefferson again added to his already extensive collection of scientific instrumentation. His purchases from the London firm of W. and S. Jones featured in particular a pair of eighteen-inch "new British Globes," Arrowsmith's 4-sheet maps of Europe, Asia and Africa, "Olmadilla's Map of South America," all to be "on Canvas and Rollers, Varnished," various and sundry slide rules, a protracting parallel ruler, a portable drawing board and "A 1 ft. Achromatic Telescope and adjustment for a Ramsdens' Equatorial."

The large maps on rollers were to equip the special map case which he had designed and had constructed in the President's House. The achromatic telescope for attachment to his Universal Equatorial Instrument was a refinement which he had designed and ordered from the Jones firm to be made to his special order.[68]

Public interest in the Lewis and Clark expedition was revived from time to time by news in the press of their progress, and by the arrival of exciting new shipments of materials from the West. The party had spent the winter encamped at River Dubois and in May proceeded by boat up the Missouri. The following winter was spent among the Mandan tribes. They were on the move again in April, and after ascending to the source of Jefferson Fork of the Missouri, they crossed the Bitter Root Mountains and descended the Columbia River, reaching the Pacific coast in November 1805.

In his message to Congress on December 2nd, Jefferson reported, "The expedition of Messrs. Lewis and Clark, for exploring the river Missouri, and the best communications from that to the Pacific ocean, has had all the success which could have been expected. They have traced the Missouri nearly to its source, descended the Columbia to the Pacific ocean, ascertained with accuracy the geography of that interesting communication across our continent, learned the character of the country, of its commerce, and inhabitants; and it is but justice to say that Messrs. Lewis and Clark, and their brave companions, have by this arduous service deserved well of their country."[69]

After wintering at Fort Clatsop on the Pacific coast, the exploring party began the long homeward journey in March, arriving in September 1806 at St. Louis, where the party disbanded. Despite the detailed instructions that Jefferson had provided to Lewis for the conduct of the expedition, he had included no instructions for the disposition of the party's equipment and collections after the expedition returned.

This was not characteristic of Jefferson, who had devoted so much personal attention to every detail of the planning for the expedition. It can be explained only by his preoccupation with the immediate crises in government, including the Burr conspiracy and Wilkinson's illegal projected expedition against the territories of Spain. He was not in fact informed of the safe return of Lewis and Clark until almost two months after they reached St. Louis.[70]

Particularly regrettable was the dispersal of the expedition's appurtenances and equipment, which would have been of enormous historical value. Included were Indian knives, tomahawks, handmade clothing, fishing gear, weapons and many other items collected on the journey, as well as the exploring party's scientific instruments, keelboat and canoes and other equipment. Inasmuch as he had received no other instructions, and in the absence of a request for Congress to appropriate money to preserve these items, Lewis followed Army procedures and arranged to sell the expedition's appurtenances and equipment at public auction.

From the sale which took place in St. Louis, a total of $408.62 was realized.[71]

Meanwhile the preserved specimens returned by the expedition were temporarily stored at St. Louis, but some of the botanical specimens were shipped to Jefferson and others were permanently lost through mishandling. No provision was made for the classification and preservation of the scientific collections, notes and journals sent or brought back by Lewis and Clark, and consequently they were dispersed to various repositories, with inadequate record keeping and consequent losses.

It must be realized, however, that at that time there was no national botanical garden or arboretum nor a national museum to serve as an official repository for such items, nor was there a national archives. Furthermore, there was no formulation of a clear policy for the handling of such materials, inasmuch as this was the first government sponsored scientific enterprise.

Nonetheless, in addition to the considerable amount of valuable information gathered and returned by the explorers about the hitherto unknown lands of the West, the expedition had two important results. It had provided Jefferson with an opportunity to enlist government sponsorship of science for the first time in the new republic, thus establishing a precedent for the future, and it served as a predecessor for future exploring expeditions to support the American position and claims to the West.[72]

Early in their journey, Lewis and Clark encountered a large number of animals and birds not previously known in the East. After spending the first winter at Fort Mandan, about fifty miles from the present city of Bismarck, North Dakota, they collected dried plants, seeds and cuttings, skins, horns and bones of animals and birds, minerals and Indian artifacts which they shipped to Jefferson.

A large consignment of natural history specimens arrived in Washington in October 1805, including a group intended for Peale's Museum, as well as a box of minerals that Lewis had specified was to go to the American Philosophical Society. In the shipment there was also another selection, described by Jefferson as "some articles I shall keep for an Indian Hall I am forming at Monticello, e.g. horns, dressed skins, utensils, etc."

Jefferson's plan was to divide his Entrance Hall in such a manner that one wall featured artifacts relating to paleontology while the other was reserved for Indian relics.

The items intended for Peale consisted of skins and skeletons of the white hare, red fox, antelope and burrowing squirrel, a skeleton of a small burrowing wolf of the prairies, a male and female burrowing prairie dog or badger called the "Blaiveau," a mammal which was found outside of Europe for the first time, and a preserved magpie. Jefferson had previously received a pair of horns described by Lewis as antelope, but which Jefferson identified as horns of the roe, because they were bony, solid and branching, while those of the antelope were hollow, annulated and single.

The shipment arrived in great disorder, because the contents had been unpacked several times along the way. The marmot or "Louisiana Badger" arrived safely but had become sleepy with the approach of winter. Peale mounted two of the bighorns, one for his Museum and another for Jefferson's Entrance Hall.[73]

Several days later Jefferson corrected his identification of the antelope horns. He had further examined "the bony prominence to the cranium on which the horn is fixed, & afterwards two pair of the horns themselves. These sufficiently prove that the animal is of the antelope family & of the chamois branch of it. This is strengthened by the dressed skin which is softer, and stronger in its texture than any chamois I have seen." He had sent along to Peale also a pair of horns of "the unknown ram" which he supposed to be "a variety of the Ovis Ammon of Linnaeus the Moufflon of the French."[74]

The matter of naming the big-horned antelope created somewhat of a problem. Peale, who always advocated the use of simple descriptive names, proposed calling it the "forked horned antelope," based on its appearance. When Peale presented a paper before the American Philosophical Society using the name he had chosen, he found objection, however. He commented to Jefferson about those "who must be humored with high-sounding names made from the dead languages." He asked Jefferson to suggest names that might be acceptable, perhaps words from the Indian languages? The mammal was formally named *Antilocapra americana americana*, and became known as the Pronghorn Antelope.[75]

The process of identification by Peale and Jefferson of examples of wild life sent or brought back from the West continued for several years after the return of the explorers. One of the animals encountered on the expedition, which Lewis called the "Fleecy Goat," puzzled Jefferson. Lewis had presented him with a skin and had given a more perfect one as well as the horns to Peale for his Museum. Wistar referred to it as the "wild sheep," but Jefferson thought it might be the llama, or *Lamae affinis*. In this connection, Jefferson was pleased to read an account about Chile by Juan Ignacio Molina, "in which, correcting Buffon's classification of the wooly animals, he speaks of one, the Chili hueco or Chili Sheep" which Jefferson thought might be identified with the "fleecy goat." He called it the "Poko-tragos."[76]

Jefferson distributed some of the seeds brought back by Lewis and Clark to Bernard McMahon, a prominent nurseryman in Philadelphia and author of the first book on gardening under American conditions.

He was made the custodian of the expedition's seeds, and arranged to have the plants sketched by the visiting English botanist, Frederick Pursh.

Of the plants returned by the expedition, Jefferson favored three which he later planted at Monticello in 1812, having obtained them from McMahon. They were the "snowberry (*Symphoricarpos aureum*), the "Missouri currant," and the "yellow currant" (*Ribes odoratum*).[77]

Notable in the shipments were six live animals and birds, consisting of four magpies, a grouse and a prairie dog. The collection of live specimens was an ambitious venture, for although Jefferson had specified that they were to observe animals and birds at close quarters, he never anticipated that the explorers would attempt to capture and send back live specimens. The prairie dog had been particularly difficult to capture, and even more difficult to name. Lewis referred to it as the "barking squirrel," Clark called it the "ground rat" and "burrowing squirrel," while Sergeant Ordway, a member of the party, named it the "prairie dog," the popular name it has retained.

The explorers encountered a new bird of the grouse family, which they captured, and later still a magpie which they shot. Although prevalent in Europe, the magpie was not previously known in the United States. Later Lewis and Clark obtained four living specimens, possibly from the Indians, and included them in the shipment to Washington. The wild life arrived at St. Louis, more than 1600 miles downstream, from which it was forwarded to New Orleans, where it arrived three weeks and another 1000 miles later. Jefferson was kept apprized of the shipment's progress all along the way. It then proceeded by water to Baltimore.

Meanwhile the grouse had died before the shipment reached New Orleans, and three of the magpies perished en route to Baltimore. The survivors arrived at the President's House in August, while Jefferson was at Poplar Forest. Étienne LeMaire, major domo of the executive mansion, informed Jefferson, describing the live specimens, and noting that he had placed them "in the room where Monsieur receives his callers."[78]

It was not until Jefferson returned to Washington that he contacted Peale on what appears to have been a prearranged plan. He forwarded the listing of the shipment's contents to Philadelphia, except for a few items he retained for himself. These consisted of some horns, dressed skins and Indian utensils which he eventually added to what he called his "Indian hall" at Monticello. Also destined for Peale's Museum were the live magpie and prairie dog.

Peale referred to the latter as "the living Marmotte, it is a handsome little animal, smaller and much more gentle than our Monax [ground hog] & I expect like it will not eat during the winter, for this eats but little at present. I shall keep it in a Warm room for a tryal. I am surprised to see the Magpie so correctly like that of Europe," he informed Jefferson, "for I have always found some difference in the Birds which has been described as belonging to both continents. It is interesting to get the living one in good condition, for a better comparison and also to give it a place near one I have from Great Britain handsomely mounted."[79]

The magpie and prairie dog arrived safely at Peale's Museum after having traveled thousands of miles over a period of some seven months from their natural home. Word of their presence circulated through the city, and they became popular exhibits. Members of the American Philosophical Society came to see them, as well as the naturalists Benjamin Smith Barton, Alexander Wilson, Alexander Lawson and George Ord.

As Peale reported to Jefferson, "The Marmot sleeps and the Magpie chatters a great deal." Despite Jefferson's expectations that the magpie would have a short life, it lived through the winter and into the following year. When it died, Peale had it mounted, and it served as a model for inclusion in Wilson's comprehensive study of American birds.[80]

In addition to the curiosities and rarities of nature which Jefferson assembled in his workshop in the President's House, there were others that had to be maintained elsewhere. Among these were two young grizzly bears which had been brought to him by Zebulon Pike on his return from his westward expedition. They were male and female and had been captured on the Rio Bravo, "from the divideing ridges of the Pacific, & Atlantic Oceans," when they were too young to feed themselves and had been kept relatively at large by the exploring party.[81]

Passersby were attracted by the animals disporting themselves in the open, on the lawn of the President's House, and often paused to watch them. At first, Jefferson had them caged, but they had soon outgrown the restraints and began to suffer as a consequence. He then had them placed together in an enclosed area, about ten feet square, on the lawn. Inevitably, the Federalists found in the young playful animals another means of deriding the President, and referred to "Jefferson's bear-garden."[82]

The bears continued to grow. Finally Jefferson concluded he could no longer maintain them in Washington, and decided to send them to Peale for the Museum. He explained, "For the first day they worried one another very much with play, but after that they played at times but were extremely happy together. When separated & put into their small cage again, one became almost furious, indeed one is much crosser than the other, but I do not think they have any idea of hurting any one. They know no benefactor but man." By sending them to Peale, he thought "They would certainly be more in the way of extending information if exhibited in your Museum to the numerous visitors." He reassured Peale that they were perfectly gentle.[83]

They did not remain "gentle" for long after they were moved to

Philadelphia, however. One of them tore off the arm and shoulder of a live monkey which had approached it too closely. Then later it broke out of its cage one night and found its way in the dark to the Peale kitchen in the basement of Independence Hall, terrorizing the Peale family. Peale managed to barricade the bear in the room for the night. The next morning he returned with his gun and shot and killed it. He also killed the mate, and then mounted the two together in a Museum display.[84]

The final Indian delegation to come to Washington during Jefferson's Presidency arrived in conjunction with the return of Lewis and Clark from the upper Missouri. The explorers had urged the Mandan chief, Shahaka (also called Sheheke), to accompany them with his wife and child to Washington in the autumn of 1806. Meanwhile, the fur trader and merchant, Pierre Chouteau, escorted another contingent of Indians to the national capital for additional consultations.

The visits were successful, but Shahaka's return to his tribe was delayed for more than two years because of war among the tribes along the upper Missouri, a circumstance which also affected other delegations to Washington. Because of the problems relating to Shahaka's return and the excessive costs of such delegations, the Jefferson administration did not authorize any more visits after 1807. Even after his return to his tribe, Shahaka experienced considerable difficulties because he had become enamoured of the white man's way of life. Yet he found it impossible to become part of it, and his continued preoccupation with this other world later caused him to lose face among his own people.[85]

Chouteau was having his own difficulties in St. Louis with Indian tribal chiefs all clamoring to be conducted to Washington. He urged most of them to return home until government authorization would be forthcoming from Washington, but with little success. Most of his time had to be directed to keeping the waiting Indians from becoming bored, and to maintaining their health while they waited. To provide variety from their endless card games, which they had learned from Canadian traders, he resorted to hiring a wagon to take them out into the countryside on hunting trips.

Chouteau also found it necessary to follow Secretary of War Dearborn's suggestion to construct a large building near his residence to accommodate the numerous Indian delegations that kept arriving. Only a few representatives from the major tribes of the Upper Louisiana were selected to go to Washington, and those not so fortunate were provided with gifts.[86]

The major problem deriving from the Indian delegations was that the government administration required that they were to be given the finest treatment on their journey and during their stay in Washington, but did not provide the funds to make it possible. Captain Amos Stoddard, lawyer and soldier in the Revolution, who now commanded a company of artillerists, was instructed that while leading the delegations, he was to camp out with them as much as possible to avoid paying costly tavern rates. Nonetheless, his allotment did not recompense for even the amount of food they consumed.

Generally, all the delegations were well received and established friendly relations wherever they went. Surprisingly, although some of the tribes were traditionally mortal enemies, there were no serious conflicts among the delegates of different tribes while in Washington.[87]

The visits of Indian delegations to the national capital helped to keep peace among them and encouraged trade, but they did not succeed in bringing about the idealistic state which Jefferson and others had envisioned and hoped to achieve. Nonetheless, he considered that the plan to civilize the Indians was far more productive than the work that was being done by religious missionaries. In his view, it was important to imbue in them a strong sense of property, which could be derived by the raising of cattle.

By teaching them arithmetic, he would enable them to calculate the value of their property, and if they were taught to write, they could keep accounts, "and here they begin to enclose farms, and the men to labor, the women to spin and weave." The Creeks and the Cherokees had already progressed this far, and he proposed "for their first delight" they should learn to read Aesop's fables and Daniel Defoe's *Robinson Crusoe.*[88]

The gap between the worlds of red men and white men was too great to be bridged merely by hospitality and ceremonies. Jefferson had long claimed that the Indians could be delivered from barbarism and protected from the problems inherent in white society, and exerted his efforts towards this aim. This might have been achieved, at least to a degree, if the white people had not continued to deceive and misuse the Indians, with the consequence that the aborigines resisted in the traditional manner known to them. The situation deteriorated even further because of the government's constant delays in fulfilling the promises it had made to the Indians.[89]

In due course the two leaders of the expedition made their way back to Washington, Lewis arriving at the end of December and Clark soon thereafter. The explorers were feted by banquets and meetings with high government officials, and the newspapers were filled with accounts of their exploits. With the departure of General Wilkinson to assume command of the military forces in the Orleans Territory, Jefferson planned to appoint Lewis as his successor as Governor of the Louisiana Territory, which was approved by the Senate. Clark was commissioned territorial agent for Indian affairs in the same Territory. Concerned that inadequate accounts of the expedition would be produced by lesser members of the expedition, Lewis at this time formally announced his intention to produce a full account and subsequently discussed the project with a printer in Philadelphia. On his departure for St. Louis in September to assume his new appointment, he took his original journals with him.[90]

Lewis at first was delighted with his appointment which would lead to a promising political career, but the developing conflicts with ambitious men and the volume of problems grew alarmingly. He proved to be an inept governor, possibly because of his military approach, making enemies of his associates, and eventually he turned to alcohol. He failed to re-establish correspondence with Jefferson and some of his drafts on government were not approved; soon he found himself out of favor with the new administration as well as with the local government. It became necessary for him to return to Washington with his fiscal records and his expedition journals by way of New Orleans. He then changed his route, arriving at Fort Pickering (now Memphis, Tennessee). There he was detained by the post commander, Captain Gilbert C. Russell, because it was apparent that he had been drinking heavily and was in no condition to travel. On October 11, 1809 Lewis died at Grinder's Tavern from gunshot wounds to the head and abdomen, which may have been self-inflicted. The circumstances were never resolved.

The expedition journals were recovered and added to those in Clark's possession, and Clark and Jefferson decided to have a narrative account produced by an experienced writer and the scientific material analyzed and published by a man of science. Nicholas Biddle, a well known Philadelphia literary figure, agreed to write the narrative and Benjamin Smith Barton the scientific report. The map was to be produced by Clark. The first two publishers selected became bankrupt after the narrative and map were published in 1814. Meanwhile Barton died before he could compile his report, and Jefferson assumed the task of assembling the materials for deposit and editing by the American Philosophical Society, a project which was to preoccupy him for some time to come.[91]

The American Philosophical Society also was seeking to make a comprehensive collection of remains of the mammoth (mastodon) and an offer to assemble such a collection for it was received from a Cincinnati physician, Dr. William Goforth. Jefferson found his terms unacceptable and refused the offer, then informed the Society that he would arrange to make such a collection at his own expense and at no cost to the Society.

Being acquainted with the proprietor of Big Bone Lick, Jefferson obtained permission to send someone there to search for such specific fossil remains as were required by the Society to complete its collection. He employed William Clark at his own cost to hire his own laborers and superintend such an excavation at the Lick. Next he arranged with

Wistar to prepare at his first convenience a list of the specific bones desired for the Society.[92]

Jefferson anxiously awaited the arrival of the fossil bones from Big Bone Lick, but had received no progress report on the venture. He again wrote to Clark, suggesting that in order to make the collection more considerable so that he would be enabled to make selections not only for the American Philosophical Society but also for the French Institut, he would like to have him send the fossil remains that he (Clark) had deposited with his brother at Clarkesville. These included the backbones, leg bones, thighs, ham hips, shoulder blades, parts of the upper and lower jaws, teeth of the "mammoth" and elephant and parts of the "mammoth" tusks. He asked that they be packed and shipped via New Orleans as before.[93]

Clark finally reported a short time later on the results of the fossil collecting enterprise commissioned by Jefferson. He informed the President that, with the assistance of ten laborers working for several weeks, he had succeeded in recovering a number of fossil remains from Big Bone Lick which he had shipped to Washington. They were contained in three large boxes sent down the Ohio River to New Orleans and would be forwarded from there by ship to Baltimore. They consisted of frontals, jawbones, tusks, teeth, ribs, a thigh, leg and some bones of the paw of the "mammoth" or American mastodon. Of the elephant he included a jawbone, tusks, teeth and ribs. Finally, he included a head and other unidentified bones "of something of the Buffalo species." Clark proved to be an excellent choice for collecting fossil remains, for he had previous experience in such an endeavor, and he was able to provide valuable descriptions with the specimens he obtained.

The three large boxes of fossil remains were shipped down the Mississippi to New Orleans and from there went by sea to Baltimore. They eventually arrived at the President's House, and Jefferson immediately informed Wistar of the fact. Among them, Jefferson noted, "There is a tusk and a femur which General Clark [George Clark] procured particularly at my request, for a special kind of cabinet I have at Monticello." His intention was to give first preference to the American Philosophical Society of those fossils not already in its collection. However, a great part of the bones shipped by Clark appeared to be duplicates of those the Society already possessed. He thereupon decided to send these to the Institut de France, inasmuch as it owned only a very few specimens of this nature.

To avoid disposing of important pieces by error, he urged Wistar to come to spend a week with him in Washington. He would be able to find lodgings in a tavern near the President's House, and was invited to take all his meals with Jefferson. He could spend time sightseeing in the city as well as in examining the bones and setting aside those required for the Society.[94]

Jefferson had spread the bones out in the large "Mammoth Room" which served as his workroom, where Wistar would be able to work undisturbed and at his own leisure from morning till night. He described the collection as containing more than three hundred specimens, few of them of large size. He reported that included were four pieces of the head, four jawbones almost complete containing several teeth and three elephant tusks, one different from the others and of excessive size, being from nine to ten feet in length.

Also in the collection were ribs, teeth of the studded and striated or ribbed varieties, a foreleg and approximately two hundred bones chiefly of the foot. An unusual item was a "horn of a colossal animal." Jefferson discovered that the bones received did not coincide entirely with those included on the list sent by Clark, so he assumed that some may have been omitted by the packers. Since he had already shipped his books to Monticello, he advised Wistar that he would be unable to provide much assistance, but noted that he had his copy of the *Encyclopédie méthodique* with him. Despite Jefferson's urgings, it was not until late June that Wistar was able to come to Washington. They began working immediately, and separated out three groups of the bones.[95]

Among the changes brought about in Paris by the National Convention after the French Revolution was the nationalization of the Cabinet du Roi, in which the natural history collections were maintained, and its name changed to the Musée National d'Histoire Naturelle. The old royal academies had been dissolved and reconstituted as different classes of the newly established Institut de France, to which in December 1801 Jefferson had been honored with an appointment as a "foreign associate."

By means of correspondence, he had continued his contacts with the French naturalists he had met in Paris, and this association, coupled with his sense of the obligation inherent in the honor bestowed upon him, led him to contribute the duplicate fossils as a gift to the Institut.

On July 14, 1808, the anniversary of the fall of the Bastille, Jefferson informed Lacépède that he was shipping the fossil bones for the Institut, inasmuch as he recalled that in the former royal cabinet of natural history the bones of the "animal incognitum of the Ohio (sometimes called mammoth)," were incomplete. He explained how Clark had assembled a collection for him, and he enclosed the catalogue which he and Wistar had compiled of the specimens being donated.

To the fossils he added from his own collection also the horns of the "Mountain Ram," so-called by the Indians, and the skin of what they described as the "Fleecy Goat," which Lewis and Clark had obtained from the Indians. He included one of the four spiral mammoth tusks thus far obtained. One had come from the north branch of the Susquehanna, another from near the Hudson River, a third was found at Big Bone Lick, which he kept at Monticello, and the fourth, which he shipped, had also come from Big Bone Lick. In his catalogue he added comments about each item, explaining features and differences. He addressed the shipment to Lacépède at the Institut through David Warden, the American consul pro tem in Paris.

The French naturalists received the fossils with considerable enthusiasm, and the specimens were promptly placed on display with labels acknowledging the donor. They were subsequently carefully studied by Cuvier, among others, who in cooperation with Lacépède, published the first description of Jefferson's gift in the second edition of his work, *Recherches sur les Ossemens Fossiles*, which appeared in 1821. From Jefferson's fossils, Cuvier was able to reconstruct two extinct species, the *Mastodon americanus* and the *Elephas primigenius*.[96]

Jefferson agreed with Peale that the distinct differences between the elephant and "our colossal animal", the so-called mammoth, entitled the latter to a name of its own. "One of those differences," he informed Peale, "& a striking one, is in the protuberances on the grinding surface of the teeth, somewhat in the shape of the mamma mastos, or breast of a woman, which has induced Cuvier to call it the Mastodonte, or bubby-toothed; which name may perhaps be as good as any another, & worthy of adoption, as it is more important that all should agree in giving the same name to the same thing, than that it should be the very best which might be given."

This appears to have been the first use, or intended use, of the name "American mastodon" for the "mammoth," an extinct species which had preoccupied American men of science since the first recovery of its bones several decades earlier.[97]

CHAPTER XV

"THE SHACKLES OF POWER" (1805–1809)

Science is more important in a republican than in any other government. And in an infant country like ours, we must depend for improvement on the science of other countries, longer established, possessing better means, and more advanced than we are. To prohibit us from the benefit of foreign light, is to consign us to long darkness.

Letter from Thomas Jefferson to
an unknown correspondent,
1821.

Although Jefferson's re-election to a second term marked the zenith of his presidency, his last years in office were not to be the most productive period of his public life. A treaty with favorable terms was signed ending the war with Tripoli, but his efforts to effect an alliance with Great Britain to offset problems with Spanish negotiations proved to be doomed to failure. Rumors of Burr's conspiracy to undertake an expedition against the Spanish territory in the Southwest and Mexico resulted in his being brought to trial for treason. Although he was acquitted, questions about Jefferson's role added fuel for Federalist criticism.

Then the country was brought to the verge of war by the British search of the American warship *Chesapeake* for supposed deserters, causing Jefferson to ban British ships from American waters. He imposed an embargo preventing American ships from sailing to foreign ports and foreign ships were barred from the United States. Equally distressing to Jefferson was the understandable negative reaction of the northeastern states to the embargo. Adopting the policy as the only alternative to war or submission, it was totally opposed to his own conviction in personal liberty in every dimension. Despite many requests that he accept a third term, Jefferson remained adamant in his refusal.

As always, Jefferson found refuge in science-related activities. His lifelong preoccupation with the compilation of statistical data was reflected in many aspects of his interests. Particularly he was fascinated with distances traveled, on his journeys between Monticello and Richmond, Washington, Poplar Forest and elsewhere. He was intrigued by the odometer, an instrument which measured distance traveled by counting and numbering the revolutions of a carriage wheel of specified circumference, and he experimented with various forms of it. He kept copious records of the distances recorded in this manner, noting them first on the ivory note leaves he always kept on his person, then transferring them to his *Memorandum Books*.

He purchased every form of odometer available. While in France in 1788, he had asked Benjamin Vaughan to investigate for him the possibility of obtaining one from London, because he had been informed by Count Francesco Verme "that they make in London an Odometer which may be made fast between the two spokes of any wheel, & will indicate the revolutions of the wheel by means of a pendulum which always keeps it's vertical position while the wheel is turning round & round." He was anxious to determine its utility and cost, but there is no evidence that he was able to acquire one.[1]

At an undetermined date, possibly while in England or later by mail order, Jefferson purchased an extremely sophisticated form of the instrument from Nairne & Blunt, which survives at Monticello. The brass movement is housed in a mahogany case with hinged front. The drive mechanism is attached to a carriage wheel or the wheel of a wayweiser by means of an attachment through the bottom of the case. Reading from the outermost circle, one sees that the dial indicates the distance traveled measured in chains, links, yards, poles, miles and furlongs. It also provides a conversion table. At home later, he purchased other odometers from Robert Leslie in 1791 and from David Rittenhouse in 1794.[2] (*Figure 30*)

Jefferson also had odometers constructed to his own design and specifications. He became extensively involved in this endeavor with James Clarke, an inventor, landowner and local politician of Powhatan, Virginia, in an association which continued until almost the end of his life. In the spring of 1807, he learned from a Mr. Stannard that

Clarke "had invented and made a machine to be fixed behind a carriage for counting the revolutions of the wheel while travelling."

The device appeared to be of a type with which Jefferson had already experimented unsuccessfully. When Stannard suggested that Clarke might not be averse to communicating it, Jefferson promptly contacted the inventor, informing him that he had himself "made an effort of the same kind & failed." He asked whether Clarke would be willing to let his instrument be copied, suggesting that it could be sent to him for that purpose through George Jefferson, his cousin who served as his agent in Richmond, from whom it would be conveyed by stage to Washington.[3]

Clarke replied in the affirmative, offering the instrument as a gift, and suggesting that he either ship it to Washington or bring it to Monticello, where he could show the President how to take it apart and put it together again, and how to install it on a carriage. He explained that the first version he had produced had a single index revolving once in ten miles but had no bell.

Since then he had developed another having two indices and a bell; one index of which denoted the number of miles traveled while the other reported the fractions of miles divided in decimals, and a bell which struck at the end of each mile. The instrument was contained within a small brass box the size of a shaving case. It was calculated for use on a wheel five feet one inch in diameter, so that it would be necessary for Jefferson to replace the hind wheels of his carriage with others of that size.

Clarke offered to show Jefferson other instruments he had made, including one "to determine the longitude by magnetick attraction and repulsion," which he had just constructed. All that remained to complete it was magnetization of the needles, for which he required a strong magnet. Although he had not been able to test the instrument as yet, he was confident that it would be successful.[4]

Jefferson explained that his wish to borrow the odometer to record the distances between Washington and Monticello, to which he planned to travel at the end of June. He invited Clarke to come to Monticello, "where I have probably the most powerful magnet in the U.S. which may answer the purpose you are at a loss for with respect to your magnetic needle. The ascertainment of the longitude by lunar observations at sea, is now rendered so practical & accurate, that any other mode must offer great precision to prevail in a competition against the lunar method. Your method will therefore have a claim to the higher merit if it should be found preferable. On land, the observation of the eclipses of Jupiter's satellites answer perfectly for the ascertainment of longitude."[5]

After he became acquainted with Clarke, Jefferson commissioned him to produce an unusual form of odometer for his use. He later described it to Dr. Thomas Cooper during a discussion of various proposals that had been made for the establishment of standard weights and measures and coinage. Jefferson suggested that each standard should be divisible decimally at the will of the individual. As an example of its popular application, he mentioned one means by which he had already tested its applicability.

"I have lately had a proof how familiar this division into dimes, cents and mills is to the people when transferred from their money to anything else. I have an odometer fixed to my carriage which gives the distances in miles, dimes & cents. The people on the road enquire with curiosity what exact distance I have found from such a place to such a place; I answer, so many miles, so many cents. I find they universally and at once form a perfect idea of the relation of the cent to the mile as an unit." He felt assured that they would do the same with yards of cloth, pounds of shot and ounces of silver or medicine, as examples.[6]

He was especially proud of this device, and described it again in his *Autobiography*, stating "I use when I travel, an odometer of Clarke's invention, which divides the mile into cents, and I find everyone comprehends a distance readily, when stated to him in miles and cents."[7]

Jefferson had been experimenting with the design of another "invention" on the principle of the odometer, to be used for surveying. After unsuccessful attempts to make it operable, he finally concluded that it was not practicable after all, and put it aside. Later he described the invention and its intended purpose to Clarke, as "a machine that could lay down the platt of a road by the traveling of a carriage over it." Clarke considered it a challenge and set to work.[8]

While engaged in these endeavors, Jefferson continued to puzzle over the origin of the North American Indians. Whether they had emigrated from another continent was a question that remained undecided, and which their traditions were was a problem too vague to resolve. He had long suspected that the solution might exist in their languages, a study of which also should show the connection between individual Indian nations.

As a young man, he had designed a vocabulary in which he had included words frequently used and names of commonplace objects that were to be found everywhere and consequently would have a name in every language. He produced a standard form for Indian languages which was then printed and distributed widely to anyone having contact with the aborigines and the willingness to complete the forms.
Included were 250 common words found in a number of Indian lan-

guages, and in an attempt to discover a relationship between them, he juxtaposed European equivalents to the Indian words.

Jefferson began collecting Indian vocabularies in about 1779 or 1780, according to his own statements, probably while compiling his notes about Virginia, and perhaps even earlier. "At a very early period of my life," he explained to Levett Harris, "contemplating the history of the aboriginal inhabitants of America, I was led to believe that if there had ever been a relation between them and the men of color of Asia, traces of it would be found in their several languages. I have therefore availed myself of every opportunity which was offered to obtain vocabularies of such tribes as have been within my reach . . . In this I made such progress that within a year or two more I think to give the public what I then have acquired."

For the compilation of his vocabularies, Jefferson had interviewed Indian traders and guides he met, and by means of correspondence consulted Indian agents such as Colonel Benjamin Hawkins and Dr. John Sibley. He also urged explorers going into Western lands to collect and record whatever they could about the languages.[9]

In his *Notes* he had proposed that the Indian languages be arranged "under the radical ones to which they may be palpably traced, and doing the same by those of the red men of Asia, there will be found probably twenty in America for one in Asia, of those radical languages, so called because, if they were ever the same, they have lost all resemblance to one another. A separation into dialects may be the work of a few ages only, but for two dialects to recede from one another till they have lost all vestiges of their common origin, must require an immense course of time; perhaps not less than many people give to the age of the earth. A greater number of these radical changes of language having taken place among the red men of America, proves them of greater antiquity than those of Asia."[10]

Similarities between Indian languages led Jefferson to conclude that the two peoples had once been in contact, but the similarities were not sufficient to identify the parent stock. From the radical differences between the languages, he theorized that the Indians had lived on the American continent long enough to have been the parent stock of Asia. His suggestion that the American Indians had a priority over Asia met with strong criticism from clergy and naturalists, including Joseph Dandridge, Clement C. Moore and Benjamin Smith Barton, among others.[11]

He was not completely convinced that the Asian population derived from America, however. He had discovered that more than half the Indian languages were as radically different as Greek and Latin, and of those that appeared to have the same basis, there was sufficient variance so that one tribe could not understand the language of another.[12]

He then suggested another solution. Having discovered that the

Indians were reluctant to use a language other than their own even when they were familar with another, and in view of their domestic feuds, he concluded that a tribal faction that had become alienated from the original tribe would be likely to form its own language.

He was never quite convinced of the inference, however, that Indians of one tribe were reluctant to use the language of another even when they were familiar with it, and that when a tribal faction fought or feuded with the main body of the tribe it formed its own language. He was aware that tribes, although having a language of their own, frequently adopted some language from other tribes. He emphasized the need to record the original language in each instance.[13]

Jefferson's long dedication to this effort was confirmed three years later, when he was about to send some fifty vocabularies he had collected to Dr. Benjamin Smith Barton. He was almost ready to proceed with their publication, but delayed because he had not yet converted the information from the vocabularies brought back by Lewis and Clark, which were to be added. He was constantly concerned over the possible loss of this work, and several times commented to Benjamin Hawkins that it was because he feared to risk the collection he had made, that he was anxious to have it printed before anything happened to it.[14]

He intended his work to be a supplement to the similar project being developed by Peter S. Pallas for "the red nations of Asia" under the patronage of the Empress of Russia. He had not seen the vocabularies collected by the Russians, but it occurred to him that a comparison of the vocabularies of the American Indians with those of Asiatic countries, would establish once and for all whether the American Indians originated in Asia, as was often conjectured.[15]

Jefferson particularly admired the ability of the Indians as artists and painters. "The Indians will crayon out an animal, plant," he wrote, "so as to prove the existence of a germ in their minds which only wants cultivation. The Indian often carves figures on their pipes not destitute of design or merit."

Jefferson's interest in the history of the American Indians led him also to collect artifacts of their culture, some of which later came to public notice. *The Monthly Magazine* in 1807 reported "Mr. Jefferson, President of the United States, possesses several busts made by Indians. The human form extends to the middle of the body, and the figures are nearly of the natural size. The lineaments are strongly marked, and such as are peculiar to the copper-coloured aboriginal inhabitants of America: among others, is one of them representing an aged savage, in which the wrinkles and look are very expressive. These busts were found by some labourers digging at a place called Palmyra, on the river Tennessee. It is not known of what materials they were made: some are of opinion, that they have been cut with a chissel, or sharp instrument, out of solid stone;

others think that they have been moulded or shaped of a soft composition, and afterwards baked. The substance is extremely hard. It has not been ascertained whether they are idols, or only images of distinguished men. It will be an interesting object of research for antiquaries, to discover who were the ancestors of the present Indians, capable of executing such a good resemblance of the human head, face, neck and shoulders."[16]

Among other Indian carvings owned by Jefferson was a clay figurine much resembling one described in a work by John Heywood. Another was the carved stone figure which he described as the "Image of Stone of a naked Woman kneeling." In addition to these, Jefferson's grandson, Thomas Jefferson Randolph, recalled seeing a carved stone Indian head mounted on a stand in the Entrance Hall at Monticello, which "had been sent to Mr. Jefferson from the West."[17]

The latter may have been one of two carved stone heads, which Jefferson believed to be of primitive Indian origin. Modern anthropologists have concluded, however, that they were produced not later than the American colonial period and were intended to represent an Indian and a Negro.

It is believed that after Jefferson's death the heads were purchased from the auction sale at Monticello in 1827 by a neighbor, Colonel John Stockton, who mounted them on gateposts. In 1861 they were discovered abandoned on the premises, and eventually found their way into museum collections.[18]

Late in 1804 the American printer, William Duane, had planned to publish a new edition of the *Notes*, but Jefferson was not ready to do so. He wished to make changes and revisions to the text before another printing. A substantial amount of time would be required, which was not then available to him. Particularly he wished to revise some of the statements in the 19th chapter, which were liable to be misconstrued.

For example, at the time that he wrote the original, he had been thinking about the larger European cities, to which the lack of food and other essentials of life had brought "a depravity of morals, a dependence and corruption, which renders them an undesirable accession to a country whose morals are sound." After publication of the *Notes*, these statements had been misquoted as referring to American cities at the present time. Instead, he said, "as yet our manufacturers are as much at their ease, as independent and moral as our agricultural inhabitants, and they will continue so as long as there are vacant lands for them to resort to; because whenever it shall be attempted by the other classes to reduce them to the minimum of subsistence, they will quit their trades and go laboring in the earth."

A question that remained unanswered in his mind was whether it was wise for the United States to receive the "dissolute and demoralized handicraftsman" who might emigrate from Europe, and if they should come, whether it would be preferable for them to establish themselves in their trades or have them turn to agriculture. A great many favorable changes had taken place in the United States since the *Notes* had been first published, and he wished he could find the time to make the necessary revisions discussing these questions. He hoped he would be able to do so for another edition after his retirement.[19]

In this period Jefferson was giving serious consideration to the best possible education of his grandson, Thomas Jefferson Randolph. He finally arranged with Peale to take him into his home and supervise his studies for a year. "I consider him as thereby placed in the best school of morality & good habits which could have been found for him, & secured against the only fears we entertained for him in your city." However, because his present tutor wished to continue with him for a year, the boy's visit had to be postponed for that period of time.

The following October Jefferson brought young "Jefferson", as Thomas Jefferson Randolph was called in the family circle, to Philadelphia to live and study with Peale, and carefully specified that he hoped the youth would "attend lectures in those branches of science which cannot be so advantageously taught anywhere else in America. These are Natural History, with the advantage of your Museum, botany aided by Mr. Hamilton's Garden, and Anatomy with the benefit of actual dissections."

He had also requested the cooperation of Wistar and Barton. He noted particularly that the youth "shall be solely occupied with his studies, that he should not be at all immersed in the society, & still less in the amusements & other abstractions of the place." He pointed out that young Jefferson was about fifteen years of age, still accustomed to being restrained, and was extremely good humored. As he advised Wistar, he did not approve of placing young men in cities, where they might acquire bad habits and inclinations.

He believed that in Philadelphia, however, there were opportunities for the study of science that were not available elsewhere in the country. "The gardens at the Woodlands for Botany," he wrote, "Mr. Peale's Museum for Natural History, your Medical School for Anatomy, and the able professors in all of them, give advantages not to be found elsewhere."[20]

He took the opportunity to express strong criticism of the profession of the physician as a healer in comparison with nature. He discussed the merits of nature in this capacity in preference to the "adventurous physician [who] goes on, and substitutes presumption for knowledge. From the scanty field of what is known, he launches into the boundless region of what is unknown. He establishes for his guide some fanciful theory of corpuscular attraction, of chemical agency, of mechanical powers, of stimuli, of irritability accumulated or exhausted, of depletion by the lancet and repletion by mercury, or some other ingenious dream, which lets him into all nature's secrets at short hand. On the principle which he thus assumes, he forms his table of nosology, arrays his diseases into families, and extends his curative treatment, by analogy, to all the cases he has thus arbitrarily marshalled together . . . I believe that we may safely affirm, that the inexperienced and presumptuous band of medical tyros let loose upon the world, destroys more of human life in one year, than all the Robinhoods, Cartouches, and Macheaths do in a century. It is in this part of medicine that I wish to see a reform, an abandonment of hypothesis for sober facts, the first degree of value set on clinical observation, and the lowest of visionary theories."[21] (*Document 10*)

The current state of medical science and the hazards of contemporary medical practice preoccupied Jefferson throughout his adult life. He demonstrated again and again his own vast knowledge of the subject, and the range of medical books in his library, which he read and used as reference, attests to his constant concern. His role in the national popularization of smallpox vaccination demonstrated his willingness to become personally involved.

There is a tradition that in an emergency Jefferson did not hesitate to engage in surgical practice as well. While visiting a neighbor on one occasion, it is told that he found a black boy suffering from a severe deep cut in the calf of his leg, which was bleeding profusely. Without any hesitation, Jefferson asked for a needle and some silk thread, skillfully sewed up the wound, and bandaged it. The account does not mention whether he first cleaned the wound and sterilized it as well as the suture material and his hands. Presumably he did not. In this period prior to modern knowledge of antiseptics, it is possible that the suture material and his hands were less liable to the presence of germs than the hands and instruments of a physician, which might have been contaminated with bacteria from treatment of previous patients. Furthermore, the soil was probably less liable to have contained septic bacteria in that period than would later be provided by developing civilization.[22]

Jefferson's ingenuity was not limited to the design of conveniences alone, but extended also to the design of his homes. Seeking to escape the great numbers of visitors who came to see him at Monticello, he resolved to build a new house for himself on a retreat he owned near Lynchburg, ninety miles away, at which he often spent weeks during the summer. Called "Poplar Forest," it consisted of a plantation of 4300 acres in the foothills of the Blue Ridge Mountains and had been part of the property inherited by his wife from her father. Probably the only previous dwelling on the property was a log cabin which he used as his summer hideaway, but over a period of time he had added tenant houses, barns for livestock and other outbuildings.

He began to prepare the design of an "octagon house" to fit the surroundings, and by 1806 he was ready to build. Turning resolution to action, he selected a high knoll surrounded by acreage on all sides and construction was begun. Years earlier, he had planned to build the first octagon-shaped house on the North American continent for his daughter Maria and her husband John Eppes at Pantops, another property he owned. Since they did not accept the property and instead settled temporarily at Mount Blanco in Chesterfield County, the house had not been built.

Although in the meantime Maria had died, and Eppes planned to remarry, Jefferson informed him that he was still willing to proceed with leveling Pantops for a house for the Eppes family, for he was anxious to have his young grandson, Francis Eppes, near him. Eppes did not accept this offer either, and therefore Jefferson proceeded with plans to build an octagon house for himself instead at Poplar Forest.[23]

Based upon an example he found in the work of Palladio, he determined that the house should be partially hidden, and appear to consist of a single story when viewed from the front, and two stories when observed from the rear. So confusing was Jefferson's plan to his mason, however, that it finally became necessary for him to lay the foundation himself.

The building was laid out with four irregular octagonal rooms pivoted around a large square central chamber. It was designed to achieve the most efficient use of light and air by means of a skylight in the center of the ceiling of the central room, with numerous windows on all four sides of the four octagonal rooms. The house was constructed like a fortress, with walls one and one-half feet in thickness.

Jefferson claimed that the octagon form provided one-fifth more interior space than did a square shape, and that it commanded twice as much sunlight. He equipped Poplar Forest with many of the same conveniences he had built into Monticello, including a dumbwaiter in a corner of the dining room. He may also have made a provision in the bedrooms for hoisting the beds to the ceiling during the day by means of pulleys.[24]

In 1810 the house was still unfinished, but it was nevertheless sufficiently complete for his periodic visits. "I have fixed myself comfortably," he informed Dr. Benjamin Rush, "keep some books here, bring others occasionally, am in the solitude of a hermit, and quite at leisure to attend absent friends." Thereafter he spent two or three weeks in his retreat every spring, another two weeks in either August or September, and he usually made a third visit in December.

Construction of the house proceeded with greater rapidity after 1812, and in time it was completely habitable, although work on the premises continued for years to come. Again he attempted to interest John Eppes in this property but without success. Finally, in April 1823, he had settled young Francis Eppes and his new bride at Poplar Forest and bequeathed it to them after his death.[25]

As with many other endeavors, in his architectural and other design enterprises, Jefferson was governed by "the eternal fitness of things." He provided the same amount of thought and consideration to the design and construction of his own office and that of the overseer as he had given to the mansion, so that although the offices's purpose was not disguised, they achieved at the same time appropriate dignity and harmonized with their surroundings.[26]

Intending to make a short visit to Monticello in March, he had to postpone his plans, first because of the illness of Thomas Mann Randolph, Jr. and then because of the onset once again of his headaches. They had become so acute that he was capable of conducting business during only one and one-half hours each morning.[27]

Despite his eager interest in scientific endeavors and his encouragement of others in these pursuits, Jefferson was nonetheless governed primarily by practical considerations. When the French naturalist, G. C. Delacoste, was contemplating the establishment of a museum of natural history in Williamsburg to be built by private contributions, Jefferson was supportive of the concept but less than enthusiastic about its prospects.

"Nobody could wish more ardently than myself," he responded to Delacoste's request for support, "to concur in whatever may promote useful science, and I view no science with more partiality than natural history. But I have ever believed that in this, as in most other cases, abortive attempts retard rather than promote this object."

He pointed out that such well-populated and wealthy cities as Boston and New York had been unable to maintain a museum, and that only in Philadelphia had a museum operation been successful. This was was due largely to the fact that the city had a wealthy, overcrowded population with a more than usual interest in the pursuit of knowledge.

Even so, the museum in Philadelphia was not entirely supported by the public, and Peale, the proprietor, frequently had to resort to his other occupation as a painter to support it. Jefferson was aware that in Williamsburg and vicinity as well there were many "who have already attained a high degree of science, and many zealously pursuing it." Even so he did not consider their number to be sufficient for the success of a museum project.[28]

It gave Jefferson particular pleasure to learn that he had been elected to membership in the Linnaean Society of Philadelphia although, as with membership in other societies, he felt frustrated that he did not have the time to contribute to their endeavors. "Sincerely associated with the friends of science," he wrote to Dr. Barton, "in spirit and inclination, I regret the constant occupations of a different kind, which put out of my power the proper co-operations with them, had I otherwise the talents for them."[29]

Jefferson's design of a mouldboard had been presented to the Société d'Agriculture de Paris by Pierre Samuel Du Pont de Nemours. For this achievement, the society presented Jefferson with a gold medal and a citation, which read, "The Society has observed with great interest that Your Excellency impelled by the desire to encourage the Agriculture in the States whose administration is entrusted to you, has not considered the improvement of the foremost tool of the laborer outside your vast schemes. It believed there should be a public expression of its appreciation of the useful work that you have done on the subject."[30]

The Société also presented him with the first four volumes of its published memoirs, and appointed him a foreign correspondent. The President acknowledged the honor with his characteristic graciousness. "Drawn to agriculture by inclination as well as by the feeling that it forms the most useful occupation of man, the circumstances of my life have not let me join my practical knowledge with my theory." Although he was not in a position to be useful to the society, he added, nonetheless he would report any contribution made to agriculture in the United States and would serve as the means of communication with its members.[31]

When Jefferson learned that the Société was sending him a plough, in accordance with his custom he decided to send a gift in return. He selected the drill developed by T. C. Martin, which he considered to be the finest yet produced. He informed John Taylor that the society was sending him "a plough supposed to be of the best construction ever known. On trial with their best ploughs, by a dynamometer, it is drawn by from one-half to two-thirds of the force requisite to their best former ploughs." As a note of interest, he added that the French were cultivating Jerusalem artichoke for feeding their animals, obtaining 10,000 pounds per acre, which was said to be three times the amount they generally obtained of the potato.[32]

Inspired by the reception with which his mouldboard had been received at home and abroad, Jefferson sought to develop it to a practical level so that it could be properly compared with the French plough he was to receive. He now required a dynamometer for testing it, and wrote to Monroe in England to "procure for me 'a machine for ascertaining the resistance of ploughs or carriages, invented and sold by Winlaw, in Margaret street, Cavendish Square.'" He estimated the cost to be between four and five guineas.[33]

His efforts to purchase or borrow a dynamometer were unsuccessful, however, until eventually David Warden managed to procure one in France and sent it back to Jefferson by General Armstrong together with the plough that had been sent to him by the Société. He would now have to wait to make his tests, nevertheless, until he was at Monticello once more.[34]

One of the inventors about whose activities Jefferson kept himself informed was Robert Fulton. He read with great interest pamphlets he received from Fulton describing the latter's invention of torpedoes. He was particularly interested in the development of the weapon and considered it to be a most valuable means of protecting harbors and urged that it should be adopted. He did not believe that the torpedo should be the sole means of defense, however, for "neither a nation nor those entrusted with its affairs, could be justifiable, however sanguine its expectations, in trusting solely to an engine not yet sufficiently tried, under all the circumstances which may occur, and against which we know not as yet what means of parrying may be used." If the torpedoes were to be transported by merely attaching them to a ship's cable, it would not be difficult to prevent their use.

Jefferson was enthusiastic also about the submarine as the means of attaching the torpedo, and because he saw no mention of it in Fulton's publications and proposal, he hoped that the submarine had not been abandoned as an impractical venture. He visualized their use with the establishment of a corps of naval engineers consisting of young men trained for the submarine service.

"I am not afraid of new inventions or improvements," Jefferson commented, "nor bigoted to the practices of our forefathers. It is that bigotry which keeps the Indians in a state of barbarism in the midst of the arts, would have kept us in the same state, even now, and still keeps Connecticut where their ancestors were when they landed on these shores. I am much pleased that Congress is taking up the business. Where a new invention is supported by well-known principles, and promises to be useful, it ought to be tried." He believed that torpedoes would be to cities what smallpox vaccination had been to mankind in general in protecting them against their gravest dangers.

He also acknowledged Fulton's attention to his query concerning the *bélier hydraulique* (hydraulic ram), and planned to have his workmen make a model of it from the drawing that Fulton had provided.[35]

Although he was frequently even too eager and enthusiastic in his support of new scientific ideas, Jefferson on other occasions proved to be inclined to be excessively skeptical and conservative. One such example related to the showers of "falling stones" (meteorites) in Weston, Connecticut, that were reported to have occurred in December 1807. Later, after reconsideration, he suggested that it might be more practical to have knowledgeable men of science investigate the matter, instead of Congressmen, to whom some of the fallen stones had been sent.

As he expressed himself to Daniel Salmon, who had obtained one of the meteorites and had written to him about it, "It's [the stone's] descent from the atmosphere presents so much difficulty as to require careful examination. But I do not know that the most effectual examination could be made by members of the National Legislature to whom you have thought of exhibiting it. Some fragments of these stones have already been handed about among them. But those most highly qualified for acting in *their* stations are not necessarily supposed most familiar with subjects of natural history; and such of them as have that familiarity are not in situations here to make the investigation. I should think that an inquiry by some one of our scientific societies, such as the Philosophical Society of Philadelphia for example, would be most likely to be directed with such caution and knowledge of the subject, as would inspire general confidence. We certainly are not to deny whatever we cannot account for. A thousand phenomena present themselves daily which we cannot explain, but where facts are suggested, bearing no analogy with the laws of nature as yet known to us, their verity needs proof proportioned to their difficulty. A cautious mind will weigh well the opposition of the phenomenon to everything hitherto observed, the strength of the testimony by which it is supported, and the errors and misconceptions to which even our senses are liable. It may be very difficult to explain how the stone you possess came into the position in which it was found. But is it easier to explain how it got into the clouds from whence it is supposed to have fallen? The actual fact however is the thing to be established, and that I hope will be done by those whose situations and qualifications enable them to do it."[36]

The phenomenon was observed in adjacent communities, including the town of Ridgefield, Connecticut, several miles distant from the site of the celestial shower. There the event was seen and later reported by the writer Samuel G. Goodrich, then a boy of fourteen, who became the author and sponsor of many instructive volumes for young people on popular history and science under the pen name of Peter Parley. He wrote:

> On the morning of the 14th of December, about daybreak, I had risen and was occupied in building a fire, this being my daily duty. Suddenly the room was filled with light, and looking up, I saw through the windows a ball of fire, nearly the size of the moon, passing across the heavens from

northwest to southeast. It was at an immense height, and of intense brilliancy. Having passed the zenith, it swiftly descended toward the earth: while still at a great elevation it burst, with three successive explosions, into fiery fragments. The report was like three claps of rattling thunder in quick succession.

My father, who saw the light and heard the sounds, declared it to be a meteor of extraordinary magnitude. It was noticed all over the town, and caused great excitement. On the following day the news came that huge fragments of stone had fallen in the adjacent town of Weston, some eight or ten miles southeast of Ridgefield. The story spread far and wide, and some of the professors of Yale College came to the place, and examined the fragments of this strange visitor from the skies. It appeared that the people in the neighborhood heard the rushing of the stones through the air, as well as the shock when they struck the earth. One, weighing two hundred pounds, fell on a rock, which it splintered—its huge fragments plowing up the ground around to the extent of a hundred feet. One piece, weighing twenty-five pounds, was taken to New Haven, where it is still to be seen, in the mineralogical cabinet of the college. The professors estimated this meteor to be half a mile in diameter, and to have traveled through the heavens at the rate of two or three hundred miles a minute.

One local theory, Goodrich related, was that "these phenomena are animals revolving in the orbits of space between the heavenly bodies. Occasionally, one of them comes too near the earth, rushing through our atmosphere with immense velocity, takes fire and explodes!" Goodrich's father, the town's Congregationalist minister, ventured the opinion that these meteorites consisted chiefly of silex, iron and nickel.[37]

Two professors of Yale College, Benjamin Silliman and James Kingsley, visited the site and examined the places where the fragments had fallen, questioned the witnesses and returned to Yale with a considerable number of specimens of the meteor. They published a full account of the phenomena in the (New Haven) Connecticut Herald, and after Silliman had an opportunity to make a chemical analysis of the fragments, he enlarged and revised their original account and sent it to the American Philosophical Society.

The paper was read also before the Royal Society of London and communicated to the Académie Royale des Sciences in Paris. It was also studied by Nathaniel Bowditch of Salem and Professor Jeremiah Day of Yale, and it was concluded that the falling stones had not come from the moon nor from the earth's volcanoes, but that they were of celestial origin, from "distant regions of space." The Silliman-Kingsley report created more interest and comment than any other scientific paper in the United States in that period.

The chemical analysis of the stones, published as a separate part of the memoir, is of considerable historical interest because it is the earliest example of that form of research of record. There were then few books on analytical chemistry, and few laboratories capable of undertaking such an analysis.[38]

Jefferson's interest in meteorites had first been aroused by a report from William Dunbar he had received in June 1800 as president of the American Philosophical Society of "a singular Phenomenon seen at Baton Rouge" on April 5, 1800. Dunbar stated that it appeared to be of "the size of a large house," and had been observed about two hundred yards above the ground.[39]

He was also aware of a communication to the Society received from John Chipchase through Leonard Snowden of October 8, 1804 reporting the meteors observed on the night of November 12, 1799 in England and France.[40]

He discussed the subject with Andrew Ellicott, who had brought to his attention a publication on meteorites published by the Institut de France. Jefferson had not seen the publication, but he had read Iram's *Léthologie Atmosphérique*, a collection of previously known facts on the subject which probably also contained the Institut's publications.

"I do not say that I disbelieve the testimony," he explained, "but neither can I say I believe it. Chemistry is too much in its infancy to satisfy us that the lapidific elements exist in the atmosphere and that the process can be compleated there. I do not know that this would be against the laws of nature, & therefore I do not say that it is impossible but as it is so much unlike any operation of nature we have ever seen, it requires testimony proportionately strong. The formation of hail in the atmosphere is entirely unaccountable, yet we have the evidence of our own senses to the fact and therefore we must believe it. A most respectable sensible and truth speaking friend of mine gave me a circumstantial account of a rain of fish to which he was an eye witness. I knew him to be incapable of speaking an untruth. How he could be deceived in such a fact was as difficult for me to account for, as how the fact should happen. I therefore prevailed on my own mind to sojourn the decision of the question till new rains of fish should take place to confirm it."[41]

The subject is of particular interest because of an oft-quoted comment on the subject which was erroneously attributed to Jefferson. Concerning the report by Silliman and Kingsley he is claimed to have stated "It is easier to believe that two professors could lie than admit that stones could fall from heaven." Investigation has revealed that the statement is a fabrication which first appeared in a work by Silliman's son published in 1874 and repeated in later biographies of Silliman.[42]

Once again as his term ended in late 1808 Jefferson attempted to resign the presidency of the American Philosophical Society, particularly since he was about to retire from public life. He informed the Society's vice presidents, "Being to remove within a few months from my present residence to one still more distant from the seat of the meetings of the American Philosophical Society, I feel it a duty no longer to obstruct it's services by keeping from it's chair members whose position, as well as qualifications, may enable them to discharge it's duties with so much more effect, begging leave therefore to withdraw from the Presidency of the Society, at the close of the present term, I avail myself of the occasion gratefully to return my thanks to the Socy. for the repeated proofs they have been pleased to give of their favor, and confidence in me, and to assure them, in retiring from the honourable station in which they have been pleased so long to continue me, I carry with me all the sentiments of an affectionate member, & faithful servant of the Society." Jefferson's wishes were ignored as usual and he was duly re-elected president of the Society early in 1809.[43]

In addition to fossil bones and other natural history artifacts, Jefferson occasionally provided the Society with examples of American and European inventions that intrigued him and that he considered might prove useful to American enterprise. Among these was a Dutch navigational sounding device called a "bathometer." It was the invention of a Delft physician and chemist named A. van Stiprian Luiscius, who published a description of it in 1805. In the same year, it was patented and manufactured by J. H. Onderdewyngaart of the same city, a maker of instruments of physics and mathematics.

The instrument consisted of two components: a fore-sound (*avant-sonde*) combining a float and a weight that separated upon contact with the ocean floor; and a bathometer, made in the same manner but having an odometer attached to the float. The visible elements were the sighting staff and flag, the float, odometer, weight and trigger rod, which extended through the weight and terminated in a pike caught within the weight between two spring hooks. Upon touching bottom, the trigger immediately extended a peg that arrested the motion of the odometer's four vanes, which had been moving by their descent through the water.

The bathometer was a mechanized refinement of the experimental forms of the sounding device, such as Robert Hooke had presented to the Royal Society on several occasions a century and a half earlier. By the middle of the 19th century, English inventors, particularly Edward Massey and Thomas Walker, had developed the sounding device into a practical form which came into general use.[44]

When Joel Barlow, the American poet and diplomat, returned to the United States after having spent a number of years on diplomatic missions in Europe, he proposed the establishment of a national institution of learning. In a manuscript prospectus which he submitted to Jefferson, Barlow described its mission to be research and instruction in the arts and sciences. After the President explained that the government could not pay for publication and distribution of the prospectus, he went on to comment on its content.

Particularly he questioned the validity of a veterinary facility which Barlow suggested as part of his institution. Although such had existed in Europe, he knew of no benefit derived from them, and in view of the number of other facilities of which the people were still in need, he doubted that one for veterinary purposes should be given a priority. The concept of a "National Institution" was not a new one, but it did not come to fruition until 1840.[45]

Among the most important scientific enterprises undertaken by the Federal government during Jefferson's Presidency was the establishment of the United States Coast Survey. Robert Patterson was probably the one who first suggested it to Jefferson, who in turn recommended it to Congress in 1806. The proposal was favorably received, and an act approved on February 10, 1807 authorized the President to have a survey made of the coasts of the United States.

The act was also to designate "the islands and shoals with the roads or places of anchorage within twenty leagues of any part of the shores of the United States; and also the respective courses and distances between the principal capes or headlands, together with such other matters as he may deem proper for completing an accurate chart of every part of the coasts." The act further authorized a survey of St. Georges Bank and other banks and shoals, as well as the soundings and currents beyond the limits already noted to the Gulf Stream.[46]

Jefferson delegated the development of the survey to Albert Gallatin, his trusted Secretary of the Treasury, who issued a descriptive circular to scientists and others inviting plans for effecting it. The project was visualized in three parts: ascertainment of the true positions of several coastal points of note to be achieved by a series of astronomical observations; a trigonometrical survey of the coastline between these points; and a nautical survey of shoals and soundings along the coast to be based upon the trigonometrical survey.

Of the plans submitted, the one proposed by Ferdinand Rudolph Hassler was selected. A Swiss-born engineer and professor of mathematics at the United States Military Academy, he had considerable experience and was appointed the first Superintendent of the U. S. Coast Survey.

The new agency had a chequered career from its very beginning, however. The required scientific instruments, many of which had to be specially designed and made for the purpose, were not available and had to be ordered from English instrument makers. It was not until 1811 that

Hassler was finally authorized to travel to Europe to purchase them. There he was detained by the War of 1812 and it was 1815 before he returned. Work with the survey was begun the following year, in the bay and harbor of New York City, but it was interrupted soon thereafter due to the failure of Congress to provide funding. The Coast Survey was not revived and reconstituted until 1832.[47]

* * *

Throughout his public career, from the days that he served as Governor of Virginia to the conclusion of his two terms in the Presidency, Jefferson was the particular target in the press of not only political opponents, but also of religious leaders and writers. He was attacked on a multitude of fronts for his political actions, for his religious beliefs, for his domestic life and particularly for his scientific interests and endeavors. To none of these did he ever reply. One of the most memorable attacks occurred as a consequence of protests from the New England states to the embargo placed on trade with England. This brought wounded outcries particularly from the northeast, for it had serious effects on the textile industry in Massachusetts and other New England states. Inevitably, Jefferson was singled out as the perpetrator. The words of a song which became popular with the Federalists of that region including the stanza:

> Our ships, all in motion,
> Once whitened the ocean,
> They sailed and returned with a cargo;
> Now doom'd to decay,
> They have fallen a prey
> To Jefferson, worms, and *Embargo*.[48]

During the same summer a satirical poem was published as a small pamphlet in Boston, a work which was to remain a permanent part of American literature. Entitled *The Embargo*, the poem was the work of a precocious boy of thirteen named William Cullen Bryant. Born in Cummington, Massachusetts, he was the son of a physician, a strong Federalist serving as a representative to the General Court of Massachusetts. Later the boy was to achieve fame as one of America's notable poets.

Becoming interested in politics because of his father's political activities despite his tender age, young William read in the press about the disastrous effects of the Embargo of 1807 on New England's foreign commerce. He wrote some lines about the President which his father admired, and encouraged him to develop the poem. The following year Dr. Bryant arranged to have it privately printed in Boston.

It received favorable notices, and the public uproar attending the passing by Congress of the 9th Embargo Act in 1809 led Dr. Bryant to induce his son to revise and enlarge the poem. He hired a printer, copyrighted the work and issued the revised poem as a pamphlet of 36 pages. The work is historically important for presenting in a succinct form the political point of view and reflecting the emotional reaction of the people to a national crisis.

Bryant represented President Jefferson as weak and erring as a ruler, and as subservient to Napoleon. He recalled the statesman's "flight" before Tarleton's raiders during the Revolution and included a sly reference to the claimed amorous association with the slave servant, Sally Hemings. Certainly this was heavy fare even for a precocious youngster, and much of the commentary in the poem unquestionably was furnished to the boy by others, probably by his father. Particularly, Jefferson was attacked for his scientific preoccupations. The stanza which was most memorable and damaging, and which has been often quoted, was

> Go, wretch, resign the presidential chair,
> Disclose thy secret measures foul or fair,
> Go, search, with curious eye, for horned frogs,
> Mongst the wild wastes of Louisiana bogs;
> Or where Ohio rolls his turbid stream,
> Dig for huge bones, thy glory and thy theme;
> Go scan, Philosophist, thy ****** charms,
> And sink supinely in her sable arms;
> But quit to abler hands the helm of state,
> Nor image ruin on thy country's fate.[49]

It is not known whether Jefferson ever saw the poem, but he was well familiar with the tenor of popular opinion in New England. Although he received abusive letters of complaint about the Embargo from time to time, based upon the opinions of friends, associates and others supporting his action, he nonetheless felt assured that it was generally approved by the public at large.

The press continued to find cause to criticize Jefferson to the very end of his administration. Early in 1809 Jefferson gave permission to two individuals in Delaware and New York to import the Merino breed of sheep obtained in Spain through France, and to several individuals in Boston to import a spinning machine for cotton, wool and flax. He ordered two tierces of cotton seed from Georgia to be sent via Baltimore and New York to the Société d'Agriculture de Paris, which had been requested for experimental purposes. His political opponents promptly informed the press of these violations of the embargo, and much was made of it.

To John Hollins, Jefferson recounted the facts and provided instances of other imports of seed sent for experimental agricultural exchange, as examples of the correspondence between scientific societies throughout the world. He wrote, "These [scientific] societies are always in peace, however their nations may be at war. Like the republic of letters, they form a great fraternity spreading over the whole earth, and their correspondence is never interrupted by any civilized nation."[50]

The Merino breed of sheep of Spain was already famous in Europe by the beginning of the nineteenth century, noted for their good health and the fine quality of their fleece. It was superior for the manufacture of woolen clothing when American farmers first became interested in acquiring and breeding the sheep. However, the Spanish maintained the strictest regulations over the breed and prohibited exportation on threat of the severest penalties.

Chancellor Robert R. Livingston of New York was interested in improving American wool production and is believed to have been the first American to succeed in importing the first pair of Merinos to the United States, in 1802 while minister to France during Jefferson's Presidency. They were not full-blooded specimens, however, or even Merinos of mixed blood. With the cooperation of David Humphreys, he was responsible for interesting American agricultural societies in the breed, and his recently published volume, Essays on Sheep: Their Varieties—Account of the Merinos of Spain, France, etc., made Americans aware of the importance of the breed.[51]

It was not until after Napoleon had invaded Spain that the breed became generally available. David Humphreys was among the first to import them, and an article which he published helped to popularize the breed in the United States. Another early importer was E. I. Du Pont de Nemours of Delaware, who succeeded in bringing a full-blooded ram with him from France for the banker Alexandre Delessert. Immediately other Americans followed suit in attempting to acquire Merino sheep. Among them was Samuel G. Wright in New Jersey.[52]

Jefferson owned a copy of Livingston's work, and also became interested, for he had been raising common sheep at Monticello for a long time when the first Merinos were imported. He raised sheep to provide food for the plantation as well as to furnish wool for the production of coarse woolens. During his second term in the Presidency he kept a whole flock of sheep on the premises of the President's House. A few weeks before he left Washington, he received a letter from William Keough informing him that the year previously while "Passing through the President's Square he was attacked and severely wounded and bruised by your excellency's ram, of which he lay ill for five or six weeks under the hands of Doctor Elsey."[53]

Although he was aware of the restrictions imposed by the Spanish government, Jefferson did what he could to assist importation of the breed. From his retirement at Monticello, he contacted the American minister to Madrid, George W. Erving, informing him that an American

ship would be calling at various Spanish ports with the intention of obtaining some Merino sheep. He cautioned that he was not asking Erving
to perform any act that would compromise him or the United States with
the Spanish government, but if he could do anything to assist in acquiring the sheep, it would be much appreciated.

Erving turned the matter over to the American consul, who succeeded in shipping twelve sheep on the vessel *Olana* to James H. Moore,
a merchant in Alexandria, Virginia. Moore was to distribute them, one
pair to go to Jefferson, another to President Madison, and the remainder
to be sold. These instructions were carried out in May 1810, and the
sheep were delivered.

While in France and England, Jefferson had made an effort to inform himself on means for improving farm livestock, particularly sheep
and cattle, and observed that it was achieved by effective inbreeding and
outcrossing to produce pedigreed herds and flocks. The supply of seed
stock derived from this program commanded high prices from farmers in
France and England, and eventually also in the United States and other
countries.

Sensing the importance of this development, after his retirement
Jefferson proposed a plan for distributing Merino sheep based on a system
of priorities which he devised. To propagate the breed throughout the
state, a program that might require as much as seven years, Jefferson
proposed that a ram be distributed to each of the counties of Virginia
without cost. He anticipated that each ram would be able to service fifty
ewes, and that the resulting rams could be sold to propagate the breed
in the country.[54]

The sheep were delivered to Jefferson and Madison, but after all the
fanfare attending the breed, Edmund Bacon, Jefferson's overseer, was
disappointed in their small size. Bacon advertised in the newspaper that
anyone wishing to improve his stock could send two ewes to Monticello,
and the owners would be given the choice of the lambs to be born, but
that the others and the two ewes were to remain at Monticello.

The excellent wool produced by Merino sheep proved to be too
fine for the manufacture of the coarse woolens produced at Monticello,
however, and as a consequence Jefferson and his neighbors lost interest
in the breed.[55]

It was not until after the end of the War of 1812 that the importation of Merino sheep became more frequent, but within the following
decade there proved to be little profit in raising them, for the breed
became so numerous in the region that the price dropped considerably.
The improvement of wool for manufacturing was considerable, and the
Merino multiplied so rapidly that every family of any size eventually prof-
ited from them.[56]

In connection with sheep culture, Jefferson had another require-ment. From Du Pont de Nemours he requested that if and when he re-turned to the United States, he would like to have him bring "a couple of pair of true-bred shepherd dogs. You will add a valuable possession to a country now beginning to pay great attention to the raising sheep."[57]

After importing "the genuine race of shepherd dogs from France" which had been selected for him by Lafayette, he attempted to propagate the breed by presenting pairs of them to those who requested them. He also kept pairs on his several farms, where he maintained no other dogs. The shepherd dogs became so popular and he received so many requests for them, however, that he rarely had any readily available.[58]

"Their extraordinary sagacity," he explained, "renders them ex-tremely valuable, capable of being taught almost any duty that may be required of them, and the most anxious in the performance of that duty, the most watchful and faithful of all servants." He warned all to whom he gave the dogs that they must be kept reasonably well fed, and if ne-glected and permitted freedom to prowl, they would become destructive, and would kill sheep and other dogs. However, they were the most watchful of watchdogs, could be taught to bring home cows and sheep in the evening, to drive fowl into their henhouses or yards and to keep other animals away from the premises.[59]

One of the purposes Jefferson had for so assiduously recording infor-mation about the weather was to correlate the data with periodic phe-nomena, such as the breeding and migration of birds and the appearance, flowering and fruiting of plants. He attempted to determine whether the large scale cutting down of forests brought about changes in climate, and he investigated the cause and effect of the flood of 1771 and the great snow of the following year, both of which had caused damage to his farm. These, the earthquake which shook Virginia two years later and the killing frost of 1779 all were manifestations of his lifelong preoccupa-tion with weather, its causes and how it affected man.

In his opinion, the healthiest and best climate was that of Albe-marle County, and he pointed out that a large number of its people lived into their nineties despite the occurrences of agues and fevers. The county was not as subject to extremes of cold and heat as were other areas. He particularly disliked the cold, as he wrote many years later, "I shudder at the approach of winter, and wish I could sleep through it with the dormouse, and only wake with him in the spring, if ever."[60]

As Jefferson's second term was coming to an end, one of his greatest disappointments was to see an end also to the possibility of achieving commercial rights through peaceful means. He managed to enact a Non-

Intercourse Act to become effective with the end of the embargo. The embargo had brought no concessions from England, while at the same time it had turned New England into a Federalist camp.

Looking forward to his return to Monticello, Jefferson informed Charles Thomson, "I am full of plans of employment when I get there,— they chiefly respect the active functions of the body. To the mind I shall administer amusement chiefly. An only daughter and numerous family of grandchildren, will furnish my great resources of happiness."[61]

In anticipation of indulging his scientific interests without interruption after leaving Washington permanently, Jefferson ordered from W. & S. Jones a Borda reflecting circle, which was then one of the more sophisticated astronomical instruments available. He felt he no longer had need of the sextant he had sent to Dr. James Small to have repaired or exchanged for him, and offered it to Small as a gift.[62]

To Humboldt, with whom he kept in correspondence, Jefferson noted, "You have wisely located yourself on the focus of the science of Europe. I am held by the cords of love to my family and country, or I should certainly join you. Within a few days I shall now bury myself in the groves of Monticello, and become a mere spectator of the passing events. On politics I will say nothing."[63]

As the conclusion of his term of office drew nearer and nearer, Jefferson calculated his income and expenses and came to the startling realization that he was already in serious financial trouble. He had to borrow $11,000 to pay just the debts he had incurred while in office. He estimated his net worth to be $225,000, which included 10,000 acres of land, a manufacturing mill, and 200 slaves, half of which were children. Two-thirds of them were house servants and/or artisans, and one-third worked in the fields.

He had owed money since before the Revolution to British firms as well as to a Dutch firm for a loan of $2,000 made in 1790. He paid these old debts by borrowing new loans, but with the increasing rates of interest he kept falling behind more and more. He immediately contacted his cousin, the Richmond merchant George Jefferson.

Jefferson asked him to use his influence with the bank on his behalf, with the greatest prudence. He added, "since I have become sensible of this deficit I have been under an agony of mortification, & therefore must sollicit as much urgency in the negociation as the case will admit. My intervening nights will be almost sleepless, as nothing could be more distressing to me than to leave debts here unpaid, if indeed I should be permitted to depart with them unpaid, of which I am by no means certain."[64]

Despite the crisis in his financial situation, Jefferson anticipated the approaching end of his second term in the Presidency with considerable relief. Two days before he left office, he wrote to his friend, Du Pont de

Nemours, "Within a few days I retire to my family, my books and farms; and having gained the harbour myself, I shall look on my friends still buffeting the storm with anxiety indeed, but not with envy. Never did a prisoner, released from his chains, feel such relief as I shall on shaking off the shackles of power. Nature intended me for the tranquil pursuits of science, by rendering them my supreme delight. But the enormities of the times in which I have lived, have forced me to take part in resisting them, and to commit myself on the boisterous ocean of political passions. I thank God for the opportunity of retiring from them without censure, and carrying with me the most consoling proofs of public approbation."[65]

Congressman William Plumer, who had been so critical of Jefferson during his administration, was led to modify his views somewhat when he learned that Jefferson did not plan to run for a third term.

The more critically and impartially I examine the character & conduct of Mr. Jefferson the more favorably I think of his integrity . . . I am really inclined to think I have done him injustice in not allowing him more credit for the integrity of heart that he possesses . . . He is a man of science. But he is very credulous—he knows little of the nature of a man—very little indeed. He has travelled the tour of Europe—he has been minister at Versailles. He has had great opportunities to know man—but he has neglected them. He is not a practical man. He has much knowledge of books—of insects—of shells—and of all that charms a virtuoso—but he knows not the human heart. He is a closet politician—but not a practical statesman. He has much *fine sense* but little of the *plain common sense* so requisite to business—& which in fact governs the world . . . An infidel in religion but in every thing else credulous to a fault! Alas man is himself a contradiction! I do not however seem to insinuate that Mr. Jefferson is a model of goodness. He has too much cunning. Still I repeat the errors of his administration proceed more often from the head than from the heart. They partake more of credulity than of wickedness . . . Mr. Jefferson is too timid—too irresolute—too fickle—he wants nerve—he wants a firmness & resolution. A wavering doubtful hesitating mind joined with credulity is oftentimes as injurious to the nation as a wicked depraved heart.[66]

Jefferson insisted on transferring his authority in the same manner in which he had received it, with the least ceremony. He remained in Washington just long enough to participate in the inaugural ceremonies for his friend and successor, James Madison. "Never will it be forgotten," stated the *National Intelligencer* on March 3rd, "as long as liberty is dear to man that it was on this day that Thomas Jefferson retired from the supreme magistracy amidst the blessings and regrets of millions."[67]

Refusing a military escort of cavalry, and accompanied only by his seventeen-year old grandson, Thomas Jefferson Randolph, Jefferson mounted his horse and they rode up Pennsylvania Avenue together from the President's House to the Capitol. There they dismounted, hitched their horses to the palings, and Jefferson entered the Capitol to witness the ceremony.

The House of Representatives was crowded as Madison made a short address in a low voice scarcely to be heard. The oath of office was administered by the Chief Justice, and after reviewing the military forces outside the Capitol, the new President proceeded to his home. There a reception was held, which Jefferson attended. People came in such great numbers that many had to wait a half hour before they could enter.

Jefferson also attended the Presidental Ball held at Long's Hotel on Capitol Hill. Admission was by ticket only, but such a great crowd filled the hall that ladies stood on benches to see the distinguished guests. The heat was so overpowering that windows were smashed to provide ventilation. The ball opened at seven o'clock, with the band playing "Jefferson's March" as the retiring President entered with a Mr. Coles. He inquired whether he was too early, and asked for advice on how to behave, inasmuch as it had been forty years since he had attended a ball. A few moments later, the band struck into "Madison's March" as the Presidential party arrived. Although the ball continued until midnight, Jefferson remained for only two hours, and "seemed in high spirits and his countenance beamed with a benevolent joy."

Jefferson was not yet ready to vacate the executive mansion, and Madison advised him to stay until he had completed his packing. He remained for one more week, then he loaded his belongings into three wagons, one of which contained his plants and another his papers.[68]

When finally he was ready to leave the city, Jefferson received visits from many of its citizens, all who came to wish him well. There were many public addresses in his honor arranged by the citizens of Georgetown and the Tammany Society of Washington, among others. He said his farewells, one of the most touching of which was to his good friend Margaret Bayard Smith.

He sent her a geranium she had agreed to accept, enclosing a note. He explained that it was in extremely poor condition, since it was not among the items he had planned to take with him, and consequently it had not been well maintained. He gave it its parting blessing by placing it in Mrs. Smith's hands, for "if plants have sensibility, as the analogy of their organization with ours seems to indicate, it cannot but be proudly sensible of her fostering attentions." Among his greatest regrets in leaving Washington was the parting from the Smiths, and they promised to visit him at Monticello.[69]

Shortly before he was about to leave Washington for the last time, Jefferson was informed that many in Albemarle County were planning to meet him on the road as a manifestation of their good will. Jefferson avoided demonstrations when possible, and as he informed Randolph, he was not certain when he could begin his journey because of details relating to the transfer of office, but expressed appreciation for the thought.

"Certainly it is the greatest consolation to me," he wrote, "to know that in returning to the bosom of my native country, I shall be again in the midst of their kind affections; and I can say with truth that my return to them will make me happier than I have been since I left them."[70]

CHAPTER XVI

THE TWILIGHT YEARS (1809–1815)

I have withdrawn from all political intermeddlings, to indulge the evening of my life with what have been the passions of every portion of it, books, science, my farms, my family and friends.

Letter from Thomas Jefferson
to James Maury, Jr., 1812

Exactly one week after the inauguration of James Madison as President of the United States had taken place, Jefferson left Washington for the last time, to settle permanently at Monticello. He was excited by the prospect that now, when he was almost sixty-six years of age, he would have all the time in the world to indulge his fancies, after having devoted such a great part of his life to public service.

At Monticello, he found himself surrounded by the children of his daughter Martha and Thomas Mann Randolph, Jr., and it was they who provided the greatest measure of comfort offsetting embarrassing debt and poor health that were to be his lot during the ensuing years.

From time to time the Randolph girls were permitted to attend social events in Charlottesville, including the annual Washington Ball. Charlottesville society may have considered the girls from Monticello to be aloof because they occasionally refused invitations to local events, and were seen too infrequently at the Sunday Episcopal services held by Mr. Hatch in the unheated Courthouse. To break the monotony of the winter months, the girls were often allowed to go on visits to cousins at Ashton or Tufton.[1]

At Monticello they did not lack companionship, for other young guests came there occasionally. Nicholas Philip and Browse Trist, sons of old friends, visited Monticello on their way north from Louisiana and remained for a prolonged stay. Nicholas left first, to enter the U. S. Military Academy, while Browse stayed on until he enrolled in a school in Charlottesville. The latter then returned every weekend, bringing five or six of his school companions to dance with the Randolph girls in the South Pavilion to the music of a black fiddler.[2]

Despite the frequent presence of young friends, the grandchildren occasionally complained about the remoteness of Monticello from other young people of their own age. Although this was true to a degree, they were not in fact isolated, as countless visitors kept arriving from every part of the country to see the elder statesman.

Scholars came from Europe as well, bringing scientific news and wishing to discuss their projects, and military heroes from South America came to pay homage to the great scribe of freedom. Equally welcomed were others coming merely out of friendship and curiosity. Among them were James Madison accompanied by Dolley and Payne Todd, her son.

Jefferson developed a routine for his day from which he rarely deviated. After devoting his early morning hours to writing, with an interruption for breakfast, he rode about the plantation, consulting with his overseer, until it was time for dinner, at approximately four o'clock in the afternoon. The only exception he made was during inclement weather. It promised to be the idyllic pastoral life for which he had yearned during the many years spent away from home, and he knew no greater pleasure.[3]

But the idyll was short-lived, for the stream of visitors arriving at his door proved to be ceaseless. Many came merely to gaze upon the venerable statesman who had played such an important role in the founding of the new republic. Others came to seek advice. The arduous journey to Monticello up the long winding road made it necessary for a polite host to offer his visitors overnight accommodations. Martha later commented that on occasion they had as many as fifty people staying on the premises. Often she had to borrow beds from the overseer's family and other sources on the plantation. In addition to the family's discomfort as a consequence of these uninvited house guests, there was the cost of feeding them and their horses, which added substantially to the household budget.

A continuous flood of mail that increased with each month of his retirement added to Jefferson's distraction. Office seekers requested recommendations; inventors sought encouragement for new inventions and often monetary support as well; men of science wrote on technical subjects. Letters came without end from historians and other writers desiring first hand information about the events and individuals in the American Revolution. There were also prolongued exchanges with his friends, Madison, Monroe and later, Adams, on government affairs, and much familial and business mail as well.

Jefferson had always considered correspondence to be among his first priorities. Inasmuch as so much of his time was spent in this endeavor, he provided himself with the maximum comfort while so engaged, designing furniture to provide the convenience he required. He continued to use the polygraph and the portable writing desk and the revolving chair he had designed for himself in 1776.

He also used a revolving chair he had purchased in 1790 from the prominent New York furniture maker, Thomas Burling. Made of mahogany and oak veneer and upholstered in red leather, it was ingeniously designed with the upper portion equipped with a center spindle and resting on four rollers sunk into each of its legs, so that it swiveled. He also had a sofa made with concave ends to fit the chair's circular base to enable the two pieces to be used together while reading and writing.

He acquired a Windsor couch to use with the chair, and it may have been at that time that he added a writing arm to the Windsor revolving chair. He modified a square top tea table with a revolving top so that it could be placed astride the couch and rolled to the foot of the couch to enable Jefferson to sit in the revolving chair while he read or wrote at the table.[4] (*Figure 31*)

Despite the annoying invasion of visitors, Jefferson's thoughts and time were chiefly preoccupied with the construction still remaining on the mansion and the needs of the plantation. His unending leisure provided him with opportunities at last to apply much of the quantitative data he had been compiling over the years in public office to practical purposes at Monticello. His alert mind readily visualized the potential relationship between a scientific principle, such as in physics, for example, and its application to the design of a piece of furniture to make it more functional, or to some useful tool for the farm. His concern for time-saving and labor-saving manifested itself in countless ways, and resulted in numerous devices he created or adapted.

It was a much more simple matter for him to do so than for many others. He was a competent draftsman, well equipped with the skills and tools necessary to render his ideas into visual form on detailed plans and in specifications for the guidance of the craftsmen who were to produce them.

There were those among the slaves he owned who had wood- and metal-working skills, which they practised in the several shops on the plantation. Finally, he was a liberal spender who never hesitated to purchase the finest materials, services or products which would provide required functions and/or pleasure.

By this time, the work force of the nailery had been reduced to six nailers, and several of those formerly so employed were now assisting other Monticello craftsmen. Although the demand for nails continued, production had to be reduced because Jefferson was experiencing difficulty in collecting payment from purchasers.[5]

One source of income had been the manufacturing mill on the banks of the Rivanna River, which he leased to Jonathan and Isaac Shoemaker. Their quarterly payments, made in either flour or currency, rarely arrived on schedule, and Jefferson received reports that their operation of the mill was steadily degenerating.

Several months after leaving Washington, Jefferson wrote an apologetic letter to his nailrod supplier, Jones and Howell, assuring them of his intention to pay them in full the several hundred dollars he owed as soon as he could. "My nails have never commanded money," he wrote "Even the merchants, if cash were demanded, would prefer importing them, because they would then make paiment by remittance of produce. Under these circumstances I am obludged to throw myself on your indulgence, with the assurance it shall never be wilfully abused. . . . while I had this [nail] business under my own direction, it was very profitable, in as much as it employed boys, not otherwise useful. During my absence it has not been so, but has been continued merely to preserve the custom. I think to try it for a year or two, in my own hands, & if I find it has become unprofitable from causes which cannot be remedied I shall abandon it."[6]

The reply from Jones and Howell was most reassuring and cited his past favorable business history with them. Taking advantage of this good will, Jefferson promptly placed new orders with them for several tons of assorted sizes of rod and other miscellaneous iron. He expected to bring the enterprise out of its doldrums with new energy now that he could personally supervise its daily operation. He was not successful, however, and within a year he temporarily suspended its operation. Since he was still unable to collect from his mill tenants, and now without nailery income, the only means he had for making payment to Jones and Howell was by the sale of produce in local markets.

He managed to restore the operation of the nailery by late 1811, and resumed his contact with Jones and Howell. The War of 1812 effectively ended the nailery as a commercial venture, however, and thereafter it was operated only for the needs of Monticello. Although he had assigned supervision of the plantation to his son-in-law, Jefferson personally took over the operation of the nailery again until about 1815. The nail-making operation may have been moved to the farm blacksmith shop thereafter, producing only such nails as were required for the premises.[7]

Jefferson enjoyed using his hands, and had always been frustrated by the lack of time to do so for the fabrication of devices and other items he conceived. While in London he had purchased a "gentleman's" tool chest made to his own specifications from the merchant Thomas Robinson. He kept his chest with him always, and in the President's House it had been stored in the unfurnished East Room with his collections of fossils and minerals.[8]

At Monticello, before he remodeled and expanded the mansion, Jefferson had kept and used his tools in his library on the second floor. Isaac, a former nailer on the plantation, recorded having observed Jefferson's activities with tools. "My Old Master was neat a hand as ever you saw to make keys and locks and small chains, iron and brass," he stated. "He kept all kind of blacksmith and carpenter tools in a great case with shelves to it in his library, an upstairs room, Isaac went up there constant; been up there a thousand times; used to car. coal up there. Old Master had a couple of small bellows up there." After the house was remodeled, Jefferson set up a work bench in the present conservatory room at the south end of the mansion. There he now made use of his tools from time to time until he experienced too much difficulty in using his hands as the result of accidents.[9]

Many of Jefferson's own "inventions," or adaptations of other existing devices, were incorporated into the mansion during the periods of construction and reconstruction. After the Entrance Hall and East Portico had been added, he moved the windvane from over the parlor to the roof of the East Portico, and had a windrose painted on its ceiling indicating wind directions by means of the wrought iron index. The design of the windrose may have been duplicated from the one painted by a Hessian officer on the ceiling of the parlor.[10]

Another of his innovations was the fireproofing of the ceilings. As he explained to his friend Benjamin Harris, he was familiar with several types of fireproofing, one of which was the use of sheet iron under floor planking, a method patented by the former minister from Great Britain, David Hartley.

At Monticello he accomplished the fireproofing "by planting slips of lath on the inside of every joist at bottom laying short planks on these and filling the interval between them & the floor with brick and mortar. This is usual to the Northward under the name of countersealing, and is used in my own house, and has once saved my house by the floor resisting taking fire from a coat of sawdust spread over it, and burning on it a whole night."[11]

This form of fireproofing, called "nogging," served to conserve heat at the same time that it fireproofed the building. It had the drawback, however, of retaining its original moisture and absorbing natural condensation which combined to accelerate the deterioration of the wooden frame.

This technique was in fact to prove to be the cause of considerable damage to the mansion after the passage of the years. The building was structurally strong enough to support the considerable weight of two layers of brick laid upon a bed of clay bonded with straw between all floor joists of yellow pine, which Jefferson had used. However, during the succeeding almost two centuries, vines growing on the outer walls found their way through the mortar joists and introduced moisture into the clay and brick nogging.

This increased the amount of moisture between floors to such an extent that it strained the timbers. When the building was restored in the early 1950's, more than one hundred tons of rubble was removed from the floors.[12]

Before Jefferson undertook weatherproofing, the building was frequently extremely cold. Once while attending to his correspondence, Jefferson discovered that the ink had frozen on the point of his pen, making it difficult to write. Turning his attention to correcting this condition, he demonstrated particular ingenuity in the design of his windows and interior doors to overcome the problem. While traveling in Holland he had observed in Amsterdam windows made in such a manner that they admitted fresh air but kept out the rain. He adopted the principle and for the second floor had windows built which provided insulation, retaining the heat inside and keeping out the cold.[13]

The three-sash windows he had built at floor level were also designed to be converted into doorways by raising the two bottom sashes to the top one. To many of the window casings he added hidden shutters. These were made in such a manner that they could be unfolded out when protection was required, and kept concealed in the casings when they were not needed. For the exterior of the house, Jefferson utilized a shutter made with fixed slats to enable sunshine and fresh air to enter, which could be shut out when desired by means of the solid folding shutters provided on the inside.

The first floor ceilings were relatively high, those of the rooms on the second floor were extremely low, and accordingly Jefferson provided the upstairs bedrooms with small windows placed just off the floor. From the outside, therefore, they appeared to be extensions of the first floor windows.[14]

For the protection of the first floor windows, Jefferson added attractive wooden lattice work which covered the bottom fourth of the glass span. An apocryphal account states that this safety measure was added after the occurrence of an accident involving one of Jefferson's most distinguished visitors, none other than President James Madison. On one occasion following dinner, when he was seated just inside the window, it is said he fell asleep in his chair. According to another version, the accident occurred because he was laughing so hard. In any case, tradition relates that he lost his balance and toppled backward, falling into the garden.[15]

Another innovation devised by Jefferson for conserving heat and maintaining the climate in the house, was the addition of two sets of pocket sliding doors, with which he doubled the entrance space. These were made with large panes of glass fitted into mullions, and originally glided smoothly into the walls when fully opened, accommodated in cavities provided for the purpose. When closed, they not only insulated the interior from the cold, but also had the virtue of providing additional privacy and freedom from noise.[16]

The mansion of Monticello survives as a three-dimensional record of Jefferson's mechanical ingenuity and his dedication to the maximum utilization of space. Particularly ingenious are the double doors separating the Entrance Hall from the parlor. This pair of glazed doors operate automatically in unison when one of them is opened or closed. This is achieved by means of a pair of wheels or drums situated under the door frame at either end of the opening. The wheels or drums are joined by a linked iron chain having a figure-eight configuration, similar to that later found on doors of trolley cars.[17]

Sixteen fireplaces served by five chimneys heated the mansion. They were constructed in such a manner that they extended into the rooms and were made with narrow throats connecting them to the flues, so that the heat was forced into the rooms. Some of the fireplaces were equipped with firebacks purchased by Jefferson before retirement from a Washington merchant. Several of the fireplaces incorporated the designs of Benjamin Thompson, Count Rumford.[18]

The building was equipped with gutters made of sheet iron and sheet copper which Jefferson purchased from Jones & Howell in Philadelphia in 1806.

A number of devices for which Jefferson made drawings and wrote specifications are not known with certainty to have been actually produced and installed at Monticello. Among these was a proposal "To fix a fan over the Dining room table." This consisted of an "axis" or bar passing from the west end of the skylight square through the east wall of the dining room, just below the cornice with its square end above the stairs. A cord was wound around a "wing wheel" having projecting teeth and was carried by means of a pulley over the stair well, terminating in a heavy weight which activated the "swing wheel" and an anchor-like escapement to operate regulated by a pendulum which was kept vibrating and which in turn caused a "fan wing" under the skylight to move. The span of the fan was to be approximately eight feet.[19] (*Document 5*)

Jefferson's insistence on the maximum utilization of space did not always produce successful results. In his design of the mansion, he directed particular attention to the area generally allotted for the great staircases in the large country houses of that period. In his view, whatever measure of architectural elegance such staircases might provide did not justify the considerable space they required. He was striving to achieve stateliness on the first floor by means of high ceilings, and avoidance of the impression that the first floor ceiling was the floor of another level, which would be created by a grand staircase. Stairs were a necessity with which he could not dispense, however, and accordingly he designed the staircase with treads only twenty-four inches in width.

"By this means," he believed, "great staircases are avoided, which are expensive and occupy a space which would make a good room in every story." He also concluded that rarely if ever did two people ascend or descend the stairs side by side. Therefore he designed them to be just wide enough for a single individual, with a right angle landing for greater economy of space. As a consequence, the treads were not only very narrow but also extremely steep.

Furthermore, although he succeeded in saving space, he had overlooked the occasional necessity to use the stairs to convey trunks and furniture from one floor to another, which was impossible with his narrow stairs. There was no alternative but to lift large objects to be moved through the windows from outside the building. In later life, Jefferson had even more cause to regret his space economy. As he became older and more crippled by rheumatism, he probably found it increasingly difficult to navigate the steep risers of the narrow stairs, and finally it became impossible for him to climb them at all.[20]

For his greater personal convenience Jefferson moved his library from the second to the first floor, to a room next to his own bedroom, with his study on the other side. Always concerned for maximum utility and space economy, he fitted his bed snugly into an alcove between the bedroom and study, an opening exactly as wide and as long as his mattress. Presumably he had his bed and mattress made to fit the space he had chosen, which was open on both sides so as to be benefited by maximum ventilation. Also, this disposition made it possible to have the bed made up easily. It also enabled him to rise on either side, depending on whether he intended to use his bedroom or his study.

Such a combination provided him with the benefits of any breeze that circulated. To avoid drafts yet permit light to filter through, however, he erected a paper-lined screen supported by a mahogany column on the study side of the alcove. In 1808 he decided to improve the screen and provided detailed instructions for doing so to Dinsmore, his master builder. The existing screen was to be replaced by a folding frame consisting of three parts made to open vertically instead of horizontally as before.[21]

All other bedrooms had "alcove beds" fitted into recesses built into the walls and enclosed by walls on three sides. Iron hooks set into the walls projected sufficiently to enable rope to be laced around them to form a mesh upon which was placed mattresses, feather beds, filled straw bedcovers and other bedclothes. The upper part of the alcove over each bed featured a closet space with a small latched door for storing bedclothes.

He also designed revolving clothes closets, none of which have survived, however. A shallow closet attached to the wall of the alcove opposite the foot of Jefferson's bed was recently discovered to have at one time served as such a revolving clothes closet. Originally a post extended from floor to the ceiling at the center of the space, with arms projecting from it, and installed in such a manner that it could revolve. Articles of clothing were hung upon the arms, and were then pushed back out of the way to make room as other arms were brought forward. Jefferson had similar revolving clothes closets installed in the President's House during his residency. No evidence of these facilities has survived later modifications and restorations of the White House.[22]

Opposite the clothes closet in his own bedroom, Jefferson installed his private privy. This consisted of two seats set at different levels. A privy was situated in the passageways and chamberpots were kept in the bedrooms. Three of the privies, including the one in Jefferson's bedroom, were connected with an underground air tunnel terminating at the east end of the building. Ropes and pulleys were used to conduct the vessels to the mouth of the tunnel, which was concealed with shrubbery. There the chamberpots were removed and emptied by servants.[23]

Determined to waste nothing in space or opportunity, Jefferson devised even the drainage to advantage. The situation of the mansion high on the mountain provided a magnificent view, but it also had attendant shortcomings, such as a limited water supply. In 1769 he had had a well dug on the western exposure to a depth of sixty-eight feet. It frequently went dry, however, and water had to be carried by hand from springs on the side of the mountain.

This constant need for more water led Jefferson to have four cisterns built at the corners of the terraces. Rainwater from the terrace surfaces was collected by means of sheet iron gutters installed at the edges of the terraces, which did double service as walkways over the all-weather passages.

They were based on a design that Jefferson had found in the works of Palladio, and which he incorporated for the terraces extending from the mansion to the South Pavilion and to the North Pavilion. The subject of cisterns in general interested Jefferson greatly, and he discussed them at some length in correspondence with Benjamin Harris.[24]

Even the location of his ice house reflected Jefferson's practical mind. It was a small building made for storage of ice cut from the Rivanna River during the winter months to be used during the following summer. In his practical manner, Jefferson situated it at the northern end of the passageway so that it would be exposed to the cold winds from the north in order to maintain the contents in as cold a climate as possible.

He had a brick-lined fish pond constructed near the South Pavilion for the purpose of conserving water but also to serve as a decorative element. Undoubtedly inspired by the Roman *piscina* (pool) from Varro's work, it was in the form of an ellipse five yards in width and ten yards in length. It was completed early in 1812 and used for temporary storage of fish for the table.

He went to great lengths to obtain fish to stock several ponds he built on his adjacent property, Tufton Farm. He purchased some carp as well as Roanoke chub from various sources, and from Captain Matthew Wills he obtained carp as well as other varieties. One shipment of fish arrived dead, he concluded, because the cask in which the fish were shipped was old and foul. Accordingly, he devised "a proper smack" for transporting fish thereafter, which could be towed behind a boat.[25]

In addition to fencing of solid wood palings, Jefferson devised an unusual form of barrier to keep undesirable animals from grazing in his garden. In 1814 he had a ditch, called a "ha ha," constructed along Mulberry Row. As described by a visitor arriving at Monticello years later, "As we approached the house we rode along a fence which was the only one of its kind I ever saw. Instead of being upright, it lay upon the ground across a ditch, the banks of the ditch raised the rails a foot or two above the ground on each side of the ditch, so that no kind of grazing animals could easily cross it, because their feet would slip between the rails. It had just the appearance of a common post and rail straight fence, blown down across a ditch."[26]

The *Farm Book* records Jefferson's varied farm activities during this period, including his application of chemistry to agriculture as well as to such domestic processes as brewing, distilling, and tanning, and to making gunpowder, building materials, coal and charcoal, among others. Like most other Virginia plantations, Monticello was large and isolated, and it was essential for it to be as self-sufficient as possible. Because of his financial strictures, it was even more necessary for Jefferson than for others to have his plantation fulfill as many of its own needs as possible.

Among these was leather for making shoes for the slaves, and for harnesses and saddles. In 1794 alone, sixty pairs of shoes were required for Jefferson's slaves. He purchased some animal hides and obtained others from his own cattle. It is not certain whether he did his own tanning but he probably did so. He ordered his men to "Get bark for tanning leather where your next clearing is to be, felling the tree and stripping it clean." At first he purchased the charcoal required by his blacksmith shop, and for fuel in the house, but in 1795 began to make his own.[27]

For the building stone and lime required for Monticello, he purchased lime from others and also quarried limestone from another of his properties called "Limestone" in Albemarle County on the Hardware River. It was transported to a small kiln in a detached piece of land on the other side of the river, where it was converted into lime. He estimated that fifteen bushels of lime were required for every thousand bricks used in building. From local merchants he purchased the gunpowder he used extensively for boring rock in building operations and similar purposes. Often the local product was of such poor quality, however, that he had to order it from the Du Pont firm in Wilmington, Delaware. To estimate the powder's power before using it he tested it with an éprouvette—a gauge for testing gunpowder—such as was used by the War Office.

Jefferson was probably propelled into the use of plaster of paris, which he applied to the soil, by a work by John A. Binns, who described his successful farming in Loudon County with the use of "gypsum, clover and deep ploughing." The statesman also derived knowledge of the use of plaster of paris from a book written at the request of George Washington by Richard Peters, a lawyer, patriot and farmer who was also a friend.[28]

As part of his enjoyment of the sweet pleasures of life as a private citizen once more, Jefferson attempted to pick up the threads of old friendships in Europe. He wrote to Lafayette, Madame de Corny and others. To General Thaddeus Kosciusko, he explained that in the past he had rarely written to him due to the necessity to avoid anything political while in public service, because it might be considered injurious to the country.

Now, however, he felt free to "talk of ploughs and harrows, of seeding and harvesting, with my neighbors, and of politics too, if they choose, with as little reserve as the rest of my fellow citizens, and feel, at length, the blessing of being free to say and do what I please, without being responsible for it to any mortal."[29]

One of his current preoccupations, he explained, was directing the studies of several young men, who found lodgings in nearby Charlottesville, and who have came to Monticello to ask for his supervision of their reading. It was a work which he greatly enjoyed.

"In advising the course of their reading," he commented, "I endeavor to keep their attention fixed on the main objects of all science, the freedom and happiness of man. So that coming to bear a share in the councils and government of their country, they will keep ever in view the sole objects of all legitimate government."[30]

Jefferson was fond of wine, ciders and malted beverages, but did not himself partake of whiskey or rum. However, he kept stocks of each for his workmen and servants "when they work in the water in cool weather . . . which might produce colds . . . & sickness." In 1813 he began to brew beer on the plantation in a brewery built for him by Captain Joseph Miller, a London brewer confined to Albemarle County as a political prisoner during the War of 1812. Miller lived at Monticello for a time, and taught the servants how to malt and brew.

From George Divers Jefferson obtained information about the best types of stills available for purchase and designed his own apple mill and press. From his copy of *The American Brewer* by Joseph Coppinger he learned how to malt corn "with perfect success." Although James River brewers used corn almost exclusively, Jefferson used wheat, which one of his slaves, Peter Hemings, became skilled in brewing. In time Jefferson became quite adept at the art of brewing and was able to advise Madison on the equipment required.[31]

Jefferson proved to be competent also in carriage design. While in France, he had made drawings for a phaeton to be built for Baron von Geismar. He assured the Baron that the plans were "made with such scrupulous exactness in every part that your workmen may safely rely on them." Later at Monticello, he experimented with a two-wheeled gig, converting it into a four-wheeled vehicle in the interests of greater safety. He prepared the plans and specifications and the conversion was made successfully by his Monticello craftsmen. He used it for many years in its modified form.[32]

The year 1811 was a particularly poor one for crops. As Jefferson complained to Monroe in the spring, "We are suffering here, both in the gathered and the growing crop. The lowness of the river, and great quantity of produce brought to Milton this year, render it almost impossible to get our crops to market. This is the case of mine as well as yours, and the Hessian fly appears alarmingly in our growing crops. Everything is in distress for the want of rain."[33]

To add to his difficulties, during the summer he suffered a severe attack of rheumatism. As soon as he was able to do so, he set out for Poplar Forest. It was a poor decision, for the journey proved to be agonizing as the carriage traveled over rough roads. Upon his arrival he immediately wrote to Dr. Rush for medical advice.

Rush sent him a variety of remedies, including the application of quilted bruised rolls of sulphur contained in pieces of muslin, rubbing the painful areas with a brush and bathing twice daily with castile soap, camphor, opium and salt in spirits. Further, he recommended internal doses of sassafras tea and spirits of turpentine.

During the most of that year, Jefferson was forced to spend much of his time in confinement. While remaining at Poplar Forest, he diverted himself by calculating its latitude, and he planned to establish the latitude of Willis's Mountain in the region if and when he could travel again on horseback.[34]

With his unlimited leisure, Jefferson returned to astronomy. Accompanied by either Payne Todd or James Madison, on September 17, 1811 he used his telescope at Monticello to observe the annular eclipse of the sun and recorded his observations with precision and modesty. He successfully made his observations without benefit of an astronomical clock, using an ordinary timepiece instead, and sent copies of his calculations to Todd and others. He explained that he had had perfect observation of the sun's passage over the meridian, and the eclipse had begun so soon thereafter "as to leave little room for error from the time-piece. Her rate of going, however, was ascertained by ten days' subsequent observation and comparison with the sun, and the times, as I now give them to you, are corrected by these."

He noted, however, that the times of the first and last contacts were not reliable since his clock was too slow, and he had not begun watching soon enough. He reported that the last contact was sufficiently well observed, however, but that it was on the forming and breaking of the annulus that he relied and was certain that there was no error in either. He had not yet calculated the longitude from them, and suggested that Todd could do this as a college exercise. He estimated that the latitude of Monticello was 39° 8′ and he was correct.

While observing the eclipse, he had used an "equatorial telescope" (probably the universal equatorial instrument) and noted that a companion had observed through a Dollond achromatic telescope. Two other companions attended the timepieces. He was pleased with the fact that as well as he knew, he had been the only one in Virginia to have made the observations.

Not feeling up to the task himself, he sent his notations to Lambert, who was to make final calculations of the longitude of Monticello. He explained, however, "I have for some time past been rubbing off the rust of my mathematics contracted during 50. years engrossed by other pursuits, and have found in it a delight and a success beyond my expectations."[35]

He also sent an account of his observations to H. A. S. Dearborn, who had sent him a copy of Nathaniel Bowditch's report on a comet which the mathematician had recently observed in New England. Jefferson hoped that from his observations and those of others it would be

possible to determine whether the comet was one that had been previously seen in America. He included the results of the observations such
as he had already provided to Payne Todd.[36]

In November Jefferson received the calculations made by Lambert,
and after reading them he realized that his plan for establishing the longitude of Monticello based on his observations of the eclipse of September
17th would not have been successful. Although he owned a universal
equatorial instrument and a theodolite, both made by Ramsden, a Borda
reflecting circle, a Hadley reflecting quadrant, and "a fine meridian and
horizon," as well as a pocket sextant, he had no telescope capable of
observing Jupiter's satellites.

He had established the latitudes of Poplar Forest and Willis Mountain by his own observations, which had been repeated and confirmed
by his grandson Thomas Jefferson Randolph. After ascertaining the dip
of his Borda circle, he discovered that he was able to use it on land
without an artificial horizon in the same manner that it was used at sea.[37]

He offered to provide the Reverend Madison with some additional
latitudes for the map the latter was preparing, adding "I have a pocket
sextant of miraculous accuracy, considering its microscopic graduation.
With this I have ascertained the latitude of Poplar Forest (say New London) by multiplied observations, and lately that of the Willis mountains
by observations of my own, repeated by my grandson, whom I am carrying on in his different studies. Any latitudes within the circuit of these
three places I could take for you myself, to which my grandson, whose
motions will be on a larger scale, would be able to add others."

He planned, as soon as he could to "fit up a room to fix my instruments" to determine Monticello's longitude by means of lunar observations, inasmuch as this method had "the advantages of multiplied repetitions & less laborious calculations."[38]

Jefferson did in fact eventually provide a place for his instruments
in his study, on the sills of the bay window on the southern exposure,
from which he had a clear view of the sky. He prepared an elaborate
"plan of a Bow window to be made at the Southern angle of my cabinet
for observing instruments," an extension to be added as an "observatory
corner" to his study. The plan included skylights to be built over both
sides of the triangular space of the extension, each of which could be
lifted on hinges.

At the apex of the triangular addition were to be placed three marble slabs at the level of the window sill, over a solid brickwork pier. The
purpose of the pier, which was to extend to basement level, was to protect the instruments from any possible vibrations from the floor. From
the level of the window sills, four sash doors four panes high would enclose the addition on each side, requiring 32 lights. They were to be
made to open on hinges. The existing windows were to be converted to

three sashes to open to the floor. In other words, the "observatory corner" was to be separated from the "cabinet" or study by the old floor-length windows as another provision to avoid distraction or vibrations from the house while observing.[39]

Despite his elaborate planning, Jefferson never constructed the "observatory corner." Instead, he continued to use the existing platform for his instruments. He had three marble slabs set into the front of the existing window embrasure, upon a brick pier extending to the basement to eliminate vibrations. The marble slabs of the existing support, which survive, were also shown on his "plan of a Bow window."[40]

While incapacitated with a bout of rheumatism at Poplar Forest, Jefferson had passed the time calculating the hour lines for a horizontal sundial for that latitude, 37° 22' 26". As he explained to Charles Clay, a neighbor of his summer residence, he had made calculations for every five minutes of time exact to within half a second of a degree.

He suggested to Clay that he might wish to have one made by "Master Cyrus." All that would be required, he advised, were a pair of dividers and a protractor or a line of chords. "A dial of size, say of from twelve inches to two feet square," he went on, "is the cheapest and most accurate measure of time for general use, and would I suppose be more common if every one possessed the proper horary lines for his own latitude."

Since Williamsburg was in almost the same parallel as Poplar Forest, he believed that his calculations would be adequate for all counties in between, including Lynchburg and Clay's home in New London as well. He recommended slate to be preferable to wood or metal for making the dial plate.[41] (Document 11)

It was Benjamin Latrobe who inspired Jefferson to design another type of sundial some time later. While engaged in the design and construction of the Capitol building, Latrobe had included corn among the iconographic features on capitals in the Senate stair vestibule. He sent a model of one to Jefferson as a gift for his garden. Later, in 1816, for the columns of the Capitol Rotunda he designed what he named "the American capital" as a new purely American architectural form with the columns featuring stalks of maize and the capital decorated with flowers and leaves of the tobacco plant.

He sent a drawing of it to Jefferson, explaining that the columns were being carved by Francisco Iardella, a sculptor recently arrived from Italy. Latrobe had another model made, which he also forwarded to Jefferson.

Jefferson found it pleasing in design, but was disturbed by the capital's lack of function. He derived considerable pleasure from inventing a purpose for it, and proceeded to put it to use as the base for a spherical sundial, a description and sketch of which he sent to Latrobe.

Latrobe was most complimentary in his comments about the sundial. "I can only say that its principles are so plain," he responded, "by its construction so easy, that dials on Your construction might be brought into very general use, if once known & introduced. They could be made so cheap, that they might be sold at every turner's, with a hole *to be bored* in the Naddir of the Latitude of the place at which they are wanted at the time of purchasing them. The only difficulty which an unskilled person would find would be to place them in the true Meridian. But a little instruction, which might be given by a bill delivered with the Dial, would enable any farmer to accomplish that object. Every common Al-manack would enable him to convert Solor into common time. You have done my Capital much honor in making it the support of your Dial." Jefferson installed the Latrobe model of the American Capital on the northwest corner of the terrace at Monticello, and surmounted it with his globe sundial.[42]

Although he did not relax his interest in the sciences after retire-ment, Jefferson was not inclined to become involved when John Camp-bell proposed to publish an edition of Jefferson's complete writings. He responded that all that had been published had been his *Notes*, which he still intended to enlarge and revise, the *Summary View*, which had not been intended for publication, and the Parliamentary Manual, which he considered to be no more than a compilation with no original contri-bution of his own. As to his official papers, he thought they might be of interest to historians but not to any one else, so that he saw no point in undertaking publication of his complete writings.[43]

He was pleasantly surprised to receive news from William Clark, then soon to become governor of the Missouri Territory. Clark's gift of the hide of a Rocky Mountain sheep had been delivered to the Presi-dent's House in Washington and forwarded by Madison to Jefferson at Monticello. Another gift from Clark was an Indian blanket made of ani-mal hide.

The remainder of the fossil remains which Clark had obtained from Big Bone Lick and sent in a second shipment of three boxes failed to reach him, however. After Jefferson received the bill of lading, he suc-ceeded in tracing the boxes as far as New Orleans. After leaving that port, the vessel put in at Havana under embargo distress and was con-demned as unseaworthy. His efforts to learn the fate of Clark's shipment thereafter were unsuccessful. He was particularly concerned because of the great scarcity of mastodon fossils.

He informed Clark of the disposition he had made of those he had previously received, noting he had "reserved a very few for myself" and explained that these bones "have enabled them [the French naturalists] to decide that the animal was neither a mammoth nor an elephant, but of a distinct kind, to which they have given the name of Mastodont, from the protuberances of its teeth. These, from their forms, and the immense mass of their jaws, satisfy me this animal must have been arbor-ivorous. Nature seems not to have provided other food sufficient for him, and the limb of a tree would be no more to him than a bough of a cotton tree to a horse."[44]

Even more disappointing to Jefferson than the disappearance of the Clark shipment was the loss of the major part of his own collection of Indian vocabularies, which occurred upon his departure from Washington. This loss destroyed a work to which he had devoted many years and during which he had collected vocabularies of Indian tribes from a multitude of sources. It was no longer possible for him even to attempt to duplicate them. Jefferson commented that he had incorporated in his vocabularies seventy-five words which were also included in the Russian vocabularies made for other parts of the world.

In preparation for his departure from Washington, he had collected all of the vocabularies and packed them together carefully with other papers into a trunk, which was shipped by water with thirty other packages of his effects. While the vessel bearing his goods was ascending the James River, a thief assumed that because of its weight, that particular trunk contained valuable articles. When he opened it, however, only to reveal papers and a few miscellaneous objects, the disappointed thief threw its contents into the river. Some pages of the vocabularies floated ashore and were found in the mud. When recovered most of them proved to have been so greatly water-damaged that they were useless, but Jefferson managed to save a few.[45]

Jefferson lost a number of other valuable items contained in the stolen trunk, including "a pocket telescope with a brass case, a Dynamometer in steel and brass instrument for measuring the exertions of draught animals."[46]

The dynamometer was an instrument which Jefferson planned to use for testing his mouldboard, and for which he had expended considerable effort to obtain. It was recently invented by Edmé Regnier, based on a concept of the French physicist, Charles Augustin de Coulomb, for ascertaining the comparative strength which individuals are capable of exerting.[47]

Jefferson had purchased one in 1808 and after its loss he sought to borrow another from friends who might own one. He queried Joel Barlow without success, and finally he managed to borrow one from Robert Fulton, who had brought it from France. Jefferson explained his need to test his mouldboard and compare its resistance to the Guillaume plough sent him by the Société d'Agriculture de la Seine.[48]

After testing his mouldboard by means of the dynamometer, he discovered that it was too long and that its square toe was liable to collect soil when damp. Accordingly he modified his original design by shortening it and making it with a sharp toe.[49]

He used the dynamometer to make other tests as well. Edmund Bacon, a Monticello overseer, recalled years later that Jefferson "had a machine for measuring strength. There were very few men that I have seen try it that were as strong in the arms as his son-in-law, Colonel Thomas Mann Randolph; but Mr. Jefferson was stronger than he."[50]

In addition to the damage to his lands during his absence due to neglect and poor management, even more had been brought about by the natural elements. The red soil of his farms had been washed away by erosion and the recurring planting of the staple crops of tobacco and corn had contributed not only to erosion but soil exhaustion as well. Jefferson attempted to counteract these conditions by adding gypsum plaster to the soil, and initiated contour ploughing by means of a hillside plough designed by Thomas Mann Randolph. He promoted conservation practises by example as well as in correspondence. He was particularly proud of the technique of side-hill ploughing developed by his son-in-law, and wrote even lyrically about it to Peale:

> The spontaneous energies of the earth are a gift of nature, but they require the labor of man to direct their operation, and the question is, so to husband his labor as to turn the greatest quantity of this useful action of the earth to his benefit.

Jefferson explained that by ploughing horizontally on hilly land following "the curvations of the hills and hollows" on the dead level, every furrow made serves as a reservoir to receive and retain rain instead of running off and taking the soil with it. Furthermore, the horses draw much easier on such a level. He went on to note that as the declivity of the hill varied in different parts of the line, the guide furrows would approach or recede from each other in different parts of the line and the parallel furrows would finally touch in one part and be far apart in others leaving unploughed gores, which had to be ploughed separately. Randolph had initiated side-hill ploughing on his own farm and later at Monticello in about 1807.[51]

During the early years of his retirement, Jefferson still maintained his dream of an agrarian nation and the development of home industries to make it independent of foreign imports. He expressed his optimistic views to David Baillie Warden, the American consul in Paris, who had originally helped him obtain his dynamometer.

"Our manufactures are spreading with a rapidity which could not have been expected," he noted. "The capital of our merchants diverted from commerce turns of necessity into the channels of manufactures. The spinning machines are getting into every farm house, and I think we cannot be far short of a million of spindles at work, which will fully clothe our 8. millions of people. The root these have taken among the body of our people is so firm that there is no danger of it's not being permanent. It's household establishment will fix the habit where no future change of employment in the mercantile capital can ever affect it."[52]

As Jefferson experimented with his astronomical instruments, he explained to Robert Patterson his particular fondness for astronomy. "Before I entered on the business of the world I was much attached to Astronomy & had laid a sufficient foundation at College to have pursued it with satisfaction & advantage. But after 40. years of abstraction from it, and my mathematical acquirements coated over with rust, I find myself equal only to such simple operations & practices in it as serve to amuse me. But they give me great amusement, and the more as I have some excellent instruments. My telescope however is not equal to the observation of the eclipses of Jupiter's satellites, nor my best time piece sufficiently to be depended on, for that purpose."

He also expressed his continued concern about the unit of measure. He commented that he did not like the new system of French measure primarily because it was based on a standard that was accessible only to the French, from whom other nations were required to obtain it.

He explained, "on examining the map of the earth, you will find no meridian on it but the one passing through their country, offering the extent of land on both sides of the 45th degree, and terminating at both ends in a portion of the ocean which the conditions of the problem for an universal standard of measures require."

He felt that other nations might just as well have adopted the French foot as the standard. He noted that the French had abandoned their "Decada Calendar" but not the centesimal division of the quadrant. Although they had not yet been published, the French astronomer Jean-Charles de Borda had calculated new trigonometrical tables according to that division.

Jefferson favored the pendulum because it was fixed not by the laws of one country but by the laws of nature to which every country had access and at a cost within the means of everyone. He still maintained the hope that one day the pendulum would be accepted as the universal basis for a common system of measures, weights and coinage, which would be generally understood.

He proposed that the literary societies of the world should adopt the seconds pendulum as the unit of measure "on the authorities of reason, convenience, and common consent," and that the American Philosophical Society should propose it to other institutions of learning by means of a circular letter.

Jefferson was pleased to learn that the Society had agreed to consider the subject of fixed standards of measures, weights and coinage, and he submitted some additional general thoughts. In his opinion, "a direct admeasurement of a line on the earth's surface and a measure derived from its motion on its axis" were those that had received most attention. Jefferson discussed their advantages and disadvantages, noting "a pendulum of such length as in the latitude of 45°, in the level of the mean, and in a given temperature, shall perform its vibrations, in small and equal arcs, in one second of mean time."

For the ratio of its parts and multiples he proposed the decimal inasmuch as arithmetic was based on decimal numeration. For measures of surface he proposed the square unit, equal to about "ten square feet or $\frac{1}{9}$th more than a square yard; a killiad was not quite a rood or quarter of an acre, and a myriad not quite 2-½ acres." For measures of capacity he proposed the cubic unit of ".1 to be about .35 cubic feet, .28 bushels dry, or ⅛ of a ton liquid. The Dime .1 would be about 3.5 cubit feet, 2.8 bushels or about ⅞ of a barrel liquid. The Cent would equal .01 or about 50 cubic inches, or ⅛ of a quart, while the Mill equaled .001 or .5 of a cubic inch or ⅔ of a gill." To incorporate weights into the same system, Jefferson proposed the use of rain water as the most nearly uniform substance to be found in nature.

For coinage, Jefferson suggested using the pure silver of the dollar fixed by law at 347-¼ grains. To apply the system universally, he proposed to establish the length of the seconds pendulum of 45° on the basis of two tables. One provided the equivalent of every different denomination of measurement, weights and coinage in the United States in the unit of that pendulum and its decimals and multiples. The other table provided the equivalent of all the decimal parts and multiples of the pendulum in the several denominations of measures, weights and coinage of the existing system.

These tables would be provided to learned institutions in every civilized country. The proposal he thought should be made with particular diplomacy to France because of its fine work in the admeasurement of a portion of the meridian, and to England because "They are the older country, the mother country, more advanced in the arts and sciences, possessing more wealth and leisure for their improvement, and animated by a pride more than laudable."[53]

In another commentary on the British, he stated, "They are all occupied in industrious pursuits. They abound with persons living on the industry of their fathers or on the earnings of their fellow citizens, given away by their rulers in sinecures and pensions. Some of these, desirous of laudable distinction, devote their time and means to the pursuit of science, and become profitable members of society by an industry of a higher order."[54]

For many years Jefferson had desired to have a regulator clock for making astronomical observations, and had in fact ordered one from David Rittenhouse in the summer of 1778, after observing an eclipse of the moon. However, at that time Rittenhouse was fully occupied with war activities and his responsibilities on the Pennsylvania Committee of Safety, and Jefferson's own political activities left little time for scientific pursuits. The project was postponed and then forgotten, although the desire for such a timepiece was revived in Jefferson's mind from time to time.

Now in corresponding with Patterson on measures, the statesman was reminded once more, and asked Patterson to investigate costs "of a clock, the time-keeping part of which should be perfect? And what the difference of cost between a wooden and a gridiron pendulum? To be of course without a striking apparatus, as it would be wanted for astronomical purposes only."[55]

Two months passed before Patterson replied, recommending "young Mr. Voigt, an ingenious artist, who would make such a clock for sixty-five dollars." Jefferson was familiar with his father, Henry Voigt, Chief Coiner of the Mint, and had previously already used the younger Voight's services. He accepted the price, and Voight was instructed to proceed with the order.

The clock was to be without ornamentation, in a plain mahogany case. In addition to using it for making celestial observations, Jefferson had in mind to utilize it also for experimentation with the pendulum as a standard of measure.

A full year passed before Jefferson was informed by Patterson that the timepiece was completed at last. The cost was $115.50, considerably more than Jefferson had anticipated, but he paid it promptly. Patterson estimated that a week or so would be required by Voight to regulate the clock before shipment. However, in view of the fact that the War of 1812 was then at its height, Patterson suggested that the risks of shipping by sea would require insurance, which Jefferson authorized, and further specified "the package should be water-tight, as it will be long exposed on our river in a boat open to rain. Perhaps it would not be amiss to roll the instrument up in what are called Dutch or striped blankets. With this precaution I once before received a clock from Philadelphia in perfect good order."[56]

Just as Patterson finished preparing the clock for shipment aboard the *Happy Return* bound for Richmond, he discovered that the river had been frozen over and the shipment had to be delayed. While waiting Patterson asked Voight to add certain elaborations to increase the clock's precision.[57]

The adventures of the clock were only just begun. No sooner had the river become free of ice and was once again navigable, than it was blockaded by the British fleet. The extremely patient Patterson unpacked the clock and set it up in his own home while awaiting further instructions from Monticello. Jefferson had informed Voight meanwhile that he had authorized Patterson to take the clock into his own home "and with the rod pendulum which I wish to be made an appendage to it, to try the experiment of the rod vibrating seconds."[58]

A month passed during which Patterson observed the clock's operation. He had noted, he informed Jefferson, that the pendulum was "suspended by a few inches of watch-spring attached to the upper end, as in a common pendulum." He had been informed by a mathematician at New Brunswick that his experiments on rod pendulums had failed because the watch-spring suspension had been used. "I presume," Patterson ventured, "the suspension spring must be abandoned, and the knife-edge substituted in its place, and with this I am persuaded (but shall test it by experiments) that theory and practice will agree."[59]

More time passed while the clock remained in Philadelphia with Patterson, and characteristically, Jefferson did not press Patterson for delivery of the timepiece while he corresponded with him on other subjects. In the summer of 1815, Patterson finally sent him a note of apology and explanation. "When (peace) had taken place," he wrote, "I perceived that some parts of the veneering were scaling off from the case. I sent it to the maker to have it repaired; and several months passed before the work was completed." Jefferson carefully wrote out shipping instructions: the clock was to be wrapped in coarse woolen blankets, placed in a well-jointed case which in turn was to be wrapped in oilcloth, and then shipped by sea to Richmond. Illness in Patterson's family occasioned another delay, and it was not until late the following month that the clock was placed aboard the *Guinea Hen* en route to Richmond.[60]

When the long-awaited clock finally arrived at Monticello, Jefferson had it placed in his study where he kept his telescopes and other instruments. He marked the inside back panel for each day of the week as indicated by the descent of the weight, so that it served as a calendar in the same manner as the Great Clock in the Entrance Hall.

Although he used the Voight clock for occasional astronomical observations, it served him primarily for regulating the times of his rising and retiring for the remainder of his life. He wound it every Sunday morning, as he did all other clocks in the mansion. (*Figure 32*)

A third clock which Jefferson modified to mark the days of the week by means of the descending weights was the mahogany eight-day clock made by Thomas Dring which he had purchased from Benjamin Ferris for his kitchen. To the back panel he attached tinned iron plates having the names of the days of the week painted on them to be indicated by the top edge of the descending weight.[61] (*Document 19*)

In his retirement, because he was nationally known as a man of science, Jefferson continued to receive countless requests for advice and information from all over the country. To each of these he responded in detail, although often annoyed that this correspondence robbed him of so much of his leisure.

For example, the artist Raphaelle Peale, one of the sons of Charles Willson Peale, while on the island of St. Helena off South Carolina, had invented an instrument to replace the octant for establishing latitudes. He was unable to find craftsmen locally to make a model for him, and now sought Jefferson's advice.[62]

Some of the inquiries interested Jefferson more than others, and he encouraged Melatiah Nash in his proposal to produce an ephemeris—a table of the position of celestial bodies for regular intervals or specified days—that would provide more astronomical information than was generally available in common almanacs, without becoming involved with "higher astronomical operations." He suggested adding the equation of time because it was necessary for the regulation of clocks and watches.

Also to be included, in his view, was the sun's declination as an element for enabling anyone to calculate the hours of the rising and setting of the sun, which would make the almanac useful in all parallels. He also suggested "to the logarithmic tangent of the latitude (a constant number) add the logarithmic tangent of the sun's declination; taking 10 from the Index, the remainder is the line of an arc which, turned into time and added to six hours, gives sunrise for the winter half and sunset for the summer half of the year, to which may be added three lines only from the table of refractions. . . ."

To provide a note of novelty which might be advantageous for promoting sales of the almanac, Jefferson suggested that with each issue Nash should include one or two useful tables that the purchaser would wish to preserve. As sources for such tables he suggested the *Connaissance des Temps* and Nicholas Pike's work on arithmetic, among others.[63]

Jefferson made a point of keeping informed on the current state of the medical sciences, and still remained extremely critical of the medical profession. After receiving a pamphlet from Dr. John Crawford on the cause, seat and cure of disease, he was unable to resist yet another attack on physicians.

"While surgery is seated in the temple of the exact sciences," he commented, "medicine has scarcely entered its threshold. Her theories have passed in such rapid succession as to prove the insufficiency of all, and their fatal errors are recorded in the necrology of man. For some forms of disease, well known and well defined, she has found substances which will restore order to the human system, and it is to be hoped that observation and experience will add to their number. But a great mass of diseases remain undistinguished and unknown, exposed to the random shot of the theory of the day. If on this chaos you can throw such a beam of light as your celebrated brother has done on the sources of animal heat, you will, like him, render great service to mankind."[64]

Following a discussion about the veterinary institutions of London and Paris with Dr. Benjamin Rush, Jefferson went on to speak about his reservations about medicine. "That there are certain diseases of the human body," he wrote, "so distinctly pronounced by well-articulated symptoms, and recurring so often, as not to be mistaken, wherein experience has proved that certain substance applied, will restore order, I cannot doubt. Such as Kinkina in Intermittents, Mercury in Syphilis, Castor Oil in Dysentery, &c. But there are also a great mass of indistinct diseases, presenting themselves under no form clearly characterized, nor exactly recognized as having occurred before, and to which of course the application of no particular substance can be known to have been made, nor its effect on the case experienced. These may be called unknown cases, and they may in time be lessened by the progress of observation and experiment. Observing that there are in the construction of the animal system some means provided unknown to us, which have a tendency to restore order, when disturbed by accident, called by physicians *vis medicatris naturae,* I think it safer to trust to this power in the unknown cases, than to uncertain conjectures built on the ever-changing hypothetical systems of medicine."[65]

Notable among Jefferson's correspondents in retirement sharing the same limitations brought on by age was his old friend John Adams. The rift in their friendship had been healed at last through the good offices of Benjamin Rush, and thereafter they enjoyed a memorable correspondence. Jefferson acknowledged the gift of some "homespun"—two volumes of his son's published lectures—Adams was sending him, and took the opportunity to discuss the status of domestic manufactures. He explained that at Monticello production was only of coarse and middling goods.

"Every family in the country is a manufactory within itself," he wrote, "and is very generally able to make within itself all the stouter and middling stuffs for its own clothing and household use. We consider a sheep for every person in the family as sufficient to clothe it, in addition to the cotton, hemp and flax which we raise ourselves. For fine stuff we shall depend on your northern manufactories. Of these, that is to say, of company establishments, we have none. We use little machinery. The spinning jenny, and loom with the flying shuttle, can be managed in a family; but nothing more complicated. The economy and thriftiness resulting from our household manufactures are such that they will never again be laid aside; and nothing more salutary for us has ever happened than the British obstructions to our demands for their manufactures."

Reminiscing about their association in the past, Jefferson commented on the conflicts with the French and British. "As for France and England, with all their preeminence in science, the one is a den of robbers, and the other of pirates. And if science produces no better fruits than tyranny, murder, rapine and destitution of national morality, I would rather wish our country to be ignorant, honest and estimable as our neighboring savages are."

He reported that he had now totally foregone the reading of newspapers and instead spent his time with Tacitus and Thucydides, Newton and Euclid, and consequently was happier than before. He explained that he spent three or four hours on horseback each day, and three or four times a year he visited Poplar Forest which was approximately ninety miles distant. In the winter he made the journey on horseback. Much as he had always enjoyed walking, now he was able to walk only a little, not even a mile a day.[66]

Another correspondence which Jefferson much enjoyed was with Judge Thomas Cooper. An English-born man of science who had studied both medicine and law, he was a well-known educator. A friend of Priestley, in 1794 he established himself at Northumberland, Pennsylvania and practised law. He was a strong Republican opponent of the Federalists and served as a state judge until he was removed by the governor in 1811.

Returning to science, Cooper began teaching, first in the chair of chemistry at Dickinson College, where he also taught mineralogy and geology, then at the University of Pennsylvania as professor of applied chemistry.[67]

When Cooper was seeking a capable geological correspondent in Virginia, he turned to Jefferson. The latter noted, however, that he could not offer himself inasmuch as it was the one science about which he knew least. "Our researches into the texture of our globe could be but superficial, compared with its vast interior construction, that I saw no safety of conclusion from the one, as to the other; and therefore have pointed my own attentions to other objects in preference, as far as a heavy load of business would permit me to attend to anything else."

He suggested that Joseph C. Cabell might serve Cooper's purpose since he had recently been in France and had accompanied the Scottish geologist, William Maclure, on some of his geological expeditions and was interested also in chemistry. When Cabell responded in the negative, Jefferson sought another correspondent for Cooper.[68]

He read with interest and approbation Cooper's published introductory lecture on chemistry, and expressed his views on the general subject. "You know the just esteem which attached itself to Dr. Franklin's science," Jefferson wrote, "because he always endeavored to direct it to something useful in private life. The chemists have not been attentive enough to this. I have wished to see their science applied to domestic objects, to malting, for instance, brewing, making cider, to fermentation and distillation generally, to the making of bread, butter, cheese, soap, to the incubation of eggs, &c." He was pleased to note that Cooper had directed some attention to these subjects in his syllabus, for it was a field in which much had still to be done.[69]

The mapping of the country remained paramount in Jefferson's mind long after he left Washington. He continued to exchange letters with Andrew Ellicott on mapping and astronomical observations, and in response to one of the latter's communications, Jefferson voiced his concerns about the future national scientific needs.

"A great deal is yet wanting to ascertain the true geography of our country; more indeed as to its longitudes than latitudes. Towards this we have done too little for ourselves and depended too long on the ancient and inaccurate observations of other nations."[70]

Humboldt periodically sent Jefferson copies of his newly published works. He was distressed to learn that Humboldt's fortunes had suffered, as the latter reported, not as much through his travels as from political upheavals. The German geographer continued to find consolation in his work, however, and in the friendships of those who appreciated his devotion to duties.[71]

To Humboldt, Jefferson expressed some of his hopes and anticipations for the future. "The European nations constitute a separate division of the globe," he wrote, "their localities make them part of a distinct system; they have a set of interests of their own in which it is our business never to engage ourselves. America has a hemisphere to itself: it must have it's separate new system of interests, which must not be subordinated to those of Europe. The insulated state in which nature has placed the American continent should so far avail it that no spark of war kindled in the other parts of the globe should be wafted across the wide oceans which separate us from them."

He wrote of the Indians, and "the benevolent plan we were pursuing here for the happiness of the Aboriginal inhabitants in our vicinities. We spared nothing to keep them at peace with each other, to teach them agriculture and the rudiments of the most miscellany arts, and to encourage industry by establishing among them separate property. In this way they would have been enabled to subsist and multiply on a moderate scale of landed· possession, they would have mixed their blood with ours and been amalgamated and identified with us within no distant period of time. On the commencement of our present war, we pressed on them the observance of peace and neutrality, but the interested and unprincipled policy of England has defected all our labors for the salvation of these unfortunate people. They have seduced the greater part of the tribes, within our neighborhood, to take up the hatchet against us, and the cruel massacres they have committed on the women and children of our frontiers taken by surprise, will oblige us now to pursue them to extermination, or drive them to new seats beyond our reach."[72]

Jefferson also commented on Humboldt's claim that the British traveler Arrowsmith had pirated his map of Mexico and apologized for Zebulon Pike's similar action. However, Jefferson wrote, "whatever he did was on a principle of enlarging knowledge and not for filthy shillings and pence of which he made none from that book. If what he has borrowed has any effect, it will be to excite an appeal in his readers from his defective information to the copious volumes of it with which you have enriched the world. I am sorry he omitted even to acknowlege the source of his information. It has been an oversight, and not at all in the spirit of his generous nature. Let me sollicit your forgiveness then of a declared hero, of an honest and zealous patriot, who lived and died for his country."[73]

Returning from a five week stay at Poplar Forest, Jefferson found awaiting him an account from Patterson of the perpetual motion machine that had been causing considerable excitement in Philadelphia. Charles Redheffer (also Redhoeffer) first appeared in Philadelphia with his invention of a perpetual motion machine. It was widely advertised and described in the press, and excited considerable comment. Installed in a house on the outskirts of the city, the inventor charged admission to view his invention, and people flocked to see it and made wagers concerning its authenticity.

Jefferson was intrigued with the description and sketch of the machine which Patterson sent him. "I had never before been able to form an idea of what his principle of deception was," he commented. "He is the first of the inventors of perpetual motion within my knowledge, who has had the cunning to put his visitors on a false pursuit, by amusing them with a sham machinery whose loose and vibratory motion might impose on them the belief that it is the real source of the motion they see. To this device he is indebted for a more extensive delusion than I have before witnessed on this point. We are full of it as far as this State, and I know not how much further. In Richmond they have done me the honor to quote me as having said that it was a possible thing. A poor Frenchman who called on me the other day, with another invention of perpetual motion, assured me that Dr. Franklin, many years ago, expressed his opinion to him that it was not impossible. Without entering into contest on this abuse of the Doctor's name, I gave him the answer I had given to others before, that the Almighty himself could not construct a machine of perpetual motions while the laws exist which He has prescribed for the government of matter in our system; that the equilibrium established by Him between cause and effect must be suspended to effect that purpose. But Redhefer seems to be reaping a rich harvest from the public deception. The office of science is to instruct the ignorant. Would it be unworthy of some one of its votaries who witness this deception, to give a popular demonstration of the insufficiency of the ostensible machinery, and of course of the necessary existence of some hidden mover? And who could do it with more effect on the public mind than yourself?[74]

When Redheffer applied to the Pennsylvania legislature for funding to develop his invention, a committee of eight experts was commissioned to report on it. The inventor set up his machine in a building near the Schuylkill, and in January 1813 the committee inspected it. One of the commissioners, Nathan Sellers, brought his young son with him. Upon their arrival, the committee found that the room containing the machine was locked and the key could not be found, so that they were able to observe the machine only through a barred window.

It was the boy who made the discovery that there was something unusual about the teeth around the periphery of the machine's rotating table, which meshed with another wheel, the axis of which was to transmit the power to another point where the work was to be done. He noticed that the faces of the two wheels demonstrated wear on the wrong sides, and pointed out to his father that the machine was in fact being operated by a concealed power source.

Sellers thereupon arranged with the well-known mechanician and engineer, Isaiah Lukens, to produce an operating model, in the base of which a concealed clockwork mechanism provided the motion. A demonstration of the model for the commissioners was arranged at a meeting to which Redheffer was also invited. Redheffer was so intrigued with the model that he offered Lukens a large sum of money to reveal how he had accomplished it, which the latter refused.[75]

After Redheffer had accumulated a considerable amount of money in Philadelphia from exhibiting his hoax, he moved on to New York where he again displayed it. There the skeptical Robert Fulton, after observing the machine in operation, concluded that it was powered by crank motion, having noticed that it did not operate at a constant speed. Suspecting that the machine was manually operated, he denounced Redheffer. Knocking away a partition between the machine and the next room, Fulton revealed a catgut belt drive connected to a back attic in which an old man provided the source of power for the machine. The crowd of onlookers that had collected demolished the machine, and Redheffer fled. Although they corresponded during this period, Jefferson was not informed of Fulton's encounter, but would have greatly enjoyed it if he had.[76]

While requesting Fulton's advice for the means of returning the dynamometer he had borrowed, Jefferson mentioned that from Abraham Howard Quincy of New York City he had learned of an improvement in fireplaces that required only one-tenth of the fuel and when used only one hour in five, maintained a room at a moderately warm temperature. He asked Fulton to look into the invention and to keep him informed. He went on to congratulate the inventor on the success of his steamboats and wished for him the same success with his torpedoes. "I have more hopes of the mode of destruction by the submarine boat than any other," he went on, "No law of nature opposes it, and in that case nothing is to be despaired of by human invention, nor particularly by yours."[77]

Jefferson continued to be interested in the submarine long after he left public service, forseeing in it a means of maritime protection. Reading Clarke's work on American naval history, Jefferson was reminded of David Bushnell's famous "Turtle". "It was excellently contrived," he commented, "and might perhaps, by improvement, be brought into real use. I do not know the difference between this and Mr. Fulton's submarine boat. But the effectual machine of that kind is not beyond the laws of nature; and whatever is within these, is not to be despaired of. It would be to the United States the consummation of their safety."[78]

For many years Jefferson had attempted to obtain cork oak trees from Europe to introduce their cultivation in the United States, but without success. He had brought a plant from Paris, but it languished for some time and then died. He obtained several parcels of its acorns from a correspondent in Marseilles, but none of them rooted. He continued his endeavors to introduce new plants from other countries, but was greatly disheartened by the apparent lack of interest and cooperation from farmers in the South, the only region in which they could thrive.

He reflected that a quarter of a century had already passed since he shipped about five hundred plants of the "Olive tree of Aix," which he considered to be the finest olives in the world, from France to Southern farmers. No orchard had been planted with them, however, and if any plants survived they were merely curiosities in someone's garden.

He had also sent a grass native to Malta called sulla (Sainfoin), which grew well even without rainfall, but none of it had survived either. Despite his disappointment with the lack of interest in the innovations he had offered, he nonetheless acknowledged the success of Southern farmers in the growing of cotton. He predicted that cotton, due to its cleanliness, would eventually supplant silk as a fiber as well as flax and hemp because of the ease with which it was spun.[79]

Jefferson was frequently asked to review manuscripts in progress as well as published works. One such manuscript was a work on travel by John Melish, a Scottish cartographer and textile manufacturer who traveled in the United States in 1807 and 1809. While Melish was in New York, the Non-Intercourse Act of 1811 effectively destroyed his business, and thereafter he established himself as a merchant in Philadelphia. Jefferson found the manuscript of interest in relation to the description of the Western states and an account of their manufactures and a report on the dispersion of carding and spinning machines. Although formerly not an advocate of great manufactures, he had changed his mind.

In response to Melish's suggestion that the *Notes* be reprinted, Jefferson responded that he no longer considered the possibility. "The work itself," he wrote, "indeed is nothing more than the measure of a shadow, never stationary, but lengthening as the sun advances, and to be taken anew from hour to hour." Someone else would have to undertake the task of bringing such a work up to date for much had changed since it had been written.[80].

In much the same vein as he had written to Melish, he communicated to General Kosciusko, discussing household manufactures. He explained that at Monticello he had acquired the following: for $60 a carding machine, an implement for collecting, cleaning and disentangling cotton fibers in preparation for spinning, which could be operated by a twelve-year-old girl; a spinning machine made for $10 with 6 spindles for wool which could also be operated by a young girl; another spinning machine of twelve spindles for cotton; and a loom and flying shuttle for $25, with which twenty yards per day could be woven. He explained that the two thousand yards of linen, cotton and woolen required each year to clothe his family and servants, he could produce with this machinery costing only $150 and operated by two women and two girls.[81]

In addition to productive farm crops, Jefferson was interested also in useful plants, some of which were poisonous. Dr. Samuel Brown of Lexington, Kentucky, was one of his most faithful correspondents, and had furnished him with many seeds, including Guinea Grass, the pod or cherry pepper, the Friholio or red bean and Capsicum and Galvance peas. He had already experimented with one variety of Capsicum which proved to be too tender for the Virginia climate. Having so many grandchildren and others who might be endangered by the presence of poisonous plants on the premises, however, he concluded that it was too risky to try to plant the Galvance, which Brown called "the round Black nut," not the pea.

He explained that the most elegant poison from plants known to him was a preparation made from jimson weed (*Datura stramonium*) which had been invented by the French at the time of Robespierre. "Every man of firmness carried it constantly in his pocket to anticipate the guillotine," he wrote. "It brings on the sleep of death as quietly as fatigue does the ordinary sleep, without the least struggle or motion. Condorcet, who had recourse to it, was found lifeless on his bed a few minutes after his landlady had left him there, and even the slipper which she had observed half suspended on his foot, was not shaken off. It seems far preferable to the Venesection of the Romans, the Hemlock of the Greeks, and the Opium of the Turks. I have never been able to learn what the preparation is, other than a strong concentration of its lethiferous principle. Could such a mendicament be restrained to self-administration, it ought not to be kept secret. There are ills in life as desperate as intolerable, to which it would be the rational relief, *e.g.* the inveterate cancer. As a relief from tyranny indeed, for which the Romans recurred to it in the times of the emperors, it has been a wonder to me that they did not consider a poignard [dagger] in the breast of the tyrant as a better remedy."[82]

Brown also provided information about the "Freezing Cave" near Winchester, and a memoir on nitre and gunpowder. He described the patented portable vapor bath apparatus devised by Samuel Kennedy Jennings for healing the sick, which was a considerable improvement over the "Indian sweats" devised by the Navajos and other Indian tribes. Brown was convinced that it would be extremely useful in the epidemic of typhoid pleurisy which had then spread through the Western country. Such an "Indian sweat" had been successfully applied to William Bratton, a member of the Lewis and Clark expedition who had become so crippled from back pains and rheumatic stiffness that he was unable to walk.[83]

Jefferson's considerable knowledge of the habits and origins of plants, and the extensiveness of his library on botany, were revealed again and again in his correspondence. As an example, upon receiving a copy of Horatio G. Spafford's *General Geography,* and thanking the author, Jefferson could not resist adding a little criticism. "In passing my eye rapidly over parts of the book," he told Spafford, "I was struck with two passages, on which I will make observations, not doubting your wish, in any future edition, to render the work as accurate as you can. In page 186 you said the potato is a native of the United States. I presume you speak of the irish potato. I have inquired much into the question, and I think I can assure you that plant is not a native of North America. Zimmerman, in his 'Geographical Zoology,' says it is a native of Guiana, and Clavigero, that the Mexicans got it from South America, its native country. The most probable account I have been able to collect is, that a vessel of Sir Walter Raleigh's, returning from Guiana, put into the west of Ireland in distress, having on board some potatoes which they called earth apples. That the season of the year, and circumstances of their being already sprouted, induced them to give them all out there, and they were no more heard or thought of, till they had been spread considerably into that island, whence they were carried over into England, and therefore called the Irish potato. From England they came to the United States, bringing their name with them."[84]

The potato in fact was native to South America from Chile to Colombia but not in Mexico. It was imported to and cultivated in Spain and Italy prior to being brought to Ireland by John Hawkins in about 1563. There it was first grown on Sir Walter Raleigh's estate near Cork and from there introduced into England. It is believed, however, that it was the sweet potato and not the common potato that was brought to Ireland.

To Peale Jefferson continued to extol the virtues of farming, and his enjoyment of it. "I have often thought that if heaven had given me choice of my position and calling," he wrote, "it should have been on a rich spot of earth, well watered, and near a good market for the production of the garden. No occupation is so delightful to me as the culture of the earth, and no culture comparable to that of the garden. Such a variety of subjects, someone always coming to perfection, the failure of one thing repaired by the success of another, & instead of one harvest a continued one through the year."[85]

Despite this optimistic outlook, the war years had brought Jefferson to extremely difficult times. Lack of rain resulted in poor crops and considerable damage to his fields and gardens. Taxes were on the rise, the market for wheat had fallen and his debts had increased alarmingly. Yet Jefferson felt assured that the future would be better.

Although he was now distant from the political scene, during these years of retirement Jefferson remained an avid observer of events overtaking his country. Although he had informed Adams that he had abandoned newspapers in favor of scholarly works, he had by no means lost interest in public affairs and was kept well informed by Madison and Monroe and other friends in government. He strongly supported the war with Great Britain and came to the conclusion that universal military training was necessary. "We must train and classify the whole of our male citizens,' he wrote, "and make military instruction a regular part of collegiate education. We can never be safe till this is done." Thus it may be said that he forecast the institution of the Reserve Officers Training Corps and the draft. His son-in-law was commissioned a colonel in the United States Army, and other members of his family were also involved.[86]

Late in 1814 Monroe informed him that negotations had been resumed at Ghent and that peace was imminent. Subsequently Andrew Jackson successfully defended New Orleans, keeping the Mississippi

River open for American trade. It was not until the summer of 1815 that Jefferson learned the details of the burning of the Capitol and the destruction of the Congressional library. Without hesitation, he offered his own collection of books to replace it, and for many months thereafter he was involved in negotiations to bring the transaction to reality.[87]

CHAPTER XVII

VENERABLE SAGE (1814–1824)

But consider that we do not expect our schools to turn out their alumni already enthroned on the pinnacles of their respective sciences; but only so far advanced in each as to be able to pursue them by themselves, and to become Newtons and Laplaces by energies and perseverances to be continued through life.

Letter from Thomas Jefferson
to Dr. John P. Emmet, 1826.

The invasion of visitors and mail which usurped much of Jefferson's time was not restricted only to the period immediately following his retirement, but continued into his final years. His scientific interests were so well known that he received mail from all parts of the country, and indeed other countries, communications which often included as examples, worms, dead birds, Indian artifacts, animalicules—minute or often microscopic organisms found in moss—and even Hessian flies, all sent for his examination and comment.

"From sunrise to one or two o'clock, and often from dinner to dark, I am drudging at the writing table," Jefferson grumbled to John Adams.[1]

One of his most valuable resources during these final years, of which he made almost daily use, was his polygraph, which he had been constantly using for a dozen years. Its pen frame had become loosened, however, but he was reluctant to attempt to repair it himself. He told Latrobe, "I consider [it] as one of the greatest inventions of the age."[2]

His scientific correspondents brought him a wide range of topics

435

with which to preoccupy his days. The Abbé Correa de Serra furnished a recipe for "purrolani" for making his cisterns impermeable to water. An ore which Jefferson believed to be antimony had been discovered in the neighborhood and he sought to have it analyzed.

The French economist, Jean Baptiste Say, was considering emigrating to the United States, and Jefferson provided him with information about land, labor and other details of the Charlottesville area, where he hoped Say would settle. He was delighted at the prospect of the Frenchman's arrival, but realistically considered him to be of too great an age to make the great change from French society to what Charlottesville had to offer.[3]

When the German geographer and scholar, Christoph Daniel Ebeling, was preparing a work on the geography of the United States, he requested information about Virginia from Jefferson. After warning his correspondent not to trust the section on Virginia in Jedidiah Morse's recent work on American geography, the statesman excused himself from participating because he lacked his library and his full schedule of work on his farm. Jefferson expressed the hope, however, that the work would be translated so that there could be a dispassionate account of the country.[4]

He became indignant over the new methods of classification being advanced in the natural sciences. "Linnaeus's method was received, understood, and conventionally settled among the learned, and was even getting into common use. To disturb it then was unfortunate. The new system attempted in botany by Jussieu, in mineralogy by Haüy, are subjects of the same regret, and so also the non-system of Buffon, the great advocate of individualism in opposition to classification. He would carry us back to the days of Aristotle and Pliny, give up the improvements of twenty centuries, and cooperate with the Neologists in rendering the science of one generation useless to the next by perpetual changes of its language. In botany Wildenow and Persoon have incorporated into Linnaeus the new discovered plants. I do not know whether anyone has rendered us the same service as to his natural history. It would be a very acceptable one."

After commenting on specific mammals that had been recently discovered, he went on, "I have not at all meant to insinuate that that [method of classification] of Linnaeus is intrinsically preferable to those of Blumenbach and Cuvier. I adhere to the Linnaean because it is sufficient as a groundwork, admits of supplementary insertions as new productions are discovered, and mainly because it has got into so general use that it will not be easy to displace it, and still less to find another which shall have the same singular fortune of obtaining the general consent . . . I am not myself apt to be alarmed at innovations recommended by reason. That read belongs to those whose interests or prejudices shrink from the advance of truth and science. My reluctance is to give up an universal language of which we are in possession, without an assurance of general consent to receive another. And the higher the character of the authors recommending it, and the more excellent what they offer, the greater the danger of producing schism."[5]

Visitors to Monticello during the last two decades of the statesman's life invariably commented, sometimes in published writings, about the museum collection he had brought together in the Entrance Hall. He had been assembling Indian artifacts and fossil remains while engaged in writing his *Notes*, and undoubtedly even before that time.

Apparently Jefferson displayed few if any of them until after he had remodeled the mansion and added the Entrance Hall, for none of the earlier visitors mentioned them. He had exhibited some of the same items in the "Mammoth Room" of the President's House during his occupancy, but it was not until his final retirement that he assembled them for display at Monticello.

The collection was well worthy of comment, for it was one of the most extensive and significant privately owned collections of Indian artifacts and natural history specimens of the period. The reactions of visitors ranged from surprise and praise to occasional criticism, but as a whole their published comments provide an invaluable identification, and the only record, of the specific scientific artifacts that Jefferson had brought together.

Among the Indian items were busts of a male and female, sitting in the Indian position; a representation of a battle between the Panis and Osage and a map of the Missouri and its tributary streams, both on dressed buffalo hides; and bows, arrows, quivers, poisoned lances, pipes of peace, wampum belts, moccasins, dresses and cooking utensils of the Mandan and other nations of the Missouri. The natural curiosities consisted of mammoth and other bones, the upper and lower jawbones and tusks of the mastodon and the elephant, horns of elk, moose and deer, a head of the prehistoric mountain ram, a bear's claw, preserved reptiles and insects, petrifactions, crystalizations, minerals and shells. To these were added paintings, engravings, a model of the great pyramid of Egypt, Mexican antiquities, a European coat of mail, a large collection of mathematical and optical instruments and sculpture, including a bust of Jefferson by Ceracchi.[6] (*Figures 33 and 34*)

Jefferson belonged to a great number of agricultural and other scientific societies, many of them foreign. To a correspondent seeking biographical information, he responded, "I could not readily make a statement of the literary societies of which I am a member, they are many and would be too long to enumerate and would savor too much of vanity and pedantry. Would it not be better to say that I am a member of many literary societies in Europe and America?"[7]

After leaving public office, Jefferson continued to receive honors for his support of the sciences. In accepting membership in the Antiquarian Society of Charleston, he noted two of his particular interests which he shared with the Society. "The works of our aboriginal inhabitants have been so perishable, that much of them must have disappeared already. The antiquarian researches, therefore, of the Society, cannot be too soon, or too assiduously directed, to the collecting and preserving what still remain."

He enclosed a sample of the *capsicum*, a genus of tropical plants of the nightshade family cultivated for their berries, which he had just received from Texas, where it was indigenous and perennial. It was a variety different from the *Capsicum minium* found in Charleston, and probably hardier. He explained, "This stimulant being found salutary in a visceral complaint known on the seacoast, the introduction of a hardier variety may be of value."[8]

He was pleased to be elected to membership in the American Antiquarian Society and to be made an honorary member of The New-York Historical Society. In accepting, he noted that "now more than a septuagenary, retired from the active scenes and business of life, I am sensible how little I can contribute to the advancement of the objects of their views; but I shall certainly, and with great pleasure, embrace every occasion which shall occur, of rendering them any services in my power."[9]

On November 23, 1814 at the age of seventy-one, Jefferson resigned as president of the American Philosophical Society, but this did not end his Society activities. In 1818 he was informed that at its recent election, the Society had "done themselves the honor of placing you at the head of the List of their Counsellors. In doing so, they had no wish but to let the world know that you are still willing to be their guide and adviser, to excite confidence, and preserve the respect which it has acquired by being presided by such men as Franklin, Rittenhouse & yourself." Jefferson was not indifferent to the unexpected honor and responded appropriately. He was re-elected Councillor in 1821 and again in 1824, remaining a member until his death.[10]

The Society honored him not only for past services and accomplishments, but also for his work in more recent years in the organization of the Society's Historical and Literary Committee. On March 17, 1815 the Society established a "Committee of History, Moral Science, and General Literature." This was a continuation or revival of the committee originally organized by Jefferson at the first meeting over which he presided in 1797 as one of the very first acts of his presidency of the Society.

This was "A plan for collecting information respecting the Antiquities of N. A."[11]

Jefferson proposed a program of work to be undertaken by the new Historical and Literary Committee to which he promised his cooperation. It was to collect "original MS. many loose sheets of no use by themselves and in the hands of the holders; but of great value when brought into a general depot, open to the use of the future historian or literary inquirer."

As a beginning, he contributed a manuscript providing a geographical and statistical account of the Creek or Muscogee Indians and their country which had been compiled in 1798–99 by Colonel Benjamin Hawkins, and he promised other materials as they came to hand. He promised also to search for the long lost manuscript journal of the Commissioners of 1728 for the North Carolina boundary written by Dr. William Byrd, and which formerly had been in the Westover family's possession. In a series of gifts made over the succeeding years, Jefferson sent the Society Indian vocabularies, documents dealing with American history and geographical descriptions, as well as the papers of the Lewis and Clark expedition.[12]

As soon as a Secretary of War was appointed, Jefferson planned to ask him to have the required calculations made at public expense from the astronomical and geographical papers so that the map of the United States could be corrected for its longitudes and latitudes, and he hoped the Society would publish a digest of the other papers. He offered to send the Indian vocabularies remaining in his possession if the Society's Historical Committee was inclined to publish them.

He explained that although originally he had collected a great number of them, only fragments survived, which Jefferson forwarded a month later. He included a description of how they had been arranged and a digest he had made of them, in addition to Clark's collection, which had been very carefully executed. He also included his own memoir about Louisiana and its boundaries.[13]

At the time that the Congress moved the government to the new Federal City in 1800, it enacted a bill to pay for the costs of transfer of the offices, with a proviso permitting the expenditure of $5000 for books and the preparation of a room to house them in the new Capitol building. The selection of the books was to be made by the Secretary of State and the Clerk of the House. The library was to be available for the use only of members of Congress, and not of the executive and judicial branches.

There was considerable discussion about the subject matter of the books to be purchased, and eventually the selection was limited to books required for making laws. In June an order was sent to London for books on the law, political science and history, and all maps available of the New World.

Jefferson appointed his close friend, John James Beckley, who was serving as Clerk of the House, as the first Congressional librarian at a salary of two dollars a day. Eventually the library grew to 4000 volumes.[14]

These were lost when British troops marched into Washington on August 24, 1814 and set fire to the Capitol building. They took special pains to destroy the national archives and every volume in the library. Within the next month, Jefferson submitted suggestions for the library's rehabilitation, pointing out the difficulties in restoring the library while the war progressed, because of the impossibility of ordering books from England.

He then proposed to make his own collection available to Congress for purchase. Having already planned to give Congress first refusal of his collection after his death, he suggested it could now avail itself of the books because of its need.

His private collection consisted of 6487 volumes, for which he had paid more than $50,000 at the time of purchase. He described his book buying to his friend Samuel Harrison Smith, who served as his agent in the sale of the library to Congress. "While residing at Paris, I devoted every afternoon I was disengaged for a summer or two, in examining all the principal bookstores, turning over every book with my own hand, and putting by everything which related to America, and indeed that was rare and valuable in every science. Besides this, I had standing orders during the whole time that I was in Europe, on it's principal book-marts, particularly Amsterdam, Frankfort, Madrid and London, for such works relating to America as could not be found in Paris."

The prices paid by Congress were based entirely on the size of each book—$10 for a folio,* $6 for a quarto, $3 for an octavo, and $1 for a duodecimo, totaling $23,950 for Jefferson's whole collection.

He was fully aware that the prices paid for the books were considerably below their market value, for he made a selection of twelve volumes as a sample, listing the prices paid for them by Congress with those being asked in London converted to dollars. The market value of the twelve volumes was $1552, for which Congress paid only $297, or approximately one-fifth of the true value.[15]

At Monticello the books had been housed in modular bookcases consisting of long pine boxes stacked one upon another and next to each other, requiring only a face board to be screwed or nailed to the front of the box to convert them into sturdy cases for transporting. The books

---

*Folio is the largest size of book based on the size of the page cut two from a sheet; quarto is the size of the page cut four from a sheet; octavo is the size of the page cut eight from a sheet; and duodecimo the smallest size, based on the size of a page cut twelve from a sheet.

were shipped in ten wagon loads, the last of which arrived in Washington in May 1815.

Jefferson had organized his library around the philosophical scheme devised by Sir Francis Bacon based on the concepts of "the three faculties needed to comprehend knowledge," namely, "Memory," "Reason" and "Imagination," with 44 sub-classifications, a system which the Library retained into the twentieth century.[16]

Despite his distance from affairs of government and of the Patent Office, Jefferson nonetheless could not resist commenting on the claims of the millwright inventor, Oliver Evans. Following the expiration of Evans's first patent for his invention of "Elevators, Conveyors and Hopper-boys," complications developed.

Jefferson engaged in a long correspondence with Isaac McPherson on the question of whether what Evans described in his patent application constituted in fact new inventions. If they were not, then he had no right to prevent others from constructing them. Jefferson pointed out that it was the invention of the machine itself, not the application made of it to any particular purpose, which could be patented. As examples he noted that if a patent were issued for a knife for pointing pens, another had no patent right to the same knife if used for pointing pencils.

In his view, the patent for an invention of a compass for navigating at sea would not allow for the use of the same compass for surveying land, for example. He raised the question of whether the string of buckets which formed part of Evans's invention was first invented by Evans. From his research into the matter, he had discovered that such buckets had been in use from time immemorial. He cited Joseph Shaw's volume of travels and his *Universal History* published in the early eighteenth century, in which he reported having seen such buckets in use in Egypt, and noted numerous other sources.[17]

As another example he mentioned Martin's seed drill, which utilized a band of buckets for elevating the grain from the box into a funnel, with different sizes of buckets for the various kinds of seed. He concluded that there was in fact nothing new in Evans's conveyors except for the fact that his buckets were strung together on a leather strap. Even so, it was to be noted that Martin had used such a leather strap on his seed drill, so that there was nothing original in Evans's invention after all. He agreed, however, that the hopper-boy was original with Evans.

In an illuminating discussion of natural rights and the rights of inventors, he commented, "It would be curious then, if an idea, the fugitive fermentation of an individual brain, could, of natural right, be claimed in exclusive and stable property. If nature had made any one thing less susceptible than all others of exclusive property, it is the action of the thinking power called an idea, which an individual may exclusively possess as long as he keeps it to himself; but the moment it is divulged, it forces itself into the possession of every one, and the receiver cannot dispossess himself of it. Its peculiar character, too, is that no one possesses the less, because every other possesses the whole of it. He who receives an idea from me, receives instruction himself without lessening mine; as he who lights his taper at mine, receives light without darkening me . . . inventions then cannot in nature, be a subject of property. Society may give an exclusive right to the profits arising from them, as an encouragement to men to pursue ideas which may produce utility, but this may or may not be done, according to the will and convenience of society, without claim or complaint from anybody."

He then went on to recount how he himself had a mill built during the period between the issuance of the first and second patents to Evans. He was living in Washington at the time, and left the construction in the hands of his millwright. He was unaware that the millwright had constructed elevators, conveyors and hopper-boys until he received a request from Evans's agent to pay the patent price. No judicial decision had as yet been rendered on the matter of Evans's patent rights, so that Jefferson did not know whether he had a rightful claim at the time. Nonetheless, he paid Evans the old patent price he was asked. Despite their differences, Jefferson esteemed Evans highly, "and deem him a valuable citizen of uncommon ingenuity and usefulness."[18]

Inevitably an exchange of communications developed between Evans and Jefferson concerning what the statesman had written to McPherson. Evans conceded that the chain of buckets and Archimedean screw were old inventions and common property, and Jefferson pointed out that consequently he had no exclusive right to them. Evans claimed that his patent was for his improvement of the manufacture of flour by the application of certain principles, and of such machinery as carried these principles into operation.

"I can conceive how a machine may improve the manufacture of flour," Jefferson responded, "not how a *principle* abstracted from any machine can do it. It must then be the machine, and the principle of that machine, which is secured to you by patent." In such a case, if anyone had the right to use the string of buckets and the Archimedean screw, did Evans then have the sole right to apply these principles to the manufacture of flour?

"But if we have the right to use these three things separately, I see nothing in reason, or in the patent law, which forbids our using them all together. A man has a right to use a saw, an axe, a plane, separately; may he not combine their uses on the same piece of wood?"[19]

He held strong convictions that "The abuse of the frivolous patents is likely to cause more inconvenience than is countervailed by those really useful. We know not to what uses we may apply implements which have been in our hands before the birth of our government, and even the discovery of America."[20]

Jefferson was provided with many opportunities to apply his mechanical ingenuity in improving and repairing equipment on the farm and shops on his premises. After receiving a new carding machine he had ordered from Aldrichs and Dixon, he discovered they had been unable to make a perfect roll. He successfully improved it by replacing the handle of the great cylinder with a six-inch whirl "to be driven by a two-foot wheel and band so that the hand will make one revolution where it now makes four. The addition will be attached by two screws only, so that if it does not answer, it will be taken off and leave the machine exactly as it is now."[21]

In Philadelphia, Charles Willson Peale had become anxious for retirement. Having reached the decision to dispose of his Museum, he consulted with Jefferson as to the best way to accomplish the task. Jefferson responded that first of all the Museum should be sold to the greatest advantage of Peale, and secondly that the collections should not be dispersed. If profit was a factor, then the purchaser must be required to keep it in Philadelphia where the residents would ensure its maintenance.

He informed Peale that inasmuch as the latter would soon be engaged in farming, he could make free use of his mouldboard, as indeed all the world might, "having never thought of monopolizing by patent any useful idea which happens to offer itself to me; and the permission to do this is doing a great deal more harm than good."

He commented "There is a late instance in this State of a rascal going through every part of it, and swindling the mill-owners, under a patent of two years old only, out of 20,000 dollars for the use of winged-gudgeons which they have had in their mills for twenty years, every one preferring to pay ten dollars unjustly rather than be dragged into a Federal court, one, two, or three hundred miles distant."

Jefferson had not yet seen an example of the corn sheller with two cylinders which Peale described to him, noting that wooden cylinders for machines had a tendency to become deranged due to the spring of the timber, particularly of white oak, for which reason he preferred pine.

He commented that a corn-crushing machine was being used in his area, for which Oliver Evans had obtained a patent, although the exact same machine had been made and marketed by a smith in Georgetown for the past sixteen years for crushing plaster. He had in fact made one for Jefferson twelve years previously, long before Evans obtained his patent. The only difference was that the smith fixed his crusher horizontally and Evans vertically. "Yet I choose to pay Evans's patent price for one rather than be involved in a lawsuit of two or three hundred dollars' cost."

For his home industries he expressed a preference for the spinning jenny over the Arkwright machines because it was simpler, cheaper and easier to repair. He also devised equipment for "fulling", by means of which "Two hands fulls 20 yards in two hours."[22]

Jefferson was particularly bothered by the fact that he knew so little about the steam engine. He was informed about its original simple form constructed by the English blacksmith Thomas Newcomen and the English military engineer Thomas Savery, but had not pursued its later advances. Consequently, when George Fleming asked him for an appraisal of his improvement of the steam engine, the elder statesman felt incapable of judging its merits, and reported he had no valid opinion on the matter.

In his view it appeared to be useful, however, and to have "the valuable properties of simplicity, cheapness and accomodation to the small and numerous calls of life." In the event that when in production the engine appeared to be feasible in operation, then "the importance of your construction will be enhanced by the consideration that a smaller agent, applicable to our daily concerns, is infinitely more valuable than the greatest which can be used only for great objects. For these interest the few alone, the former many."

He added that at one time he had contemplated the possibility of utilizing the steam from a pot kept boiling on the kitchen stove until it had accumulated enough to provide a sufficient number of strokes to raise the water from an adjacent well. This would furnish an adequate amount of water for the daily chores of the kitchen, such as washing linen, kneading bread, beating the hominy, churning the butter, turning the spit and such other activities as required a mechanical motion. If this were possible, he thought, the labor saved in the kitchen could be employed in the fields.

When he had suggested it to the mechanical engineer James Rumsey, the latter concurred that it had possibility and promised to explore it. However, Rumsey's death came too soon thereafter. Such an application, Jefferson considered, would be even more valuable to ordinary life than the thirty pairs of millstones that Boulton and Watt turned by one of their steam engines.

In time Jefferson discovered that flax had proven to be harmful to the fields and was of relatively little production, so he turned to the cultivation of hemp. This, he noted, was not only abundantly productive, but would continue to grow on the same spot permanently. However, the breaking up and beating of it by hand had proven to be so slow and laborious that he had resorted to purchasing cotton for the shirts of his farm hands. Recently the price of cotton had risen so high, though, that he was forced to resort once more to hemp culture.

He invented a hemp-break, a device which rendered the procedure simple and inexpensive, to be attached to a threshing machine, and he illustrated how it could be done. He placed a wallower and shaft upon the cogs on the horizontal horse-wheel's upper face, thus giving motion to the threshing apparatus. He placed another wallower and shaft on the opposite side of the same wheel, through which, and near its outer end, he passed a cross-arm which projected fifteen inches on each side. He situated a heavy duty hemp break with a particularly massive head block four feet high nearly under the cross-arm. He then fixed a strong pin in front near its upper end by means of which the cross-arm lifted and let fall the break twice in every revolution of the wallower. Hemp stalks were fed manually into the break, and, he noted, "a little person holds under the head block a large twist of the hemp which has been broken, resembling a twist of tobacco, but larger, where it is more perfectly beaten than I have ever seen done by hand. If the horse-wheel has one hundred and forty-four cogs, the wallower eleven rounds, and the horse goes three times round in a minute, it will give about eighty strokes in a minute."

Jefferson had arranged a break to be moved by means of the gate of his saw-mill, which broke and beat at the rate of two hundred pounds a day. To overcome the inconveniences of such an arrangement, he eventually successfully substituted a horse. He noted that such a device had been long needed by hemp growers, and after he had tested it thoroughly he planned to describe it in an anonymous article in the public papers to make certain that it would not be pre-empted by "some interloping patentee."[23]

During these years of permanent residency, Jefferson directed his attention to his home's indoor needs as well as those of the plantation. He continued to search for a clockmaker and watchmaker who would be willing to settle in Charlottesville. He was impelled as much by his own multiple needs for such a craftsman as his desire to have all the necessary crafts represented in his neighboring community. On his own account, the necessity for shipping his numerous timepieces for cleaning and repair to Philadelphia was time consuming, expensive and hazardous to the mechanisms.

He was hopeful of success at last when he was informed by his old friend Peale that he had finally managed to interest a young watchmaker in Philadelphia named McIlhenny in coming to Charlottesville. After having heard nothing further on the matter for some time, Jefferson became anxious to know whether the watchmaker was still planning to come, since, as he informed Peale, "I have a good deal also which might employ him until work should come in."[24]

Finally he received a letter from McIlhenny confirming that he planned to move, and Jefferson looked forward to his arrival. McIlhenny remained as an overnight guest at Monticello, then Jefferson took him into Charlottesville, where he presented the young man with his recommendation to the principal citizens. He found him a shop he could rent in a desirable location, and arranged with the landlord for his year's rent and board. He assured McIlhenny that he would provide any further necessary assistance until he could stand on his own feet.

When he left, McIlhenny promised that he would report to Monticello on Monday to repair several clocks and as many watches as needed attention. On Sunday morning, however, without a word of explanation, McIlhenny departed on the stage with his baggage. On his way through Staunton he called upon the local clockmaker Logan and then went on. He had left a letter for Jefferson informing him of his decision not to settle in Charlottesville, but the letter was not received at Monticello until a month later.[25]

Jefferson was forced to continue to avail himself of the services of Logan, the only clockmaker in Albemarle County. Soon, however, he was able to report to Peale that despite McIlhenny's defection, all was well because of the arrival in Charlottesville of Louis Leschot, a Swiss watchmaker.

Leschot arrived with recommendations from Patterson and a Mr. Harlaer, and "he completely knocks down the opposition bungler who comes from Staunton [Logan] to contest the ground with Mr. McIlhenny, gets more work than he can do, and sells more watches than he could have done in Philadelphia. Brought up among the mountains of Switzerland he is delighted with ours." Upon their deaths, Leschot and his wife were buried in the family burial ground at Monticello.[26]

Jefferson was repeatedly consulted by others on the subject of surveying and mapping. Captain A. Partridge of the Corps of Engineers at West Point sent him calculations of the altitudes of some of the mountains in the north just at the time that Jefferson was inquiring about the height of the White Mountains in New Hampshire, presumed to be the highest in the maritime states. He was planning to measure the height of the Peaks of Otter in Virginia, which he believed were the highest of any east of the Mississippi except for the White Mountains when measured from their base, and not much shorter.

In Jefferson's view, the method of measuring heights by means of the barometer was convenient, although just what degree of accuracy it furnished was not yet known. He considered that this manner of measuring the height of a mountain from its base achieved a different degree of merit than the measurement of the mountain's height above sea level when that is distant. As an example he had noted that the height of Monticello from its base to be 580 feet, and its base to be 310 feet 8 inches above sea level. He believed the former to be accurate, but knowledge of the different falls of water from Monticello to Richmond, a distance of some seventy-five miles, was but 170 or 180 feet, and from Richmond to the sea was a distance of one hundred miles, all tide-water and through level country. He did not believe it was 435 feet, as theory indicated, and not even a quarter of it.

He concluded that Jonathan Williams's calculations reckoned at the foot of the Blue Ridge could not be accurate. He was convinced that "Results so different prove that for distant comparisons of height, the barometer is not to be relied on according to any theory yet known." Whereas measurements of the summit of a mountain from its base were reliable, those between its summit and sea level were not.

After having read Williams's barometrical estimates of the heights of mountains, Jefferson realized that his own calculations had made the Blue Ridge Mountains somewhat higher than the heights achieved by Williams. On the basis of his own observations and those made by others, he concluded that the Blue Ridge, on its south side, "is the highest ridge in our country compared with it's base."[27]

At the time that Jefferson was preoccupied with these observations, Thomas W. Maury consulted Jefferson with a proposal for a geographical map of the United States that would include a mineralogical survey and statistical tables. Jefferson expressed some doubts about the desirability of the undertaking as an excessively ambitious combination of objectives.

As to statistical tables, he believed that the recent government census provided the best model, except that it was not sufficiently comprehensive, and should also have indicated the proportion of the population employed in agriculture and in trades. Such a listing might present difficulties, however, inasmuch as some of the population had double employment. Finally, he advised that to compile the geographical content required assembling private surveys for each region, as well as supplementary surveys indicating roads, towns, habitations and water courses.[28]

When the Virginia legislature directed that a general map of the state of Virginia be made, Governor Wilson C. Nicholas also turned to Jefferson for advice about how to proceed. Jefferson suggested that it should consist of a combination of four surveys, i.e., a topographical survey by county, a general survey of the state's boundaries and its prominent features such as rivers and mountains, an astronomical survey made to correct the other surveys and a mineralogical survey. He cautioned that the competence of surveyors to be employed should first be determined by the mathematical faculty of the College of William and Mary. He provided specifications for each type of survey, the scales in which they were to be drawn, and the instruments to be used. He proposed that the engineer, Ferdinand Rudolph Hassler, who had been appointed to make a comprehensive survey of the coastal United States, might be able to undertake the state map using the instruments he had purchased for the government in England.

Jefferson considered the astronomical survey to be the most important of all. "Measures and rhumbs taken on the spherical surface of the earth," he advised, "cannot be represented on a plane surface of paper without astronomical corrections; and paradoxical as it may seem, it is nevertheless true, that we cannot know the relative position of two places on the earth, but by interrogating the sun, moon, and stars. The observer must, therefore, correctly fix, in longitude and latitude, all remarkable points from distance to distance."

He could not resist the temptation to suggest that the universal equatorial instrument might be required. "This instrument set to the observed latitude," he noted, "gives the meridian of the place." Although observation of lunar distances did not provide it at sea or on land in Europe, "here, where our geography is still to be fixed by a portable apparatus only, we are obliged to resort, as at sea, to the lunar observations, with the advantage, however, of a fixed meridian. And although the use of a meridian in these observations is a novelty yet, placed under new circumstances, we must countervail their advantages by whatever new resources they offer."[29]

Among Jefferson's most prized possessions was a traveling thermometer, which enabled him to continue to conduct climatological observations even while traveling and away from home. Made by Dollond, the eminent London maker, it was little larger than a mechanical pencil or fountain pen, and would fit into any pocket with ease. It was the first such instrument Jefferson could use during travel, and he was delighted with it. He may have purchased it in 1786 when he visited Dollond's shop in London, or it may in fact be the gift of a thermometer he received from Payne Todd.

Jefferson gracefully acknowledged "the handsome keep-sake which has amused me much, and not the less by the puzzle it has afforded me, to find out the method of rectifying it. I at length discovered it, and that it was only necessary to loosen a little a single screw to throw it out of geer [sic] and to throw it again after setting the index, it was exactly 10 [degrees] wrong."[30]

In 1817 Jefferson became involved with the Albemarle County Agricultural Society, organized by a group of his friends and neighbors. James Madison, Thomas Mann Randolph and later his grandson, Thomas Jefferson Randolph, were members. He drew up a platform for the new organization, entitled "Objects for the Attention and Enquiry of Agriculture." These included the production of such staples as wheat, tobacco and hemp, improvement of the soil, care of livestock and development of farm machinery as well as "the destruction of noxious quadrupeds, fowls, insects, and reptiles." He insisted that members should file reports of bad practices as well as good ones. The Society prospered as similar societies elsewhere in the state and in other states began to cooperate with it and exchanged publications.

Based on the success of the meetings held in Albemarle County, Jefferson proposed a "Scheme for a System of Agricultural Societies." A centrally located society would serve as a repository for communications from the others, select those communications that were generally useful, extract and digest useful data from them and then condense the information into a practical form for distribution at a reasonable cost. In this proposal was the genesis of what later would be established as the Department of Agriculture under the Federal government. The connected system of agricultural societies that he visualized in fact reflects the present system of extension agencies of the state Department of Agriculture and the affiliated state Grange societies.

The Society's primary purpose was to share information on agricultural topics and to encourage research and publication for the common good of the agricultural community. Active in the early stages of the formation of the Society, Jefferson became less so as he became increasingly preoccupied with the design of the University of Virginia.[31]

Jefferson had made considerable use of the odometer he had obtained from James Clarke in 1807, and a decade later the inventor communicated with him concerning a device that Jefferson had visualized based on the principle of the odometer, for use in surveying. He had described it as a "machine that could lay down the platt of a road by the traveling of a carriage over it." Having concluded after extensive experimentation that it was not practical, he discussed it with Clarke, who eventually succeeded in producing an instrument to be attached to a carriage wheel that fulfilled the purpose Jefferson intended.[32]

As might be anticipated, Jefferson responded with enthusiasm. "I have but occasionally looked at the subject as a desideratum; but never seriously aiming at it's solution myself," he responded.

When Clarke proposed to apply for a patent for his original form of the odometer, he asked Jefferson for comments on its performance from his own experience. The statesman was enthusiastic in its praise. "I think it is as simple as we can expect such a machine to be," he wrote. "I can only say I have known no Odometer either in Europe or America, resembling it in any degree, or at all to be compared with it in all its characters and merits taken together." Clarke was granted a patent in 1818.[33]

When Jefferson's Clarke odometer was damaged the following year, he requested replacement parts from the inventor. He had lost the rod and ratchet wheel connecting the carriage wheel to the odometer and asked Clarke for a measured sketch so that he could have them replaced. Clarke responded by sending him the parts required which could be shaped to fit.[34]

Several months later Jefferson was delighted to receive from Clarke samples of cotton and coffee grown in Liberia, that part of Africa that was then being colonized with free blacks from the United States.[35]

It is a curious coincidence that in 1820 another Virginia inventor, James Deneale of Dumfries County, claimed to have perfected and patented a "land mapper" or instrument for mapping lands, similar to the one proposed by Jefferson to Clarke. Deneale asked Jefferson's evaluation of the instrument, which he had previously sent for comments to someone in Fredericksburg. The recipient, Deneale reported, had returned it with the words, "the Idea of the Mapper I am Inclined is not a new one. Mr. Girardin was at my house 6 or seven years ago he lived at that time in the neighborhood of Monticello and was intimate with Mr. Jefferson as near as my Recollections favors me at so remote a period. I think it was [he who told me] that Mr. Jefferson used something similar to your Mapper in plotting fields."

Deneale then explained that he could in good conscience have claimed to have been the inventor of the instrument before receiving the information from Fredericksburg. He felt, however, that inasmuch as it had been suggested that the instrument was based on Jefferson's method of surveying, he felt compelled to inform him of it. After examining the Deneale instrument, Jefferson concluded that it was in no way similar to the method of plotting he had discussed with Girardin some years previously. (Document 13)

"That was on the usual mode of course & distance, and was merely a substitution of East & West lines instead of Meridians, transforming these lines from station to station by the triangular parallel ruler, & applying the protractor to the edge of the ruler, at the new station instead of drawing the line actually on the paper. This method is quicker, neater, and less liable to error than the common, but is a more manual abridgement of trouble, not at all claiming the honors of invention. Having never been in the practice of plotting in the way to which your instrument is applicable, I cannot judge of the degree of convenience to be derived from its use."[36]

Deneale was granted a patent for his invention of a "Mapping Land Instrument" in August 1820, a month after Jefferson's communication. Although apparently it was a most ingenious and useful advance in surveying and mapping, nothing more is known of it, and neither descriptions nor examples have survived.[37]

From this time on, Jefferson turned his attention almost exclusively to the subject of education, and to the planning of the new University he had conceived. In this connection he expressed himself also on education for women, a subject which had not been widely discussed in his time. "A plan of female education has never been a subject of systematic contemplation with me," he confessed to Nathaniel Burwell. He was concerned with it only to the degree that it related to the education of his daughters. Since he assumed that they would be spending their lives in a country environment with little opportunity for further study, he had attempted to obtain for them the most solid education possible which would enable them to train their own children.[38]

Jefferson had first begun to contemplate the establishment of a new institution of learning for Virginia as early as 1779. He visualized a university "in which all the branches of science useful to *us*, and *at this day*, should be taught in their highest degree, and that this institution should be incorporated with the College and funds of William and Mary. But what are the sciences useful to us, and at this day thought useful to anybody? A glance over Bacon's *arbor scientiae* will show the foundation for this question, and how many of his ramifications of science is now lopped off as nugatory."

Jefferson explained that in preparation for the new University, he was taking the trouble to determine which branches of science were considered useful, and asked others who were concerned with education, such as Dr. Thomas Cooper, for suggestions.[39]

From about 1819 onwards, Jefferson's attention was directed for the most part to the realization of his final dream. A state university in Virginia, he hoped, would succeed and take its place among the foremost institutions of learning in the country. He assisted in the revival of the Albemarle Academy, which had been chartered in 1803 and converted to Central College in 1816 by act of the Virginia Assembly.

The cornerstone was laid in the following year, but before students were admitted, the Assembly passed a bill for the establishment of a state university, and Jefferson concentrated his efforts to make certain that Central College would become that university. In February 1818, the General Assembly appropriated $15,000 to found the state university, and appointed a commission with Jefferson as chairman to proceed with the project.

Despite strong opposition from other counties, the Rockfish Gap Report was adopted in in the following year, Albemarle County was chosen as the site and Jefferson's designs were accepted. Jefferson was elected to the Board of Visitors and later was named Rector of the new University, a position which enabled him to supervise the construction, to choose the faculty and contents of the library and to prescribe the courses of study.[40]

He became in effect the self-appointed architect of the University at every level. He not only chose the site, but personally wrote the deed for the land and himself laid out the grounds. Jefferson went into the field with Dinsmore, his master builder, and with Bacon, his overseer, to look over the area and survey it. After Dinsmore managed to find some shingles which he split to make pegs, Jefferson placed the first peg and directed the line to be carried to a second peg, and in this manner the foundation of the building was outlined. He then instructed Bacon to assemble ten able-bodied men, presumably from the farm staff at Monticello, and to commence work. Jefferson also supplied the bricks and supervised the construction.

The corner stone for what is now Pavilion VII was laid by President Monroe on October 6, 1817. Thereafter Jefferson rode to the site every day—except in inclement weather—to observe the construction.[41]

When Jefferson had conceived his plan for building the University some years earlier, he expressed the view that the greatest danger inherent in new colleges "will be their overbuilding, many attempting a large house in the beginning, sufficient to contain the whole institution. Large houses are always ugly, inconvenient, exposed to accident by fire, and bad in cases of infection. A plain small house for the school and lodging of each professor is best, these connected by covered ways out of which the rooms of the student should open would be best. These may then be built only as they shall be wanting. In fact an University should not be a house but a village," which was to become known as his "Academic Village."[42]

He consulted both William Thornton and Benjamin Henry Latrobe while preparing his design of the University. He asked Thornton to submit sketches, explaining "what we wish, is that these pavilions, as they will show themselves above the dormitories, shall be models of taste and good architecture, and of a variety of appearance, no two alike, so as to serve as specimens for the architectural lecturer." Thus they would serve a double purpose. Since Thornton's sketches did not meet entirely with his approval, he then discussed the project with Latrobe. The architect suggested the addition of a dominant central building, from which the concept of the Rotunda emerged.

Jefferson situated the Rotunda at the summit, with a view of the great space below it overlooked through its columns. For the one end of the quadrangle which remained open, Jefferson proposed the addition of an arboretum of exotic trees and shrubs. It never materialized, however, because other buildings eventually usurped the intended space.

The Rotunda was conceived as a temple of learning, in which the library would be housed. Its domed roof was to be surmounted with a wind vane in the form of a great quill pen. The large circular room above the main floor became the library, the columns of which supported an upper gallery where the books were shelved. It was lighted by fourteen windows and a skylight. The working tables and benches were curved to conform with the shape of the room. Three oval rooms in the basement were set aside for religious worship, drawing, music and related endeavors.

For the capitals of the columns of the Rotunda, Jefferson had planned to use native stone, but after several experimental samples were cut, he discovered that "on trial the stone we had counted on in the neighborhood of the University was found totally unsusceptible of delicate work." Consequently, marble capitals were ordered from Italy. When they arrived in 1825, a heavy duty was imposed by the government on the imported stone, a duty which was eventually remitted in a special bill passed by Congress.[43]

The planning for the University provided Jefferson at last with an opportunity to design not only the observatory he had failed to build on Montalto, but also an unusual teaching dome. Reflecting on the strong interest he had maintained in astronomy throughout his life, he found the subject to be beneficial at three levels. First of all, he explained, astronomy provided a means of understanding the architecture of the universe, a preoccupation fundamental to the study of natural philosophy in his time. Secondly, observational astronomy was to be indulged in as a pleasurable avocation as and when time and facilities permitted.

Finally and most importantly, he stressed, astronomy provided the means for achieving greater precision in surveying and mapping required not only for the definition of personal properties but also of national boundaries. He was among the handful of men of his time who combined an understanding of the theoretical with a competent practical knowledge of the subject, and an awareness of its potential applications.

It is not surprising, therefore, that in his Rockfish Gap Report for the projected University, Jefferson had emphasized the study of astronomy, which he considered to be quite as important as the study of architecture. He did not at that time propose the erection of an astronomical observatory, but instead he contemplated the utilization of one of the University buildings for teaching astronomy by object lesson. He selected the interior of the dome of the Rotunda for the purpose, and visualized it as a form of planetarium.

In a notebook entry, he sketched the concave ceiling, proposing that it was "to be painted sky-blue, and spangled with gilt stars in their position and magnitude copied exactly from any selected hemisphere of our latitude." He may have been inspired by the imaginary cenotaph dedicated to Isaac Newton designed by Étienne-Louis Boullée.

He also proposed the construction of an elaborate teaching device by means of which the instructor would be seated in an ordinary saddle attached to the end of a boom which would enable him to move about to any point of the ceiling to adjust the stars in their appropriate positions, and to lecture while doing so.

On his sketch, he marked off the inner surface of 90° of the dome, and designated the boom to be made of a white oak sapling of proper strength, "its heel working in the center of the sphere, by a compound joint admitting motion in any direction like a ball and socket." A rope suspending the small end of the boom passed over a pulley attached to the ceiling at the zenith and the excess hung to the floor so that by its means the boom could be raised or lowered.

An ordinary saddle with stirrups was fixed, in which the operator was seated and could, by manipulating the rope, move himself to any point of the concave. He described the machinery for locating the stars in excruciating detail.[44] (*Document 18*)

This teaching device was never installed in the Rotunda, but it is interesting to trace its concept from its inspiration derived from Jefferson's reading at an early age. The dome was a deliberate imitation of the Pantheon in Rome, with which Jefferson was familiar from his reading of Dio Cassius, in which the author suggested that the Pantheon "is called thus possibly because it included images and many gods in its statues, amongst them those of Ares and Aphrodite; but I believe that the reason is the similarity of its cupola-form to the heavens."

An undocumented source for the quotation by Cassius states that the coffers of the dome had been decorated with stars. Because the coffer decoration ended some distance beyond the skylight, it was suggested by restorers that originally the Pantheon had a canopy or shell.

The use Jefferson planned for the ceiling of the Rotunda may also have been inspired by an arrangement which he undoubtedly recalled from his reading about the *tholus* with moving stars described in Varro's work on agriculture. He certainly was familiar with its description in the later work by Robert Castell on Roman architecture.[45]

Another source of inspiration may have been Seneca, an author whose works were never far from Jefferson's hand. The Roman author described the *Domus aurea* of the large octagonal domed dining hall of the "Golden House" of Nero in Rome, the hall of which revolved like the world. Seneca described a mechanism by means of which both the paneling and the framework below it revolved, moving in opposite directions. He wrote about "a ceiling of movable panels that it presents one appearance after another, thereof changing as often as the courses."

This is a prospect that would have delighted Jefferson, and the fact that he did not install it at the University could only have been due to the difficulty of construction and the excessive cost of such a project.[46]

This teaching "dome of heaven" in the Rotunda was quite distinct from Jefferson's other astronomical project for the university—an observatory—a project which had been at the back of his mind throughout the years of planning and construction. Undoubtedly he was influenced to proceed slowly with this addition because of the cost involved in constructing such a structure which would at the same time be suitable for its intended purpose and yet be proportionate to other parts of the University complex.

In 1820 Jefferson calculated the probable cost of the observatory to be at least $10,000 and possibly $12,000. The only means of realizing such a sum was to utilize the remainder of the subscription funds, and supplement them with the rents anticipated from the dormitories and hotels after the University was open. Although he might have been inclined to follow this plan, others did not agree, and it was not long before any prospect of using this income for an observatory had diminished.[47]

Three years later, Jefferson again turned his attention to the construction of an observatory. He realized that the erection of a new building for the purpose was out of the question because of lack of funds, so he considered the possibility of converting for the purpose a house on Monroe Hill belonging to the University which was then occupied by the Proctor. Because of its elevation and isolation, its situation made it particularly adaptable. This possibility was not to materialize either, however.[48]

During the next several years Jefferson made an intensive study of all the principal astronomical observatories then existing throughout the world, with a view to identifying and selecting their best features to be incorporated in his design for an observatory for the University. His plan specified that the structure should be "so solid in its construction, with a foundation and walls so massive as not to be liable to tremble with the wind, walking, &c." or affected by vibration from any possible source.

The installation was to terminate in a cupola high enough to house long telescopes and protect them from the weather. The cupola also must have ample apertures in all directions so that observations could be made of all points of the horizon. Withal, the building was to be of the least height possible.[49]

He proceeded to lay out his plan on grille paper, dividing the interior into four angular rooms. On the reverse side of his paper he noted his specifications. Each of the rooms was to be eighteen feet in diameter and eighteen feet in height, dimensions that he specified were to determine all others. He then listed his specific requirements. He noted that the observatories of the major European cities were necessarily tall in order to overlook adjacent buildings. As an example, the Paris Observatory was eighty feet high.

The observatory building was to be surrounded by a *terras* [terrace] seventy feet square, four and one-half feet high, to be filled solidly with stone laid dry and compact, and the surface of which was to be paved. He prescribed the same treatment for the floors of the rooms, the doors of which were to be arched in such a manner as to unite the four octagonal rooms to form a solid body.

The walls were to be two and one-half feet in thickness, those of the middle rooms to be vaulted together at the top, and the hollow between the hemisphere and the square formed by the walls was to be honeycombed with cross arches having crowns that were straight and level with the vault's crown.

The crown of the vault was to rise a little above the top of the roof, providing a paved and solid terrace which commanded a wide horizon. Of particular interest was Jefferson's requirement that

"the Cupola cover should have a cylindrical body of thin light frame moveable on pulley wheels at bottom in a circular groove, the top a hollow hemisphere, lightly ribbed and covered with tin, the two together high enough to cover a long refractor, of 15 f. for example, this moveable cover should be cut vertically into 2. halves from top to bottom, and the radius of one half should be less than that of the other, and move in an inner groove so that one may be shut into the other, leaving half of the vault of the heavens open to view, thus [DRAWING]. Over the wall of the mural quadrant must be a fissure in the roof closed with shutters water tight.[50]

Whether this design was entirely his conception, which seems likely, or based on others already existing in Europe, cannot be determined. In any case, it is intriguing in that it anticipated the astronomer's every need. "This building is proposed for the ordinary use of the Astronomical professor and his school," Jefferson went on to explain, "and should be placed on the nearest site proper for it, & convenient to the University. The hill on which the old buildings stand seems to be the best . . . The mountain belonging to the University was purchased with a view to a permanent establishment of an Observatory, with an Astronomer resident at it, employed solely in the business of Observation. But I believe a site on the nearest mountain in the s.w. ridge, Montalto for example, would be better, because of its command of the fine horizon to the East."[51]

At some later date Jefferson added a note to the margin of this sketch, "See an infinitely better plan by Hassler" which had been published in the *Transactions* of the American Philosophical Society. As a consequence of interest expressed by President James Madison and former Secretary of the Treasury Alexander J. Dallas, in 1816 Hassler, as Superintendent of the U.S. Coast Survey, had designed an astronomical observatory to be erected in a small building on the hill north of the Capitol building in what was then the center of the city of Washington.

It was to accommodate a five-foot transit instrument, an astronomical clock, two eighteen-inch repeating circles, "the large telescopes," a six-foot zenith sector, all of which had already been ordered by Hassler from the London instrument maker, Edward Troughton. The observatory was to serve as a center for the storage of the government's chronometers and other instruments when not in use, and for housing the government's standard weights and measures as well as an appropriate library.[52]

In his article Hassler included drawings and specifications for a building forty-two feet in the direction of the parallel and twenty-eight feet in the direction of the meridian. The featured instrument was to be the transit instrument which was to occupy the center of the space. He provided careful specifications for the construction of the building and every part of it including bases, placement of instruments and the location and construction of windows and the roof. Like Jefferson, he visualized a roof that could be opened, although Hassler's consisted of five double shutters of strong sheet tin, which would slide out from the center to both sides.[53]

Jefferson was pleased to receive a copy of Hassler's published papers. "Attentive, in everything, to what I can find in it which may be useful to our university (now the only object and occupation of my life)," he informed Hassler, "I singled out your plan for an observatory, which, for its simplicity, solidity, and every aptitude for its purposes, and for its economy, presents at once what I had, for some time, thought of requesting some kind friend in Europe to procure for me."[54]

He eventually deposited the copy of the *Transactions* in the University library, with a note recommending Hassler's plan as eminently appropriate for the university whenever it became possible to consider the construction of an observatory. He discussed Hassler's design of a flat roof, and suggested replacing it with one of a different form, similar to the roof at Monticello. Hassler later noted that in his paper the flat roof was only hinted at, inasmuch as he agreed that such a type of roofing was not appropriate for an observatory.[55]

Jefferson finally reached the conclusion that it was not necessary for the site of the observatory to be at a very high altitude, inasmuch as the skyline of the University was sufficiently elevated above other interfering habitations and obstructions. A site on the reservoir mountain suggested itself because it had all the requisites, except that the most remote limit of the eastern skies would be obscured by the mountains of the Southwest Range. At one point, Jefferson apparently considered the likelihood of placing the observatory on the top of one of the peaks in this Range. (*Document 16*)

As part of this project, Jefferson provided Charles Bonneycastle with a copy of his "Ideas on the subject of a Meridian for the University." Bonnycastle, the son of a noted mathematician, had been appointed professor of natural philosophy of the new University.[56] (*Document 17*)

The observatory was not to materialize within Jefferson's lifetime, despite the considerable effort he had expended on the project. In about March 1828 a small observatory building was erected on the reservoir mountain, but it was never properly equipped for making observations. In 1859 the building was torn down and the building materials carted away to be used for construction elsewhere.[57]

A small brick building was subsequently erected on a knoll just south of Monroe Hill to serve the University for astronomical observations. It was equipped with the necessary instruments and apparatus made by Isaiah Lukens of Philadelphia, and placed in the charge of Professor Robert Patterson, who made observations from this facility and used it extensively also for his classes in natural philosophy.[58]

Jefferson's dream for a University observatory was eventually realized with the dedication in 1885 of the Leander McCormick Observatory. It was erected on Mount Jefferson on the site which he had designated for the purpose. It was equipped with a 26¼-inch objective lens and telescope made by Alvin Clark & Sons and a dome forty-five feet in diameter made by Warner & Swasey.

As the construction of the University was nearing completion, Jefferson was alarmed by the news that a proposal had been made to move the College of William and Mary to Richmond, there to re-found the University with schools of theology and medicine. Jefferson had visualized Norfolk as the potential center for training in medicine. Acting quickly, he led such a skillful and vigorous opposition that the proposal to move the College to Richmond was defeated.[59]

Plans for a two-year medical school at the University of Virginia were developed, although no provision was made for a hospital. It was the first full-time, state-supported university-based chair of medicine. In 1825 Jefferson arranged to bring Dr. Robley Dunglison from England to be the University of Virginia's first and only professor of medicine. Dunglison was given responsibilities for anatomy, surgery, the history of the progress and the theories of medicine, materia medica, physiology and pharmacy. He conducted his classes in Pavilion X on the Lawn until the first medical building, the Anatomical Theatre designed by Jefferson, was completed in 1827.[60]

Another of the candidates proposed for the faculty was Dr. Robert Adrain, professor of mathematics at Columbia College in New York. His name was suggested to Jefferson by the New York physician Dr. David Hosack. Jefferson responded with regret that it was not the University's plan to attempt to entice capable faculty from other institutions of learning, even though Adrain's "mathematical talents are well known to be of the first grade of that science in the US," the University was committed beyond retraction.

"The [Board of] Visitors of our University," he went on, "at their last session, came to a determination to open the institution at the beginning of the next year. They did not think it honorable, or even moral, to allure from other sister-seminaries the distinguished characters engaged with them . . . nor did they see in the unemployed portion of science in the US. a prospect of obtaining among them Professors of the first grade of qualifications in their several lines. they took measures therefore for procuring such from Europe, which measures are . . . too far advanced to be changed, & not leaving them therefore at liberty to accept of any particular offers."[61]

His choice for the astronomy post was Nathaniel Bowditch. Jefferson was greatly impressed with Bowditch's achievements, and delighted that the United States had such a capable observer. "On the other side of the water they have great advantages in their well-established observatories," he wrote, "the magnificent instruments provided for them, and the leisure and information of their scientific men. The acquirements of Mr. Bowditch in solitude and unaided by these advantages, do him great honor."

After acknowledging a copy of Bowditch's pamphlet on Stewart's formula for determining the sun's distance from the motions of the moon's apsides, Jefferson admitted it to be "much above my mathematical stature." He described to Bowditch the plan for the University, and then went on to report on the soil of Albemarle County, its temperatures, snowfall, and other related data. The purpose of this information was to acquaint the astronomer with the region, and to entice him to accept a professorship. Bowditch was not interested in moving to Virginia, however.[62]

When the Legislature appropriated $50,000 for the purchase of a library and its apparatus for the University, Jefferson promptly opened an account with Boston booksellers to supply "desirable volumes covering every field of learning." He then proceeded to compile his own list of more than 7000 volumes. He recommended approximately 300 works dealing with history, combined with works on ancient history.

He personally owned more than 450 books on the law, and for the University he ordered approximately 370 books on the subject. Having been schooled in the classic tradition, his list of works on belles lettres were chiefly in Greek and Latin. He also included approximately 180 works on ecclesiastical history or religion for the University.

All three of the libraries he had assembled for himself in his lifetime contained numerous works on agriculture, mathematics, natural philosophy, geology, rhetoric, chemistry, horticulture, botany, zoology, mineralogy, music, medicine, physiology and related subjects. When grouped together, the 800 or more scientific books in his own libraries outnumbered those on history. In his list for the University, he included approximately 1000 works on scientific subjects.

This was the fourth library that Jefferson assembled in his lifetime, the other three having been personal collections. The first consisted of the books he purchased to supplement the nucelus he had inherited from his father, and which were lost in the fire that destroyed Shadwell. Although without formal education, Peter Jefferson was, as his son later wrote, a man of "strong mind, sound judgement, and eager after information . . . [who] read much and improved himself." His collection of forty-two volumes was then considered to be one of the most substantial in his region.

Jefferson's second library, which he sold to the Congress in 1815, was begun soon after the Shadwell fire, and totalled 3200 works in some 6500 volumes, which was undoubtedly the best for its size in the country. No sooner had it been removed to Washington, that he began to assemble a third library for himself, as he said, for the amusement of his old age, and managed to bring together some 900 volumes before his death.[63]

Although Jefferson's libraries contained a number of rare books, be did not purchase them for their antiquarian value but for their content. He did not use a bookplate, and instead initialed the books internally on the signatures marked by the printer "I" and "T"; the letter "J" was not used at that time.

He explained his book collecting to a bookseller, "my own collection furnishing things *old* and my time not permitting me to read but what is *good*, the title will enable me to judge whether the subject interests me."

"It almost seems as if some ghostly pyromaniac had pursued Mr. Jefferson all his days," wrote the librarian, Randolph G. Adams, some years ago. The statesman's first library, including his father's books, was totally destroyed in a fire that consumed Shadwell in 1770. A fire in the Library of Congress in 1851 destroyed more than two-thirds of his major library which he had sold to the government in 1815. Of his "fourth" library—the books he selected for the University of Virginia, more than half were burned in the fire of the Rotunda which occurred in 1895.[64]

The great fire occurred on the morning of October 27th, and was discovered shortly after ten o'clock. Faculty and students rushed to assist in bringing out the University's fire engine and hoses and reels, and were forced to chop down the engine room door in order to do so. Hoses were run the distance to the small lake nearby, and then it was discovered that the engine, having no suction pump, could not be used, and hoses had to be attached to a plug, which yielded a stream that ranged only four or five feet. By this time the fire was well under way. In the Public Hall, the fire had progressed rapidly and the great overhead beam to which lights and reflectors were attached dropped to the ground.

Meanwhile students and others were desperately carrying books from the Law Library, then housed in the Annex next door, to a place of safety. They also brought out "the instruments from the physical and mechanical laboratories, also at that time in the Annex, but, as one might expect, these instruments, when removed, were in a woefully delapidated condition." Faculty members had brought one hundred pounds of dynamite to the site with which they attempted to bring down the four columns to weaken the roof sufficiently to keep the fire confined, and thus save the books on the second floor.[65]

CHAPTER XVIII

THE DREAM FULFILLED (1824–1827)

I was bold in the pursuit of knowledge, never fearing to follow the truth and reason to whatever results they led, and bearding every authority which stood in their way.

Letter from Thomas Jefferson
to Dr. Thomas Cooper, 1818.

Now entering his eighties, Jefferson's preoccupation with time became all the more relevant. Among the earliest of Jefferson's book purchases, made when he was twenty-one, had been a copy of E. F. Young's *Night Thoughts*. One passage in the work that particularly impressed him to the extent that he copied it into his *Literary Bible*, summarized his concern with time:

> Youth is not rich in time; it may be poor;
> Part with it as with money, sparingly; pay
> No moment but in purchase of its worth;
> And what it's worth, ask death-bells; they can tell.
> Part with it as with life, reluctant; big
> With holy hope of nobler time to come.[1]

In his final days, as his physical disabilities increased, Jefferson likened himself to a timepiece, an image which came readily to his mind. When his grandson, Thomas Jefferson Randolph, remarked that he appeared somewhat better, the statesman responded, "Do not imagine for a moment that I feel the smallest solicitude about the result: I am like an old watch, with a pinion worn out here, and a wheel there, until it can go no longer."[2]

461

It is not surprising that Jefferson's preoccupation with time and the most gainful use of it led him, during the second part of his life, to present pocket watches as tokens of esteem to members of his family and occasionally to others. As each of his daughters, and later his granddaughters, reached the age of sixteen, for example, he deemed that she had achieved the status of a young lady with certain responsibilities. On that birthday, he gave each of them a gold ladies' watch, and a servant whom she was required to train by herself. He chose each timepiece and each young servant carefully, to reflect as much as possible the personality of the recipient.

To his daughter, Martha, for example, he gave a watch made by the eminent Swiss watchmaker, Coulin, which he probably purchased in France. His granddaughter Ellen Wayles Randolph received a particularly handsome timepiece on her sixteenth birthday, while her sister Cornelia also was given a small gold ladies' watch, rimmed front and back with pearls.[3]

John Garland Jefferson, son of the statesman's cousin, George Jefferson, and for whom Jefferson had assumed responsibility when the youth was left without means, was studying law. He too expected to receive the gift of a watch from his patron, and inquired, "my Benefactor, if the request seems not unreasonable [would you] furnish me with a watch? It gives me pain to add to the obligation I am already under by such an act; but I am persuaded you are so well convinced of the convenience and even the necessity of one it will plead my excuse for writing to you." It is not known whether Jefferson obliged. He may have given him a watch he already owned, but he did not purchase a new one for him at that time.[4]

This practise was reflected in Jefferson's last will and testament. It specified, "I give a gold watch to each of my grandchildren, who shall not already have received one from me, to be purchased and delivered by my executor to my grandsons at the age of twenty-one, and granddaughters at that of sixteen." It is doubtful that this provision could have been fulfilled, however, in view of the reduced circumstances of Jefferson's estate.

For his executor and favorite grandson, Thomas Jefferson Randolph, however, Jefferson made special provision, and to him he bequeathed "my silver watch in preference of the golden one, because of it's superior excellence." This may have been the famous timepiece that had figured in the incident of the "Midnight Appointments."[5]

In view of his lifelong preoccupation with time, it seems particularly appropriate that among the last projects with which Jefferson was involved at the close of his life was the public clock for the University which had been his creation. Early in 1825, as the work on the construction of the University was progressing, Arthur P. Brockenbough,

FIGURE 26. Unguals, phalanges, and metacarpals of the *Megalonyx jeffersonii*, found in West Virginia and presented by Jefferson to the American Philosophical Society. The extinct mammal was later named for Jefferson. Courtesy of the Academy of Natural Sciences of Philadelphia.

FIGURE 27. The "Great Clock" made by Peter Spurck to Jefferson's specifications and mounted over the main entrance in the Entrance Hall of Monticello. Courtesy of the Thomas Jefferson Memorial Foundation.

FIGURE 28.   Polygraph, a writing machine with two pens, invented by John Isaac Hawkins, manufactured by Charles Willson Peale, and used by Jefferson in Washington and at Monticello. Courtesy of the Thomas Jefferson Memorial Foundation.

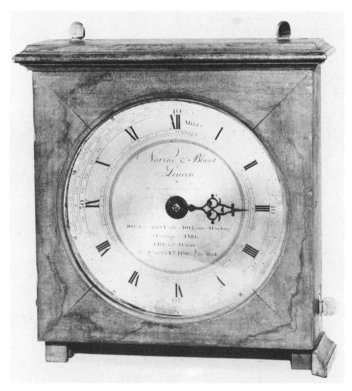

FIGURE 30.   Odometer for a wayweiser or carriage wheel made by Nairne & Blunt of London and used by Jefferson. Courtesy of the Thomas Jefferson Memorial Foundation.

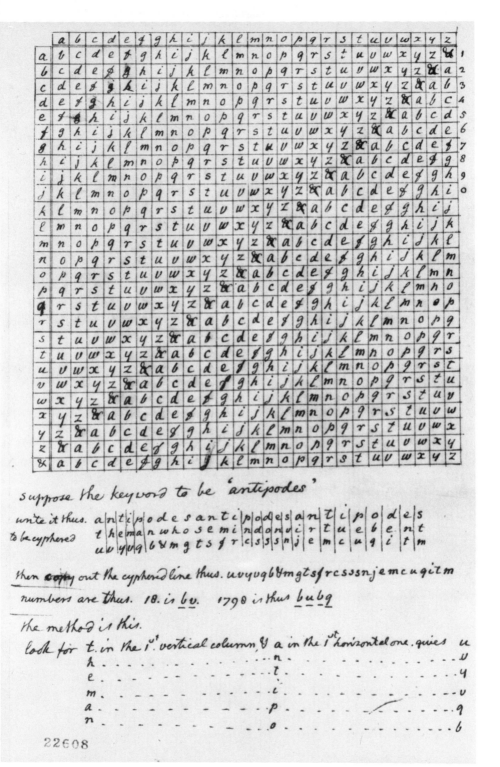

FIGURE 29. Cipher devised by Jefferson for confidential communications with Lewis and Clark on their expedition. Courtesy of the Library of Congress.

FIGURE 31.   Jefferson's writing furniture combination including the Burling revolving chair, the chaise longue, and converted tea table. Courtesy of the Thomas Jefferson Memorial Foundation.

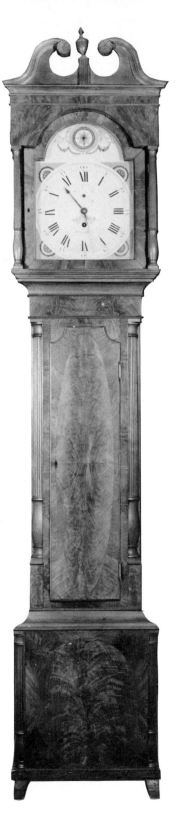

FIGURE 32. Astronomical regulator clock
made by Thomas Voight of Philadelphia to
Jefferson's specifications in 1811 and used by
Jefferson in his study. The backboard is
marked with the days of the week indicated
by the descent of the weight. Courtesy of the
Historical Society of Pennsylvania.

FIGURE 33.   Main doorway into the Entrance Hall at Monticello, where Jefferson kept his natural history collections, showing the Great Clock and elk antlers. Courtesy of the Thomas Jefferson Memorial Foundation.

FIGURE 34.   Buffalo robe of the Mandan tribe, painted with the scene of a battle fought in 1797 by the Sioux and Arikaras against the Mandans, Minnetarees, and Ah-wah-har-ways tribes. It was sent to Jefferson by Lewis and Clark in 1805, and he first displayed it in the White House and later at Monticello. The robe measures 5 feet by 6 feet. Sixty-four figures of Indians are shown. Courtesy of the Peabody Museum of Ethnology, Harvard University.

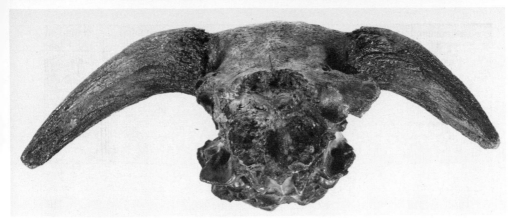

FIGURE 35. Holotype cranium of *Boothe-rium bombifrons* (Harlan 1825), an extinct musk ox, collected by William Clark for Thomas Jefferson. It retains most of the horn cores but lacks the facial and palatal bones. Courtesy of the Academy of Natural Sciences of Philadelphia.

FIGURE 36. Lower mandible of the *Mammut americanum* (American mastodon) from Jefferson's personal collection and displayed in the Entrance Hall at Monticello during his later years. Courtesy of the University of Virginia and the Thomas Jefferson Memorial Foundation.

A table of thermometrical observations, made at Monticello, from January 1, 1810, to December 31, 1816.

	1810.			1811.			1812.			1813.			1814.			1815.			1816.			mean of each month.
	max.	mean	min.	max.	mean	min.	max.	mean	min.	max.	mean	min.	max.	mean	min.	max.	mean	min.	max.	mean	min.	
Jan.	5½	38	66	20	39	68	5½	34	53	13	35	59	16½	36	55	8½	35	60	16	34	51	36
Feb.	12	43	73				21	40	75	19	38	65	14	42	65	16	36	57	15½	41	62	40
Mar.	20	41	61	28	44	78	31½	46	70	28	48	71	13½	43	73	31	54	80	25	48	75	46
April	42	55	81	36	58	86	31	56	86	40	59	80	35	59	82	41	60	82	30	49	71	56½
May	43	64	88	46	62	79	39	60	86	46	62	81	47	65	91	37	58	77	43	60	79	61½
June	53	70	87	58	73	89	58	74	92½	54	75	93	57	69	87	54	71	88	51	70	86	72
July	60	75	88	60	76	89½	57	75	91	61	75	94½	60	74	89	63	77	89	51	71	86	75
Aug.	55	71	90	59	75	85	61	71	87	62	74	92	56	75	88	58	72	84	51	73	90	73
Sep.	50	70	81	50	67	81	47	68	75	54	69	83	52	70	89	45	61	82	54	63	90½	67
Oct.	32	57	82	35	62	85	39	55	80	32	53	70	37	58	83	38½	59	76	37	57	73	57
Nov.	27	44	69	32	45	62	18	43	76	20	48	71	23	47	71	20	46	70	24	46	71	45½
Dec.	14	32	62	20	38	49	13	35	63	18	37	53	18	38	59	12	36	57	23	43	69	37
mean of clear weather.	55			58			55			56			56⅓			55½			54½			55½

FIGURE 37. "A table of thermometrical observations, made at Monticello, from January 1, 1810, to December 31, 1816," from *The Virginia Literary Museum, and Journal of Belles Lettres, Arts, Sciences, etc.* Courtesy of the Library of Congress.

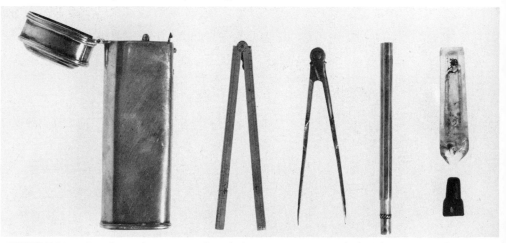

FIGURE 38. Cased set of miniature silver drafting instruments made by John Letelier of Philadelphia and used by Jefferson while traveling. Courtesy of the Thomas Jefferson Memorial Foundation.

of the Board of Visitors, unsuccessfully sought a maker of public clocks to produce the one to be installed in the Rotunda. Jefferson took over the project and enlisted the assistance of Joseph Coolidge, Jr., his grandson-in-law in Boston. He prepared detailed specifications; the clock required an eight-day movement, a dial seven feet in diameter and a fifteen hundred pound bell. "We want a bell," he wrote, "that can GENERALLY be heard at a distance of two miles, because this will ensure its being ALWAYS heard at Charlottesville."[6]

Several months passed before Coolidge provided "the name of the best clockmaker of this place," Simon Willard. He reminded Jefferson that while he had been Secretary of State, he had awarded Willard several patents for horological inventions. Willard submitted an estimate of $800, which appeared to be reasonable. (*Document 18*)

Final negotiations for the project were completed in February 1826, with Coolidge acting as the intermediary between Jefferson and the clockmaker, and the contract was finalized in June. The clock was to be ready by September. Jefferson received the letter on July 1st, three days before his death, and did not live to see the timepiece in place. Willard later commented that the plans and specifications that Jefferson had prepared for the clock and bell were the only ones he had ever received throughout his career that had been so well designed that when the time came for installation, everything fitted to the sixteenth of an inch.[7]

Arrangements for installation of the clock did not proceed as planned, however, and the project seemed fraught with problems. Jefferson's order to Willard for the bell was countermanded by John Hartwell Cocke of the University's Board of Governors, and at first it was planned to substitute a triangle. Eventually the purchase of the bell was approved, and ordered from a New York founder. The bell proved to be unsatisfactory, and another founder had to be sought. The clock movement was damaged in transit, and had to be returned to Boston for repair. It was probably early in 1827 that the clock was finally installed.[8] (*Documents 14 and 15*)

It was when he first began to plan the University of Virginia that Jefferson's health began to deteriorate, at about the age of seventy-five. After attending the conference in the early months of 1818 held at Rockfish Gap to plan for a state university, he suffered another severe attack of rheumatism. When it took a turn for the worse, Jefferson sought relief at Warm Springs. Instead of healing, however, the waters of the sulphur springs created another affliction. He returned to Monticello wracked with a severe intestinal disturbance. Treatment only aggravated the condition and for a time he was in danger of losing his life. The modern gastroenterological diagnosis is "irritable colon," due to severe periodic episodes of bacterial infection (dysentery), or even viral gastroenteritis. He suffered for many months from this new problem, and never fully recovered. To this distress was added the consequences of a fall, in which he broke his left arm at the same time that his right hand and wrist became severely swollen.[9]

Nonetheless, to most of his friends he consistently reported improvement in health, although on occasion he became depressed. "When all our faculties have left," he commented during one such interlude to John Adams, "or are leaving us, one by one—sight, hearing, memory—every avenue of pleasing sensation is closed, and . . . debility and malaise left in their places—when friends of our youth are gone, and a generation is risen around us whom we know not, is death an evil?"[10]

When Dr. Vine Utley inquired concerning his health, he responded in detail with candor. "I live so much like other people," he stated, "that I might refer to ordinary life as the history of my own. Like my friend the Doctor [Benjamin Rush], I have lived temperately, eating little animal food, and that not as an aliment, so much as a condiment for the vegetables, which constitute my principal diet. I double, however, the Doctor's glass and a half of wine, and even treble it with a friend; but halve its effects by drinking the weak wines only. The ardent wines I cannot drink, nor do I use ardent spirits in any form. Malt liquors and cider are my table drinks, and my breakfast, like that also of my friend, is of tea and coffee. I have been blest with organs of digestion which accept and concoct, without ever murmuring, whatever the palate chooses to consign to them, and I have not yet lost a tooth by age. I was a hard student when I entered on the business of life, the duties of which leave no idle time to those disposed to fulfill them; and now, retired, and at the age of seventy-six, I am again a hard student. Indeed, my fondness for reading and study revolts me from the drudgery of letter-writing. And a stiff wrist, the consequence of an early dislocation, makes writing both slow and painful. I am not so regular in my sleep as the Doctor says he was, devoting to it from five to eight hours, according as my company or the book I am reading interests me; and I never go to bed without an hour, or half hour's previous reading of something moral, whereon to ruminate in the intervals of sleep. But whether I retire to bed early or late, I rise with the sun. I use spectacles at night but not necessarily in the day unless reading small print. My hearing is distinct in particular conversation but confused when several voices cross each other, which unfits one for the society of the table . . . so free from catarrhs that I have not had one on an average of eight to ten years. I ascribe this exemption partly to the habit of bathing my feet every morning for sixty years past."[11]

Despite his increasing years and infirmities, Jefferson continued to live dangerously for a man of his age. Still an excellent horseman, he rode his fine bay horse, Eagle, every day, even when he had to be helped into the saddle. During the cold weather he often took long forays on horseback along the mountain roads. He made several visits to his beloved Natural Bridge, a journey of four or five days. On one occasion he was forced to spend two days in extreme cold at the site without even his greatcoat, because he had forgotten to bring it with him.[12]

From time to time, however, serious accidents befell him. Several years previously he stepped on a rotted tread in a flight of steps and fell and broke his arm, rendering his left hand permanently almost useless. On another occasion he was thrown while riding. Not long afterwards, venturing out without the servant who customarily attended him, and with his arm still in a sling, he almost drowned while fording a river.[13]

In the last year of his life, Jefferson's health deteriorated even more rapidly, and between the end of May and late September 1825 Dr. Robley Dunglison made thirty visits to Monticello. Other factors in addition to health combined to fill Jefferson's twilight years with grief and sadness. Martha's husband, Thomas Mann Randolph, Jr., whose family he supported at Monticello, was hopelessly in debt, and had become eccentric and unstable; by 1825 he had become entirely alienated from his wife and children. For his considerable financial problems, he blamed his son, Thomas Jefferson Randolph, and his wife's family.[14]

The national depression following the crash of 1819 had reduced Jefferson's resources to the very minimum. The money received from the sale of his books to the Library of Congress erased only half of his debts. Interest due on his loan from the Dutch firm doubled the amount of the original loan. Failure of crops and lack of production of his mill and nailery had forcd him to borrow again, from the Bank of the United States, of which his friend, Wilson Cary Nicholas, was the president.

His financial burden was substantially increased after he had cosigned two $10,000 notes for Nicholas and again two more for the same amount some time later, for Nicholas subsequently became bankrupt and his property was turned over to trustees. Although Jefferson sold parcels of land from time to time, the income derived did little to meet the demands of the increasing number of creditors.[15]

Beset with growing debts and the burden of his farms, Jefferson finally turned the management of all of his affairs over to his competent grandson, Thomas Jefferson Randolph, whom he later designated in his will as executor of his estate. Young Randolph also assisted him in carrying on matters relating to the University.

His final years provided Jefferson with occasional opportunities for reflection on historical events. Commenting on William Wirt's recently published biography of Patrick Henry to his old friend Waterhouse, he considered the matter as to who had commenced the American Revolution. The question, he explained, "is as difficult as that of the first inventors of a thousand good things . . . I suppose it would be as difficult to trace the Revolution to its first embryo . . . This question of priority is as the inquiry would be, who first of the three hundred Spartans offered his name to Leonidas? The fact is, that one new idea leads to another, that to a third, and so on through a course of time until some one, with whom no one of these ideas was original, combines all together, and produces what is justly called a new invention." As to the Revolution, he noted that no one knew how long it may have been hatching in the British Cabinet before the government made the first of the "experiments" which were eventually to ignite the conflagration.[16]

Now, several decades after having expedited his "corps of discovery," Jefferson had an opportunity to summarize his vision of the new republic which had led him to undertake the exploration of the Western lands. "I had long deemed it incumbent on the authorities of our country," he stated, "to have the great western wilderness beyond the Mississippi, explored, to make known its geography, its natural productions, its general character and inhabitants."

His first attempt to achieve this, he explained, was by means of the Lewis and Clark expedition, and his decision to establish longitudes by means of observations of lunar distances. Although he had recommended the use of a universal equatorial instrument with a portable pendulum, "astronomical friends" he had consulted suggested several other methods. "Those deserts are yet to be explored," he added, "and their geography given to the world and ourselves with a correctness worthy of the science of the age."[17]

The mapping of the country continued to preoccupy him. When John Wood was commissioned to prepare an accurate map of Virginia, he combined maps of individual counties, surveys made with chain and compass, on the assumption that the earth was a plane. "To fit them together," Jefferson advised, "they must be accomodated to its real spherical surface; and this can be done only by observations of latitude and longitude, taken at different points of the area to which they are to be reduced."

He suggested that for the lower parts of the state observations could be made of lunar distances with the Borda circle or sextant and a timekeeper. However, when it came to the regions beyond the Allegheny and Missouri, the question arose whether or not the equatorial instrument without a timekeeper would not have been preferable for ascertaining longitudes on land, where a fixed meridian could always be obtained. He commented, "As to myself, I am an astronomer of theory only, little versed in practical observations, and of the minute attentions and corrections they require."[18]

Jefferson continued to be equally concerned about weather observation on a national scale. For him it was not merely a hobby nor just a matter of scientific curiosity. He was aware that climatic conditions and the manner in which they varied from one part of the country to another were of considerable importance and affected the progress of the American population and the cultivation of a variety of plants and crops. One of the best informed Americans on the subject, he took the lead in making meteorological investigations. He became, in effect, an unofficial weather bureau and shared his knowledge with the many who wrote to him for information.

Early in his career, even before the American Revolution, he had visualized the institution of a weather service on a national scale. The slow advancement of the science of meteorology distressed him, and he continued to hope that some means of recording observations with exactitude could be developed in each of the states.

He had been encouraged to learn that in 1814 Dr. James Tilton, the newly appointed Surgeon General of the Army, had ordered that as part of their duties, hospital surgeons were required to keep diaries of the weather, providing information of observations made at many points throughout the country under the auspices of the government. Two years passed before the order could be fully implemented; the first of the reports was submitted in March 1816 by Jefferson's old friend, Dr. Benjamin Waterhouse. Under the guidance of Tilton's successor, Dr. Joseph Lovell, the program flourished and the data collected was eventually prepared for publication.

Meanwhile, Josiah Meigs, Commissioner of the Land Office, proposed that meteorological registers should be maintained by that office, and accordingly in 1817 forms were distributed to all Land Office Registers. The data collected in this manner was never evaluated, however.

Although some states also expressed interest in the development of a weather observation system, no major advance was made until later in the century. Then Joseph Henry, first Secretary of the Smithsonian Institution, developed a means for systematic collection and evaluation of meteorological data from stations throughout the country.

It was not until the second half of the nineteenth century, however, that a systematic survey of climatological conditions was attempted, initially inspired by the foreign Societa Meteorologica Palatina, which maintained two stations in the United States. In 1870 the Smithsonian's operation was superseded by the formation of the United States Weather Bureau, a full century after Jefferson had first visualized such a government service.[19]

The aged statesman's dedication to weather observation continued to the last years of his life. In response to a comparative statement he received from Jacob Bigelow, of the climate of the several northern states based on observations of the flowering of trees in the same year, Jefferson sent him a compilation made over a period of the past seven years of the climate of Virginia, including mean temperatures, dates of frosts, rainfall, snowfall, prevailing winds, the flowering of plants, ripening of fruit, arrival of birds and related data.[20]

After reading a manuscript on the subject intended for publication by George F. Hopkins, he commented, "Of all the departments of science, no one seems to have been less advanced for the last hundred years than that of meteorology. The new chemistry indeed has given us a new principle of the generation of rain, by proving water to be a composition of different gases, and has aided our theory of meteoric lights. Electricity stands where Dr. Franklin's early discoveries placed it, except with its new modification of galvanism. But the phenomena of snow, hail, halo, aurora borealis, haze, looming, &c. are as yet very imperfectly understood. I am myself an emperic in natural philosophy, suffering my faith to go no further than my facts. I am pleased, however, to see the efforts of hypothetical speculation because by the collisions of different hypotheses, truth may be elicited and science advanced in the end."[21]

Jefferson was particularly impressed with a recently published pamphlet about the climate of the Midwest compiled by Lewis Beck, a physician and man of science, a work that added substantially to existing knowledge of the American climate. In acknowledging it, Jefferson described his own long-cherished hopes for bringing together all the known facts about the climate of the American continent, a project which had been interrupted by the American Revolution and to which he had been unable to return. His own earlier efforts he stated to be "perhaps the first attempt, not to form a theory, but to bring together the few facts then known, and suggest them to public attention."

Since then the Western lands had been opened, and he conceived that eventually a theory could be developed with a solid foundation in fact. He noted, however, that "years are requisite for this steady attention to the thermometer, to the plants growing there, the times of their leafing and flowering, its animal inhabitants, beasts, birds, reptiles and insects; its prevalent winds, quantities of rain and snow, temperature of fountains, and other indexes of climate." He advised that similar observations would have to be collected for every State, and repeated once or twice a century, to "show the effect of clearing and culture towards changes of climates. My Notes give a very imperfect idea of what our climate was, half a century ago, at this place, which being nearly central to the State may be taken for its medium."

More recently he had made a survey of Virginia's climate over a seven year period, which might be added to his earlier work, adding the hope that "Something like this is doing in the other States, which, when all shall be brought together, may produce theories meriting confidence." Jefferson's survey was published in *The Virginia Literary Museum* with the title "A Table of Thermometric Observations, Made at Monticello, From January 1, 1810, to December 31, 1816."[22] (*Figure 37*)

As the months advanced Jefferson became too weak to walk beyond his garden without suffering, but nonetheless he continued to ride six to eight miles a day without experiencing fatigue, and sometimes he was able to ride as much as twenty miles in the same day.[23]

As a consequence, during this period he made frequent use of the last of his "inventions," a walking-stick chair. As described by his grandson, Thomas Jefferson Randolph, it was made as "a walking stick . . . composed of three sticks, which being spread out and covered with a piece of cloth made a tolerable seat."

Whenever a minister came into the region Jefferson attended church services in the courthouse at Charlottesville, as well as meetings of a Baptist preacher named Hiter. A servant carried his folding camp-stool since the available seating often proved to be insufficient for the size of the congregation. During his later years Jefferson used the folding stool almost daily. When he went on walks around Monticello, he was customarily accompanied by a servant carrying the folding stool for his frequent periods of rest. Each morning he mounted his horse, taking the stool with him, and rode off down the mountain into Charlottesville to the building site of the University. There he would sit upon his camp-stool for hours, supervising the construction in progress.[24]

One of the greatest moments in Jefferson's saddened last years was the visit to Monticello of his old friend, Lafayette. Upon learning of the impending visit, he wrote to Lafayette, "What recollections, dear friend, will this call up to you and me! What a history have we run over from the evening that yourself, Mousnier, Bernan, and other patriots settled, in my house in Paris, the outlines of the constitution you wished. And to trace it through all the disastrous chapters of Robespierre, Barras, Bonaparte, and the Bourbons!"[25]

The great day came at last three weeks later. As the French general's barouche swept up the winding road to the top of the "low mountain" escorted by an entourage of one hundred twenty men with unfurled banners, some two hundred onlookers had collected to observe the historic reunion. The aged general stepped from his carriage when it halted on the east lawn, where Jefferson was eagerly awaiting him.

Now feeble and worn with age, the statesman tottered slowly down the portico steps. Instead of the burly dynamic figure he remembered from Paris, he saw instead only another old man like himself, made lame and in poor health by his imprisonment by the Bourbons. Martha Randolph recalled the scene as the two venerable patriots drew near to each other. "Their uncertain gait quickened itself into a shuffling run," she wrote, "and exclaiming, 'Ah, Jefferson!' 'Ah, Lafayette!' they burst into tears as they fell into each other's arms."

There was not a dry eye among the spectators, Thomas Jefferson Randolph later reported, and only occasional sobs broke the silence. During the several days that Lafayette remained as a guest at Monticello, the old comrades reviewed many years of their past together.[26]

Lafayette was the guest of honor at a banquet held in the Rotunda of the University, which was still under construction with scaffolding all about. Jefferson, although quite ill at the time, attended and was one of the three former Presidents at the head table, the others being James Madison and James Monroe.

He had prepared a brief address of tribute to "our benefactor in peace as well as in war," but he was too weak to deliver it, and it was read by another guest. Jefferson's speech ended with a strong support of the University.

"Could I live to see it once enjoy the patronage & cherishment of our public authorities with undivided voice," he had written, "I should die without a doubt of the future fortunes of my native state."[27]

With each passing month, Jefferson's health deteriorated more and more. By the autumn of 1825, he was confined to his house by prostatic hypertrophy, which plagued him increasingly during the past four months. He was forced to spend long sessions on a couch, suffering considerable pain. Nonetheless, he was still often in the saddle or in his carriage overviewing the progress of work at the University. As he noted in October of that year, "The little of the powers of life which remains to me I consecrate to our University."[28]

On his return from a visit some distance away, possibly to Poplar Forest, Jefferson developed an itch which Dunglison treated with mercury. This brought on a reaction causing salivation, annoying him greatly. When he complained about it to Governor Coles one day, the latter commented, "Mr. Jefferson, you are the last man in the world, from your hatred of physic, of whom I would have expected any excess in taking physic." To which Jefferson responded, "Yes, but I would rather have *the devil than the itch!*"[29]

Despite his negative feelings about physicians in general, he had the highest respect and admiration for young Dunglison, and was a most cooperative patient despite his melancholy suffering. Dunglison refused to submit a bill for his services because he claimed that as Rector of the University Jefferson was his employer. Jefferson found himself placed under great embarrassment. "The fragment of life remaining to me is likely to be passed in sickness and suffering," he informed Dunglison. "The young physicians in our neighborhood will probably be good ones in time. But time & experience as well as science are necessary to make a skillful physician, and Nature is preferable to an unskilled one. I had therefore made up my mind to trust to her altogether, until your arrival gave me better prospects." Dunglison eventually accepted a single payment of fifty dollars for his services.[30]

Although his body was fast failing and constantly racked with rheumatism and chronic diarrhea, and although he chafed at his forced inactivity, Jefferson's mind remained clear and fully alert. He demonstrated considerable courage despite his health afflictions and financial problems, and accepted his conditions with fortitude, directing all his energies to the completion of the University.

The opening of the University was scheduled for February 1, 1825, but it had to be postponed because of the delayed arrival of three of the professors coming from England. As a consequence, some of the applicants enrolled in other colleges, and by March 7th only forty students had arrived for the beginning of classes. It was an unprepossessing scene that greeted them, for all of Albemarle was a sea of mud from the heavy spring rains, and the college premises were filled with scattered debris and other evidences of construction.

In attempting to build a faculty, Jefferson had refused to raid American colleges by luring their outstanding staff away, stating it was neither "honorable or moral to seduce them from their stations." Inasmuch as it had not been possible to attract qualified professors for the faculty from within the United States, it had been decided to send Francis Walker Gilmer as an agent to Europe to scout and recruit them. Jefferson warned that he would not be satisfied with staff of less than the highest quality, noting, "we all, from the beginning considered the high qualifications of our professors as the only means by which we can give to our institution splendor and preeminence over all its sister seminaries."

Gilmer visited the English universities of Cambridge, Oxford and Edinburgh, with little success at the first two, but he managed to recruit the first professor of English, Thomas Hewlett Key. Others followed, including George Long, Charles Bonneycastle, Robley Dunglison, John Patton Emmet and George Blaetterman. It was a remarkable triumph for Gilmer to have accomplished so much during a short visit. His choices did not meet with universal approval, however, and the Boston press in particular was critical of a "foreign" faculty.[31]

In March 1825 Jefferson saw his dream fulfilled as the University of Virginia finally opened its doors and the forty students were enrolled. Jefferson's hope that the University would attract serious students, however, was not to be realized in its initial period.

The students first enrolled were not particularly prepossessing and were poorly prepared for their curriculum of studies. For the most part, they were scions of prominent and wealthy Virginia families, accustomed to drinking and gambling, and it was discovered that some of them carried weapons. From the very beginning, they were responsible for a number of disturbances on the campus.

No strict rules of behavior had as yet been formulated, and most of the young men who enrolled took great advantage of the loose code of discipline that prevailed. They frequently became drunk in the local taverns, gambled in the dormitories, walked out of classrooms without permission and even threw stink bombs into the professors's rooms. The "foreign" professors had been selected to become their unanimous target.

One night a group of fourteen students, "animated first with wine," and wearing masks, cavorted on the main lawn with considerable noise and uproar, shouting, "Down with the European professors!" When two professors emerged to investigate, they were met with insults, and bricks and sticks were thrown at them. They each captured one of the offenders and attempted to determine their identity, but were unable to do so before the imprisoned culprits were rescued by their companions and all fled to the dormitories.[32]

It was a shocking experience, particularly for Jefferson, who had not visualized the possibility of such behavior, although he had observed similar conditions when he was a student at William and Mary. On the following day a meeting was called of the Board of Visitors, and all the students were summoned to an assembly in the Rotunda. The three former Presidents were present—Jefferson, Madison and Monroe.

Jefferson was the first to address them, and as he rose slowly and in obvious pain and stood before them, he spoke with difficulty. "It was one of the most painful events of my life," he began, but became so overcome with emotion that he was unable to continue. Although his lips continued to move, no words could be heard. Tears came to his eyes, and he finally sat back into his seat.

Everyone, including the students, was so moved that when Chapman Johnson, another member of the Board of Visitors, rose and asked the rioters to come forward, almost all of them stood up and did so. As one of the students later commented, "It was not his words, but Mr. Jefferson's tears that melted their stubborn purpose."

Jefferson later described the occurrence to Joseph Coolidge, Jr. "The University had gone on with a degree of order and harmony," he wrote, "which had strengthened the hope that much of self government might be trusted to the discretion of the Students at the age of 16. and upwards, until the lst instant."

In his view, there could be but one solution. "Coercion must be resorted to where confidence has been disappointed." The Board established a stricter code of discipline in lieu of self-government.[33]

Jefferson's efforts were now all concentrated on the University. He cooperated closely with Dunglison to provide the School of Medicine

with all the equipment it required. Dunglison prepared a list of anatomical preparations, which Jefferson attempted to acquire with the assistance of Dr. Robert Greenhow of New York. They experienced difficulty
in obtaining some of the items, however, such as the dried preparation
of the female genital organs and adjacent parts.

Greenhow complained that what was available "does not exhibit
the parts properly and is liable to be destroyed by flies." He had no difficulty obtaining the fetal circulation and the penis, but "the heart with
the adjacent vessels and thoracic duct cannot be obtained unless the
vertebral column is attached."[34]

It was Jefferson's suggestion to establish a dispensary at the School
of Medicine supervised by the medical faculty, with a clinic to be open
one-half hour a day three days of the week. To this resource could come
all the poor free persons who "disordered in body, topically or generally,
applying for advice, shall receive it gratis."

All others, bonded or free, were to pay fifty cents on each visit.
Vaccination was to be free to all. In return for the use of these facilities
by the public, medical students were to be allowed to attend, to prepare
medicine and to examine patients. The fees received would be used for
the purchase of dispensary medicines.[35]

In a discussion of the curriculum with John Brazier, reviewer of a
work on Greek pronunciation, Jefferson pointed out that the teaching
of Greek and Latin provided "models of pure taste in writing," and that
from them in fact was derived "the rational and chaste style of modern
composition which so much distinguishes the nations to whom these
languages are familiar." Without such models, he believed that the people would have continued to use "the inflated style of our northern ancestors, or the hyperbolical and vague ones of the east." He extolled "the
innocent and elegant luxury" of being able to read the Greek and Latin
writers in the original.

"I think myself more indebted to my father for this," he stated,
"than for all the other luxuries his cares and affections have placed
within my reach; and more now than when younger, and more susceptible of delights from other sources."

Of further value, he noted, was the store of knowledge of real science, history, mathematics, ethics, arithmetic, geometry, astronomy and
natural history to be found in the works of these authors. In summation,
he concluded, "it may truly be said that the classical languages are a solid
basis for most, and an ornament to all the sciences."[36]

One of the last letters he was to write was also concerned with the
curriculum. He pointed out to Dr. John Emmet that the educational
product to be derived was proportional to the investment in funding
and faculty. It was necessary, therefore, to distribute the branches of the
sciences to be taught into as many groups as professors could be hired,

the number of hours that would be available to students for study and the segment of time that each professor could assign to each of the branches.

He compared the University with established academies and universities in both the United States and Europe, where the faculty numbered as many as twenty or thirty professors. The Virginia legislature had appropriated $15,000 for the employment of ten professors, but in fact it had been possible to hire only eight for the amount of funding available. Accordingly, there was no alternative but to divide between them the sciences to be taught.

Jefferson then speculated on the amount of time that students could give to their education. He estimated that three years should be allowed for a general education, and two or perhaps three for the particular profession for which a student was preparing. The first year might be devoted to Languages and Mathematics, the second to Mathematics and Physics, and the third year to Physics and Chemistry.

The sciences to be taught were Botany, Zoology, Mineralogy, Chemistry, Geology and Rural Economics, the last-named of which included Agriculture. Assuming that twelve dozen lectures were presented during an academic year, he suggested that two dozen each should be devoted to Botany and Zoology, and Mineralogy and Geology, and eight dozen to Chemistry; or if Mineralogy, Geology and Chemistry were combined into one, the student's year should be divided into two parts, one-third to Botany and Zoology, and two-thirds to Chemistry, Mineralogy and Zoology.

He proposed that the least amount of time be devoted to Geology. "To learn as far as observation has informed us," he wrote, "the ordinary arrangement of the different strata of minerals in the earth, to know from their habitual collocations and proximities, where we find one mineral, whether another, for which we are seeking, may be expected to be in its neighborhood, is useful. But the dreams about the modes of creation, inquiries whether our globe has been formed by the agency of fire or water, how many millions of years it has cost Vulcan or Neptune to produce what the fiat of the Creator would effect by a single act of will, is too idle to be worth a single hour of any man's life."

To the supposition that two-thirds of a year could provide only an inadequate knowledge of chemistry, he responded that "we do not expect our schools to turn out their alumni enthroned on the pinnacles of their respective sciences; but only so far advanced in each as to be able to pursue them by themselves, and to become Newtons and Laplaces by energies and perseverances to be continued through life."[37]

There was little that escaped Jefferson's attention in the planning for the University. He proposed that "manual exercises, military manoeuvres, and tactics generally should be the frequent exercises of the students in their hours of recreation. It is at that age of aptness, docility, and emulation of the practices of manhood that such things are soonest learned and longest remembered."

He also encouraged instruction in the use of tools of the manual arts, as well as what he called "the arts which embellish life," such as dancing, music and drawing. However, the University was not to provide staff but only space for these activities, which were to be taught by "accessory teachers," who would be paid by the students.[38]

The Board of Visitors had not yet established a style of student diet because the "hotels"—the student boarding houses—had not yet been completed, whereupon Jefferson proposed a menu which he believed would meet with the Board's approval.[39]

Scarcely more than two months before his death, Jefferson addressed Professor Emmet once more, this time on the subject of botany as it related to the University. "It is time to think of the introduction of the School of Botany into our Institution," he advised. Although it would not be possible to begin the lectures that year, he suggested that preparations should be made for introducing them in the following year, because botany could be taught to the greatest advantage only during the months of April and May, requiring Emmet to suspend teaching of other subjects during that period.

He also proposed the most practical manner of developing a six-acre botanical garden, noting that a greenhouse was out of the question due to lack of funds. Emmet was to compile a list of trees and plants he considered to be most desirable for the project, and Jefferson assured him of his own assistance and that of his friends in providing seeds. The garden should be developed on that part of the University premises that had been set aside for the purpose, and it should have good soil. It was to be enclosed with a serpentine wall seven feet high, the construction of which Jefferson estimated would require about 80,000 bricks. Such walls were partly for economy, being one brick in thickness yet sufficiently strong. He conceived it as an artistic element which would throw interesting shadows upon the paths and would provide a sense of life and movement in the gardens.

Inspired by similar walls he had observed during his tour of English gardens, he made drawings delineating how to make straight and serpentine walls of brick. Two years prior to planning the walls for the University, he had designed serpentine walls for "Folly," the residence of his friend, Joseph Smith, near Staunton.

"The trees I should propose would be exotics of distinguished usefulness, and accomodated to our climate," he noted, and proceeded to list "larch, Cedar of Libanus, Cork oak, the Marronier, mahogany, caoutchouc, teak, and various trees of Brazil." Seeds for some of these trees could be acquired from several sources in the United States, he explained, and others would have to be obtained through the government's foreign service. The hillside was to be leveled into terraces, and the level ground divided into beds and allées.[40]

In landscaping, Jefferson disavowed the geometric patterns, such as he had seen in English gardens, which were favored by the French landscape architect André Le Nôtre. Instead he visualized the use of lines and masses, "winding walks and serpentine rivers." Just as he had been strongly influenced in architectural design by Andrea Palladio, Jefferson was equally influenced in landscape design by William Hogarth's *The Analysis of Beauty*, with which he had been familiar since 1771, when he had purchased a copy of the work.

In and around Paris he had observed early vegetables planted in beds along walls in order to provide them with the radiant heat stored in the brick or stone during the day. Elsewhere in France he had seen trees trained as espaliers along similar walls, which made possible the harvesting of early peaches, pears and figs.

Undoubtedly all these considerations figured in his selection of serpentine walls for the University. After such walls had been constructed, the recesses did indeed serve as windbreaks, and concentrated the sun's rays on the plants, just as had those he had observed in France.[41]

Jefferson was already permanently confined to his bed when he received an invitation from General Roger Weightman to attend the celebration in Washington of the fiftieth anniversary of the signing of the Declaration of Independence. In declining, he carefully worded what was to be his last public statement.

"I should, indeed, with peculiar delight, have met and exchanged there, congratulations personally, with the small band, the remnant of the host of worthies, who joined with us, on that day, in the bold and doubtful election we were to make for our country, between submission, or the sword; and to have enjoyed with them the consolatory fact that our fellow citizens, after half a century of experience and prosperity, continue to approve the choice we made. May it be to the world, what I believe it will be . . . the Signal of arousing men to burst the chains, under which Monkish ignorance and superstition had persuaded them to bind themselves, and to assume the blessing & security of self government . . . All eyes are opened, or opening to the rights of man. The general spread of the light of science has already laid open to every view the palpable truth that the mass of mankind has not been born, with saddles on their backs, nor a favored few booted and spurred, ready to ride them legitimately, by the grace of god. For ourselves let the annual return of this day, for ever refresh our recollections of these r[ights,] and an undiminished devotion to them." Much as he regretted his inability to attend the ceremonies, he awaited the day of anniversary with great expectation.[42]

The last description of Jefferson's physical appearance was provided by the rising young politician, Daniel Webster, who visited him at Monticello. He described the aging statesman as tall and thin, with a wiry and limber neck and his head set forward on his shoulders, his hair long and graying.

"His eyes are small," wrote Webster, "very light, and now neither brilliant nor striking. His chin is rather long, but not pointed. His nose small, regular in its outline, and the nostrils a little elevated. His mouth is well-formed and still filled with teeth; it is strongly compressed, bearing an expression of contentment and benevolence. His complexion, formerly light and freckled, now bears the marks of age and cutaneous affection. His limbs are uncommonly long; his hands and feet very large, and his wrists of an extraordinary size. His walk is . . . easy and swinging. He stoops a little . . . When sitting, he appears short, partly from a rather lounging habit of sitting and partly from the disproportionate length of his limbs."

Webster considered Jefferson's dress to be neglected but not slovenly, and he customarily wore his surtout or long gray overcoat with two waistcoats underneath it even inside the house. He wore pantaloons of the same color as his coat, and loose and long.

The aged statesman's hearing continued to be excellent and he wore glasses only while reading at night. With an easy and natural conversation that touched on all subjects with lightness and grace, Webster considered that he demonstrated "an extraordinary degree of health, vivacity, and spirit."[43]

When Samuel Whitcomb, Jr., a book peddler, visited Jefferson in the spring of 1824, he described his physical appearance in virtually the same words as had been used by Webster. "I should not take him for a generous man," he went on, "He is more positive, decided and passionate than I had expected. I should think him less of a philosopher than a partizan. His manners are much the most agreeable part of him. They are artifical [sic], he shrugs his shoulders when talking, has much of the Frenchman, is rapid, varying, volatile, eloquent, amusing. I should not think him (did I not know his age) much over 60 or 65 years . . .

"When speaking of the Indians he observed that in a conversation with a Chief he had told him that both his daughters married descendants of Pocahontas. This he evidently is proud of.

"His house is rather old and going to decay; appearances about his yard and hill are rather slovenly. It commands an extensive prospect but it being a misty cloudy day, I could see but little of the surrounding scenery."

After a visit to James Madison immediately thereafter, Whitcomb made a comparison between him and Jefferson. "Mr. Madison appears less studied, brilliant and frank but more natural, candid and profound than Mr. Jefferson. Mr. Jefferson has more imagination and passion, quicker and richer conceptions. Mr. Madison has a sound judgement, tranquil temper and logical mind. Mr. Jefferson excites interest immediately on entering his presence."[44]

It was at about this time that Jefferson permitted a mask to be made of himself by J. H. I. Browere, an event which was to usurp even more of his failing strength. Although the sculptor had assured Jefferson that the process would require not more than twenty minutes, in actuality it required hours of agony for the sitter as the sculptor resorted to removing the plaster with which he had coated Jefferson's head, and which had hardened too quickly, with a mallet and chisel. Jefferson complained to Madison that he thought his ears would part from his head before the plaster did.[45]

In his last months, Jefferson continued his desperate attempts to find means to provide for his family after his demise. His efforts to sell some of his land had been unsuccessful, for increasing taxes and falling prices rendered Virginia agriculture a poor investment in this time. He sent his grandson to Richmond to obtain authorization from the legislature for a lottery in which the land and slaves would be sold. There was strong opposition, however, but the lottery was finally approved, and newspapers offered tickets for sale. Meanwhile many private individuals promised funds, so that the lottery was cancelled.[46]

As Jefferson's health by the spring of 1826 was reduced to almost total debility, he responded at last to entreaties from his family and summoned Dr. Dunglison. The physician responded at once, and after an examination, prescribed medication. Dunglison noted in his autobiography that by the end of June the affliction was sapping the aged statesman's bodily powers. He became "apprehensive that the attack would prove fatal. Nor did Mr. Jefferson himself indulge in any other opinion. From this time his strength gradually diminished and he had to remain in bed. The evacuations became less numerous, but it was manifest that his power was failing."[47]

Soon after he learned that his grandfather had summoned a physician, Thomas Jefferson Randolph hurried to Monticello from his home at Tufton. There he remained as part of the permanent household with his mother and brothers and sisters until the end came. His father, however, was not among them, and remained in seclusion at Milton.

Nicholas and Virginia Trist and their young child were living in the Law Office, and four of the late Anne Cary Randolph Bankhead's children and Jefferson's sister, Anna Scott Marks, were also at Monticello. For an unexplained reason, the horde of uninvited visitors who generally came to Monticello in this season was notably absent.[48]

In late June, Henry Lee III, grandson of the Revolutionary War patriot, asked to see Jefferson to discuss certain events for the publication of a new edition of his father's *Memoirs*. Trist called on him to inform him that such a meeting would not be possible, but invited him to dinner at Monticello. Nonetheless Lee called in the early forenoon with the hope that Jefferson might have recovered sufficiently for an interview.

When Jefferson learned of his presence, he insisted upon seeing him and Lee was conducted to his bedroom, where the statesman lay on his alcove bed. Lee recalled the the room's furnishings had changed little since Jefferson's return from Washington. On the alcove wall at the foot of the bed was the black pyramid clock, and below it was an Arabian sword with a blade of Damascus steel. Jefferson told him that the sword had been the gift of an Arabian prince whom he had long forgotten.

Lee also commented that on the other side of the alcove was a small recess in which was "a convenient contrivance on which to hang clothes." Other furniture consisted of a mirror on the east wall beneath which was a dressing table, a bureau in the northeast corner, with a small bookcase and chair beside it. Through the alcove the combination writing furniture was visible in the study.[49]

Although Jefferson appeared to be feeble, his conversation with Lee touched on many subjects and he was urged to stay for dinner. Lee was the last of the countless visitors to Monticello to see the venerable sage.

Jefferson's faithful body servant, Burwell, slept on a pallet in the same room with his master, and among Jefferson's nurses in his final days were his daughter Martha, Thomas Jefferson Randolph, Nicholas P. Trist, and Dr. Dunglison.

At Jefferson's explicit direction, Martha and other women of the household sat with the patient only during the daylight hours. Throughout this period, Jefferson talked freely with all. As the end neared, he held a final interview with the family, speaking calmly as he gave them encouragement and advice. Although he had several spells of unconsciousness, he remained lucid until July 1st.[50]

During one of his brief periods of wakefulness on July 2nd, Jefferson handed Martha a small casket, which she did not open until after his death. Therein she found a touching souvenir of his last hours, a poem he had written to her. Few of Jefferson's poetical writings have survived, if indeed there had been more than those that are known. These are the verses in Jefferson's hand:

A Death Bed Adieu from T.J. to M.R.

> Life's visions are vanished, its dreams are no more,
> Dear friends of my bosom, why bathed in tears,
> I go to my fathers, I welcome the shore,
> Which crowns all my hopes, or buries my cares.
>
> Then farewell my dear, my loved daughter adieu,
> The last pang of life is in parting from you.
> Two seraphs await me long shrouded in death,
> I will bear them your love on my last parting
> breath.[51]

The forthcoming anniversary weighed heavily on Jefferson's mind in his final hours. He lapsed into a stupor on the night of July 2nd, and during the next day he had intervals of wakefulness and unconsciousness. At about seven o'clock that evening, he asked Dunglison, "Is it the Fourth?"

After consulting the Voight clock around the corner of the room, the physician quietly replied, "It soon will be." A short time later he informed the family that Jefferson might be expected to expire any time thereafter.

Trist, who maintained the vigil with Dr. Dunglison, watched the clock during the last hours of the 3rd of July. One time Jefferson awoke and inquired again whether it was yet the 4th. Trist ignored the question but when he was asked one more time, he nodded. "Ah," murmured the statesman, "just as I wished."

When the hour of midnight had passed, Trist knew that Jefferson's last wish had been fulfilled. Jefferson slept until four o'clock in the morning and then summoned the servants, and when they had gathered by the bed, he spoke to them. These were the last words he spoke. He attempted to speak again later in the morning, but although his lips moved, no words came.

He lapsed into total unconsciousness, with his open eyes staring at the ceiling. As Dunglison checked his pulse from time to time, he found the heart beat erratic, and it finally stopped at 12:50 p.m. on July 4th. Thomas Jefferson Randolph, who had been standing woodenly by, then moved forward and closed his grandfather's eyes. Locks of hair were cut at this time for souvenirs, it is believed by Trist. The mortal remains of the venerable statesman were then laid out in a shroud and the last offices performed. [52]

That afternoon the bells of Charlottesville began tolling for the passing of the old patriot. At the University down in the valley, the faculty and the students were deeply affected. Those who had known him personally grieved and afterwards wore black crepe as did many of the citizens of Charlottesville, where all business was suspended for a day.

The family respected the statesman's wishes to have a private internment without a parade. No invitations were issued and no details of the service were publicized, but it was made known that anyone who came would be welcome. The coffin was undoubtedly constructed by John Hemings in the Monticello cabinet shop, and it was kept in the parlor through July 5th and 6th.

It had been raining all day, and at five o'clock the coffin was carried by servants to the family burial ground, There the gardener, Wormley, had dug the grave, and had placed narrow planks across it to hold the coffin during the service.

As the servants brought the coffin within the enclosure inside the low stone wall and placed it upon the planks, the family gathered at the graveside. At the head of the grave was Thomas Mann Randolph, Jr., who had come out of his seclusion for the occasion, and at the foot was his son, Thomas Jefferson Randolph.[53]

The Reverend Frederick Hatch, rector of the Episcopalian church in Charlottesville, of which Jefferson had been the designer, seeing the coffin placed, began the service. It was at a most unfortunate moment, however. Despite the statesman's request, the family had been prevailed upon to postpone services until the arrival of a procession which had assembled at the courthouse in Charlottesville.

The procession had been delayed due to an argument that ensued concerning who should lead it, the townspeople or the students. Meanwhile Randolph and his son had disagreed as to which of them was to inform Mr. Hatch that a procession would be coming, with the consequence that the minister had not been informed at all.

The service was over, the grave was being filled and the family mourners were leaving the graveyard, when the procession first straggled into view over the hillside through the rain. The latecomers were considerably irked to find that they had arrived too late, and some made it known.

According to the only account of the event, "Among those students present there was one described as 'a highminded and honourable young man, though one easily persuaded to his wrong.' This was Edgar Allan Poe."[54]

Jefferson had left specific written instructions for his gravestone, with a sketch. He wished to have a simple grave in the family burial plot on the hillside with a plain monument. He wrote:

the following would be to my Manes* the most
    gratifying.
  On the grave
      a plain die or cube of 3. f[eet] without any mouldings, surmounted
by an Obelisk of 6. f[eet] height, each of a single stone; on the faces of
the Obelisk the following inscription, & not a word more:

Here was buried
Thomas Jefferson
Author of the Declaration of American Independance
of the Statute of Virginia for religious freedom
& Father of the University of Virginia

---

*"to appease the Manes" is to do after a person's death what would have pleased him or was due him.

because by these, as testimonials that I have lived, I wish most to be remembered. To be of the coarse stone of which my columns are made, that no one might be tempted hereafter to destroy it for the value of the materials. My bust by Ciracchi, with the pedestal and truncated column on which it stands, might be given to the University if they would place it in the Dome room of the Rotunda.
on the Die of the Obelisk might be engraved

Born Apr. 2. 1743. O.S.
Died——.[55]

It is to be noted that Jefferson used the actual date of his birth, according to the Old Style, not as later revised to April 13th.

Following her father's death, Martha was overcome with grief, her daily vigil at her father's bedside over at last, but she was unable to cry. Shortly after Jefferson's burial, with her daughters Cornelia and Septimia and the boys she left Monticello for the last time. Taking only a few treasured possessions, they joined Nicholas and Virginia Trist in Washington. Monticello was abandoned, the pavilions fell into ruin, and the gardens became choked with weeds.

Jefferson's precautions against vandalism were in vain. In 1844, when the Prussian historian, Friedrich von Raumer, visited Monticello, he sought out the statesman's gravesite. He found himself before "a place enclosed with a half-decayed wall. . . . A half sunken tomb, neglected and in disorder was there; and a damaged granite pyramid, already inclined to one side, with a partly defaced inscription containing the date of a birth and a death."

He was mortified to find in such a state the tomb of the author of "the memorable declaration of 1785, even grander and more comprehensive than the Declaration of Independence . . . He was a man who would have torn the sword from the hands of Albas and Torquemadas." In the course of the years the obelisk was overthrown and broken, and it was not until 1883 that it was replaced with a copy.[56]

During the weeks following the passing of his grandfather, Thomas Jefferson Randolph, serving as his executor, began to look through his possessions to arrange for their disposition. He found 26,000 letters that Jefferson had received and filed, and copies of 16,000 letters he had sent.

He collected all the scientific instruments and natural history specimens—"the natural and artificial curiosities"—at Monticello, which Jefferson had bequeathed to the University. After packing them, Randolph informed the University, and provision was made for receiving them.

Three months later, in early October, the Board of Visitors "resolved that the faculty be requested forthwith to cause the small room on the first floor of the Rotunda to be finished & fitted for the reception of the natural and artificial curiosities given to the University by the late venerable Rector; and to have them suitably arranged for preservation & exhibition." The Librarian was designated to be in charge of Jefferson's collections.[57]

Young Randolph arranged for the transfer to the University of Virginia, but apparently made no inventory of the collection at the time, nor was one compiled upon their arrival at the University. Two years later, the Board resolved "that the objects of Mr. Jefferson's donation be removed from the small oval room on the first floor of the Rotunda, to the small oval room in the basement story of the same building."

In 1829 the collection was removed to the custody of the Professor of Natural History and Chemistry, and installed on the upper gallery of the Library in the Rotunda. In 1831 the Board commissioned Franklin Peale of Philadelphia to come to the University to "annex nomenclature to the objects of natural . . . curiosity," but whether Peale did so is not recorded.

At some time within the next decade, a "Jefferson Museum" was established as part of the University. In 1840 the Professor of Natural History was authorized to procure "a press for holding such of the objects . . . as cannot otherwise be properly preserved." Later that year the collection was again moved, this time to the "opposite of western hall," probably still within the confines of the library.

Then in 1848 the Board resolved "that such Dormitories on the lawn as the Executive Committee deem most suitable for the purpose be appropriated for the reception of the objects in the Jefferson Museum, the mineralogical and geological collections now in the Rotunda, and those which may hereafter be presented to the University." This is the last certain information about the location of the Jeffersonian materials in the University, but its adventures were not yet over.[58]

In about 1853 an Annex was constructed on the north side of the Rotunda, which was to contain lecture halls, exhibition rooms and a museum. Presumably the Jefferson collection joined other collections in this new building. The natural history artifacts may also have formed part of the museum in the old Chemical Hall constructed in 1868 and 1869, which consisted of choice assemblages of "wonders and beauties of nature," including mineral specimens, many of them analyzed by Professor Dunnington and his students.

The Lewis Brooke Museum was constructed in 1876, but the inventory of its contents published at that time did not include specimens from either the Jefferson or other older collections. Presumably those remained in the Annex or in the museum in Chemical Hall.

According to later records, however, the collections were eventually transferred to the Lewis Brooke Museum, and thus escaped destruction by the fire of the Rotunda in 1895, during which the Annex was totally destroyed with all of its contents.

The old Chemical Hall was destroyed early in the present century. The repeated moves had the unfortunate consequence of dispersing any surviving fossil bones, minerals, Indian artifacts and scientific instruments, and of integrating them into existing collections, so that most of the items lost any identification of their Jefferson association.[59]

The only paleontological specimens documented with certainty to have been part of Jefferson's collection are several which are dramatically displayed on the walls of the Entrance Hall and elsewhere at Monticello. Among them are the upper jawbone and lower mandible of the mastodon, and the antlers of the elk. The source of the mastodon jawbone and mandible is not known with certainty, but it is believed that Jefferson acquired them from Shawungunk, New York, and not from Big Bone Lick. (*Figures 35 and 36*)

A number of the scientific instruments have been preserved at the University or by descendants, and are now displayed at Monticello. Included are two of Jefferson's theodolites, two Dollond pedestal telescopes, an odometer, a polygraph, and a few other items. Regrettably, all trace of his universal equatorial instrument, of which he was so proud, has been lost.

Jefferson had maintained a selection of Indian artifacts at Poplar Forest, where they remained after his death. He had bequeathed the summer residence to his grandson, Francis Eppes, and it may have been assumed that the contents were included in the bequest. On the other hand, because of their distance they may have been overlooked by T. J. Randolph when assembling the materials for the University.

When Eppes later sold Poplar Forest, some of Jefferson's Indian collection remained in the house, and a subsequent owner donated them to the Peale Museum in Philadelphia. Among them were approximately thirty-five Indian artifacts and a group of minerals from the West. Included was the great Mandan buffalo robe with a battle scene. A number of these were purchased from the Peale Museum by Moses Kimball for his museum in Boston, from which they were later acquired by Harvard University.[60]

In Philadelphia on July 8th, four days after Jefferson's death, seventeen members of the American Philosophical Society assembled in Philosophical Hall, with Peter Stephen Du Ponceau in the chair. On a motion made by Robert Patterson, they resolved that the President's chair which Jefferson had occupied for so many years be draped in black for six months and that a public discourse commemorating Jefferson be presented by a member to be appointed. A letter of condolences was to be sent to his family, with a certified copy of the proceedings, and a similar letter was to be sent to the Royal Academy of Inscriptions and Belles Lettres in Paris, of which he had been a member, informing its members of Jefferson's death. Nicholas Biddle was chosen as orator, and similar resolutions were passed on member John Adams, who had died the same day.[61]

Many orations to commemorate Jefferson were delivered throughout the country during the ensuing months, but the only one which dealt adequately with Jefferson's contributions to science was made by Dr. Samuel Latham Mitchill, the invited speaker at the New York Lyceum of Natural History, of which Jefferson had been elected a member.

On October 11, 1826, Mitchill presented "A Discourse on the Character and Services of Thomas Jefferson, more especially as a promoter of Natural and Physical Science." In addition to listing the many important contributions made by Jefferson, Mitchill also mentioned the limitations and faults of some of his scientific endeavors, and particularly extolled the visionary character of some of the statesman's views.[62]

The official eulogium was delivered before the American Philosophical Society by Biddle on April 11, 1827. His theme was that in Jefferson's view, "the highest studies are those which advance man's moral dignity and improve his intellectual and physical condition." In this manner he explained Jefferson's comparative neglect of metaphysics and the purely theoretical sciences. He also pointed out the character of his destiny, about which Jefferson had said to a friend, "The whole of my life has been at war with my natural tastes, feelings and wishes. Circumstances have led me along the path I have trodden, and like a bow bent I resume with delight the character and pursuits for which nature designed me."[63]

Jefferson's passing was mourned by the world of science in many countries. In France, Baron Cuvier, in the fifth volume of his monumental work, praised Jefferson as "the former President of the United States, whose virtues and talents have done so much for the happiness of the people who have chosen him as their leader, who has won the admiration of all the friends of mankind and in whom these superior qualities were combined with an enlightened love for the sciences and a broad knowledge of scientific subjects to which he has made notable contributions."[64]

Charles Lemesle presented before the Société Linnéanne de Paris an "Elogé de Thomas Jefferson ancien Président des États-Unis de l'Amérique du Nord, Membre honoraire de la Société Linneanne de Paris," which was published in the fifth volume of the society's Mémoires in 1827.

Lemesle recalled Cuvier's tribute to the statesman, and noted particularly that he had presented the fine collection of fossils to the Institut de France, that he had sent the model of his mouldboard to the Société d'Agriculture de la Seine, of which he was a member, that he had assisted the refugee Joseph Priestley in his flight from England and that he had maintained correspondence with many scientific societies in Europe.[65]

In retrospect, Jefferson was a perennial student, constantly endeavoring to absorb the entire range of earthly wisdom and to transmit it to others. His ventures into specialized fields, because he was a layman, must be considered objectively in relation to the achievements of the professionals in those fields. In his scientific convictions he was totally unafraid, daring to dispute with and correct the great French naturalists, and to disparage the medical practices of his time, for which he had ample justification.

Although he never acquired the degree of proficiency in some of the sciences as did a few of his contemporaries, because of the priorities of his public service, Jefferson nonetheless had a wider overall knowledge of every branch of science and education, and specifically of their potential national utility, than did any other American of the period in which he lived.

Nor did anyone have as wide an acquaintance among contemporary men of science at home and abroad. His mind touched upon almost everything that was human, as reflected in his surviving papers and letters, the memoranda of his studies and the library collections he assembled.

Jefferson was one of the first Americans to apply the word "civilization," a word that first came into being in the mid-eighteenth century, in his interpretation of the history that had been made or was about to be made. In doing so, he proved himself to be an eminently civilized man with a worldview of civilization, and one who worked creatively for civilization.

Jefferson's chief intellectual preoccupation was the discovery and presentation of new truths. A disciple of the Enlightenment and proponent of the Newtonian philosophy, he was unceasingly dedicated to the application of science in its most general meaning, as the most certain means of advancing progress and human happiness in the new republic.

Of past American presidents, he was the most versatile in the range of his knowledge and interests. When in 1775 he first appeared at the Continental Congress, John Adams had noted that the young lawyer had already gained "a reputation for literature, science and a happy talent of composition . . . Writings of his were handed about, remarkable for the peculiar facility of expression."

As Jefferson's interests developed and his preoccupation with the world around him expanded, he emerged as a catalyst and promoter of the sciences, few of which escaped his attention. Some have claimed that he was reminiscent of Descartes, because like the French scientist and philosopher, he believed that there was no problem in science that could not be simplified or quantitatively analyzed.[66]

Reflected in his papers is the lifelong mental struggle he endured, on the one hand to pursue as a private citizen the scientific interests for which he felt he was destined, and on the other hand to fulfill as well as he was able the patriotic obligations to serve his state and the new republic of which he was an architect.

As a man of science, from the time of his youth, Jefferson embraced and absorbed all that was science that came within his purview, and which he sought from correspondents and publications not only at home but also abroad. As such, he maintained weather records for the greater part of his life, and built a network with other observers in various parts of the country. He personally made surveys of various topographical features to obtain a better knowledge of his state, capably using the most sophisticated instruments then available. During all his life he sought and acquired a collection of the finest mathematical instruments available, and had others made to his specifications for particular purposes. He did not collect these as artifacts, but because he required them for his own experimentation and field use.

Throughout his lifetime Jefferson served as observer and informer of the sciences, and literally became the information center for both sides of the Atlantic. As a promoter of science, he had no equal, collecting scientific information at home and abroad by means of a network of associates and correspondents and by conveying it to those who could best benefit from the information and apply it.

In addition to this self-assigned purpose, he made it his mission to bring information about American achievements to the attention of others in foreign countries to demonstrate with understandable pride the talents of his countrymen. He was the first to provide government support of science and to anticipate the formation of the government's scientific agencies long before they came into being.

While countless volumes attest to Jefferson's public career in government, none have attempted to provide a comprehensive account of his unceasing dedication to the application of science as the most certain means of national advancement and human happiness in the new republic. Not only did he advocate the pursuit of the practical sciences for the improvement of the work and condition of his fellow countrymen. he also commended their use to inform the rest of the world about the free republic. Not only was he a statesman in his country's diplomatic service, but he was also a statesman in the service of science.

Jefferson was interested in and preoccupied with all aspects of the sciences then known, including what is now generally known as "technology." In his time, however, the word had not come into common usage, and its substance was included in "science." The word "science," which originally was another word for "knowledge," was then more encompassing than in its present use, and included as well the application of the physical sciences, agriculture, health and medicine, the mechanical arts and in fact all that is now included in "technology."

The word "technology" has an early history, and Captain John Smith may have been the first to use it in his account of his travels in the early seventeenth century. Although its use recurred occasionally since then, it was not until the beginning of the Industrial Revolution in America in the early decades of the nineteenth century that "technology" came to mean the application of the sciences.

It was first used in this manner in 1816 by Professor Jacob Bigelow at Harvard College in his inaugural address when assuming the Rumford Chair of the Application of Science, and it was in connection with his teaching of mechanics that he "invented" the word. The publication of his Rumford lectures in 1829 in a volume entitled *Elements of Technology* popularized the word.[67]

In Jefferson's view, only the practical sciences merited consideration in the service of mankind. These included cartography, surveying, navigation, science teaching and the making of mathematical instruments required to fulfill these needs. Among them he included also agriculture. On the seventy-fifth anniversary of the establishment of the land-grant colleges and of the U. S. Department of Agriculture, Secretary of Agriculture Henry A. Wallace laid upon Jefferson's tomb at Monticello a wreath made symbolically of cereals and plants produced by general science.

In his keynote address later at the University of Virginia, Wallace commented, "It was Jefferson more than any other man of his time who foresaw the fruitfulness of the application of science to agriculture."[68]

Jefferson advocated the precept that in science there must be absolute freedom of inquiry, and that the only legitimate conclusions were those based on careful observation and experiment. He expressed these beliefs in a letter to a young friend, advising "when your mind shall be well improved with science, nothing is necessary to place you in the highest points of view, but to pursue the interests of your country, the interests of your friends, and your own interests also with the purest integrity, the most chaste honor." These words reflected his own total lifelong dedication to science, which had been pre-ordained by the totality of the influences brought to bear upon him from every direction since childhood.[69]

As reflected in many of his writings, Jefferson's preoccupation with the sciences was primarily utilitarian, particularly botany, chemistry, mineralogy, physics and the natural sciences. He considered them worthy of study only insofar as they fulfilled a useful purpose, including the advancement of agriculture and such technical arts as the preparation of food and other domestic products to supply the needs of the family and community.

He graded geology as the least useful of the sciences except for its economic and practical aspects, but speculation "about the modes of creation . . . is too idle to be worth a single hour of any man's life." Nevertheless, he proved to be somewhat latitudinarian by emphasizing always the utilitarian, for in his *Notes*, he engaged in speculation again and again on such topics as the origin of fossil marine shells found on mountaintops, and of the fossil remains of ancient fauna.[70]

Nor did Jefferson's lack of interest in geology ever prevent him, however, from observing natural wonders and appreciating the awesome mystery of their creation and their breathtaking beauty. His facility with language created vivid pictures which are unsurpassed. The "Jefferson Rock" at Harpers Ferry, which lies at the junction of the Potomac and Shenandoah Rivers, for example, was such a scene that he masterfully described.

"The passage of the Potomac through the Blue Ridge is, perhaps, one of the most stupendous scenes in nature. You stand on a very high point of land. On your right comes up the Shenandoah, having ranged along the foot of the mountain an hundred miles to seek a vent. On your left approaches the Potomac, in quest of a passage also. In the moment of their junction, they rush together against the mountain, rend it asunder, and pass off to the sea. The first glance of this scene hurries our senses into the opinion, that this earth has been created in time, that the mountains were formed first, that the rivers began to flow afterwards, that in this place, particularly, they have been dammed up by the Blue Ridge of mountains, and have formed an ocean which filled the whole valley; that continuing to rise they have at length broken over at this spot, and have torn the mountain down from its summit to its base."

He was as excited about the Natural Bridge, situated on land which he owned, and which he considered to be one of the greatest wonders of nature. "It is on the ascent of a hill," he wrote, "which seems to have been cloven through its length by some great convulsion . . . Though the sides of this bridge are provided in some parts with a parapet of fixed rocks, yet few men have resolution to walk to them and look over into the abyss. You voluntarily fall on your hands and feet, creep to the parapet and peep over it. Looking down from this height about a minute, gave me a violent head ach. (This painful sensation is relieved by a short, but pleasing view of the Blue Ridge along the fissure downwards, and upwards by that of the Short hills, which, with the Purgatory mountain, is a divergence from the North ridge; and descending then to the valley below, the sensation becomes delightful in the extreme.) It is impossible for the emotions, arising from the sublime, to be left beyond what they are here: so beautiful an arch, so elevated, so light and spring-ing, as it were, up to heaven, the rapture of the Spectator is really inde-scribable."[71]

In evaluating Jefferson's descriptions of geographical features and natural phenomena in his *Notes*, General A. W. Greely pointed out that although the work had been written half a century before Humboldt's *Kosmos*, the *Notes* had been produced along the lines formulated by Humboldt for scientific geography.

Jefferson, he noted, "described not only its rivers, but their relations to commerce, and especially their possible utility in trade with Ohio, the Great Lakes and the Mississippi Valley. The plants and trees are classified as to their value for ornamental, medicinal and esculent pur-poses. Comparative views are given to native birds and animals with those of Europe. The subject of climate is handled admirably for such an early date. The pressure, rain, temperature and wind are treated briefly and clearly in their general aspects. The effect of seawinds on sail-mak-ing, the prevalence of sunshine, the temperature at which frosts occur and their effect on plant-life, and other similar notes evidence the acute-ness of Jefferson's observations and his happy powers of generalization. If he had exclusively applied himself to geography, there is little doubt he would have distinguished himself in the science."[72]

Jefferson's utilitarian outlook on science was necessarily prompted by the requirements of an emerging new nation having tremendous but unstudied natural resources remaining to be developed. It was an attitude reflecting the times in which he lived, with the discarding of long estab-lished political preponderant influences and with the emergence of new scientific beliefs which gradually replaced other tenaciously held surviv-als from the past. He lived in the time that witnessed the greatest up-heavals in the world of science.

It was the period during which Stahl's phlogistic doctrine, the hypo-thetical principle of fire formerly regarded as a material substance, was pre-empted by Lavoisier's modern system. Haüy's crystallographic order replaced the traditional mixed methods of mineralogical classification, just as Jussieu's natural system replaced the artificial arrangement of Lin-naeus, and de Saussure overthrew the doctrine of the formation of min-eral constituents through forces of vitalization by proving instead that they originated in the soil.

Jefferson remained an interested but conservative spectator of the scientific controversies that raged at home and abroad, keeping himself as well informed as possible, but refraining from conclusions, believing "it is laudable to encourage investigation, but to hold back conclusion." Jefferson warned that although chemistry was "among the most useful of sciences, and big with future discoveries for the utility and safety of the human race," it was still in an embryonic state, "its principles are contested; experiments seem contradictory; their subjects are so minute as to escape our senses; and their results too fallacious to satisfy the mind."[73]

In the same manner he was opposed to the changes being made in scientific nomenclature because he considered them to be premature. He complained that Buffon, "the great advocate of individualism in opposition to classification," would cause a return to the confused days of the Greeks and Romans, foregoing the developments in science of two thousand years by cooperating with "the neologists in rendering the science of one generation useless to the next by perpetual change of language."[74]

Jefferson's insatiable curiosity brought his mind to bear on every science known in his time, but he never posed as an expert in any, although his knowledge of meteorology, geology, botany, astronomy, paleontology, geography and other natural sciences was far greater than superficial. He repeatedly claimed that he was no more than an amateur, but nonetheless he brought to these sciences a wide philosophical interpretation, maintaining a cosmic outlook always, in contrast to other contemporary writers on these subjects.

A few years after his death, M. Conseil in the introduction to his work, *Mélanges politique et philosophique*, acknowledged Jefferson as "the master of the liberal school which had assumed the name "école américaine."[75]

Inevitably he made errors, which were immediately realized and magnified by his critics. It was pointed out that his paper on the *Megalonyx,*, for example, was prepared without the requisite scientific analysis and care. He might have excused his errors in scientific matters in the same words of his message to both houses of Congress in 1801 which so suitably expressed his personality:

> I shall often go wrong, through defect of judgement. When right, I shall often be thought wrong to those whose positions will not command a view of the whole ground. I ask your indulgence for my own errours, which will never be intentional; and your support against the errours of others, who may condemn what they would not, if seen in all its parts. The approbation implied by your suffrage is a great consolation to me for the past; and my future solicitude will be, to retain the good opinion of those who have bestowed it in advance, to conciliate that of others by doing them all the good in my power, and to be instrumental to the happiness and freedom of all.[76]

Jefferson cannot be described as a "scientist," nor was he only a "man of science," but he was above all a "statesman of science." As such, Jefferson's greatest achievement was the promotion of the sciences in the embryonic new republic, for which he used every opportunity and every means available to him in private life and in public office.

While minister to France, he kept the four major American colleges—Harvard, Yale, the University of Pennsylvania and the College of William and Mary—informed of scientific activities in Europe. He was awarded honorary degrees by four American colleges—William and Mary in 1783, Yale in 1786, Harvard in 1787 and Princeton in 1791— and received numerous foreign honors for his scientific endeavors and contributions.

Occasionally inaccurate, impractical, and accused of being too visionary in his science-related endeavors, he was nevertheless responsible for the first government support of science, and for the support of government by science. Jefferson conceived the establishment of scientific agencies in the government, several of which came into being in his time and others which were realized thereafter on principles he had proposed.

Notable among these was the national weather bureau, a proposal he had described to Count Volney as early as 1797. He may be considered to have been the father of the Bureau of Standards, having established the system of weights and measures for the government. He was closely involved with the founding and management of the first United States Mint at Philadelphia, and devised the first system of coinage and currency.

Jefferson was among the first in the American colonies to conduct meteorological studies, maintaining and distributing records from his student days to the last years of his life. He encouraged others to do the same, and established what constituted a virtual weather service with the assistance of many. He believed that only by means of simultaneous observations made at considerable distances could knowledge of weather be derived that would be useful.

Throughout his long career in public office, Jefferson remained nonetheless a practical farmer. He was widely read on all aspects of agriculture, and his library included 78 books on the subject, 48 of which were in English, 24 in French, 5 in Italian and 1 in Latin, all of which he could read. His farming activities reported in his *Farm Book* and *Garden Book* reveal that he was also an agricultural engineer, competent in fencing, roadbuilding and bridging as well as in developing farm crops and in planting.

As a horticulturist he experimented with many varieties of plants and vegetables. He was at the same time a conservationist, advocating the rotation of crops and the amelioration of soils by a variety of means. He was among the first to undertake contour ploughing to prevent soil erosion, and initiated gall and gulley control and controlled woodland cutting.

He converted his lands into progressive experimental farms for the testing of new machinery, new agricultural methods and new crops. One of his principal contributions to agriculture was his design of a mouldboard based on mathematical principles which could be readily duplicated "by the coarsest workman, by a process so exact that it's shape shall never be varied by a single hair's breadth."[77]

Considering agriculture to be the basic industry of the new nation, he advocated instruction in agriculture in the colleges, and he promoted the formation of agricultural societies as a means of developing and communicating good farming techniques. He exchanged plants and methods of husbandry as well as innovative ideas with correspondents at home and overseas, and introduced many new plants to the United States.

He strongly advocated mandatory teaching of the practical sciences in the schools and colleges throughout the country. From his earliest years he was influenced by books, the collecting of which became a lifelong passion. He read much of history from Tacitus to Macauley. He learned to use his sources as evidenced during his study of law, when he approached the dusty tomes of the profession as an archeologist, digging as far back as the Saxon ancestors.

Throughout his life he drew inspiration from the books he had studied as a youth—Homer, Epicurus, Epictetus, Cicero, Shakespeare and the Bible. In the sciences, his greatest inspiration came from the works of Lord Francis Bacon, Isaac Newton and John Locke. To John Trumbull he had written, "I consider them [Bacon, Newton and Locke] as the three greatest men that have ever lived, without any exception, and as having laid the foundation of those super structures which have been raised in the Physical and Moral Sciences."[78]

With his inventive mind, Jefferson produced various utilitarian devices and improved others that already existed. Of particular importance was his invention of the cryptographic device he called his "wheel cipher" for secret diplomatic communication. Although it was not applied in his time, it served the American military forces for several decades in the twentieth century. His design of a mouldboard for the wooden plough would have advanced agriculture considerably had it not been replaced by the introduction of the iron plough a short time later.

In medicine, Jefferson was an innovator. Encouraging research in all its aspects, he advocated education in medicine, and was a promoter of public health. He was greatly opposed to the inexpert and unschooled medical practises of the physicians of his time, and spoke out against the usage of bleeding in particular. He played a significant role in establishing vaccination as a preventative against smallpox on a national scale by distributing the vaccine among physicians in the mid-Atlantic and Southern states, and later initiating vaccination among the Indians.

He deserves the title of the first scientific archeologist for his excavation of an Indian mound in his region, applying for the first time the principles of stratification which became and remain standard professional practice, a technique with which he was almost a century ahead of his time.

Often called "the father of American paleontology" for the important role he played in popularizing almost single-handedly that emerging new science in the United States, he made it a respectable pursuit. His unending efforts to collect, preserve and study fossil remains, often at substantial personal cost, distributing many specimens to institutions where others could study them, were responsible for preserving many specimens that otherwise would have been ignored or destroyed.

In Jefferson's time it was not yet known that the scientific examination of ambient technologies would be so difficult and relatively unproductive of technological advance as it proved to be in later generations. It was not until long after Jefferson's death that enough was known about chemistry, for example, to comment usefully on iron smelting. Certainly it was not until very recently that there was any basic science for understanding why textile materials, as another example, worked as they did.

Not knowing the difficulties, and not yet reaching even the stage that Josiah Wedgwood had in systematic technological experimentation to produce fine china, the natural philosophers of the late seventeenth and early eighteenth centuries indulged in an orgy of turning all available technologies into subject matter for their natural philosophy.

A particularly fine example is the sort of investigations made by Robert Hooke and other Fellows of the Royal Society of the felt industry of London. This was precisely the type of philosophy that Francis Bacon had fondly imagined would provide some sort of science of felt-making with resulting increase of the economy and quality of the land. This pathetically over-simplified hopefulness extended all the way from Bacon to today's Vannevar Bush.

It is into this tradition in the natural philosophy of technology that Jefferson fitted so magnificently. He was interested equally in the technical aspects of ice houses and of clocks, not so much for their practical returns, but in the same manner that he was intrigued by a fine scientific instrument or an astronomical observation.

Recognition of Jefferson's scientific endeavors came in two ways. On the negative side, he was maliciously vilified again and again by political opponents, men of religion and the press, beginning during his Vice Presidency and increasing apace during the Presidential campaigns of 1800 and 1804.

Much of the antagonism of which he became the target reflected the strong feeling against the Republican party of which he emerged as the leader. He became the prime target for everything from his political theories, his religious beliefs and his private life to his philosophy and scientific activities.

A favorite claim was that a "philosopher" could only be incompetent in fulfilling the requirements of the nation's highest offices. His sponsorship of French arts in particular became anathema to the syncophants of British monarchy among the Federalists.

After his retirement, Jefferson had occasion to make one of the few responses he ever made on the accusations and criticisms which had been brought against him during public office. "Of all the charges brought against me by my political adversaries," he commented, "that of possessing some science has probably done them the least credit. Our countrymen are too enlightened themselves, to believe that ignorance is the best qualification for their service." Later he noted, "Even science itself as well as my affection for it is a fit object of ridicule and a disqualification for the affairs of government."[79]

On the other hand, this calumny was counteracted by favorable recognition which came in the form of many honors and memberships in scholarly societies at home and abroad. In addition to honorary degrees from four of the foremost American colleges, he was the first American to be made an associate of the Institut de France, and elected to membership in many agricultural societies in the United States and Europe.

One of his earliest biographers, Henry S. Randall, noted that he had seen in the aged stateman's possession "A large collection of diplomas, in almost every language in Europe, conferring degrees, honorary memberships, &c. on him." These included the Dutch Royal Institute of Sciences, Literature and the Fine Arts, the Linnaean Society of Paris, the Agronomic Society of Bavaria, the Board of Agriculture of London, an agronomic society in Florence and numerous others.

In his own country, he was honored with membership in the American Academy of Arts and Sciences, The New-York Historical Society, the American Antiquarian Society, the Society of Artists of the United States, the Virginia Society for the Promotion of Useful Knowledge, the Linnaean Society of Philadelphia, the South Carolina Agricultural Society and the Agricultural Society of the Valley, among many others.[80]

The organization to which he devoted the most time and attention was the American Philosophical Society, of which he was a member for forty-six years and president for seventeen years. He made numerous contributions of specimens to its collections, and presented two important papers which were published in the Society's *Transactions*.

Despite the calumny heaped upon him by politicians, religious leaders and the newspapers, contemporary men of science nonetheless held him in high esteem. An impressive tribute was the renaming of the genus *Podophyllum diphyllum* to *Jeffersonia binata* by Dr. Benjamin Smith Barton. In a paper read before the American Philosophical Society, Barton wrote, "Having not found it described by any authors, except Linnaeus and Clayton, neither of whom had seen the flowers, and as it is, certainly, a new family, I take the liberty of making it known to the botanist by the name of JEFFERSONIA in honor of Thomas Jefferson, Esq., Secretary of State to the United States.

"I beg leave to observe to you, in this place, that in imposing upon this genus the name of Mr. Jefferson, I have had no reference to his political character, or to his reputation for general science, and for literature. My business was with his knowledge of natural history. In the various departments of this science, but especially in botany and zoology, the information of this gentleman is equalled by that of few persons in the United-States." Barton also dedicated to Jefferson his work, *New Views of the Origins of the Tribes and Nations of America.*[81]

Jefferson's lifelong preoccupation with science and his confidence in the American future was most succinctly stated in a comment to Dr. Benjamin Waterhouse:

> When I contemplate the immense advances in sciences and discoveries in the arts which have been made within the period of my life, I look forward with confidence to equal advances by the present generation, and have no doubt they will consequently be as much wiser than we have been as we than our fathers were, and they than the burners of witches.[82]

ABBREVIATIONS

AHR	American Historical Review
APS	American Philosophical Society
Autobiography	In *The Complete Jefferson*, ed. by Saul K. Padover
Bixby	*Thomas Jefferson Correspondence*, Bixby Collection
Boyd	*The Papers of Thomas Jefferson*, edited by Julian P. Boyd
Calendar	*Calendar of the Correspondence of Thomas Jefferson*, State Department Library
CSmH	Henry E. Huntington Library and Art Gallery
DAB	*Dictionary of American Biography*
DLC	The Library of Congress, Manuscripts Division, *The Papers of Thomas Jefferson*
DNB	*Dictionary of National Biography*
Force	*American Archives*, edited by Peter Force
Farm Book	*Thomas Jefferson's Farm Book*, edited by Edwin M. Betts
Ford	*The Writings of Thomas Jefferson*, edited by Paul Leicester Ford
Garden Book	*Thomas Jefferson's Garden Book*, edited by Edwin M. Betts
HAW	*The Writings of Thomas Jefferson*, edited by Henry A. Washington
L&B	*The Writings of Thomas Jefferson*, edited by A. Lipscomb and A. E. Bergh
Letters	*The Letters of the Lewis and Clark Expedition*, edited by Donald Jackson
Malone	*Jefferson and His Time* (6 vols.) by Dumas Malone
Memorandum	*Memorandum Books:*
Book	1767–1770: DLC
	1771 : MHi
	1772 : MHi
	1773 : DLC
	1774 : MHi
	1775 : CSmH
	1776–1778: MHi
	1779–1782: DLC
	1783–1790: MHi
	1791–1803: NN
	1804–1808: NHi
MHi	Massachusetts Historical Society, *The Coolidge-Jefferson Papers*
MoHSi	Missouri Historical Society
NHi	The New-York Historical Society
NN	New York Public Library
Notes	*Notes On the State of Virginia* by Thomas Jefferson
PHi	Historical Society of Pennsylvania

NOTE: In citing Jefferson's correspondence, only the name of the originator or recipient is provided with the understanding that the other correspondent is Jefferson.

PMHB	*Pennsylvania Magazine of History and Biography*
PPAmP	American Philosophical Society, Collections
Randall	*The Life of Thomas Jefferson* by Henry S. Randall (3 vols.)
SNR	*The Domestic Life of Thomas Jefferson* by Sarah N. Randolph
TJ	Thomas Jefferson as originator or recipient of correspondence
TJR	Thomas Jefferson Randolph
TMR	Thomas Mann Randolph, Jr.
ViU	University of Virginia, Alderman Library, Manuscripts Division
VMHB	*Virginia Magazine of History and Biography*
VQR	*Virginia Quarterly Review*
WMQ	*William and Mary Quarterly*
WMQHM	*William and Mary College Quarterly and Historical Magazine*

APPENDIX
DOCUMENTS

DOCUMENT 1. Amendment to act concerning surveyors. *Virginia Gazette*, June 1, 1773.

Surveyors are directed and obliged, under a certain Penalty, to return (plat or Protract) all new surveys by the true and not by the artificial or magnetic Meridian. By the true Meridian is meant that line or Direction in which the Surveyor's Needle is generally supposed to lie, or point in, when at Rest, but which, from some unknown Cause, it does not, and from which indeed it is constantly varying, vibrating imperceptibly between certain hitherto unknown Limits eastward and westward of that Direction; or in other Words, it is the Direction in which Shadows are cast by the Meridian Sun; or, it is the true north and South Line. By the magnetick or artificial Meridian is meant a north and South Line found by a Magnet, or Surveyor's Compass. Now this line is constantly varying, sometimes to the West and sometimes to the East of the true Meridian; and as the Bounds of our Lands are always run, or taken, by a magnetick Needle, and are laid down, or plat[ted], as making certain Angles with the Direction of the Needle, or magnetick Meridian; these Bounds must likewise vary, running my Land upon my Neighbor's, and his upon mine. This has often happened, and been productive of Lawsuits and much Confusion. But when Surveyors will take the Pains to find the Variation of their Needles, and protract their Surveys by the true Meridian, which never changes, their Surveys must always agree with a correct Survey reduced to the true Meridian, and their Courses will always be found to run in the same Direction; and then, if there should but one Tree be found in a given Course, and all the bounds are lost, they will easily find them, because then the old Courses may be reduced to the true Meridian and may be found by the Compass corrected.

There are many methods proposed and practised for finding the true Meridian Line, but none more, simple, or better adapted to a Surveyor's Purpose, than that proposed by Mr. THOMAS MARSHALL of Fauquier, who first proposed the Amendment of the Act directing Surveys of Land. His instrument is cheap and portable, and the Method of using it may be easily learned.

It may be had of Mr. *Dickinson* in Williamsburg. You may, if you please, and will probably oblige many of your Readers by it, to publish out of Ferguson's Astronomy, and out of his Lectures, his Method of providing a Meridian Line.

DOCUMENT 2. Description of a hygrometer invented by David Rittenhouse. Letter from Jefferson to Benjamin Vaughan, December 29, 1786 (Boyd, vol. 10, p. 647).

I think Mr. Rittenhouse never published an invention of his in this way, which was a very good one. It was of a hygrometer, which like the common ones was to give the actual moisture of the air. He had two slips of mahogany about 5. I. long, ¾ I. broad and ¹⁄₁₀ I. thick, the one having the grain running lengthwise, and the other crosswise. These are glued together by their faces, so as to form a piece 5. I. long, ¾ I. broad and ⅕ I. thick. which is stuck, by its lower end, into a little plinth of wood thus [DRAWING 1] presenting their edges to the view. The fibres of wood you know are dilated but not lengthened by moisture. The slip therefore whose grain is lengthwise, becomes a standard, retaining always the same precise length. That which has it's grain crosswise, dilates with moisture and contracts with the want of it. If the right hand peice above represented be the cross grained one, when the air is very moist, it lengthens and forces it's companion to form a kind of interior annulus of a circle on the left thus [DRAWING 2]. When the air is dry, it contracts, draws it's companion to the right, and becomes itself the inner annulus, thus [DRAWING 3]. In order to shew this dilation and contraction, an index is fixed on the upper end of the two slips: a plate of metal or wood is fastened to the front of the plinth so as to cover the two slips from the eye. A slit, being nearly the portion of a circle, is cut in this plate so that the shank of the index may play freely through it's whole range. On the edge of the slit is a graduation, so that the instrument shews somewhat thus [DRAWING 4]. The objection to this instrument is that it is not fit for comparative observations, because no two peices of wood being of the same texture exactly, no two will yeild exactly alike to the same agent. However it is less objectionable on this account than most of the substances used. Mr. Rittenhouse had a thought of trying ivory: but I do not know whether he executed it. All these substances not only vary from one another at the same time, but from themselves at different times. All of them however have some peculiar advantages, and I think this on the whole appeared preferable to any other I had ever seen.

DOCUMENT 3. "Mathematical Apparatus" owned by Jefferson. Listing made by Jefferson at some time after 1786. MHi, *Coolidge-Jefferson Papers*.

		£	s.	
A case of pocket instruments	cost	4	4	Ster.
A pair of [Jones's?] globes 18 I[nches] diam. in Wainscot frames		9	7	
Martin's—portable air pump & apparatus Jones		12	12	
An Electrical apparatus				
A best Barometer		1	11	6
Farenheit's thermometer with Reaumur's scale on one side				
Pocket thermometer with Farenheit's & Reaumur's scales				
An Ombrometer of glass		0	– 5	
Hydrostatic balance by Dollond		1	– 16	
Hydrometer by Dollond		1	11	6
An Achromatic telescope with three object glasses by Dolond		10	– 10	
A Telescope of Iceland chrystal by the Abbés Rochon & Herbage				
A Compound microscope by Jones		4	– 7	
Solar microscope in brass by Dollond		5	16	6
Scioptric ball and socket. by Dollond			10	6
A Botanical microscope			10	
A Cloth microscope			3	
A Concave mirrour 12. I[nches]		2	5	
3 prisms & stand by Dollond		1	7	6
a Theodolite by Ramsden. the spirit level 2-1/2 I[nches]		26	5	
*an Equatorial by Ramsden		40	13	
*a Hadley's circle of Borda by Jones 10 I[nches]		26	15	6
*a pocket graphometer by Cole 3-7/8 I[nches] diam.		4	11	6
*a common Theodolite or Graphometer 8 I[nches]		54	D.	
a Gunter's chain			4	
*a 3 I[nch] pocket box Sextant by Jones with platina limb		3	6	

In Jefferson's manuscript inventory items marked with < > were deleted by a line drawn through them. The list includes purchases made in England during Jefferson's visit in 1786 and later by correspondence, as well as several instruments purchased in the United States. The latter are marked with an *.

	£	s.	
Perambulator			
⟨a pocket level by Shuttleworth	1	1⟩	
*⟨a spirit level⟩			
*Marshall's meridian instrument mahogany 20/# currency			
⟨ by Ramsden ⟩			
⟨an Astronomical Quadrant by Bird⟩			
⟨Apparatus for sketching of the mechanical p[apers?]⟩			
a Pantographer for reducing drawings by Shuttleworth	1	11	6
a Ring dial 5 I[nches] diam.	0	14	0
⟨a second clock⟩			
a clock with the grid-iron pendulum			

DOCUMENT 4. Instructions from Jefferson to William Short for the construction of the Pyramid Clock. Letter dated after March 12, 1790, College of William and Mary, Library.

This, mr. Short may recollect, was the form of the little clock which was stolen from the chimney of my study. the parts, a, b, c, d were parts of a cone, being round and tapering to the top, [DRAWING] where a gilt head was put on. I would wish one to be made like that as to the pedestal part, but with obelisks as is represented here. a. b. c. d. instead of conical columns as the former had. no gilt head to be on the obelisk, but to be in plain marble, cut off obliquely as is always done in the obelisk. the section of an obelisk, you know, is a square; I mean its ichnography. the clock to have a pendulum vibrating half seconds exactly. to have a second hand, but none for the days of the week, month or moon. to strike the hours and half hours. the dial plate to be open work, or as the French workmen say, le cadran a jour. of black marble, the superintendent of the Salle des vents (where I bought mine) undertook to have a clock on the above plan made for me, for either 12. or 15. guieas, I forget which. he required only three or four weeks. I shall be obliged to mr. Short to have one made immediately, for me, that it may be done in time to come with my other things. . . . [DRAWING]

DOCUMENT 5. "Mechanism for the table." Letter from James Madison to Jefferson May 1, 1791, (Boyd vol. 20, pp. 337–38). 2 drawings.

A thought has occurred on the subject of your mechanism for the table, which in my idle situation will supply me with another paragraph, if of no other use. The great difficulty incident to your contrivance seemed to be that of supporting the weight of the Castor without embarrassing the shortening and lengthening of the movable radius. Might not this be avoided by suspending the Castor by a chain or chord on a radius above, and requiring nothing more of yours than to move the swinging apparatus: thus. A.B. moveable on a shoulder at A. would be a necessary brace, and must allow C.D. to pass thro' it and play from a to b as the tongs are shortened or lengthened. The use of C.D. would be to connect F.G. and the tongs, so as to make them move together on the common perpendicular axis. As the distance from C to D must vary with the protraction of the tongs, the connecting bar ought to be long accordingly, and pass through without being fixed to the tongs. Its office would in that state be sufficiently performed. The objections to this plan are 1. The height of the perpendicular axis necessary to render the motion of the Castor easy, and to diminish the degree in which it would mount up at the end of the table. Perhaps this objection may be fatal. 2. The necessity of adjusting the friction of the tongs so as not to be inconvenient to the hand, and be sufficient to stop and hold the castor at any part of the table. In this point of view perhaps a slide on a spring would be better than the tongs. In that case C.D. might be fixed, and not moveable in the brace.—By projecting F.G. to H. the castor might be made to swing perpendicularly not at the part of the table least distant, but at the mean distance from the Center, and the difference between its greatest and least elevation and pressure diminished. But inconveniences of another sort might be increased by this expedient. If the tongs or slide were to be placed not horizontally, but inclining so as to lessen the effect of the pressure of the Castor without being less moveable by the hand, the 2nd objection might be lessened. It would in that case be of less consequence to project the upper radius as proposed. [DRAWINGS]

DOCUMENT 6. Subscription list for proposed André Michaux expedition to explore the West, January 1793. In the hand of Thomas Jefferson. American Philosophical Society.

Whereas Andrew Michaux, a native of France, and inhabitant of the United States has undertaken to explore the interior country of North America from the Mississippi along the Missouri, and Westwardly to the Pacific ocean, or in such other direction as shall be ordered by the American Philosophical society, & on his return to communicate to the said society the information he shall have acquired of the geography of the said country it's inhabitants, soil, climate, animals, vegetables, minerals & other circumstances of note: We the Subscribers, desirous of obtaining for ourselves relative to the land we live on, and of communicating to the world, information so interesting to curiosity, to science, and to the future prospects of mankind, promise for ourselves, our heirs, executors & administrators, that we will pay the said Andrew Michaux, or his assigns, the sums herein affixed to our names respectively, one fourth part thereof on demand, the remaining three fourths whenever, after his return, the said Philosophical society shall declare themselves satisfied that he has performed the s[ai]d journey & that he has communicated to them freely all the information which he shall have acquired & they demanded of him: or if the s[ai]d Andrew Michaux shall not proceed to the Pacific ocean and shall reach the sources of the waters running into it, then we will pay him such part only of the remaining three fourths, as the said Philosophical society shall deem duly proportioned to the extent of unknown country explored by him in the direction prescribed as compared with that omitted to be explored. And we consent that the bills of exchange of the s[ai]d Andrew Michaux, for monies said to be due him in France, shall be received to the amount of two hundred Louis, & shall be negotiated by the s[ai]d Philosophical society, and the proceeds thereof retained in their hands, to be delivered to the said Andrew Michaux, on his return, after having performed the journey to their satisfaction, or if not to their satisfaction, then to be applied towards reimbursing the subscribers the fourth of their subscription advanced to the said Andrew Michaux. We consent also that the said Andrew Michaux shall take himself all benefit arising from the publication of the discoveries he shall make in the three departments of Natural history, Animal, Vegetable and Mineral, he concerting with the said Philosophical society such measures for securing to himself the said benefit as shall be consistent with the due publication of the sd discoveries. In witness we have hereto subscribed our names and affixed the sums we engage respectively to contribute.

The first signature is that of George Washington, subscribing $100, followed by John Adams $20, and among the others are Henry Knox, Jefferson and Alexander Hamilton, each subscribing $50. There is a total of thirty-eight signatures. The document was presented to Michaux on April 30, 1793. In a letter of the same date Jefferson provided specific objectives for the expedition and instructions for achieving them.

DOCUMENT 7. "Project of a cypher." Library of Congress, Manuscripts Division, *The Papers of Thomas Jefferson*, fol. 22608. Rough draft copy, fol. 41575. Undated.

Turn a cylinder of white wood about 2. I[nches] diameter & 6. or 8. I[nches] long. bore through its center hole sufficient to recieve an iron spindle or axis of ⅛ or ¼ I.[nches] diam. divide the periphery into 26. equal parts (for the 26. letters of the alphabet) and, with a sharp point, draw parallel lines through all the points of division from one end to the other of the cylinder, & trace those lines with ink to make them plain. then cut the cylinder crosswise into pieces of about ⅙ of an inch thick.

they will resemble back-gammon men with plane sides. number each of them, as they are cut off, on one side, that they may be arrangeable in any order you please. on the periphery of each, and between the black lines, put all the letters of the alphabet, not in their established order, but jumbled & without order, so that no two shall be alike, now string them in their numerical order on an iron axis, one end of which has a head, and the other a nut and screw; the use of which is to hold them firm in any given position when you chuse it. they are now ready for use, your correspondent having a similar cylinder, similarly arranged.

Suppose I have to cypher this phrase, "Your favor of the 22.d is recieved."
I turn the lst wheel till the letter y. presents itself
I turn the 2nd and place it's . o. by the side of the y. of the lst wheel.
I turn the 3rd & place it's . u. by the side of the o. of the 2nd

4th . . . . r. by the side of the 3rd
5th . . . . f. by the side of the 4th
6th . . . . a. by the side of the 5th

and so on until I have got all the words of the phrase arranged in one line. fix them with the screw. you will observe that the cylinder then presents 25. other lines of letters, not in any regular series, but jumbled, & without order or meaning. copy any one of them in the letter to your correspondent, when he recieves it, he takes his cylinder and arranges the wheels so as to present the same jumbled letters in the same order in one line. he then fixes them with his screw, and examines the other 25 lines and finds one of them presenting him these letters:
"yourfavorofthe22isrecieved." which he writes down. as the others will be jumbled & have no meaning, he cannot mistake the true one intended. so proceed with every other portion of the letter. numbers had better be represented by letters with dots over them; as for instance, by the 6 vowels & 4 liquids. because if the periphery were divided into 36. instead of 26. lines for the numerical, as well as alphabetical characters, it would increase the trouble of finding the letters on the wheels.

When the cylinder is fixed, with the jumbled alphabets on their peripheries, by only changing the order of the wheels of the cylinder, an immense variety of different cyphers may be produced for different correspondents. for whatever be the number of wheels, if you take all the natural numbers from unit to that inclusive, & multiply them successively into one another, their product will be the number of different combinations of which the wheels are susceptible, and consequently of the different cyphers they may form for different correspondents, entirely unintelligible to each other. for the every one possesses the cylinder, and with the alphabets similarly arranged on the wheels, yet if the order be interverted, but one line similar through the whole cylinder can be produced on any two of them.

DOCUMENT 8. "The Great Clock." Manuscript specifications. Library of Congress, Manuscripts Division, *The Papers of Thomas Jefferson*, fol. 41588. Undated, [1793].

the works are 15, I[nches] deep, from the plate to the farthest point in the back.

a circle of 12 I.[nches] radius round the center of the hour circle, will barely cover the remotest point of the works.

the center of vibration of the pendulum is 7 I.[nches] above the point back end of the axis of the hour hand.

the arc of vibration is (at the bob) 18 I.[nches]

the same arc, at 7 I.[nches] below the center, will be 3 I.[nches]-

then a toothed wheel of 2 I.[nches]on the back-end of the axis of the hour hand, taking in an equal wheel whose axis will be of course 2 I.[nches] horizontally from that of hour hand, will be clear of the vibration of the pendulum, and may turn an hour hand on the reverse of the wall on a wooden hour plate of 12 I.[nches] radius. there need be no minute hand, as the hour figures will be 6 I.[nches] apart. but the interspace should be divided into quarters and 5. minute marks. the fore & back hour plates will not be concentric. The center axis of the second hand 4-⅙ I.[nches] from that of the hour hand (i. e., their centers) the radius of the second circle (i.e. length of hand) 1-¾ I.[nches].

DOCUMENT 9. "Notes for the use of Borda's circle." University of Virginia, Alderman Library, *Accession 5533*, Box 3161. Undated.

the whole periphery is divided into $720 = 360 \times 2$.

the graduation is numbered to 160 on each side of the zero.

The under with adjusting screws works on the numbered gradua[tio]n from zero upwards or towards the long handle for direct observa[tio]n and from zero downwards, or towards the short handle, [*illegible*] artificial horizon is used. When the observ[atio]n is direct, i.e., on the ascend[in]g graduat[io]n, count the Nonius ascendingly from the lower zero on it, commands it by the upper screw.

DOCUMENT 10. Letter from Jefferson to Caspar Wistar, June 21, 1807. The Library of Congress, Manuscripts Division, *The Papers of Thomas Jefferson*.

We know, from what we see and feel, that the animal body is in its organs and functions subject to derangement inducing pain, and tending to its destruction. In this disordered state, we observe nature providing for the re-establishment of order, by exciting some salutary evacuation of the morbid matter or by some other operation which escapes our imperfect senses and researches. She brings on a crisis, by stools, vomiting, sweat, urine, expectoration, bleeding, &c., which, for the most part, ends in the restoration of healthy action. Experience has taught us also, that there are certain substances, by which, applied to the living body, internally or externally, we can at will produce these same evacuations, and thus do, in a short time, what nature would do but slowly, and do effectually, what perhaps she would not have the strength to accomplish. Where, then, we have seen a disease, characterized by specific signs or phenomena, and relieved by a certain natural evacuation or process, whenever that disease recurs under the same appearances, we may reasonably count on producing a solution of it, by the use of such substances as we have found produce the same evacuation or movement. Thus, fulness of the stomach we can relieve by emetics; diseases of the bowels, by purgatives; inflammatory cases, by bleeding; intermittents, by the Peruvian bark; syphilis, by mercury; watchfulness, by opium; &c. So far, I bow to the utility of medicine. It goes to the well-defined forms of disease, and happily, to those most frequent. But the disorders of the animal body, and the symptoms indicating them, are as various as the elements of which the body is composed. The combinations, too, of these symptoms are so infinitely diversified, that many associations of them appear too rarely to establish a definite disease; and to an unknown disease there cannot be a known remedy. Here then, the judicious, the moral, the human physician should stop. Having been so often a witness to the salutory effects which nature makes to re-establish the disordered functions, he should rather trust to their action, than hazard the interruption of that, and a greater derangement of the system, by conjectural experiments on a machine so complicated and so unknown as the human body, and a subject so sacred as human life. Or, if the appearance of doing something be necessary to keep alive the hope and spirits of the patient, it should be of the most innocuous nature. One of the most successful physicians I have ever known, has assured me, that he has used more bread pills, drops of colored water, and powders of hickory ashes, than of all other medicines put together. It was certainly a pious fraud. But the adventurous physician goes on, and substitutes presumption for knowledge. From the scanty field of what is known, he launches into the boundless region of what is unknown. He establishes for his guide some fanciful theory of corpuscular attraction, of chemical agency, of mechanical powers, of stimuli, of irritability accumulated or exhausted, of depletion by the lancet and repletion by mercury, or some other ingenious dream, which lets him into all nature's secrets at short hand. On the principle which he thus assumes, he forms his table of nosology, arrays his diseases into families, and extends his curative treatment, by analogy, to all the cases he has thus arbitrarily marshalled together. I have lived myself to see the disciples of Hoffman, Boerhaave, Stahl, Cullen, Brown, succeed one another like the shifting figures of a magic lantern, and their fancies, like the dresses of the annual doll-babies from Paris, becoming, from their novelty, the vogue of the day, and yielding to the next novelty their ephemeral favor. The patient, treated on the fashionable theory, sometimes gets well in spite of the medicine. The medicine, therefore, restored him, and the young doctor receives new courage to proceed in his bold experiments on the lives of his fellow-creatures. I believe we may safely affirm, that the inexperienced and presumptuous band of the medical tyros let loose upon the world, destroys more human life in one year, than all the Robinhoods, Cartouches, and Macheaths do in a century. It is on this part of medicine that I wish to see a reform, an abandonment of hypothesis for sober facts, the first degree of value set on clinical observation, and the lowest on visionary theories. I would wish the young practitioner, especially, to have deeply impressed on his mind, the real limits of his art, and that when the state of his patient gets beyond these, his office is to be a watchful, but quiet spectator of the operations of nature, giving them fair play by a well-regulated regimen, and by all the aid they can derive from the excitement of good spirits and hope in the patient. I have no doubt, that some diseases not yet understood may in time be transferred to the table of those known. But, were I a physician, I would rather leave the transfer to the slow hand of accident, than hasten it by guilty experiments on those who put their lives into my hands. The only sure foundations of medicine are, an intimate knowledge of the human body, and observation on the effects of medical substances on that. The anatomical and clinical schools, therefore, are those in which the young physician should be formed. If he enters with innocence that of the theory of medicine, it is scarcely possible he should come out untainted with error. His mind must be strong indeed, if, rising above juvenile credulity, it can maintain a wise infidelity against the authority of his instructors, and the bewitching delusions of their theories.

DOCUMENT 11. "Instructions for installing a sundial." University of Virginia, Alderman Library, *Jefferson Transcripts*, undated.

To set the Dial the first and all important object is to have the top of the dial post perfectly horizontal, without this it never can be true one moment. To this end, after the post is immovably fixed in the ground, the log should be tried with a [DRAWING] level and planed to the true horizontal level in every direction. It will take a butt of a tree 28 or 28 I[nches] in diameter. When planed, place the dial on it concentrically with the post, fix the gnomon of the dial in it's groove truly, the toe at the 6 o'clock mark, the heel at/on the 12 o'clock or meridian line. Test the perpendicularity of the gnomon by the walnut square sent; (which square had better be kept to rectify the perpendicularity occasionally when by an accident it gets bent.) Set the dial time as nearly right as you can, by a watch, or by a guess. About 9 o'clock in the forenoon stick a bit of wax, of the size and form of a Bristol drop shot on the upper edge of the gnomon, sliding it up or down on the edge until it's shadow shall fall exactly on the outer circle of the dial. Mark that point in the circle slightly with the point of a pin. Let the wax stay on exactly in the same place, and in the afternoon, watch when it's shadow shall be crossing the same circle on the other side, and mark the circle there again with the point of a pin. If these two *points* are equidistant from the 12 o'clock, or meridian line, the dial is right: if not, take half the difference between their two distances from the meridian line, and twist the dial plate around on the block exactly that much from the nearest point. Do the same the next day, and the 3rd, 4th etc. days until the shadow of the wax pellet shall cross the circle exactly equidistantly from the meridian, your dial will then be accurately true.

Have 2 nails ready entered in the North and South nail holes in the margin and tap them alternately that they may fix the dial firmly to the block without jostling it out of place, and when driven home secure it by screws thro' the other holes.

The gnomon being of sheet lead and liable to be bent is made to take out easily to be straitened again between two boards.

DOCUMENT 12. Proposal for dry docks. Letter from Jefferson to Lewis M. Wiss November 27, 1825. (L&B vol. XVI pp. 136–38).

I learnt that, in Venice, there were then ships, lying on their original stocks, ready for launching at any moment, which had been so for eighty years, and were still in a state of perfect preservation; and that this was effected by disposing of them in docks pumped dry, and kept so by constant pumping. It occurred to me that this expense of constant pumping might be saved by combining a lock with the common wet dock, wherever there was a running stream of water, the bed of which, within a reasonable distance, was of a sufficient height above the high-water level of the harbor. This was the case at the navy yard on the eastern branch at Washington, the high water line of which was seventy-eight feet lower than the ground on which the Capitol stands, and to which it was found that the water of the Tyber creek could be brought for watering the city. My proposition then was as follows: Let $a b$ be the high water level of the harbor, and the vessel to be laid up draw eighteen feet water. Make a chamber A twenty feet deep below high water and twenty feet high above it, as $c d e f$, and at the upper end make another chamber, B, [DRAWING] the bottom of which should be in the high-water level, and the tops twenty feet above that. $g h$ is the water of the Tyber. When the vessel is to be introduced, open the gate at $c b d$. The tide-water rises in the chamber A to the level $b i$, and floats the vessel in with it. Shut the gate C $b d$ and open that of $f i$. The water of the Tyber fills both chambers to the level $c f g$, and the vessel floats into the chamber B; then opening both gates C $b d$ and $f i$, the water flows out, and the vessel settles down on the stays previously prepared at the bottom *i h* to receive her. The gate at *g h* must of course be closed, and the water of the feeding stream be diverted elsewhere. The chamber B is to have a roof over it of the construction of that over the meal market at Paris, except that that is hemispherical, this semi-cylindrical. For this construction see Delenne's [Delormé's?] architecture, whose invention it was. The diameter of the dome of the meal market is considerably over one hundred feet.

It will be seen at once that instead of making the chamber B of sufficient width and length for a single vessel only, it may be widened to whatever span the semi-circular framing of the roof can be trusted, and to whatever length you please, so as to admit two or more vessels in breadth, and as many in length as the localities render expedient.

DOCUMENT 13. Platting survey courses. Letter from Jefferson to Louis Hue Girardin, March 18, 1814. (Lipscomb & Bergh, vol. XIV pp. 124–25).

you likewise requested for the use of your school, my explanation of a method of platting the courses of a survey, which I mentioned to you as of my own practice. This is so obvious and simple, that as it occurred to myself so I presume it has to others, although I have not seen it stated in any of the books. For drawing parallel lines, I use the triangular rule, the hypothenusal side of which being applied to the side of a common straight rule, the triangle sides on that, as thus, [DRAWING] always parallel to itself. Instead of drawing meridians on his paper, let the pupil draw a parallel of latitude, or east and west line, and note in that a point for his first station, then applying to it his protractor, lay off the first course and distance in the usual way to ascertain his second station. For the second course, lay the triangular rule to the east and west line, or first parallel, holding the straight or guide rule firmly against its hypothenusal side. Then slide up the triangle (for a northerly course) to the point of his second station, and pressing it firmly there, lay the protractor to that, and mark off the second course, and distance as before, for the third station. Then lay the triangle to the first parallel again, and sliding it as before to the point of the third station, there apply to it the protractor for the third course and distance, which gives the fourth station; and so on. Where a course is southwardly, lay the protractor, as before, to the northern edge of the triangle, but prick its reversed course, which reversed again in drawing, gives the true course. When the station has got so far from the first parallel, as to be out of the reach of the parallel rule sliding on its hypothenuse, another parallel must be drawn by laying the edge, or longer leg of the triangle to the first parallel as before, applying the guide-rule to the end, or short leg, (instead of the hypothenuse,) as in the margin, and sliding the triangle up to the point for the new parallel. I have found this, in practice, the quickest and most correct method of platting which I have ever tried, and the neatest also, because it disfigures the paper with the fewest unnecessary lines.

DOCUMENT 14. "Clock for University. Note to Mr. Coolidge." [1825/26]. Massachusetts Historical Society, *The Coolidge-Jefferson Papers.*

A clock is wanting for the Rotunda of the University; the size and strength of it's works must be accomodated to two data.
1. the bell weighs 400 lb. and it is to be heard with certainty 1-½ miles.
2. The dial-plate is to be *about* 6 feet 3 I.[nches] diameter, it is to be fixed in the tympanum of the Pediment of the Portico. the triangle of this tympanum has not been measured exactly yet, therefore we cannot exactly ascertain the size of the dial plate it will admit.
the bell is to remain free to be rung. the bell ropes for the weights will have to go directly back about 30 f.[eet] then turn off at a right angle horizontally about 21. f.[eet] to the hole of their descent, consequently upwards of 100. f.[eet] long the rope for swinging must do the same, but on the opposite side, where there are stairs it must be wound up on the back or inside.
and the hands must be set right by a key at the back or inside

What will such a clock cost?
the tympanum is 9. f.[eet] 4. I.[nches] in the
            perpendicular   )
            42 feet in the span) measured
                                within the
                                cornice.
the hole for the descent of the weights is 5.
f.[eet] in the clear opening
            48. f.[eet] depth, i.e. from the
            level of the axis of the dial plate
            to the ground

within the naked of the [DRAWING] forms. the tympanum, a circle of 52. I.[nches] rad. may be obtained if necessary for the pendulum, the whole interior of the roof of the Portico being vacant.
allowing the dial plate 5. f.[eet] diam. clear within the tympanum, accomodated within the architrave of 10 f.[eet] breadth, there will still be a space or margin 12. I.[nches] wide in its narrowest parts.

the dial plate must be of metal, of course, as wood would soon rot, in addition therefore to the 5. foot of dial plate which will show there must be additional margin to be imbedded in a rabbet of suff[icien]t breadth to hold it form within the architrave.

The weights of the striking as well as the going parts descend in the same cylinder, but the ringing rope may go down the opposite cylinder at f., which is occupied by winding stairs. The winding up of the clock must be at the back side of the works within the hollow of the roof. And there also means must be furnished for setting the hands.

DOCUMENT 15. "Instructions for the Government of the Artist in Making the Clock for the University of Virginia." Accompanying letter from Jefferson to Joseph Coolidge, Jr., June 4, 1826. University of Virginia, Alderman Library, *University Archives.*

The bell is to weight 400 lbs., which it is supposed will insure its being heard 1-½ miles under any circumstances of weather. The distance of the hollow cylinder in which the weights are to descend, and its oblique direction from the dial-plate has rendered necessary an outline of the ground plate and elevation of the parts of the building where it will be placed; this is drawn on lined paper, in which every line counts a foot, and every 10th line is more strongly drawn to facilitate counting, by which the measures are taken and not all by scale and compass. The cylindrical space in which the weights descend is of 5 ft. diameter and 48 ft. depth, that is to say from the level of the center of the dial-plate to the ground. The tympanum of the pediment, in the center of which the dial-plate is to be placed, is 42 ft. in the span, and 9 ft. 4 in. in its perpendicular at the apex, that is to say the naked of the tympanum within its cornice. Such a triangle admits a circle of 52 in. radius, to be inscribed within it, so that describing its center in its center the dial-plate of 30 in. radius, and around that the architrave and cornice of the pediment of 12 in. in the points where they approach nearest. But the dial-plate must be as much wider than the 5 ft. which it shows as to fill a rabbet of ½ in., at least in the back face of the architrave in which it may be firmly imbedded. It must be of metal, of course, as wood would go too soon into decay.

The face of the tympanum will be exactly over the line a, b, and c in the center of the cylinder of descent for the weights. The direction of the cord is supposed may be from d to where an aperture in the wall may pass it on to the pulley or point of suspension, thus requiring but a single change of direction. This, however, is for the consideration of the artist.

The bell is to be suspended on an iron gallows sufficiently strong, mounted on the ridge pole of the pediment, perpendicularly over the clock works; no ornament is to be given to it, nothing which may attract notice, or withdraw the attention of the observer from its principal object, somewhat in this simple style. it must be free to be rung independently of the clock.

The weights of the striking as well as the going parts descend in the same cylinder, but the ringing rope may go down the opposite cylinder at f, which is occupied by the winding stairs. The winding up of the clock must be on the back side of the works within the hollow of the roof. And there also means must be furnished for setting the hands.

DOCUMENT 16. "Ideas on the subject of a Meridian for the University." From Jefferson to Charles Bonneycastle, September 30, 1825. University of Virginia, Alderman Library, *University Archives*, FC 3078).

The small mountain a little to the West of the South from the University was purchased for the purpose of an Observatory, whenever the establishment of one may become desirable. It is proposed than whenever the meridian from that may cross the South West ridge of mountains, to cut a vista through the woods across the ridge in the direction of the meridian, and in that Vista erect an Obelisk with an iron needle in the top. This will give a meridian of probably 7. or 8. miles in length.

In the mean time however one will be wanting at the University. For this I propose to use the Portico of the Rotunda in this way. In the center between the two middle columns, make fast to the soffite a strap of strong hoop iron in the form [DRAWING] securing the limb a.b. across the bottom of the Soffite by screws, and making an eyelet hole in the limb b.c. for a ray of the sun to pass through. Perpendicularly under the eyelet hole, drill in the pavement as small a hole as can be drilled, and plug it with an iron pin, filed down to the level of the surface of the pavement. On this, as a center, draw several concentric portions of circles, tracing them very slightly on the pavement, and, by repeated observations, before and after noon, for several days, mark the points at which the solar ray crosses them, and the middle point between these crossings of every circle, and average the whole for a true meridian line. Draw it strongly on the pavement, from the iron plug to the wall of the house, and perpendicularly up the wall, as far as the meridian altitude of the sun at the winter solstice shall require. But this cannot be done until the pavement of the Portico shall be laid.

Until it is done, the rising or setting sun will give time by the clock, with sufficient accuracy for meals and meetings of the different schools.

For the plan of an Observatory see a late Vol. of the A. P. Transactions which I sent to Mr. Keane for the Library.

DOCUMENT 17. Specifications for the Observatory. University of Virginia, Alderman Library, *University Archives*.

> For an Observatory the material attentions are 1. that it be so solid in it's construction, with a foundation and walls so massive as not to be liable to tremble with the wind, walking, etc. 2. That it have ample apertures in every direction. 3. That it have some one position perfectly solid which may command the whole horizon and heavens; with a cupola cover, movable and high enough to protect long telescopes from the weather. As to height of the building, the less the solider. The Observatories in the considerable cities of Europe are high of necessity to overlook the buildings of the place. That of Paris is 80. f. high, but so much the worse, if avoidable. In the design on the other side, the body of the building is surrounding with a terras of 70. f. square, 4-½ f. high, to be filled solidly with stone laid dry and compact, in like manner to the floors, which should be paved. the doors of the 4 passages to be arched in order to unite the 4 octagon rooms together, and to form them into one solid body, all the walls to be 2-½ bricks thick. those of the middle rooms to be vaulted together at top, and the hollow between the hemisphere and the square of the walls to be honeycombed with cross arches their crowns being made strait and level with the crown of the vault. this should rise a little above the top of the roof, so as to give a whole paved terras on the top which may command the whole horizon. the Cupola cover should have a cylindrical body of thin light frame work moveable on pulley wheels at bottom in a circular groove, the top a hollow hemisphere, lightly ribbed and covered with tin, the two together high enough to cover a long refractor, of 15 f. for example. this moveable cover should be cut vertically into 2. halves from top to bottom, and the radius of one half should be less than that of the other, and move in an inner groove so that one may be shut into the other, leaving half of the vault of the heavens open to view, thus. over the wall of the mural quadrant must be a fissure in the roof closed with shutters water tight.
>
> The building is proposed for the ordinary purposes of the Astronomical professor and his school, and should be placed on the nearest site proper for it, & convenient to the University. the hill on which the old buildings stand seem to be the best.
>
> The mountain belonging to the University was purchased with a view to the permanent establishment of an Observatory, with an Astronomer resident at it, employed solely in the business of Observation. but I believe a site on the nearest mountain in the S. W. ridge, Montalto for example would be better, because of it's command of the fine horizon to the East.

DOCUMENT 18. Planetarium for dome of the Rotunda, University of Virginia, at and for the College. University of Virginia, Alderman Library. *JP–1518*, 3rd, 4th and 39th pages. Undated.

The Concave ceiling of the Rotunda is proposed to be painted skyblue and spangled with gilt stars in their position and magnitude copied exactly from any selected hemisphere of our latitude. a seat for the Operator moveable and fixable at any point in the concave will be necessary, and means of giving every star its exact position.

[DRAWING]

Machinery for moving the Operator. a.b.c.d.e.f.g. is the inner surface of 90° of the dome.

o.p. is a boom, a white oak sapling of proper strength, it's heel working in the center of the sphere, by a compound joint admitting motion in any direction liker a ball and socket.

p.q.r. is a rope suspending the small end of the boom, passing over a pulley in the zenith at g. and hanging down to the floor by which it may be raised or lowered to any altitude.

at p. a common saddle with stirrups is fixed for the seat of the operator and seated on that he may by the rope be presented to any point of the concave.

Machinery for locating the stars.

a. s. is the horizontal plane passing thro' the center of the sphere o. an annular ream of wood, of the radius of the sphere must be laid on this plane and graduated to degrees and minutes, the graduation beginning in the North rhomb of the place. call this the circle of amplitude. a movable meridian meridien of 90°, must then be provided, it's upper end moving on a pivot in the zenith, it's lower end resting on the circle of amplitude, this must be made of thin flexible white oak like the ream of a cotton spinning wheel, and fixed in it's curvature, in a true quadrant by a similar lath of white oak as it's chord a. n. their ends made fast together by clamps, this flexible meridian may be 6. i. breadth and graduated to degrees and minutes. the zenith distance and amplitude of every star must then be obtained from the astronomical tables. place the foot of the movable meridian in that of the North rhomb of the place, and the polar star at it's zenith distance, and so of every other star of that meridian. then move the foot to another meridian at a convenient interval, mark it's stars by their zenith distance and so go round the circle.

bh. ci. dk. el. fm. are braces of window cord for keeping the meridian in it's true curve. perhaps the rope had better be attached to the boom at s. instead of p. to be out of the way of the operator perhaps also the chord an had better present it's edge to the meridian than it's side. if the meridian ark and it's chord be 6.i. wide and ½ i. thick they will wiegh about 135. lb. and consequently be easily manageable.

if the boom op. be 35 f. long, 6 i. at the but and 3. i. at the small end, it might weigh about 100 lb. and be manageable also.

Rotunda notes.

the rule for apportioning the area of windows to the volume of the room is to take the cubic contents of the room in feet, and the square root of that for the area of all its windows.the large oval room below has 17,600 cu. f. contents.

the sq. root of that is 132 sq. f. for all it's windows, each of the 4. windows then must be 132/4 = 33. f. or say they must be 4. f. wide, & 8. f. high. the body of the house (shaft & entablature) being 34 f. − 1-½ high & the voids of the 2. windows (below & above) being 16. f. is in good proportion, being nearly one half.

DOCUMENT 19. Disposition of Jefferson's clocks after his death.

In January 1827 an auction was held of the furnishings of Monticello, attended by many of Jefferson's friends and neighbors who came to purchase souvenirs and mementos of the statesman. A number of the more important pieces were retained by members of the family, but three of the clocks were sold.

1. Martha Jefferson Randolph paid one hundred dollars for one of the clocks, which has not been identified.

2. General John Hartwell Cocke, a friend of the family, purchased a mahogany eight-day clock made by Thomas Dring of West Chester, Pa. which had been purchased for Jefferson by Isaac Briggs from Benjamin Ferris. Cocke paid fifty-five dollars for the timepiece. Jefferson had added tin plates to the backboard on which the days of the week were painted, and which were indicated by the descent of the weight. Shortly after the sale R. S. Jones, presumably a local clockmaker, wrote to Cocke on January 27th to advise,

> I have gotten the clock from Monticello, and indeed it was the most smoke dried thing of the kind that I ever saw. Ned gave the case a rubbing over with hot water and soap which helped it but a little—I find the cap of the case to be mahogany, the other parts walnut. I shall take it in hand the first [opportunity] . . . The face and inside works of the clock were almost as badly smoked as the case and it is a task to get them in order, I have however gotten Cullen at work on the clock who says it is the most excellent piece of work . . .

On July 28th Cocke noted in his day book "By House Expense for Clock . . . purchased at Thos. Jefferson Sale. . . ."

The Dring clock was in the Monticello kitchen. According to the plantation servant Isaac, Jefferson never entered the kitchen except to wind the clock, which he customarily did on Sunday.

3. The third timepiece sold was the astronomical regulator made by Thomas Voight. Three individuals bid on it, Cocke, who bid one hundred forty-five dollars, Dr. Robley Dunglison, who bid one hundred and

fifty dollars, and Nicholas P. Trist, who obtained the clock for one hundred and fifty-five dollars. After the sale Dunglison apologized to Trist for having bid against him, but Trist assured him it was quite all right inasmuch as he had purchased the clock in order to present it to Dunglison as a gift of the Jefferson family! The timepiece was subsequently presented to Dunglison by Martha Jefferson Randolph, and the physician cherished it during the remainder of his life. It remained in the family until 1894, when a descendant presented it to the Historical Society of Pennsylvania.

[Communications to the writer from Mr. Charles L. Granquist; letter from R. S. Jones to John Hartwell Cocke, January 27, 1827 and entry in Cocke daybook for July 28, 1827, ViU, Alderman Library, *Cocke Papers*; "Memoirs of a Monticello Slave," edited by Rayford W. Logan, in James A. Bear, Jr., ed., *Jefferson at Monticello* (Charlottesville: The University Press of Virginia, 1951), p. 23; Robley Dunglison, *Diary*, PPAmP, pp. 328ff.].

BIBLIOGRAPHY

Abrahams, Harold D. 1961–63. "Thomas Jefferson's Library of Applied Chemistry," *Journal of the Elisha Mitchell Scientific Society*, vols. 77–79, pp. 267–74.

"Account of a new Machine for raising Water by Wind," taken from *Gentleman's Magazine*, February 1787, *Columbian Magazine*, vol. II, June 1787.

[Adams, Abigail]. 1947. *New Letters of Abigail Adams, 1788–1801*. Edited by Stewart Mitchell. Boston: Houghton Mifflin Company.

Adams, Dickinson W. 1983. *Jefferson's Extracts From the Gospels. "The Philosophy of Jesus" and "The Life and Morals of Jesus." The Papers of Thomas Jefferson*. Second Series. Princeton: Princeton University Press.

Adams, Elizabeth L. 1943. "The Jefferson Bicentenary," *The Bulletin of the Boston Public Library*, vol. XVIII, No. 4, April, pp. 153–58.

Adams, Henry, ed. 1879. *The Life of Albert Gallatin*. Philadelphia: J. B. Lippincott & Co.

Adams, Herbert Baxter. 1887. *The College of William and Mary. Circular of Information No. 1*. Washington, D.C. Bureau of Education.

———. 1888. *Thomas Jefferson and the University of Virginia*. U. S. Bureau of Education Circular of Information No. 1. Washington, D.C.: Government Printing Office.

———. 1898. *Phi Beta Kappa Address At the College of William and Mary*. Richmond: Whittet & Shepperson.

[Adams, John Quincy]. 1874–77. *Memoirs of John Quincy Adams*, edited by C. F. Adams. 12 vols. Philadelphia: J. B. Lippincott & Co.

Adams, Randolph G. 1939. *Three Americanists—Henry Harrisse, Bibliographer, George Brinley, Book Collector, Thomas Jefferson, Librarian*. Philadelphia: University of Pennsylvania Press.

"Advertisement of the Reverend W. S.," *Virginia Gazette*, May 2, 1771.

Albemarle County Will Book. No. 2. 1757. Inventory of Peter Jefferson's Estate. Filed August 17, 1757, p. 41.

Allen, John Logan. 1975. *Passage Through The Garden. Lewis and Clark and the Image of the American Northwest*. Urbana, Ill.: University of Illinois Press.

American State Papers. 1793. *Foreign Relations*.

Anbury, Thomas. 1791. *Travels Through the Interior Parts of America*. London. For W. Lane.

Appleton's Encyclopedia of American Biography. 1894–1896. 6 vols. New York: D. Appleton & Co.

Ardrey, R. L. 1894. *American Agricultural Implements*. Chicago: The author.

Armstrong, Edward, ed. 1826. *Memoirs*. Philadelphia: McCarty & Davis.

Arrêté relatif à la fabrique de platines du Citoyen Le Blanc à Roanne. 1791.

Auger, Helen. 1946. *Passage to Glory: John Ledyard's America*. Garden City, N.Y.: Doubleday & Company.

[Bailey, Francis]. 1785. *Francis Bailey's Pocket Almanac, Being an American Annual Register for the Year of Our Lord 1785*.

Baker, Marcus. 1894. "Surveys and Maps of the District of Columbia," *National Geographic Magazine*, vol. 6, pp. 149–66.

Ball, Sidney H. 1941. *The Mining of Gems and Ornamental Stones by American Indians*. Bulletin of the American Bureau of Ethnology No. 120. Washington, D.C.: Government Printing Office.

[Banneker, Benjamin]. 1792. *Copy of a Letter from Benjamin Banneker, to the Secretary of State, with his Answer*. Philadelphia: David Lawrence.

Barnard, Ella Kent. 1912. "Isaac Briggs, A.M., F.A.P.S.," *Maryland Historical Magazine*, vol. VII, pp. 409–19.

Baron, Sherry. 1975. "Thomas Jefferson: Scientist as Politician," *Synthesis*, vol. 3, No. 1, pp. 6–21.

Barrett, Clifton Waller. 1973. "The Struggle to Create a University," *Virginia Quarterly Review*, vol. 49, No. 4, Autumn, pp. 494–506.

Barton, Benjamin Smith. 1793. "A Letter to Chas. Peter Thunberg. A Botanical Description of the *Podophyllum Diphyllum*," *Transactions of the American Philosophical Society*, vol. III, pp. 334–48.

———. 1798. *New Views of the Origin of the Tribes and Nations of America*. Philadelphia: John Bioren for the author.

———. 1799. "Observations and Conjectures concerning certain articles which were taken out of an ancient Tumulus or Grave at Cincinnati. Letter from Benjamin Smith Barton to Dr. Joseph Priestley." *Transactions of the American Philosophical Society*, vol. IV, pp. 179–81.

Barton, William. 1813. *Memoirs of the Life of David Rittenhouse, LLD., F.R.S.. . . .* Philadelphia: Edward Parker.

Bathe, Greville and Bathe, Dorothy. 1935. *Oliver Evans. A Chronicle of Early American Engineering*. Philadelphia: Historical Society of Philadelphia.

Battison, Edward A. 1976. *Muskets to Mass Production. The Men & the Times that Shaped American Manufacturing*. Windsor, Vt.: The American Precision Museum.

Battle, John D., Jr. 1984. "Periodical Headaches of Thomas Jefferson," *Cleveland Clinic Foundation*, pp. 531–39.

Bazeries, Commandant Étienne. 1901. *Les Chiffres secrets dévoilés*. Paris: Librairie Charpentier et Fasquelle.

Bean, William B. 1960. "Mr. Jefferson's Influence on American Medical Education," *Virginia Medical Monthly*, vol. 87, December, pp. 669–80.

Bear, James A., Jr. 1958. "Mr. Jefferson's Nails," *The Magazine of Albemarle County History*, vol. XVI, pp. 47–52.

———. 1961. "Thomas Jefferson, Manufacturer," *The Iron Worker*, vol. 25, Autumn, pp. 1–11.

———. ed. 1967. *Jefferson At Monticello*. Charlottesville: The University Press of Virginia.

———. 1974. "The Last Few Days in the Life of Thomas Jefferson," *The Magazine of Albemarle County History*, vol. 32, pp. 62–79.

Becker, George F. 1895. "Gold Fields of the Southern Appalachians," *Sixteenth Annual Report of the United States Geological Survey. . .*, Part III, Mineral Resources of the United States, 1894, Mineral Products. Washington, D.C.: Government Printing Office.

Bedini, Silvio A. 1957. "Thomas Jefferson and His Watches," *Hobbies Magazine*, vol. 61, February, pp. 38–39.

———. 1964. "Thomas Jefferson, Clock Designer," *Proceedings of the American Philosophical Society*, vol. 108, No. 3, June, pp. 163–80.

———. 1972. *The Life of Benjamin Banneker*. New York: Charles Scribner's Sons.

———. 1975. *Thinkers and Tinkers. Early American Men of Science*. New York: Charles Scribner's Sons.

———. 1976. "Andrew Ellicott, Surveyor of the Wilderness," *Surveying and Mapping*, vol. XXXVI, No. 2, June, pp. 113–35.

———. 1978. "Godfather of American Invention," in *The Smithsonian Book of Invention*, edited by T. Edwards Park. Washington, D.C.: Smithsonian Institution Press, pp. 82–85.

———. 1981. *Declaration of Independence Desk. Relic of Revolution*. Washington, D. C.: Smithsonian Institution Press.

———. 1981–82. "Jefferson: Man of Science," *Frontiers* (Annual of the Academy of Natural Sciences of Philadelphia), vol. III, pp. 10–23.

———. 1984. *Thomas Jefferson and His Copying Machines*. Charlottesville: The University Press of Virginia.

———. 1984. "The Scientific Instruments of the Lewis and Clark Expedition," *Great Plains Quarterly*, vol. 4, No. 1, Winter, pp. 54–69; reprinted in *Mapping the Plains* edited by Frederick C. Luebke, Frances Kaye and Gary E. Moulton (1987), Norman, Okla.: University of Oklahoma Press.

———. 1985. *Thomas Jefferson and American Vertebrate Paleontology*. Virginia Division of Mineral Resources Publication 61. Charlottesville: Division of Mineral Resources.

————. 1986. "That Awfull Stage (The Search for the State House Yard Observatory)," in *Science and Society in Early America. Essays in Honor of Whitfield J. Bell, Jr.* edited by Randolph S. Klein. Philadelphia: American Philosophical Society, pp. 169–73.

————. 1986. "[Thomas Jefferson], Man of Science," in *Thomas Jefferson. A Reference Biography,* edited by Merrill D. Peterson. New York: Charles Scribner's Sons, pp. 253–76.

————. 1987. "Marshall's Meridian Instrument," *Professional Surveyor,* vol. 7, No. 4, July-August, pp. 26–27, 60.

————. 1987. "The Marshall Mystery," *Professional Surveyor,* vol. 7, No. 5, September-October. p. 60.

Bell, Whitfield J., Jr. 1949. "A Box of Old Bones: A Note on the Identification of the Mastodon, 1766–1806," *Proceedings of the American Philosophical Society,* vol. 93, pp. 169–77.

————. 1974. "Addenda to Watson's Annals of Philadelphia. Notes By Jacob Mordecai, 1836," *The Pennsylvania Magazine of History and Biography,* April, pp. 131–170.

Bendikson, L. 1937. "The Restoration of Obliterated Passages and of Secret Writing in Diplomatic Missives," *American Review,* Revised. vol. 1, pp. 243–56.

Berkhofer, Robert F., Jr. 1972. "Jefferson, the Ordnance of 1784, and the Origins of the American Territorial System," *William and Mary Quarterly,* 3rd series, vol. XXIX, No. 2, April, pp. 231–32.

Betts, Edwin M., ed. 1944. *Thomas Jefferson's Garden Book 1766–1824.* Philadelphia: American Philosophical Society.

————. 1944. "The Correspondence Between Constantin Samuel Rafinesque and Thomas Jefferson," *Proceedings of the American Philosophical Society,* vol. 87, No. 5, May 5, pp. 368–80.

————, ed. 1953. *Thomas Jefferson's Farm Book With Commentary and Relevant Extracts from Other Writings.* Princeton: Princeton University Press, for the American Philosophical Society.

Betts, Edwin Morris and Bear, James A., Jr. 1966. *The Family Letters of Thomas Jefferson.* Columbia, Mo.: University of Missouri Press.

[Biddle, Charles]. 1883. *Autobiography of Charles Biddle, Vice-President of the Executive Council of Pennsylvania, 1745–1821.* Philadelphia: E. Claxton and Company.

Bigelow, Jacob. 1829. *Elements of Technology, taken chiefly from a course of lectures delivered at Cambridge, on the application of the sciences to the useful arts.* Boston: Hilliard, Gray, Little & Wilkins.

Biographie universelle et portative des contemporains [*Biographie Rabbé*]. 1826. 4 vols. Paris: Au Bureau de la Biographie.

Biographie universelle ancienne et moderne. 1843–45. 45 vols. Paris: R. T. Desplaces.

Blair, James. 1691. *Memorial Concerning A Colege in Virginia,* December 11.

Blake, John B. 1957. *Benjamin Waterhouse and the Introduction of Vaccination.* Philadelphia: University of Pennsylvania Press.

Blanc, Honoré. 1790. *A l'Assemblé Nationale. Mémoire important sur la Fabrication des Armes de Guerre.* Paris: Imprimerie de L. M. Cellot.

[Blanc, Honoré]. N.D. "France. Nécrologie. Sur le C. Blanc." *Le Magazin Encyclopédique.* 7th année, Tome V, pp. 512–13.

Blanton, Wyndham B. 1931. *Medicine in Virginia in the Eighteenth Century.* Richmond: Garrett & Massie.

Boller, Paul F., Jr. 1981. *Presidential Anecdotes.* Oxford: Oxford University Press.

"Books in Colonial Virginia," 1903. *Virginia Magazine of History and Biography,* vol. X, pp. 389–92.

Bore, Henry. 1890. *The Story of the Invention of the Steel Pen.* New York: Irison, Blakeman & Co.

Boorstin, Daniel J. 1948. *The Lost World of Thomas Jefferson.* New York: Henry Holt and Company.

[Bossu, Jean-Bernard]. 1962. *Jean-Bernard Bossu's Travels in the Interior of North America 1751–1762.* Translated and edited by Seymour Feiler. Norman, Okla.: University of Oklahoma Press.

[Boulton, Matthew]. Birmingham Engineering Reference Library, Birmingham, Eng.. *The Boulton-Watt Papers.*

Boulton-Watts Papers. Birmingham, Eng. Birmingham Reference Library.

[Bowditch, Nathaniel]. 1815 [1809?]. "An Estimate of the Height, Direction, Velocity and Magnitude of the Meteor, that Exploded Over Weston in Connecticut, December 4, 1807. With methods of calculating observations made on such bodies. By Nathaniel Bowditch, A.M., A.A.S., and member of the American Philosophical Society," *Memoirs of the American Academy of Arts and Sciences,* vol. 3, part 2, No. XXXII, pp. 213–36.

Boyd, H. S. 1968. *The History of Montgomery County, Maryland.* Baltimore: Regional Publishing Co.

Boyd, Julian P., ed. 1943– . *The Papers of Thomas Jefferson*. 22 vols. to date. Princeton: Princeton University Press.

———. "Horatio Gates Spafford," *Proceedings of the American Philosophical Society*, vol. 87, No. 1, July, pp. 47–50.

———. 1943. *The Declaration of Independence. The Evolution of the Text As Shown in Facsimiles of Various Drafts By Its Author Thomas Jefferson.*. . . .Washington, D.C.: The Library of Congress.

———. 1958. "Two Diplomats Between Revolutions. John Jay and Thomas Jefferson," VMHB, vol. 66, No. 2, April, pp. 134–35.

———. 1958. "The Megalonyx, the Megatherium and Thomas Jefferson's Lapse of Memory," *Proceedings of the American Philosophical Society*, vol. 102, No. 5, October 20, pp. 420–35.

———. 1976. "The Declaration of Independence: The Mystery of the Lost Original," *Pennsylvania Magazine of History and Biography*, vol. c, No. 4, October, pp. 438–67.

Bridges, Peter. 1980. "A Triumphant Failure," *Dartmouth Alumni Magazine*, October, pp. 30–35.

Brook, Barry S. 1962. *La Symphonie Française dans la seconde moitié du XIIIe siècle*. Paris: Institut de Musicologie de la Université de Paris, vol. I, Annexe III.

Brown, Elizabeth Gaspar. 1969. "A Jeffersonian's Recommendation for a Lawyer's Education, 1802," *American Journal of Legal History*, vol. 13, April, pp. 139–44.

Brown, Everett Somerville, ed. 1923. *William Plumer's Memorandum of Proceedings in the United States Senate, 1803–1807*. New York: The Macmillan Company.

———. 1943. "Jefferson"s Manual of Parliamentary Practice," *Michigan Alumnus Quarterly Review*, vol. XLIV, February 20, p. 148.

Brown, Margaret W. 1954. "The Story of the Declaration of Independence Desk and How It Came to the National Museum," *Annual Report of the Smithsonian Institution for 1953*. Washington, D.C.: Government Printing Office, pp. 455–62.

Browne, Charles A. 1944. "Thomas Jefferson and the Scientific Trends of His Time," *Chronica Botanica*, vol. 8, No. 3, Summer, pp. 363–423.

Bruce, Philip A. 1920. *History of the University of Virginia, 1819–1919. The Lengthened Shadow of One Man*. Volume I. New York: The Macmillan Company.

Bryan, W. B. 1916. *History of the National Capitol*. 2 vols. New York: The Macmillan Company.

Bullock, Helen Duprey. 1941–42. "A Dissertation on Education in the Form of a Letter from James Maury to Robert Jackson, July 17, 1762," *Papers of the Albemarle County Historical Society*, vol. II, pp. 36–60.

———. N.D. *On Music in Colonial Williamsburg*. Williamsburg: Colonial Williamsburg Foundation, Inc. (Unpublished manuscript).

———. 1941. "The Papers of Thomas Jefferson," *American Archivist*, vol. 4, pp. 243–44.

———. *My Head and My Heart*. New York: G. P. Putnam's Sons.

Burk, John Daly. 1804. *History of Virginia*. 4 vols. Petersburg, Va.: For the author by Dickson & Peseud.

Burnaby, Andrew. 1775, repr. 1798. *Travels Thru the Middle Settlement of Virginia in the Years 1759 and 1760*. 4 vols. London: For T. Payne.

Burnett, Edmund C., ed. 1904–1936. *Journals of the Continental Congress*. 34 vols. Washington, D.C.: Government Printing Office.

———, ed. 1921–1936. *Letters of the Continental Congress*. 8 vols. Washington, D.C.: Carnegie Institution.

[Burwell, William A.]. Library of Congress, Manuscripts Division, *The William A. Burwell Papers*.

Bushnell, David I. 1930. "Five Monocan Towns in Virginia, 1607," *Smithsonian Miscellaneous Collections*, vol. 82, No. 12, pp. 1–40.

———. 1933. "Evidence of Indian Occupancy in Albemarle County, Virginia," Publication 3217, *Smithsonian Miscellaneous Collections*, vol. 89, No. 7, pp. 1–24.

Butterfield, L. H. 1952. "Elder John Leland Jeffersonian Itinerant," *Proceedings of the American Antiquarian Society*, vol. 62, part 2, pp. 119–27.

Butterfield, L. H. and Rice, Howard C., Jr. 1948. "Jefferson's Earliest Note to Maria Cosway with Some New Facts and Conjectures on His Broken Wrist," *William and Mary Quarterly*, 3rd series, vol. V, January, pp. 31–32.

Cabell, Nathaniel Francis, ed. 1856. *Early History of the University of Virginia, as Contained in the Letters of Thomas Jefferson and Joseph C. Cabell*. Richmond: J. W. Randolph.

Cajori, Florian. 1890. *The Teaching and History of Mathematics in the United States*. Washington, D.C.: Government Printing Office.

Caldwell, John Edward. 1810, repr. 1951. *A Tour Through Part of Virginia, In the Summer of 1808. Also, Some Account of the Islands of the Azores.* Edited by William M. E. Rachal. Belfast: Smyth & Lyons; Richmond: The Dietz Press.

Caldwell, L. K. 1942–43. "The Jurisprudence of Thomas Jefferson," *Indiana Law Journal,* vol. 18, pp. 193–213.

Calendar of Virginia State Papers. 1875. vol. I, pp. 239–40.

Cantwell, Robert. 1961. *Alexander Wilson: Naturalist and Pioneer.* Philadelphia: J. B. Lippincott & Co.

Cappon, Lester J., ed. 1959. *The Adams-Jefferson Letters. The Complete Correspondence Between Thomas Jefferson and Abigail Adams.* 2 vols. Chapel Hill: University of North Carolina Press.

Carozzi, Marguerite. 1984. *Voltaire's Attitude Towards Geology.* Geneva: Société de Physique et d'Histoire Naturelle (Musée de Genève).

Carrière, Joseph M. 1946. "Mr. Jefferson Sponsored A New French Method," *French Review,* vol. XIX, May, pp. 398–99.

———. 1948. "The Manuscripts of Jefferson's Unpublished Errata List for Abbé Morellet's Translation of the *Notes on Virginia*," *Studies in Bibliography. Papers of the Bibliographical Society of the University of Virginia,* edited by Fredson Bowers, pp. 4–24.

Carrière, Joseph M. and Moffat, L. G. 1943–44. "A Frenchman Visits Albemarle," *Magazine of the Albemarle County Historical Society,* vol. 4, pp. 39–55.

Carter, Clarence C. and Bloom, John Porter, eds. 1934–■■■. *Territorial Papers of the United States.* 25 vols. Washington, D.C.: Government Printing Office.

Cary, Wilson Miles. 1904. "Some Family Letters of Thomas Jefferson," *Scribner's Magazine,* vol. XXXVI, November, pp. 573–86.

Castell, Robert. 1728. *The Villas of the Antients.* London: Printed for the author.

Catesby, Mark. 1743. *The Natural History of Carolina, Florida, and the Bahamas Islands.* 2 vols. London: For B. White.

Ceram, C. W. 1971. *The First American.* New York: Harcourt, Brace & Jovanovich.

———. 1971. "Mr. Jefferson's Dig," *American History Illustrated,* vol. VI, No. 7, November, p. 41.

Chamberlain, Alexander F. 1907. "Thomas Jefferson's Ethnological Opinions and Activities," *American Anthropologist,* New series, vol. 9, pp. 499–509.

Champier, Victor. 1900. *Le Palais Royal.* Paris: N.P.

Chandler, J. A. C. 1934. "Jefferson and William and Mary," *William and Mary Quarterly,* 2nd series, vol. XIV, pp. 304–7.

Chapin, Seymour L. 1972. " 'In a Mirror Brightly': French Attempts to Build Reflecting Telescopes Using Platinum," *Journal for the History of Astronomy,* vol. 3, part 2, No. 7, June, pp. 87–104.

Chaseboeuf, Constantin François, Comte de Volney. See *Volney.*

Chastellux, Marquis de. 1787. *Travels in North America in the Years 1780, 1781, and 1782.* 2 vols. London: G. C. J. and J. Robinson.

Chief Signal Officer, U. S. War Department. 1922. *Instructions for Using Cipher Device Type M-94.* Washington, D.C.: Government Printing Office.

Chinard, Gilbert, ed. 1926. *The Commonplace Book of Thomas Jefferson. A Repertory of His Ideas On Government.* With an Introduction and Notes by Gilbert Chinard. Baltimore: Johns Hopkins Press.

———. 1923. *Volney et l'Amérique.* Baltimore: Johns Hopkins University Press.

———. 1927. *Trois Amitiés Françaises de Jefferson.* Paris: Société d'Edition "Les Belles Lettres."

———, ed. 1928. *The Literary Bible of Thomas Jefferson. His Commonplace Book of Philosophers and Poets.* Baltimore: Johns Hopkins University Press.

———. 1929. *Thomas Jefferson, Apostle of Americanism.* Boston: Little, Brown and Company.

———, ed. 1929. *The Letters of Lafayette and Jefferson.* Baltimore: Johns Hopkins University Press.

———. 1943. "Jefferson and the American Philosophical Society," *Proceedings of the American Philosophical Society,* vol. LXXXVII, pp. 264–65.

———. 1957. "André and François-André Michaux and Their Predecessors," *Proceedings of the American Philosophical Society,* vol. 101, No. 4, August 16, pp. 344–68.

Chuinard, K. G. 1975. "Thomas Jefferson and the Corps of Discovery. Could He Have Done More?" *The American West,* vol. 12, November-December, pp. 4–13.

Churchman, John. 1789. "An Address to the members of the different learned Societies in America and Europe, in support of the Principles of Magnetic Variation and their application in Determining the Longitude at Sea," *The American Museum or Repository of Ancient and Modern Fugitive Pieces,* vol. V, pp. 496–500.

————. 1790. *An Explanation of the Magnetic Atlas, or Variation Chart, Hereunto Annexed: Projected on a Plan Entirely New*. Philadelphia: James & Johnson.

————. 1794, repr. 1800. *Magnetic Atlas or Variation Chart of the Whole Terraqueous Globe, Comprising a System of the Variation and Dip of the Needle, by which the Observations being truly made . . . the Longitude may be Ascertained*. London: Darton & Harvey; Gaines & Ten Eyck.

————. 1804. " "Essay on the improvement of Geography," *Transactions of the Society Instituted at London for the Encouragement of the Arts, Manufactures, and Commerce; With the Premiuns Offered for the Year 1804*, vol. XXII, pp. 221–29.

Clark, James C. 1985. *Faded Glory. Presidents Out of Power*. New York: Praeger Publishers.

Clarke, Charles G. 1970. *The Men of the Lewis and Clark Expedition*. Glendale, Cal.: The Arthur H. Clark Company.

Cohn, L. 1979. "Contributions of Thomas Jefferson to American Medicine," *The American Journal of Surgery*, vol. 138, August, pp. 286–292.

Cohen, Morris L. 1971. "Thomas Jefferson Recommends a Course of Study," *University of Pennsylvania Law Review*, vol. 119, pp. 823–44.

Colden, Cadwallader D. 1817. *The Life of Robert Fulton*. New York: Kirk & Mercein.

Coleman, George P. 1916. *The Flat Hat Club and the Phi Beta Kappa Society. Some New Light on Their History*. Richmond: The Dietz Press.

[College of William and Mary]. *Archives*. Commission of Thomnas Jefferson as Surveyor of Albemarle County, June 6, 1773.

"Papers Relating to the College. Letter from T. B. Smith," 1908, *William and Mary College Quarterly Historical Magazine*, vol. XVI, No. 3, January, pp. 162–73.

Collinson, Peter. 1767. "An account of some very large fossil teeth, found in North America," *Philosophical Transactions*, vol. LVII, 1767 (1768), pp. 464–67.

————. 1767. "Sequel to the foregoing account of the large fossil teeth," *Philosophical Transactions*, vol. LVII, 1767 (1768), pp. 468–69.

Cometti, Elizabeth, ed. 1946. "Mr. Jefferson Prepares an Itinerary," *Journal of Southern History*, vol. XII, February, pp. 89–106.

Corner, George W., ed. 1948. *The Autobiography of Benjamin Rush: His 'Travels Through Life', Together with His Commonplace Book for 1789–1813*. Memoirs vol. 25. Philadephia: American Philosophical Society.

Cotter, Charles H. 1968. *A History of Nautical Astronomy*. New York: Elsevier Publishing Company, Inc.

Coues, Elliott, ed. 1893, repr. 1965. *History of the Expedition Under the Command of Lewis and Clark*. 3 vols. New York: Dover Publications.

Council Journals, Colonial Virginia. 1768.

Cousins, Peter A. 1976. "The plowmaker from Monticello: America's First Agricultural Engineer," *The Herald* (Greenfield Village), vol. 5, No. 1, January, pp. 34–37.

Couture, Richard T. 1980. *Powhatan: A Bicentennial History*. Richmond: The Dietz Press.

Cox, John Redman. 1802. *Practical Considerations on Vaccination: or Inoculation for the Cow-Pock*. Philadelphia: James Humphreys.

Cripe, Helen. 1974. *Thomas Jefferson and Music*. Charlottesville: The University Press of Virginia.

Crouch, Tom D. 1983. *The Eagle Aloft. Two Centuries of the Balloon in America*. Washington, D. C.: Smithsonian Institution Press.

Culley, Frank L. 1936. "Meridians of Washington," *Geodetic Letter*, vol. 3, No. 1, March, p. 56.

Curtis, William Eleroy. 1901. *The True Thomas Jefferson*. Philadelphia. J. B. Lippincott & Co.

Cuthbert, Norma B. 1943. "Poplar Forest," *Huntington Library Quarterly*, vol. VI, No. 3, May, pp. 333–356.

Cutler, William Parker and Cutler, Julia Perkins. 1888. *Life, Journals and Correspondence of Reverend Manassah Cutler*. 2 vols. Cincinnati: R. Clarke & Co.

Cutright, Paul Russell. 1967. "The Odyssey of the Magpie and the Prairie Dog," *Bulletin of the Missouri Historical Society*, vol. XXIII, No. 3, April, pp. 215–28.

————. 1969. *Lewis and Clark. Pioneering Naturalists*. Urbana, Ill.: University of Illinois Press.

————. 1966. "Thomas Jefferson's Instructions to Lewis and Clark," *Bulletin of the Missouri Historical Society*, vol. XXII, No. 3, April, pp. 304–7.

————. 1982. "Contributions of Philadelphia to Lewis and Clark History," *We Proceeded On*, Publication No. 6, pp. 1–43.

[Cutting. Nathaniel]. Massachusetts Historical Society, Manuscripts Division. *The Papers of Nathaniel Cutting*.

Cuvier, Georges Leopold Chrétien. 1796. "Notice sur le squelette d'une grande espèce de quadrupède inconnue jusqu'à présent, trouvé au Paraguay, déposé au cabinet d'Histoire naturel de Madrid," *Magasin encyclopédique*, Deuxieme annee, vol. I, pp. 303–10, 2 pl.

———. 1796. "Notice concerning the Skeleton of a very large Species of a Quadruped, hitherto unknown, found at Paraguay, and deposited in the Cabinet of Natural History at Madrid," *The Monthly Magazine, and British Register for 1796*, vol. 2, September, pp. 637–38.

———. 1804. "Sur le megalonyx, animal de la famille des paresseux, mais de la taille de boeuf, dont les ossmens ont été découverte en Virginie, en 1796," *Annales du Museum d'Histoire Naturelle*, vol. V, pp. 538–76.

———. 1821. *Recherches sur les Ossemeus Fossiles, ou l'on rétablit les caractères de plusiers animaux dont les Révolutions du globe ont distruit les espèces. 10 vols. Paris/Amsterdam: G. Defour et d'Ocagne. 2nd edition.*

[L. D.]. 1951. "A Life Portrait of Jefferson," *Worcester Art Museum News Bulletin and Calendar*, vol. 17, No. 3, pp. 9–10.

Dabney, Virginius. 1928. "Jouett Outrides Tarleton," *Scribner's Magazine*, vol. 83, June, pp. 690–98.

Dabney, Virginius. 1981. *The Jefferson Scandals. A Rebuttal.* New York: Dodd, Mead & Company.

Darlington, William M., ed. 1893. *Christopher Gist's Journals, with historical Geographical and Ethnological Notes, and Biographies of His Contemporaries.* Pittsburgh: J. R. Weldon & Co.

Daubenton, Louis Jean Marie. 1762. "Mémoire sur des os et des dents remarquables pour leur grandeur," *Mémoires de l'Académie Royale des Sciences*, An 1762 (1764), pp. 206–29.

Daumas, Maurice. 1953. *Les instruments scientifiques aux XVIIe et XVIIIe.* Paris: Presses Universitaires de France.

Davis, Charles H. 1849. *Remarks Upon the Establishment of an American Prime Meridian.* Cambridge: Metcalf and Company.

Davis, John. 1803. *Travels of Four Years and a Half in the United States of America, during 1798–99–1800–1–2.* London: For R. Edwards, Bristol.

Davis, Richard Beale. 1961. "Jefferson as a Collector of Virginiana," in *Studies in Bibliography. Papers of the Bibliographical Society of the University of Virginia.* Edited by Fredson Bowers. Charlottesville: Bibliographical Society of the University of Virginia, pp. 137–38.

———. 1972. *Intellectual Life in Jefferson's Virginia 1790–1830.* Knoxville, Tenn.: University of Tennessee Press.

Department of State, *Records*. 1790. *Miscellaneous Letters.*

DeRosier, Arthur H., Jr. 1972. "Natchez and the Formative Years of William Dunbar," *The Journal of Mississippi History*, vol. XXXIV, No. 1, February, pp. 29–47.

Desmarest, Anselme. 1822. *Mammologie ou description des espèces de Manniferes.* Paris: Veuve Agasse.

De Sassure, Henry W. 1800. *Address to the Citizens of South Carolina.* Charleston, S.C.: For W. D. Young.

Dewey, Frank L. 1977. "Thomas Jefferson's Law Practice," *Virginia Magazine of History and Biography*, vol. 85, No. 3, July, pp. 289–301.

———. 1986. *Thomas Jefferson Lawyer.* Charlottesville: The University Press of Virginia.

Diamond, Sigmund, ed. 1941. "Some Jefferson Letters," *Mississippi Valley Historical Review*, vol. XXVIII, September, pp. 225–42.

Diaz del Castillo, Bernal. 1568, repr. 1928. *The True History of the Conquest of Mexico.* New York: Harper & Bros.

Dick, Stephen J. 1980. "How the U. S. Naval Observatory Began, 1830–65," *Sky and Telescope*, December, pp. 466–71.

Dictionary of American Biography. 1934–44. 11 vols. New York: Charles Scribner's Sons.

The Diplomatic Correspondence of the United States of America from the Signing of the Definitive Treaty of Peace 10 September 1783 to the Adoption of the Constitution, March 4, 1789. . . . 1837. 3 vols. Washington, D.C.: Blair & Rives.

Disbrow, Natalie J. 1941. "Thomas Walker of Albemarle," *Papers of the Albemarle County Historical Society*, vol. I, pp. 5–18.

"Documents Relating to the Boundary of Northern Neck," 1920 *Virginia Magazine of History and Biography*, vol. XXVIII, pp. 297–99.

Dodsley, Robert. 1764–1769. Description of "The Leasowes," in William Shenstone, *The Collected Works in Prose and Poetry of William Shenstone, Esq.* 3 vols. London: R. J. Dodsley.

"Don Pedro Theme for Hagley's Christmas," 1985. *Hagley Museum and Library Newsletter*, vol. 14, No. 4, Winter, unpaginated.

Dorfman, Joseph. 1946. *The Economic Mind in American Civilization*. New York: Viking Press.

Dorsey, John M., ed. 1960. *The Jefferson-Dunglison Letters*. Charlottesville: The University Press of Virginia.

Dos Passos, John. 1959. *The Head and Heart of Thomas Jefferson*. Garden City, N. Y.: Doubleday & Co.

Dumbauld, Edward. 1946. *Thomas Jefferson, Tourist*. Norman, Okla.: University of Oklahoma Press.

————. 1979 *Thomas Jefferson and the Law*. Norman, Okla.: University of Oklahoma Press.

Dunbar, William. 1809. "Meteorological Observation for One Year from Jan. 31, 1800, Made at The Forest Four and a Half Miles Northeast of the Mississippi," *Transactions of the American Philosophical Society*, old series, vol. 6, pp. 9–24.

[Dunglison, Robley]. 1963. *The Autobiographical Ana of Robley Dunglison M.D.* Edited by Samuel X. Radbill. *Transactions of the American Philosophical Society*, vol. 53, part 8.

Duparc, L. and Tikhonovich, M. N. 1920. *Le platine et les gîtes platinifères de l'Oural et du Monde*. Geneva: Impr. et lith. Sonor.

Dupree, A. Hunter. 1957. *Science In the Federal Government. A History of Policies and Activities to 1940*. Cambridge: The Belknap Press, Harvard University Press.

Durfee, W. F. 1892–1893. "The History and Development of the Art of Interchangeable Construction in Mechanism," *Transactions of the American Society of Mechanical Engineers*, vol. 14, pp. 1225–27.

————. 1894. "The First Systematic Attempt at Interchangeability in Firearms," *Cassier's Magazine*, vol. V, April, pp. 469–77.

Duveen, Denis I. and Glickstein, Herbert. 1955. "Alexandre-Marie Quesnay de Beaurepaire's 'Mémoire 1788' ", VMHB, vol. LXIII, pp. 280–85.

Earle, Alice Morse. 1902. *Sun-dials and Roses of Yesterday*. New York: The Macmillan Company.

Eaton, Clement. 1951. "A Mirror of the Southern Colonial Lawyer. The Fee Books of Patrick Henry, Thomas Jefferson and Waightstill Avery," *William and Mary Quarterly*, 3rd series, vol. 8, pp. 520–34.

Eckhardt, George H. 1935. *Pennsylvania Clocks and Clockmakers*. New York: Devin-Adair Company.

"Education in Colonial Virginia," 1898, *William and Mary College Quarterly Historical Magazine*, vol. VII, No. 2, October, pp. 73–74.

Edwards, Edward E., ed. 1943. *Jefferson and Agriculture*. Agricultural History Series No. 7, U. S. Department of Agriculture. Washington, D.C.: N.P.

Ehrenberg, Ralph H. 1971. "Nicholas King: First Surveyor of the City of Washington, 1803–1812," *Records of the Columbia Historical Society of Washington, D. C.*, pp. 31–65.

Elgan, Marcus C., Jr., ed. 1961. "Peter Jefferson and Joshua Fry—Mapmakers," *The Iron Worker*, vol. XXVI, No. 4, Autumn, pp. 13–19.

Ellicott, Andrew. 1803. repr. 1962. *The Journal of Andrew Ellicott. . . .* Chicago: Quadrangle Books.

Ellis, K. L. 1958. "British Communication and Diplomacy in the Eighteenth Century," *Bulletin of the Institute of Historical Research*, vol. XXXI, No. 84, November, pp. 159–67.

Encyclopedia Britannica. 1788. 10 vols. 2nd edition. Edinburgh: Colin MacFauquhar.

Encyclopedia Britannica, 1943. 24 vols. 14th edition.

Encyclopédie ancienne. 1771. Paris: N. Diderot.

L'Encyclopédie méthodique. 1790. Paris: Chez Panckoucke, etc.

Ewers, John C. 1966. " 'Chiefs from the Missouri and Mississippi' and Peale's Silhouettes of 1806," *The Smithsonian Journal of History*, vol. 1, No. 1, Spring, pp. 12–19.

Ewing, Galen W. 1938. "Early Teaching of Science at the College of William and Mary," *Journal of Chemical Education*, vol. 15, No. 1, January, pp. 3–13.

Faden, William and Jeffreys, Thomas. 1774. *A Catalogue of Modern and Correct Maps, Plans, and Charts, Chiefly Engraved by the Late T. Jeffreys*. London: "Sold by Faden & Jeffreys."

Fauque, Danielle. 1985. "Alexis-Marie Rochon (1741–1817), savant astronomique et opticien," *Revue d'Histoire des Sciences*, Tome XXXVIII, pp. 3–36.

[Fauquier, Francis]. 1758. "An Account of an extraordinary Storm of Hail in Virginia. By Francis Fauquier, Esq. Communicated by William Fauquier, Esq., F.R.S.," *Philosophical Transactions of the Royal Society of London*, vol. L, part II for 1758 (1759), pp. 746–47.

[Fauquier, Francis]. Colonial Williamsburg Foundation, Inc., Manuscripts Collection, *Papers of Robert Carter III*, 1770.

Fay, Bernard. 1927. *The Revolutionary Spirit in France and America*. New York: Harcourt, Brace & Javanovich.

Featherstonhaugh, G. W. 1831. "The Journal of Col. Groghan," *Monthly American Journal of Geological and Natural Sciences*, vol. I, pp. 257–72.

Federico, Pasquale J. 1936. "Origin and Early History of Patents," *Journal of the Patent Office Society*, vol. XVIII, No. 7, July, pp. 292–305.

———. 1936. "Operation of the Patent Act of 1790," *Journal of the Patent Office Society*, vol. XVIII, No. 4, April, p. 237–51.

Ferguson, Eugene S. 1951, " "Mr. Jefferson's Dry Docks," *The American Neptune*, vol. XI, pp. 108–14.

Fessenden, Thomas Green. 1806. *Democracy Unveiled, or the Tyranny Stripped of the Garb of Patriotism by Christopher Caustic*. New York: Printed for J. Riley & Co.

Fetis, F-J. 1875, repr. 1963. *Biographie universelle des musiciens et bibliographie général de la musique*. Paris: Culture et Civilization.

Field, James A., Jr. 1969. *America and the Mediterranean World, 1776–1882*. Princeton: Princeton University Press.

Filson, John. 1784. *The Discovery, Settlement, and Present State of Kentucke*. Wilmington, Del.: James Adams.

Fitzpatrick, John C., ed. 1925. *Diaries of George Washington*. 4 vols. Boston: Houghton Mifflin Company.

———., ed. 1931–1940. *The Writings of George Washington*. 39 vols. Washington, D. C.: G.P.O.

John P. Foley, ed. 1900, repr. 1967. *The Jeffersonian Encyclopedia. A Comprehensive Collection of the Views of Thomas Jefferson*. 2 vols. New York: Russell & Russell.

Foley, William E. and Rice, Charles David. 1979. "Visiting the President. An Exercise in Jeffersonian Diplomacy," *The American West*, vol. XVI, No. 6, November-December, pp. 4–15, 56.

Foley, William E. and Rice, Charles David. 1979. "The Return of the Mandan Chief," *Montana, The Magazine of Western History*, vol. 29, Summer, pp. 2–15.

Force, Peter. 1837–1853. *American Archives*. 9 vols. Washington, D. C.: Prepared and published by authority of Congress.

Ford, Worthington and Fitzpatrick, John C., eds. 1904–37. *Journals of the Continental Congress*. 34 vols. Washington, D.C.: Government Printing Office.

Ford, Paul Leicester, ed. 1892–99. *The Writings of Thomas Jefferson*. 10 vols. New York: G. P. Putnam's Sons.

———. 1892. "Thomas Jefferson in Undress," *Scribner's Magazine*, vol. XII, No. 4, pp. 509–16.

Ford, W. C., ed. 1916, repr. 1936. *Thomas Jefferson Correspondence, Printed from the Originals in the Collection of William K. Bixby*. Boston: Privately printed; St. Louis, Mo.: Jefferson Memorial.

Forman, Sidney. 1947. "Thomas Jefferson on Universal Military Training," *Military Affairs*, vol. 11, Fall, pp. 177–78.

[Foster, Sir Augustus John]. 1954. *Jeffersonian America: Notes on the United States of America Collected in the Years 1805–06–07 and 11–12 by Sir Augustus John Foster, Bart*. Edited by Richard Beale Davis. San Marino, Cal.: Huntington Library.

Fouts, Levi N. 1922. "Jefferson the Inventor, and His Relations to the Patent System," *Journal of the Patent Office Society*, vol. I, No. 7, March, pp. 316–31.

[Franklin, Benjamin]. 1904. *The Works of Benjamin Franklin*. Edited by John Bigelow. 10 vols. New York: G. P. Putnam's Sons & the Knickerbocker Press.

[Franklin, Benjamin]. American Philosophical Society, Manuscripts Division. *The Papers of Benjamin Franklin*.

Fraser, Alexander David. 1934–35. "Thomas Jefferson As Field Archeologist," *Four Arts: Dedicated to Artistic Virginia*, vols. 1–2, pp. 3–4.

Friis, Herman R. 1951. "Cartographic and Geographic Activities of the Lewis and Clark Expedition," *Journal of the Washington Academy of Sciences*, vol. 44, No. 11, November 1954, pp. 338–51.

———. 1959. "Alexander von Humboldts Besuch in den Vereinigten Staaten von America vom 20. Mai bis zum 30. Juni 1804," in *Alexander von Humboldt. Studien zu seiner universalen Geisteshaltung*, edited by Joachim H. Schultze. Berlin: Verlag Walter de Grutter & Co., pp. 145–95.

———. 1960–62. "Baron Alexander von Humboldt's Visit to Washington, D. C. June 1 through June 13, 1804," *Records of the Columbia Historical Society of Washington, D.C.*, ., pp. 6–18.

Fulling, E. H. 1944 and 1945. "Thomas Jefferson: His Interest in Plant Life as Revealed in His Writings," *Bulletin of the Torrey Botanical Club*, vol. 71, No. 6, November 1944, pp. 563–98, vol. 72, (1945), pp. 248–70.

528 BIBLIOGRAPHY

Fulton, John F. and Thomson, Elizabeth H. 1947. *Benjamin Silliman, Pathfinder in American Science*. New York: Henry Schuman.

Gaines, Richard Hayward. 1891. "Richmond's First Academy, Projected by M. Quesnay de Beaurepaire," *Virginia Historical Society Collections*, new series, vol. II, pp. 167–75.

Gaines, William H., Jr. 1948. "An Unpublished Jefferson Map, With a Petition for the Division of Fluvanna from Albemarle County, 1777," *Papers of the Albemarle County Historical Society*, vol. VII, 1946–47 (1948), pp. 23–28.

————. 1955. "Thomas Jefferson's Favorite Hideaway," *Virginia Cavalcade*, vol. 5, pp. 36–39.

Ganter, Herbert L. 1947. "William Small, Jefferson's Beloved Teacher," *William and Mary Quarterly*, 3rd series, vol. IV, No. 4, pp. 505–11.

Garlick, Richard C., Jr. 1933. *Philip Mazzei, Friend of Jefferson*. Baltimore: Johns Hopkins University Press.

Garriga, Jose. 1796. *Descripcion del esqueletto de un quadropedo muy corpulento y raro que se conserva en el Real Gabinete de Historia Natural de Madrid*. Madrid: Iberra.

[Gassendi, Genl.] 1819. *Aide-Mémoire à l'usage des officiers d'artillerie de France. Attachés au service de Terre*. Paris: Chez Magimel, Anselin et Pochard. 5th edition.

Gaynor, Jay. 1985. "Mr. Hewlett's Tool Chest. Part I," *Chronicle of the Early American Industries Association*, vol. 38, No. 4, December, pp. 57–60.

Geer, Henry Burns. 1902. "Thomas Jefferson and Pre-historic Americans," *The American and Oriental Journal*, vol. XXIV, January-November, pp. 224–28.

Gibbs, James. 1728. *Book of Architecture, Containing Designs of Buildings and Ornaments*. London: N.P.

"The George Wythe House." N.D. Williamsburg: Colonial Williamsburg, Inc.

Glisson, L., ed. *1000 Years, A Bicentennial Illustrated History of the United States*. 2 vols. Washington, D.C.: U.S. News & World Report, Inc.

Goff, Frederick R. 1972. "Jefferson the Book Collector," *Journal of the Library of Congress*, January, pp. 32–47.

Goldsborough, Charles W. 1824. *The United States Naval Chronicle*. Washington, D.C.: J. Wilson.

Good, R. N.D. "John Harrison's Last Timekeeper of 1770," in *Pioneers of Precision Timekeeping*. Monograph No. 3. London: Antiquarian Horological Society.

Goodrich, Samuel G. 1857. *Recollections of a Lifetime, or Men and Things I Have Seen: In a Series of Familiar letters to a friend, Historical, Biographical, Anecdotal, and Descriptive*. 2 vols. New York/ Auburn: Miller, Orton & Mulligan.

Goodwin, Rutherford. 1941. *A Brief and True Report Concerning Williamsburg in Virginia: Being an Account of the Most Important Occurrences in That Place From Its Beginning to the Present Time. . . .* Richmond: The Dietz Press, for Colonial Williamsburg, Inc.

Goodwin, W. A. R. 1903. *Historical Sketch of Bruton Church*. Petersburg, Va.: Franklin Press.

Gould, Rupert T. 1958. *John Harrison and His Timekeepers*. London: National Maritime Museum.

Granquist, Charles L. 1976. "Thomas Jefferson's 'Whirligig Chairs,'" *Antiques*, vol. 109, No. 5, May, pp. 1056–60.

————. 1977. "Cabinetmaking at Monticello." Unpublished thesis for M.A., Cooperstown Graduate Programs, Oneonta, New York.

Green, Constance McL. 1956. *Eli Whitney and the Birth of American Technology*. Boston: Little, Brown and Company.

————. 1962. *Washington Village and Capital, 1800–1878*. Princeton: Princeton University Press.

Grégoire, Henri. 1808. *De la littérature des Nègres, ou Recherches sur leur facultés intellectuelles, leurs qualités morales et leur littérature; suivies de Notices sur la vie et les ouvrages des Nègres qui se sont distingués dans les Sciences, les Lettres et les Arts*. Paris: Chez Maradan, Libraire.

Gregory, Richard Claxton. 1971. "The Myth of the Founding Fathers," in *No More Lies: The Myth and Reality of American History*. New York: Harper & Row, pp. 64–100.

Guettard, Jean Étienne. 1752. "Mémoires dans lequel on compare le Canada e la Suisse par rapport a ses minéraux," *Mémoires de l'Académie Royale des Sciences*, An 1752 (1756), pp. 189–220.

Guillaumin, A. and Chaudun, V. 1944. "La collection de modèles réduits d'instruments agricoles et horticoles du Museum à propos d'une lettre inédite de A. Thouin," *Bulletin du Museum National d'Histoire Naturelle*, 2nd series, Tome XVI, No. 2, Mars-Avril, pp. 137–41.

Guinness, Desmond and Sadler, Julius Trousdale, Jr. 1973. *Mr. Jefferson Architect*. New York: Viking Press.

Hagerty, J. H. 1962. "Dr. James Tilton: 1745–1822," *Weatherwise*, vol. 15, pp. 124–25.

Hall, Francis. 1818, 1819. *Travels In Canada and the United States in 1816 and 1817.* Boston: Wells & Lilly. London: For Longman, Hurst, Rees, and Orme & Brown.

Hall, Gordon Langley. 1966. *Mr. Jefferson's Ladies.* Boston: Beacon Press.

Hart, Andrew DeJarnette, Jr. 1938. "Thomas Jefferson's Influence on the Foundation of Medical Instruction at the University of Virginia," *Annals of Medical History,* pp. 47–60.

Halsey, Robert H. 1936. *How the President, Thomas Jefferson, and Doctor Benjamin Waterhouse Established Vaccination As a Public Health Procedure.* New York: The author, auspices of the New York Academy of Medicine.

Hamilton, Alexander, Jay, John and Madison, James. 1941. *The Federalist. A Commentary on The Constitution of the United States.* New York: The Modern Library.

Hamlin, Talbot. 1955. *Benjamin Henry Latrobe.* New York: Oxford University Press.

Harrison, Fairfax. 1924. "The Northern Neck Maps of 1737–1747," *William and Mary College Quarterly Historical Magazine,* 2nd series, vol. IV, No. 1, January, pp. 1–24.

———. 1924. "A Portrait of Governor Fauquier," Bulletin No. 4, *Fauquier Historical Society,* July, pp. 343–51.

Hart, James. 1948. *The American Presidency in Action, 1789.* New York: The Macmillan Company.

Hartnagel, C. A. and Bishop, Sherman C. 1921. "The Mastodons, Mammoths and Other Pleistocene Mammals of New York State," *New York State Museum Bulletin,* Nos. 241–242, January-February, p. 63.

Hartwell, Henry et al. 1940. *The Present State of Virginia and the College,* edited by H. D. Parish. Williamsburg: Colonial Williamsburg, Inc.

Hassler, Ferdinand Rudolph. 1825. "Survey of the Coast of the United States," *Transactions of the American Philosophical Society,* New series, vol. 2, "Plan of an Observatory to be built in Washington," pp. 365–85.

———. 1834–36. *Principal Documents Relating to the Survey of the Coast of the United States Since 1816.* New York: J. Windt.

Hastings, G. 1926. *Life and Works of Francis Hopkinson.* Chicago: University of Chicago Press.

Hawes, Lloyd E. 1974. *Benjamin Waterhouse, M. D. First Professor of the Theory and Practice of Physic at Harvard.* Boston: The Francis A. Countway Library of Medicine.

[Hawtrey, F. M. 1765]. 1908. "Description of William and Mary College, 1765," (From *The Hawtrey Family* by F. M. Hawtrey, London: G. Allen, 1903, vol. I, p. 146), *Virginia Magazine of History and Biography,* vol. XVI, No. 2, October, pp. 209–10.

Hazelton, J. H. 1906. *Declaration of Independence. Its History.* New York: Dodd, Mead & Company.

Heal, Sir Ambrose. 1953. *The London Furniture Makers From the Renaissance to the Victorian Era, 1560–1840.* London: Batsford.

Heller, Francis H. 1948. "Monticello and the University of Virginia, 1825: A German Prince's Travel Notes," *Papers of the Albemarle County Historical Society,* vol. 7, 1946–47, pp. 34–35.

Hemphill, John M., II, ed. 1959. "Edmund Randolph Assumes Thomas Jefferson's Practice," *Virginia Magazine of History and Biography,* vol. LXVII, pp. 170–71.

Hening, William Waller, ed. 1809–23. *The Statutes At Large, Being A Collection of All the Laws of Virginia. . . .* New York, Philadelphia and Richmond: Printed for Samuel Pleasants, Jr. by the Printer of the Commonwealth.

Henry, Joseph. 1848. *First Report of the Secretary of the Smithsonian Institution.* Appendix. Washington, D.C.: Government Printing Office.

Heywood, John. 1823. *Natural and Aboriginal History of Tennessee.* Nashville, Tenn.: G. Wilson.

Hillairet, Jacques. 1963. *Dictionnaire historique des rues de Paris.* Paris: Les Editions de Minuit. 4th edition.

Hindle, Brooke. 1956. *The Pursuit of Science in Revolutionary America, 1735–1785.* Chapel Hill: University of North Carolina Press.

———. 1964. *David Rittenhouse.* Princeton: Princeton University Press.

Hines, Christian. 1866. *Early Recollections of Washington City.* Washington, D.C.: Chronicle Book & Job Print.

"The History of the United States Patent Office," 1936, *Journal of the Patent Office Society,* vol. XVIII, No. 7, July, pp. 5–144.

Hitt, Parker. 1916. *Manual For the Solution of Military Ciphers.* Fort Leavenworth, Kansas: Press of the Army Service Schools.

Holland, C. C. 1978. "Albemarle County Settlements: A Piedmont Model," *Quarterly Review of the Archeological Society of Virginia,* vol. 33, No. 2, December, pp. 29–32.

Honeywell, 1931. *The Educational Work of Thomas Jefferson.* Harvard Studies in Education, vol. 16. Cambridge: Harvard University Press.

Hopkins, Samuel. 1791. *An Address to the Manufacturers of Pot and Pearl Ash, With an Explanation of Samuel Hopkins's Patent Method of Making the Same . . . Also a Copy of the Patent Granted to Samuel Hopkins.* New York: Childs and Swaine.

Hopper, Margaret G. and Bollinger, G. A. 1971. *The Earthquake History of Virginia—1774 to 1900.* Blacksburg, Va.: Virginia Polytechnic Institute and State Library. Department of Geological Sciences.

The (Virginia) *House of Burgesses. Journal,* 1727–40. p. 379; 1752–55, 1756–58.

Hughes, Sarah S. 1980. *Surveyors and Statesmen; Land Measuring in Colonial Virginia.* Richmond: Virginia Surveyors Association of Surveyors and Virginia Surveyors Foundation.

Hummel, Charles F. 1965. "English Tools in America: The Evidence of the Dominys," *Winterthur Portfolio,* vol. 2, pp. 27–46.

Hunt, Gaillard. 1901. *The Department of State.* Washington, D.C.: Government Printing Office.

Hunter, Clark. 1983. *The Life and Letters of Alexander Wilson.* Memoirs, Vol. 154. Philadelphia: American Philosophical Society.

Hunter, William. 1768. "Observations on the Bones commonly supposed to be Elephant's Bones, which have been found near the river Ohio in America," *Philosophical Transactions,* vol. 58, pp. 34–45.

Huntington Library and Art Gallery. Manuscripts Division. *The Papers of Thomas Jefferson.*

Hurd, Charles. 1966. *The White House. A Biography.* New York: Harper & Bros.

Index Biographique des Membres et Correpondants de l'Académie des Sciences. 1954. Paris: Gauthier-Villars.

Index to the Thomas Jefferson Papers. 1976. Washington, D.C.: The Library of Congress.

Institut de France, Académie des Sciences. 1808–1811. *Procès-verbaux des séances de l'Académie depuis la fondation de l'Institut jusqu'à mois d'aout 1835,* vol. IV.

Isaac [slave]. 1967. "Memoirs of a Monticello Slave as dictated to Charles Campbell by Isaac," in *Jefferson at Monticello,* edited by James A. Bear, Jr. Charlottesville: The University Press of Virginia.

Jackson, Donald. 1961. *Thomas Jefferson & the Stony Mountains. Exploring the West from Monticello.* Urbana, Ill.: University of Illinois Press.

———, ed. 1966. *The Journals of Zebulon Montgomery Pike.* 2 vols. Norman, Okla.: University of Oklahoma Press.

———. 1974–75. "Thomas Jefferson and the Pacific Northwest," *We Proceeded On,* vol. 1, No. 1, Winter, pp. 5–6.

———. 1978. "Ledyard and Lapérouse: A Contrast in Northwestern Exploration," *The Western Historical Quarterly,* vol. 9, October, pp. 495–508.

———. 1978. *The Letters of the Lewis and Clark Expedition, With Related Documents 1783–1854.* 2 vols. Urbana, Ill.: University of Illinois Press.

———. 1980. "Jefferson, Meriwether Lewis and the Reduction of the United States Army," *Proceedings of the American Philosophical Society,* vol. 124, pp. 91–96.

Jackson (Whitney), Lois Fell. 1941. *Colonel Joshua Fry, Albemarle's Soldier-Statesman.* (Master's Thesis, August 1941), University of Virginia.

Janson, Charles William. 1807, repr. 1935. *The Stranger in America, 1794–1806.* London: For J. Cundee; New York: Press of the Pioneers.

The Papers of Thomas Jefferson, Library of Congress, Manuscripts Division. Paul G. Sifton, "Introduction."

"The Jefferson Family," *Tyler's Quarterly Historical Magazine,* vol. II, pp. 264–65.

Jefferson, Thomas. "A Summary View of the Rights of British America," in *The Complete Jefferson,* edited and arranged by Saul K. Padover, pp. 5–19.

———. 1787, repr. 1955. *Notes On the State of Virginia.* With an Introduction by William Peden. Chapel Hill; University of North Carolina Press.

———. 1790. *Report on the Method for Obtaining Fresh Water from Salt.* Washington, D.C.: For the House of Representatives.

———. 1799. "Letter to Sir John Sinclair, containing a description of the mould-board of the least resistance, and of the easiest and most certain construction," *Transactions of the American Philosophical Society,* Old series, vol. 4, pp. 313–22.

————. 1799. "A Memoir on the discovery of certain bones of an animal of the clawed kind in the Western parts of Virginia," *Transactions of the American Philosophical Society*, vol. 4, No. 30, pp. 246–60.

————. *Parliamentary Manual*. (L&B II pp. 333–50).

————. 1802. "D'une oreille de charrue, offrant le moins de resistance possible, et dont l'exécution est aussi facile que certaine. Par M. Jefferson, président des États-Unis d'Amérique," *Annales du Museum d'Histoire Naturelle*, vol. I, pp. 322–31.

————. 1802. "On the Necessity of establishing a Point of Time for taking the Vaccine Virus for the Purpose of Inoculation, as a Popular Criterion," *Medical Repository*, vol. V, pp. 348–49.

————. 1803. "An Account of Louisiana, being an abstract of documents, in the offices of the Departments of State and of the Treasury," a report made to Congress on November 14, 1803, *American State Papers, Miscellaneous*, vol. 10, pp. 344–64.

————. 1829. "A Table of Thermometric Observations Made at Monticello, From January 1, 1810, to December 31, 1816," *The Virginia Literary Museum, and Journal of Belles Lettres, Arts, Sciences, &c.* vol. 1, No. 1, p. 26.

————. 1829. *A Catalogue of the Valuable and Extensive Library of the Late President Jefferson.* Washington: Gales & Seaton.

————. 1851. *An Essay Towards Facilitating Instruction in the Anglo-Saxon and Modern Dialects of the English Language. For the Use of the University of Virginia.* New York: J. F. Trow.

————. *Fee Book.* CSmH.

————. *Nailery Account Book.* William Andrews Clark Memorial Library, University of California at Los Angeles.

————. 1943. *Autobiography.* In *The Complete Jefferson*, edited and arranged by Paul K. Padover. New York: Tudor Publishing Company.

————. *Weather Memorandum Book.* Library of Congress, Manuscripts Division, *The Papers of Thomas Jefferson*.

[Jefferson, Thomas]. 1854. *The Youth of Jefferson. A Chronicle of College Scrapes at Williamsburg, in Virginia, A.D. 1764.* New York: Redfield.

[Jefferson, Thomas]. "When Jefferson Lived in New York," editorial. 1929. *The New York Times*, April 15, 1929.

Jennings, Walter Wilson. 1921. *The American Embargo, 1807–1809.* University of Iowa Studies in the Social Sciences. Iowa City, Ia.: University of Iowa Press.

Jillson, Willard Rouse. 1936. *Big Bone Lick. An Outline of Its History Geology and Paleontology.* Big Bone Lick Association Publications No. 1. Louisville, Ky.: The Standard Printing Co.

Jodoin, Alex and Vincent, J. L. 1889. *Histoire de Longueuil et de la famille de Longueuil.* Montreal: Gebhardt-Berthianne.

Johnston, Henry P. 1882. "The Secret Service of the Revolution," *The Magazine of American History*, vol. VIII, pp. 95–105.

Johnston, W. D. 1904. *History of the Library of Congress.* Washington, D.C.: Government Printing Office.

Jones, Anna Clark. 1939. "Antlers for Mr. Jefferson," *The New England Quarterly*, vol. XII, pp. 333–48.

Jones, Charles C. 1873. *Antiquities of the Southern Indians, Particularly of the Georgia Tribes.* New York: D. Appleton & Co.

[Jones, John]. 1787. *The Description and Use of a New Portable Orrery . . . To Which is prefixed, a Short Account of the Solar System, or the True System of the World.* London: John Jones, 3rd edition.

Jones, Robert. 1976. "Thomas Jefferson and Pecan Breeding," *67th Report of the Proceedings of the Northern Nut Growers Association*, pp. 123–26.

Jones, Hugh. 1724. *The Present State of Virginia.* London: For J. Clarke.

Journal Encyclopédique. 1781.

Journal of the Twentieth House of Representatives of the Commonwealth of Pennsylvania. 1809. Lancaster, Pa.

Journals of the Meetings," 1894–95. *William and Mary College Quarterly Historical Magazine*, series 1, vol. 3, p. 129.

Kahn, C. 1963. "History of Smallpox and Its Prevention," *American Journal of Diseases of Children*, vol. 106, No. 597, pp. 597–609.

Kahn, David. 1967. *The Code Breakers.* New York: The Macmillan Company.

Kallen, Horace M. 1944. "Jefferson's Garden Wall," *American Bookman*, vol. I, Winter, pp. 78–82.

Kean, Robert H. 1972. *History of the Graveyard at Monticello*. Charlottesville: Thomas Jefferson Memorial Foundation.

Keene, John T., Jr. 1972. "The Nail Making Industry in Early Virginia," *The Chronicle of the Early American Industries Association, Inc.*, vol. XXV, No. 1, March, pp. 1–9.

Kelso, M. 1982. "Jefferson's Garden: Landscape Archeology at Monticello," *Archeology*, vol. 35, July-August, pp. 43–44.

Kennedy, John P. 1849. *Memoirs of William Wirt*. 2 vols. Philadelphia: Lea & Blanchard.

Kimball, Fiske. 1916. *Thomas Jefferson, Architect. Original Designs in the Collection of Thomas Jefferson Coolidge, Junior, With an Essay and Notes by Fiske Kimball*. Boston: For private distribution.

———. 1917. "The Genesis of the White House," *The Century Illustrated Monthly Magazine*, vol. XCV, New Series, vol. LXXIII, November 1917–April 1918, pp. 523–28.

———. 1925. "Thomas Jefferson's Windsor Chairs," *The Pennsylvania Museum Bulletin*, vol. 21, No. 98, December, pp. 58–60.

———. 1943. "In Search of Jefferson's Birthplace," *The Virginia Magazine of History and Biography*, vol. LI, No. 4, October, pp. 313–25.

———. 1943. "Jefferson and the Arts," *Proceedings of the American Philosophical Society*, vol. CXXX-VII, p. 239.

Kimball, Marie. 1929. "Thomas Jefferson's French Furniture," *Antiques*, vol. XIV, No. 2, February, pp. 23–28.

———. 1929. "Jefferson's Furniture Comes Home to Monticello," *House Beautiful*, vol. 66, August, pp. 164–65, 186, 188, 190.

———. 1929. "The Original Furnishings of the White House," *Antiques*, vol. 15, June, pp. 481–86; July, pp. 33–37.

———. 1933. "The Epicure of the White House," *Virginia Quarterly Review*, vol. 9, No. 1, January, pp. 71–81.

———. 1940. *The Furnishings of Monticello*. Philadelphia: N.P.

———. 1943. *Jefferson, The Road To Glory. 1743–1776*. New York: Coward-McCann, Inc.

———. 1947. *Jefferson, War and Peace, 1776 to 1784*. New York: Coward-McCann, Inc.

———. 1949. *The Furnishings of Monticello*. Charlottesville: Thomas Jefferson Memorial Foundation.

Kindle, E. M. 1931. "The Story of the Discovery of Big Bone Lick," *Kentucky Geological Survey*, Series VI, vol. XLI, pp. 195–212.

King, Henry C. 1955. *The History of the Telescope*. London: Charles Griffin & Co., Ltd.

———. 1978. *Geared To the Stars. The Evolution of Planetariums, Orreries and Astronomical Clocks*. Toronto/Buffalo: University of Toronto Press.

Lacépède, Bernard-Germain Étienne de and Cuvier, Georges. 1808. "Des os fossiles trouvés dans l'Amérique-septentrionale," *Journal de physique*, vol. 67, pp. 331–33.

Lambeth, William Alexander and Manning, Warren H. 1913. *Thomas Jefferson As An Architect and a Designer of Landscape*. Boston: Houghton Mifflin Company.

Landsberg, H. E. 1964. "Early Stages of Climatology in the United States," *Bulletin of the American Meteorological Society*, vol. 45, No. 5, May, pp. 268–75.

La Pérouse, Jean François de Galaup, Comte de. 1807. *A Voyage Round the World Performed in the Years 1785, 1786, 1787, and 1788, By the Boussole and Astrolabe*. 3 vols. and atlas. London: Hackington.

Larch, Alice H. 1943. "Who Was the Printer of Jefferson's *Notes?*" *Bookman's Holiday* (New York Public Library), pp. 45–46.

La Rochefoucauld-Liancourt, François Alexandre, Duc de. 1800. *Travels Through the United States of North America . . . in the Years 1795, 1796 and 1797. . . . 2 vols.* London: R. Phillips.

"Last Scenes of Mr. Jefferson's Life, etc." 1826. *Richmond Enquirer*, August 27, 1826.

[Latrobe, Benjamin Henry]. Maryland Historical Society, Manuscripts Division. *The Papers of Benjamin Henry Latrobe*.

[Latrobe, Benjamin Henry]. 1984. *The Papers of Benjamin Henry Latrobe. Correspondence and Miscellaneous Papers, 1781–1804*. Edited by John C. Van Horne et al. New Haven: Yale University Press.

Lavoisier, Antoine. 178?. *The Art of Manufacturing Alkaline Salts and Potashes*, translated by Charles Williamos. Paris: N.P.

Leavell, Byrd S. 1977. "Jeffersonian Ideals Endowed the University of Virginia," *Virginia Medical*, vol. 104, No. 2, February, pp. 91–96.

Ledyard, John. 1783. *A Journal of Captain Cook's Last Voyage to the Pacific Ocean in the Years 1776, 1777, 1778 and 1779*. Hartford, Conn.: Nathaniel Patten.

Lehmann, Karl. 1945. "The Dom of Heaven," *Art Bulletin*, vol. XXVII, pp. 19–20.

———. 1947. *Thomas Jefferson, Humanist*. Chicago: University of Chicago Press.

Lehmann-Haupt, Karl. 1943. "Thomas Jefferson, Archeologist," *American Journal of Archeology*, vol. XLVII, No. 2, April-June, pp. 161–63.

Leighton, Ann. 1981. "Thomas Jefferson As a Gardener," *Country Life*, vol. 170, November 5, pp. 1556–58.

Le Magazin Encyclopédique, pp. 512–13, "France. Nécrologie. Sur le C. Blanc."

Le Roy, Jean Baptiste, Laplace, Pierre-Simon, Coulomb, Charles-Augustin and Borda, Jean-Charles de la. 1791. *Rapport fait à l'Académie Royale des Sciences, le Samedi 19 Mars 1791, d'une Mémoire Important, de M. Blanc, sur la fabrication des armes de guerre*. Paris: Imprimerie de Moutard.

Levasseur, August. 1829. *Lafayette in America in 1824 and 1825, or Journal of Travels in the United States*. 2 vols. New York: W. B. Gilley, Collins & Co.

Levene, John R. 1977. *Clinical Refraction and Visual Science*. London: Batsford.

Levy, Leonard W. 1988. *Original Intent and the Framers' Constitution*. New York: The Macmillan Pub Company.

Lewis, B. R. 1949. "The First U.S. Repeaters," *American Rifleman*, vol. 97, December, pp. 38–42.

Lewis, Grace. 1954. "Financial Records, 'Expedition to the Pacific Ocean,' " *Bulletin of the Missouri Historical Society*, vol. 10, No. 4, July, pp. 465–89.

[Lewis, Thomas]. 1925. *The Fairfax Line—Thomas Lewis's Journal of 1746*. With Footnotes and an Index by John W. Wayland. New Market, Va.: The Henkel Press.

Lewis, William Draper, ed. 1907. *Great American Lawyers*. 2 vols. Philadelphia: John C. Winston Company.

Link, Patricia. 1978. "The Chien des Bergères of Thomas Jefferson," *Pure-Bred Dogs American Kennel Gazette*, vol. 93, August, pp. 25–28.

Lipscomb, Andrew A. and Bergh, Albert E. 1903–4. *The Writings of Thomas Jefferson*. 20 vols. Washington, D.C.: The Thomas Jefferson Memorial Foundation.

Lockwood, Luke Vincent. 1926. "The St.-Mémin Indian Portraits," The *New-York Historical Society Quarterly Bulletin*, vol. 12, pp. 3–26.

Long, E. John. 1961. "Shadwell—Jefferson's Birthplace," *The Iron Worker*, vol. XXVI, No. 4, Autumn, pp. 1–7.

Looney, Jefferson J. N.D. "Joseph Gaston Chambers," in *Princetonians: A Biographical Dictionary. Princetonians 1776–1783*. Princeton: Princeton University Press (In preparation).

Loos, John Louis. 1954. "William Clark's Part in the Preparation of the Lewis and Clark Expedition," *Bulletin of the Missouri Historical Society*, vol. X, July, pp. 490–511.

Lossing, Benson J. 1853. "Monticello," *Harper's New Monthly Magazine*, vol. VII, No. 38, July, pp. 145–51.

———. 1859–60. *Pictorial Field Book of the Revolution*. 2 vols. New York: Harper & Bros.

Lovell, Joseph. 1826. *Meteorological Register 1822–1825*. Washington: Government Printing Office.

Lovering, J. 1850. "On the American Prime Meridian," *The American Journal of Science and Arts*, 2nd series, vol. IX, May, pp. 184–98.

Lowrie, Walter and Franklin, Walter S., eds. 1834. *Documents, Legislative and Executive, of the Congress of the United States From the First Session of the Eleventh to the Second Session of the Seventeenth Congress, Inclusive. . . .* Washington: Gale and Seaton.

Luiscius, A. van Stiprian. 1805. *Beschrijving van een zeepeiler of bathometer*. 's Gravenhage.

Mabbot, T. O. 1955. *The Embargo of William Cullen Bryant*. Gainsville, Fla.:Scholarly Facsimiles & Reprints.

McAdie, Alexander. 1894. "A Colonial Weather Service," *The Popular Science Monthly*, vol. XLV, July, pp. 336–37.

———. 1930. "Thomas Jefferson at Home," *Proceedings of the American Antiquarian Society*, new series, vol. 40, part 1, April, pp. 27–46.

MacCarthy, Gerald R. 1964. "A Descriptive List of Virginia Earthquakes Through 1960," *Journal of the Elisha Mitchell Scientific Society*, vol. 80, No. 2, December, supplement, pp. 82–84.

McDermott, John Francis. 1959. "The Western Journals of Dr. George Hunter, 1796–1805," *Proceedings of the American Philosophical Society*, vol. 103, No. 6, December 15, pp. 770–73.

Mackenzie, Alexander. 1801. *Voyages from Montreal, on the River St. Lawrence, through the continent of North America, to the frozen . . . and Pacific Ocean; in the years 1789 and 1793.* 2 vols. London: For T. Cadell & W. Davies.

McKnight, John L. N.D. "The Scientific Instruments on Display in the Wythe House." Williamsburg: Colonial Williamsburg, Inc. (Unpublished manuscript).

McLaughlin, Jack. 1988. *Jefferson and Monticello. The Biography of a Builder.* New York: Henry Holt & Company.

Malone, Dumas. 1931. "Polly Jefferson and Her Father," *Virginia Quarterly Review*, vol. 7, January, pp. 81–95.

———. 1948. *Jefferson and His Time. Volume One. Jefferson the Virginian.* Boston: Little, Brown and Company.

———. 1950. *The Fry & Jefferson Map of Virginia & Maryland: Facsimile of the first edition with introduction by Dumas Malone.* Princeton: Princeton University Press.

———. 1951. *Jefferson and His Time. Volume Two. Jefferson and the Rights of Man.* Boston: Little, Brown & Company.

———. 1957. "Jefferson Goes to School in Williamsburg," *Virginia Quarterly Review*, vol. 33, No. 4, Autumn, pp. 482–96.

———. 1962. *Jefferson and His Time. Volume Three. Jefferson and the Ordeal of Liberty.* Boston: Little, Brown and Company.

———. 1970. *Jefferson and His Time. Volume Four. Jefferson the President. First Term, 1801–1805.* Boston, Little, Brown and Company.

———. 1974. *Jefferson and His Time. Volume Five. Jefferson the President Second Term, 1805–1809.* Boston: Little, Brown and Company.

———. 1981. *Jefferson and His Time. Volume Six. The Sage of Monticello.* Boston: Little, Brown and Company.

[Manly, John M.]. University of Chicago, The Joseph Regenstein Library, *The Papers of John M. Manly.*

Mansfield, Edward. 1863. "The Military Academy at West Point," *American Journal of Education*, vol. 30, pp. 17–24.

Marraro, Howard R., ed. 1942. *Memoirs of Philip Mazzei 1730–1816.* New York: Columbia University Press.

[Marshall, Christopher]. 1877. *Extracts from the Diary of Christopher Marshall, Kept in Philadelphia and Lancaster, During the American Revolution 1774–1781,* edited by William Duane. Albany, N.Y.: Joel Munsell.

Martin, Edwin T. 1946. "Thomas Jefferson's Interest in Science and the Useful Arts," *Emory University Quarterly*, vol. 2, June, pp. 65–73.

Martin, Edwin T. 1952. "Thomas Jefferson, A Scientist in the White House," *Emory University Quarterly*, vol. 8, March, pp. 46–47.

———. 1952. *Thomas Jefferson, Scientist.* New York: Henry Schuman.

Martin, Henry A. 1881. "Jefferson As a Vaccinator," *North Carolina Medical Journal*, vol. 7, No. 1, January, pp. 1–34.

Marx, Rudolph. 1960. *The Health of the Presidents.* New York: G. P. Putnam's Sons.

Massachusetts Historical Society, Manuscripts Division. *The Coolidge-Jefferson Papers.*

[Mather, Cotton]. "An Extract of Several Letters from Cotton Mather to John Woodward, M.D. and Richard Waller, Esq.", *Philosophical Transactions*, vol. 29, pp. 61–71.

Matthews, Albert. 1918. "Journal of William Loughton Smith, 1790," *Proceedings of the Massachusetts Historical Society*, vol. LI, pp. 36–39.

[Maury, Anne Fountaine]. University of Virginia, Alderman Library, Manuscripts Division. *Maury Deposit.* (MS). Anne Fountaine Maury, "Intimate Virginians: A Century of Maury Travels by Land and Sea."

Mayer, Brantz. 1851. *Tah-Gah-Jute.* Baltimore: T. Murphy & Co.

Mayo, Barbara. 1941. "Twilight at Monticello," *Virginia Quarterly Review*, vol. 17, pp. 502–15.

Mayo, Bernard, ed. 1942. *Jefferson Himself: The Personal Narrative of a Many-Sided American.* Charlottesville: The University Press of Virginia.

———. 1943. "A Peppercorn for Mr. Jefferson," *Virginia Quarterly Review*, vol. XIX, pp. 222–28.

Meade, William. 1857. *Old Churches, Ministers, and Families of Virginia.* Philadelphia: J. B. Lippincott & Co.

Medlin, Dorothy. 1978. "Thomas Jefferson, André Morellet, and the French Version of Notes on the State of Virginia," *William amd Mary Quarterly*, vol. 35, January, pp. 85–99.

Metral, Denyse. 1939. *Blaise de Vigénère: Archéologue et Critique d'Art*. Paris: Librairie E. Droz.

Milham, Willis I. 1938. *Early American Observatories. Which Was the First Astronomical Observatory in America?* Williamstown, Mass.: Williams College.

Miller, John Chester. 1977. *The Wolf by the Ears. Thomas Jefferson and Slavery*. New York: The Free Press.

Mirsky, Jeanette and Nevins, Allan. 1962. *The World of Eli Whitney*. New York: Collier Books.

Mitchill, Samuel L. 1826, repr. 1982. *A Discourse on the Character and Services of Thomas Jefferson, More Especially as a Promoter of Natural and Physical Science*. Charlottesville: University of Virginia, Division of Humanities.

Molina, Juan Ignacio. 1776. *Compendio della storia geografica naturale, e civile, del regno di Chile*. Traducido per Nareiso Cueto. Bologna: Stamperia di S. Tommaso d'Aquino.

Montlezun, Baron de. 1818, repr. 1828. *Voyage fait dans les années 1816 et 1817 de New Yorck la Nouvelle-Orleans, et de l'Orenoque au Mississippi, par les Petites et les Grandes-Antilles*. 2 vols. Paris: Librairie de Gide Fils.

Moore, Clement C. 1804. *Observations Upon Certain Passages in Mr. Jefferson's Notes on Virginia*. New York: N.P.

Moore, T. C. and Shield, J. A. 1969. "Medical Education of America's First University," *The Journal of Medical Education*, vol. 44, pp. 241 et seq.

Moore, John Hammond. 1976. *Albemarle, Jefferson's County, 1727–1976*. Charlottesville, Va.: The University Press of Virginia.

Morgan, Gerald, Jr. 1965. "Nicholas, Philip and Virginia Jefferson Randolph Trist," *Collected Papers of the Monticello Association of the Descendants of Thomas Jefferson*, edited by George Green Shackelford. Princeton: Princeton University Press.

Morris, Mabel. 1945. "Jefferson and the Language of the American Indian," *Modern Language Quarterly*, vol. 6, March, pp. 31–34.

Morris, Roland S. 1943. "Jefferson As a Lawyer," *Transactions of the American Philosophical Society*, vol. 87, No. 3, pp. 211–15.

Morrison, A. J. 1922. "Virginia Patents," *William and Mary College Quarterly Historical Magazine*, 2nd series, vol. II, No. 3, July, pp. 149–56.

Morveau, L. B. Guton de. 1805. *Traité des moyens de désinfecter l'air*. Paris: Chez Bernard.

Multhauf, Robert P. 1961. *Catalogue of Instruments and Models in the Possession of the American Philosophical Society*. Memoirs, vol. 53. Philadelphia: American Philosophical Society.

———. 1975. "Potash," in *Material Culture in the Wooden Age*, edited by Brooke Hindle. Tarrytown, N.Y.: Sleepy Hollow Restorations, pp. 227–40.

[Nettleton, Thomas]. 1725. "Observations concerning the Height of the Barometer, at different Elevations above the Surface of the Earth, in a Letter to the Publisher from the Learned Dr. Nettleton," *Philosophical Transactions*, vol. 33, pp. 308–12.

Nichols, Frederick Doveton and Bear, James A. Jr. 1982. *Monticello. A Guidebook*. Charlottesville: Thomas Jefferson Memorial Foundation.

Nichols, Frederick Doveton. 1974. "Jefferson's Retreat: Poplar Forest," *The Iron Worker*, vol. XXXVIII, No. 2, Spring, pp. 2–13.

———. 1984. *Thomas Jefferson's Architectural Drawings*. Charlottesville: The University Press of Virginia.

Nicholson, Michael. 1796, repr. 1826. *The Carpenter's and Joiner's Companion*. London: Caxton Press.

Nicholson, Peter. 1796. *The New and Improved Builder and Workman's Companion*. 3 vols. London: Thomas Kelly.

———. 1815. *The Carpenter and Joiner's Assistant*. 4th edition. London: For J. Taylor.

Norfleet, Fillmore. 1942. *Saint-Mémim in Virginia: Portraits and Biographies*. Richmond: The Dietz Press.

Norton, Paul F. 1956. "Jefferson's Plans for Mothballing the Frigates," *Proceedings of the United States Naval Institute*, vol. 81, pp. 737–41.

Nourse, J. E. 1873. *Memoir of the Founding and Progress of the United States Naval Observatory. Washington Observations for 1871*. Washington, D.C.: Government Printing Office.

Nouvelle Biographie Général sous la direction de M. le Dr. Hofer. 1859. 46 vols. Paris: Firmin Didot Frères.

Office of Naval Records and Library. 1939–44. *Naval Documents Relating to the United States Wars with the Barbary Powers*. 5 vols. Washington, D.C.: Government Printing Office.

Onderdewyngaart, J. H. 1805. *Beschrijving van sen zeepeiler of bathometer*. s'Gravenhage.

Ord-Hume, Arthur W. J. G. 1977. *Perpetual Motion: The History of An Obsession.* New York: St. Martin's Press.

Osborn, Henry Fairchild. 1929. "Thomas Jefferson, the Pioneer of American Paleontology," *Science,* vol. 69, No. 1790, pp. 410–13.

———. 1935. "Thomas Jefferson as Paleontologist," *Science,* vol. 82, No. 2136, pp. 533–38.

"Outline of the History of the United States Patent Office." 1936. *Journal of the Patent Office Society,* 1936, vol. xviii, No. 7, July, pp. 5–144.

Padgett, James A., ed. 1937. "The Letters of Dr. Samuel Brown to President Jefferson and James Brown," *Register of the Kentucky Historical Society,* vol. 35, No. 111, April, pp. 99–130.

Padover, Saul K., ed. 1943. *The Complete Jefferson.* New York: Tudor Publishing Company.

———., ed. 1946. *Thomas Jefferson and the Nation's Capital 1783–1818.* Washington, D.C.: Government Printing Office.

Pannekeok, A. 1961. *A History of Astronomy.* New York: Interscience Publishers, Inc.

[Page, John]. 1850. "John Page on William Small," *Virginia Historical Register,* July, pp. 150–51.

Paltsits, Victor Hugo. 1935. "The Use of Invisible Ink for Secret Writing During the American Revolution," *New York Public Library Bulletin,* vol. XXXIX, May 1935, pp. 361–65.

Paris, Archives Affaires Etrangères, *Correspondence Political, Etats-Unis.*

Parker, Rosane Strong. 1941. *Colonel William Mayo, F.R.S. Soldier and Promoter of the Virginia Piedmont 1684–1744.* (Master's thesis, August 1941), University of Virginia.

Parker, William B. and Viles, Jonas, eds. 1905. *Letters and Addresses of Thomas Jefferson.* New York: The Unit Book Publishing Co.

Parton, James. 1872. "College Days of Thomas Jefferson," *Atlantic Monthly,* vol. XXIX, January, pp. 26–77.

———. 1872. "Thomas Jefferson As a Student of Law," *Atlantic Monthly,* February, pp. 179–97.

———. 1872. "Thomas Jefferson As a Virginia Lawyer," *Atlantic Monthly,* March, pp. 320.

———. 1874. *Life of Thomas Jefferson, Third President of the United States.* Boston: James R. Osgood & Co.

Patterson, C. Perry. 1950. "Jefferson the Lawyer," *University of Pittsburgh Law Review,* vol. 11, No. 3, Spring, pp. 369–96.

[Patterson, Robert]. 1794. "An easy and accurate method of adjusting the glasses of the Hadley quadrant on land for back observation; letter from Robert Patterson to David Rittenhouse, April 10, 1794," *Transactions of the American Philosophical Society,* vol. 4, pp. 154–61.

[Patterson, Robert]. American Philosophical Society, Manuscripts Division. *The Papers of Robert Patterson.*

Paullin, Charles O. 1923. "Early Movements for a National Observatory," *Records of the Columbia Historical Society of Washington, D. C.,* vol. 25, pp. 36–56.

Peale, Charles Willson. N.D. American Philosophical Society, Peale Family Papers. *Autobiography.* Typescript.

———. American Philosophical Society, Manuscript Division, *The Peale Family Papers, Diary.* (MS).

Peckham, Howard H. 1937–38. "British Secret Writing in the Revolution," *Michigan Alumni Quarterly Review,* vol. XLVI, pp. 126–31.

Peden, William. 1941. *Some Aspects of Jefferson Bibliography.* Lexington, Va.: Washington and Lee University.

———. 1942. "Thomas Jefferson: Book Collector." (Doctoral dissertation, University of Virginia).

———. 1944. "Some Notes Concerning Thomas Jefferson's Libraries," *William and Mary Quarterly,* 3rd series, vol. I, July, pp. 265–74.

———. 1949. "A Book Peddler Invades Monticello," *William and Mary Quarterly,* 3rd series, vol. VI, No. 1, October, pp. 631–36.

Pennypacker, Morton. 1939. *George Washington's Spies on Long Island and in New York.* Brooklyn, Long Island Historical Society.

Perry, William Stevens, ed. 1870–78. *Historical Collections Relating to the American Colonial Church.* 2 vols. Hartford: Printed for the Subscribers.

Peterson, Merrill D. 1960. *The Jefferson Image in the American Mind.* New York: Oxford University Press.

———. 1970. *Thomas Jefferson and the New Nation.* Oxford: Oxford University Press.

———, ed. 1986. *Thomas Jefferson. A Reference Biography.* New York: Charles Scribner's Sons.

Philip, Cynthia Owen. 1985. *Robert Fulton. A Biography.* New York: Franklin Watts.

[Phillips, Henry, Jr.]. 1885. "Early Proceedings of the American Philosophical Society For the Promotion of Useful Knowleddge Compiled by Henry Phillips, Jr. from Manuscript Minutes of Its Meetings from 1744 to 1838," *Proceedings of the American Philosophical Society*, vol. 22, No. 119, part 3.

Phillipps, Philip Lee. 1896. "Virginia Cartography," *Smithsonian Miscellaneous Collections*, vol. 37, No. 4. Washington, D. C.: Government Printing Office, pp. 1–85.

Pickens, Buford. 1975. "Mr. Jefferson as Revolutionary Architect," *Journal of the Society of Architectural Historians*, vol. XXXIV, No. 4, December, pp. 260–66.

Pierson, Hamilton Wilcox. 1862, repr. 1967. *Jefferson at Monticello. The Private Life of Thomas Jefferson*. Edited, with an introduction, by James A. Bear, Jr. Charlottesville: The University Press of Virginia.

Pi-Sunyer, Oriol. 1964. "Thomas Jefferson, Reluctant Manufacturer," *Janus*, vol. 51, No. 3, pp. 226–34.

"Plan of the Virginia Society for the Promotion of Usefull Knowledge." 1772. Williamsburg: Colonial Williamsburg Foundation, Inc.

[Plumer, William]. Library of Congress, Manuscripts Division, *The Papers of William Plumer*.

Prager, Frank D. 1944. "A History of Intellectual Property from 1545 to 1787," *Journal of the Patent Office Society*, vol. XXVI, No. 11, November, pp. 711–60.

Pratt, Joseph Hyde. 1942. "American Prime Meridians," *The Geographical Review*, vol. XXXII, pp. 234–35.

Preston, Howard W. 1916. "Washington's Visits to Providence," *Rhode Island Historical Society Collections*, vol. XIX, No. 4, October, pp. 109–15.

Preston, John Raine, ed. 1973. "Correspondence Between Thomas Jefferson and John Stuart," *Greenbrier Historical Society*, vol. 2, No. 5, pp. 4–13.

M. Prevost and Roman d'Amat, eds. 1959. *Dictionnaire de Biographie Française*. Paris: Letouzey et Ane.

Price, William Jennings. 1927. " 'The Characteristic Bent of A Lawyer' in Jefferson," *Georgetown Law Journal*, vol. 16, pp. 41–54.

Prime, Phoebe Phillips, compl. 1960. *The Alfred Coxe Prime Directory of Craftsmen*. (MS). American Philosophical Society, Manuscripts Division.

Procès-verbal des Comités d'agriculture et de commerce de la Constituante, de la Législature et de la Convention. 1790. Paris: F. Gerbaux et Ch. Schmidt.

Procès-verbal de l'Assemblée nationale (constituante). 1791. Paris: Imprimerie par son ordre.

Procès-verbal de l'Assemblée (législative). 1792. Paris: Imprimerie par son ordre.

Procès-verbal de la Convention nationale. 1794. Paris: Imprimerie per son ordre.

Prucha, Francis P. 1962. *American Indian Policy in the Formative Years*. Cambridge: Harvard University Press.

———. 1971. *Indian Peace Medals in American History*. Madison, Wisc.: Wisconsin State Historical Society.

Quaife, Milo M., ed. 1916. *The Journals of Captain Meriwether Lewis and Sergeant John Ordway kept on the Expedition of Western Exploration, 1803–1806*. Madison, Wisc.: State Historical Society of Wisconsin.

[Quesnay de Beaurepaire, Alexandre-Marie]. 1788. *Memoire and Prospectus Concerning the Academy of Sciences and Fine Arts of the United States of America, established at Richmond, the Capital of Virginia, By the Chevalier Quesnay de Beaurepaire*. Paris.

Radbill, S. X. 1969. "Thomas Jefferson and the Doctors," *Transactions and Studies of the College of Physicians of Philadelphia*, 4th series, vol. 37, No. 2, October, pp. 106–14.

Ramsden, Jesse. 1771. *Description of a New Universal Instrument*. London: Privately printed.

———. 1791. *Description of the Universal Equatorial and of the New Refraction Apparatus*. London: Privately printed.

Ramsey, George. 1936. "The Historical Background of Patents," *Journal of the Patent Office Society*, vol. XVIII, No. 1, January, pp. 14–15.

Randall, Henry S. 1858. *The Life of Thomas Jefferson*. 3 vols. New York: Derby & Jackson.

Randolph, Edmund. 1935. "Essay on the Revolutionary History of Virginia, 1774–1782," *Virginia Magazine of History and Biography*, vol. XLIII, p. 123.

———. 1970. *Revolutionary History of Virginia*. Edited by Arthur Harvey Shaffer. Charlottesville: The University Press of Virginia.

Randolph, Fred. J. and Francis, Fred. L. 1895. "Thomas Jefferson as Meteorologist," *Monthly Weather Review*, vol. 23, December, pp. 456–58.

Randolph, Sarah N. 1871, repr. 1978. *The Domestic Life of Thomas Jefferson*. Charlottesville: The University Press of Virginia.

Randolph, Thomas Jefferson, ed. 1829. *Memoir, Correspondence and Miscellanies from the Papers of Thomas Jefferson*. 4 vols. Charlottesville: F. Carr and Co.

[Randolph, Thomas Jefferson]. University of Virginia, Alderman Library, Manuscripts Division. *Edgehill Randolph Papers*. "Memoirs of Thomas Jefferson Randolph."

Raphael, Henry. 1943. "Thomas Jefferson, Astronomer," *Astronomical Society of the Pacific. Leaflet No. 17*. August, p. 7.

Raumer, Frederich von. 1846. *America, and the American People*. Translated by W. W. Turner. New York: S. & H. G. Langley.

Rawlings, Mary. 1925. *The Albemarle of Other Days*. Charlottesville, Va.: The Michie Company.

Rayner, B. L. 1832. *Sketches of the Life and Writings of Thomas Jefferson*. New York: Francis & Boardman.

Recueil des Actes du comité de salut publique. 1794.

[Redheffer, Charles]. 1812. *An Accurate Delineation of Readheffers Perpetual Motion*. (Broadside).

[Redheffer, Charles]. 1812. *Whereas the interference of the Legislature of Pennsylvania is causing an inquiry to [be] made, relative to the perfection or imperfection of the newly invented machinery, is not without precedent. . . .* Harrisburg, Pa.: State of Pennsylvania.

[Redheffer, Charles]. 1828. *Documents For and Against Charles Redheffer As It Respects His Alleged Invention of Perpetual Motion. Collected from Authentic Sources*. Philadelphia: N.P.

Rees, Abraham. 1819. *The Cyclopaedia; or, Universal Dictionary of Arts, Sciences. and Literature*. 45 vols. London: For Longman, Hurst, Rees, Orme & Brown.

Rees, John E. 1970. *Madame Charbonneau: The Indian Woman Who Accompanied the Lewis and Clark Expedition*. Salmon, Idaho: Lemhi County Historical Society.

Reese, A. L. N.D. *Transcripts from the Papers of George Washington*. (MS). Library of Congress.

[Regnier, Edmé]. 17 . . . "Description et usage du dynamometre . . . par le C[itoy]en Regnier," *Journal de l'Ecole Polytechnique*, vol. 2, pp. 160–78.

Regnier, Edme. N.D. *Description et usage du cadenas de Sûrété, à combinaisons*, Paris: Imprimerie de Madame Huzard.

Report of the Chief Signal Officer to the Secretary of War. 1919. Washington, D.C.: Government Printing Office.

Report of the Secretary of State, on the Subject of Establishing a Uniformity in the Weights, Measures and Coins of the U. S. 1790. New York.

Rice, Howard C., Jr. 1947. *L'Hôtel de Langeac, Jefferson's Paris Residence*. Paris: H. Lefebure and Charlottesville: Thomas Jefferson Memorial Foundation.

———. 1951. "An Album of Saint-Mémin Portraits," *Princeton University Library Chronicle*, vol. 13, No. 1, pp. 23–31.

———. 1951. "Jefferson's Gift of Fossils to the Museum of Natural History in Paris," *Proceedings of the American Philosophical Society*, vol. 95, pp. 597–627.

———. 1953–54. "Les Visites de Jefferson au Mont-Valerien," *Bulletin de la Société d'Histoire de Suresnes*, vol. III, No. 13, pp. 46–49.

———. 1954. *The Rittenhouse Orrery*. Princeton: Princeton University Press.

———. 1976. *Thomas Jefferson's Paris*. Princeton: Princeton University Press.

Richmond Enquirer, August 25, 1805.

Rickman, John. 1783. *An Authentic Voyage to the Pacific Ocean. By an Officer on Board the Discovery*. Philadelphia: Robert Ball.

[Riedesel, Maj. Genl.]. 1866. *Memoirs, and Letters and Journals Relating To the War of the American Revolution*. Translated by W. L. Stone. 2 vols. Albany, N.Y.: Times.

[Riedesel, Mrs. Genl.] 1867. *Letters and Journals Relating to the War of the American Revolution*. Translated from the German by W. L. Stone. Albany, N.Y.: J. Munsell.

Ritchie-Calder, Lord. 1982. "The Lunar Society of Birmingham," *Scientific American*, vol. 246, No. 6, June, pp. 136–45.

Robbins, Roland Wells. 1955/56. *Report on 1955 Archeological Exploration at Shadwell, Birthplace of Thomas Jefferson*. (MS). Charlottesville: The Thomas Jefferson Memorial Commission.

Robillard, Walter G. and Bouman, Lane J. 1987. *A Treatise On the Law of Surveying and Boundaries*. Fifth edition. Charlottesville: The Michie Company.

Robins, F. W. 1939. *The Story of the Lamp*. Oxford: Oxford University Press.

Robinson, Morgan P. 1905. "The Burning of the Rotunda," *University of Virginia Magazine*, series 3, October, pp. 2–23.

Rochon, Alexis. 1801. "Mémoire sur les verres acromatiques adapté a la mesure des angles, et sur les avantages que l'on peut retirer de la double refraction pour la mesure precise des petits angles," *Journal de Physique, de Chemie, et d'Histoire Naturelle et des Arts*, Fructidor An 9 (1801), pp. 169–99.

[Rochon, Alexis]. 1866. *Nouvelle Biographie Générale, vol. 38. pp. 466–68.*

Rowland, Mrs. Dunbar. 1930. *Life, Letters and Papers of William Dunbar.* Jackson, Miss.: Mississippi Historical Society.

Rudd, Velva E. 1954. "Botanical Contributions of the Lewis and Clark Expedition," *Journal of the Washington Academy of Sciences,* vol. 44, No. 11, November, pp. 351–56.

[Rush, Benjamin]. 1948. *The Autobiography of Benjamin Rush; His 'Travels Through Life', Together With His Commonplace Book for 1789–1813.* Memoirs vol. 25. Philadelphia: American Philosophical Society.

Rutland, Robert Allen. 1987. *James Madison The Founding Father.* New York: The Macmillan Company.

Sadie, Stanley, ed. 1980. *The New Grove Dictionary of Musical Instruments.* 20 vols. 6th edition. New York: Grove Publishing Co.

Saint-Marc, Agricol Bynet. 1881. *Chroniques du Palais-Royal.* Paris: T. Belin.

Sanchez-Saavedra, E. M. 1975. *Description of the Country. Virginia's Cartographers and Their Maps 1607–1881.* Charlottesville: University Press of Virginia.

Sarton, George. 1942–43. "Aimé Bonpland, 1773–1850," *Isis,* vol. 34, No. 5, pp. 385–99.

Saxe-Weimar Eisenbach, Bernhard Karl, Duke of. 1828. *Travels in North America in 1825 and 1826.* Philadelphia: Lea & Carey.

Schachner, Nathan. 1957. *Thomas Jefferson A Biography.* New York: Thomas Yoseloff.

Schapley, Harlow. 1943. "Thomas Jefferson As a Natural Philosopher," *Transactions of the American Philosophical Society,* vol. 87, No. 3, pp. 234–37.

Scharf, J. Thomas and Westcott, Thompson. 1884. *History of Philadelphia 1609–1884.* 2 vols. Philadelphia: L. H. Everts and Company.

Scheffel, Richard L. 1961. "Presidential Bird Watcher," *Audubon Magazine,* vol. 63, May-June, pp. 138–39.

Schofield, Robert E. 1963. *The Lunar Society of Birmingham. A Social History of Provincial Science and Industry in Eighteenth-Century England.* Oxford: Oxford University Press.

Sellers, Charles Coleman. 1947. *Charles Willson Peale.* 2 vols. Philadelphia: American Philosophical Society.

———. 1980. *Mr. Peale's Museum. Charles Willson Peale and the First Popular Museum of Natural Science and Art.* New York: W. W. Norton & Co.

Sellers, Horace W. 1904. "Letters of Thomas Jefferson to Charles Willson Peale, 1796–1823," *Pennsylvania Magazine of History and Biography,* vol. 28, pp. 136–54, 295–319, 403–19.

Setzer, Henry W. 1954. "Zoological Contributions of the Lewis and Clark Expedition," *Journal of the Washington Academy of Sciences,* vol. 44, No. 11, November, pp. 356–57.

Severance, Frank H. 1904. "A Bundle of Thomas Jefferson Letters Now First Published," *Publications of the Buffalo Historical Society,* vol. 7, pp. 1–32.

Shackelford, George G., ed. 1965. *Collected Papers to Commemmorate Fifty Years of the Monticello Association of the Descendants of Thomas Jefferson.* Princeton: Princeton University Press.

Shapely, Harlow. 1943. "Notes on Thomas Jefferson as a Natural Philosopher," *Proceedings of the American Philosophical Society,* vol. 87, pp. 234–37.

Shayt, David H. *The Nailery of Thomas Jefferson: Ironworking in America.* George Washington University. Master's thesis. Unpublished.

Sheehan, Bernard W, 1973. *Seeds of Extinction. Jeffersonian Philanthropy and the American Indian.* Chapel Hill: University of North Carolina Press.

Shenkir, William G,. Welsch, Glenn A. and Bear, James A. Jr. 1972. "Thomas Jefferson: Management Accountant," *The Journal of Accountancy,* April, pp. 33–47.

Shenstone, William. 1764–1769, repr. 1773. "Unconnected Thoughts on Gardening," in [Shenstone, William]. *The Collected Works in Prose and Poetry of William Shenstone, Esq.* London: R. J. Dodsley. Jefferson owned the 1773 edition.

Shepherd, Henry E. 1882. "Thomas Jefferson As a Philologist," *American Journal of Philology,* vol. 3, pp. 211–14.

[Silliman, Benjamin and Kingsley, J.]. 1810. "An Account of the Meteor, Which Burst Over Weston in Connecticut, in December 1807, and of the falling of Stones on that occasion. By Professors Silliman and Kingsley. With a Chemical Analysis of the Stones, by Professor Silliman, *Memoirs of the Connecticut Academy of Arts and Sciences*, vol. I, Part l, No. XV, pp. 141–61.

Simpson, George Gaylord. 1942. "The Beginnings of Vertebrate Paleontology in North America," *Proceedings of the American Philosophical Society*, vol. 86, No. 1, September, pp. 130–88.

Singleton, Esther. 1907. *The Story of the White House*. 2 vols. New York: The McClure Company.

Slaughter, Rev. P. S. 1880. *Memorial of Colonel Joshua Fry, Sometime Professor in William and Mary College, Virginia, and Washington's Senior in Command of Virginia Forces, 1754 etc*. N.P.

[Smith, Abigail Adams]. 1841. *Letters and Correspondence of Miss Adams, Daughter of John Adams, edited by Her Daughter*. New York: Wiley & Putnam.

Smith, David Eugene. 1934. "The Poetry of Mathematics and Other Essays," *The Scripta Mathematica Library No. 1*. New York: Scripta Mathematica, pp. 49–70.

Smith, Genl. Francis H. 1874. *The Schools and Schoolmasters of Virginia In the Olden Time*. Richmond: Clemmit & Jones.

Smith, Glenn Curtis. 1951. "Notes on Thomas Jefferson's 'Summary View of the Rights of British America,'" *Virginia Magazine of History and Biography*, vol. LIX, pp. 494–98.

Smith, Jane Blair. *The Carys of Virginia*. (Diary of Mrs. Jane B. Smith, copied by Captain Wilson Miles Cary. University of Virginia, Alderman Library, Manuscripts Division.

Smith, Margaret Bayard. 1824. *A Winter in Washington, or, Memoirs of the Seymour Family*. 3 vols. New York: E. Bliss & E. A. White.

———. 1906, repr. 1965. *First Forty Years of Washington Society*. Edited by Gaillard Hunt. 2 vols. New York: Charles Scribner's Sons; Frederick Unger Publishing Co.

———. 1906. "Washington in Jefferson's Time From the Diaries and Family Letters of Mrs. Samuel Harrison Smith (Margaret Bayard)," edited by Gaillard Hunt, *Scribner's Magazine*, vol. XL, July-December, pp. 292–310.

Smith, Marie. 1970. *Entertaining in the White House*. New York: MacFadden-Bartell Corporation.

Smith, William Loughton. 1796. *The Pretensions of Thomas Jefferson to the Presidency Examined: and the Charges Against John Adams Refuted. Addressed to the Citizens of America in General; and Particularly to the Electors of the President*. Philadelphia: N.P.

Smyth, Albert Henry. 1905–7. *The Writings of Benjamin Franklin*. 10 vols. New York: The Macmillan Company.

Smyth, J. F. D. 1784. *A Tour In the United States of America*. 2 vols. London: For G. Robinson.

Sowerby, E. Millicent. 1955. *Catalogue of the Library of Thomas Jefferson*. 5 vols. Washington, D.C.: The Library of Congress.

———. 1956. "Thomas Jefferson and His Library," *The Papers of the Bibliographical Society of America*, vol. 50, 3rd quarter, pp. 215–16.

Sparks, Jared. 1828, repr. 1847. *Memoirs of the Life and Travels of John Ledyard*. London: H. Colburn; Boston: N.P.

[Sparks, Jared]. Harvard College Library, *Sparks Manuscripts*.

Spafford, Horatio Gates. 1809. *General Geography and Rudiments of Useful Knowledge*. Hudson: Croswell & Frary.

Sprat, H. Philip. 1958. *The Birth of the Steamboat*. London: Charles Griffin & Company, Ltd.

"Statutes of William and Mary College," 1966. *William and Mary College Quarterly Historical Magazine*, series I, vol. 2, pp. 56 ff., vol. IV, p. 44, vol. XVI, No. 3, pp. 164–68, 247.

Stearn, E. Wagner and Stearn, Allen E. 1945. *The Effect of Smallpox on the Destiny of the Amerindian*. Boston: Bruce Humphries, Inc.

Steibing, William H., Jr. 1981. "Who First Excavated Stratigraphically?" *Biblical Archeological Review*, vol. 7, January-February, pp. 52–53.

Stimpson, George W. 1930. *Popular Questions Answered*. New York: George Sully and Company, Inc.

Stoddard, Amos. 1812. *Sketches historical and descriptive of Louisiana*. Philadelphia: Matthew Carey, A. Small.

Stolba, K. Marie. 1974. "Music in the Life of Thomas Jefferson," *Daughters of the American Revolution Magazine*, vol. 108, No. 3, March, pp. 197–202.

[Stuart, Archibald]. University of Virginia, Alderman Library, *Stuart Papers*.

Swanstrom, Roy, compl. 1985. *The United States Senate 1787–1801. A Dissertation on the First Fourteen Years of the Upper Legislative Body*. Washington, D.C.: Government Printing Office.

Swem, E. G. 1914. "Maps Relating to Virginia in the Virginia State Library and Other Departments of the Commonwealth," *Bulletin of the Virginia State Library*, vol. VII, Nos. 2–3, April-July, pp. 37–233.

Tableau du Nouveau Palais-Royal. 1788. Paris.

Tarleton, Banastre. 1787. *History of the Campaign of 1781 and 1782.* Dublin: Printed for Colles.

Taylor, E. G. R. 1966. *The Mathematical Practitioners of Hanoverian England 1714–1840.* Cambridge: Cambridge University Press.

Taylor, Olivia. 1965. "The Ancestry of Thomas Jefferson," in *Collected Papers To Commemmorate Fifty Years of the Monticello Association of the Descendants of Thomas Jefferson.* Princeton: Princeton University Press, pp. 39–44.

Taylor, Robert J. et al, eds. 1977–. *The Papers of John Adams.* 8 vols. to date. Cambridge, Mass./ London: The Belknap Press.

Terra, Helmut de. 1959. "Alexander von Humboldt's Correspondence With Jefferson, Madison, and Gallatin," *Proceedings of the American Philosophical Society,* vol. 103, No. 6, December, pp. 783–806.

Thacker, William C. 1955. *The Structural Preservation of Monticello.* Charlottesville: Jarman Printing Company.

"Thomas Jefferson: The Sheepman," 1976. *National Wool Grower,* vol. 66, April, pp. 10–11, 24–25.

Thomas, Selma. 1979. " 'La plus grande économie et la précision la plus exacte.' l'oeuvre d'Honoré Blanc," *Le Musée d'Armes,* 7 année, No. 24, Juin, pp. 1–43.

Thompson, Holland. 1921. *The Age of Invention. A Chronicle of Mechanical Conquest.* New Haven: Yale University Press.

Thorup, Oscar A. 1972. "Jefferson's Admonition," *Mayo Clinic Proceedings,* vol. 47, March, pp. 199–201.

Thurlow, Constance E. and Berkeley, Francis L., Jr., eds. 1950. *Jefferson Papers at the University of Virginia; A Calendar.* Charlottesville: The University Press of Virginia.

Thwaites, Reuben Gold, ed. 1904–5. *The Original Journals of the Lewis and Clark Expedition 1804–1806.* 8 vols. New York: Dodd, Mead & Company.

[Ticknor, George]. 1876. *Life, Letters and Journals of George Ticknor.* Edited by George S. Hillard et al. 2 vols. Boston: James R. Osgood and Company.

Tomlinson, Charles, ed. 1853. *Rudimentary Treatise on the Construction of Locks.* London: John Weale.

True, Rodney. 1916. "Thomas Jefferson In Relation to Botany," *Scientific Monthly,* vol. 3, pp. 345–60.

————. 1921. "Early Days of the Albemarle Agricultural Society," *Annual Report of the American Historical Association for the Year 1918,* vol. I, pp. 243–59.

————. 1928. "Some Neglected Botanical Results of the Lewis and Clark Expedition," *Proceedings of the American Philosophical Society,* vol. 67, No. 1, pp. 1–19.

Trumbull, John. 1841. *Autobiography, Reminiscences, and Letters 1756–1841.* New York: Wiley & Putnam.

"The Truth About the Signing of the Declaration of Independence," 1915. *The Sunday Star* (Washington, D.C.), July 4, Part 4, p. 2.

Tucker, George. 1837. *The Life of Thomas Jefferson.* 2 vols. Philadelphia: Carey, Lea & Blanchard; London: C. Knight & Co..

Turner, Katherine. 1965. "Federalist Policy and the Judiciary Act of 1801," *William and Mary Quarterly,* vol. 22, No. 1, January, pp. 23–30.

Tuttle, Kate A. 1899. "The First Bell and Clock of the University," *University of Virginia Alumni Bulletin,* February, pp. 111–13.

Tyler, Lyon G. 1884–96. *Letters and Times of the Tylers.* 2 vols. Richmond: Whittet & Shepperson.

————. 1907. *Williamsburg the Colonial Capitol.* Richmond: Whittet & Shepperson.

————. 1892. "Early Presidents of William and Mary, by the Editor: Lyon G. Tyler," *William and Mary College Quarterly Historical Magazine,* vol. I, No. 2, October, pp. 63–65.

University of Virginia, Alderman Library, Manuscripts Division, *Virginia Gazette.* Daybooks.

————, Alderman Library, *Board of Visitors,* Minutes.

Upton, Harriet Taylor. 1891. *Our Early Presidents, Their Wives and Children, From Washington to Jackson.* Boston: D. Lothrop. "The Family of Jefferson," pp. 149–88.

U. S. House of Representatives. 1939. *House Manual, 75th Congress, 3rd Session, House Document No. 700.*

Varro, Marcus Terentius. 1728, 1783. *De res rusticas. Libri III.* Venice: T. Bettinelli.

Van Doren, Carl. 1948. *The Great Rehearsal.* New York: Viking Press.

Verner, Coolie. 1951. "The Maps and Plates Appearing With the Several Editions of Mr. Jefferson's 'Notes on the State of Virginia'," *Virginia Magazine of History and Biography*, vol. 59, No. 1, January, pp. 21–33.

———. 1959. "Mr. Jefferson Makes A Map," *Imago Mundi*, vol. XIV, pp. 96–108.

———. 1967. "The Fry and Jefferson Map," *Imago Mundi*, vol. XXI, pp. 70–94.

Viola, Herman J. 1981. *Diplomats in Buckskins. A History of Indian Delegations to Washington City.* Washington, D.C.: Smithsonian Institution Press.

Virginia Council Journal. 1781.

Virginia Gazette, January 5, 1738.

Virginia House of Delegates, Journal.

Vogel, Virgil J. 1970. *American Indian Medicine.* Norman, Okla.: University of Oklahoma Press.

Volney, Constantin François Chaseboeuf, Comte de. 1803. *Tableau du climat et du sol des États-Unis d'Amérique.* Paris: Courcier, etc.

Waddell, Gene. 1987. "The First Monticello," *Journal of the Society of Architectural Historians*, vol. XLVI, No. 1, pp. 5–29.

Wallace, Henry A. 1937. Keynote address, November 17, 1937, *Proceedings of the Association of Land-Grant Colleges and Universities*, vol. 51, pp. 336–46.

Walters, Raymond, Jr. 1957. *Albert Gallatin: Jeffersonian Financier and Diplomat.* New York: The Macmillan Company.

Warner, Charles Willard Hoskins. 1961. *Road To Revolution. Virginia's Rebels From Bacon to Jefferson (1676–1776).* Richmond: Garrett & Massie.

Warren, Charles. 1945. "Fourth of July Myths," *William and Mary Quarterly*, 3rd series, vol. 2, No. 3, July, pp. 237–72.

Washington, Henry A., ed. 1853–54. *The Writings of Thomas Jefferson.* 9 vols. Washington: Taylor & Maury.

Waterhouse, Benjamin. 1800, 1802. *A Prospect of Exterminating the Smallpox; Being a History of the Varioliae Vaccinae or Kine-pox, Commonly Called the Cow-pox As It Has Appeared in England: With an Account of a Series of Inoculations Performed for the Kine-pox in Massachusetts.* Parts I and II.

Waterman, T. T. 1945. *The Mansions of Virginia 1706–1776.* Chapel Hill: University of North Carolina Press.

Watrous, Stephen D., ed. 1966. *John Ledyard's Journey Through Russia and Siberia, 1787–1788.* Madison, Wisc.: University of Wisconsin Press.

Watson, Lucille McWane. 1957. "Thomas Jefferson's Other Home," *Antiques*, vol. 71, pp. 342–46.

Watts, George B. 1965. "Thomas Jefferson, His 'Encyclopédie' and the 'Encyclopédie méthodique'," *The French Review*, vol. XXXVIII, No. 3, January, pp. 318–25.

Weber, Gustavus A. 1923. *The Coast and Geodetic Survey. Its History, Activities and Organization.* Service Monographs of the U. S. Government No. 16. Baltimore: Johns Hopkins University Press.

Weber, Ralph E. 1979. *United States Diplomatic Codes and Ciphers 1775–1938.* Chicago: Precedent Publishing, Inc.

[Webster, Daniel]. 1974. *Papers: Correspondence.* Volume I, edited by Charles M. Wiltse and Harold D. Moser. Hanover, N.H.: University Press of New England.

Webster, Fletcher, ed. 1857. *The Private Correspondence of Daniel Webster.* Boston: Little, Brown & Company.

Webster's Dictionary, 2nd International Unabridged Edition. 1947.

Weis, Frederick Lewis. 1950. *The Colonial Clergy of Maryland, Delaware, and Georgia.* Lancaster, Mass.: Society of the Descendants of Colonial Clergy.

Weld, Isaac, Jr. 1799. *Travels Through the States of North America and the Provinces of Upper and Lower Canada During the Years 1795, 1796 and 1797.* 2 vols. London: John Stockdale.

Wharton, F., ed. 1889. *The Revolutionary Diplomatic Correspondence of the United States.* 2 vols. Washington, D.C.: Govt. Printing Office.

Williams, Jonathan. 1799. "Barometrical Measurement of the Blue-Ridge, Warm Spring, and Alleghany Mountains, in Virginia, taken in the Summer of 1791," *Transactions of the American Philosophical Society*, vol. IV, pp. 216–23.

"Williamsburg—the Old Colonial Capitol," 1907. *William and Mary College Quarterly Historical Magazine*, vol. XVI, No. 1, July, pp. 10–34.

Willich, A. F. M., ed. 1803–4. *Domestic Encyclopedia, or, A Dictionary of Facts, and Useful Knowledge*. 5 vols. Philadelphia: Birch & Small.

Willard, John Ware. 1911, repr. 1962. *Simon Willard and His Clocks*. Mamaroneck, N.Y.: Paul P. Appel.

Wilson, Douglas L. 1985. "Thomas Jefferson's Early Notebooks," WMQ, Third series, vol. XLII, No. 4, October, pp. 433–52.

Wilson, M. L. 1942. "Survey of Scientific Agriculture," *Proceedings of the American Philosophical Society*, vol., 86, No. 1, September 25, pp. 52–62.

———. 1943. "Jefferson and His Mouldboard Plow," *The Land*, vol. III, No. 1, Summer, pp. 59–64.

———. 1943–44. "Thomas Jefferson—Farmer," *Proceedings of the American Philosophical Society*, vol. 87, pp. 216–20.

Wilstach, Paul. 1925. *Jefferson and Monticello*. Garden City, N.Y.: Doubleday and Co.

———. 1928. "Thomas Jefferson's Secret Home," *Country Life*, vol. 53, April, pp. 41–43.

Wing, DeWitt C. 1944. "Thomas Jefferson: Pioneer in Genetic Science," *Journal of Heredity*, vol. 35, June, pp. 173–74.

Wirt, William C. 1832, repr. 1903. *The Life of Patrick Henry*. New York: A. L. Burt and Company.

Wissler, Clark. 1919. "An Indian Peace Medal," *Natural History*, vol. XIX, No. 1, January, pp. 113–14.

Wistar, Caspar. 1799. "A Description of the bones deposited, by the president, in the Museum of the Society, and represented in the annexed plates. By C. Wistar, M.D., Adjunct Professor of Anatomy, &c. in the University of Pennsylvania," *Transactions of the American Philosophical Society*, vol. 4, No. 71, pp. 526–31, pls. X–XI.

Woodbury, Robert S. 1960. "The Legend of Eli Whitney and Interchangeable Parts," *Technology and Culture*, vol. I, No. 3, Summer, pp. 235–53.

Woods, Edgar. 1901. *History of Albemarle County, Virginia*. Charlottesville: The Michie Company.

Wright, Louis B. 1943. "Thomas Jefferson and the Classics," *Proceedings of the American Philosophical Society*, vol. 87, No. 3, July, pp. 223–33.

Wright, Louis B. and Macleod, Julia H. 1944. "Mellimelli, a Problem for President Jefferson in North African Diplomacy," *Virginia Quarterly Review*, vol. 20, pp. 555–65.

———. 1945. *The First Americans in North Africa: William Eaton's Struggle for a Vigorous Policy against the Barbary Pirates, 1799–1805*. Princeton: Princeton University Press.

Wright, John Kirkland. 1966. *Human Nature in Geography*. Cambridge: Harvard University Press.

Wyman, William I. 1918. "Legislative Beginnings of the Federal Patent System," *Journal of the Patent Office Society*, vol. I, No. 2, October, pp. 51–54.

———. 1918. "Thomas Jefferson and the Patent System," *Journal of the Patent Office Society*, vol. 1, No. 1, September, pp. 5–8.

[Wythe, George]. Haverford College, Manuscripts Division, *Quaker Collection*. Correspondence of George Wythe, 1755? (1785?).

[Wythe, George]. 1772. Colonial Williamsburg Foundation, Inc., Manuscripts Division. *Correspondence of George Wythe*.

EPIGRAM
SOURCES

Front Matter. Letter from Thomas Jefferson to Pierre Samuel Du Pont de Nemours, March 2, 1809, L&B, vol. XII, p. 260.

Chapter I. Letter from Thomas Jefferson to the Reverend Samuel Knox, December 18, 1818, DLC.

Chapter II. Letter from Thomas Jefferson to Peter Carr, August 19, 1785, Boyd, vol. 8, pp. 405–6.

Chapter III. Letter from Thomas Jefferson to Thomas Mann Randolph, Jr., May 30, 1790, Boyd, vol. 16, p. 449.

Chapter IV. Letter from Thomas Jefferson to Dr. Joseph Willard, March 24, 1789, Boyd, vol. 14, p. 699.

Chapter V. Letter from Thomas Jefferson to Dr. John P. Emmet, May 2, 1826, L&B, vol. XVI, p. 171.

Chapter VI. Letter from Thomas Jefferson to Charles Bellini, September 30, 1785, Boyd, vol. 8, pp. 568–69.

Chapter VII. Letter from Thomas Jefferson to Charles Bellini, September 30, 1785, Boyd, vol. 8, pp. 568–69.

Chapter VIII. Letter from Thomas Jefferson to an unidentified correspondent, September 28, 1821, L&B, vol. XV, p. 339.

Chapter IX. Letter from Thomas Jefferson to Elbridge Gerry, January 26, 1799, L&B, vol. X, p. 78.

Chapter X. Letter from Thomas Jefferson to David Williams, November 14, 1803, L&B, vol. X, p. 429.

Chapter XI. Letter from Thomas Jefferson to Elbridge Gerry, 1797, L&B, vol. IX, pp. 380—86.

Chapter XII. Letter from Thomas Jefferson to Robert Fulton, March 17, 1810, L&B, vol. XII, pp. 380—81.

Chapter XIII. Thomas Jefferson, *Notes On the State of Virginia* (1955), p. 65.

Chapter XIV. Letter from Thomas Jefferson to Andrew Ellicott, June 24, 1812, L&B, vol. XIX, p. 185.

Chapter XV. Letter from Thomas Jefferson to an unidentified correspondent, September 28, 1821, L&B, vol. XV, p. 339.

Chapter XVI. Letter from Thomas Jefferson to James Maury, April 25, 1812, L&B, vol. XIII, pp. 148–49.

Chapter XVII. Letter from Thomas Jefferson to Dr. John P. Emmet, May 2, 1826, L&B, vol. XVI, p. 171.

Chapter XVIII. Letter from Thomas Jefferson to Dr. Thomas Cooper, February 10, 1814, L&B, vol. XIV, p. 85.

NOTES

CHAPTER I. FRONTIER GENTRY

1. Rawlings, pp. 1–11; Hughes, pp. 1–27; Moore, pp. 5–30; Randall, vol. I, pp. 6–7.
2. Randall, vol. I, p. 6; Hughes, pp. 86–90, 147–48, 159–63; M. Kimball, *Road*, pp. 8–12.
3. *Tyler's*, vol. VII, pp. 264–65; Taylor, in *Collected Papers*, pp. 39–44; M. Kimball, *Road*, pp. 12–14.
4. Randall, vol. I, pp. 12–15; Malone, *Jefferson*, vol. I, pp. 11–13; M. Kimball, *Road*, p. 14.
5. *Tyler's*, vol. VII, pp. 121–22, 264–65; M. Kimball, *Road*, pp. 14–15; Malone, *Jefferson*, vol. I, pp. 12–13; Randall, vol. I, pp. 8–10.
6. Goochland County Courthouse, Marriage bond; Randall, vol. I, pp. 10—11; M. Kimball, *Road*, pp. 16–18; Malone, *Jefferson*, vol. I, pp. 17–18, 35–36, 309–10n.
7. Randall, vol. I pp. 10–11; M. Kimball, *Road*, p. 18.
8. F. Kimball, "Search," pp. 313–25; Long, pp. 1–7; Robbins, "Report," pp. 33–35.
9. Randall, vol. I pp. 13–15; Malone, *Jefferson*, vol. I, pp. 17–18.
10. Parker, pp. 59–73; Randall, vol. I, p. 6.
11. Elgan, pp. 13–19; Jackson (Whitney), pp. 1–31; pp. 14–29; Rawlings, pp. 11–14.
12. Randall, vol. I, pp. 11–12; M. Kimball, *Road*, pp. 26–30; Malone, *Jefferson*, vol. I, pp. 19–20.
13. SNR, p. 23; Randall, vol. I, p. 11; Malone, *Jefferson*, vol. I, p. 21.
14. Malone, *Jefferson*, vol. I, pp. 19–20; M. Kimball, *Road*, pp. 26–29; Anburey, vol. II, pp. 318–19; Waterman, pp. 85–92.
15. F. H. Smith, pp. 8–9.
16. Randall, vol. I, p. 18; Cripe, pp. 12–13; Stolba, pp. 197–202.
17. Harrison, "Northern Neck Maps," pp. 1–24; Malone, *Jefferson*, vol. I, pp. 21–27; Whitney, pp. 11–14; M. Kimball, *Road*, pp. 28–30.
18. [Lewis], *Fairfax Line*, pp. 29, 46, 54, 58.
19. "Documents Relating to . . . Northern Neck," pp. 297–99; Harrison, "Northern Neck Maps," pp. 10—11; [Lewis], pp. 41–42, 44, 88; *Calendar of Virginia State Papers*, vol. I, 1875, pp. 239–40; Harrison, "Northern Neck Maps," pp. 8–15; Whitney, pp. 11–12; *Journals of the House of Burgesses*, 1727–40, p. 379; *Virginia Gazette*, January 5, 1738; M. Kimball, *Road*, pp. 29–30; Randall, vol. I, pp. 11–12; Verner, "Fry and Jefferson Map," pp. 70—94; Sanchez-Saavedra, pp. 25–30; Phillips, "Virginia Cartography," p. 46; [Malone], *Fry & Jefferson Map*, pp. 7–12.
20. Harrison, "Northern Neck Maps," p. 10; Faden and Jeffreys, *Catalogue*.
21. Elgan, pp. 13–19; SNR, pp. 391–92; Malone, *Jefferson*, vol. I, pp. xvii, 33; Randall, vol. I p. 373; *Albemarle County Will Book*, No. 2, p. 41, Inventory of Peter Jefferson's Estate. filed August 17, 1757; "Books in Colonial Virginia," pp. 389–92; Schachner, p. 61.
22. Malone, *Jefferson*, vol. I, pp. 60—61; Schachner, p. 19; SNR, p. 23.
23. *Albemarle City Will Book No. 2*, pp. 41, 59; M. Kimball, *Road*, pp. 12–13.
24. Whitney, pp. 32–54; Slaughter, pp. 29–39.
25. *Journals of the House of Burgesses*, 1752–55, 1756–58, pp. vii, 211, 214, 235, 484; Malone, *Jefferson*, vol. I, pp. 26–27.
26. Meade, vol. I, pp. 457–59; Rawlings, p. 38; Malone, *Jefferson*, vol. I, pp. 39–40.
27. "Advertisement of W. S.," pp. 178–79.

28. Schachner, pp. 18–19; Randall, vol. I, pp. 17–18; Malone, *Jefferson*, vol. I, pp. 39–40.
29. Malone, *Jefferson*, vol. I, p. 46; *Edgehill Randolph Papers*, "Memoirs of T. J. Randolph," ViU, p. 31.
30. Letter to Peter Carr, August 19, 1785, Boyd, vol. 8, pp. 405–8.
31. "A Decalogue of Canons for Observation in Practical Life," accompanying letter to Thomas Jefferson Smith, February 21, 1825, Padover. *Complete Jefferson*, pp. 1038–39.
32. CSmH, Peter Jefferson's Account Book; F. Kimball, *Architect*, pp. 314–15.
33. *Ibid.*
34. F. Kimball, *Architect*, p. 314.
35. *Albemarle County Will Book No. 2*, pp. 32–34, 41–47, Last will and testament of Peter Jefferson filed August 17, 1757; Malone, *Jefferson*, vol. I, pp. 31–32.
36. *Ibid*; M. Kimball, *Road*, pp. 32–34.
37. Disbrow, pp. 5–18; M. Kimball, *Road*, pp. 24–25.
38. Bullock, "Dissertation," pp. 36–60; Rawlings, pp. 95–96.
39. Bullock, "Dissertation," pp. 39–60.
40. ViU, *Maury Deposit*, A. F. Maury, "Intimate Virginians," p. 12; letter to James Maury, April 25, 1812, L&B, vol. XIII, pp. 144–49.
41. Letter to James Maury, April 25, 1812, L&B, vol. XIII pp. 144–49.
42. Randolph, pp. 45–47; *Garden Book*, p. 44; Randall, vol. I, pp. 83–84; Malone, *Jefferson*, vol. I, pp. 160—61, 431.
43. Letter to John Harvie, January 14, 1760, Boyd, vol. I, p. 3.
44. SNR, p. 45.
45. Letter to John Harvie, January 14, 1760, Boyd, vol. I, p. 3.

CHAPTER II. TOWN AND GOWN

1. "Williamsburg," WMCQHM, vol. XVI, No. 1, July 1907, pp. 10—34; Jones, *Present State*, pp. 31–32, 45, 66, 213; Tyler, *Colonial Capitol*, pp. 134–38.
2. Burnaby, 2nd edition, p. 163; 3rd edition, 1798, pp. 215–51, Appendix 5, Fauquier weather diary; J. F. D. Smyth, *Tour*, vol. I, pp. 20—23; "Williamsburg," p. 38; H. B. Adams, *Phi Beta Kappa Address*, p. 29; H. B. Adams, *College*, Circular No. 1, pp. 20, 39–47; M. Kimball, *Road* pp. 39–47; "Williamsburg," p. 38; Schachner, pp. 30—34; DAB, vol. VII, pp. 137–38.
3. Malone, *Jefferson*, vol. I, pp. 56–58; letter to Dr. Vine Utley, March 21, 1819, Ford, vol. X, p. 126.
4. *Notes*, p. 153; Parton, "College Days," pp. 26–77.
5. F. H. Smith, *Schools*, pp. 6–7; Tyler, "Early Presidents," pp. 63–65.
6. "Education in Colonial Virginia," pp. 73–74; F. H. Smith, pp. 6–7; Parton, "College Days," pp. 27–28.
7. Parton, "College Days," p. 28; Chandler, pp. 304–7; Malone, "Jefferson Goes to School," pp. 482–96.
8. [Hawtrey], "Description," pp. 209–10.
9. "Statutes of William and Mary College," WMCHQ, Series I, vol. II, pp. 55 ff., vol. XVI, No. 3, pp. 164–68, 247, vol. 4, p. 44; M. Kimball, *Road*, pp. 42–43.
10. "Journals of the Meetings," WMCHQ, series 1, vol. 3, pp. 60—64, 128–32, 195–97, 262–65; M. Kimball, *Road*, pp. 41–42.
11. "Statutes," WMQ, series 1, vol. XVI, p. 247; Malone, *Jefferson*, vol. I, pp. 51–52.
12. M. Kimball, *Road*, pp. 41–42; R. Goodwin, pp. 194–95; Perry, vol. I (Virginia), p. 517; "Statutes," WMCQHM, Series 1, vol. III, p. 129.
13. Hawtrey, pp. 209–10.
14. SNR, pp. 45–47; M. Kimball, *Road*, pp. 42–47; Malone, *Jefferson*, vol. I, pp. 58–59; DAB, vol. IV, pp. 554–59, vol. VII, pp. 137–38.
15. Ganter, pp. 505–ll; Dos Passos, pp. 85–100; Schachner, p. 29.
16. Letter to L. H. Girardin, January 15, 1815, L&B, vol. XIV, pp. 231–32.
17. Ewing, pp. 3–13.
18. DAB, vol. V, p. 175.
19. Cajori, pp. 33–36.
20. Letter to Colonel William Duane, October 1, 1812, DLC; Randall, vol. I, p. 24n.; letter to Dr. Benjamin Rush, August 17, 1811, Ford, vol. IX, p. 328.

21. Perry, vol. I, pp. 470—72, 517-18; W. A. R. Goodwin, p. 44.
22. "Description of William and Mary College," (See Note 8); Schachner, pp. 29-30; Warner, *Road*, pp. 131-40.
23. Burk, vol. III, 333-34; letter to L. H. Girardin, January 15, 1815, L&B, vol. XIV, p. 232; Randall, vol. I, pp. 31-32.
24. W. D. Lewis, vol. I, pp. 51-90, DAB, vol. X, pp. 586-89.
25. [Harrison], "Portrait," pp. 343-351; DAB, vol. III, p. 301; Burk, vol. III, pp. 333-34.
26. Randall, vol. I, pp. 34-35; Malone, *Jefferson*, vol. I, p. 48.
27. Letter to Louis H. Girardin, January 15, 1819, L&B, vol. XIV, pp. 231-32; Schachner, pp. 37-39.
28. Letter to Henry Lee, May 8, 1825, L&B, vol. XVI, pp. 118-19.
29. *The George Wythe House*, pp. 3-15; McKnight, unpublished manuscript.
30. Colonial Williamsburg Foundation, Inc., Manuscripts Collection, Correspondence of Wythe with John Norton & Sons, September and December 1772; Haverford College Library, *Quaker Collection*, letter from Wythe relating to purchase of instruments from Nairne and Blunt, July 10, 1755 (1785?); Hemphill, "Colonial Briton," MS, unpaginated.
31. L. W. Tazewell, "Family," MS. unpaginated.
32. Wythe, last will and testament, February 21 and June 1, 1806, DLC, fols. 27971-72; letters from William DuVal, June 19 and July 12, 1806, DLC.
33. [Fauquier], "Extraordinary Storm," pp. 746-47.
34. Colonial Williamsburg Foundation, Inc., Manuscripts Collection. Letters from the executors of the estate of Francis Fauquier to Francis Fauquier, Jr., August 31, 1769, letter from Francis Fauquier, Jr. to Robert Carter III, May 31, 1770.
35. Bullock, "On Music;" Cripe, pp. 6-7; Stolba, pp. 197-202; Malone, *Jefferson*, vol. I, p. 79.
36. Coleman, unpaginated; letter to John Walker, September 3, 1769, Boyd, vol. I, p. 32.
37. Letter to W. Taylor, February 13, 1821, NHi; letter to Thomas McCauley, June 14, 1819, DLC.
38. [Page], pp. 150—51.
39. Letter to T. J. Randolph, November 24, 1808, L&B, vol. XII, pp. 196-202.
40. Letter to John Adams, June 11, 1812, L&B, vol. XIII, p. 160; DAB, vol. VII, pp. 111-12.
41. Letter to John Sanderson, August 31, 1820, DLC; "Notes Relating to Some of the Students Who Attended the College of William and Mary 1752-1770, WMQ, 2nd series, vol. I, No. 1, January 1921, pp. 27-41; Schachner, pp. 32-33.

CHAPTER III. LAW AND LEARNING

1. M. Kimball, *Road* p. 65.
2. Letter to John Page, December 25, 1762, Boyd, vol. I, pp. 3-6; Randall, vol. I, pp. 32-35; SNR, pp. 31-33; M. Kimball, *Road*, pp. 63-66.
3. SNR, pp. 33-34.
4. Letter to John Page, January 20, 1763, Boyd, vol. I, pp. 7-9.
5. Randall, vol. I, pp. 15-17; Malone, *Jefferson*, vol. I, pp. 37-38.
6. Letter to John Page, July 15, 1763, Boyd, vol. I, pp. 9-11.
7. Letter to William Fleming, c. October 1763, Boyd, vol. I, pp. 12-13; letters to John Page, December 25, 1762, January 10, July 15, and October 7, 1763, Boyd, vol. I, pp. 9-12; letter to William Fleming, March 20, 1764, Boyd, vol. I, pp. 15-17.
8. *Correspondence*, Bixby, pp. 19-22; M. Kimball, *Road*, p. 78.
9. Parton, "Student of Law," pp. 179-97; Randall, vol. I, pp. 30—35; M. Kimball, *Road*, pp. 83-88; Malone, *Jefferson*, vol. I, pp. 67, 74.
10. Letter to T. J. Randolph, November 24, 1808, Ford, vol. IX, p. 231; Meade, vol. I, pp. 106-8; Malone, Jefferson, vol. I, pp. 83-84.
11. Letter to Charles MacPherson, February 25, 1773, Boyd, vol. I, pp. 96-97; letter from Charles McPherson, August 12, 1773, Boyd, vol. I, pp. 101-2; letter to John Trumbull, February 15, 1789, Boyd, vol. 14, p. 561; letter to Benjamin Rush, January 16, 1811, Ford, vol. IX, p. 296; Wright, "Jefferson and Classics," pp. 223-33.
12. Letter to Louis H. Girardin, January 15, 1815, L&B, vol. XIV, p. 231; SNR, p. 31.
13. Eaton, pp. 520—22; Dumbauld, *Jefferson and the Law*, pp. 3-17; Parton, "Student," pp. 186-87.

14. Jefferson, "Essay Towards Facilitating Instruction." The original was written by Jefferson to a friend in 1798, L&B, vol. XVIII, pp. 365–411; L. K. Caldwell, pp. 193–213; Price, pp. 41–54; Shepherd, pp. 211–14.
15. Parton, "Student," pp. 188–89.
16. *Ibid.*
17. Parton, "Student," pp. 189–91.
18. Letter to Frank Willis, July 23, 1766, Boyd, vol. I, p. 21; letters to William Wirt, August 5, 1815 and September 4, 1816, Ford, vol. IX, pp. 339–45, 475–76n.; Tyler, *Letters*, vol. I, p. 55; *Virginia Gazette* daybooks (on deposit at ViU), entries for February 20, 1764 and April 3, 1765; Randall, vol. I, p. 40.
19. Randall, vol. I, pp. 20—21.
20. Letter to John Page, April 9, 1764, Boyd, vol. I, pp. 17–18; Malone, *Jefferson*, vol. I, pp. 115–16.
21. Jefferson, *Fee Book*, CSmH, account of estate; *Garden Book*, pp. 1–3; Malone, *Jefferson*, vol. I, pp. 114–15, Appendix B, pp. 439–40.
22. Dos Passos, pp. 96–99; Schofield, pp. 37–38; Boyd, vol. 1, p. 166n.
23. Schofield, pp. 67–73; Dos Passos, pp. 279–83.
24. "Papers Relating to the College," WMCQHM, vol. XVI, January 1908, pp. 162–73, "Dr. William Small's Accounts (1758–1767), Portion of Physical Apparatus Purchased by Dr. William Small in 1767;" Ewing, p. 5.
25. *Garden Book*, pp. vii–viii.
26. Schofield, pp. 33–38, 67–73; Ritchie-Calder, pp. 136–45.
27. Letter to Bernard Moore, c. 1765, Ford, vol. IX, p. 480; "Education for a Lawyer," Padover, *Complete Jefferson*, pp. 1043–47; Kimball, p. 79–84; Parton, "Student," pp. 185–87; Cohen, pp. 823–44; Elizabeth G. Brown, pp. 139–44.
28. Project for Making the Rivanna River Navigable (1771?), Boyd, vol. I, pp. 87–88; Woods, pp. 83–85; Malone, Jefferson, vol. I, pp. 115–16; Jefferson, "List of Services," Ford, vol. VII, pp. 475–77.
29. Randall, vol. I, pp. 40—41; SNR, pp. 38–39.
30. *Garden Book*, pp. vii, 1–3.
31. Letter to John Page, May 25, 1766, Boyd, vol. 1, pp. 18–20; Randall, vol. I, p. 46.
32. Letter from Dr. George Gilmer to Dr. John Morgan, May 11, 1766, Boyd, vol. 1, p. 18; Blanton, pp. 23, 34; F. Kimball, "Arts," p. 239; Malone, *Jefferson*, vol. 1, pp. 99–100.
33. Letter to John Page, May 25, 1766, Boyd, vol. 1, pp. 18–20; letter to Francis Willis, July 23, 1766, Boyd, vol. I, p. 21; *Garden Book*, pp. 1, 3; M. Kimball, *Road*, pp. 137–39; Malone, *Jefferson*, vol. 1, pp. 104–5.
34. Chinard, *Literary Bible*; Peden, "Book Collector"; Peden, "Some Notes," pp. 265–74; Malone, *Jefferson*, vol. 1, pp. 104–5.
35. Letter to Joseph Priestley, January 27, 1800, L&B, vol. X, pp. 146–47.
36. *Virginia Gazette* daybooks, February 4, 1764; letter to Herbert Croft, October 30, 1798 L&B, vol. XVIII, p. 363; Jefferson, "Essay Towards Facilitating Instruction," L&B, vol. XVIII, pp. 365–411 (See Note 14); M. Kimball, *Road*, pp. 106–7.
37. Jefferson, "Autobiography," Padover, *Complete Jefferson*, p. 1120.
38. Letter to Thomas Turpin, February 5, 1769, Boyd, vol. I, pp. 23–24.
39. Randall, vol. I, pp. 50—52; Edmund Randolph, "Essay," p. 123; Parton, "Virginia Lawyer," p. 320.
40. Malone, *Jefferson*, vol. I, pp. 66–69.
41. Letter to George Wythe, January 16, 1796, DLC; Bullock, "Papers," pp. 243–44; letters to Ebenezer Hazard, April 30, 1775 and February 18, 1791, Boyd, vol. I, p. 164, vol. 19, pp. 287–88; Bedini, *Copying Machines*, pp. 1–3; Parton, "Lawyer," pp. 320—21.
42. Hening, pp. vii–viii; Bullock, "Papers," p. 244.
43. Dewey, "Law Practice," pp. 289–301; C. P. Patterson, pp. 369–96; Parton, "Virginia Lawyer," pp. 319–21.
44. *Case Book* and *Fee Book*, CSmH; "Memoirs of Thomas Jefferson Randolph," ViU, *Edgehill Randolph Papers*, pp. 12–14; Randall, vol. I, pp. 47–51.
45. Randall, vol. I, p. 57–58; *Council Journals, Colonial Virginia*, ViU, October 27 and November 1, 1768; *Memorandum Book*, DLC, entries for March 22 and September 21, 1769.

46. *Memorandum Book*, DLC, May 15, 1768; *Garden Book*, p. 6, entry for August 3, 1767; pp. 12–18, 21; M. Kimball, Road, pp. 135, 149–62; F. Kimball, *Architect*, pp. 22–29; Pickens, pp. 260—66.

47. Letter to John Page, July 15, 1763, Boyd, vol. I, pp. 9–11.

48. Dodsley, *Description*; Shenstone, *Unconnected Thoughts*; James, *Gardening*; *Virginia Gazette* day-books, entries for August 6 and October 10, 1765; M. Kimball, *Road*, pp. 147–49, 160—65.

49. M. Kimball, *Road*, pp. 149–57; *Garden Book*, pp. 33–34; *Memorandum Book*, DLC, entry for July 23, 1772.

50. *Garden Book*, pp. 33–34.

51. *Garden Book*, p. 42.

52. *Virginia Gazette* (Purdie & Dixon), February 22, 1770.

53. Randall, vol. I, pp. 2–3; F. Kimball, "Search," pp. 313–25.

54. *Edgehill Randolph Papers*, "Memoirs of Thomas Jefferson Randolph," ViU, p. 2; SNR, p. 43; letter to John Page, February 21, 1770, Boyd, vol. I, pp. 34–36; letters from Thomas Nelson, Sr., Thomas Nelson, Jr., and John Page, March 6, 1770; letter from George Wythe, March 9, 1770, Boyd, vol. I, pp. 37–38.

55. *Memorandum Book*, DLC, entries for October 17, 1769 and c. June 1, 1770; Randall, vol. I, pp. 2–3; letter to Robert Walsh, April 5, 1823, ViU.

56. Letter to James Ogilvie, February 20, 1771, Boyd, vol. I, pp. 62–64; M. Kimball, *Road*, pp. 156–65; *Garden Book*, pp. 18, 322; letter to James Madison, July 26, 1806, DLC.

57. *Garden Book*, pp. 6, 13–28; SNR, pp. 43–45; Randall, vol. I, pp. 62–66.

58. Randall, vol. I, p. 64.

59. M. Kimball, *Road*, pp. 169–71; *Memorandum Book*, entries for October 6, 1770; letter to James Ogilvie, February 20, 1771, Boyd, vol. I, pp. 62–64.

60. Randall, vol. I, pp. 62–65; Lossing, *Field Book*, vol. II, p. 443; *Memorandum Book*, entries for December 1771 and January 1772; *Virginia Gazette*, January 2, 1772; SNR, pp. 43–44.

61. *Case Book No. 612*; Randall, vol. I, pp. 49, 64.

62. SNR, pp. 44–45. M. Kimball, *Road*, pp. 176–79.

63. *Garden Book*, pp. 33, 35; Randall, vol. 1, pp. 64–65; M. Kimball, *Road*, 176–79.

64. *Garden Book*, pp. 35–36; Malone, *Jefferson*, vol. I, p. 160.

65. Letter to T. M. Randolph, Jr., October 19, 1792, DLC; Malone, *Jefferson*, vol. I, p. 160.

CHAPTER IV. CLIMATE FOR GREATNESS

1. R. B. Davis, pp. 168, 178; Hindle, *Pursuit* pp. 213–15; *Virginia Gazette* (Purdie & Dixon), November 19, 1772 and June 16, 1774; "Plan of Virginia Society," November 20, 1772; Francis Hargreaves, CWF, Manuscript on the Society for the Advancement of Useful Knowledge, cited in WMQ, 1st series, vol. 4, 1896, p. 201; Randall, vol. I, pp. 83–84; SNR, pp. 45–47; letter to William Fleming, May 19, 1773, Boyd, vol. I, pp. 97–98.

2. *Garden Book*, pp. 40—42.

3. Malone, *Jefferson*, vol. 1, pp. 441–45, Appendix II; Randall, vol. I, pp. 65–66; M. Kimball, *Road*, pp. 178–81.

4. College of William and Mary, Archives, "Commission of Thomas Jefferson as Surveyor of Albemarle County," June 6, 1773, and blank commission to employ an assistant surveyor, *Faculty Minutes*, October 14, 1773, *Albemarle County Surveyor's Book*; Boyd, vol. I, pp. 99–100; Hughes, pp. 90—91, 97.

5. Hartwell et al, pp. 90—92; James Blair, "Memorial Concerning a Coledge in Virginia," December 11, 1691; Hughes, pp. 12, 23–27.

6. General Assembly, Act of February 1772, amendment to laws affecting "The Duty of Survey-ors," effective June 1, 1773, published in the *Virginia Gazette* (Purdie & Dixon), June 1, 1773, "To the Printer;" advertisement of Edmund Dickinson, *Virginia Gazette* (Purdie & Dixon), April 13, 1772; Bedini, "Marshall's Meridian Instrument," pp. 26, 26, 60.

7. Hughes, pp. 127–28; Bedini, "The Marshall Mystery," p. 60.

8. Garlick, pp. 40—47; Marraro, pp. 164–67, 190–93; *Garden Book*, pp. 56–59.

9. *Farm Book*, pp. vii–viii; *Garden Book*, pp. 47–48, 56–57; D. L. Wilson, pp. 433–52.

10. *Memorandum Book*, MHi, entries for February 21, February 22, March 1, March 6, March 7, 1774; Hopper and Bollinger, pp. 3–4; *Garden Book*, p. 57.

11. Malone, *Jefferson*, vol. I, pp. 165–66; *Memorandum Book*, MHi, March 1, March 7 and March 10, 1774.

12. *Memorandum Book*, MHi, entries for March 6 and 7, 1774.

13. SNR, pp. 57–58; Malone, *Jefferson*, vol.I, p. 165.

14. *Journals of the House of Burgesses, 1773–1776*, pp. ix–xi, 28, 41–43, 124, 138; letter to S. A. Wells, May 12, 1819, Ford, vol. X, p. 128; Jefferson, *Autobiography*, pp. 1122–23; Malone, *Jefferson*, vol. I, pp. 170—71.

15. Jefferson, *Autobiography*, p. 1124; Randall, vol. I, pp. 86–95; [Chinard], *Commonplace Book*, pp. 24–28, 41–44, 54; [Jefferson], *Summary View*, pp. 5–19; G. C. Smith, pp. 494–98.

16. *Memorandum Book*, MHi, entries for 1774; Jefferson, *Autobiography*, pp. 1121–24; Randall, vol. I, pp. 77–88; Schachner, p. 95; Hemphill, pp. 170—71; "Law Practice," p. 295; Dumbauld, *Law*, pp. 89, 158.

17. Malone, *Jefferson*, vol. I, p. 171; Schachner, p. 95.

18. *Journals of the House of Burgesses, 1773–1776*, p. 138; *Virginia Gazette* (Purdie & Dixon), June 2, 1774; Jefferson, *Autobiography*, pp. 1122–24; Randall, vol. I, p. 86; Ford, vol. I, p. 418; Malone, *Jefferson*, vol. I, pp. 171–73; "Continental Association," Boyd, vol. I, pp. 149–54; letters to Archibald Cary and Benjamin Harrison, December 9, 1774, Boyd, vol. 1, pp. 154–55.

19. *Virginia Gazette* (Purdie & Dixon), July 14 and August 4, 1774; Malone, *Jefferson*, vol. I, p. 180.

20. *Summary View*, Boyd, vol. 1, pp. 121–37; Padover, pp. 5–19; Randall, vol. I, pp. 86–98; Malone, *Jefferson*, vol. I, 181–90.

21. Wirt, *Henry*, vol. I, p. 260; E. Randolph, "Essay," p. 223; Ford, vol. I, pp. 451–52; "Draft of Resolution," Boyd, vol. I, pp. 159–60.

22. "Virginia's Resolutions on Lord North's Conciliatory Proposal, June 10, 1775," Boyd, vol. I, pp. 170—74; *Gilmer Papers*, pp. 75–85; Jefferson, *Autobiography*, p. 1125; letter to François Soules, September 13, 1786, Boyd, vol. 10, p. 363; Burk, pp. 2–3, 14.

23. Randall, vol. I, pp. 111–12; Malone, vol. I, p. 202.

24. Randall, vol. I, p. 112–13; *Memorandum Book*, CSmH, entries for June 20, 1775, July 9 and July 29, 1775; Ford and J. C. Fitzpatrick, *Journals*, vol. II, p. 101; letter from John Adams to Abigail Adams, June 23, 1775, Burnett, *Letters*, vol. I, pp. 139, 142.

25. Jefferson, *Autobiography*, pp. 1125–27; Burnett, *Journals*, vol. II, pp. 106–8, 128–39.

26. Jefferson, *Autobiography*, p. 1127; "Jefferson's Draft Resolutions, July 25, 1775," Boyd, vol. I, pp. 225–29.

27. Force, vol. 4, series III, pp. 365–97; *Memorandum Book*, CSmH, entry for August 17, 1775; letter to John Randolph, August 25, 1775, Boyd, vol. I, pp. 240—43; letter from John Randolph, August 31, 1775, Boyd, vol. I, p. 244.

28. Randall, vol. I, p. 133; Commission as Lieutenant of Albemarle, September 26, 1775, Boyd, vol. I, p. 246.

29. Letter to Thomas Nelson, May 16, 1776, Boyd, vol. I, pp. 292–93; *Memorandum Book*, CSmH, entry for October 22, 1775; letter to Joseph Delaplaine, July 26, 1816, Ford, vol. X, p. 55.

30. Letter to John Randolph, August 25, 1775, Boyd, vol. 1, pp. 240—43.

31. Letter to John Page, October 31, 1775, Boyd, vol. I, pp. 250—51; letter to Francis Eppes, November 7, 1775, Boyd, vol. I, p. 252.

32. Randall, vol. III, pp. 568–70; Randall, vol. I, p. 134; *Memorandum Book*, CSmH, entry for March 31, 1776; letter to William Randolph, c. June 1776, Boyd, vol. I, pp. 408–10; SNR, pp. 49–50.

33. *Farm Book*, p. 92; "Report of a Committee to Prepare a Plan for a Militia, March 25, 1775," Boyd, vol. 1, pp. 160—62.

34. Letter to Thomas Nelson, May 16, 1776, Boyd, vol. 1, pp. 292–93.

35. Randall, vol. I, p. 177; Scharf and Westcott, vol. I, p. 320; *Memorandum Book*, CSmH, entries for May 24, May 31, June 1, 1776; Bedini, *Desk*, p. 5.

36. "The Virginia Constitution," Boyd, vol. I, pp. 329–65; "The Constitution as Adopted by the Convention, June 29, 1776," Boyd, vol. I, pp. 377–86.

37. *Journals of the Continental Congress*, vol. V, p. 429; Randall, vol.I, pp. 164–68; Hazelton, pp. 141–46; Bedini, *Desk*, pp. 5–10.

38. *Memorandum Book*, CSmH, September 1, 1776; Bedini, *Desk*, p. 6; M. W. Brown, pp. 455–62.

39. Bedini, *Desk*, pp. 6–7; Granquist, "Chairs," pp. 1056–60; F. Kimball, "Chairs," pp. 58–60; letter from John Kintzing Kane to the president of the American Philosophical Society, April 20, 1838, PPAmP.

40. Letter to Henry Lee, May 8, 1825, Ford, vol. X, pp. 343; "The Declaration of Independence," Boyd, vol. I, pp. 413–28.

41. Letter to John Vaughan, September 16, 1825, Ford, vol. X, pp. 345–46; letter to Ellen Wayles Randolph Coolidge, November 14, 1825, MHi; Randall, vol. I, pp. 177–78.

42. Letter to Richard Henry Lee, July 8, 1776, Boyd, vol. 1, pp. 455–56; Boyd, *Declaration* (1945), pp. 9–12; Boyd, "Declaration . . . Mystery," pp. 438–67.

43. *Memorandum Book*, CSmH, entry for July 4, 1776; Boyd, "Declaration," vol. 1, pp. 413–17; Bedini, *Desk*, p. 10.

44. *Memorandum Book*, CSmH, entry for July 4, 1776; Randall, vol. I, p. 179; Bedini, *Desk*, p. 15.

45. Warren, pp. 237–72; "The Truth About the Signing," p. 2; Bedini, *Desk*, pp. 10—15.

46. Boyd, *Declaration*, pp. 9–12; Boyd, "Declaration . . . Mystery," pp. 438–67.

47. Bedini, "Awfull Stage," pp. 169–73; Armstrong, pp. xlv–xlvi, "Logan and Penn Correspondencel;" p. 86; Duane, ed., p. 83.

48. R. J. Taylor et al, vol. 4, pp. 372–73.

49. Randall, vol. I, p. 179; Malone, *Jefferson*, vol. 1, p. 229.

50. Randall, vol. I, pp. 197–232; Boyd, vol. I, pp. 525–64; Jefferson, *Autobiography*, pp. 1139–50; Malone, *Jefferson*, vol. 1, p. 251.

51. *Weather Memorandum Book*, DLC, entry for September 15, 1776; [Nettleton], "Observations," pp. 308–12. The U. S. Geodetic Survey shows the base of Monticello to be 300 feet and a height of 867 feet.

52. "Petition," Boyd, vol. 2, pp. 14–15, 208; Gaines, "Unpublished Jefferson Map," pp. 23–28; Swem, "Maps," vol. VII, 1914, Map 254.

53. M. Kimball, *War and Peace*, pp. 24–27; Mazzei, *Memoirs*, pp. 185–86, 199; letter from Giovanni Fabbroni, September 15, 1776 Boyd, vol. 1, pp. 519–20.

54. Letter to Giovanni Fabbroni, June 8, 1778, Boyd, vol. 2, pp. 195–97.

55. Letter from Rev. James Madison, July 26, 1778, Boyd, vol. I, pp. 205–6; letter from John Page, August 19, 1778, Boyd, vol. 2, p. 210; letter to David Rittenhouse, July 19, 1778, Boyd, vol. I, pp. 202–3; McAdie, pp. 336–37.

56. *Notes*, p. 73.

57. *Notes*, pp. 80—81.

58. *Memorandum Book*, CSmH, entry for January 1778; *Garden Book*, pp. 80, 84–85.

59. HSP, *Jacobs Papers*, Rittenhouse, "Little Paper," February 1771; Rittenhouse, "Description," March 1767, pp. 1–3; Babb, pp. 193–224; Rice, Orrery, pp. 28–41; Hindle, pp. 27–30, 72–75.

60. Letter to Rittenhouse, July 19, 1778, Boyd, vol. 1, pp. 202–3.

61. Pickens, pp. 269–71; F. Kimball, Architect, pp. 1293–35, drawings K 38 and K 39; Farm Book, pp. 32, 127.

62. Randall, vol. I, pp. 232–37; letter to Patrick Henry, March 27, 1779, Boyd, vol. 2, pp. 237–44; Mazzei, *Memoirs*, pp. 224–26; Stone, *Memoirs . . . of Major General Riedesel*, vol. II, p. 65; Stone, *Letters of Mrs. General Riedesel*, p. 154–57.

63. Letter to Richard Henry Lee, April 21, 1779, Boyd, vol. 2, p. 255; letter from Richard Henry Lee, May 22, 1779, Boyd, vol. 2, pp. 270–71; letter from General Riedesel, June 13, 1780, Boyd, vol. 3, p. 440; letter from General Geismar, February 26, 1780, Boyd, vol. 3, pp. 304–5; letter from John Lewis de Unger, November 13, 1780, Boyd, vol. 4, p. 117; letter to Unger, November 30, 1780, Boyd, vol. 4, p. 171.

64. Randall, vol. I, pp. 238–60; Malone, *Jefferson*, vol. 1, pp. 314–29.

65. Letter from Jacob Rubsamen, January 1, 1780, with enclosure from a Hamburg newspaper, Boyd, vol. 4, p. 174.

66. Varro, *De res rusticus*; Castell, *Villas*; Lehmann, "Dom," pp. 19–20; F. Kimball, *Architect*, figs. 38–39; Lehmann, *Humanist*, pp. 184, 187, 254.

67. Chandler, pp. 304–7; letters from Samuel Stanhope Smith, March ?, 1779 and April 19, 1779, Boyd, vol. 2, pp. 246–49, 252–55; "A Bill for the More General Diffusion of Knowledge," Boyd, vol. 2, pp. 526–35; Jefferson, *Autobiography*, pp. 1055–57, 1148–49.

68. "A Bill for Amending the Constitution of the College of William and Mary . . .," Boyd, vol. 2, pp. 535–43; *Autobiography*, pp. 1148–49; Randall, vol. I, pp. 223–26.
69. Chinard, "Jefferson and the American Philosophical Society," pp. 264–65; H. Phillips, entry for January 21, 1780.
70. Letter from John Page, December 9, 1780, Boyd, vol. 4, pp. 191–93.
71. Letter from Joseph Reed, January 8, 1780, Boyd, vol. 3, pp. 262–3n; letter to Joseph Reed, July 17, 1780, Boyd, vol. 1, p. 459; letter to Joseph Reed, April 17, 1781, Boyd, vol. 5, p. 478.
72. Letter from Joseph Reed, February 26, 1781, Boyd, vol. 5, p. 13; *Virginia Council Journal*, vol. II, p. 324; letter to James Madison and Robert Andrews, March 31, 1781, Boyd, vol. 5, pp. 303–4; letter from Joseph Reed, May 14, 1781, Boyd, vol. 5, p 650; letter from Robert Andrews, April 4, 1781, Boyd, vol. 5, p. 339.
73. Letter to Timothy Matlack, April 18, 1781, Boyd, vol. 5, p. 490.
74. "Notes and Documents Relating to the British Invasion . . .," Boyd, vol. 4, pp. 256–78; Randall, vol. I, pp. 321–35;
75. *Delegates's Journal*, June 4, 1781; Randall, vol. I, pp. 335–39.
76. "Depositions," Boyd, vol. 4, pp. 271–77, 278n; Tarleton, pp. 302–5; Dabney, "Jouett," pp. 690—98; Randall, vol. I, pp. 335–39.
77. Letter to Dr. William Gordon, July 16, 1788, Boyd, vol. 13, pp. 362–65; Deposition of Christopher Hudson, July 26, 1805, Boyd, vol. 4, pp. 277–78; Randall, vol. I, p. 341–42.
78. Letter to George Nicholas, July 28, 1781, Boyd, vol. 6, pp. 104–5; letter from George Nicholas, July 31, 1781, Boyd, vol. 6, pp. 105–6; charges Advanced by Nicholas with Jefferson's Responses, Boyd, vol. 6, pp. 106–11; *Journal of the House of Delegates*, June 12, 1781; E. Randolph, "Essay," pp. 320—21.
79. Letter to Thomas Turner, in Richmond Enquirer, August 25, 1805.
80. Letter from the President of Congress, June 15, 1781, Boyd, vol. 6, pp. 94–95; letter to Lafayette, August 4, 1781, Boyd, vol. 6, pp. 111–12; letter from John Harvie, enclosing Resolution of the House, November 27, 1781, Boyd, vol. 6, pp. 133–34; *Journal of the House of Delegates*, November 26 and December 12, 1781; "Resolution of Thanks," Boyd, vol. 6, pp. 135–37.

CHAPTER V. "MEASURE OF A SHADOW"

1. "Marbois's Queries," Boyd, vol. 4, pp. 166–67.
2. Boyd, vol. 4, p. 167n.
3. Letter from Marbois, February 5, 1781 (now missing); letter to Marbois March 4, 1781, Boyd, vol. 5, p. 58–59n; letter to Chevalier Charles F. D'Anmours, November 30, 1780, Boyd, vol. 4, pp. 167–68; letter to Monroe May 20, 1782, Boyd, vol. 6, p. 186.
4. *Memorandum Book*, DLC, April 15, 1781; letter to David Jamieson, April 16, 1781, Boyd, vol. 5, pp. 468–69n; Malone, *Jefferson*, vol. 1, p. 434.
5. *Notes*, p. v; Randall, vol. I, pp. 363–64; Malone, *Jefferson*, vol. I, pp. 373–74; M. Kimball, *War and Peace*, pp. 262–63.
6. *Autobiography*, pp. 1158–59.
7. Peden, "Some Notes," pp. 265–74; *Virginia Gazette* daybooks (deposited in ViU), entries for 1764.
8. Bullock, "Papers," pp. 243–44; letter to Ebenezer Hazard, February 18, 1791, Boyd, vol. 19, pp. 287–88.
9. *Autobiography*, pp. 1158–59; MHi, Manuscript memoranda for Notes.
10. Letter from Archibald Cary, October 12, 1783, Boyd, vol. 6, pp. 342–44; letter to Dr. Thomas Walker, September 25, 1783, Boyd, vol. 6, pp. 339–40.
11. Letter to Thomas Walker, September 25, 1783, Boyd, vol. 6, pp. 339–40; letter from James Madison, July 3, 1784, Boyd, vol. 7, p. 362; letter to George Rogers Clark, November 26, 1782, Boyd, vol. 6, pp. 204–5; M. Kimball, *War and Peace*, pp. 270–73; letter from Archibald Cary, October 12, 1783, Boyd, vol. 6, pp. 342–44; letter from General John Sullivan, March 12, 1784, Boyd, vol. 7, pp. 21–24; letter from General William Whipple, March 14, 1784, Boyd, vol. 7, pp. 28–30; letter from Thomas Hutchins, February 11, 1784, Boyd, vol. 6, pp. 535–37.
12. Letter to Charles Thomson, December 20, 1781, Boyd, vol.6, pp. 142–43.
13. Letter from Charles Thomson, March 9, 1782, Boyd, vol. 6, pp. 163–64.

14. *Autobiography*, p. 1159; letter to Charles Thomson, May 21, 1784, Boyd, vol. 7, pp. 281–82.
15. Chinard, *Apostle*, p. 118; Fay, *Revolutionary Spirit*, p. 202.
16. DSB, vol. ll, pp. 576–82; *Notes*, pp. 55, 272.
17. *Notes*, pp. 53–58.
18. *Notes*, pp. 50–52, 66–70, 49.
19. *Notes*, p. 43.
20. Letter to George Rogers Clark, November 26, 1782, Boyd, vol. 6, pp. 204–5.
21. Ball, pp. xi–xii, 1–77; Simpson, "Beginnings," pp. 133–34; Diaz del Castillo, p. 143; [Mather], "Extract," pp. 61–71; *Bossu's Travels*, p. 104; Jodoin and Vincent, Simpson, pp. 135–39; Catesby, vol. II, Appendix, p. vii; Darlington, pp. 57–58; Jillson, pp. 27–28; Simpson, pp. 134, 139; Guettard, "Memoires," pp. 189–220, 323–60; Simpson, p. 144; Daubenton, "Mémoire su des os," pp. 206–29; Simpson, pp. 144–45.
22. Filson, *Discovery*; Jillson, pp. 32–34; Featherstonhaugh, pp. 257–72; Kindle, pp. 195–212; Jillson, pp. 27–30; Bigelow, vol. IV, pp. 303–4; Simpson, pp. 141–44; Hunter, pp. 34–45; Simpson, pp. 148–50; PPAmP, Peale Papers, C. W. Peale, *Autobiography*, p. 107; Bell, "Box of Old Bones," pp. 171–72; Sellers, *Museum*, pp. 10–11.
23. Collinson, "Account," pp. 464–69; Collinson, "Sequel," pp. 468–69; Simpson, p. 148.
24. *Notes*, pp. 44–45.
25. Hunter, *op. cit.*; Collinson, *op. cit.*
26. Notes, pp. 43–47.
27. *Notes*, pp. 53–54.
28. *Notes*, p. 45.
29. *Notes*, pp. 48–49.
30. Letter to George Rogers Clark, December 19, 1781, Boyd, vol. 6, p. 139.
31. Letter from George Rogers Clark, February 20, 1782, Boyd, vol. 6, pp. 159–60.
32. *Notes*, pp. 38–43; letter to James Madison, July 11, 1788, Boyd, vol. 13, p. 379.
33. *Notes*, p. 199.
34. *Notes*, p. 48.
35. *Notes*, pp. 73–81.
36. *Notes*, pp. 198–99.
37. *Notes*, p. 26; G. F. Becker, p. 256.
38. *Notes*, p. 47.
39. *Notes*, pp. 31, 265–66.
40. *Notes*, pp. 32–33.
41. *Notes*, pp. 97–100, 281.
42. *Notes*, pp. 98–100; C. C. Jones, pp. 193–94; Lehmann-Hartleben, pp. 161–63; Steibing, pp. 52–53; Ceram, *First American*, pp. 8–9; Ceram, "Jefferson's 'Dig'," pp. 38–41.
43. Holland, pp. 29–32; Bushnell, "Five Monocan Towns," pp. 17–25; Bushnell, "Evidence of Indian Occupancy," pp. 1–40; Fraser, pp. 3–4, 15; Geer, pp. 224–28.
44. *Notes*, pp. 58–60. Buffon based his conclusions about the North American Indian from the work by the Spanish naval officer Antonio de Ulloa, *Notiçias Americanas*, describing the Indians of South America.
45. *Notes*, pp. 59–60.
46. *Notes*, Appendix No. I, pp. 199–202.
47. *Notes*, pp. 174–75.
48. Letter to Marbois, December 20, 1781, Boyd, vol. 6, pp. 140–42; letter from Marbois January 29, 1782, Boyd, vol. 6. pp. 149–50; letter from Jacquelin Ambler, March 16, 1782, Boyd, vol. 6, p. 165.
49. *Notes*, pp. 24–25, 263–64; Chastellux, vol. II, p. 55.
50. Chastellux, vol. II, pp. 40–46; Randall, vol. I, pp. 373–74.
51. Randall, vol. I, pp. 362–63, 380–83; SNR, pp. 62–63; Pierson, pp. 106–7.
52. Letter to James Monroe, May 20, 1782, Boyd, vol. 6, pp. 184–86; letter to the Speaker of the House of Delegates, May 6, 1782, Boyd, vol. 6, p. 179; letter from John Tyler, May 16, 1782 Boyd, vol. 6, pp. 183–84.
53. SNR, pp. 62–63; Randall, vol. I, pp. 380–83.
54. *Memorandum Book*, DLC, entry for September 6, 1782; Randall, vol. I, p. 382; SNR, pp. 62–63.
55. Tucker, vol. I, p. 158; Randall I p. 382.

56. SNR, p. 64; Randall, vol. I, p. 383.
57. Letter to Elizabeth Wayles Eppes, October 3, 1782, Boyd, vol. 6, pp. 198–99.
58. SNR, p. 67; Randall, vol. I, p. 384.
59. Randall, vol. I, pp. 384–85; Burnett, *Letters*, vol. VI, p. 539; letter from James Madison to Edmund Randolph, November 12, 1782; letter from Robert R. Livingston enclosing Jefferson's appointment as a Peace Commissioner, November 13, 1782, Boyd, vol. 6, p. 202; letter to Chastellux, November 26, 1782, Boyd, vol. 6, pp. 203–4. 60. *Autobiography*, p. 1151; Randall, vol. I, pp. 386–88; letter to Robert R. Livingston, November 26, 1782, Boyd, vol. 6, p. 206; letter to James Madison, November 26, 1782, Boyd, vol. 6, pp. 206–7.
61. Letter from Arthur Campbell, November 11, 1782, Boyd, vol. 6, pp. 201, 208–9.
62. Letters to George Rogers Clark, November 26, 1782 and January 6, 1783, Boyd, vol. 6, pp. 204–5, 218–19.
63. Honorary Degree, Boyd, vol. 6, pp. 221–22.
64. *Notes*, pp. 64–65, 276–77.
65. *Notes*, pp. 64–65.
66. Letter to Francis Hopkinson, December 23, 1783 (Not found); Boyd, vol. 6, p.418; [Henry Phillips], *Early Proceedings*, pp. 115–16.
67. Letter from the Reverend James Madison, January 22, 1784, Boyd, vol. 6, pp. 507–8; letter from Anne Cèsar, Comte de La Luzerne to the Reverend William White, September 1783, PPAmP; Hindle, *Rittenhouse*, pp. 244–45; Rice, *Orrery*, pp. 48–51; Wharton, vol. 2, p. 214; King, *Geared*, pp. 270–76.
68. Letter from La Luzerne to Vergennes, December 25, 1783, Archives Affaires Etrangères, *Correspondence Political, États-Unis*, vol. XXVI, pp. 252–53.
69. PPAmP, *Minutes*, entries for January 18, March 6, September 26, 1783.
70. Rice, *Orrery*, pp. 51–52; Hindle, *Pursuit*, p. 227; Chastellux, p. 112.
71. William Barton, pp. 218–20, 230–31; King, *Geared*, pp. 271–72.
72. MHi, [Jefferson], "Catalogue of books," 1783; R. G. Adams, pp. 72–83; Peden, "Book Collector," Chapter 8; Peden, "Some Notes," pp. 265–72; W. D. Johnston, vol. I, pp. 143–45, letter to George Watterson, May 7, 1815; letter to Augustus B. Woodward, March 21, 1824, L&B, vol. XVI, pp. 17–20.
73. *Memorandum Book*, MHi, entry for November 4, 1783; letter to Francis Eppes, November 10, 1783, Boyd, vol. 6, pp. 349–50; letter to Benjamin Harrison, November 11, 1783, Boyd, vol. 6, pp. 351–53.
74. Letter to Martha Jefferson, November 28, 1783, Boyd, vol. 6, pp. 359–60; Hastings, pp. 331–35; letter to Martha Jefferson, January 15, 1784, Boyd, vol. 6, pp. 465–66.
75. Letter to Robert Morris, August 15, 1783, Boyd, vol. 15, pp. 608–9; [Jefferson], "Summary Journal of Letters Sent," entry for December 5, 1783, Boyd, vol. 6, p. 373.
76. Letter from Robert Morris to Benjamin Franklin, September 17, 1783, PPAmP, *Franklin Papers*; Boyd, vol. 15, pp. 608–9; Herries & Co. to W. T. Franklin, April 13, 1784; W. T. Franklin to Benjamin Franklin, October 13, 1784, *Franklin Papers*, PPAmP; Bedini, *Copying Machines*, pp. 13–18; letter to Robert Morris, July 3, 1784, Boyd, vol. 7, p. 362.
77. Report of committee on arrangements, December 22, 1783, Boyd, vol. 6, p. 409; Washington's address, December 23, 1783, Boyd, vol. 6, pp. 411–12; letter to Benjamin Harrison, December 24, 1783, Boyd, vol. 6, p. 419.
78. Letter to Francis Hopkinson, December 23, 1783 (not found), Boyd, vol. 6, pp. 418–19; letter from Francis Hopkinson, January 4, 1783, Boyd, vol. 6, pp. 443–45.
79. Letter to Thomas Walker, September 23, 1783, Boyd, vol. 6, pp. 339–40; letter from Archibald Cary, October 12, 1783, Boyd, vol. 6, pp. 342–44.
80. Letter to George Rogers Clark, December 4, 1783, Boyd, vol. 6, p. 371.
81. Bedini, *Thinkers*, pp. 299–304.
82. Letter to Isaac Zane, November 8, 1783, Boyd, vol. 6, pp. 347–49.
83. Letter from the Reverend James Madison, January 22, 1784, Boyd, vol. 6, pp. 507–8.
84. Letter to the Reverend James Madison, April 28, 1784, Boyd, vol. 7, pp. 133–34.
85. Letter to James Madison, March 16, 1784, Boyd, vol. 7, pp. 30–32; letter from James Madison April 25, 1784, Boyd, vol. 7, p. 122.
86. Letter from Reverend James Madison, April 27, 1785, Boyd, vol. 8, p. 115.
87. Letter to Francis Eppes, March 2, 1784 (not found), Boyd, vol. 7, p. 3; letters to Martha Jefferson, April 4 and April 17, Boyd, vol. 7, pp. 62, 110; Rickman, *An Authentic Voyage*; Ledyard, *Journal*.

88. Letter to James Madison, January 1,1784, Boyd, vol. 6, pp. 436–38; letter to Francis Hopkinson, February 18, 1784, Boyd, vol. 6, pp. 541–52, 107.
89. Plan for Government of the Western Territory, February 3, April 23, 1784, Boyd, vol. 6, pp. 581–617.
90. *Jefferson-Hartley Map*, Boyd, vol. 6, pp. 592–95; "A Map of the United States of N. America" in *Bailey's Pocket Almanac*.
91. Berkhofer, pp. 231–32.
92. Letters to James Madison, December 16, 1786 and June 20, 1787, Boyd, vol. 10, pp. 481, 603.
93. Letter to Francis Hopkinson, February 18, 1784, Boyd, vol. 6, pp. 541–42.
94. *Ibid*; Crouch, pp. 44–45.
95. Letter from Francis Hopkinson, March 31, 1784, Boyd, vol. 7, p. 57.
96. Letters to James McClurg, March 17 and April 24, 1784 (not found), Boyd, vol. 7, pp. 40, 115; letter from the Reverend James Madison, April 28, 1784, Boyd, vol. 7, pp. 133–34.
97. Letter to Philip Turpin, April 28, 1784, Boyd, vol. 7, pp. 134–37.
98. Letters to James Monroe, January 14, 1784, Boyd. vol. 7, pp. 607–8; letter of May 21, 1784, Boyd, vol. 7, pp. 279–81.
99. Letter to Charles Thomson, May 21, 1784, Boyd, vol. 7, pp. 281–82.
100. *Memorandum Book*, MHi, entries for July 5–August 6, 1784; letter to ——— Cabot, July 24, 1784 (not found), Boyd, vol. 7, p. 383; SNR, p. 73; Randall, vol. I, pp. 411–12.

CHAPTER VI. THE VAUNTED SCENE

1. *Memorandum Book*, MHi, entry for August 26, 1784; [Abigail Adams Smith], *Letters*, pp. 14, 16, 20–27; Rice, *Paris*, pp. 13–14, 51–54.
2. *Memorandum Book*, MHi, entry for August 26, 1784; Rice, *Paris*, pp. 64–68.
3. Carriere, "New French Method," pp. 398–99; letter to Eliza House Trist, August 18, 1785, Boyd, vol. 8, pp. 403–5; letter to James Currie, September 27, 1785, Boyd, vol. 8, pp. 558–60.
4. *Memorandum Book*, MHi, entries for September 5 and October 12, 1787; Randall, vol. I, p. 437; Rice, *Paris*, pp. 105–7; Rice, "Les Visites," pp. 46–49.
5. Randall, vol. I, p. 413; *Diplomatic Correspondence*, vol. I, pp. 534–40; letter from Benjamin Franklin to Charles Thomson, October 16, 1784, Bigelow, *Works*, vol. IX pp. 65–66.
6. Letter to James Monroe, June 17, 1785, Boyd, vol. 8, p. 233.
7. Letter to Charles Bellini, September 30, 1785, Boyd, vol. 8, pp. 568–70.
8. Letter from William Temple Franklin to Benjamin Franklin, October 13, 1784, Letter from Joseph Moore to W. T. Franklin, December 24, 1784, Philippe-Denis Pierres to Benjamin Franklin, February 21, 1785, Edward Bancroft to W. T. Franklin, February 24, 1785, PPAmP, *Franklin Papers*; letters from Jefferson to Jean Holker, December 15 and 29, 1784, March 24 and May 20, 1785, Boyd, vol. 7, pp. 575, 586, vol. 8, pp. 55, 93, 159; letters from Jean Holker, December 30, 1784, March 12 and April 25, 1785, vol. 7, pp. 579, 587, vol. 8, pp. 22–24, 67, 103, 162–63, 304–5.
9. Letter to Jean-Baptiste Henri Barre, June 3, 1785, Boyd, vol. 8, pp. 176–77, earliest extant letter Jefferson copied with copying press; Bedini, *Copying Machines*, p. 17.
10. Letter to James Madison, September 1, 1785, Boyd, vol. 8, pp. 460–64; letter from James Madison, March 18, 1786, Boyd, vol. 9, pp. 333–36.
11. Letter to the Reverend James Madison, October 2, 1785, Boyd, vol. 8, pp. 574–77.
12. Parker and Cutler, vol. I, p. 269, entry for July 13, 1787; Fitzpatrick, *Writings*, vol. I, p. xlviii, vol. 24, pp. 149, 356, vol. 35, p. 492, vol. 36, pp. 19–20, 57; Reese, p. 285; Fitzpatrick, *Diaries*, vol. 3, p. 76.
13. Letter from Dr. James Currie, November 20, 1784, Boyd, vol. 7, pp. 538–39; SNR, pp. 101–02.
14. Letters to Dr. James Currie and Francis Eppes, February 5, 1785, Boyd, vol. 7, p. 635–36; Randall, vol. I, p. 415; J. Q. Adams, vol. I, pp. 15–19; Abigail A. Smith, *Letters*, pp. 65–68.
15. Letters to Francis Eppes, May 11 and August 30, 1785, Boyd, vol. 8, pp. 141–42, 451.
16. Letter to Elizabeth Eppes, September 22, 1785, Boyd, vol. 8, pp. 539–40.
17. Letter to Mary Jefferson, September 20, 1785, Boyd, vol. 8, pp. 532–33.
18. Letter from John Jay, March 15, 1785, Boyd, vol. 8, p. 33.

19. Letter from John Jay, March 22, 1785, Jefferson's attestations, March 22, 1785, Boyd, vol. 8, pp. 54–55; *Memorandum Book*, MHi, entry for May 17, 1785; letter to John Jay, June 17, 1785, Boyd, vol. 8, pp. 226–27; Randall, vol. I, p. 415.

20. Letter to John Fitzgerald, February 27, 1781, Boyd, vol. 5, p. 15; letter from John Fitzgerald, April 1, 1781, Boyd, vol. 5, pp. 311–12; Report of a Committee to Prepare a List of Books for Congress, January 24, 1783, Boyd, vol. 6, p. 216; letter to David S. Franks, March/April 1783, Boyd, vol. 6, p. 258; letter from the Reverend James Madison, April 10, 1785, Boyd, vol. 8, pp. 73–75; Watts, pp. 318–25.

21. Letter to Charles Thomson, May 21, 1784, Boyd, vol. 7, p. 282; letter to James Monroe, December 10, 1784, Boyd, vol. 7, p. 563; letter to Philippe-Denis Pierres, January 12, 1787, Boyd, vol. 11, pp. 38–39; letter from Philippe-Denis Pierres, January 15, 1787, Boyd, vol. 11, p. 45; Lerch, pp. 45–46.

22. Letter to James Madison, May 11, 1785, Boyd, vol. 8, pp. 147–48; letter to James Monroe, June 17, 1785, Boyd, vol. 8, p. 229.

23. Letter to James Madison, May 11, 1785, Boyd, vol. 8, pp. 147–48.

24. Letter to James Monroe, June 11, 1785, Boyd, vol. 8, p. 229.

25. Letter from Chastellux, June 2, 1785, Boyd, vol. 8, pp. 174–75; letter to Chastellux, June 7, 1785, Boyd, vol. 8, pp. 184–86; letter to Edward Bancroft, February 26, 1786, Boyd, vol. 9, pp. 299–300; letter to James Madison, February 8, 1786, Boyd, vol. 9, pp. 264–67; letter to C. W. F. Dumas, February 2, 1786, Boyd, vol. 9, pp. 243–44.

26. Letter to Edward Bancroft, February 26, 1786, Boyd, vol. 9, pp. 299–300; letter to William Short, March 28, 1786, Boyd vol. 9, p. 362–64.

27. etter to Edward Bancroft, February 26, 1786, Boyd, vol. 9, pp. 299–300; letter from John Page, April 28, 1785, Boyd, vol. 8, pp. 116–20; letter to John Page, August 20, 1785, Boyd, vol. 8, pp. 417–19; letter to David Rittenhouse, January 25, 1786, Boyd, vol. 9, pp. 215–16; letter to Francis Hopkinson, August 14, 1786, Boyd, vol. 10, p. 249.

28. Verner, "Mr. Jefferson Makes a Map," pp. 96–108; Verner, "Maps and Plates," pp. 21–33.

29. Letter from the Abbé Morellet, January 11, 1787 (?), Boyd, vol. 11, p. 37; Carriere, "Manuscripts," pp. 4–24.

30. Letter to James Madison, November 11, 1784, Boyd, vol. 7, p. 504; letter to David Rittenhouse, November 11, 1784, Boyd, vol. 7, p. 517; letter to Charles Thomson, November 11, 1784, Boyd, vol. 7, p. 518; letter from James Currie, August 5, 1785, Boyd, vol. 8, p. 342.

31. Letter to James Monroe, May 21, 1784, Boyd, vol. 7, pp. 280; letter to Francis Hopkinson, January 13, 1785, Boyd, vol. 7, pp. 602–3; letter to James Monroe, January 14, 1784 [1785], Boyd, vol. 7, p. 608; letter to St. John de Crèvecoeur, January 14, 1785 (not found), Boyd, vol. 7, p. 604; letter to Niel Jamieson, January 3, 1785 (not found), Boyd, vol. 7, p. 603.

32. Letter to James Monroe, June 17, 1785, Boyd, vol. 8, p. 233; letter to Joseph Jones, June 19, 1785, Boyd, vol. 7, p. 237; letter to Abigail Adams, June 21, 1785, Boyd, vol. 8, p. 241; letter to Charles Thomson, June 21, 1785, Boyd, vol. 8, p. 245.

33. Letter to Francis Hopkinson, September 25, 1785, Boyd, vol. 8, pp. 550–51; letter to Ralph Izard, September 26, 1785, Boyd, vol. 8, pp. 552–54; letter to James Currie, September 27, 1785, Boyd, vol. 8, p. 559; letter to the Reverend James Madison, October 2, 1785, Boyd, vol. 8, p. 576; letter to Charles Thomson, October 8, 1785, Boyd, vol. 8, pp. 598–99.

34. Letter to James Madison, November 11, 1784, Boyd, vol. 7, pp. 503–7; letter to Charles Thomson, November 11, 1784, Boyd, vol. 7, pp. 518–19; letter from James Madison, April 27, 1785, Boyd, vol. 8, p. 111; Robins, pp. 112–14.

35. Letter from Charles Thomson, March 6, 1785, Boyd, vol. 8, pp. 15–16; letter to Charles Thomson, October 8, 1785, Boyd, vol. 8, pp. 598–99; Boyd, vol. 8, p. 599n; letter to John Vaughan, May 16, 1791, Boyd, vol. 20, p. 420.

36. Letter to James Currie, November 11, 1784 (not found), Boyd, vol. 7, p. 500; letter to James Madison, November 11, 1784, Boyd, vol. 7, pp. 503–7; letter to John Page, November 11, 1784, Boyd, vol. 7, pp. 514–15; letter to Charles Thomson, November 11, 1784, Boyd, vol. 7, pp. 518–19; letter from Charles Thomson, March 6, 1785, Boyd, vol. 8, pp. 15–16.

37. Drawing and description in the Bixby Collection, MoHi; Jefferson's note of an article in *Columbian Magazine*, vol. II, June 1787, of an "Account of a new Machine for raising Water by Wind" in *Gentleman's Magazine* for February 1787, DLC, *Jefferson Papers* following fol. 41675.

38. Letter to Hugh Williamson, February 6, 1785, Boyd, vol. 7, pp. 642–43.

39. Letter to the Reverend Ezra Stiles, July 17, 1785, Boyd, vol. 8, pp. 298–300.
40. Letter from General Samuel Holden Parsons to the Reverend Ezra Stiles, April 27, 1786, Boyd, vol. 9, pp. 477–78; letter to the Reverend Ezra Stiles, September 1, 1786, Boyd, vol.10, pp. 311–16.
41. Rochon, pp. 169–199; Daumas, pp. 356–57; Fauque, pp. 3–36; King, Telescope, pp. 152, 155, 197, 231.
42. Letter to David Rittenhouse, November 11, 1784, Boyd, vol. 7, p. 517.
43. Letter to the Reverend James Madison, November 11, 1784, (not found), Boyd, vol. 7, p. 508; letter from the Reverend James Madison, April 10, 1785, Boyd, vol. 8, p. 73; letter to the Reverend James Madison, October 2, 1785, Boyd, vol. 8, p. 575.
44. Letter to Francis Hopkinson, January 3, 1786, Boyd, vol. 9, pp. 146–49; letter to David Rittenhouse, January 25, 1786, Boyd, vol. 9, pp. 215–17; letter to Benjamin Franklin, January 27, 1786, Boyd, vol. 9, pp. 232–33; letter to the Reverend Ezra Stiles, September 1, 1786, Boyd, vol. 10, p. 317; Chapin, pp. 87–104.
45. Duparc and Tikhonovich, passim; Encyclopedia Brittanica, 14th edition. vol. 18, p. 45.
46. Letter from the Reverend James Madison, March 27, 1786, Boyd, vol. 9, p. 356.
47. Letter to Robert Patterson, December 27, 1812, HAW, vol. VI, pp. 83–84.
48. Letter to Peter Carr, August 19, 1785, Boyd, vol. 8, pp. 405–8.
49. Letter from James Madison, May 12, 1786, Boyd, vol. 9, pp. 517–22; letter to James Madison, May 3, 1788, Boyd, vol. 13, p. 132.
50. Letter to James Madison, January 30, 1787, Boyd, vol. 11, p. 97.
51. Letter to John Jay, August 30, 1785, Boyd, vol. 8, pp. 453–56.
52. Aide-Mémoire Tome II, pp. 591–93.
53. Blanc, l'Assemblée Nationale, pp. 3–21; "Blanc, N."; Biographie universelle, anciénne, Tome XVII, pp. 473–75, "Gribeauval, Jean Baptiste Vaquette de;" Nouvelle Biographie Général, Tome XXII, cols. 19–24; Durfee, pp. 469–77; Thomas, "Plus grand économie," pp. 1–4.
54. Letter to Patrick Henry, January 24, 1786, Boyd, vol. 9, pp. 212–15; Ford, vol. IV, pp. 134–37.
55. Memorandum Book, MHi, entry for September 5, 1789.
56. Letter to Henry Knox, September 12, 1786, Boyd, vol. 15, pp. 421–23.
57. Ibid.
58. Letter to William Short, April 6, 1790, Boyd, vol. 16, p. 316; letters from William Short, August 4, August 22 and October 27, 1790, Boyd, vol. 17, pp. 317–18, 412, 642.
59. Procès-verbal des Comités d'Agriculture, Tome I, pp. 623, 632; Le Roy, Laplace, Coulomb, Borda, pp. 11; Procès-verbal de l'Assemblée nationale, Tome 53, 28 Avril 1791, p. 10; Laboratoires Central, Archives, 6–c-5, 6th division, lst Chap. File 6202; Procès-verbal de l'Assemblée, (legislative), Tome 7, 8 avril 1792, p. 130; Procès-verbal de la Convention nationale, Séances de 4 brumaire an II (1794), p. 96, Séances de 11 brumaire An II (1794), pp. 254–56. AF(II)214B), pl. 1841, piece 45. Arrête relatif à la fabrique de platines du Citoyen Le Blanc à Roanne (18 ventose An I); Recueil des Actes du comife de salut publique, 16 decembre 1794, p. 755; [Géneral Gassendi], Aide-Mémoire, 5th édition, Tome II, pp. 591–93; Magazin Encyclopédique, 7th année, Tome V, pp. 512–13, "France. Necrologie. Sur le C. Blanc;" Mirsky and Nevins, pp. 152–55; Woodbury, "Legend," p. 241.
60. Fetis, vol. VII, p. 229; "Lettre sur un instrument ou pendule nouveau," p. 539; Sadie, vol. 2, p. 647; B. S. Brook, vol. I, pp. 502–10.
61. Letter to Francis Hopkinson, January 31, 1786, Boyd, vol. 9, pp. 146–47; Memorandum Book, MHi, entry for December 17, 1785.
62. Letter to the Reverend James Madison, October 2, 1785, Boyd, vol. 8, pp. 575–76; Raphael, p. 7; letter from Benjamin Vaughan, February 16, 1787, Boyd, vol. 11, p. 162.
63. Letter to Francis Hopkinson, January 3, 1786, Boyd, vol. 9, pp. 146–49; Notes, p. 39; Garden Book, pp. 268–70, 378; R. Jones, pp. 123–26; True, "Botany," pp. 345–60; Fulling, pp. 248–70.
64. Letter to Francis Hopkinson, August 14, 1786, Boyd, vol. 9, p. 250; letter from Francis Hopkinson, December 9, 1786, Boyd, vol. 10, p. 587.
65. Letter to David Rittenhouse, January 25, 1786, Boyd, vol. 9, pp. 215–17.
66. Letter to the Reverend Madison, October 2, 1785, Boyd, vol. 8, pp. 574–76.
67. Letter to James Madison, December 16, 1786, Boyd, vol. 10, pp. 604–5; letter to James Madison, August 2, 1787, Boyd, vol. 11, p. 664.

68. Letter to the Reverend Ezra Stiles, September 1, 1786, Boyd, vol. 10, p. 317; "Polytype," Boyd, vol. 10, pp. 318–25; "Estimate for Printing," Boyd, vol. 10, p. 325.
69. Letter to Benjamin Hawkins, August 13, 1786, Boyd, vol. 10, pp. 240—41; letter from Benjamin Hawkins, October 6, 1789, Boyd, vol. 15, pp. 506–7.
70. Letter to William Drayton, May 6, 1786, Boyd, vol. 9, p. 461; Browne, p. 411.
71. Letter to John Adams, August 27, 1786, Boyd, vol. 10, pp. 302–3.
72. Letter to Jean Baptiste Le Roy, November 13, 1786, Boyd, vol. 10, pp. 524–26.
73. Letter from General John Sullivan, March 12, 1784, Boyd, vol. 7, pp. 21–24; letter from William Whipple, March 15, 1784, Boyd, vol. 7, pp. 28–30; letter from General John Sullivan, June 22, 1784, Boyd, vol. 7, pp. 317–20.
74. Letter from Buffon, December 31, 1785, Boyd, vol. 9, pp. 130—31; letter to Francis Hopkinson, December 23, 1786, Boyd, vol. 10, p. 625; Webster, vol. I, pp. 371–72.
75. Letter to John Sullivan, January 7, 1786, Boyd, vol. 9, p. 160; letter to William Whipple, January 7, 1786, Boyd, vol. 9, pp. 161–62; letter from John Sullivan, April 16, 1787, Boyd, vol. 11, pp. 295–96; letter from John Sullivan, May 9, 1787, Boyd, vol. 11, p. 359; letter to Archibald Cary, January 7, 1786, Boyd, vol. 9, pp. 158–59.
76. Letters from John Sullivan, January 26, April 16, May 9, and May 29, 1787, Boyd, vol. 11, pp. 68, 295–96, 359, 384; letters to John Sullivan, August 15 and October 5, 1787, Boyd, vol. 12, pp. 41–42, 208–9; letter from John Rutledge, Jr., September 4, 1788, Boyd, vol. 13, pp. 567–68; letter to John Rutledge, Jr., September 9, 1788, Boyd, vol. 13, pp. 593–94; letter from John Sullivan, April 26, 1787, Boyd, vol. 11, pp. 320—21.
77. Letter to Buffon, October 1, 1787, Boyd, vol. 12, pp. 194–95; letter to L.J.M. Daubenton, October 1, 1787, Boyd, vol. 12, pp. 195–96; letter from L.J.M. Daubenton, October 2, 1787, Boyd, vol. 12, p. 197.
78. Letter to John Rutledge, Jr., September 9, 1788, Boyd, vol. 13, pp. 593–94; letter from Bernard Germain Étienne de la Ville-sur-Ilon, Comte de Lacépède, October 25, 1787, Boyd. vol. 12, pp. 287–88; Webster, vol. I, pp. 364, 371–72; A. C. Jones, pp. 333–48.
79. Letter to Archibald Stuart, January 25, 1786, Boyd, vol. 9, pp. 217–19; letter to James Currie, January 28, 1786, Boyd, vol. 9, p. 240; letter from James Currie, May 2, 1787, Boyd, vol. 11, p. 328.
80. Memorandum Book, MHi, entries for March 21, April 4, April 11, April 12, April 15, April 22, April 26, 1786.
81. Bedini, Copying Machines, pp. 20—25; letter from William Stephens Smith May 21, 1786, Boyd, vol. 9, pp. 554–55; letter from John Paradise, May 23, 1786, Boyd, vol. 9, p. 557; letter to William Stephens Smith, July 9, 1786, Boyd, vol. 10, pp. 115–17.
82. Letter from Jean Baptiste Leroy, September 28, 1786, Boyd, vol. 10, pp. 410—11; letter to Jean Baptiste Le Roy, November 13, 1786, Boyd, vol.10, pp. 524–30; Prévost and d'Amat, s. v. "Charpentier, François-Philippe."
83. Letter to William Carmichael, December 26, 1786, Boyd, vol. 10, p. 632–34; letters from Miguel de Lardizábal y Uribe, January 17 and May 10, 1787, Boyd, vol. 11, pp. 52–53, 236–38; letter from William Carmichael, March 25, 1787, Boyd, vol. 11, p. 384; letter to Miguel de Lardizabel y Uribe, July 6, 1787, Boyd, vol. 11, pp. 553–54.
84. Letter to James Madison, January 30, 1787, Boyd, vol. 11, pp. 92–97.
85. Letter from William Temple Franklin to Benjamin Franklin, October 13, 1784, PPAmP, Franklin Papers.
86. Letter from Andrew Cabrit to James Watt, June 12, 1786, Boulton-Watt Papers, Birmingham Engineering Reference Library; Heal, p. 58.
87. Letter to LouisDominique Ethis de Corny, December 17, 1787, Boyd, vol. 12, pp. 430—31.
88. Boyd, vol. 15, p. 521n; "Jefferson's Instructions to William Short for procuring household goods," enclosure with letter to Short, April 6, 1790, Boyd, vol. 16, pp. 321–24.
89. Verner, "Map," pp. 96–108; letter to Edward Bancroft, February 26, 1786, Boyd, vol. 9, pp. 299–300; letter from Samuel J. Neele, December 21, 1786, Boyd, vol. 10, pp. 621–22; letter to William Stephens Smith, August 9 (10), 1786, Boyd, vol. 10, p. 212; letter from William Stephens Smith, September 18, 1786, Boyd, vol. 10, p. 393; letter to William Stephens Smith, October 22, 1786, Boyd, vol. 10, pp. 478–79; letter to William Faden, Boyd, vol. 9, pp. 300, 342; letter to William Faden, Boyd, vol. 10, p. 226; letter from S. J. Neele, December 31, 1786, Boyd. vol. 10, pp. 621–22; letter to William Stephens Smith, January 15, 1787, Boyd, vol. 11, p. 46; letter from William Stephen Smith, January 29, 1787, Boyd, vol. 11, p. 91; Notes, "Introduction," p. xviii, n. 24.

90. Letter from John Stockdale, August 8, 1786, Boyd, vol. 10, p. 210; letter to John Stockdale, July 1, 1787, Boyd, vol. 11, pp. 521–22; letter to Abbé André Morellet, July 2, 1787, Boyd, vol. 11, pp. 529–30; letter from Abbé André Morellet, July 3, 1787, Boyd, vol. 11, p. 542; letter from William Short, May 29, 1787, Boyd, vol. 11, p. 383; letter to Thomas Mann Randolph, July 6, 1787, Boyd, vol. 11, p. 559; Memorandum for John Trumbull, c. February 15, 1788, Boyd, vol. 12, pp. 597–98; letter from John Stockdale, February 22, 1788, Boyd, vol. 12, pp. 621–22; letter from John Trumbull, February 22, 1788, Boyd, vol. 12, p. 622.
91. Letter to Alexander Donald, September 17, 1787, Boyd, vol. 12, pp. 132–34; Verner, "Map," pp. 96–108; Clement C. Moore, passim; Mayer, passim; Fay, p. 202.
92. Letter to Mme. Anne Mangeot Ethis de Corny, June 30, 1787, Boyd, vol. 11, p. 509.
93. Letter to Charles Thomson, April 22, 1786, Boyd, vol. 9, pp. 400—1; letter to John Page, May 4, 1786, Boyd, vol. 9, p. 444; letter to Charles Thomson, December 17, 1786, Boyd, vol. 10, pp. 609–10; letter to Charles Thomson, September 20, 1787, Boyd, vol. 12, pp. 159–61.
94. Trumbull, Autobiography, pp. 95–96, 108, 117–19; letter to Antoine Jean Marie Thevenard, May 5, 1786, Boyd, vol. 10, pp. 458–59; letter to William Stephens Smith, September 23, 1786, Boyd, vol. 10, p. 400; letter to James Madison, February 8 1786, Boyd, vol. 9, p. 265.
95. Chinard, Trois Amitiés, Chapter IV; letter to Maria Cosway, October 13, 1786, Boyd, vol. 10, pp. 458–59; Bullock, Head and Heart, passim; Butterfield and Rice, "Earliest Note," pp. 31–32.
96. Letter to William Stephen Smith, October 22, 1786, Boyd, vol. 10, pp. 478–79.
97. Letter to Maria Cosway, October 5, 1786, Butterfield and Rice, pp. 26–29; letter to Maria Cosway, October 12, 1786, Boyd, vol. 10, pp. 443–55; SNR, pp. 85–87.
98. Letter to Chrétien Guillaume de Lamoignon de Malesherbes, May 5, 1786, Boyd, vol. 9, pp. 452–53; letter to George Wythe, August 13, 1786, Boyd, vol. 10, p. 243.

CHAPTER VII. THE VIRGINIAN ABROAD

1. Letter from James Madison, October 24, 1787, Boyd, vol. 12, pp. 270—86; letter to James Madison, December 20, 1787, Boyd, vol. 12, pp. 438–42.
2. Extensively described, with documents, in F. Kimball, First Monument; F. Kimball, Architect, pp. 40–43, 142–48; letter to Madame de Tesse, March 20, 1787, L&B, vol. VI, p. 102.
3. Sparks, Ledyard, p. 212; Randall, vol. I, pp. 443–44; Auger, pp. 167–82; Jackson, Stony Mountains, pp. 45–48.
4. Letter to Ezra Stiles, September 1, 1786, Boyd, vol. 10, pp. 316–18; letter to John Banister, Jr., June 19, 1787, Boyd, vol. 11, pp. 476–77; letter to Charles Thomson, September 20, 1787, Boyd, vol. 12, pp. 159–61; Auger, pp. 167–82; Randall, vol. I, p. 507; letter to George Rogers Clark, December 4, 1783, Boyd, vol. 6, p. 371.
5. Letter to John Jay, August 14, 1785, Boyd, vol. 8, p. 373; La Perouse.
6. Sparks, pp. 192–99; Watrous, p. 108; MHi, Cutting Papers, Diary of Nathaniel Cutting, Ms.
7. Letter to John Ledyard, August 16, 1786, Boyd, vol. 10, p. 258; letter from John Ledyard, November 25, 1786, Boyd, vol. 10, pp. 548–49.
8. Letter to Reverend James Madison, July 19, 1788, Boyd, vol. 13, p. 382; D. Jackson, "Ledyard and La Pérouse," pp. 495–508; Bridges, pp. 30—35.
9. Jefferson, Autobiography, pp. 1163–64.
10. Jefferson, Observations on the Whale Fishery, Boyd, vol. 13, pp. 52n., vol. 14, pp. 226–34, 242–56; Malone, Jefferson, vol. 2, pp. 16–41.
11. Letter from Benjamin Franklin to Edward Nairne, October 18, 1783, A. H. Smyth, vol. IX, p. 109.
12. Letter to Benjamin Vaughan, December 29, 1786, Boyd, vol. 10, pp. 637–47; Hindle, Rittenhouse, pp. 84–85; W. Barton, pp. 139n, 207n, 585–86.
13. Letters from Benjamin Vaughan, January 26 and February 16, 1787, Boyd, vol. 10, pp. 69–77, vol. 11, p. 162; letters to Benjamin Vaughan, July 2 and July 23, 1787, Boyd, vol. 11, p. 532, 13 pp. 394–98; letter from Benjamin Vaughan, August 2, 1788, Boyd, vol. 13, pp. 459–61.
14. Letter to Michel Guillaume St. John de Crèvecoeur, January 15, 1787, Boyd, vol. 11, pp. 43–44.
15. Letter to John Jones, January 22, 1787, Boyd, vol. 11, p. 61; letter to William Stephens Smith, February 19, 1787, Boyd, vol. 11, p. 168.

16. Letter to James Madison, January 30, 1787, Boyd, vol. 11, pp. 92–97.
17. "Memoranda," Boyd, vol. 11, pp. 415–64; Randall, vol. I, pp. 466–77.
18. Letter to William Short, March 27, 1787, Boyd, vol. 11, p. 249.
19. Letter to John Trumbull, February 23, 1787, Boyd, vol. 11, p. 181; letter to François Jean de Beauvoir, Chevalier de Chastellux, April 4, 1787, Boyd, vol. 11, pp. 261–62.
20. Letter to Lafayette, April 11, 1787, Boyd, vol. 11, pp. 283–85.
21. "Memoranda," in Padover, pp. 759–61.
22. Notes, pp. 265–66; letter from the Abbé André Morellet, [1] September ?, 1786, Boyd, vol. 10, p. 350.
23. Notes, pp. 31–33, 265; letter to David Rittenhouse, January 28, 1786, Boyd, vol. 9, p. 216; letter to Chastellux, April 4, 1787, Boyd, vol. 11, pp. 262; "Memoranda," Boyd, vol. 11, pp. 460—61; Carozzi, passim.
24. "Memoranda," Padover, Complete Jefferson, pp. 793–94; Notes, p. 33.
25. "Memoranda," Boyd, vol. 11, pp. 460—61.
26. Letter to David Rittenhouse, September 18, 1787, Boyd, vol. 12, p. 144; Felix François Le Royer d'Artezet de La Sauvagère (1707–1781), Recueil de Dissertations, ou recherches historiques et critiques sur le temps ou vivait le solitaire saint Florent, au mont Gionne en Anjou. . . . (1776). Nouvelle Biographie Générale, vol. 19, cols. 736–37.
27. Letter to William Short, April 12, 1787, Boyd, vol. 11, p. 287; letter to William Drayton, July 20, 1787, Boyd, vol. 11m pp. 644–50; letter to William Drayton, July 30, 1787, Boyd, vol. 11, pp. 644–50.
28. Cometti, p. 99; "Memoranda," Padover, Complete Jefferson, pp. 776; letter to John Jay, May 4, 1787, L&B, vol. 6, pp. 112–13; Fulling, pp. 563–98.
29. Letter to Edward Rutledge, July 14, 1787, Boyd, vol. 11, pp. 587–89.
30. Letter to George Wythe, September 16, 1787, Boyd, vol. 12, p. 127.
31. Letter to William Drayton, July 30, 1787, Boyd, vol. 11, pp. 644–50; letter to William Drayton, July 17, 1787 (8), DLC; letter to Charles C. Pinckney, October 8, 1792, L&B, vol. 8, pp. 412–14; letter to Stephen Cathalan, December 2, 1792, L&B, vol. 19, pp. 98–101; letter to James Ronaldson, January 12, 1813, L&B, vol. 13, pp. 204–5.
32. Letter to William Drayton, July 30, 1787, Boyd, vol. 11, pp. 644–50.
33. "Memoranda," Padover, Complete Jefferson, pp. 773–74.
34. "Memoranda," Padover, Complete Jefferson, p. 773.
35. Letter to Martha Jefferson, May 21, 1787, Boyd, vol. 11, pp. 369–70.
36. "Memoranda," Padover, 784–85; Boyd, vol. 11, pp. 415–64.
37. Letter to Lafayette, April 21, 1787, Boyd, vol. 11, pp. 369–70.
38. Letter to G. K. van Hagendorp, October 13, 1785, Boyd, vol. 8, p. 633.
39. Letter to Jeudy de l'Hommande, August 9, 1787, Boyd, vol. 12, p. 11.
40. Letter to Isaac McPherson, August 13, 1813, L&B, vol. 13, pp. 326–38.
41. Letter to Thomas Digges, June 19, 1788, Boyd, vol. 13, pp. 260—61.
42. Letter to the Reverend James Madison, July 19, 1788, Boyd, vol. 13, pp. 379–83.
43. Letter from John Churchman, June 6, 1787, Boyd, vol. 11, pp. 397–99; Churchman, "Address," pp. 496–500; Churchman, Explanation; Bedini, Thinkers, pp. 349–51; Dupree, pp. 9–11.
44. Letter from David Rittenhouse, April 14, 1787, Boyd, vol. 11, pp. 293–94; letter from Francis Hopkinson, July 8, 1787, Boyd, vol. 11, pp. 561–62.
45. Letter to Benjamin Vaughan, July 2, 1787, Boyd, vol. 11, pp. 532–33; letter to Charles Thomson, September 20, 1787, Boyd, vol. 12, pp. 159–61.
46. Letter from John Churchman, June 6, 1787, Boyd, vol. 11, pp. 397–99; letter to John Churchman, August 8, 1787, Boyd, vol. 12, p. 5.
47. Churchman, Magnetic Atlas; Nova Acta, vol. X, 1791, p. 16, vol. XIII, 1795–96, p. 14; Churchman, "Essay," pp. 221–29; Dupree, pp. 9–11.
48. Letter from Andrew Ramsay, July 6, 1787, Boyd, vol. 11, p. 556; letter to Madame de Corny, June 30, 1787, Boyd, vol. 11, pp. 509–10; letters from Abigail Adams, June 26 and July 6, 1787, Boyd 11, pp. 501–2, 550—52; Randall, vol. I, pp. 480—82; Malone, "Polly Jefferson," pp. 81–95.
49. Letter to Abigail Adams, July 16, Boyd, vol. 11, p. 592, and October 4, 1787, Boyd, vol. 12, pp. 201–2; letter to Elizabeth Eppes, July 12, 1788, Boyd, vol. 13, pp. 347–48; SNR, p. 128.

50. Letter to James Madison, October 24, 1787, Boyd, vol. 12, pp. 270—82; letter to James Madison, August 28, 1789, Boyd, vol. 15, pp. 367–68.
51. Letter to James Madison, December 20, 1787, Boyd, vol. 12, pp. 438–43; letter to James Madison July 19, 1788, Boyd, vol. 13, pp. 379–83; letter to James Madison, March 15, 1789, vol. 14, pp. 483–84; letter to James Madison, August 28, 1789, Boyd, vol. 15, pp. 364–69.
52. Letter to James Madison, August 28, 1789, Boyd, vol. 15, pp. 364–69.
53. Van Doren, pp. 30—35, 138–41; Levy, pp. 147–66.
54. Hamilton, Jay and Madison, No. 43, p. 279; Wyman, pp. 51–54.
55. Federico, "Origin," pp. 292–305; Federico, "Operation," pp. 237–51.
56. Letter to the Reverend James Madison, August 13, 1787, Boyd, vol. 12, pp. 30—31.
57. Letter to David Rittenhouse, September 18, 1787, Boyd, vol. 12, pp. 144–45.
58. Letter to George Wythe, September 16, 1787, Boyd, vol. 12, pp. 127–30.
59. Letter to Charles Thomson, September 20, 1787, Boyd, vol. 12, pp. 159–61.
60. Letter from Thomas Mann Randolph, Jr., April 14, 1787, Boyd, vol. 11, pp. 291–93; letter to Thomas Mann Randolph, Jr., July 6, 1787, Boyd, vol. 11, pp. 556–59.
61. Letter to Peter Carr, August 10, 1787, Boyd, vol. 12, pp. 14–18.
62. Letter to Jean Baptiste Le Roy, November 13, 1786, Boyd, vol. 10, p. 529.
63. Letter to Jean Baptiste Le Roy, November 13, 1786, Boyd, vol. 10, pp. 524–30; letter to William Carmichael, December 15, 1787, Boyd, vol. 12, pp. 423–27; letter to William Carmichael June 3, 1788, Boyd, vol. 13, pp. 229–34.
64. Letter from John Jones, January 2, 1788, Boyd, vol. 14, pp. 411–12; [John Jones], Description, 3rd edition; Encyclopaedia Britannica, vol. I, pp. 556 ff.; letter to William Jones, December 10, 1788, Boyd, vol. 14, p. 346.
65. Memorandum for John Trumbull, c. February 15, 1788, Boyd, vol. 12, pp. 597–98.
66. Letter to the Reverend James Madison, July 19, 1788, Boyd, vol. 13, p. 381.
67. Ibid.
68. Ibid; letter to James Currie, December 20, 1788, Boyd, vol. 14, pp. 366–67; Lavoisier, Traité élémentaire de chimie.
69. Letter to the Reverend James Madison, July 19, 1788, Boyd, vol. 13, p. 381; letter to James Currie, December 20, 1788, Boyd, vol. 14, p. 367.
70. Letter to the Reverend James Madison, July 19, 1788, Boyd, vol. 13, pp. 379–81; letter from the Reverend James Madison, February 10, 1789, Boyd, vol. 14, pp. 535–36.
71. Letter to Benjamin Vaughan, July 23, 1788, Boyd, vol. 13, pp. 394–98. The clergyman-inventor was the Rev. John Prince (1751–1836) of Salem, Massachusetts, Bedini, Early American Scientific Instruments, pp. 24–25.
72. Letter from Benjamin Vaughan, August 2, 1788, Boyd, vol. 13, pp. 459–61.
73. Letter from Benjamin Vaughan, April 5, 1788, Boyd, vol. 13, p. 37; letter to Benjamin Vaughan, July 23, 1788, Boyd, vol. 13, pp. 395–97; letter from Benjamin Vaughan, August 2, 1788, Boyd, vol. 13, pp. 459–60.
74. Letter from Benjamin Vaughan, August 2, 1788, Boyd, vol. 13, p. 460.
75. Letter to Benjamin Vaughan, July 23, 1788, Boyd, vol. 13, pp. 395–97.
76. Letter to Thomas Paine, December 23, 1788, Boyd, vol. 14, pp. 372–77.
77. Letter to Thomas Paine, December 23, 1788, Boyd, vol. 14, pp. 372–77.
78. Letter from Joseph Willard, September 24, 1788, Boyd, vol. 13, pp. 637–38.
79. Letter to Joseph Willard, March 24, 1789, Boyd, vol. 14, pp. 697–99.
80. Letter to John Jay, March 13, 1788, Boyd, vol. 12, p. 661; letter to John Jay, March 16, 1788, Boyd, vol. 12, pp. 671–76.
81. Jefferson, "Memorandums on a Tour," in Padover, Complete Jefferson, pp. 799–819; Boyd, vol. 13, pp. 8–36.
82. "Memorandums," Padover, Complete Jefferson, pp. 803–806; letter to Jean Jacques Peuchen, April 7, 1788, Boyd, vol. 13, p. 43; letter to Nicholas and Jacob van Staphorst, April 7, 1788, Boyd, vol. 13, p. 44.
83. "Memorandums," Boyd, vol. 11, pp. 415–64.
84. Letter to Baron von Geismar, March 18, 1788, Boyd, vol. 12, p. 680; letter to William Short, April 9, 1788, Boyd, vol. 13, pp. 48–49; Randall, vol. I, p. 500; Dumbauld, Tourist, pp. 116–17, 120—21; 122–23.
85. "Memoranda," Padover, Complete Jefferson, pp. 814–15.
86. Letter to John Adams, August 30, 1787, Boyd, vol. 12, pp. 66–69.

87. Randall, vol. I, pp. 538–39; SNR, p. 146.
88. Letter to Ralph Izard, November 10, 1787, Boyd, vol. 12, pp. 338–40; *Memorandum Book*, MHi, entry for April 20, 1789, Randall, vol. I, pp. 538–39.
89. Letter from George Washington, November 27, 1788, Boyd, vol. 14, p. 295; letter from George Washington, February 13, 1789, Boyd, vol. 14, pp. 546–49; letter to George Washington, May 10, 1789, Boyd, vol. 15, pp. 117–19.
90. Letter to Jean Baptiste Le Roy, November 13, 1786, Boyd, vol. 10, pp. 524–30.
91. Letter to James Madison, May 3, 1788, Boyd, vol. 13, p. 132.
92. Rice, "A 'New' Likeness," pp. 84–89; L. D., "A Life Portrait of Jefferson," *Worcester . . . Bulletin*, pp. 9–10; Bedini, *Copying Machines*, p. 35.
93. Boyd, vol. 14, p. xliv; Norfleet, pp. 11–33; Rice, "Album," pp. 23–31; Bedini *Copying Machines*, p. 35.
94. [Governeur Morris], *Diary*, July 4, 1789, quoted in Randall, vol. I, p. 514.
95. Bernard Mayo, *Jefferson Himself*, pp. 147–48.
96. SNR, pp. 154–68.
97. Letter to John Jay, July 19, 1789, Boyd, vol. 15, pp. 284–91.
98. Jefferson, *Autobiography*, in Padover, *Complete Jefferson*, p. 1192.
99. SNR, pp. 154–68; Randall, vol. I, pp. 551–52; letters to William Short, October 4, October 7, November 21, 1789, Boyd, vol. 15, pp. 506, 508–09, 552–53.
100. Letter to Michel Guillaume St. John de Crèvecoeur, January 15, 1787, Boyd, vol. 11, pp. 43–45; letter from Jean Nicolas Démeunier, January 21, 1786, Boyd, vol. 9, pp. 382–83; letter to George Washington, November 14, 1786, Boyd, vol. 10, pp. 531–35; letter to the *Journal de Paris*, August 29, 1787, L&B, vol. XVII, pp. 148–53; Chinard, "Influence," pp. 171–86; Jefferson, *Autobiography*, in Padover, *Complete Jefferson*, p. 1192.
101. (Bills of credit to Démeunier), letter to Démeunier, January 24, 1786, Boyd, vol. 10, pp. 11–29; (Comments on Francois Soulès's *Histoire*), September 1786, Boyd, vol, 10, p. 367.

CHAPTER VIII. THE SHIP OF STATE

1. Letter to John Trumbull, November 25, 1789, Boyd, vol. 15, pp. 559–61; Randall, vol. I, pp. 551–52; SNR, pp. 150–52.
2. Letters from George Washington, October 13 and November 30, 1789, Boyd, vol. 15, pp. 519–20, Boyd, vol. 16, pp. 8–9; letter to George Washington, December 15, 1789, Boyd, vol. 16, pp. 34–35; letter from James Currie, November 27, 1789, Boyd, vol. 15, p. 562; letter to William Short, December 14, 1789, Boyd, vol. 16, pp. 24–28; *New-York Gazette of the United States*, September 30 and December 12, 1789.
3. Randall, vol. I, pp. 558–59; SNR, pp. 172–73.
4. SNR, pp. 152–53.
5. *Garden Book*, pp. 148–49.
6. Letter to James Madison, August 29, 1789, Boyd, vol. 15, p. 369; letter from James Madison to George Washington, January 4, 1790, Fitzpatrick, *Writings*, vol. XXX, p. 448n; letter from George Washington, January 21, 1790, Fitzpatrick, *Writings*, vol. XXX, pp. 509–11.
7. Letter to George Washington, February 14, 1790, Boyd, vol. 16, p. 184; Hall, pp. 104–5.
8. Randall, vol. I, pp. 558; SNR, pp. 172–73; *Memorandum Book*, MHi, entries for February 23 and February 27, 1790; Betts and Bear, pp. 49–50.
9. Letter to Thomas Mann Randolph, Jr., March 28, 1790, Boyd, vol. 16, pp. 277–79; letter from Thomas Mann Randolph, Jr., May 25, 1790, Boyd, vol. 16, pp. 441–42; Randall, vol. I, p. 558; SNR, pp. 173–75; *Garden Book*, p. 149.
10. Letter to Francis Willis, April 18, 1790, Boyd, vol. 16, pp. 352–53; Randall, vol. I, pp. 560–62; letter to Martha Jefferson Randolph, April 4, 1790, Boyd, vol. 16, p. 300; Dumbauld, *Tourist*, p. 155; "When Jefferson Lived in New York," editorial, *The New York Times*, April 15, 1929.
11. Letter to Nicholas Lewis, March 7, 1790, Boyd, vol. 16, pp. 210–12.
12. Boyd, vol. 17, p. 288n; Bedini, *Copying Machines*, pp. 25–26.
13. Letter to William Short with "Instructions," April 6, 1790, Boyd, vol. 16, pp. 321–24.
14. Letter to T. M. Randolph, Jr., April 18, 1790, Boyd, vol. 16, pp. 351–52.

15. Letter from T. M. Randolph. Jr., April 30, 1791, Boyd, vol. 20, pp. 327–30; letter from David Rittenhouse, May 8, 1791, DLC.
16. Jefferson's report of his conversation with George Washington, February 26, 1792, Ford, vol. I, p. 176; Hart, Chapter VII; Hunt, *Department of State*, Chapters III and IV.
17. Letter to T. M. Randolph, Jr. May 30, 1790, Boyd, vol. 16, pp. 448–50.
18. Letter to William Short, May 27, 1790, Boyd, vol. 16, pp. 443–45; letter to William Short, January 8, 1825, Ford, vol. X, p. 333; letter from Abigail Adams to Mrs. Cranch, April 3, 1790, Mitchell, *New Letters*, p. 44; letter to Elizabeth Eppes, June 13, 1790, Boyd, vol. 16, p. 489; letters to M. J. Randolph, May 16 and June 6, 1790, Betts and Bear, pp. 56–58; letter to William Short, June 6, 1790, Boyd, vol. 16, pp. 475–76.
19. Letter to Thomas Cooper, October 27, 1808, L&B, vol. XII, p. 180; letter to Peter Carr, June 13, 1790, Boyd, vol. 16, pp. 487–88; Hart, Chapter VII.
20. Letter to Robert Leslie, June 27, 1790, Boyd, vol. 16, p. 576; letters to David Rittenhouse, June 12, June 14 and June 26, 1790, Boyd, vol. 16, pp. 484–85, 509–10, 574; letter from David Rittenhouse, June 21, 1790, Boyd, vol. 16, pp. 545–47.
21. "Report of the Secretary of State, on the Subject of Establishing a Uniformity in the Weights, Measures and Coins of the U. S," Boyd, vol. 16, pp. 602–75.
22. "Jefferson's Notes on Coinage," Boyd, vol. 7, pp. 150–202; text, Boyd, vol. 7, pp. 175–85.
23. Ramsey, "Historical Background," pp. 14–15; Federico, "Operation," p. 237, Boyd, vol. 15, pp. 170–72; Henry Remsen, Jr., "The Board of Arts," c. 1792, Boyd, vol. 17, pp. 384–85.
24. Federico, "Operation," pp. 237–51.
25. Letter to Benjamin Vaughan, June 27, 1790, Boyd, vol. 16, pp. 578–80.
26. Letter to Robert R. Livingston, February 4, 1791, Boyd, vol. 19, pp. 240–41; Ramsay, "Historical Background," pp. 14–15.
27. Federico, "Operation," vol. XVIII, pp. 248–51; Prager, "Intellectual Property," pp. 248–51.
28. Letter to Robert R. Livingston, February 4, 1791, Ford, vol. V, p. 276; Wyman, "Patent System," pp. 7–8; Federico, "Act of 1793," p. 69].
29. Letter to Thomas Cooper, January 16, 1814, L&B, vol. XIV, pp. 62–63.
30. DAB, vol. III, pp. 208–9; letters from James B. Pleasants, May 5, 1790, Boyd, vol. 16, pp. 412–13, and August 6, 1790, Boyd, vol. 17, p. 320; letter from James McHenry. April 18, 1791, Boyd, vol. 16, pp. 412–13; letter from Tobias Lear, August 30, 1791, Boyd, vol. 22, p. 10 (?); Fouts, pp. 325–29; Wyman, "Patent System," pp. 7–8; Federico, "Operation," p. 247–48.
31. Federico, "Operation," pp. 248–51.
32. "A Bill to Promote the Progress of the Useful Arts," Padover, *Complete Jefferson*, pp. 995–97; Federico, "The Patent Act of 1793," pp. 77–81.
33. Letters to Hugh Williamson, November 13 (DLC) and April 1, 1792, Ford, vol. V, pp. 492, 392–93.
34. Letter to Robert R. Livingston, February 4, 1791, Ford, vol. V, pp. 276–77.
35. Letter to Isaac McPherson, August 13, 1813, L&B, vol. XIII, pp. 333–34; Fouts, p. 331.
36. Letters to James Hutchinson, March 12, 1791 and March 25, 1791, Boyd, vol. 19, pp. 614, 616; letters from Caspar Wistar, March 19, 1791 and March 20, 1791, Boyd, vol. 19, pp. 614–15, 616; letter to Caspar Wistar, March 20, 1791, Boyd, vol. 19, pp. 615–16; "Affidavit of the Secretary of State on the Results of the Experiments," March 26, 1791, Boyd, vol. 19, pp. 617–18; letters to Isaac Senter, March 26, 1791 and May 10, 1791, Boyd, vol. 19, pp. 618–19, 621–22.
37. "Experiments in Desalination of Sea Water to Test the Claim of Jacob Isaacks," (Editorial Note), Boyd, vol. 19, pp. 608–14.
38. "Report On the Methods for Obtaining Fresh Water From Salt," Padover, *Complete Jefferson*, pp. 970–74.
39. Jefferson, "Notes on the Permanent Seat of Congress," pp. 6–9, "Note on Residence Bill," pp. 11–12; "The President of the United States," pp. 21–27, Padover, *National Capital*; Malone, *Jefferson*, vol. II, pp. 297–303, 371–87.
40. Letter to Andrew Ellicott, February 2, 1791, Padover, *National Capital*, pp. 40–41; *Georgetown Weekly Ledger*, March 12, 1791; letter from George Washington to Daniel Carroll, November 28, 1791, Fitzpatrick, *Writings*, vol. XXXI, pp. 429–31; letter from George Washington to Pierre Charles L'Enfant, November 28, 1791, Fitzpatrick, *Writings*, vol. XXXI, pp. 429–31; Bedini, *Banneker*, pp. 103–36; Malone, *Jefferson*, vol. II, pp. 371–84.

41. Letter to L'Enfant, April 10, 1791, Padover, *National Capital*, pp. 58–59, letter from Andrew Ellicott, January 12, 1793, letter to Andrew Ellicott, January 13, 1793, Padover, *National Capital*, pp. 169–70.

42. Jefferson, "Note: Proceedings to be had under the Residence Act," Padover, *National Capital*, pp. 30–36; letter from George Washington, January 2, 1791, Padover, *National Capital*, p. 36; letter to P. C. L'Enfant, April 10, 1791, Padover, *National Capital*, pp. 58–59.

43. "Notes on Commissioners' Meeting, September 8, 1791, letter from the Commissioners to P. C. L'Enfant, September 9, 1791, Padover, *National Capital*, pp. 70–75.

44. Letter from the Commissioners to George Washington, November 25, 1791, Padover, *National Capital*, pp. 78–79; letter from George Washington, November 30, 1791, letter to Pierre Charles L'Enfant, December 1, 1791, letter from the Commissioners, December 8, 1791, Jefferson, "Opinion on the L'Enfant letter," letter from Pierre Charles L'Enfant, February 26, 1792, Padover, *National Capital*, pp. 79–100.

45. Letter to the Commissioners, March 6, 1792, Padover, pp. 103–6, Letter to Daniel Carroll, February 1, 1793, Padover, p. 171; Malone, *Jefferson*, vol. II, pp. 384–Design of Capitol building; "Draft of Competition for Plan of a Capitol," Padover, *National Capital*, pp. 119–20; letter to George Washington, March 26, 1794, p. 180, letter from Washington, June 30, 1794, pp. 181–82, letter from Commissioners, July 7, 1794, p. 183, letter to George Washington, July 17, 1794, 184–85, Padover, *National Capital*, pp. 180–85.

46. "A Premium . . . to the person . . . who shall produce the most approved plan for a President's house. . . .," March 6, 1792, DLC; letter from the Commissioners of the District, July 5, 1792, letter to the Commissioners, July 16, 1792, National Archives, *Commissioners' Letterbooks*, vol. I, 1791–1793; F. Kimball, *Jefferson, Architect*, pp. 52–53, 154–55; F. Kimball, "Genesis," pp. 523–28.

47. Letter from Maria Cosway, April 6, 1790, Boyd, vol. 16, pp. 312–13; letter to Maria Cosway, June 23, 1790, Boyd, vol. 16, pp. 550–51.

48. Letter to Martha Randolph, May 16, 1790, Boyd, vol. 16, p. 429; letter from James Monroe, May 20, 1790, Boyd, vol. 16, p. 432; letter to Maria Jefferson, May 23, 1790, Boyd, vol. 16, p. 435; letter to T. M. Randolph, May 23, 1790, Boyd, vol. 16, p. 436; letter to William Short, May 27, 1790, Boyd, vol. 16, p. 443.

49. Letter to William Short, August 12, 1790, Boyd, vol. 17, p. 342; *New-York Gazette of the U. S.*, August 18, 21, 22, 1790; letter to Martha Randolph, August 22, 1790, Boyd, vol. 17, p. 402; Preston, pp. 109–15; Dumbauld, *Tourist*, pp. 156–58; Matthews, pp. 36–39; "Journal of William Loughton Smith," pp. 37–38.

50. Jefferson, "Recipe," DLC. For a medical analysis of Jefferson's headaches see Battle, pp. 531–39.

51. Letters to Thomas Leiper, August 4 and 24, 1791 and December 16, 1792, MHi, *Jefferson-Coolidge Papers*; DAB, vol. VI, p. 154.

52. M. Kimball, "French Furniture," p. 128; letter to T. M. Randolph, Jr., May 30, 1790, Boyd, vol. 16, p. 448; *Memorandum Book*, entries for December 11, 17 and 19, 1790, and January 8, 11 and 20, 1791; letter to Maria Jefferson, December 7, 1790, Boyd, vol. 18, pp. 141–42; letter to Thomas Leiper, August 16, 1791, Boyd, vol. 22, pp. 44–45; Dumbauld, *Tourist*, pp. 160–66; F. Kimball, *Architect*, pp. 151–54, figs. 122–124.

53. Letter to Martha Randolph, February 9, 1791, Betts and Bear, pp. 71–72.

54. Jefferson, *Garden Book*, p. 158; *Memorandum Book*, NN entry for September 2, 1791 ("pd. Leslie for an odometer 10 D."), entry for October 5, 1791.

55. [Phillips], *Early Proceedings*, January 7, 1791, p. 187.

56. "Report on the Fisheries," Boyd, vol. 19, pp. 140–237; see particularly pp. 206–20.

57. Letter to Robert R. Livingston, February 4, 1791, Boyd, vol. 19, pp. 240–41.

58. Letter to T. M. Randolph, Jr., February 24, 1791, Boyd, vol. 19, pp. 328–31; letter to David Rittenhouse, May 8, 1791, Boyd, vol. 20, pp. 382–83.

59. Letter from Harry Innes, July 8, 1790, Boyd, vol. 17, p. 20; letter to Harry Innes, March 7, 1791, Boyd, vol. 19, pp. 521–22; H. Phillips, *Early Proceedings*, p. 196.

60. Letter to Dr. David Ramsay, October 27, 1786, DLC; letter to George Wythe, June 13, 1790, DLC; letter to Benjamin Waterhouse, December 1, 1808, L&B, vol. 12, pp. 204–5.

61. [Phillips] *Early Proceedings*, pp. 193, 195, "Resolution" circular, April 17, 1792, APS, *Benjamin Smith Barton Papers*; *General Advertiser*, August 23, 1792; letter to Charles Thomson, April 20, 1791, Boyd, vol. 20, pp. 244–45.

62. Letter to T. M. Randolph, Jr., May 1, 1791, Boyd, vol. 20, pp. 341–42.

63. Letter to Benjamin Smith Barton and others, May 12, 1791, Boyd, vol. 20, p. 395; [Barton on Hessian fly], Boyd, vol. 20, pp. 245n, 395, 446–47; *Notes on the Northern Journey*," Boyd, vol. 20, pp. 445–62; Dumbauld, *Tourist*, pp. 172–76.
64. Letters to Mary Jefferson, May 8 and May 30, 1791, letter to M. J. Randolph, May 31, 1791, Betts and Bear, pp. 83–84, 84–85.
65. Letter to William Prince, July 6, 1791, MHi; letter from Joseph Fay, August 9, 1791, MHi; *Garden Book*, p. 159, 166–68; letter to William Drayton, May 1, 1791, DLC.
66. [Jefferson], "Notes on the Northern Journey," Boyd, vol. 20, pp. 445–62; Dumbauld, *Tourist*, pp. 172–77.
67. Letter to M. J. Randolph, June 23, 1791, Betts and Bear, pp. 85–86; Bemis, p. 83; Bowers, p. 79.
68. Letter from Benjamin Banneker, August 19, 1791, Boyd, vol. 22, pp. 49–54; letter to Benjamin Banneker, August 30, 1791, Boyd, vol. 22, pp. 97–98; Bedini, *Banneker*, pp. 150–62, 279–83; "Locating the Federal District," Boyd, vol. 19, pp. 41–43, fn. 119.
69. Letter to Condorcet, August 30, 1791, Boyd, vol. 22, pp. 98–99; Bedini, *Banneker*, pp. 158–59.
70. *Notes*, pp. 162–63; Chill, pp. 6–7; Miller, *Wolf*, pp. 100–103.
71. Letter from Condorcet, May 3, 1791, Boyd, vol. 20, pp. 353–60.
72. Bedini, *Banneker*, pp. 158–62; *Encyclopedia Brittanica*, 14th edition, vol. VI, pp. 222–23; *Index Biographique*, pp. 118–19.
73. Bedini, *Banneker*, pp. 280–83; 287–89; W. L. Smith, *Pretensions*, pp. 7–14; De Saussure, *Address*, p. 16; Fessenden, *Democracy Unveiled*, vol. II, p. 52n; Gregory, "Myth of the Founding Fathers," pp. 64–100; Miller, pp. 74–78.
74. *Notes*, pp. 162–63, 292; letter to Jean Pierre Brissot de Warville, February 11, 1788, Boyd, vol. 12, p. 577; Gregoire, pp. 211–12; letter to Henri Gregoire, February 25, 1809, Ford, vol. XI, pp. 99–100; letter to Joel Barlow, October 8, 1809, HAW, vol. V, 475–76; J. C. Miller, pp. 76–78.
75. *Memorandum Book*, entries for October 12–22, 1791; *Garden Book*, p. 172; Randall, vol. II, p. 23.
76. Letter to Daniel Hylton, January 20, 1783, Boyd, vol. 6, pp. 220–21.
77. Letter to Willian Ronald, September 20, 1790, Boyd, vol. 17, pp. 512–13; letter to Francis Eppes, October 8, 1790, Boyd, vol. 17, p. 581; letters to T. M. Randolph, Jr., February 13, 1792, DLC, and October 12, 1792, ViU; *Farm Book*, pp. 12–16.
78. Letters to Henry Remsen, Jr., November 13 and November 25, 1792, September 11, 1793, DLC; letter from Henry Remsen, Jr., November 19, 1792 and August 1, 1793, DLC; *Farm Book*, pp. 500–503; McLaughlin, pp. 318–19.
79. *Letter* to Samuel Biddle, December 12, 1792, MHi.
80. *Ibid.*
81. Sellers, *Museum*, pp. 57–58.
82. B. S. Barton, APS, Transactions, vol. 3, pp. 334–47.
83. Letter to Martha J. Randolph, January 15, 1792, Betts and Bear, p. 93; SNR, p. 200.
84. Letters from Joseph Gaston Chambers, August 13, October 10, and November 20, 1792, DNA; letter to Joseph Gaston Chambers, November 5, 1792, DLC; letter to J. W. Kittera, January 24, 1793, DLC.
85. Looney, "Joseph Gaston Chambers," (in preparation); B. R. Lewis, "Repeaters," pp. 38–42; Griffin, pp. 31–37, 41, 44.
86. "Astronomical Equatorial Instrument," UK Patent No. 1112, April 27, 1776; Ramsden, *Universal Equatorial*; Rees, *Cyclopaedia*, vol. XIII, unpaginated, "Ramsden's portable equatorial instrument;" DAB, vol. III, 182–83.
87. Letter to David Rittenhouse, August 12, 1792, DLC. DAB, vol. III, pp. 182–83. In his manuscript "List of Mathematical Instruments" Jefferson listed "An Equatorial by Ramsden 40–13." The sum of $102.67 was equal at that time to "23.6.4.
88. King, *Telescope*, pp. 162–70.
89. "Design for telescopic attachment to Universal Equatorial Instrument," N.D., MoHi; Invoice from W. & S. Jones, July 23, 1805.
90. Letter to Thomas Leiper, December 3, 1792, MHi; letter to George Washington, July 31, 1793, L&B, vol. 9, pp. 173–74; Jefferson, *Anas*, August 6, 1793, Ford, vol. I, pp. 310–15.
91. Letters to M. J. Randolph, December 31, 1792 and January 14, 1793, Betts and Bear, pp. 108–9.

CHAPTER IX. THE VEILING OF DIPLOMACY

1. *Memorandum Book*, NN, entries for January 9 and April 7, 1793; letter to Martha Jefferson Randolph, January 14, 1793, Betts & Bear, *Family Letters*, pp. 108–9; Randall, vol. II, p. 191; Scharf and Westcott, vol. I, p. 471.
2. Letter to George Washington, July 31, 1793, DLC; letter from George Washington, August 12, 1793, DLC; letter to Stephen Willis, November 12, 1792, MHi; *Garden Book*, p. 173.
3. Letter from Caspar Wistar to Moses Marshall, June 20, 1792, Jackson, *Letters*, vol. 2, p. 675; letter to Benjamin Smith Barton, December 2, 1792, DLC.
4. Subscription agreement, PPAmP, instructions to André Michaux, 30 April 1793, Jackson, *Letters*, vol. 2 pp. 669–73.
5. Chinard, "André and François-André Michaux," pp. 344–68; Malone, *Jefferson*, vol. 3, pp. 104–8; Turner, A. H. R. Report, vol. III, pp. 650—71.
6. H. P. Johnston, "Secret Service," pp. 95–105; Weber, pp. 118–24.
7. Peckham, "British Secret Writing," pp. 126–31; K. L. Ellis, "British Communication," pp. 159–67; Harvard College Library, *Sparks Manuscripts*, letter from George Washington to Benjamin Tallmadge, July 25, 1779; Weber, pp. 59, 71–72n, 77; Victor Hugo Paltsits, "The Use of Invisible Ink for Secret Writing During the American Revolution," *NYPL Bulletin*, vol. XXXIX, May 1935, pp. 361–65; Fitzpatrick, *Diaries*, vol. 2, p. 214; Morton Pennypacker, George Washington's Spies on Long Island and in New York (Brooklyn: L I Hist Soc, 1939), pp. 51 ff.; L. Bendikson, "The Restoration of Obliterated Passages and of Secret Writing in Diplomatic Missives," *Franco-American Review*, Revised, vol. I, 1937, pp. 243–56.
8. Kahn, pp. 181–86; Weber, pp. 27–35.
9. Burnett, p. 331; Peckham, pp. 128–29; DAB, vol. VI, pp. 438–39; Burnett, *Letters*, vol. VI, pp. 328–33; Weber, pp. 35–36, 82–86, 184–85.
10. Weber, pp. 56–59, 102–5, Kahn, p. 185.
11. Weber, pp. 102–5.
12. Letter from William Carmichael, June 25, 1785, Boyd, vol. 8, p. 251.
13. Metral, *Blaise de Vigenere*; Kahn, pp. 191–92.
14. Tomlinson, pp. 16–26.
15. *Encyclopédie anciénne*, vol. II (1751), vol. IX (1771); *Encyclopédie méthodique*; Tomlinson, pp. 16–26.
16. Communication from Julian P. Boyd, September 26, 1977.
17. *Memorandum Book*, entry for April 21, 1792; [P. P. Prime], *Prime Directory*, Ms. PPAmP; W. J. Bell, "Addenda," pp. 131–70.
18. Communications from Mr. Charles L. Granquist, Jr., then Assistant Director, Thomas Jefferson Memorial Foundation.
19. Bedini, *Desk*, pp. 5–7; Campbell, [Isaac], p. 18.
20. Letter to Robert Patterson, March 22, 1802, DLC letter from Robert Patterson, December 19, 1801; letters from Robert Patterson, April 12 and April 17, 1802; letter to Robert Patterson, April 17, 1802; letter from Patterson, April 24, 1802, DLC, f. 21071, ff. 21119–20, 27086–8; Weber, pp. 170—7. Kahn, pp. 194–95.
21. Kahn, p. 195; Weber, pp. 183–84.
22. Letter to Robert Patterson, March 22, 1802, DLC.
23. Letter from Robert Patterson, April 12, 1802, DLC; letter to Robert R. Livingston, April 18, 1802, DLC; Weber, pp. 175–77.
24. Letter from Hugh Williamson [date uncertain, 1785 or 1802]; letter to Hugh Williamson, December 11, 1784, Boyd, vol. 7, pp. 569–70; letter to Hugh Williamson, February 6, 1785, Boyd, vol. 7, pp. 641–43; Weber, pp. 178, 189.
25. DLC, f. 22138, f. 41575.
26. Communication from the late Julian P. Boyd, September 26, 1977.
27. Weber, pp. 147–48n, 152.
28. Bazeries, *Chiffres secrets*; Kahn, pp. 246–50
29. Memorandum from Colonel Parker Hitt to the Director, Army Signal School, December 19, 1914, *Hitt Papers*, Kahn, pp. 324–25.
30. Letter from Major General Joseph O. Mauborgne, USA Ret., to Colonel William F. Friedman, August 16, 1945, The George C. Marshall Memorial Library, *Friedman Collection*, Kahn, p. 325.

31. Letter from Major General Joseph O. Mauborgne, USA Ret., August 16, 1947, to Colonel William F. Friedman, The George C. Marshall Memorial Library, *Friedman Collection*.
32. Signal Corps, U. S. Army, Specifications No. 72–26, May 20, 1921, The George C. Marshall Memorial Library, *Friedman Collection*; Kahn, p. 585.
33. Letters from Edmund C. Burnett to Professor John M. Manly, February 13 and March 14, 1922, The University of Chicago, The Joseph Regenstein Library, *Manly Papers*.
34. Letter from William F. Friedman to John M. Manly, April 12, 1922, University of Chicago, The Joseph Regenstein Library, *Manly Papers*.
35. *Report of the Chief Signal Officer to the Secretary of War* (Washington, Government Printing Office, 1919); Kahn, p. 385.
36. Chief Signal Officer, United States War Department, *Instructions for Cipher Device Type M-94*; Kruh, pp. 20—21; Kahn, p. 585.
37. Letter to George Washington, September 9, 1792, Ford, vol. VI, p. 108; [Malone, *Jefferson*, vol. III, pp. 8–20, 69–73; Schachner, pp. 503–6.
38. Schachner, pp. 507–8.
39. Letter to T. M. Randolph, Jr. August 25, 1793, DLC; letters to James Madison, September 1, 1793, September 8, 1793, Ford, vol. VIII, pp. 11–14, 32–34; letter to James Madison, September 12, 1793, DLC; letter to Martha J. Randolph, September 8, 1793, Morgan Library, *Jefferson Papers*; letter to George Washington, September 15, 1793, Ford, vol. VIII, 45–46.
39. Letter to T. M. Randolph, Jr. September 15, 1793, DLC; Schachner, p. 508.
40. Letter from Andrew Ellicott, November 26, 1792, DLC; letter to Andrew Ellicott, January 15, 1794, DLC.
41. Bedini, "Clock Designer," p. 166.
42. DAB, vol. VI, pp. 184–5; Eckhardt, pp. 182, 193; *Philadelphia City Directory*, 1794 to 1806; "The Great Clock," Ms. DLC, 233 fol. 41588; Bedini, "Clock Designer," pp. 165–67.
43. Letter from Robert Leslie, July 10, 1793, DLC; letter to Robert Leslie, December 12, 1793, DLC, ViU, *Edgehill Randolph Papers*.
44. Bedini, "Clock Designer," p. 168; letter from Robert Leslie, July 10, 1793, DLC; letter to Robert Leslie, December 12, 1793, DLC; letter from Robert Leslie, February 13, 1803, DLC; *Memorandum Book*, NN, entry for April 27, 1793.
45. Letter to Moses Cox, September 17, 1793, MHi; letter from George Washington, August 12, 1793, HAW, vol. XXXIII, p. 45.
46. Letter from Edmond C. Genêt, September 18, 1793, *American State Papers*, Foreign Relations, vol. I, pp. 173–74; letter to Genêt, September 15, 1793, Ford, vol. VIII, pp. 46–47; Jefferson to Genêt, Georg Hammond, et al, November 8, 1793, Ford, vol. VIII, pp. 60—63; letter to Genêt, December 31, 1793, Ford, vol. VIII, pp. 135–36.
47. Letter to Thomas Pinckney, November 27, 1793, DLC.
48. Letter to John Jones, December 26, 1792, DLC; letter from William and Samuel Jones, March 9, 1793, DLC.
49. Letter to David Rittenhouse, September 6, 1793, letter sold at auction sale as Lot 331 on March 11, 1970 by Samuel Freeman of Philadelphia.
50. Letter to Martha Jefferson Randolph, December 22, 1793, Ford. vol. VIII, pp. 124–25; letter to T. M. Randolph, Jr., December 30, 1793, DLC; letter from George Washington, January 1, 1794, HAW, vol. XXXIII, p. 231.
51. Letter to Eli Whitney, November 16, 1793, Ford, vol. VIII, pp. 70—71; letter from Eli Whitney, November 24, 1793, quoted in Mirsky and Nevins, pp. 88–89; Mirsky and Nevins, pp. 90—93; Battison, pp. 8–10.

CHAPTER X. ROSINANTE STABLED

1. Letter to George Washington, May 14, 1794, L&B, vol. IX, p. 287.
2. *Notes*, pp. 166–68; 180–84; letter to George Washington, June 28, 1793, L&B, vol. IX, pp. 141–42; letter to James Madison, June 29, 1793, DLC; letter to T. M. Randolph, Jr., July 28, 1793, DLC; letter to John Taylor, May 1, 1794, Ford, vol. VIII, pp. 145–46; *Farm Book*, p. 188–92.
3. *Garden Book*, pp. 208, 211–12; Farm Book, p. 78, 314–16; Kelso, pp. 43–44.
4. [Isaac], *Memoirs*, p. 18.

5. Letter to Philip Mazzei, May 30, 1795, DLC; letter to Henry Knox, June 1, 1795, MHi.
6. Letter to George Washington, April 25, 1794, L&B, vol. IX, pp. 283–84.
7. Letter to George Wythe, October 24, 1794, DLC.
8. *Farm Book*, pp. 68–74; letter from George Washington, August 21, 1791, DLC; letter to Thomas Pinckney, June 24, 1792, CtY; letter to Thomas Pinckney, November 8, 1792, DLC; letter from Thomas Pinckney, February 10, 1793, DLC; letter to Thomas Pinckney, April 12, 1793, DLC; letter to Thomas Pinckney, December 12, 1793, CtY; letter from Thomas Pinckney, January 29, 1794, DLC; letter to Thomas Pinckney, September 8, 1795, DLC; *Memorandum Book*, NN, entry for December 12, 1793.
9. Letter to George Washington, June 19, 1796, L&B, vol. IX, pp. 342–43.
10. Letter to Thomas Mann Randolph, January 11, 1796, DLC; letter to Edward Rutledge, December 27, 1796, DLC. letter to Mr. Booker, October 4, 1796, MHi; *Farm Book*, pp. 68–69.
11 *Farm Book*, p. 77.
12. Letter from John Taylor, May 1, 1794, Ford, vol. VIII, pp. 145–46; letter from John Taylor, November 19, 1797, DLC; *Memorandum Book*, NN, entry for December 21, 1797; letter from John Taylor, March 25, 1798, DLC; letter to John Taylor, April 6, 1798, DLC.
13. Letter to Henry Remsen, October 30, 1794, Yale University, *Franklin Collection*, Papers of Thomas Jefferson; letter to Joseph Leacock, November 24, 1792, DLC; letters from Joseph Leacock, November 25 and December 10, 1792, DLC; *Farm Book*, pp. 495–500; Lavoisier, *Art of manufacturing alkaline salts and potashes*; [Samuel Hopkins], "Address;" Multhauf, "Potash," pp. 227–40.
14. Letter to Caleb Lownes, December 18, 1793, DLC; *Farm Book*, pp. 426–53; Keene, pp. 7–9; Bear, "Nails," p. 47.
15. *Farm Book*, p. 427; letter to James Lyle, July 10, 1795, MHi; "Agreement with James Anderson for Nailers," February 9, 1781, Boyd, vol. 4, p. 566.
16. "Memorandum to Edmund Bacon," Pierson, p. 53; letter to T. M. Randolph, Jr., January 23, 1801, MHi; Oriol Pi-Sunyer, pp. 226–34; Shayt, *Nailery*, unpublished manuscript; Kelso, p. 44.
17. *Nailery Account Book*, Clark Memorial Library, UCLA; *Memorandum Book*, NYHS; Bear, "Nails," pp. 49–50; *Farm Book*, pp. 426–52; Keene, pp. 3–8.
18. Letter to Jean N. Démeunier, April 29, 1795, Ford, vol. VIII, pp. 174–75; letter to William Temple, April 26, 1795, MHi; letter to James Lyle, July 10, 1795, MHi; *Farm Book*, p. 426.
19. *Nailery Account Book*; Shayt, pp. 75–76; letter to Archibald Stuart, January 3, 1796, ViHi, *Papers of Archibald Stuart*; *Farm Book*, pp. 431–32.
20. Letter to William Temple, April 26, 1795, MHi; letter to James Lyle, July 10, 1795, MHi; letter to Henry Remsen, July 1795, Shayt, pp. 80–81; letter from Henry Remsen, April 30, 1795 and letter to Henry Remsen, June 18, 1795, quoted in Shayt, pp. 80–81; letter to Archibald Stuart, February 22, 1796, VHi, *Stuart Papers*; letter from Benjamin Perkins, May 15, 1801, MHi; *Farm Book*, pp. 427–28.
21. Letter to Archibald Stuart, June 11, 1795, VHi, *Stuart Papers*; letter to T. M. Randolph, January 11, 1796, DLC; letter to Benjamin Jones, March 4, 1815, MHi; letter from Benjamin Jones, March 25, 1815, MHi; *Farm Book*, p. 428.
22. Letter to David Williams, November 14, 1803, L&B, vol. X, p. 429.
23. *Ibid*, p. 431; *Farm Book*, pp. 464–65; letter to William Maclure, September 10, 1811, MHi; letter to William Thornton, January 14, 1812, DLC; letter to Thaddeus Kosciusko, June 28, 1812, DLC; Pierson, p. 69.
24. Letter to Henry Remsen, October 30, 1794, CtY; letter to Mann Page, August 30, 1795, L&B, vol. IX, p. 306; letter to Thomas Mann Randolph, January 11, 1796.
25. Letter to Colonel Samuel Blackden, December 11, 1794, DLC; *Garden Book*, p. 212.
26. *Garden Book*, pp. 226–27; letter to George Wythe, April 18, 1795, DLC; letters to T. M. Randolph, Jr., February 12, and February 19, 1795, DLC; *Farm Book*, facsimile, pp. 45–47.
27. H. B. Adams, pp. 21–30; *Virginia Gazette*, July 1, 1786; Quesnay de Beaurepaire, *Memoir and Prospectus Concerning the Academy of Sciences and Fine Arts in the United States of America, Established at Richmond, the Capital of Virginia, by the Chevalier Quesnay de Beaurepaire* (Paris, 1788) [copy in the Virginia State Library]; Richard H. Gaines, pp. 167–75.
28. H. B. Adams, pp. 45–46; R. B. Davis, pp. 59–61; Duveen and Glickstein, pp. 280–85.
29. Letter to François d'Ivernois, February 6, 1795, Ford, vol. VII, pp. 2–4.
30. H. B. Adams, p. 45.

31. Patterson, "An Easy and accurate method," pp. 154–61; *Garden Book*, pp. 226–31.
32. Letter from Jonathan Williams, January 24, 1796, DLC; Williams, "Barometrical Measurement," APS *Transactions*, vol. 4, pp. 216–23.
33. Letter to Jonathan Williams, July 3, 1796, L&B, vol. IX, pp. 346–48.
34. *Ibid.*
35. *Notes*, pp. 80–81, 280.
36. Letter to Jonathan Williams, July 3, 1796, DLC.
37. "*Memorandums*," Boyd, vol. 11, pp. 415–64; Ardrey, pp. 5–9; M. L. Wilson, "Mouldboard Plow," pp. 59–64; Willich, vol. IV, pp. 288.
38. "Memoranda," Boyd, vol. 11, pp. 415–64; letter to John Taylor, December 29, 1794, MHi; Cousins, "Plowmaker," pp. 34–37; M. L. Wilson, "Farmer," pp. 216–20.
39. Letter from Robert Patterson, March 29, 1798, MHi; letter to John Taylor, December 29, 1794, L&B, vol. XVIII, p. 199; letter to Robert Patterson, March 27, 1798, L&B, vol. X, pp. 15–16; letters to Robert Patterson, March 30 and March 31, 1798, DLC; letter to John Taylor, June 4, 1798, MHi.
40. Letter to John Taylor, June 8, 1795, DLC; letter to Robert Patterson, March 27, 1798 L&B, vol. X, pp. 15–16; letter to Sir John Sinclair, March 23, 1798, APS *Transactions*, Old series, vol. 4, 1799, pp. 313–222.
41. Letter from William Strickland, July 16, 1798, DLC; letter to A. F. Sylvestre, May 29, 1807, Padover, *Complete Jefferson*, pp. 997–98; letter to A. F. Sylvestre, July 15, 1808 L&B, vol. 12, pp. 88–90; "D'une oreille de charrue," pp. 322–31; Guillaume and Chaudun, pp. 137–41.
42. Letter to M. Giroud, May 22, 1797, L&B, vol. IX, pp. 387–88; letter from Allen Jones, August 20, 1797, MoHi; letter from Samuel Maverick, March 4, 1822, *Garden Book*, p. 602.
43. "Diary for 1796," *Farm Book*, facsimile, p. 54; letter to T. M. Randolph, Jr., February 29, 1796, DLC; letter to John Taylor, April 6, 1798, DLC.
44. Letter to Volney, April 10, 1796, DLC; *Garden Book*, pp. 240–41.
45. Letter to T. M. Randolph, Jr., November 28, 1796, MHi; letter to James Madison, December 17, 1796, L&B, vol. IX, p. 352.
46. Hillairet, p. 224; Champier, p. 116; Tableau, Tome I, pp. 55–61; Nichols and Bear, *Monticello*, p. 39; Pierson, p. 125, n. 40; McLaughlin, pp. 256, 412.
47. Nichols and Bear, p. 39; M. B. Smith, *First Forty Years*, pp. 387–77.
48. [Isaac], *Memoirs*, p. 12, Pierson, p. 125, n. 40.
49. M. B. Smith, *First Forty Years*, p. 392.
50. [Isaac], *Memoirs*, p. 18; M. B. Smith, *First Forty Years*, pp. 384–86; M. B. Smith, "Winter," p. 227; McLaughlin, pp. 321–23, 373.
51. Randall, vol. II, pp. 302–7; *Garden Book*, pp. 241–45; Weld, *Travels*, vol. I, pp. 206–8; Chinard, *Volney et l'Amerique*, pp. 38–40.
52. W. L. Smith, *Pretensions*; letters to T. M. Randolph, Jr., April 11 and November 28, 1796, DLC and MHi; letter to James Madison, December 17, 1796, Ford, vol. VII, p. 92.
53. Letter to Edward Rutledge, December 27, 1796, [L&B, vol. XVIII, p. 352] Ford, vol. VII, p. 93; letter to Dr. Benjamin Rush, January 1797, Ford, vol. VII, p. 113.
54. Letter to James Madison, January 1, 1797, Ford, vol. VII, p. 98.
55. Letter from John Stuart, July 13, 1796, Preston, p. 8.
56. Letter from John Stuart, April 11, 1796, Preston, p. 6; letter to John Stuart, May 26, 1796, Preston, p. 7.
57. Letter to John Stuart, November 10, 1796, Ford, vol. VII, pp. 90–91.
58. Letter to David Rittenhouse, July 3, 1796, PPAmP; letter from Benjamin Smith Barton, August 1, 1796, PPAmP; H. F. Osborn, "Pioneer," pp. 410–13.
59. Jefferson, "Memoir on the discovery," pp. 255–56; Boyd, "Megalonyx," pp. 420–35; H. F. Osborn, "Paleontologist," p. 537.
60. Letter from Thomas Pinckney, enclosing letter from Louis, Prince of Parma, May 29, 1797, L&B, vol. IX, p. 388; letter to Charles Willson Peale, June 5, 1796, Sellers, PMHB, p. 136; letter from Charles Willson Peale, June 22, 1796, DLC.
61. Letter to Louis, Prince of Parma May 23, 1797, L&B, XIX, pp. 115–19.
62. Letter from the Prince of Parma, March 30, 1798, DLC; letter from Peale to the Prince of Parma, February 21, 1799, PPAmP, *Peale Papers*; C. W. Peale, *Diary*, entries for June 28 and June 29, 1804, PPAmP, *Peale Papers*; Prince of Parma's list of desiderata, Smithsonian Institu-

tion Archives, *Peale Papers*; letter to the Prince of Parma, February 25, 1799, DLC; C. W. Peale, *Diary*, May 30, 1804, PPAmP, *Peale Papers*; C. C. Sellers, *Museum*, pp. 163–64.

63. Letters to James Madison, January 22 and January 30, 1797, Ford, vol. VII, pp. 107, 116; letter to T. M. Randolph, Jr., January 22, 1797, DLC; *Minerva* (Philadelphia), March 4, 1797; *Memorandum Book*, entries for March 3 to March 13, 1797; Randall, vol. 2, p. 334.

64. Boyd, vol. 14, pp. xxv–xxxiv, 504–5; Boyd, "Megalonyx," pp. 425–32; Preston, pp. 10–11.

65. Jefferson, "Memoir on the discovery," pp. 246–60; Boyd, vol. 14, pp. 504–5.

66. Letter from William Carmichael, January 26, 1789, Boyd, vol. 14, pp. xxv–xxxiv, 498–505; letter to William Carmichael, May 8, 1789, L&B, vol. 7, pp. 335–38.

67. Letter from American Philosophical Society, January 7, 1797, APS *Transactions*, vol. 4, 1799, pp. xi–xii; letter from Benjamin Rush, January 4, 1797, DLC; Randall, vol. II, p. 334.

68. Jefferson, " "Memoir on the discovery," pp. 259–60; Boyd, "Megalonyx," pp. 433–34.

69. Wistar, "Description of the bones," pp. 526–31.

70. [Garriga], Boyd, vol. 14, xxix–xxxi.

71. Cuvier, "Squelette fossile," pp. 637–38; Desmarest, Part II, p. 366.

CHAPTER XI. "HONORABLE AND EASY"

1. *Memorandum Book*, NN, entries for March 10 and March 13, 1797; Randall, vol. II. pp. 199–200.

2. Notice from APS, January 7, 1797; letter to secretary of the APS, January 28, 1797, APS, *Transactions*, vol. IV, pp. xi–xiii.

3. [H. Phillips], *Early Proceedings*, p. 258.

4. *Memorandum Book*, NN, entry for June 14, 1797.

5. Letter to John Wise, February 12, 1798, *American Historical Review*, vol. III, pp. 488–89.

6. Letter to Elbridge Gerry, June 21, 1797, L&B , vol. IX, p. 405.

7. Letter to Elbridge Gerry, June 21, 1797, L&B, vol. IX, p. 405.

8. Letter to Elbridge Gerry, January 28, 1799, L&B, vol. X, p. 78.

9. Letter to James Madison, July 24, 1797, Ford, vol. VIII, p. 321.

10. Letter to Maria Jefferson, March 11, 1797, Betts and Bear, p. 141; letter to Martha Jefferson Randolph, June 8, 1797, Betts and Bear, pp. 145–47; letters to Maria Jefferson, June 14, 1797 and January 7, 1798, Betts and Bear, *Family Letters*, pp. 148–49, 151–53.

11. Letter from Mary Jefferson Eppes, December 8, 1797, Betts and Bear, pp. 149–50; *Memorandum Book*, NN, entry for October 13, 1797.

12. [H. Phillips], *Early Proceedings*, January 19, 1798, pp. 266–67; *Transactions*, APS, vol. 4, pp. xxxiv–xxxv.

13. Letter to Thomas Willing, February 23, 1798, DLC.

14. *Notes*, pp. 225–58, 298–301; Randall, vol. III, pp. 206–10; Schachner, pp. 228–29.

15. Letter to the Reverend James Madison, March 4, 1798, DLC; letter from the Reverend James Madison, March 13, 1798, DLC; letter to the Reverend James Madison, April 1, 1798, DLC; letter from the Reverend James Madison, April 15, 1798, DLC; letter from Joseph Elgar, Jr., November 24, 1801, DLC.

16. Malone, *Jefferson*, vol. 3, pp. 397–409; [Phillips], *Early Proceedings*, pp. 258.

17. [Phillips], *Early Proceedings*, February 19, 1796, p. 237; Barton, "Observations and Conjectures," APS *Transactions*, vol. IV, 1799, pp. 179–81.

18. H. E. Osborn, 1935, p. 535; letter from the Reverend Ezra Stiles, July 7, 1785, Boyd, vol. 8, p. 300; letter to Robert R. Livingston, December 14, 1800, Ford, vol. IX, pp. 150–54; letter to Caspar Wistar, February 3, 1801, DLC; [H. Phillips], *Early Proceedings*, p. 258; Bedini, "Paleontology," pp. 10–12.

19. Letter to John Taylor, December 29, 1794, DLC, *Garden Book*, pp. 220–23; DAB, vol. IX, pp. 331–33.

20. Letter to John Taylor, October 8, 1797, MHi, *Garden Book*, p. 258.

21. Letter from John Taylor, March 23, 1798, DLC; letter to John Taylor, April 6, 1798, DLC; *Farm Book*, pp. 74–75; letter to John Taylor, June 4, 1798, L&B, vol. XVIII, pp. 205–9.

22. *Farm Book*, pp. 426–53; letter to Samuel Clarke, September 25, 1798, MHi; letters to John McDowell, September 25, October 22, 1798, February 1 and November 12, 1800, DLC.

23. Letter to Robert R. Livingston, February 28, 1799, L&B, vol. X, pp. 117–18; [Phillips], *Early Proceedings*, p. 280.
24. *Farm Book*, pp. 325, 334–35, 351–53, 363–65; letter to David Call, September 28, 1799, Boston Public Library, Manuscripts Collection; E. L. Adams, "Bicentenary," pp. 153, 157–58.
25. Letter to Joseph Priestley, December 18, 1799, Ford, vol. VII, pp. 404–09; letter to Joseph Priestley, January 18, 1800, L&B, vol. X, pp. 138–43; letter to Joseph Priestley, January 27, 1800, L&B, vol. X, pp. 146–48; letter from Joseph Priestley, enclosing "Hints Concerning Public Education," May 8, 1800, DLC.
26. Letters to Pierre Samuel Du Pont de Nemours, January 17 and April 12, 1800, DLC; letters from Pierre Samuel Du Pont de Nemours, April 21, June 15, August 14, and November 8, 1800, DLC; letter to Pierre Samuel Du Pont de Nemours, December 12, 1800, DLC; Bruce, vol. I, pp. 63–65.
27. Letter to George Wythe, January 22, 1797, L&B, vol. IX, p. 370; letter from George Wythe, February 1, 1797, DLC.
28. Jefferson, *Manual*, MHi; Randall, vol. II, p. 356.
29. Letter to George Wythe, February 18, 1800, Ford, vol. IX, pp. 113–17; letter to George Wythe, April 7, 1800, DLC; letter from George Wythe, December 8, 1800, DLC; letter to Edmund Pendleton, April 19, 1800, DLC; letter from Edmund Pendleton, June 17, 1800, DLC; Randall, vol.II, pp. 356–57.
30. Swanstrom, *Senate*, pp. 6–8; Malone, *Jefferson*, vol. III, pp. 452–53; E. S. Brown, "Manual," p. 148; Jefferson, *Manual*, L&B, vol. II, pp. 331–450; M. B. Smith, *First Forty Years*, pp. 6–8.
31. U. S. H. R., *Manual*, p. 105n; E. S. Brown, *Manual*, pp. 144–48.
32. Letter to T. M. Randolph, Jr., May 7, 1800, DLC; J. C. Miller, *Hamilton*, pp. 520–24; *Aurora* (Philadelphia), October 22, 1800; letter to T. M. Randolph, Jr, November 30, 1800, DLC; D. W. Adams, *Jefferson's Extracts*, pp. 4–12.
33. [H. Phillips, *Early Proceedings*, p. 307; letter to APS, January 25, 1801, PPAmP.
34. Letter to Hugh Williamson, January 10, 1801, Ford, vol. VII, pp. 479–81.
35. Letter to William Dunbar, January 12, 1801, L&B, vol. X, pp. 191–93.
36. Letter from Andrew Ellicott, May 28, 1800, DLC; letter to Andrew Ellicott, December 18, 1800, L&B, vol. XIX, pp. 121–22.
37. Letter to Samuel Smith, August 22, 1798, L&B, vol. X, pp. 55–59.
38. *City Gazette and Daily-Advertiser* (Charleston, S. C.), May 5, 1801; June 24, 1801; July 13, 1801; *Aurora* (Philadelphia), September 8, 1800; February 23, 1801, DAB, vol. IX, pp. 530–31; letter from George Helmbold, Jr., April 3, 1801, National Archives and Records Service, Record Group 59, Letters of Application and Recommendation.
39. M. B. Smith, *First Forty Years*, p. 12.
40. Smith, *First Forty Years*, pp. 13–15.
41. Letter to Jonathan Williams, January 10, 1801, Ford, vol. VII, pp. 479–81; letter to William Dunbar, January 12, 1801, L&B, vol. X, pp. 191–93; letter to Benjamin Hawkins, November 6, 1800, DLC.
42. Letter to William Dunbar, January 12, 1801, L&B, vol. X, pp. 192–93.
43. Letter to Robert R. Livingston, February 24, 1801, L&B, vol. X, p. 210; letter from Robert R. Livingston, January 7, 1801, DLC; letter to Caspar Wistar, February 3, 1801, L&B, vol. X, pp. 196–97.
44. Mirsky and Nevins, pp. 216–21; C. McL. Green, *Whitney*, pp. 55–62, 100–109, 118–43.
45. Letter to Meriwether Lewis, February 23, 1801, Jackson, *L & C Letters*, vol. I, pp. 2–3.
46. 52. *Ibid*; letter to General James Wilkinson, February 23, 1801, Jackson, *L & C Letters*, vol. I, pp. 1–3.
47. Letter from Meriwether Lewis, March 10, 1801, Jackson, *L & C Letters*, vol. I, p. 3.
48. [M. Lewis], Roster, DLC; Jackson, "Reduction of the United States Army," pp. 91–96.
49. Jefferson, Farewell Speech as Vice-President, February 28, 1801, Padover, *Complete Jefferson*, pp. 383–84.
50. Letter to John W. Eppes, March 27, 1801, ViU; SNR, pp. 307–8; Schachner, pp. 670–72.
51. Letter from Abigail Adams, May 10, 1804, Cappon, vol. I, pp. 268–69; letter to Abigail Adams, June 13, 1804, Cappon, vol. I, p. 270.
52. *Jeffersonian Democrat* (Charlottesville), January 19, 1876.
53. Letter to John Dickinson, March 6, 1801, L&B, vol. X, pp. 217–18.

CHAPTER XII. "SPLENDID MISERY"

1. Dispatch from Edward Thornton to Lord Grenville, March 4, 1801, *Dispatches of the British Ministers*; *National Intelligencer*, March 6, 1801; J. Davis, *Travels*, p. 177; Stimpson, pp. 267–68; Randall, vol. 2, pp. 630–31.
2. [Jefferson], Inaugural Address, March 4, 1801, Padover, *Complete Jefferson*, pp. 384–87; *National Intelligencer*, March 6, 1801; M. B. Smith, *First Forty Years*, pp. 25–26; *The Daily Advertiser* (New York), March 2, 1801.
3. Bryan, *History*, vol. 1, p. 406; Davis, *Travels*, pp. 171–72; M. B. Smith, *First Forty Years*, p. 384; Abigail Adams, *Letters*, pp. 382–88; Abigail Adams, *New Letters*, pp. 255–60; Hurd, pp. 30–36; Singleton, vol. I, pp. 15–16.
4. Letter to Benjamin Rush, December 20, 1801, L&B, vol. X, p. 303–4; Hurd, pp. 30–33; Randall, vol. 2, pp. 666–67.
5. A. Foster, pp. 10–11; Thomas Moore, "Epistle VII. To Thomas Hume, Esq., M.D.," Epistles, pp. 209–15.
6. M. B. Smith, *First Forty Years*, pp. 398–400; L. H. Butterfield, "Leland," pp. 214–23; J. Davis, *Travels*, pp. 329–30; *Commercial Advertiser* (New York), December 7, 1801.
7. Letter to T. M. Randolph, Jr., January 1, 1802, DLC; Singleton, vol. 1, pp. 42–54; *Memorandum Book*, NN, entry for January 4, 1802; L. H. Butterfield, "Leland," pp. 223–29; *Impartial Observer* (Providence, R. I.), August 8, 1801; *Hampshire Gazette*, August 18, 1801; poem in the *Mercury and New-England Palladium*, September 8, 1801; H. T. Upton, pp. 165–66; Boller, pp. #35–36.
8. B. Mayo, "Peppercorn," pp. 222–28; *National Intelligencer*, January 20, 1802; *New York Evening Post*, March 5, 1802; letter from the Reverend Manasseh Cutler to Dr. Joseph Torrey, January 4, 1802, in Cutler and Cutler, *Life*, vol. II, pp. 66–67.
9. SNR, pp. 288–90; *Farm Book*, pp. 99–101; Malone, *Jefferson*, vol. 4, p. 41; M. B. Smith, *First Forty Years*, pp. 394–95.
10. M. B. Smith, *First Forty Years*, p. 393.
11. Letter from William Plumer to Jeremiah Smith, December 9, 1802, DLC, *Papers of William Plumer*.
12. E. S. Brown, pp. 245–46, 212–13; Upton, pp. 165–66; M. Smith, pp. 34–37; letter from Anthony Merry to Lord Hawkesbury, December 6, 1803, *Dispatches of the British Ministers to the United States from the Foreign Office, 1801–1805*, vol. V, p. 41; letter from Rufus King to Christopher Gore, January 4, 1804, King, vol. IV, p. 340; letter to William Short, January 23, 1804, *American Historical Review*, July 1928, p. 833; letter from S. L. Mitchill to his wife, January 10, 1802, *Harper's New Monthly Magazine, vol. LVIII*, 1879, pp. 743–44; Hurd, White House, pp. 30–32; M. Kimball, "Epicure" pp. 72–73.
13. Letter from William Short, February 11, 1789, Boyd, vol. 14, pp. 540–41; Bernard Mayo, "Peppercorn," p. 231; M. Kimball, "Epicure," pp. 71–81.
14. M. B. Smith, *First Forty Years*, pp. 37, 387–92; M. Kimball, "Epicure," p. 80; Singleton, vol. 1, pp. 31–39.
16. M. B. Smith, *First Forty Years*, pp. 387–88; M. Smith, p. 37; letter from William Short, August 4, 1790, Boyd, vol. 17, pp. 315–18; Granquist, *Furniture*, pp. 33–35, 58–59; M. Kimball, "Epicure," p. 80.
17. M. B. Smith, *First Forty Years*, pp. 387–88, 392; M. B. Smith, *A Winter in Washington*, vol. II, p. 34; Bryan, vol. 1, p. 406; *Alexandria Advertiser*, May 25, 1801; [Jefferson], Memorandum to Commissioners of Public Buildings, August 19, 1801, Padover, *Complete Jefferson*, pp. 226–27.
18. M. B. Smith, *First Forty Years*, p. 384; Klapthor, "First Lady," *Historic Preservation*, vol. XV, No. 3, 1963, pp. 88–93; M. Kimball, "White House Furnishings," *Antiques*, June 1929, pp. 485–86; letter to Gouverneur Morris, May 8, 1801, Ford, vol. VIII, pp. 48–50; letter to Gouverneur Morris, November 1, 1801, DLC.
19. M. B. Smith, *First Forty Years*, p. 385.
20. "Surveyorship of Public Buildings," Latrobe, *Correspondence*, vol. 1, pp. 259–60; Scheffel, pp. 138–39, 178–80; *Garden Book*, pp. 42, 93; letter to M. J. Randolph, June 10, 1793, Betts and Bear, p. 120; letter to Martha Jefferson Randolph, May 21, 1787, Betts and Bear, pp. 41–42; M. B. Smith, *First Forty Years*, p. 385.
21. M. Smith, *A Winter in Washington*, p. 38; McLaughlin, p. 372; E. T. Martin, "Scientist," p. 46.

22. M. B. Smith, *First Forty Years*, p. 385; Monticello, *Construction Files*, communication from Charles L. Granquist, April 13, 1981.

23. Letter from T. M. Randolph, Jr., April 22, 1798, ViU, Alderman Library; *Farm Book*, p. 436.

24. *Medical Repository*, vol. 4, 1801, pp. 211–14; C. C. Sellers, *Museum*, pp. 113–14; letter to C. W. Peale, July 29, 1801, Sellers, "Letters," (hereafter PMHB), p. 137; letters from C. W. Peale, June 29 and July 25, 1801, PPAmP, *Peale Papers*

25. C. C. Sellers, *Museum*, pp. 142–48.

26. Letter from C. W. Peale, January 12, 1802, DLC.

27. Letter to C. W. Peale, January, 16, 1802, Sellers, PMHB, pp. 138–39.

28. C. C. Sellers, *Museum*, pp. 151–54; "The Substance of an address intended to be presented to the Legislature of Pennsylvania. in 1802 by C. W. Peale," DLC; letter from C. W. Peale to Andrew Ellicott, February 28, 1802, PPAmP, Peale Papers; *Poulson's American Daily Advertiser*, February 19 and 27, March 24, 1802; C. W. Peale to the Councils, March 1802; PPAmP, *Peale Papers*; letter from C. W. Peale to Samuel Wetherill, March 24, 1802, PPAmP, *Peale Papers*.

29. Letter to C. W. Peale, May 5, 1802, Sellers, PMHB, p. 139.

30. C. Kahn, "History of Smallpox," pp. 597–609; Bernstein, pp. 228 et seq.; Stearn and Stearn, pp. 34–65.

31. Rochefoucauld-Liancourt, *Travels*, vol. III, pp. 79–80; Blanton, pp. 60–66.

32. DAB, vol. X, pp. 529–32; Hawes, pp. 7–50; *Columbian Centinel*, March 12, 1799.

33. Letter from Dr. Benjamin Waterhouse to John Adams, September 2, 1800; letter from John Adams to Dr. Benjamin Waterhouse, September 10, 1800, Harvard University, Countway Library.

34. Letter from Dr. Benjamin Waterhouse, December 1, 1800, DLC; letter to Dr. Benjamin Waterhouse, December 25, 1800, MHi; H. A. Martin, pp. 19–21.

35. Letter from Dr. Benjamin Waterhouse, May 28, 1801, DLC; letter from Benjamin Waterhouse, June 8, 1801, DLC; letter to Benjamin Waterhouse, June 26, 1801, Harvard University, Countway Library; Reverend Dr. Edward Gantt (1746–1837), Appleton, vol. 2, p. 590; Weis, p. 44.

36. Letter from Dr. Benjamin Waterhouse, July 17, 1801, DLC.

37. Letter to Martha Jefferson Randolph, July 16, 1801, Betts and Bear, *Family Letters*, pp. 207–8.

38. Letter to Dr. Benjamin Waterhouse, July 25, 1801, Harvard University, Countway Library.

39. Letter from Dr. Benjamin Waterhouse, July 26, 1801, DLC; letters to Benjamin Waterhouse, August 8 and 14, 1801, Harvard University, Countway Library; Hening, *Statutes*, vols. VIII and IX.

40. Letter to Dr. Benjamin Waterhouse, August 14 and August 21, 1801, Harvard University, Countway Library; letters from Dr. Benjamin Waterhouse August 28, September 2 and September 4, 1801, DLC.

41. Letter to Benjamin Waterhouse. September 17, 1801, Harvard University, Countway Library; letter to Dr. Shore, September 12, 1801; letter to John Vaughan, November 5, 1801, DLC; letter to Dr. Benjamin Rush, December 20, 1801, L&B, vol. X, pp. 303–4; letter from Dr. John Redman Coxe, January 15, 1803, DLC; letter to Dr. J. R. Coxe, April 30, 1802, College of Physicians, Library.

42. Letter to John Vaughan, November 5, 1802, DLC; letter to Dr. Benjamin Waterhouse, December 25, 1801, Countway Library; [Jefferson], "On the Necessity," *Medical Repository*, vol. V, 1802, p. 348.

43. Letter from Dr. Benjamin Waterhouse to Dr. Edward Jenner, April 8, 1802, Halsey, pp. 55–56; *Columbia Centinel*, July 11 and September 26, 1801; *New-England Palladium*, July 7, 1801 and February 26, 1802; *Independent Chronicle*, May 20, 1802; Blake, *Waterhouse*, p. 42; DAB, vol. VI, p. 300; Waterhouse, *Prospect*, pp. 37–38.

44. J. R. Coxe, *Practical Considerations*, pp. 120–21; letter to John Redman Coxe, July 15, 1802, College of Physicians Library.

45. Letter to John Redman Coxe, December 6, 1802, College of Physicians Library; letter from J. R. Coxe, December 10, 1802, College of Physicians Library.

46. Letter from Dr. Benjamin Waterhouse, March 1, 1803, DLC; Waterhouse, *Prospect*, Part II, pp. 22–39; H. A. Martin, "Vaccinator," pp. 1–34; Halsey, *VACCINATION AS A PUBLIC HEALTH PROCEDURE*; Coxe, *Considerations*, pp. 135–38.

47. Letter to Benjamin Rush, March 24, 1801, L&B, vol. X, pp. 241–44.

48. Letter to James Madison, January 13, 1821, Ford, vol. X, pp. 181–82; Blanton, pp. 187–200.
49. Letter to Dr. Benjamin Rush, December 20, 1801, L&B, vol. X, p. 304.
50. Letter to Caspar Wistar, June 21, 1807, Ford, vol. IX, pp. 78–85.
51. Radbill, p. 106.
52. *Daily Advertiser*, September 15, 1802; H. S. Boyd, *History*, pp. 90–92. Thomas Moore (1755–1818) of Brookville, Maryland, worked first as a cabinetmaker in Loudon County, Va. then moved to Maryland where he became a prominent agriculturist. He published pamphlets on agriculture, refrigerators and ice-houses, constructed the causeway between Mason's Island and the Virginia shore, was chief manager of the Union Manufacturing Works near Ellicott City, chief engineer of the James River Canal and later of the Chesapeake and Ohio Canal.
53. Letter to C. W. Peale, November 3, 1802, Sellers, PMHB pp. 139–40; letter to Michael Bowyer, November 3, 1802, DLC.
54. Letter from William Thornton, July 28, 1802, DLC.
55. E. S. Ferguson, "Dry Docks," pp. 108–14.
56. P. F. Norton, "Mothballing the Frigates," pp. 737–41.
57. Report of B. H. Latrobe, *American State Papers*, Naval Affairs, class 6, vol. I, pp. 104–7; Latrobe, *Correspondence*, vol. I, pp. 219–20, 237–43.
58. Jefferson, Second Annual Message to Congress, December 15, 1803, L&B, vol. III, pp. 347–48.
59. Letters from Robert Leslie, January 10, January 26, February 13, 1803, DLC; letters to Robert Leslie, January 27, DLC; Goldsborough, *Naval Chronicle*, p. 355.
60. *Naval Documents Relating to the United States Wars with the Barbary Powers*, vol. II, pp. 202, 308–9.
61. *Memorandum Book*, NN, entry for July, 1802.
62. Letter to John Adams, November 1, 1822, L&B, vol. XV, pp. 401–3.
63. Letter to Lewis M. Wiss, November 27, 1825, L&B, vol. XVI, pp. 135–38.
64. Patent to Richard Claiborne, February 22, 1802, Howard-Tilton Memorial Library, Tulane University; letter from Richard Claiborne, August 22, 1802, DLC; *New-York Herald*, September 8, 1802; *Memorandum Book*, NN, entry for October 7, 1802; letter from Richard Claiborne, December 12, 1802, DLC; letter from Richard Claiborne to John Stevens, May 18, 1811.
65. H. P. Sprat, pp. 28–58.
66. Letter from Richard Claiborne, July 4, 1817, DLC
67. Letter to Marc Auguste Pictet, February 5, 1803, L&B, vol. X, pp. 355–57.
68. Letter to Joseph C. Cabell from Col. Isaac A. Coles, 1807, H. B. Adams, pp. 51–52.
69. DAB, vol. 2, pp. 387–88.
70. Mansfield, "Military Academy," pp. 17–24; Forman, pp. 177–78.
71. Letter to Patrick K. Rogers, June 23, 1819, DLC; letter from Patrick K. Rogers, January 14, 1824, DLC; letter to Patrick K. Rogers, January 29, 1824, DLC; letter from Patrick K. Rogers, March 14, 1824, DLC.
72. D. E. Smith, "Poetry of Mathematics," pp. 49–70.
73. Letter to Andrew Ellicott, January 19, 1802, DLC; letters from Andrew Ellicott, February 7 and February 14, 1802, DLC.
74. Letter from Andrew Ellicott, March 10, 1802, DLC.
75. Letter from James Call, December 5, 1801, DLC; letter from Matthew Groves, August 2, 1802, DLC; letter to Robert Patterson, October 16, 1802, PPAmP.
76. Letter from Robert Patterson, November 1, 1802, PPAmP; letter to Matthew C. Groves, November 7, 1802, DLC.
77. "Double Reflection," *Mercantile Advertiser* (New York), September 12, 1803.
78. Letter from Matthew Groves, October 11, 1808, DLC; letter to Matthew Groves, October 19, 1808, L&B, vol. XII, pp. 175–78.
79. Letter to Thomas Perkins, March 24, 1801, *Pennsylvania Magazine of History and Biography*, vol. 27, 1903, pp. 251–52; Bear, "Nails," pp. 47–52.
80. Letter from T. M. Randolph, Jr., May 30, 1803, ViU, *Jefferson Papers*. Bear, "Nailery," pp. 47–52; *Memorandum Book*, entry for September 7, 1802; *Farm Book*, p. 427; letter to Richard Richardson, February 25, 1801, MiHi; letter to James Madison, March 6, 1796, DLC.

CHAPTER XIII. PHILOSOPHER PRESIDENT

1. *Garden Book*, pp. 291–94; Letter to Timothy Bloodworth, January 29, 1804, L&B, vol. X, p. 443.
2. Letter from Isaac Briggs, May 2, 1803, DLC; *Memorandum Book*, NN, entry for June 8, 1803, payment to Benjamin Ferris for a clock to be forwarded to Monticello; entry for February 15, 1817, for repairs of this and other clocks; [Isaac] *Memoirs*, pp. 12–13; Bedini, "Clock Designer," pp. 170–71.
3. Letter to James Dinsmore, January 28, 1804, TJMF, *Construction File*; original sold as lot No. 87 in Sotheby Parke Bernet auction sale No. 4998 in New York City on January 26, 1983; Nichols and Bear, *Monticello*, p. 24–26; Bedini, "Clock Designer," pp. 165–67.
4. Nichols and Bear, *Monticello*, p. 26, figs. 14, 15; TJMF, *Construction File*; Bedini, "Clock Designer," p. 168.
5. Letter to Archibald Stuart, May 23, 1795, ViU, *Stuart Papers*; *Memorandum Book*, NN, *entry for July 9, 1804, May 8, 1807 and July 10, 1807; Bedini, "Clock Designer," p. 168.*
6. Letter from James Dinsmore, February 24, 1809, letter to James Dinsmore, February 27, 1809, TJMF, *Construction File*; Bedini, "Clock Designer," p. 170.
7. Bedini, *Copying Machines*, pp. 40–58.
8. Hamlin, pp. 189–214; letter from Charles Willson Peale to Benjamin Henry Latrobe, September 24, 1803, PPAmP, *Peale Papers*, Letterbooks.
9. Letter from Benjamin Henry Latrobe to Charles Willson Peale, February 22, 1804, MdHi, *Latrobe Papers*, Letterbooks; letter from Peale to Latrobe, February 26, 1804, PPAmP, *Peale Papers*, Letterbooks.
10. Letter from C. W. Peale, February 26, 1804, DLC; letter from C. W. Peale to J. I. Hawkins, April 22, 1804, PPAmP, *Peale Papers*, Letterbook; Bedini, *Copying Machines*, pp. 62–63.
11. Letters from C. W. Peale, March 5 and March 13, 1804, DLC; letter to C. W. Peale, October 5, 1807, Sellers, PMHB, p. 312; letter to Latrobe, July 16, 1817, DLC; Bedini, *Copying Machines*, pp. 154–59.
12. Letter to C. W. Peale, November 22, 1806, Sellers, PMHB, pp. 308–9; Bedini, Copying Machines, pp. x, 130–32.
13. Letters to Charles Willson Peale, February 27 and March 1, 1804, H. W. Sellers, PMHB, pp. 141–42; letters from C. W. Peale, March 5 and March 13, 1804, DLC; letter to C. W. Peale, March 1 and March 30, 1804, Sellers, PMHB, pp. 142–43; letter from William Lyman, July 11, 1807, DLC; letter to C. W. Peale, October 5, 1807, DLC; Bore, pp. 3–36; Bedini, *Copying Machines*, pp. 153–59.
14. *Poulson's American Daily Advertiser*, December 6, 1804; Bedini, *Copying Machines*, pp. 98–99.
15. Letter to Samuel Hawkins, November 30, 1808, L&B, vol. XII, pp. 203–4.
16. Letter from Edward Preble to Robert Smith, May 18, 1805, DLC; letter to Robert Smith, May 31, 1805, DLC; letter to C. W. Peale, June 9, 1805, DLC.
17. Letter from Edward Preble, July 30, 1805, DLC.
18. Letter to C. W. Peale, November 14, 1804, DLC; letter to Volney, February 8, 1805, L&B, vol. XI, pp. 62–69; letter to James Bowdoin, July 10, 1806, HAW, vol. VI, p. 17.
19. Wright and Macleod, *First Americans*, pp. 76–100; Field, pp. 27–66; Bedini, *Copying Machines*, pp. 134–42.
20. Singleton, vol. 1, pp. 45–46; Hines, p. 85.
21. Bedini, *Copying Machines*, p. 135.
22. Wright and Macleod, "Mellimelli," pp. 555–65.
23. Janson, *Stranger*, pp. 220–33; Foster, *Jeffersonian America*, pp. 204–5.
24. Janson, *Stranger*, pp. 225–29; Ewers, "Chiefs,", pp. 12–19.
25. Wollon, "Sir Augustus Foster," pp. 199–200.
26. Letter to C. W. Peale, January 1, 1806, Sellers, PMHB, pp. 305–6.
27. Letter from C. W. Peale, January 12, 1806, DLC.
28. [Jefferson], "Address to the Chiefs of the Osages," *Complete Jefferson*, pp. 476–78; Janson, *Stranger*, pp. 230–31.
29. *Aurora & General Advertiser* (Philadelphia), February 22, 1806; *Columbian Centinel, Massachusetts Federalist*, March 5, 1806; Janson, *Stranger*, p. 232.
30. Janson, *Stranger*, pp. 230–31; *Aurora, General Advertiser*, January 16, 1806; Ewers, pp. 21–24.

31. Letters from James Leander Cathcart to James Madison, April 26 and May 5, 1806; letter from Cathcart to Jacob Wagner, July 20, 1806; letters from Mellimelli to James Madison, August 21 and August 23, 1806; letter from Cathcart to James Madison, August 27, 1806; all the foregoing in the National Archives and Records Service, Record Group 217, microfilm roll 3; Foster, *Jeffersonian America*, pp. 48–50.
32. Bedini, *Copying Machines*, pp. 151–52, 187–88.
33. Letter from Benjamin H. Latrobe, July 25, 1817, DLC; Bedini, *Copying Machines*, pp. 172–73; Hamlin, pp. 479–80.
34. Letter to C. W. Peale, December 28, 1820, Sellers, PMHB, pp. 413–14.
35. Letter to David Williams, November 14, 1803, L&B, vol. X, pp. 428–31.

CHAPTER XIV. "THE CORPS OF DISCOVERY"

1. Letter from Carlos Martinez de Yrujo to Pedro Cevallos, January 31, 1803, Jackson, *Letters*, vol. I, pp. 14–15; letter from Louis André Pichon to the Minister of Foreign Affairs, March 4, 1803, Jackson, *Letters*, vol. I, pp. 22–23; letter from Louis André Pichon, March 4, 1803, Jackson, *Letters*, vol. I, pp. 21–22.
2. Letter to Meriwether Lewis, February 13, 1801, DLC, Jackson, *Letters*, vol. 1, pp. 42; letter to Paul Allen, August 18, 1813, with biographical sketch of Meriwether Lewis, c. August 18, 1815, Jackson, *Letters*, vol. 2, pp. 585–94.
3. Letter to W. A. Burwell, March 26, 1804, Bixby, pp. 105–6.
4. Estimate of expenses by M. Lewis, 1803, Jackson, *Letters*, vol. 1, pp, 8–9, 69–74; estimate of overall cost of the expedition, G. Lewis, pp. 465–89.
5. President's message to Congress, January 18, 1803, Ford, vol. VIII, pp. 191–202; Jackson, *Letters*, vol. 1, pp. 10–14n.
6. Letters to Benjamin Smith Barton, February 27, 1803, Caspar Wistar, February 18, 1803, Benjamin Rush, February 28, 1803, Robert Patterson, March 2, 1803, Jackson, *Letters*, vol. 1, pp. 16–19, 21.
7. Letter to William Dunbar, May 25, 1805, Jackson, *Letters*, vol. 1, pp. 244–45; letter from Isaac Briggs, May 17, 1803, Jackson, *Letters*, vol. 1, p. 45, Item 32n and Item 33n; letters from Albert Gallatin, March 14 and April 13, 1803, Jackson, *Letters*, vol. 1, pp. 27–28, 32–34.
8. Letter to Benjamin Smith Barton, February 27, 1803, Jackson, *Letters*, vol. 1, pp. 16–17.
9. Letter to Robert Patterson, March 2, 1803, Jackson, *Letters*, p. 21.
10. Letter to Andrew Ellicott, February 26, 1803 (letter not found); letter from Andrew Ellicott, March 6, 1803, Jackson, *Letters*, vol. 1, pp. 23–25.
11. Letter from Robert Patterson, March 15, 1803, Jackson, *Letters*, vol. 1, pp. 28–31.
12. Letter from Andrew Ellicott, March 6, 1803, Jackson, *Letters*, vol. 1, pp. 23–25.
13. Letters from Joseph Wingate to Israel Whelan and William Irvine, March 14, 1803, Jackson, *Letters*, vol. 1, p. 76. Wingate was chief clerk of the War Department.
14. Letter from Meriwether Lewis, April 20, 1803, Jackson, *Letters*, vol. 1, pp. 37–40.
15. Bedini, "Ellicott," pp. 113–35.
16. Letters from Albert Gallatin, March 14 and April 13, 1803, Jackson, *Letters*, vol. 1, pp. 27–28, 32–34; Allen, *Passage*, pp. 97–102.
17. Summary of Purchase, Jackson, *Letters*, vol. 1, p. 96, vol. 2, pp. 738–39; letter to James Cheetham, June 17, 1803, Jackson, *L & C Letters*, vol. 1, p. 56n.; letter from Albert Gallatin, March 14, 1803, Jackson, *Letters*, vol. 1, pp. 27–28.
18. Letter to Robert Patterson, November 16, 1803, Jackson, *Letters*, vol. 1, p. 270; Cotter, pp. 180–92; Pannekeok, pp. 276–81.
19. Ramsden, *New Universal Equatorial Instrument*; Ramsden, *Universal Equatorial*; King, *Telescope*, pp. 162–63.
20. Letter to William Dunbar, May 25, 1805, Jackson, *Letters*, vol. 1, pp. 244–46; letter from William Dunbar, July 9, 1805, Jackson, *Letters*, vol. 1, 250–51; letter to William Lambert, December 22, 1804, DLC; letter to William Dunbar, January 12, 1806, Jackson, *Letters*, vol. 1, pp. 290; letter from Andrew Ellicott, March 6, 1805, Jackson, *Letters*, vol. 1, pp. 23–25; letter from Robert Patterson, March 15, 1805, Jackson, *Letters*, vol. 1, pp. 28–31.
21. Letter to unknown correspondent (believed to be William Lambert), November 16, 1805, Jackson, *L & C Letters*, vol. 1, p. 270. [November 29, 1821, L&B, vol. XV, pp. 342–49].
22. Letter to Meriwether Lewis, April 30, 1803, Jackson, *Letters*, vol. 1, pp. 44–45.

23. Letter from Meriwether Lewis, May 14, 1803, Jackson, *Letters*, vol. 1, pp. 48–49.

24. Letter to Meriwether Lewis, May 16, 1803, Jackson, *Letters*, vol. 1, p. 49.

25. Letter to Meriwether Lewis, April 27, 1803, Jackson, *Letters*, vol. 1, p. 44.

26. Letter from Andrew Ellicott, April 18, 1803, Jackson, *Letters*, vol. 1, pp. 36–37.

27. Letters from Andrew Ellicott to John Vaughan and Robert Patterson, May 7, 1803, Jackson, Letters, vol. 1, pp. 45–46.

28. Lewis's list of requirements, Jackson, *Letters*, vol. 1, p. 69.

29. An early example of the surveying tape of English manufacture c. 1846 is in the collections of the Science Museum, South Kensington, London.

30. Bedini, *Early American Scientific Instruments*, pp. 30–31.

31. Letter from Meriwether Lewis, May 14, 1803, Jackson, *Letters*, pp. 48–49; invoices to Israel Whelan from Thomas Parker, May 19, 1803, and from Henry Voigt, June 10, 1803, Jackson, *Letters*, vol. 1, pp. 88, 90; Eckhardt, p. 187; Good, *Harrison*, pp. 19–30.

32. Letter from Andrew Ellicott, March 6, 1803, Jackson, *Letters*, vol. 1, pp. 23–25.

33. Letter to Meriwether Lewis, June 20, 1803, Jackson, *Letters*, vol. 1, pp. 61–66.

34. R. E. Weber, pp. 178, 190–91; Jackson, *Letters*, vol. 1, pp. 9–10.

35. Original Journals (1905), vol. 5, pp. 15–16; Wissler, pp. 113–14; Prucha, vol. 1, pp. 205–8, 303, vol. 2, pp. 388, 433, 453; Jackson, *Letters*, vol. 1, pp. 72–73.

36. Letter to Meriwether Lewis, June 20, 1803, Jackson, *Letters*, vol. 1, p. 63.

37. Letter from Meriwether Lewis to William Clark, June 19, 1803, Jackson, *Letters*, vol. 1, pp. 57–60; letters from William Clark to Meriwether Lewis, July 18 and July 24, 1803, Jackson, *Letters*, vol. 1, pp. 110–11, 112–13.

38. Letter from Meriwether Lewis, September 8, 1803, Jackson, *Letters*, vol. 1, p. 121–22; letter from Caspar Wistar, October 6, 1803, Jackson, *Letters*, vol. 1, p. 133; Loos, pp. 490–511.

39. Letter from Meriwether Lewis, October 3, 1803, Jackson, *Letters*, vol. 1, pp. 126–32; letter to Caspar Wistar, February 25, 1807, L&B, vol. XI, pp. 158–59.

40. Letter to W. C. C. Claiborne, May 24, 1803, L&B, vol. X, pp. 390–96; letter from Isaac Briggs, January 2, 1804, DLC; letter to Wilson C. Nicholas, April 22, 1803, "Glimpses of the Past," *Missouri Historical Society*, vol. III, Nos. 4–6, April-June 1936, pp. 90–91; Barnard, pp. 409–19.

41. Letter to Andrew Ellicott, December 22, 1803, DLC.

42. Lockwood, "St.-Memin," pp. 3–26; *Washington Advertiser and the National Intelligencer*, October 12, 1804.

43. Coues, vol. 1, p. 257; Thwaites, vol. 2, pp. 197–99; Rees, *Madame Charbonneau*; R. B. Betts, pp. 20–21, 26–27, 43–55; C. G. Clarke, p. 38.

44. Letters from Isaac Briggs, March 1, May 2 and May 17, 1803, DLC; [Phillips], *Early Proceedings*, pp. 337–38.

45. Letters from Isaac Briggs, February 27 and May 25, 1804, DLC; Barnard, pp. 411–12; *American State Papers*, vol. 19, Claims, Washington, 1834, p. 362.

46. De Terra, pp. 783–86; letters from Vincent Gray to James Madison, April 28 and May 8, 1804, letter from von Humboldt to James Madison, May 24, 1804, DLC, *Madison Papers*.

47. Sarton, "Bonpland," pp. 385–99; Corner, p. 325; *Ralph's Philadelphia Gazette and Daily Advertiser*, vol. 21, No. 4815, May 26, 1804, p. 3; "Private memoir written at the request of a friend—by William Burwell . . ." DLC, *William A. Burwell Papers*.

48. Letter from Alexander von Humboldt, May 24, 1804, DLC; letter to Alexander von Humboldt, May 28, 1804, DLC.

49. Friis, "Humboldts Besuch," pp. 145–62; Friis, "Humboldt's Visit," pp. 6–18; C. C. Sellers, *Museum*, pp. 160–64; letter from Albert Gallatin to his wife, June 6, 1804, H. Adams, *Gallatin*, pp. 323–24; Peale, *Diary*, June 5, 1804, PPAmP, *Peale Papers*.

50. Letter to Alexander von Humboldt, June 9, 1804, De Terra, p. 789; M. B. Smith, *First Forty Years*, pp. 396–97; letter from Alexander von Humboldt, December 20, 1811, DLC; letter to Alexander von Humboldt, December 6, 1813, DLC.

51. [Jefferson], "Louisiana-Texas by Pages, Nolan, Sibley, Humboldt," DLC.

52. Letter to Isaac Briggs, June 11, 1804, DLC; letter from Isaac Briggs, March 1, 1805, DLC.

53. Letters to William Dunbar, March 13, April 15, and May 25, 1804, DLC.

54. E. M. Betts, "Rafinesque-Jefferson Correspondence," pp. 368–80.

55. Letter from Alexander Wilson, February 6, 1806, letter from Alexander Wilson to William Duncan, February 26, 1806, Clark Hunter, pp. 249–54; Cantwell, *Wilson*, p. 136.

56. Letters to William Dunbar, March 13, April 15, 1804, May 25, 1805, L&B, vol. XI, pp. 74–78; letters to William Dunbar, October 8, 1805, February 6, 1806, March 28, 1806; DLC; letters from William Dunbar, May 13, 1804, October 8, 1805, March 17, 1806, DLC; Rowland, *Life*, pp. 327–30.

57. Letter from William Dunbar, May 13, 1804, DLC; Cox, "Early Explorer," pp. 73–77; Jackson, *Stony Mountains*, pp. 227–41.

58. Letter from William Dunbar, June 9, 1804, DLC; Rowland, pp. 133–35; Jackson, *Stony Mountains*, pp. 224–25, 238–39, 10n.

59. Letter to William Dunbar, April 15, 1804, DLC.

60. Letter to William Dunbar, July 17, 1804, *Territ. Papers*, vol. 13, pp. 31–32; Jackson, *Stony Mountains*, pp. 225–26; letter from William Dunbar, November 9, 1804, DLC; *National Intelligencer*, October 15, 27, 31 and November 10, 12, 1806; McDermott, "Western Journals," pp. 770–73

61. Jackson, *Stony Mountains*, pp. 225–36.

62. Letter from Benjamin Hawkins, August 4, 1804, DLC.

63. Jackson, *Pike Journals*, vol. 1, pp. 134–89; Jackson, *Stony Mountains*, pp. 246–48; letter from Henry Dearborn, February 11, 1807, DLC.

64. Letter to Henry Dearborn, October 27, 1818, DLC Jackson, *Pike Journals*, vol. 1, pp. 285–86, vol. 2, p. 191n.; Jackson, *Stony Mountains*, pp. 250–54.

65. Letter to Dunbar, May 25, 1805, Jackson, *Letters*, vol. 1, pp. 244–45.

66. Letter from William Dunbar, July 9, 1805, Jackson, *Letters*, vol. 1, pp. 250–51.

67. Letters to William Dunbar, May 25, 1805, L&B, vol. XI, pp. 74–78, and January 12, 1806, Jackson, *Letters*, vol. 1, p. 245.

68. Letters to William Tunnicliff, April 25, 1805, CSmH; letter from William Tunnicliff, May 19, 1805, MoHi; invoice of W. & S. Jones, London, July 23, 1805, MoHi; *Memorandum Book*, entry for December 12, 1805.

69. [Jefferson], 6th Annual Message to Congress, December 2, 1806, *Complete Jefferson*, pp. 423–24.

70. Letter to Meriwether Lewis, October 26, 1806, Jackson, *Letters*, vol. 1, pp. 350–51; Chuinard, "Jefferson and the Corps," pp. 4–13; Malone, *Jefferson*, vol. 4, pp. 208–12.

71. Letter from J. L. Donaldson, January 11, 1807, letter to Meriwether Lewis, June 4, 1807, letter from Meriwether Lewis, June 27, 1807, Jackson, *Letters*, vol. 1, p. 360, vol. 2, pp. 415, 418; Snow, pp. 36–41; Appleman, pp. 235, 375 n. 150. One of the pocket compasses made by Thomas Whitney and which, according to Clark family tradition, was carried on the expedition by William Clark, is in the collections of the National Museum of American History, Smithsonian Institution.

72. Chuinard, "Jefferson and the Corps," pp. 4–13; Friis, "Activities," p. 339; Rudd, pp. 351–56; Setzer, pp. 356–57; Malone, *Jefferson*, vol. 4, pp. 208–12.

73. Letter to C. W. Peale, October 6, 1805, Sellers, PMHB, pp. 302–4; Peale, *Museum Record Book*, PPAmP, *Peale Papers; Poulson's American Daily Advertiser*, March 1, 1810; letters from C. W. Peale, October 22 and November 3, 1805, Jackson, *Letters*, vol. 1, pp. 267–68.

74. Letters to C. W. Peale, October 9 and October 21, 1805, Sellers, PMHB, pp. 304–5.

75. Letter from C. W. Peale, July 4, 1806, Jackson, Letters, vol. 1, pp. 308–9.

76. Letter to Caspar Wistar, December 19, 1807, L&B, vol. XI, pp. 403–4; letter to C. W. Peale, January 15, 1809, Sellers, PMHB, pp. 317–18; letter to T. M. Randolph, Jr., January 31, 1808, MHi. Ref. Juan Ignacio Molina, *Compendio della storia geografica, naturale, e civile del regno del Chile* (Bologna, 1776).

77. Letters to Bernard McMahon, January 6, March 20, March 22, 1807, Jackson, Letters, vol. 2, pp. 388–89; letter to William Hamilton, November 6, 1805, Jackson, *Letters*, vol. 1, pp. 269–70; letter to William Hamilton, March 22, 1807, Jackson, *Letters*, vol. 2, 388–89; letter from Bernard McMahon, December 26, 1806, Jackson, *Letters*, vol. 1, pp. 354–55; letter from Bernard Macmahon, December 24, 1809, Jackson, *Letters*, vol. 2, pp. 484–86; letters from Bernard MacMahon, March 27, April 10, 1807, June 28, 1808, January 17, 1809, DLC; letter from William Hamilton, February 5, 1808, DLC; True, "Neglected Botanical Results," pp. 1–19; Rudd, pp. 351–56; letter from Bernard McMahon, February 28, 1812, DLC; letter to Bernard McMahon, October 11, 1812, DLC; letter to Bernard Macmahon, May 30, 1813, Jackson, *Letters*, vol. 2, pp. 582–84; letter to Mme. Noailles de Tesse, December 8, 1813, DLC; Leighton, pp. 1556–58.

78. Letter from Meriwether Lewis, April 7, 1805, Jackson, *Letters*, vol. 1, pp. 231–242n; letter from Étienne Lemaire, August 17, 1805, DLC; Peale, *Museum Record Book*, PPAmP, *Peale Papers; Poulson's American Daily Advertiser*, March 1, 1810.
79. Letters to C. W. Peale, October 6, 1805, Jackson, *Letters*, vol. 1, pp. 260–61; October 9 and October 21, 1805, PPAmP, *Peale Papers*; letter from C. W. Peale, October 22, 1805, Jackson, *Letters*, vol. 1, pp. 163–64, 267; Cutright, "Odyssey." pp. 215–28.
80. Letter to C. W. Peale, January 12, 1806, PPAmP, *Peale Papers*; letter from C. W. Peale, April 5, 1806, Jackson *Letters*, vol. 1, pp. 301–2; Thwaites, vol. VI, p. 130, vol. VII, p. 317; Cutright, pp. 215–28.
81. Letter from Zebulon M. Pike, October 29, 1807, DLC; letter to Zebulon M. Pike, November 5, 1807, DLC; letter to C. W. Peale, November 5, 1807, PPAmP, *Peale Papers*.
82. Letter to Anne Cary Randolph, November 1, 1807, Betts and Bear, pp. 312–13; M. B. Smith, *First Forty Years*, p. 393.
83. Letters to C. W. Peale, November 6, 1807, January 6, and February 6, 1808, PPAmP, *Peale Papers*; Jackson, *Pike Journals*, vol. II, pp. 275–76, 278–79, 294; letter from Pike, February 6, 1808, DLC; letter from C. W. Peale, January 29, 1808, Jackson, *Letters*, pp. 439–40.
84. Letter from C. W. Peale, March 8, 1808, DLC; Peale, *Museum Record Book*, p. 28, PPAmP, *Peale Papers*; C. C. Sellers, *Peale*, vol. 2, p. 228; C. C. Sellers, *Museum*, pp. 206–7.
85. Letter from William Clark to Charbonneau, August 20, 1806, MoHi; letter to Meriwether Lewis, July 17, 1808, DLC; Foley and Rice, "Visiting the President," pp. 4–15, 56; Foley and Rice, "Return of the Mandan Chief," pp. 2–14. Jackson, *Stony Mountains*, pp. 270–71.
86. Letter from Pierre Choteau to William Eustis, December 14, 1809, Jackson, Letters, vol. 2, pp. 479–84.
87. Viola, pp. 22–30, 42–45.
88. Letter to James Jay, April 7, 1809, L&B, vol. XII, p. 270.
89. Letter to William Henry Harrison, February 27, 1803, DLC; letter to the Society of Friends of Philadelphia, November 13, 1807, DLC.
90. *National Intelligencer*, December 31, 1806 and January 21, 1807; Chuinard, "Jefferson and the Corps of Discovery," pp. 12–13; Janson, pp. 235–37; Jackson, *Stony Mountains*, pp. 268–69.
91. Letters from Captain Gilbert C. Russell, November 13, 1809 and January 31, 1810, DLC; letters to Captain Russell, April 18, 1810 and November 23, 1809 and April 18, 1810, DLC; letter to Peter S. Du Ponceau, November 7, 1817, letter from Peter S. Du Ponceau, December 5, 1817, PPAmP; Jackson, *Stony Mountains*, pp. 269–72.
92. Letters from William Gofroth, December 1, 1806 and January 23, 1807, APS; letter to Caspar Wistar, February 25, 1807, L&B, vol. XI, pp. 158–59.
93. Letter to William Clark, December 19, 1807, L&B, vol. 11, pp. 404–5.
94. Letters from William Clark, October 10 and November 10, 1807, DLC; letters to Caspar Wistar, William Clark and George Rogers Clark, December 19, 1807, L&B, vol. XI, pp. 403–5, vol. XII, pp. 15–16.
95. Letter to Caspar Wistar, March 20, 1808, L&B, vol. XII, pp. 15–16.
96. Wistar *Letterbook, 1794–1817*, PPAmP; letter to Lacépède, July 14, 1808, Jackson, *Letters*, vol. 2, pp. 442–43; Rice, "Gift of Fossils," pp. 597–627.
97. Letter to C. W. Peale, May 5, 1809, Sellers, PMHB, pp. 318–19.

CHAPTER XV. "THE SHACKLES OF POWER"

1. Letter to Benjamin Vaughan, July 23, 1788, Boyd, vol. 13, pp. 394–98.
2. *Memorandum Book*, NN, entry for September 2, 1791, paid to Robert Leslie for odometer, $10; entry for January 3, 1794, paid David Rittenhouse for an odometer and camera obscura, $39.94. Purchase of the Nairne & Blunt odometer is not recorded.
3. Letter to James Clarke, May 22, 1807, DLC.
4. Letter from James Clarke, May 27, 1807, MHi.
5. Letter to James Clarke, June 5, 1807, DLC.
6. Letter to Thomas Cooper, October 27, 1808 L&B. vol. XII, pp. 180–82.
7. *Autobiography*, in Padover, *Complete Jefferson*, p. 1153.
8. Letter from James Clarke, July 6, 1817, DLC; letter to James Clarke, August 1, 1817, DLC.

9. Letter to Dr. John Sibley, May 27, 1805, L&B, vol. XI, pp. 79–81; letter to Levett Harris, April 18, 1806, L&B, XI, pp. 101–3; letter to Benjamin Smith Barton, September 21, 1809, L&B, vol. XII, pp. 312–14.

10. *Notes*, pp. 101–2, 282.

11. Letter to the Reverend Ezra Stiles, September 1, 1786, Boyd, vol. 10, p. 316; letter to Charles Thomson, September 20, 1787, Boyd, vol. 12, p. 159.

12. *Notes*, pp. 100–102.

13. *Notes*, p. 282, n. 12.

14. Letter to Benjamin Hawkins, August 13, 1786, Boyd, vol. 10, pp. 240–41; letter from Benjamin Hawkins, May 3, 1791, Boyd, vol. 20, pp. 360–61.

15. Boyd, vol. 11, pp. 218, 638.

16. Letter to John Adams, Cappon, vol. 2, p. 287; *The Monthly Magazine*, vol. 24, part I, 1807, p. 74; C. C. Jones, *Antiquities*, 436–37.

17. Heywood, pp. 123–24, noted in Jones (see Note 16); Boyd, vol. 17, p. xxx, letter from Harry Innes, July 8, 1790, Boyd, vol. 17, p. 20; letter to Harry Innes, March 7, 1791, Boyd, vol. 19, pp. 521–22.

18. U. S. National Museum, Accession File No. 3689, 1875; Valentine Museum, Accession File No. X51.1.512; Woods, p. 321.

19. Randall, vol. 3, p. 354.

20. Letter to C. W. Peale, August 24, 1808, PPAmP, *Peale Papers*; letter from C. W. Peale, September 1, 1808, DLC; letter to C. W. Peale, October 12, 1808, PPAmP, *Peale Papers*; letter to Casper Wistar, October 12, 1808, PPAmP, *Wistar Papers*; Memorandum to Thomas Jefferson Randolph, October 13, 1808, DLC.

21. Letters to Caspar Wistar, June 21, 1807, Ford, vol. 9, pp. 78–85; February 25, 1807, L&B, vol. XV, pp. 158–59; December 19, 1807, L&B, vol. XI, pp. 403–4.

22. Marx, p. 49. No source is provided for the statement that Jefferson on one occasion sewed up the wound of a slave boy; no mention has been found in other sources.

23. Letter to Martha Randolph, June 16, 1806, Betts & Bear, p. 284; Cuthbert, "Poplar Forest," pp. 333–356; Randall, vol. III, pp. 342–44; W. H. Gaines, "Hideaway," pp. 36–39; Wilstach, "Secret Home," pp. 41–43; Randall, vol. III, pp. 342–44.

24. Nichols, "Jefferson's Retreat," pp. 2–13; L. M. Watson, pp. 342–46; N. Cuthbert, pp. 333–56.

25. Letter to John W. Eppes, July 28, 1822, W. M. Cary, p. 586; Jefferson's will, Ford, vol. X, pp. 392–96.

25. Letter to Benjamin Rush, August 17, 1811, L&B, vol. 13, pp. 74–77.

26. Lambeth and Manning, p. 79.

27. Letter to Ellen Wayles Randolph, March 29, 1808, Betts and Bear, p. 338; letter to Cornelia Jefferson Randolph, April 3, 1808, Betts and Bear, p. 339.

28. Letter from G. C. Delacoste, April 10, 1807, DLC; letter to G. C. Delacoste, May 24, 1807, L&B, vol. XI, pp. 206–8.

29. Letter to Benjamin Smith Barton, October 18, 1807, L&B, vol. XI, pp. 382–83.

30. Letter to Augustin-François Silvestre, May 29, 1807, L&B, vol. XI, pp. 212–13.

31. *Ibid.*

32. Letter to John Taylor, January 4, 1808, L&B, vol. XI, pp. 413–14.

33. Letter to James Monroe, May 29, 1807, L&B, vol. XI, p. 211.

34. Letter to John Armstrong, March 5, 1809, L&B, vol. XII, pp. 260–62.

35. Letters to Robert Fulton, August 16, 1807, L&B, vol. XI, p. 328, March 17, 1810, L&B, vol. XII, pp. 380–81.

36. Letter to David Salmon, February 15, 1808, DLC; Shapely, "Natural Philosopher," pp. 234–37.

37. S. G. Goodrich, *Recollections*, vol. I, pp. 276–82.

38. Silliman and Kingsley, pp. 141–61; Fulton and Thomson, pp. 76–78; [Bowditch], "Estimate of the Height," pp. 213–36.

39. Letter from Dunbar, April-June 1800, PPAmP; "Dunbar's Meteorological Observations, 1800," [Phillips], *Early Proceedings*, pp. 308, 323.

40. Letter from John Chipchase through Leonard Snowden, October 8, 1804, PPAmP; [Phillips], *Early Proceedings*, pp. 319, 349.

41. Letter to Andrew Ellicott, October 25, 1805, DLC.

42. Fulton and Thompson, *Benjamin Silliman*, pp. 76–78.

43. Letter to the vice presidents of the American Philosophical Society, November 30, 1808, L&B, vol. XII, p. 202; APS *Minutes*, January 6, 1809, PPAmP.
44. Luiscius, *Beschrijving*; Multhauf, *Catalogue*, pp. 29–30; E. G. R. Taylor, *Mathematical Practitioners*, pp. 92, 369–70.
45. Letter to Joel Barlow, December 12, 1808, DLC; letter to Joel Barlow, December 25, 1808, L&B, vol. XII, pp. 216–17.
46. Dupree, p. 29; G. A. Weber, pp. 1–5
47. Hassler, DAB, vol. 4, pp. 385–86.
48. *Port Folio*, July 30, 1808; *Boston Repertory*, July 15, 1808; W. W. Jennings, *Embargo*, pp. 128–29.
49. Mabbot, pp. 9–15, 23–24.
50. Letter to John Hollins, February 19, 1809, L&B, vol. XII, pp. 252–53.
51. "Thomas Jefferson: The Sheepman," pp. 10–11, 24–25; *Farm Book*, pp. 111–13.
52. Letter from E. I. Du Pont de Nemours, February 23, 1809, DLC.
53. *Farm Book*, pp. 111–16; letter from William Keough, February 15, 1809, DLC.
54. Letter to George Erving, November 23, 1809, DLC; letter from William Thornton, May 10, 1810, DLC; letters from Joseph Dougherty, May 14 and June 1, 1810, DLC; letter to Joseph Dougherty, May 24, 1810, DLC; letter to John Hollins, February 19, 1809, L&B XII pp. 252–53; letters from James Madison, May 7 and May 25, 1810, DLC; letter to James Madison May 13, 1810, L&B, vol. X, pp. 389–91; "Thomas Jefferson, The Sheepman," pp. 10–11, 24–25.
55. Pierson, pp. 58–59; Wing, pp. 173–74.
56. Letter to Joseph Dougherty, December 25, 1812, DLC; "Don Pedro Theme," unpaginated.
57. Letter to Pierre Samuel Du Pont de Nemours, March 2, 1809, DLC; letter to Judge Harry Innes, September 18, 1813, MHi; Link, "Chien des Bergères," pp. 25–28.
58. Letter to William Thornton, April 27, 1810, *Farm Book*, pp. 126–27.
59. Letter to Joseph Dougherty, May 24, 1810, *Farm Book*, pp. 130–31; letter to Harry Innes, September 18, 1813, *Farm Book*, p. 140.
60. Letter to Volney, April 9, 1797, DLC; *Garden Book*, p. 255; Cutright, "Instructions," pp. 304–5.
61. Letter to Charles Thomson, December 25, 1808, L&B, vol. XII, pp. 217–18.
62. Letter to Dr. James Small, January 20, 1809, MHi.
63. Letter to Alexander von Humboldt, March 6, 1809, L&B, vol. XII, pp. 263–64.
64. Letter to George Jefferson, December 24, 1808, sold as Lot 100 at Sotheby Parke Bernet auction sale in New York, October 31, 1985; J. C. Clark, *Faded Glory*, pp. 14–19.
65. Letter to Pierre Samuel Du Pont de Nemours, March 2, 1809, L&B, vol. XII, pp. 258–60.
66. E. S. Brown, "Plumer's Memorandum," pp. 453–55.
67. Randall, vol. III, pp. 303–6; M. B. Smith, *First Forty Years*, pp. 55, 409–12; *Weather Book*, DLC, March 11, 1809.
68. B. Mayo, "Peppercorn," pp. 234–35.
69. Note from M. B. Smith, N.D., MHi; note to M. B. Smith, March 6, 1809, *Garden Book*, pp. 382–83.
70. Randall, vol. 3, pp. 305–6.

CHAPTER XVI. THE TWILIGHT YEARS

1. Pierson, pp. 85–87; Randall, vol. 3, pp. 342–44; Barbara Mayo, "Twilight," pp. 502–6, 512–14.
2. Letters from H. Browse Trist to Nicholas P. Trist, May 13, 1819 and October 19, 1819, DLC, *Trist Papers*; letter to James Madison, July 7, 1819, DLC; letter to M. Laporte, June 4, 1819, Koch and Peden, pp. 692–93; letter from Alexander Garrett to J. H. Cocke, June 4, 1819, ViU, *Cocke Papers*; Malone, *Jefferson*, vol. VI, 371–73.
3. Letter to Thaddeus Kosciusko, February 26, 1810, L&B, vol. XII, pp. 365–70; letter to Dr. Benjamin Rush, January 16, 1811, L&B, vol. XIII, pp. 1–2; Randall, vol. 3, pp. 322–23.
4. S. N. Randolph, pp. 401–4; Wilstach, *Jefferson and Monticello*, pp. 110, 134–42; M. Kimball, *Furnishings of Monticello*, p. 23; Bedini, *Copying Machines*, pp. 167–68; Granquist, "Cabinet-making," pp. 36–37, pl. 6.
5. *Farm Book*, pp. 7–9, 29, 426–28; Shayt, unpaginated.

6. Letter from Edmund Bacon, January 19, 1809, ViU, Alderman Library; letter to Jones and Howell, August 10, 1809, MHi; *Farm Book*, pp. 341–43, 369–76; Pierson, pp. 64–68; Malone, *Jefferson*, vol. VI, pp. 37–38.

7. Letter to Jones and Howell, August 10, 1809, MHi; letter from Martha Jefferson Randolph, August 7, 1819, Betts and Bear, pp. 429–30; *Farm Book*, pp. 341–43; Shayt, *Nailery*; Oriol Pi-Sunyer, "Reluctant Manufacturer," pp. 226–34; Bear, "Manufacturer," pp. 1–11.

8. Letter from Thomas Robinson, March 25, 1786, ViU; *Memorandum Book*, MHi, entry for April 4, 1786; Gaynor, "Tool Chest," pp. 57–60; Hummel, "English Tools," pp. 27–46.

9. M. B. Smith, Winter, vol. III, p. 265; [Isaac], "Memoirs," p. 18.

10. [Isaac], *Memoirs*, pp. 12, 125 fn. 38, fn. 41; Sowerby, "Library," p. 87; letter from Jacob Rubsamen, December 1, 1780, Boyd, vol. 4, p. 174.

11. Letter to Benjamin Harris, August 3, 1812, DLC.

12. Thacker, unpaginated.

13. Letter to Thomas Mann Randolph, Jr., November 28, 1796, L&B, vol. XVIII, p. 200; "Memoranda," Padover, *Complete Jefferson*, p. 799

14. McLaughlin, pp. 163–64, 252–53; Nichols and Bear, *Monticello*, p. 46.

15. McLaughlin, pp. 252–55, 293–94, 320–21, 329–31, 446–47; Nichols and Bear, *Monticello*, p. 21.

16. Nichols and Bear, pp. 17, 19.

17. M. Nicholson, *The Carpenter and Joiner's Companion*; Nichols and Bear, *Monticello*, p. 21.

18. Letter to B. H. Latrobe, November 3, 1804, DLC; Thomas Appleton, May 18, 1824, MHi; letters from Thomas Appleton, July 28, 1824, May 8, 1825, June 22, 1825, MHi; McLaughlin, pp. 305–10, 438.

19. Letter from James Madison, May 1, 1791, vol. 20, pp. 335–39; Nichols, *Drawings*, No. 171.

20. McLaughlin, pp. 5–7, 36, 163, 252, 255–56, 412, 426–27; Nichols and Bear, p. 49.

21. Letter to James Dinsmore, December 30, 1808, MHi; letter from James Dinsmore, January 19, 1809, MHi; letter to James Dinsmore, January 30, 1809, MHi; M. B. Smith, *First Forty Years*, pp. 71–72; Malone, *Jefferson*, vol. VI, pp. 170–71; Nichols and Bear, *Monticello*, pp. 28–33; McLaughlin, p. 444; communication from Lucia C. Stanton, June 19, 1986.

22. McMaster, vol. II, p. 605; M. B. Smith, *First Forty Years*, pp. 387, 392; Nichols and Bear, *Monticello*, pp. 44–46; McLaughlin, pp. 7–9, 444–45.

23. McLaughlin, pp. 195, 416.

24. Letter to Benjamin Harris, August 9, 1812; letter to William Thornton, February 9, 1815, MHi; *Garden Book*, p. 427; McLaughlin, pp. 302–3, 436.

25. *Garden Book*, pp. 278, 281, 400, 476, 485–87, 631; McLaughlin, pp. 296, 301–2, 433–36.

26. Kelso, "Jefferson's Garden," pp. 38–45; *Farm Book*, pp. 78.

27. Letter to John W. Campbell, September 3, 1809, L&B, vol. XII, pp. 307–9; *Farm Book*, pp. 453–56.

28. *Farm Book*, pp. 195–96, 337–39, 364–65, 412–13.

29. Letter to Thaddeus Kosciusko, February 26, 1810, L&B, vol. XII, pp. 365–70.

30. *Ibid.*

31. Letter to George Divers, November 26, 1792, DLC; letter to Joseph Coppinger, April 25, 1815, DLC; letter to Captain Joseph Miller, June 26, 1815, DLC; *Farm Book*, pp. 413–21.

32. Letter from Baron von Geismar, April 13, 1789, Boyd, vol. 15, p. 49; letter to Baron von Geismar, November 20, 1789, L&B, vol. XIX, p. 71–72; drawings are in ViU, Alderman Library.

33. Letter to James Monroe, May 5, 1811, L&B, vol. XIII, pp. 59–60.

34. Letter to William A. Burwell, August 19, 1811, MoHi; letter from Benjamin Rush, August 26, 1811, DLC.

35. Letter to Payne Todd, October 10, 1811, L&B, vol. XIII, pp. 95–95; letter to William Lambert, December 29, 1811, DLC.

36. Letter from H. A. S. Dearborn, October 14, 1811, DLC; letter to H. A. S. Dearborn, November 15, 1811, L&B, vol. XIII, pp. 110–12.

37. Letters to William Lambert, September 19, 1811 and December 29, 1811, DLC; letters from William Lambert, November 14 and November 22, 1811, DLC.

38. Letter from the Reverend James Madison, November 19, 1811, DLC; letter to the Reverend James Madison, December 28, 1811, L&B, vol. XIX, pp. 183–84.

39. Nichols, *Architectural Drawings*, K154a, "Instrument bay," MHi.

40. TJMF, *Construction File*; communications to the writer from Mr. Charles L. Granquist, November 27, 1980.
41. Letter to Charles Clay, August 23, 1811, L&B, vol. XIII, pp. 80–81.
42. Letter from Benjamin Henry Latrobe, August 28, 1809, DLC; letter to Benjamin Henry Latrobe, August 27, 1816, DLC; Hamlin, *Latrobe*, pp. 270, 446, 454, 533; letter from Benjamin Henry Latrobe, November 5, 1816, MdHi, *Latrobe Papers*, Letterbooks.
43. Letter to John W. Campbell, September 9, 1809, L&B, vol. XII, pp. 307–9.
44. Letter to William Clark, September 10, 1809, L&B, vol. XII, pp. 309–11.
45. Letter from Isaac A. Coles, March 13, 1809, DLC; letter to Benjamin Smith Barton, September 21, 1809, L&B, vol. XII, pp. 312–14; letter to J. S. Barnes, August 3, 1809, DLC; *Memorandum Book*, entries for March 14 and 15, 1809; Randall, vol. 3, pp. 321–22.
46. Letter to George Jefferson, May 18, 1809, MHi; letters from George Jefferson, June 12, June 26, and July 21, 1809, MHi.
47. "An Apparatus for measuring power, especially muscular effort of men and animals, or the power developed by a motor, or that required to operate machinery. It commonly embodies a spring to be compressed or a weight to be sustained by the force applied, combined with an index, or automatic recorder, to show the work performed," *Webster's Dictionary*, 2nd International Unabridged Edition, 1947.
48. Letter from William Strickland, May 20, 1796, DLC; letter to David Baillie Warden, May 1, 1808, DLC; letter to T. M. Randolph, Jr., October 11, 1808, letter from T. M. Randolph, Jr., December 14, 1808, ViU, Alderman Library; letter to Joel Barlow, December 31, 1809, DLC; letter from Joel Barlow, January 15, 1810, DLC; letter to Joel Barlow, January 24, 1810, DLC; letter to Dabney Carr, Jr., January 17, 1810, MHi; letter to Robert Fulton, April 16, 1810, L&B, vol. XIX, pp. 172–73.
49. Letter to James Madison, April 16, 1810, DLC.
50. Pierson, p. 71; letter from T. M. Randolph, Jr., October 14, 1808, ViU, Alderman Library; letter to Robert Fulton, March 8, 1813, DLC.
51. Letter to Charles Willson Peale, April 17, 1813, Sellers PMHB pp. 403–5; letter to Richard Peters, March 6, 1816, DLC; *Farm Book*, pp. 48, 56.
52. Letters to David Baillie Warden, July 15, 1810 and December 23, 1813, *Mississippi Valley Historical Review*, vol. XXVIII, 1941–42 (1965), pp. 227, 230–33; DAB vol. XIX, pp. 443–44.
53. Letter to Robert Patterson, November 10, 1811, L&B, vol. XIII, pp. 95–112.
54. *Ibid*, p. 105.
55. Letter to David Rittenhouse, July 19, 1778, Boyd, vol. 2, pp. 202–3; letter to Robert Patterson, September 11, 1811, L&B, vol. XIII, pp. 85–89.
56. Letter from Robert Patterson, November 11, 1811, PPAmP, *Patterson Papers*; letter to Robert Patterson, November 10, 1811, L&B, vol. XIII, pp. 95–112; Eckhardt, pp. 195–96; letter from Robert Patterson, November 30, 1812, DLC; letter to Robert Patterson, December 27, 1812, PPAmP, *Patterson Papers*.
57. Letter from Robert Patterson, January 12, 1813, DLC; letter to Thomas Voight, April 9, 1813, PPAmP. The reference is to a description of "Dr. Rittenhouse's Chronometer" written by Henry Voigt, featuring the pendulum and its construction, in Barton, *Rittenhouse*, pp. 584–85.
58. Letter from Robert Patterson, April 24, 1813, DLC; letter to Robert Patterson, April 9, 1813, PPAmP, *Patterson Papers*.
59. Letter from Robert Patterson, September 3, 1813, PPAmP, *Patterson Papers*.
60. Letter from Robert Patterson, August 25, 1815, PPAmP; letter to Robert Patterson, October 13, 1815, PPAmP, *Patterson Papers*.
61. Letter from Isaac Briggs, May 2, 1803, DLC; *Memorandum Book*, NN, entry for June 8, 1803.
62. Letter from Raphaelle Peale, January 19, 1806, PPAmP, *Peale Papers*.
63. Letter to Melatiah Nash, November 15, 1811, L&B, vol. XIII, pp. 112–14.
64. Letter to Dr. John Crawford, January 2, 1812, L&B, vol. XIII, pp. 117–19.
65. Letter to Dr. Benjamin Rush, March 6, 1813, L&B, vol. XIII, pp. 222–26.
66. Letter to John Adams, January 21, 1812, L&B, vol. XIII, pp. 122–25.
67. DAB, vol. 2, pp. 414–16.
68. Letter to Dr. Thomas Cooper, August 10, 1810, L&B, vol. XII, pp. 401–3.
69. Letter to Dr. Thomas Cooper, July 10, 1812, L&B, vol. XIII, pp. 176–78.
70. Letter to Andrew Ellicott, June 24, 1812, L&B, vol. XIX, p. 185.
71. Letter to Alexander von Humboldt, December 6, 1813, Ford, vol. IX, pp. 430—33.

72. *Ibid*, pp. 431–32.
73. *Ibid*, pp. 432–33; Jackson, *Stony Mountains*, pp. 273–74.
74. Letter from Robert Patterson, with encl., November 30, 1812, DLC; letters to Robert Patterson, December 12 and December 27, 1812, L&B, vol. XIII, pp. 191–93.
75. *An Accurate Delineation of Readheffers Perpetual Motion* (Broadside, c. 1812); *Documents For and Against Charles Redheffer*, pp. 1–24; "Whereas the interference of the Legislature of Pennsylvania is causing an inquiry to [be] made, relative to the perfection or imperfection of the newly invented machinery, is not without precedent. . . ." (Harrisburg, Pa.: State of Pennsylvania, 1812); E. S. Ferguson, ed., *Engineering Reminiscenses*, pp. 79–86; Ord-Hume, pp. 125–33.
76. Colden, *Fulton*, pp. 216–20.
77. Letter to Robert Fulton, March 8, 1813, L&B, vol. XIX, pp. 187–89.
78. Letter to Robert Fulton, July 21, 1813, Yale, *Franklin Papers*.
79. Letter to James Ronaldson, January 12, 1813, L&B, vol. XIII, pp. 204–6.
80. Letter to John Melish, January 13, 1813, L&B, vol. XIII, pp. 206–8.
81. 81. Letter to Thaddeus Kosciusko, June 28, 1812, L&B, vol. XIII, pp. 168–72.
82. Letter to Dr. Samuel Brown, July 14, 1813, L&B, vol. XIII, pp. 310–11.
83. Padgett, "Letters of Dr. Samuel Brown," pp. 99–130; Vogel, pp. 256–57.
84. Letter to Horatio Spafford, May 14, 1809, L&B, vol. XII, pp. 278–82; Spafford, *General Geography*; Boyd, "Horatio Gates Spafford," pp. 47–50.
85. Letter to C. W. Peale, August 30, 1811, L&B, vol. XIII, p. 79.
86. Letters to James Monroe, June 18, 1813, L&B, vol. XIII, p. 261; letter to James Monroe, October 16, 1814, Ford, IX, pp. 492–04; letter to W. H. Crawford, February 11, 1815, Ford, vol. IX, pp. 502–3.
87. Letters to Samuel Harrison Smith, September 21, 1814, Ford, vol. IX, pp. 485–88; letter to James Monroe, September 24, 1814, Ford, vol. IX, pp. 488–89.

CHAPTER XVII. VENERABLE SAGE

1. Letter to John Adams, January 11, 1817, L&B, vol. XV, pp. 97–100.
2. Letter to Benjamin Henry Latrobe, July 16, 1817, DLC.
3. Letter to Correa de Serra, December 27, 1814, L&B, vol. XIV, pp. 221–25; letter to Jean Baptiste Say, March 2, 1815, L&B, vol. XIV, pp. 258–67.
4. Letter to William Bentley, December 28, 1815, L&B, vol. 14, pp. 363–65.
5. Letter to Dr. John Manners, February 22, 1814, L&B, vol. XIV, pp. 97–103.
6. J. E. Caldwell, *Tour*, pp. 39–40; M. B. Smith, *First Forty Years*, pp. 71–72; M. B. Smith, *Winter in Washington*, vol. III, pp. 260–67; "Washington in Jefferson's Time from the Diaries and Family Letters of Mrs. Samuel Harrison Smith," pp. 304–309; G. Tucker, *Life of Thomas Jefferson*, vol. I, pp. 472–74; Ticknor, *Life*, vol. I, pp. 34–36; F. Hall, *Travels*, pp. 225–31; Randall, vol. III, p. 346; Montlezun, *Voyage*, vol. I, pp. 75–86; Carriere and Moffat, pp. 39–55; J. B. Smith, "The Carys of Virginia," MS.; Levasseur, vol. I, pp. 214–15; French, *Travels*, passim; Rayner, *Sketches*, pp. 519–26; Kennedy, *Wirt*, vol. II, p. 203; Lossing, "Monticello," pp. 145–51; Lossing, *Field-Book*, vol. II, pp. 341–42; SaxeWeimar Eisenach, *Travels*, vol. I, pp. 197–200; Heller, pp. 34–35.
7. Letters to Joseph Delaplaine, April 12, October 30, November 10, 1817, DLC.
8. Letter to John L. E. Shecut, June 29, 1813, L&B, vol. XIII, pp. 295–96.
9. Letter to Samuel M. Burnside, January 9, 1814, L&B, vol. XIV, pp. 53–54; Letter to John Pintard, January 9, 1814, L&B, vol. XIV, p. 53.
10. Letter from Peter S. Du Ponceau, January 24, 1818, DLC; letter to Robert Patterson, February 15, 1818, PPAmP, *Patterson Papers*.
11. Circular, *Transactions of the American Philosophical Society*, vol. IV, 1799, p. xxxvii.
12. Letter to P. S. Du Ponceau, January 22, 1816, L&B, vol, XIX, pp. 231–33.
13. Letters to P. S. Du Ponceau, November 7 and December 30, 1817, L&B, vol. XV, pp. 150–53, 157–60.
14. Johnston, *Library*, pp. 23–27.
15. Letter to Samuel Harrison Smith, September 21, 1814, L&B, vol. XIV, pp. 190–94; letter to James Madison, September 24, 1814, L&B, vol. XIV, p. 176; *Annals of the 13th Congress, 3rd session*, pp. 23–26, 29–30; Goff, pp. 32–47.
16. Letter to M. de Lomerie, April 3, 1813, L&B, vol. XIII, pp. 226–27.

17. Letter to Isaac McPherson, August 13, 1813, L&B, vol, XIII, pp. 326–28.
18. *Ibid.*
19. Letter to Oliver Evans, January 16, 1814, L&B, vol. XIV, pp. 63–67.
20. Letter to Dr. Thomas Cooper, January 16, 1814, L&B, vol. XIV, pp. 54–63.
21. Letter to Aldrichs & Dixon, January 14, 1813, L&B, vol. XIX, pp. 186–87.
22. Letter to Charles Willson Peale, June 13, 1815, with drawing, L&B, vol. XVIII, pp. 287–90.
23. Letter to William J. Coffee, November 22, 1821, DLC. Coffee was a New York sculptor and dealer in building ornaments, and furnished some of the latter for Monticello, Poplar Forest and the University of Virginia.
24. Letter to Charles Willson Peale, August 17, 1816, Sellers, PMHB, p. 409.
25. Letter to Charles Willson Peale, December 24, 1816, Sellers, PMHB, pp. 409–10. A clock-maker named J. E. McIlheny was listed in the Philadelphia city directories from 1818 to 1822 as a member of the firm of McIlheny & West, and a clockmaker named Joseph McIlheny was listed in 1825.
26. Letter to Charles Willson Peale, March 15, 1817, Sellers, PMHB, p. 411; letter to F. X. Zeltner, July 23, 1818, MoHi; Bedini, "Clock Designer," pp. 166, 171–72.
27. Letter to Captain A. Partridge, October 12, 1815, L&B, vol. XIV, pp. 352–54; letters from Captain A. Partridge, November 23 and December 9, 1815; letter to Captain A. Partridge, January 2, 1816, L&B, vol. XIV, pp. 374–79.
28. Letter to Thomas W. Maury, February 3, 1816, L&B, vol. XIV, pp. 428–30.
29. Letter to Governor Wilson C. Nicholas, April 19, 1816, L&B, vol. XIV, pp. 471–87.
30. Letter to Payne Todd, August 15, 1816, MoHi; the original was sold as Lot 118 at auction by Christie, Manson & Woods in New York in recent years.
31. Jefferson, "Scheme for a System of Agricultural Societies," March 1811, L&B, vol. XVII, pp. 404–10; True, "Albemarle Agricultural Society," pp. 243–59.
32. Letter from James Clarke, July 6, 1817, DLC.
33. Letter to James Clarke, August 1, 1817, DLC.
34. Letter from James Clarke, September 1, 1818, DLC.
35. Letters to James Clarke, September 5, 1820, January 19, April 2 and August 15, 1821, DLC; A. J. Morrison, "Virginia Patents," p. 152; Couture, pp. 423–26.
36. Letter from James Deneale, July 2, 1820, DLC; letter to James Deneale, July 8, 1820, DLC.
37. Morrison, p. 153.
38. Letter to Nathaniel Burwell, March 14, 1818, L&B, vol. XV, p. 165.
39. Letter to Dr. Thomas Cooper, August 25, 1814, L&B, vol. XIV, pp. 199–202.
40. [Rockfish Gap Report], *Manual of the Board of Visitors of the University of Virginia*, pp. 41–77; Pierson, p. 32.
41. Pierson, pp. 31–34; Bruce, vol. I, pp. 88, 164–72, 209, 236; Honeywell, *Educational Work*, Appendix J, pp. 248–60.
42. Letter to Littleton Waller Tazewell, January 5, 1805, ViU, Alderman Library.
43. Letter to William Thornton, May 9, 1817, L&B, vol. XVII, p. 396; letter from William Thornton, May 17, 1817, DLC; letters to B. H. Latrobe, June 12 and August 3, 1817, DLC; letter from B. H. Latrobe, June 17, 1817, DLC; F. Kimball, *Architect*, pp. 75–80.
44. Jefferson, *Notebook*, Drawing N 317, ViU, Alderman Library; Bruce, *History*, vol. I, pp. 52, 270, fig. 7; Lambeth and Manning, pp. 74–78.
45. Dio. Cassius, *History*, LIII, 27; Lehmann, "Dome," pp. 22, 25–26; Lehmann, *Humanist*, pp. 187–88.
46. Seneca, trans. by R. M. Gummere, Loeb Classical Library, pp. 90, 115; Lehmann, "Dome," p. 22.
47. Nichols, *Drawings*, N 381, "Observatory," p. 42; Lambeth and Manning, pp. 80–84; Hassler, "Plan of an Observatory," APS *Transactions*, new series, vol. II, plate X.
48. Bruce, vol. I, pp. 270–72.
49. Lambeth and Manning, pp. 80–84.
50. Nichols, *Drawings*, N 381, "Observatory," p. 42
51. Lambeth and Manning, pp. 80–81.
52. Jefferson, *Notebook*, ViU, Alderman Library; Hassler, *Principal Documents*, vol. 3, pp. 49–50; Hassler, "Plan," pp. 365–70, plate X.
53. Hassler, "Plan," pp. 365–70.
54. Letter to Ferdinand Rudolph Hassler, December 3, 1825, DLC.
55. Hassler, *Principal Documents*, vol. 3, p. 51.

56. Letter to Charles Bonnycastle, September 30, 1825, ViU, Alderman Library.
57. Bruce, *History*, vol. I, pp. 170–72.
58. Bruce, *History*, vol. I, pp. 272–73.
59. Letters to Joseph C. Cabell, May 16, 1824 (Cabell, pp. 305–13), December 22, 1824 (Cabell, pp. 316–18), January 22, 1824 (Cabell, pp. 324–29); letter from Cabell, January 30, 1825 (Cabell, pp. 336–37).
60. Bean, pp. 669–72; Hart, pp. 51–59; letter to Dr. David Hosack, May 12, 1824, DLC.
61. Letter to Nathaniel Bowditch, October 26, 1818, L&B, vol. XIX, pp. 264–68; letter to H. A. S. Dearborne, April 3, 1821, L&B, vol. XIII, pp. 110–13.
62. Letter to David Baillie Warden, June 6, 1817, in Diamond, ed., "Some Jefferson Letters," p. 239; *A Catalogue of the Extensive and Valuable Library of the Late President Jefferson* (Washington, 1829).
64. Peden, *Some Aspects*; Peden, "Some Notes," pp. 265–72; letter to Samuel Harrison Smith, July 23, 1815, DLC, cited in Sowerby,"Thomas Jefferson and His Library," pp. 215–16; R. G. Adams, *Three Americanists*, pp. 72–95.
65. M. P. Robinson, "Burning of the Rotunda," pp. 2–23.

CHAPTER XVIII. THE DREAM FULFILLED

1. Letter to Martha Jefferson Randolph, May 5, 1787, Betts and Bear, p. 40; G. L. Hall, pp. 220–22; Edward F. Young, *Night Thoughts* (London: J. and F. Rivington, 1777).
2. G.L. Hall, pp. 220–22.
3. S. N. Randolph, p. 345; letter from Henry Voigt, December 19, 1807, letter to Henry Voigt, January 6, 1808, PPAmP; Bedini, "His Watches," pp. 38–39.
4. Letter from John Garland Jefferson, February 26, 1791, ViU, Alderman Library.
5. Randall, vol. 3, pp. 665–67; Malone, *Jefferson*, vol. 6, pp. 488–89.
6. Letter to Arthur S. Brockenbough from Coleman Sellers, October 4, 1825, enclosing letter from Joseph Saxton, HSP, Manuscripts Division; letter to Joseph Coolidge, Jr., April 12, 1825, with enclosure, ViU, Alderman Library, *Edgehill Randolph Papers*; Bedini, "Clock Designer," pp. 172–79.
7. Letters from Joseph Coolidge, Jr., August 5, 1825 and February 27, 1826, MHi, *Coolidge-Jefferson Papers*; letter to Joseph Coolidge, Jr., June 4, 1826, with enclosure, letter from Coolidge, June 15, 1826, ViU, Alderman Library; letter from Coolidge to John H. Cocke, October 31, 1826, MHi, *Coolidge-Cocke Papers*; Bruce, *History*, vol. I, pp. 274–75 280–81; K. A. Tuttle, p. 111–13.
8. A. B. Philip, vol. I, pp. 274–75; Bedini, "Clock Designer," pp. 177–78.
9. Letter from Dr. R. G. Watkins, May 11, 1825, DLC; Dunglison, *Ana*, p. 26; M. Peterson, *New Nation*, p. 1005.
10. Letter to John Adams, June 1, 1822, DLC.
11. Letter to Dr. Vine Utley, March 21, 1819, L&B, vol. XV, pp. 186–88.
12. Letter to William Short, November 24, 1821, MHC, *Garden Book*, pp. 594–95.
13. Letter to John W, Eppes, July 28, 1822; Martha Randolph to Nicholas Trist, November 12, 1822, DLC; letter to Joseph Cabell, December 28, 1822, DLC; Randall, vol. 3, p. 538.
14. Letter from Dr. Robley Dunglison to James Madison, July 1, 1826, Dorsey, *The Jefferson-Dunglison Letters*, pp. 66–67; letter to Samuel Smith, October 22, 1825, MHi.
15. Letters to Remsen, October 26 and December 19, 1823, Yale University, *Franklin Papers*; letter to Thomas Leiper, May 31, 1823, Ford, vol. XII, pp. 286–89; Randall, vol. III, pp. 532–37; S. N. Randolph, pp. 406–7.
16. Letter to Dr. Benjamin Waterhouse, March 3, 1818, L&B, vol. XV, p. 163.
17. Letter to an unidentified correspondent (William Lambert?), November 29, 1821, L&B, vol. XV, pp. 342–49.
18. *Ibid*, p. 345.
19. Landsberg, pp. 268–71; DAB, vol. 18, pp. 550–51, vol. 11, pp. 440–41; Hagerty, pp. 124–25; Lovell, *Meteorological Register*.
20. Letter to Jacob Bigelow, April 11, 1818, L&B, vol. XIX, pp. 257–61.
21. Letter to George F. Hopkins, September 5, 1822, L&B, vol. XV, pp. 394–95.
22. Letter to Lewis Beck, July 16, 1824, DLC; *Virginia Literary Museum*, vol. 1, No. 1, p. 26.
23. Letter to Charles Willson Peale, October 23, 1822, Sellers, PMHB, p. 218.

24. Pierson, p. 74.
25. Letter to Lafayette, September 3, 1824, DLC.
26. *Richmond Enquirer*, November 16, 1824; S. N. Randolph, pp. 389–91.
27. S. N. Randolph, pp. 395–96; speech on Lafayette, Padover, *Complete Jefferson*, pp. 447–48.
28. Letter to Robley Dunglison, November 26, 1825; *Jefferson-Dunglison Letters*, pp. 45–46.
29. Bean, "Influence on American Medical Education," pp. 669–80; Thorup, pp. 199–201.
30. Letter from Dunglison, July 2, 1825, letters to Dunglison, July 4 and November 26, 1825, *Jefferson-Dunglison Letters*, pp. 35, 38–39, 44–45; *Memorandum Book*, entry for November 27, 1825.
31. Letter to James Madison, November 6, 1823, DLC; minutes of the meeting of the Board of Visitors, April 5–7, 1824, ViU; letter to Francis Walker Gilmer, June 5, 1824, DLC.
32. Barrett, "Struggle," pp. 494–506.
33. *Minutes of the Faculty, September 20–October 1, 1825*, ViU; Letter to Joseph Coolidge, Jr., October 13, 1825, L&B, vol. 18, pp. 342–46; M. B. Smith, *First Forty Years*, pp. 228–30; Bruce, vol. II, pp. 298–301.
34. Letters to Dr. Robert Greenhow, March 8, April 14, 1825; letters from Dr. Greenhow, March 22, April 23 and June 16, 1825, *Jefferson-Dunglison Letters*, pp. 17–25, 27–29.
35. Letter to Robley Dunglison, November 25, 1825, *Jefferson-Dunglison Letters*, pp. 47–48; Bean, p. 671; Leavell, p. 96; Cohn, p. 291.
36. Letter to John Brazier, August 24, 1819, L&B, vol. XV, pp. 207–11. Brazier was the author of a review on a work about Greek pronunciation by Pickering.
37. Letter to Dr. John Emmet, May 2, 1826, L&B, vol. XV, pp. 168–72.
38. H. B. Adams, *Jefferson and the University*, pp. 94–96.
39. Letter to Mr. La Porte, June 4, 1819, Harvard University Library. He specified:
    "For breakfast. Wheat or corn bread, at the choice of each particular, with butter, and milk, or Coffee-au-lait, at the choice of each, no meat.
    "For dinner. A soup, a dish of salt meat, a dish of fresh fruit & as great a variety of vegetables well cooked as you please.
    "For supper. Corn or wheat bread at their choice, & milk, or Coffee-au-lait, also at their choice. But no meat.
    "Their drink at all times water, a young stomach needing no stimulating drinks, and the habit of using them being dangerous.
    "And I should recommend as late a dinner as the rules of their school will permit.
    "No games of chance to be permitted in the house."
40. Letter to Dr. John P. Emmet, April 27, 1826, L&B, vol. XVI, pp. 163–67; True, "Botany," pp. 359–60.
41. Kallen, "Garden Wall," pp. 78–82; Bruce, vol. I, p. 273; Guiness and Sadler, Jr., pp. 109–50.
42. Letter from Roger C. Weightman, June 14, 1826, DLC; letter to Roger C. Weightman, June 24, 1826, DLC.
43. Randall, vol. III, pp. 505–6; M. Peterson, *Thomas Jefferson and the Nation*, p. 1006.
44. Peden, "A Book Peddler," pp. 631–36.
45. Letter from Virginia Trist to Ellen Wayles Coolidge, October 16, 1825, MHi, *Coolidge Papers*; letter to James Madison, October 18, 1825, L&B, vol. XIX, p. 287; Randall, vol. 3, p. 540.
46. Letter to Thomas Jefferson Randolph, February 8, 1826, DLC; Jefferson, "Thoughts on Lotteries," DLC; *Richmond Enquirer*, February 9, 11, and 21, and April 4, 1826.
47. Robley Dunglison, *Ana*, p. 32–33; letter to Henry Randall from Thomas Jefferson Randolph, N.D., Randall, vol. 3, pp. 543–44.
48. Randall, vol. 3, pp. 540–41; G. Morgan, *Collected Papers*, p. 104.
49. Randall, vol. 3, pp. 660–64; "Last Scenes of Mr. Jefferson's Life, etc.", *Richmond Enquirer*, August 27, 1826; M. Peterson, *Jefferson Image*, pp. 116–22.
50. Randall, vol. 3, pp. 545–50.
51. Randall, vol. 3, p. 545; SNR, p. 429.
52. Letter from Robley Dunglison to James Madison, July 1, 1826, DLC, *Madison Papers*; Dunglison, *Ana*, pp. 32–33; Randall, vol. 3, pp. 544–49.
53. Randall, vol. 3, p. 545; Bear, "Last Few Days," pp. 77–79.
54. Bear, "Last Few Days," p. 78.
55. Letter from Thomas Jefferson Randolph to John M. Perry and James Dinsmore, August 3, 1826, ViU, *Edgehill-Randolph Papers*; Randall, vol. 3, pp. 563–64; Kean, pp. 7–18.

56. Von Raumer, p. 427.
57. University of Virginia, Alderman Library, *Minutes of the Board of Visitors*, October 3–7, 1826, October 3, 1828, July 20, 1831, June 28, 1848; letter to the writer from Dr. Richard S. Mitchell, Department of Environmental Sciences, ViU, June 23, 1977.
58. *Ibid.*
59. ViU, Board of Visitors, *Minutes* (typescript), vol. I, p. 131, vol. II, pp. 10, 65, vol. III, pp. 45, 56.
60. Sellers, *Museum*, pp. 258–60, 353 n. 8; HSP, Peale Papers, *Museum Record Book*, pp. 137–38.
61. [Phillips], *Early Proceedings*, entry for July 8, 1826, pp. 555–56; Chuinard, "and Society," p. 272.
62. Mitchill, *Discourse*, pp. 1–44.
63. [Phillips], *Early Proceedings*, entry for April 13, 1827, p. 565; Chuinard, "and Society," pp. 273–74.
64. Cuvier, *Annales du Museum d'Histoire Naturelle*, Tome V, 1804, p. 358; also in Tome V of his major work.
65. Charles Lemesle, "Éloge de Thomas Jefferson,. . . .," *Mémoires de la Société Linneanne*, Tome V, 1827; Chuinard, "and Society," p. 275.
66. Glisson, vol. I, pp. 70–71.
67. DAB, vol. I, pp. 257–58; Bigelow, *Elements of Technology*.
68. H. A. Wallace, Keynote Address, pp. 336–46.
69. Letter to Peter Carr, August 19, 1785, L&B, vol. V, pp. 82.
[70. Letter to Dr. Thomas Cooper, July 10, 1812, H. J. Abrahams, "Library of Applied Chemistry," p. 267].
70. Letter to Dr. John P. Emmet, May 2, 1826, L&B, vol. XVI, p. 171.
71. *Notes*, pp. 19, 24–25.
72. A. W. Greely, L&B, vol. XIII, pp. iii–iv.
73. Letter to the Reverend James Madison, July 19, 1788, Boyd, vol. 13, pp. 379–83.
74. Letter to John Manners, February 22, 1814, Boyd, vol. 14, pp. 97–104.
75. M. Conseil, *Mélanges politique*, introduction.
76. [Jefferson], First Inaugural Address, December 8, 1801, Padover, *Complete Jefferson*, p. 387.
77. H. Thompson, *Age of Invention*, pp. 111–13.
78. Letter to John Trumbull, February 15, 1789, DLC; letter to Dr. Benjamin Rush, January 16, 1811, L&B, vol. 13, pp. 1–9.
79. E. T. Martin, *Thomas Jefferson: Scientist*, p. 216.
80. Among Jefferson's greatest honors was his election as foreign associate of the Institut de France. Other candidates being considered at the time of his election included Christoph Ebeling, Johann Gottfried von Herder, Immanuel Kant, David Ramsay, James Rennell, Count Rumford, Dugald Stuart and Arthur Young. Elected at the same time as Jefferson were James Rennell of England, Ouvaroff of Russia, Sestini of Italy, Arnold Heeren of Göttingen, Friedrich Creuzer of Heidelberg and Wilhelm von Humboldt of Berlin.
81. B. S. Barton, "A Letter," pp. 334–48.
82. Letter to Benjamin Waterhouse, March 3, 1818, L&B, vol. XV, pp. 162–64.

INDEX

INDEX